AN INTRODUCTION TO LANGUAGE

AN INTRODUCTION TO LANGUAGE

SECOND CANADIAN EDITION

Victoria Fromkin
UNIVERSITY OF CALIFORNIA, LOS ANGELES

-

Robert Rodman
NORTH CAROLINA STATE UNIVERSITY, RALEIGH

-

Neil Hultin
EMERITUS, UNIVERSITY OF WATERLOO

-

Harry Logan
EMERITUS, UNIVERSITY OF WATERLOO

THOMSON

NELSON

Australia   Canada   Mexico   Singapore   Spain   United Kingdom   United States

For more information contact
Nelson, 1120 Birchmount Road, Scarborough, Ontario, M1K 5G4.
Or you can visit our Internet site at http://www.nelson.com

Canadian Cataloguing in Publication Data

Main entry under title:

An introduction to language

2nd Canadian ed.
Includes index.
ISBN 0-7747-3723-9

1. Linguistics.   2. Language and languages.
I. Fromkin, Victoria.

P106.I57   2001   410   C00-932399-6

Acquisitions Editor: Anne Williams
Senior Developmental Editor: Martina van de Velde
Production Editor: Emily Ferguson
Production Coordinator: Cheri Westra
Copy Editor: Dallas Harrison
Permissions Editor: Cindy Howard
Cover Design: Sonya V. Thursby, Opus House Incorporated
Typesetting and Assembly: Bookman Typesetting Co.
Printing and Binding: Transcontinental Printing Inc.

Cover Art: Open Air Café by Yana Headford. 20" ¥ 24", oil on canvas, © copyright Yana Headford. Reproduced by permission of the artist.

This book was printed in Canada.

4 5   05 04

Preface

Many of the questions discussed in this book have been asked for thousands of years. What is language? What do you know when you know a language? What is the origin of language? Is language unique to the human species? Why are there many languages? Where do they come from? How are they related? How do children learn language? Are some languages (or dialects) superior to others? Are some languages simpler than others? What do all languages have in common? What is the neurological basis of human language? What parts of the brain are concerned with language? Can computers be taught to speak and understand human language? These are only a few of the questions that have piqued human curiosity about language.

In addition to a philosophical interest in such questions, there are many reasons why linguists, psychologists, educators, sociologists, legal experts, neurologists, communication engineers, and computer scientists need to understand the nature of human language. Linguistics provides a theoretical basis for practical applications that include the diagnosis and treatment of language disorders such as aphasia and dyslexia, the planning of "language arts" curricula in schools, the fight against illiteracy, the learning of foreign languages, the simplification of legal language, and the development of computerized speech products.

This book has been used in both linguistics and non-linguistics courses, at all levels from first-year through graduate courses, for majors in fields as diverse as computer science, English, foreign languages, speech pathology, anthropology, communications, and philosophy. The second Canadian edition reflects linguistics issues and developments in Canada.

The text is divided into five parts: "The Nature of Human Language," "Grammatical Aspects of Language," "Social Aspects of Language," "Biological Aspects of Language," and "Language in the Computer Age."

Part 1, Chapter 1, establishes the framework for what follows by discussing linguistic knowledge, grammars, linguistic creativity, language universals, non-human communication, and the origin of language.

Part 2, Chapters 2 through 6, examines the kinds of linguistic knowledge that speakers of all languages, from Arabic to Zulu, possess. There are chapters on words and word formation (morphology), sentence structure (syntax), meaning (semantics), and the sound patterns of language (phonetics and phonology). Greater emphasis has been placed on linguistic data and less on the formalisms used in different theories, since these theories are usually covered in more advanced courses.

In Part 3, Chapter 7, we consider language variation and the study of ethnic minority and social dialects in Canada. Attitudes toward language and how it reflects the views and mores of society are included. Another section, on language and sexism, reflects a growing concern with this topic. Chapters 8 and 9 discuss language change or historical linguistics and the nature and development of writing.

Part 4 reflects the rapid changes occurring in our understanding of the biological basis of language. Chapter 10 covers acquisition of spoken and sign languages by hearing and deaf infants, respectively. The section on attempts to teach language to chimpanzees (and one gorilla) traces the entire 50-year history of this endeavour, from the outset to the present. Chapter 11, on brain, mind, and language, and, in Part 5, Chapter 12, on computer processing of human language, reflect exciting discoveries in these research areas.

Canadians abroad are often mistaken for their more numerous "American" neighbours, and we have tried to explain both how Canadian English differs from and why it is so similar to "American English." Of course, in an introductory text devoted to such basic issues, much must be simplified or entirely omitted. We hope, however, that issues such as the complexities of Canadian spelling (Chapter 9), the nature of "Canadian raising," and the summary of the origins of Canadian English (Chapter 7) will stimulate interest and discussion among readers. What is found here is merely a beginning.

The primary concern of this text is with basic ideas rather than detailed expositions. The textbook assumes no previous knowledge of linguistics on the part of the reader. A list of references at the end of each chapter is included to accommodate any reader who wishes to pursue the subject in more depth. Each chapter concludes with a summary and exercises to enhance the student's interest in and comprehension of the textual material. Students may find some of the exercises particularly challenging or problematic. For this reason, we have included answers to these exercises, marked with an asterisk (*). Thus, students can establish immediately whether they have understood the materials. To further assist learning, a glossary of the technical terms introduced in each chapter can be found at the end of the book.

Acknowledgements

We would like to thank Martina van de Velde for her editorial assistance in putting together this second Canadian edition — and for putting up with us. We are also indebted to those instructors who, on the basis of their use of the book in their classrooms, provided us with thought-provoking questions and comments: Carol Fraser (York University) and Madga Stroinska (McMaster University). In particular, we are obliged to Robert I. Binnick (University of Toronto) for his careful reading of the first Canadian edition. We have benefited from his observations and suggestions. The responsibility for errors in fact or judgement is, of course, ours alone.

Victoria Fromkin
Robert Rodman
Neil Hultin
Harry Logan

A Note from the Publisher

Thank you for selecting *An Introduction to Language*, Second Canadian Edition, by Victoria Fromkin, Robert Rodman, Neil Hultin, and Harry Logan. The authors and publisher have devoted considerable time to the careful development of this book. We appreciate your recognition of this effort and accomplishment.

Contents

CHAPTER 3   **Syntax: The Sentence Patterns of Language**   **78**

CHAPTER 4   **Semantics: The Meanings of Language   128**

PART 3
Social Aspects of Language

CHAPTER 9   Writing: The ABCs of Language   385

PART 4
Biological Aspects of Language

CHAPTER 10   **Language Acquisition   419**

PART 5
Language in the Computer Age

PART 1
The Nature of Human Language

Reflecting on ... Noam Chomsky's ideas on the innateness of the fundamentals of grammar in the human mind, I saw that any innate features of the language capacity must be a set of biological structures, selected in the course of the evolution of the human brain. . . .

S.E. Luria, *A Slot Machine, a Broken Test Tube, an Autobiography*

Language is not an abstract construction of the learned, or of dictionary-makers, but is something arising out of the work, needs, ties, joys, affections, tastes, of long generations of humanity, and has its bases broad and low, close to the ground.

Walt Whitman

CHAPTER 1
What Is Language?

When we study human language, we are approaching what some might call the "human essence," the distinctive qualities of mind that are, so far as we know, unique to man.

Noam Chomsky, *Language and Mind*

Calvin and Hobbes
by Bill Watterson

Whatever else people do when they come together — whether they play, fight, make love, or make automobiles — they talk. We live in a world of language. We talk to our friends, our associates, our wives and husbands, our lovers, our teachers, and our parents and in-laws. We talk to bus drivers and total strangers. We talk face to face and over the telephone, and everyone responds with more talk. Television and radio further swell this torrent of words. Hardly a moment of our waking lives is free from words, and even in our dreams we talk and are talked to. We also talk when there is no one to answer. Some of us talk aloud in our sleep. We talk to our pets and sometimes to ourselves.

The possession of language, perhaps more than any other attribute, distinguishes humans from other animals. To understand our humanity, we must understand the nature of language that makes us human. According to the philosophy expressed in the myths and religions of many peoples, it is language that is the source of human life and power. To some people of Africa, a newborn child is a *kuntu*, a "thing," not yet a *muntu*, a "person." Only by the act of learning does the child become a human being. Thus, according to this tradition, we all become "human" because we all know at least one language. But what does it mean to "know" a language?

Linguistic Knowledge

When you know a language, you can speak and be understood by others who know that language. This means you have the capacity to produce sounds that signify certain meanings and to understand or interpret the sounds produced by others. We are, of course, referring to normal-hearing individuals. Deaf persons produce and understand sign languages just as hearing persons produce and understand spoken languages.

Everyone knows a language. Five-year-old children are almost as proficient at speaking and understanding as are their parents. Yet the ability to carry out the simplest conversation requires profound knowledge that most speakers are unaware of. This is as true of speakers of Japanese as of English, of Armenian as of Navajo. A speaker of English can produce a sentence having two relative clauses without knowing what a relative clause is; for example,

> My goddaughter, who was born in Sweden and who now lives in Vermont, is named Disa, after a Viking queen.

In a parallel fashion, a child can walk without understanding or being able to explain the principles of balance and support or the neurophysiological control mechanisms that permit one to do so. The fact that we may know something unconsciously is not unique to language.

What, then, do speakers of English or Quechua or French or Mohawk or Arabic know?

Knowledge of the Sound System

Knowing a language means knowing what sounds (or signs, in the case of sign languages of the deaf) are in that language and what sounds are not. This unconscious knowledge is revealed by the way speakers of one language pronounce words from another language. If you speak only English, for example, you may substitute an English sound for a non-English sound when pronouncing "foreign" words. Most English speakers pronounce the name *Bach* with a final *k* sound because the sound represented by the letters *ch* in German is no longer an English sound. If you pronounce it as the Germans do, you are using a sound outside the English sound system. Many French Canadians, though otherwise fluent in English, pronounce words such as *this* and *that* as if they were spelled *dis* and *dat*. The English sound represented by the initial letters *th* is not part of the French sound system, and the French "mispronunciation" reveals the speakers' unconscious knowledge of this fact.

Knowing the sound system of a language includes more than knowing the inventory of sounds: sounds may start a word, end a word, or follow each other. The name of a former president of Ghana was *Nkrumah*, pronounced with an initial sound identical with the single sound spelled *ng* in the English word *sing*. While this sound does appear in English medially and finally before *k*, no word in English begins with it. As a result, most speakers of English mispronounce Mr. Nkrumah's name (by Ghanaian standards) by inserting a short vowel before or after the nasal (*n*) sound.

Children who learn English discover this restriction of *ng* to medial or final positions, while Ghanaian children learn that words in their language may begin with the *ng* sound.

We will learn more about sound systems in Chapters 5 and 6.

Knowledge of the Meaning of Words

> The minute I set eyes on an animal I know what it is. I don't have to reflect a moment; the right name comes out instantly.... I seem to know just by the shape of the creature and the way it acts what animal it is. When the dodo came along he [Adam] thought it was a wildcat.... But I saved him.... I just spoke up in a quite natural way . . . and said, "Well, I do declare if there isn't the dodo!"
>
> Mark Twain, *Eve's Diary*

Knowing the sounds and sound patterns in our language constitutes only one part of our linguistic knowledge. In addition, knowing a language is knowing that certain sound sequences signify certain concepts or meanings. Speakers of English know what *boy* means and that it means something different from *toy* or *girl* or *pterodactyl*. Knowing a language is therefore knowing how to relate sounds and meanings.

If you do not know a language, the sounds spoken to you will be mainly incomprehensible, because the relationship between speech sounds and the meanings they represent in the languages of the world is, for the most part, **arbitrary**. You have to learn (when you are acquiring the language) that the sounds represented by the letters *house* (in the written form of the language) signify the concept 🏠; if you know French, this meaning is represented by *maison*; if you know Twi, it is represented by *ɔdaŋ*; if you know Russian, by *dom*; if you know Spanish, by *casa*. Similarly, the concept ✋ is represented by *hand* in English, *main* in French, *nsa* in Twi, and *ruka* in Russian.

The sounds of words are given meaning only by the language in which they occur, despite what Eve says in Mark Twain's satire *Eve's Diary*. As Shakespeare has Juliet say,

> What's in a name: That which we call a rose
> By any other name would smell as sweet.

What's in a name, as Steven Pinker (1999) points out, is that a language community tacitly agrees to use a particular sound to convey a certain idea — that is, the linguistic sign is not only arbitrary but also conventional.

This arbitrary relationship between the **form** (sounds) and the **meaning** (concept) of a word in spoken language is also true of the sign languages used by the deaf. If you see someone using a sign language you do not know, it is doubtful you will understand the message from the signs alone (see Figure 1.1). A person who knows Chinese Sign Language would find it difficult to understand American Sign Language. Signs that may have originally been **mimetic** (similar to miming) or **iconic** (with a non-arbitrary relationship between form and meaning) change

FIGURE 1.1

Arbitrary relationship between gestures and meanings of the signs for *father* and *suspect* in ASL and CSL.

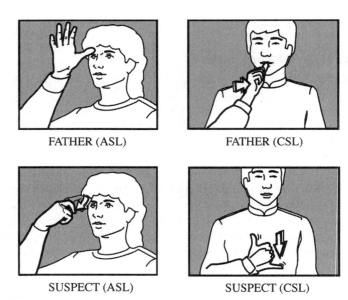

FATHER (ASL)   FATHER (CSL)

SUSPECT (ASL)   SUSPECT (CSL)

Copyright © 1987 by Massachusetts Institute of Technology. From *What the Hands Reveal about the Brain* by Howard Poizner, Edward S. Klima, and Ursula Bellugi, 1987.

historically as do words, and the iconicity is lost. These signs become **conventional**, so knowing the shape or movement of the hands does not reveal the meaning of the gestures in sign languages.

There is some iconicity in language. **Sound symbolism** is found in words whose pronunciation suggests the meaning; for example, the sounds *sn* are associated with the nose as in *sneer, snarl, sneeze, snoot(y), snot,* and *snore.* Other words with this combination — *snow, snip,* and *snoop,* for example — have no such association. A few words in most languages are **onomatopoeic** — the sounds of the words supposedly imitate the sounds of nature. Even here, the sounds differ from one language to another, reflecting the particular sound system of the language. In English, we say *cockadoodledoo* to represent the rooster's crow, but in Russian they say *kukuriku;* dogs bark *amh-amh* in Irish, while pigs "oink" *boo-boo* in Japanese.

Sometimes particular sound sequences seem to relate to a particular concept. In English, many words beginning with *gl* relate to sight, such as *glare, glint, gleam, glitter, glossy, glaze, glance, glimmer, glimpse,* and *glisten.* However, such words are a very small part of any language, and *gl* may have nothing to do with "sight" in another language, or even in other words in English, such as *gladiator, glucose, glory, glycerin, globe,* and so on.

English speakers know the *gl* words that relate to sight and those that do not; they know the onomatopoeic words and all the words in the basic vocabulary of the language. There are no speakers of English who know all the words listed in *Webster's Third New International Dictionary* or even the many fewer that appear in desk dictionaries such as *The Concise Oxford Dictionary* or *The Gage Canadian Dictionary*; but even if they did know all the words, they would not know English. Imagine trying to learn a foreign language by buying a dictionary and memorizing words. No matter how many words you learned, you would not be able to form the simplest phrases or sentences in the language or understand a native speaker. No one speaks in isolated words. (Of course, you could search in your traveller's dictionary for individual words to find out how to say something such as "car — gas — where?" After many tries, a native speaker might understand this question and then point in the direction of a gas station. If you are answered with a sentence, however, you probably will not understand what was said or be able to look it up, because you will not know where one word ended and another began.) Chapter 4 will further explore word meanings.

The Creativity of Linguistic Knowledge

Knowledge of a language enables you to combine words to form phrases and phrases to form sentences. You cannot buy a dictionary of any language with all its sentences, because no dictionary can list all the possible sentences. Knowing a language means being able to produce new sentences never spoken before and to understand sentences never heard before. Noam Chomsky refers to this ability as part of the **creative aspect** of language use. Not every speaker of a language can create great literature, but you, and all persons who know a language, can and do create new sentences when you speak and understand new sentences created by others.

This creative ability is due to the fact that language use is not limited to stimulus–response behaviour. If someone steps on our toes, we will automatically respond with a scream or gasp or grunt, but these sounds are not part of language; they are involuntary reactions to stimuli. After we automatically cry out, we might say "That was some clumsy act, you big oaf," or "Thank you very much for stepping on my toe, because I was afraid I had elephantiasis, and now that I can feel it hurt I know it isn't so," or any one of an infinite number of sentences, because the particular sentence we produce is not controlled by any stimulus.

Even some involuntary cries such as *ouch* are constrained by our own language system, as are the filled pauses sprinkled throughout conversational speech — *er* or *uh* or *you know* in English. They contain only the sounds found in the language. French speakers, for example, often fill their pauses with the vowel sound that starts their word for egg — *oeuf* — a sound that does not occur in English.

Knowing a language includes knowing what sentences are appropriate in various situations. Saying "Roast beef costs $12.50 a kilo" after someone has just stepped on your toe would hardly be an appropriate response, although it would be possible.

Consider the following sentence:

> Jacques Cartier decided to become a pioneer because he dreamed of pigeon-toed giraffes and cross-eyed elephants dancing in pink shirts and green berets on the wind-swept prairies.

You may not believe the sentence; you may question its logic; but you can understand it, although you probably never heard or read it before now.

Knowledge of a language, then, makes it possible to understand and produce new sentences. If you counted the number of sentences in this book that you have seen or heard before, the number would be small. The next time you write an essay or a letter, see how many of your sentences are new. Few sentences are stored in your brain, to be pulled out to fit some situation or matched with some sentence that you hear. Novel sentences never spoken or heard before cannot be in your memory.

Simple memorization of all the possible sentences in a language is impossible in principle. If for every sentence in the language a longer sentence can be formed, then there is no limit to the length of any sentence and therefore no limit to the number of sentences. In English, you can say

> This is the house.

or

> This is the house that Jack built.

or

> This is the malt that lay in the house that Jack built.

or

> This is the dog that chased the cat that killed the rat that ate the malt that lay
> in the house that Jack built.

You need not stop there. How long, then, is the longest sentence? A speaker of English can say

> The old man came.

or

> The old, old, old, old, old man came.

How many "olds" are too many? Seven? Twenty-three?

The longer these sentences become, the less likely we would hear or say them. A sentence with 276 occurrences of "old" would be highly unlikely in either speech or writing, even to describe Methuselah, but such a sentence is theoretically possible. If you know English, you have the knowledge to add any number of adjectives as modifiers to a noun.

All human languages permit their speakers to form indefinitely long sentences; creativity is a universal property of human language.

To memorize an infinite set of sentences would require an infinite storage capacity. However, the brain is finite, and even if it were not we could not store novel sentences.

Knowledge of Sentences and Non-Sentences

When you learn a language, you must learn something that is finite — your vocabulary, for example, is finite however large it may be — and that can be stored in the brain. If sentences in a language were formed by putting one word after another in any order, then language could simply be a set of words, but you can see that words are not enough by examining the following strings of words.

(1)   (a)   John kissed the little old lady who owned the shaggy dog.
     (b)   Who owned the shaggy dog John kissed the little old lady.
     (c)   John is difficult to love.
     (d)   It is difficult to love John.
     (e)   John is anxious to go.
     (f)   It is anxious to go John.
     (g)   John, who was a student, flunked his exams.
     (h)   Exams his flunked student a was who John.

If you were asked to put a star or asterisk before the examples that seem to be "odd" or "no good" (the conventional way of indicating unacceptable examples), you would probably select (b), (f), and (h). Our "intuitive" knowledge of what is or is not an acceptable sentence in English allows us to recognize such ungrammatical sentences with little difficulty. Most fluent speakers of English will agree that the following starred strings of words are unacceptable sentences even if they have difficulty explaining why this is so.

(2)   (a)   What he did was climb a tree.
     (b)   *What he thought was want a sports car.
     (c)   Drink your beer and go home!
     (d)   *What are drinking and go home?
     (e)   I expect them to arrive a week from next Thursday.
     (f)   *I expect a week from next Thursday to arrive them.
     (g)   Linus lost his security blanket.
     (h)   *Lost Linus security blanket his.

As you can see, not every string of words constitutes a well-formed sentence in a language. Knowledge of a language determines which strings of words are sentences and which are not. Therefore, in addition to knowledge of the words of the language, linguistic knowledge includes **rules** for forming sentences and making judgements such as those made about the examples in **(1)** and **(2)**. These rules must be finite in length and finite in number so that they can be stored in our finite brains; yet they must permit us to form and understand an infinite set of new sentences. They are not rules determined by a judge or a legislature or even rules taught in a grammar class. They are unconscious constraints on sentence formation that children discover about the language.

A language, then, consists of all the sounds, words, and possible sentences. When you know a language, you know the sounds, the words, and the rules for their combination.

Linguistic Knowledge and Performance

"What's one and one and one and one and one and one and one and one and one and one?"

"I don't know," said Alice. "I lost count."

"She can't do Addition," the Red Queen interrupted.

Lewis Carroll, *Through the Looking-Glass*

Speakers' linguistic knowledge permits them to form longer and longer sentences by joining sentences and phrases together or adding modifiers to a noun. Whether you stop at three, five, or eighteen adjectives, it is impossible to limit the number you could add if desired. Very long sentences are theoretically possible, but they are highly improbable. Evidently, there is a difference between having the knowledge necessary to produce sentences of a language and applying this knowledge. It is a difference between what you *know*, which is your **linguistic competence**, and how you *use* this knowledge in actual speech production and comprehension, which is your **linguistic performance**.

Speakers of all languages have the knowledge to understand or produce sentences of any length. When they attempt to use that knowledge, though — when they perform linguistically — there are physiological and psychological reasons that limit the number of adjectives, adverbs, clauses, and so on. They may run out of breath, their audience may leave, they may lose track of what they have said, and, of course, no one lives forever.

When we speak, we usually wish to convey some message (although it seems that some of us occasionally like to talk just to hear our own voices). At some stage in the act of producing speech, we must organize our thoughts into strings of words. But sometimes the message gets garbled. We may stammer, or pause, or produce **slips of the tongue**. We may even sound like Tarzan in the cartoon by Gary Larson, who illustrates the difference between linguistic knowledge and the way we use that knowledge in performance.

For the most part, linguistic knowledge is not conscious knowledge. The linguistic system — the sounds, structures, meanings, words, and rules for putting them all together — is learned subconsciously with no awareness that rules are being learned. Just as we may be unconscious of the rules that allow us to stand or walk, to crawl on all fours if we choose, to catch a baseball, or to ride a bicycle, our unconscious ability to speak and understand and to make judgements about sentences reveals our knowledge of the rules of our language. This knowledge represents a complex cognitive system. The nature of this system is what this book is all about.

THE FAR SIDE © 1991 FARWORKS Inc. Distributed by Universal Press Syndicate. Reprinted with permission. All rights reserved.

What Is Grammar?

We use the term "grammar" with a systematic ambiguity. On the one hand, the term refers to the explicit theory constructed by the linguist and proposed as a description of the speaker's competence. On the other hand, . . . [it refers] to this competence itself.

N. Chomsky and M. Halle, *The Sound Pattern of English*

Descriptive Grammars

The sounds and sound patterns, the basic units of meaning, such as words, and the rules to combine them to form new sentences constitute the **grammar** of a language. The grammar, then, is what we know; it represents our linguistic competence. To understand the nature of language, we must understand the nature of this internalized, unconscious set of rules, which is part of every grammar of every language.

Every human being who speaks a language knows its grammar. When linguists wish to describe a language, they attempt to describe the grammar of the language that exists in the minds of its speakers. There may be some differences among speakers' knowledge, but there must be shared knowledge, because it is this grammar that makes it possible to communicate through language. To the extent that the linguist's description is a true model of the speakers' linguistic capacity, it will be a successful description of the grammar and of the language itself. Such a model is called a **descriptive grammar**. It does not tell you how you should speak; it describes your basic linguistic knowledge. It explains how it is possible for you to speak and understand, and it tells what you know about the sounds, words, phrases, and sentences of your language. Some linguists, however, consider descriptive grammar to be concerned with describing the patterns and constructions that occur in a language whether or not the specific descriptions mirror those in your mind.

We have used the word *grammar* in two ways: the first in reference to the **mental grammar** speakers have in their brains; the second as the model or description of this internalized grammar. Almost 2000 years ago, the Greek grammarian Dionysius Thrax defined grammar as that which permits us either to speak a language or to speak about a language. From now on, we will not differentiate these two meanings, because the linguist's descriptive grammar is an attempt at a formal statement (or theory) of the speakers' grammar.

When we say in later chapters that there is a rule in the grammar — such as "Every sentence has a noun phrase subject and a verb phrase predicate" — we posit the rule in both the mental grammar and the model of it, the linguist's grammar. When we say that a sentence is **grammatical**, we mean that it conforms to the rules of both grammars; conversely, an **ungrammatical** (unacceptable) sentence deviates in some way from these rules. If, however, we posit a rule for English that does not agree with your intuitions as a speaker, then the grammar we are describing is in some way different from the grammar that represents your linguistic competence — that is, your language is not the one described. No language or variety of a language (called a **dialect**) is superior to any other in a linguistic sense. Every grammar is equally complex and logical and capable of producing an infinite set of sentences to express any thought. If something can be expressed in one language or one dialect, then it can be expressed in any other language or dialect. It might involve different means and different words, but it can be expressed.

No grammar, therefore no language, is superior or inferior to any other. A dialect may assume a privileged position in a community, but its status is the consequence of the political, social, or economic power of its speakers, not the linguistic merit of the dialect. Languages of technologically undeveloped cultures are not primitive or ill formed in any way.

Prescriptive Grammars

This is the sort of English up with which I will not put.

Winston Churchill, marginal comment on state document

I don't want to talk grammar. I want to talk like a lady.

George Bernard Shaw, *Pygmalion*

The views expressed in the section above are not those of all grammarians now or in the past. From ancient times until the present, "purists" have believed that language change is corruption and that there are certain "correct" forms that all educated people should use in speaking and writing. The Greek Alexandrians in the first century, the Arabic scholars at Basra in the eighth century, and numerous English grammarians of the eighteenth and nineteenth centuries held this view. They wished to prescribe rather than describe the rules of grammar, which gave rise to the writing of **prescriptive grammars**.

With the rise of capitalism, a new middle class emerged who wanted their children to speak the dialect of the "upper" classes. This desire led to the publication of many prescriptive grammars. In 1762, an influential grammar, *A Short Introduction to English Grammar with Critical Notes*, was written by Bishop Robert Lowth. Lowth, influenced by Latin grammar, logic, and personal preference, prescribed a number of new rules for English. Before the publication of his grammar, practically everyone — upper-class, middle-class, and lower-class speakers of English — said *I don't have none, You was wrong about that,* and *Mathilda is fatter than me.* Lowth, however, decided that "two negatives make a positive" and therefore that one should say *I don't have any;* that even when *you* is singular it should be followed by the plural *were;* and that *I* not *me, he* not *him, they* not *them,* and so forth, should follow *than* in comparative constructions. Many of these prescriptive rules were based on Latin grammar, which had already given way to different rules in the languages that developed from Latin. Because Lowth was influential and because the rising new class wanted to speak "properly," many of these new rules were legislated into English grammar, at least for the **prestige dialect**.

The view that dialects that regularly use double negatives are inferior cannot be justified if one looks at the standard dialects of other languages in the world. Romance languages, for example, commonly utilize double negatives, as in Italian: *Non voglio parlare con nessuno,* literally, "not I-want to-speak with no-one" (i.e., "I don't want to speak with anyone.")

Grammars such as Lowth's — with their appeal to Latin, logic, and writing — are different from the descriptive grammars we have been discussing. Their goal is not to describe the rules people know but to tell them what rules they should know.

In 1908, a grammarian, Thomas R. Lounsbury, wrote that "There seems to have been in every period in the past, as there is now, a distinct apprehension in the minds of very many worthy persons that the English tongue is always in the condition approaching collapse and that arduous efforts must be put forth persistently to save it from destruction."

Today our bookstores are filled with books by language "purists" attempting to do just that. Edwin Newman, for example, in his books *Strictly Speaking* and *A Civil Tongue*, rails against those who use the word *hopefully* to mean "I hope," as in "Hopefully, it will not rain tomorrow," instead of using it "properly" to mean "with hope." What Newman fails to recognize is that language changes in the course of time and that words change meaning, and the meaning of *hopefully* has been broadened for most English speakers to include both usages. Incidentally, neither "I hope" nor "with hope" captures the useful sense of this sentence adverb (like *incidentally*, incidentally) in making a hopeful prediction (*I say/pray hopefully . . .*). Other "saviours" of the English language blame television, the schools, and even teachers of English for failing to preserve the standard language, and they mount attacks against those college and university professors who suggest that other dialects are viable, living, complete languages. The authors of this textbook would clearly be among those criticized by these new prescriptivists.

There is even a literary organization in the United States dedicated to the proper use of the English language, called the Unicorn Society of Lake Superior State College, that issues an annual "dishonour list" of words and phrases of which the members do not approve, including the word *medication*, which they say "We can no longer afford. It's too expensive. We've got to get back to the cheaper 'medicine' " (*Los Angeles Times* 1978). At least these guardians of the English language have a sense of humour; but they as well as the other prescriptivists are bound to fail. Language is vigorous and dynamic and constantly changing. All languages and dialects are expressive, complete, and logical, as much so as they were 200 or 2000 years ago. If sentences are muddled, it is not because of the language but because of the speakers. Prescriptivists should be concerned more about the thinking of the speakers than about the language they use. Hopefully, this book will convince you of this idea.

Linguists object to prescriptivism for a number of reasons. Prescriptivists assume that one variety of language has an inherently higher value than others and that it ought to be imposed on all speakers of the language. The variety favoured in this way is the standard written language, especially as found in literature. This standard formal written variety is then considered "correct," and all other varieties, such as informal spoken English, are considered "incorrect," no matter how appropriate for the occasion that variety might be (Crystal 1987). Prescriptivists, for the most part, seem to have little knowledge of the history of the language and less about the nature of language. They seem to be unaware of the fact that all dialects are rule-governed and that what is grammatical in one language may be ungrammatical in another (equally prestigious) language.

The **standard** dialect may indeed be a better dialect for someone wishing to obtain a particular job or achieve a position of social prestige, but linguistically it is not a better form of the language.

Teaching Grammars and Reference Grammars

The descriptive grammar of a language attempts to describe everything speakers know about their language. It is different from a **teaching grammar**, which is used to learn another language or dialect. Teaching grammars are those we use in school to fulfil language requirements. They can be helpful to those who do not speak the standard or prestige dialect but find it would be advantageous socially and economically to do so. Teaching grammars state explicitly the rules of the language, list the words and their pronunciations, and aid in learning a new language or dialect. It is often difficult for adults to learn a second language without being instructed, even when living for an extended period in a country where the language is spoken. Teaching grammars assume that the student already knows one language and compare the grammar of the target language with the grammar of the native language. The meaning of a word is given by providing a **gloss** — the parallel word in the student's native language, such as *maison*, "house" in French. It is assumed that the student knows the meaning of the gloss "house" and so the meaning of the word *maison*.

Sounds of the target language that do not occur in the native language are often described by reference to known sounds. Thus, the student might be aided in producing the French sound *u* in the word *tu* by instructions such as "Round your lips while producing the vowel sound in *tea*."

The rules on how to put words together to form grammatical sentences also refer to the learners' knowledge of their native language. Thus, the teaching grammar *Learn Zulu* by Sibusiso Nyembezi states that "The difference between singular and plural is not at the end of the word but at the beginning of it" and warns that "Zulu does not have the indefinite and definite articles 'a' and 'the.'" Such statements assume that students know the rules of English. Although such grammars might be considered prescriptive in the sense that they attempt to teach the student what is or is not a grammatical construction in the new language, their aim is different from grammars that attempt to change the rules or usage of a language already learned.

Another kind of grammar that might be mentioned here is a **reference grammar**, which tries to be as comprehensive as possible so that it might serve as a reference for those interested in establishing grammatical facts (Crystal 1987). Examples include several great European grammars of English, especially Otto Jespersen's seven-volume *Modern English Grammar on Historical Principles* (1909–49) and the monumental English grammar of Randolph Quirk et al., *A Comprehensive Grammar of the English Language* (1985), some 1779 pages in length.

This book is not primarily concerned with either prescriptive or teaching grammars. The matter is considered in Chapter 7, however, in the discussion of standard and non-standard dialects.

Language Universals

In a grammar there are parts which pertain to all languages; these components form what is called the general grammar. In addition to these general (universal) parts, there are those which belong only to one particular language; and these constitute the particular grammars of each language.

Du Marsais (c. 1750)

The way we are using the word *grammar* differs in another way from its most common meaning. In our sense, the grammar includes everything speakers know about their language — the sound system, called **phonology**; the system of meanings, called **semantics**; the rules of word formation, called **morphology**; and the rules of sentence formation, called **syntax**. It also, of course, includes the vocabulary of words — the dictionary or **lexicon**. Some people think that the word *grammar* applies primarily to morphology and claim that Latin has "more grammar" than English because of its many grammatical endings (inflections). Still others think of the grammar of a language as referring solely to the syntactic rules. This latter sense is what students usually mean when they talk about "English grammar."

Our aim is more in keeping with that stated in 1784 by John Fell in his *Essay towards an English Grammar*: "It is certainly the business of a grammarian to find out, and not to make, the laws of a language." This business is just what the linguist attempts — to find out the laws of a language and the laws that pertain to all languages. Those laws that pertain to all human languages, representing the universal properties of language, constitute a **Universal Grammar**.

About 1630, J.H. Alsted, a German philosopher, first used the term *general grammar* as distinct from special grammar. He believed that the function of a general grammar was to reveal those features "which relate to the method and etiology of grammatical concepts. They are common to all languages." Pointing out that "general grammar is the pattern 'norma' of every particular grammar whatsoever," he implored "eminent linguists to employ their insight in this matter" (Salmon 1969).

Three and a half centuries before Alsted, Robert Kilwardby held that linguists should be concerned with discovering the nature of language in general. So concerned was Kilwardby with universal grammar that he excluded considerations of the characteristics of particular languages, which he believed to be as "irrelevant to a science of grammar as the material of the measuring rod or the physical characteristics of objects were to geometry" (Salmon 1969). Kilwardby was perhaps too much of a universalist; the particular properties of individual languages are relevant to the discovery of language universals, and they are of interest for their own sake.

Someone attempting to study Latin, Greek, French, or Swahili as a second language may assert, in frustration, that those ancient scholars were so hidden in their ivory towers that they confused reality with idle speculation; yet the more we investigate this question, the more evidence accumulates to support Chomsky's view that there is a universal grammar that is part of the human biologically endowed **language faculty**. It may be thought of "as a system of principles which characterizes the class of possible grammars by specifying how particular grammars are organized (what are the components and their relations), how the different rules of these components are constructed, how they interact, and so on" (Chomsky 1979).

To discover the nature of this universal grammar whose principles characterize all human languages is the major aim of **linguistic theory**. The linguist's goal is to discover the "laws of human language," as the physicist's goal is to discover the "laws of the physical universe." The complexity of language, a product of the human brain, undoubtedly means that this goal will never be fully achieved. But all scientific theories are incomplete; new hypotheses are proposed to account for more data. Theories are continually changing as new discoveries are made. Just as Newtonian physics was enlarged by Einsteinian physics, so the linguistic theory of universal grammar develops, and new discoveries, some of which are discussed in this book, shed new light on what human language is.

Sign Languages: Evidence for Language Universals

> It is not the want of organs that [prevents animals from making] . . . known their thoughts . . . for it is evident that magpies and parrots are able to utter words just like ourselves, and yet they cannot speak as we do, that is, so as to give evidence that they think of what they say. On the other hand, men who, being born deaf and mute . . . are destitute of the organs which serve the others for talking, are in the habit of themselves inventing certain signs by which they make themselves understood.
>
> René Descartes, *Discourse on Method*

The **sign languages** of the deaf provide some of the best evidence to support the notion that humans are born with the ability to acquire language and that these languages are governed by the same universal properties.

Deaf children, who are unable to hear the sounds of spoken language, do not acquire spoken languages as hearing children do. However, deaf children of deaf parents who are exposed to sign language learn it in stages parallel to language acquisition by hearing children learning oral languages. These sign languages are human languages that do not utilize sounds to express meanings. Instead, sign languages are visual–gestural systems that use hand and body gestures as the forms used to represent words. Sign languages are fully developed languages, and those who know sign language are capable of creating and comprehending an unlimited number of new sentences, just like speakers of spoken languages.

Current research on sign languages has been crucial in the attempt to understand the biological underpinnings of human language acquisition and use. Some understanding of sign languages is therefore essential.

About one in a thousand babies is born deaf or with a severe hearing deficiency. One major effect is the difficulty the deaf have in learning a spoken language. It is nearly impossible for those unable to hear language to learn to speak naturally. Normal speech depends to a great extent on constant auditory feedback. Hence, a deaf child will not learn to speak without extensive training in schools or programs designed especially for them.

Although deaf persons can be taught to speak a language intelligibly, they can never understand speech as well as a hearing person can. Seventy-five percent of the words spoken cannot be read on the lips with any degree of accuracy. The ability of many deaf individuals to comprehend spoken language is therefore remarkable; they combine lip reading with a knowledge of the structure of language, as well as an awareness of semantic redundancies in language.

If, however, human language is universal in the sense that all members of the human species have the ability to learn a language, then it is not surprising that non-spoken languages have developed as a substitute for spoken languages among non-hearing individuals. The more we learn about the human linguistic ability, the clearer it is that language acquisition and use are dependent not on the ability to produce and hear sounds but on a much more abstract cognitive ability, biologically determined, that accounts for the similarities between spoken and sign languages.

American Sign Language (ASL)

The major language used by the deaf in North America is **American Sign Language** (or **ASL** or **AMESLAN**). ASL is an independent, fully developed language that is an outgrowth of the sign language used in France and brought to the United States in 1817 by the great educator Thomas Hopkins Gallaudet. Gallaudet was hired to establish a school for the deaf, and, after studying the language and methods used in the Paris school founded by the Abbé de l'Epée in 1775, he returned to the United States with Laurent Clerc, a young deaf instructor, and established the basis for ASL.

ASL, like all human languages, has its own grammar that includes everything signers know about their language — the system of gestures equivalent to the phonology of a spoken language, the morphological, syntactic, and semantic systems, and a mental lexicon of signs. The term *phonology*, first used to describe the sound systems of language, has here been extended to include the gestural systems of sign languages.

The other sign language used in North America is called **Signed English** (or **Siglish**). Essentially, it consists of the replacement of each spoken English word (and grammatical elements such as the -*s* ending for plurals or the -*ed* ending for past tense) by a sign. The syntax and semantics of Signed English are thus approximately the same as those of ordinary English. The result is unnatural in that it is similar to speaking French by translating every English word or ending into its French counterpart. Problems result because there are not always corresponding forms in the two languages.

If there is no sign in ASL, signers utilize another mechanism, the system of **finger spelling**. This method is also used to add new proper nouns or technical vocabulary. Sign interpreters of spoken English often finger spell such words. A manual alphabet consisting of various finger configurations, hand positions, and movements gives visible symbols for the alphabet and ampersand.

Signs, however, are produced differently than are finger-spelled words. "The sign DECIDE cannot be analyzed as a sequence of distinct, separable configurations of the hand. Like all other lexical signs in ASL, but unlike the individual finger-spelled letters in D-E-C-I-D-E taken separately, the ASL sign DECIDE does have an essential movement, but the hand shape occurs simultaneously with the movement. In appearance, the sign is a continuous whole" (Klima and Bellugi 1979). This sign is shown in Figure 1.2.

FIGURE 1.2

The ASL sign DECIDE. (a) and (c) show transitions from the sign; (b) illustrates the single downward movement of the sign.

transition   sign   transition
a.   b.   c.

Reprinted by permission of Harvard University Press from *The Signs of Language* by E.S. Klima and U. Bellugi. Cambridge, MA: Harvard University Press. Copyright © 1979 by the President and Fellows of Harvard College.

An accomplished signer can sign at a normal rate, even when there is a lot of finger spelling. Television stations sometimes have programs that are interpreted in sign in a corner of the TV screen. If you have ever seen such a program, you may have noted how well the interpreter kept pace with the spoken sentences.

Language arts are not lost to the deaf. Poetry is composed in sign language, and stage plays such as Richard Brinsley Sheridan's *The Critic* (1779) have been translated into sign language and acted by the National Theatre of the Deaf (NTD).

Animal "Languages"

> No matter how eloquently a dog may bark, he cannot tell you that his parents were poor but honest.
>
> Bertrand Russell

Whether language is the exclusive property of the human species is an interesting question. The idea of talking animals probably is as old and as widespread among human societies as is language itself. No culture lacks a legend in which some animal plays a speaking role. All over West Africa, children listen to folk tales in which a "spider-man" is the hero. "Coyote" is a favourite figure in many Native North American tales, and there is hardly an animal who does not figure in Aesop's famous fables. Hugh Lofting's fictional Doctor Doolittle's major accomplishment is his ability to communicate with animals.

If language is viewed only as a system of **communication**, then many species communicate. Humans also use systems other than language to relate to each other and to send "messages." The question is whether the kinds of grammars that represent linguistic knowledge acquired by children with no external instruction, and that are used creatively rather than as responses to internal or external stimuli, are unique to the human animal.

"Talking" Parrots

Most humans who acquire language utilize speech sounds to express meanings, but such sounds are not a necessary aspect of language, as evidenced by sign language. The use of speech sounds is therefore not a basic part of what we have been calling language. The chirping of birds, the squeaking of dolphins, and the dancing of bees may potentially represent systems similar to human languages. If animal communication systems are not like human language, it is not due to a lack of speech.

Conversely, when animals vocally imitate human utterances, it does not mean they possess language. Language is a system that relates sounds (or gestures) to meanings. "Talking" birds such as parrots and mynah birds are capable of faithfully reproducing words and phrases of human language that they have heard; but when a parrot says "Polly wants a cracker," she may really want a ham sandwich or a drink of water or nothing at all. A bird that has learned to say "hello" or "goodbye" is as likely to use one as the other, regardless of whether people are arriving or departing. The bird's utterances carry no meaning. The birds are speaking neither English nor their own language when they sound like us.

Talking birds do not dissect the sounds of their imitations into discrete units. *Polly* and *Molly* do not rhyme for a parrot. They are as different as *hello* and *goodbye* (or as similar). One property of all human languages (discussed further in Chapter 5) is the discreteness of the speech or gestural units, which are ordered and reordered, combined and split apart. Generally, a parrot says what it is taught, or what it hears, and no more. If Polly learns "Polly wants a cracker" and "Polly wants a doughnut" and learns to imitate the single words *whiskey* and *bagel*, she will not spontaneously produce, as children do, "Polly wants whiskey" or "Polly wants a bagel" or "Polly wants whiskey and a bagel." If she learns *cat* and *cats* and *dog* and *dogs* and then learns the word *parrot*, she will be unable to form the plural *parrots*, as children do by the age of three; nor can a parrot form an unlimited set of utterances from a finite set of units or understand utterances never heard before. Recent reports of an African grey parrot named Alex studied by Dr. Irene M. Pepperberg of the University of Arizona suggest that new methods of training may result in more learning than was previously believed possible. When the trainer uses words in context, Alex seems to relate some sounds with their meanings. This is more than simply imitation, but it is not in any way similar to the way children acquire the complexities of the grammar of any language. It is more like a dog learning to associate certain sounds with meanings, such as *heel, sit, fetch,* et cetera. Alex's ability may go somewhat beyond that. Therefore, the ability to produce sounds similar to those used in human language, even if meanings are related to these sounds, cannot be equated with the ability to acquire the complex grammar of a human language.

The Birds and the Bees

> The birds and animals are all friendly to each other, and there are no disputes about anything. They all talk, and they all talk to me, but it must be a foreign language for I cannot make out a word they say.
>
> Mark Twain, Eve's Diary

Most animals possess some kind of "signalling" communication system. Among spiders, there is a complex system for courtship. The male spider, before he approaches his lady love, goes through an elaborate series of gestures to inform her that he is indeed a spider and not a crumb or a fly to be eaten. These gestures are invariant. One never finds a creative spider changing or adding to the particular courtship ritual of his species.

A similar kind of gesture language is found among fiddler crabs. There are 40 different varieties, and each variety uses its own particular claw-waving movement to signal to another member of its "clan." The timing, movement, and posture of the body never change from one time to another or from one crab to another within the particular variety. Whatever the signal means, it is fixed. Only one meaning can be conveyed. There is not an infinite set of fiddler crab sentences.

The imitative sounds of talking birds have little in common with human language, but the calls and songs of many species of birds do have a communicative function, and they resemble human languages in that there may be "dialects" within the same species. **Bird calls** (consisting of one or more short notes) convey messages associated with the immediate environment, such as danger, feeding, nesting, and flocking. **Bird songs** (more complex patterns of notes) are used to stake out territory and to attract mates. There is no evidence of any internal structure to these songs, nor can they be segmented into independently meaningful parts as words of human language can be. In a study of the territorial song of the European robin, it was discovered that rival robins paid attention only to the alternation between high-pitched and low-pitched notes, and which came first did not matter (Busnel and Bremond 1962). The message varies only to the extent of how strongly the robin feels about its possession and to what extent it is prepared to defend it and start a family in that territory. The different alternations therefore express intensity and nothing more. The robin is creative in its ability to sing the same thing in many different ways but not creative in its ability to use the same units of the system to express many different messages with different meanings.

Despite certain superficial similarities to human language, bird calls and songs are fundamentally different kinds of communicative systems. The number of messages that can be conveyed is finite, and messages are stimulus controlled.

This distinction is also true of the system of communication used by honeybees. For a long time, it has been believed that a forager bee is able to return to the hive and tell other bees where a source of food is located. It does so by forming a dance on a wall of the hive that reveals the location and quality of the food source. For one species of Italian honeybee, the dancing behaviour may assume one of three possible patterns: round (which indicates locations near the hive, within six metres or so), sickle (which indicates locations at six to eighteen metres from the hive), and tail-wagging (for distances that exceed eighteen metres). The number of repetitions per minute of the basic pattern in the tail-wagging dance indicates the precise distance; the slower the rate of repetition, the longer the distance.

The dance is an effective system of communication for bees. It is capable, in principle, of infinitely many different messages, like human language; but unlike human language, the system is confined to a single subject — distance from the hive. The inflexibility was shown by an experimenter who forced a bee to walk to the food source. When the bee returned to the hive, it indicated a distance 25 times farther away than the food source actually was. The bee had no way of communicating the special circumstances in its message. This absence of creativity makes the bees' dance qualitatively different from human language (Von Frisch 1967).

In the seventeenth century, the philosopher and mathematician René Descartes pointed out that the communication systems of animals are qualitatively different from the languages used by humans:

> It is a very remarkable fact that there are none so depraved and stupid, without even excepting idiots, that they cannot arrange different words together, forming of them a statement by which they make known their thoughts; while, on the other hand, there is no other animal, however perfect and fortunately circumstanced it may be, which can do the same. (Descartes 1967)

Descartes goes on to state that one of the major differences between humans and animals is that human use of language is not just a response to external, or even internal, emotional stimuli, as are the sounds and gestures of animals. He warns against confusing human use of language with "natural movements which betray passions and may be . . . manifested by animals."

To hold that animals communicate by systems qualitatively different from human language systems is not to claim human superiority. Humans are not inferior to the one-celled amoeba because they cannot reproduce by splitting in two; they are just different sexually. All the studies of animal communication systems, including those of chimpanzees (discussed in Chapter 10), provide evidence for Descartes's distinction between other animal communication systems and the linguistic creative ability possessed by the human animal.

In the Beginning: The Origin of Language

> Nothing, no doubt, would be more interesting than to know from historical documents the exact process by which the first man began to lisp his first words, and thus to be rid for ever of all the theories on the origin of speech.

M. Muller (1871)

If language is unique to our species, then a natural question is how it arose. All religions and mythologies contain stories of language origin. Philosophers through the ages have argued the question. Scholarly works have been written on the subject. Prizes have been awarded for the "best answer" to this eternally perplexing problem. Theories of divine origin, evolutionary development, and language as a human invention have all been suggested.

The difficulties inherent in answering this question are immense. Anthropologists think that the species has existed for at least one million years and perhaps for as long as five or six million years. But the earliest deciphered written records are barely six thousand years old, dating from the writings of the Sumerians of 4000 B.C.E. These records appear so late in the history of the development of language that they provide no clue to its origin.

For these reasons, scholars in the latter part of the nineteenth century, who were only interested in "hard science," ridiculed, ignored, and even banned discussions of language origin. In 1886, the Linguistic Society of Paris passed a resolution "outlawing" any papers concerned with this subject.

Despite the difficulty of finding scientific evidence, speculations on language origin have provided valuable insights into the nature and development of language, which led Otto Jespersen (1964 [1921]) to remind us that "linguistic science cannot refrain forever from asking about the whence (and about the whither) of linguistic evolution." A brief look at some of these notions will reveal something of both the difficulty and the value in such speculations.

God's Gift to Humanity?

> And out of the ground the Lord God formed every beast of the field, and every fowl of the air, and brought them unto Adam to see what he would call them; and whatsoever Adam called every living creature, that was the name thereof.
>
> Genesis 2:19

According to Judeo–Christian beliefs, God gave Adam the power to name all things. Similar beliefs are found throughout the world. According to the Egyptians, the creator of speech was the god Thoth. Babylonians believed the language giver was the god Nabu, and the Hindus attributed our unique language ability to a female god; Brahma was the creator of the universe, but language was given to us by his wife, Sarasvati.

Belief in the divine origin of language is closely intertwined with the magical properties that have been associated with language and the spoken word. Children in all cultures utter "magic" words such as *abracadabra* to ward off evil or bring good luck. Despite the childish jingle "Sticks and stones may break my bones, but names will never hurt me," name-calling is insulting, cause for legal punishment, and feared. In some cultures, when certain words are used, one is required to counter them by "knocking on wood."

In many religions, only special languages may be used in prayers and rituals. The Hindu priests of the fifth century B.C.E. believed that the original pronunciations of Vedic Sanskrit had to be used. This led to important linguistic study, since their language had already changed greatly since the hymns of the Vedas had been composed. The first linguist known to us is Panini, who, in the fourth century B.C.E., wrote a detailed grammar of Sanskrit in which the phonological rules revealed the earlier pronunciation for use in religious worship.

While myths and customs and superstitions do not tell us very much about language origin, they do tell us about the importance ascribed to language.

There is no way to prove or disprove the divine origin of language, just as one cannot argue scientifically for or against the existence of God.

The First Language

Imagine the Lord talking French! Aside from a few odd words in Hebrew, I took it completely for granted that God had never spoken anything but the most dignified English.

Clarence Day, *Life with Father*

Among the proponents of the divine origin theory, a great interest arose in the language used by God, Adam, and Eve. For millennia, experiments have reportedly been devised to verify particular theories of the first language. In the fifth century B.C.E., the Greek historian Herodotus reported that the Egyptian Pharaoh Psammetichus (664–610 B.C.E.) sought to determine the most primitive "natural" language by experimental methods. The monarch was said to have placed two infants in an isolated mountain hut, to be cared for by a mute servant. The pharaoh believed that without any linguistic input the children would develop their own language and would thus reveal the original human language. The Egyptian waited patiently for the children to become old enough to talk. According to the story, the first word uttered was *bekos*, the word for "bread" in Phrygian, the language spoken in a province of Phrygia in the northwest corner of what is now modern Turkey. This ancient language, which has long since died out, was thought, on the basis of this "experiment," to be the original language.

History is replete with other proposals. In the thirteenth century, the Holy Roman Emperor Frederick II of Hohenstaufen was said to have carried out a similar test, but the children died before they uttered a single word. James IV of Scotland (1473–1513), however, supposedly succeeded in replicating the experiment with the surprising results, according to legend, that the Scottish children "spak very guid Ebrew," providing "scientific evidence" that Hebrew was the language used in the Garden of Eden.

But J.G. Becanus in the sixteenth century argued that German must have been the primeval language, since God would have used the most perfect language. In 1830, Noah Webster asserted that the "proto-language" must have been Chaldee (Aramaic), the language spoken in Jerusalem during the time of Jesus. In 1887, Joseph Elkins maintained that "there is no other language which can be more reasonably assumed to be the speech first used in the world's gray morning than can Chinese."

The belief that all languages originated from a single source — the **monogenetic theory of language origin** — is found not only in the Tower of Babel story in Genesis but also in a similar legend of the Toltecs, early inhabitants of Mexico, and in the myths of other peoples as well.

Clearly, we are no farther along in discovering the original language (or languages) than was Psammetichus, given the obscurities of prehistory.

Human Invention or the Cries of Nature?

> Language was born in the courting days of mankind; the first utterances of speech I fancy to myself like something between the nightly love lyrics of puss upon the tiles and the melodious love songs of the nightingale.
>
> Otto Jespersen, *Language: Its Nature, Development, and Origin*

The Greeks speculated about everything in the universe, including language. The earliest surviving linguistic treatise that deals with the origin and nature of language is Plato's *Cratylus*. A common view among the classical Greeks, expressed by Socrates in this dialogue, was that at some ancient time there was a "legislator" who gave the correct, natural name to everything and that words echoed the essence of their meanings.

Despite all the contrary evidence, the idea that the earliest form of language was imitative, or "echoic," was proposed up to the twentieth century. Called the *bow-wow* theory, it claimed that a dog would be designated by the word *bow-wow* because of the sounds of its bark.

A parallel view states that language at first consisted of emotional ejaculations of pain, fear, surprise, pleasure, anger, and so on. That the earliest manifestations of language were "cries of nature" was proposed by Jean-Jacques Rousseau in the middle of the eighteenth century.

Another hypothesis suggests that language arose out of the rhythmical grunts of people working together. A more charming view was suggested by Jespersen, who proposed that language derived from song as an expressive rather than a communicative need, with love being the greatest stimulus for language development.

Just as with the beliefs in a divine origin of language, these proposals are untestable. Other approaches to the evolution of language as part of the science of biology are discussed in Chapter 11.

What We Know about Language

There are many things we do not yet know about human languages, their origins, structures, and use. The science of linguistics is concerned with these questions. The investigations of linguists throughout history and the analysis of spoken languages date back at least to 1600 B.C.E. in Mesopotamia. We have learned a great deal since that time. A number of facts pertaining to all languages can now be stated.

1. Wherever humans exist, language exists.
2. There are no "primitive" languages — all languages are equally complex and equally capable of expressing any idea in the universe. The vocabulary of any language can be expanded to include new words for new concepts.
3. All languages change over time.
4. The relationships between the sounds and meanings of spoken languages and between the gestures and meanings of sign language are for the most part arbitrary.
5. All human languages utilize a finite set of discrete sounds (or gestures) that are combined to form meaningful elements or words, which themselves form an infinite set of possible sentences.
6. All grammars contain rules for the formation of words and sentences of a similar kind.
7. Every spoken language includes discrete sound segments such as *p, n,* or *a* that can all be defined by a finite set of sound properties or features. Every spoken language has a class of vowels and a class of consonants.
8. Similar grammatical categories (e.g., noun, verb) are found in all languages.
9. There are semantic universals, such as "male" or "female," "animate" or "human," found in every language in the world.
10. Every language has a way of referring to past time, negating, forming questions, issuing commands, and so on.
11. Speakers of all languages are capable of producing and comprehending an infinite set of sentences. Syntactic universals reveal that every language has a way of forming sentences such as the following:

    Linguistics is an interesting subject.
    I know that linguistics is an interesting subject.
    You know that I know that linguistics is an interesting subject.
    Cecilia knows that you know that I know that linguistics is an interesting subject.
    Is it a fact that Cecilia knows that you know that I know that linguistics is an interesting subject?

12. Any normal child, born anywhere in the world, of any racial, geographical, social, or economic heritage, is capable of learning any language to which he or she is exposed. The differences we find among languages cannot be due to biological reasons.

It seems that Alsted and De Marsais — like many other universalists from all ages — were not spinning idle thoughts. We all speak "human language."

Summary

We are all intimately familiar with at least one language — our own. Yet few of us ever stop to consider what we know when we know a language. There is no book that contains the English or Russian or Zulu language. The words of a language can be listed in a dictionary, but not all the sentences, and a language consists of sentences as well as words. Speakers use a finite set of rules to produce and understand an infinite set of possible sentences.

These rules comprise the **grammar** of a language, which is learned when you acquire the language and includes the sound system (the **phonology**), the structure of words (the **morphology**), how words may be combined into phrases and sentences (the **syntax**), the ways in which sounds and meanings are related (the **semantics**), and the words or **lexicon**. The sounds and meanings of these words are related in an **arbitrary** fashion. If you had never heard the word *syntax*, you would not, by its sounds, know what it meant. The gestures used by deaf signers are also arbitrarily related to their meanings. Language, then, is a system that relates sounds (or hand and body gestures) to meanings; when you know a language, you know this system.

This knowledge (linguistic **competence**) is different from behaviour (linguistic **performance**). If you woke one morning and decided to stop talking (as the Trappist monks did after they took a "vow of silence"), you would still have knowledge of your language. This ability or competence underlies linguistic behaviour. If you do not know the language, you cannot speak it; but if you know the language, you may choose not to speak it.

Grammars are of different kinds. The **descriptive grammar** of a language represents the unconscious linguistic knowledge or capacity of its speakers. Such a grammar is a model of the **mental grammar** every speaker of the language knows. It does not teach the rules of the language; it describes the rules that are already known. A grammar that attempts to legislate what your grammar should be is called a **prescriptive grammar**. It prescribes; it does not describe, except incidentally. **Teaching grammars** are written to help people learn a foreign language or a dialect of their own language. **Reference grammars** are written to help people find out the grammatical facts of a language.

The more linguists investigate the thousands of languages of the world and describe the ways in which they differ from one another, the more they discover that these differences are limited. There are linguistic universals that pertain to all parts of grammars, the ways in which these parts are related, and the forms of rules. These principles comprise **Universal Grammar**, which forms the basis of the specific grammars of all possible human languages.

If language is defined merely as a system of communication, then language is not unique to humans. There are, however, certain characteristics of human language not found in the communication systems of any other species. A basic property of human language is its **creative aspect** — a speaker's ability to combine the basic linguistic units to form an *infinite* set of "well-formed" grammatical sentences, most of which are novel, never before produced or heard.

The fact that deaf children learn **sign language** shows that the ability to hear or produce sounds is not a necessary prerequisite for language learning. All the sign languages in the world, which differ as spoken languages do, are visual–gestural systems that are as fully developed and as structurally complex as spoken languages. The major sign language used in North America is **American Sign Language** (also referred to as **ASL** or **AMESLAN**). Talking birds imitate sounds but cannot segment these sounds into smaller units, understand what they are imitating, or produce new utterances to convey their thoughts.

Birds, bees, crabs, spiders, and most other creatures communicate in some way, but the information imparted is severely limited and stimulus-bound, confined to a small set of messages. The system of language represented by intricate mental grammars, which are not stimulus-bound and which generate infinite messages, is unique to the human species.

The idea that language was God's gift to humanity is found in religions throughout the world. The continuing belief in the miraculous powers of language is tied to this notion. The assumption of the divine origin of language stimulated interest in discovering the first primeval language. There are legendary "experiments" in which children were kept in isolation in the belief that their first words would reveal the original language.

Opposing views suggest that language is a human invention. The Greeks believed that an ancient "legislator" gave the true names to all things. Others have suggested that language developed from "cries of nature," "early gestures," **onomatopoeic** words, or even songs to express love.

All of these proposals are untestable. The cooperative efforts of linguists and evolutionary biologists and neurologists may in time provide some answers to this intriguing question. Because of linguistic research throughout history, we have learned much about Universal Grammar, the properties shared by all languages.

Exercises

1. An English speaker's knowledge includes the sound sequences of the language. When new products are put on the market, the manufacturers have to think up new names for them that conform to the allowable sound patterns. Suppose you were hired by a manufacturer of soap products to name five new products. What names might you come up with? List them.

   We are not interested in the spelling of the words but in how they are pronounced. Therefore, describe in any way you can how the words you list should be pronounced. Suppose, for example, you named one soap powder *Blick*. You could describe the sounds in any of the following ways:

   bl as in *blood*, *i* as in *pit*, *ck* as in *stick*
   bli as in *bliss*, *ck* as in *tick*
   b as in *boy*, *lick* as in *lick*

*2. Consider the following sentences. Put an asterisk (*) before those that do not seem to conform to the rules of your grammar, that are ungrammatical for you. State, if you can, why you think the sentence is ungrammatical.

   a.   Robin forced the sheriff go.
   b.   Napoleon forced Josephine to go.

   c. The Devil made Faust go.
   d. He passed by a large sum of money.
   e. He came by a large sum of money.
   f. He came a large sum of money by.
   g. Did in a corner little Jack Horner sit?
   h. Elizabeth is resembled by Charles.
   i. Nancy is eager to please.
   j. It is easy to frighten Emily.
   k. It is eager to love a kitten.
   l. That birds can fly amazes.
   m. The fact that you are late to class is surprising.
   n. Has the nurse slept the baby yet?
   o. I was surprised for you to get married.
   p. I wonder who and Mary went swimming.
   q. Myself bit John.

3. We pointed out in this chapter that a small set of words in languages may be onomatopoeic — that is, their sounds "imitate" what they refer to. *Ding-dong, tick-tock, bang, zing, swish,* and *plop* are such words in English. Construct a list of ten new words. Test them on at least five friends to see if they are truly "non-arbitrary" as to sound and meaning.

4. Although sounds and meanings of most words in all languages are arbitrarily related, there are some communication systems in which the "signs" unambiguously reveal their "meaning."

   a. Describe (or draw) five different signs that directly show what they mean. Example: a road sign indicating an S curve.
   b. Describe any other communication system that, like language, consists of arbitrary symbols. Example: traffic signals, where red means stop and green means go.

5. Consider these two statements:

I learned a new word today.
I learned a new sentence today.

Do you think the two statements are equally probable? If not, why not?

6. What do the barking of dogs, the meowing of cats, and the singing of birds have in common with human language? What are some of the basic differences?

7. A wolf is able to express subtle gradations of emotion by different positions of the ears, the lips, and the tail. There are eleven postures of the tail that express emotions, such as self-confidence, confident threat, lack of tension, uncertain threat, depression, defensiveness, active submission, and complete

submission. This system seems to be complex. Suppose there were a thousand different emotions that the wolf could express in this way. Would you then say the wolf had a language similar to a human's? If not, why not?

8. Suppose you taught a dog to *heel, sit up, beg, roll over, play dead, stay, jump,* and *bark* on command, using the italicized words as cues. Would you be teaching it language? Why or why not?

9. State a "rule of grammar" that you have learned is the "correct" way to say something but that you do not generally use in speaking. For example, you may have heard that *It's me* is incorrect and that the correct form is *It's I.* Nevertheless, you always use *me* in such sentences, your friends do also, and, in fact, *It's I* sounds odd to you.

   Write a short essay presenting arguments against someone who tells you that you are wrong. Discuss how this disagreement demonstrates the difference between descriptive and prescriptive grammars.

Works Cited

Busnel, R.G., and J. Bremond. 1962. "Recherche du support de l'information dans le signal acoustique de défense territoriale de rougegorge." *C.R. Acad. Sci. Paris* 254: 2236–38.

Chomsky, Noam. 1979. *Language and Responsibility.* New York: Pantheon.

Crystal, David. 1987. *The Cambridge Encyclopedia of Language.* Cambridge, UK: Cambridge University Press.

Descartes, René. 1967. "Discourse on Method." In *The Philosophical Works of Descartes.* Vol. 1. Trans. by E.S. Haldane and G.R. Ross. Cambridge, UK: Cambridge University Press.

Jespersen, Otto. 1964. *Language: Its Nature, Development, and Origin.* 1921. Reprint. New York: W.W. Norton.

Klima, Edward S., and Ursula Bellugi. 1979. *The Signs of Language.* Cambridge, MA: Harvard University Press.

Los Angeles Times, 2 Jan. 1978, Part 1: 21.

Pinker, Steven. 1999. *Words and Rules: The Ingredients of Language.* London: Weidenfeld & Nicolson.

Salmon, V. 1969. "Review of *Cartesian Linguistics* by N. Chomsky." *Journal of Linguistics* 5: 165–87.

Von Frisch, K. 1967. *The Dance Language and Orientation of Bees.* Trans. by L.E. Chadwick. Cambridge, MA: Belknap Press of Harvard University Press.

Further Reading

Bolinger, Dwight. 1980. *Language — The Loaded Weapon: The Use and Abuse of Language Today.* London: Longman.

Chomsky, Noam. 1972. *Language and Mind.* Enlarged ed. New York: Harcourt Brace Jovanovich.

———. 1975. *Reflections on Language.* New York: Pantheon Books.

———. 1986. *Knowledge of Language: Its Nature, Origin, and Use.* New York: Praeger.

Crystal, David. 1984. *Who Cares about Usage?* New York: Penguin.

Gould, J.L., and C.G. Gould. 1983. "Can a Bee Behave Intelligently?" *New Scientist* 98: 84–87.

Hall, Robert A. 1950. *Leave Your Language Alone.* Ithaca, NY: Linguistica.

Jackendoff, Ray. 1994. *Patterns in the Mind: Language and Human Nature.* New York: Basic Books.

Lane, Harlan. 1984. *When the Mind Hears: A History of the Deaf.* New York: Random House.

Milroy, James, and Lesley Milroy. 1985. *Authority in Language: Investigating Language Prescription and Standardisation.* London: Routledge & Kegan Paul.

Newmeyer, Frederick J. 1983. *Grammatical Theory: Its Limits and Possibilities.* Chicago: University of Chicago Press.

Nunberg, Geoffrey. 1983. "The Decline of Grammar." *Atlantic Monthly*, Dec: 31–46.

Pinker, Steven. 1994. *The Language Instinct.* New York: William Morrow.

Safire, William. 1980. *On Age.* New York: Avon Books.

Sebeok, T.A., ed. 1977. *How Animals Communicate.* Bloomington: Indiana University Press.

Shopen, Timothy, and Joseph M. Williams, eds. 1980. *Standards and Dialects in English.* Rowley, MA: Newbury House.

Stam, J. 1976. *Inquiries into the Origin of Language: The Fate of a Question.* New York: Harper & Row.

Sternberg, Martin L.A. 1987. *American Sign Language Dictionary.* New York: Harper & Row.

Stokow, William. 1960. *Sign Language Structure: An Outline of the Visual Communication System of the American Deaf.* Silver Springs, MD: Linstok Press.

PART 2
Grammatical Aspects of Language

We may think of a grammar, represented somehow in the mind, as a system that specifies the phonetic, syntactic, and semantic properties of an infinite class of potential sentences. The child knows the language so determined by the grammar that . . . [has been] acquired. This grammar is a representation of . . . "intrinsic competence."

Noam Chomsky, "On Cognitive Structures and Their Development: A Reply to Piaget"

CHAPTER 2
Morphology: The Words of Language

A word is dead
When it is said,
Some say.
I say it just
Begins to live
That day.

Emily Dickinson, "A Word"

Every speaker of every language knows thousands of words, but none know all of the words of their native language. *Webster's Third International Dictionary of the English Language*, for example, has more than 450 000 entries, but it is estimated that the average high school graduate knows about 60 000 words. The university graduate should, we assume, know more words than that, including many in this book. It has been estimated that children of 6 know as many as 13 000 words. If they produced their first word at the age of 2, then they have learned 3250 words a year, an average of nine new words a day.

Words are an important part of linguistic knowledge and constitute a component of our mental grammars. But one can learn thousands of words in a language and still not know the language. Those who have tried to make themselves understood in a foreign country by simply using a dictionary know this to be true. On the other hand, without words we would be unable to convey our thoughts through language.

What is a word? What do you know when you know a word? Suppose you hear someone say *morpheme* and haven't the slightest idea what it means, and you don't know what the "smallest unit of linguistic meaning" is called. Then you don't know the word *morpheme*. A particular string of sounds must be united with a meaning, and a meaning must be united with specific sounds, in order for the sounds or the meaning to be a **word** in our mental dictionaries. Once you learn both the sounds and their related meaning, you know the word. It becomes an entry in your mental **lexicon** (the Greek word for *dictionary*).

Someone who doesn't know English would not know where one word begins or ends in an utterance such as *Thecatsatonthemat*. We separate written words by spaces, but in the spoken language there are no pauses between most words. Without knowledge of the language, one can't tell how many words are in an utterance. A speaker of English has no difficulty in segmenting the stream of sounds into six individual words: *the*, *cat*, *sat*, *on*, *the*, and *mat*. Similarly, a speaker of the American

Aboriginal language Potawatomi knows that *kwapmuknanuk* (which means "they see us") is just one word.

The lack of pauses between words in speech has provided humorists and songwriters with much material. During World War II, the chorus of one of the top ten tunes used this fact about speech to amuse us:

Mairzy doats and dozy doats   (Mares eat oats and does eat oats,
And liddle lamzy divey,   And little lambs eat ivy,
A kiddley-divey too,   A kid'll eat ivy too,
Wooden shoe?   Wouldn't you?)

The fact that the same sounds can be interpreted differently, even between languages, gave birth to an entertaining book. The title, *Mots d'heures: Gousses, rames* (see Van Rooten 1993), was derived from the fact that *Mother Goose Rhymes*, spoken in English, sounds to a French speaker like the French words meaning "Words of the Hours: Root, Branch." The first rhyme in French starts with

Un petit d'un petit
S'etonne aux Halles.

When interpreted as if it were English, it would sound like

Humpty dumpty
Sat on a wall.

This shows that in a particular language the form (sounds or pronunciation) and the meaning of a word are inseparable; they are like two sides of a coin. *Un petit d'un petit* in French means "a little one of a little one," but in English the sounds represent the name *Humpty Dumpty.*

Similarly, in English the sounds of the letters *bear* and *bare* represent four **homophones** (different words with the same sounds but different meanings), as shown in the following sentences:

She can't bear (tolerate) children.
She can't bear (give birth to) children.
Exit, pursued by a bear.
He stood there — bare and beautiful.

Couch, sofa, chesterfield, and *davenport,* though they have the same meaning, are called **synonyms** because they are represented by four different strings of sounds. The nineteenth-century Swiss linguist Ferdinand de Saussure (1916) pointed out the important principle of "the arbitrariness of the sign," the wholly conventional pairing of a sound (form) with a meaning (concept).

Sometimes we think we know a word even though we don't know what it means. It is hard to find an English speaker who hasn't heard the word *antidisestablishmentarianism,* and most will tell you that it is the longest word in the English language. Yet many of these persons are unsure about its meaning. According to the way we have defined what it means to "know a word" — pairing a string of sounds with a particular meaning — such individuals do not really know this word.

Information about the longest or shortest word in the language is not part of the linguistic knowledge of a language but general conceptual knowledge *about* a language. Children do not learn such facts the way they learn the sound–meaning correspondences of the words *of* their language. Both children and adults have to be told that *antidisestablishmentarianism* is the longest word in English or discover it through an analysis of a dictionary. Actually, should they wish to research this question, they would find that the longest word in *Webster's Seventh International Dictionary* is *pneumonoultramicroscopicsilicovolcanoconiosis*, a disease of the lungs. As we shall see in Chapter 10, children learn words such as *elephant, disappear, mother*, and all the other words they know without being taught them explicitly.

Since each word is a sound–meaning unit, each word stored in our mental dictionaries must be listed with its unique phonological representation, which determines its pronunciation, and with its meaning. For literate speakers, the spelling or **orthography** of most of the words we know is also in our lexicons.

Each word listed in your mental dictionary must include other information as well, such as whether it is a noun, a pronoun, a verb, an adjective, an adverb, a preposition, or a conjunction. That is, it must specify its **grammatical category** or **syntactic category**. You may not consciously know that a form such as *love* is listed as both a verb and a noun, but a speaker has such knowledge, as shown by the phrases *I love you* and *You are the love of my life*. If such information were not in your mental dictionary, you would not know how to form grammatical sentences or be able to distinguish grammatical from ungrammatical sentences. The classes of words, the syntactic categories — such as nouns, verbs, adjectives — and the semantic properties of words, which represent their meanings — will be discussed in later chapters. The semantic properties of words, which represent their meanings, will be discussed in Chapter 4.

Dictionaries

Dictionary, n. A malevolent literary device for cramping the growth of a language and making it hard and inelastic.

Ambrose Bierce, *The Devil's Dictionary*

B.C. by permission of Johnny Hart and Creators Syndicate, Inc.

The dictionaries that one buys in a bookstore contain some of the information found in our mental dictionaries. But this information appeared only gradually in the development of dictionaries (Landau 1984; Murray 1970). Dictionaries grew out of the earlier practice of writing words as translations or "glosses" above especially difficult words in Latin texts and, later, in French ones. Students may still do this as an aid for their own translations or as a way of remembering the meaning of an unusual word in an English text. Words and their glosses might then be listed separately as a "glossary"; from this developed bilingual Latin and English dictionaries. The earliest proper dictionaries in English were alphabetical lists of "hard words" with glosses of their meanings in ordinary words. The first, by Robert Cawdrey, appeared in 1604 with the title *A Table Alphabetical, Containing and Teaching the True Writing, and Understanding of Hard Usuall English Words, etc.* It listed some 2500 "hard words" with their explanations in ordinary language. They ranged alphabetically from *Abandon*, "cast away, or yeelde up, to leave, or forsake," to *Zodiack*, "a circle in the heaven, wherein be placed the 12 signes, and in which the Sunne is moved." About twenty years later, H. Cockeram's *English Dictionarie* of 1623 included not only a list of hard words but also a list going the other way, giving an ordinary word its hard-word equivalent — small talk with big words. Thus, for *abound,* one could use "exuperate"; for *youthful babbling*, "juvenile inaniloquence"; for *baked*, "pistated." Later in the seventeenth century, technical dictionaries giving new terms appeared, such as that of Edward Philips (1671), Milton's nephew, who listed technical consultants such as Robert Boyle for chemistry and Izaak Walton for fishing. He also indicated the subject field of each term and gave the language of origin.

It was not until the next century that anyone thought of including in the dictionary *all* words in the language, common words as well as hard words. Nathanael Bailey first included ordinary words in his *Universal Etymological English Dictionary* (1721) as much for his interest in etymology as for completeness. The aim of most early lexicographers, whom Samuel Johnson called "harmless drudges," was to "prescribe" rather than "describe" the words of a language, to be, as in the stated aim of one of Noah Webster's dictionaries, the "supreme authority" of the "correct" pronunciation and meaning of a word. Johnson's great *Dictionary of the English Language*, published in 1755 in two volumes, with its wealth of illustrative quotations, mostly drawn from literary sources, was intended to serve as such a standard, and indeed it did for over a century (Murray 1970). But Johnson himself soon gave up on the possibility of standardizing the language, seeing it as constantly changing. He stated that he could not construct the language but only "register the language." Moreover, his dictionary was always personal, as seen in his definition of *excise*, "a hateful tax levied upon commodities, and adjudged not by the common judges of property, but wretches hired by those to whom excise is paid." Still a pretty good definition of the GST! By the end of the eighteenth century, pronouncing dictionaries appeared to show not only how words such as *colonel, enough,* or *phthisical* were spelled but also how they were pronounced, and pronunciations became a regular part of dictionaries (e.g., Thomas Sheridan 1780; John Walker 1791).

In the United States, Noah Webster attempted to rival Johnson's dictionary in his *An American Dictionary of the English Language* in two volumes (1828). Webster was fired with the idea that the United States should have its own form of English, distinct from British usage, and included many new words and senses that had originated or been changed by usage in the United States. He also included a number of new scientific and technical terms among the 70 000 entries. The latest revision of Merriam–Webster is *Webster's Third New International Dictionary of the English Language: Unabridged* (1961), containing some 450 000 entries.

The end of the nineteenth century saw the beginning of the monumental *Oxford English Dictionary: A New English Dictionary on Historical Principles* (often referred to as *OED*), called the greatest lexicographic work in English produced to date. The second edition appeared in 1989 in twenty volumes (see Murray et al. 1989) and since then in an electronic version, a second CD-ROM version, and now on the World Wide Web. As Sidney Landau (1984) has said,

> The *OED* not only provides a historical record of the development of the meaning of each word, with illustrative quotations and definitions for each sense, it also shows the changes in spelling, the different forms each word assumed during its history. It gives by far the most complete and authoritative etymologies that existed up until that time, a body of information that is still unchallenged as a whole.

A Dictionary of Canadianisms on Historical Principles appeared in Canada's centennial year of 1967. Modelled on the *OED*, it is an indispensable source for the study of Canadian language and its development and for cultural information about Canada's past.

All dictionaries, from the *OED* to the more commonly used "collegiate dictionaries," provide the following information about each word: (1) spelling, (2) the "standard" pronunciation, (3) definitions to represent the word's one or more meanings, and (4) parts of speech — for example, noun, verb, preposition. Other information may be included, such as the etymology or history of the word, whether the word is non-standard (e.g., *ain't*) or slang, vulgar, or obsolete. Many dictionaries provide quotations from published literature to illustrate the given definitions, as was first done by Johnson.

In recent years, perhaps due to the increasing specialization in science and the arts or the growing fragmentation of the populace, we have seen the proliferation of hundreds of specialty and subspecialty dictionaries. Dictionaries of slang and jargon have been around for many years, as have multilingual dictionaries, but the shelves of bookstores and libraries are now filled with dictionaries written specifically for biologists, engineers, agriculturists, economists, artists, architects, printers, gays and lesbians, transvestites, athletes, tennis players, and almost any group that has its own set of words to describe what its members think and do. These dictionaries partly reflect the information in our mental dictionaries, stored in highly complex ways. Our own mental dictionaries probably include only a small number of the entries in these dictionaries, but each word is in someone's lexicon.

Classes of Words

Calvin and Hobbes
by Bill Watterson

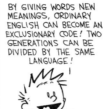

CALVIN AND HOBBES copyright 1992 Watterson. Reprinted with permission of Universal Press Syndicate. All rights reserved.

The words in our mental lexicons are not organized alphabetically or randomly but fall into classes or categories. These have traditionally been called "parts of speech," which can be divided into major classes of words — lexical content words or open classes of words that have referential meaning and function words that express grammatical meanings and relations.

Lexical Content Words

In English, nouns, verbs, adjectives, and adverbs make up the largest part of the vocabulary. They are the **content words** of a language and are sometimes called **open class words** because we can and regularly do add new words to this class. *New Age* and *New Wave* are new nouns associated with a new lifestyle and music, as is *cocooner*, described by the *Sunday Express* (1990) as "a rich yuppie who escapes the violence of society by shutting himself up with his designer wife and baby behind a screen of security alarms" (Tulloch, *Oxford Dictionary of New Words* 1991). *Yuppie* and *designer* in this quotation are also recent nouns. A new verb, *download*, which means to transfer information from a large computer to a smaller computer, entered English with the computer revolution. New adverbs such as *weatherwise* and *saleswise* have been added in recent years, as have adjectives such as *biodegradable*.

Lexical content words are said to have referential meanings. They refer to entities, events, qualities, and circumstances in our experience of the world. Notionally, nouns indicate entities and include proper nouns or names as well as words for humans, animals, other living things, inanimate objects, or abstract ideas: *Sam, Marilyn Monroe, Fido, Saskatchewan, man, dog, tree, desk, rock, music, peace.* Verbs refer to events or happenings, actions of sentient beings, states, or processes (changes of states): *explode, kiss, know, improve.* Adjectives refer to qualities or properties of entities: *red, small, quiet, honest, true*. Adverbs refer to the circumstances of time, place, or manner of events: *frequently, clockwise, slowly*.

Function Words

Other syntactic categories include **grammatical words** or **function words**. In contrast to content words, function words express grammatical rather than referential meanings. The word *dog* may be said to have lexical meaning or content because it can refer to an animal (or metaphorically a human) that we can point to, but what is a *to* or *than* or *or*? In *Mary is taller than John*, the words *Mary, tall*, and *John* are referable to human experience, but *than* is not. It has grammatical or structural function, however, since without it *Mary is taller John* means nothing; *than* is necessary to relate the terms of a comparison. Because they signal relations rather than carry information, function words also differ in being less stressed than content words, as in *the MAN on the STREET* (where stress is indicated by capital letters). Function words are also few in number (e.g., there are only three articles, *a, an,* and *the*, and only four conjunctions, *and, or, but,* and *nor*), but they occur frequently.

Conjunctions, such as *and* and *or*, prepositions, such as *in* or *of*, the articles *the* and *a/an*, and pronouns have been referred to as **closed class words**. It is not easy to think of new conjunctions or prepositions or pronouns that have recently entered the language. The small set of personal pronouns such as *I, me, mine, he, she,* and so on is part of this class. With the growth of the feminist movement, some proposals have been made for adding a new neutral singular pronoun, which would be neither masculine nor feminine and could be used as the general, or **generic**, form. If such a pronoun existed, then it might have prevented the department chairperson in a large university from making an incongruous statement: "We will hire the best person for the job regardless of his sex." Donald MacKay has suggested that we use *e*, pronounced like the letter name, for this pronoun, with various alternative forms; others point out that *they* and *their* are already being used as neutral third-person singular forms, as in "Anyone can do it if they try hard enough" or "Everyone can do their best." Use of the various forms of *they* is reported to be Standard British English used on the BBC (British Broadcasting Corporation), with *anyone* and *everyone* now considered either singular or plural, similar to words such as *committee* or *government*.

These classes of content and function words appear to have psychological and neurological validity. Some brain-damaged patients have greater difficulty in using or understanding or reading function words than content words. Some are unable to read function words such as *in* or *which* but can read the lexical content words *inn* and *witch*. Other patients do just the opposite. The two classes of words also seem to function differently in **slips of the tongue** produced by normal individuals. For example, a speaker may inadvertently switch words, producing "the journal of the editor" instead of "the editor of the journal," but the exchanging of function words has not been observed. The important feature of these two classes is their function rather than their degrees of "openness." What is an open class in one language may be closed in another. In Akan, the major language spoken in Ghana, for example, there are only a handful of adjectives; most English adjectives are in the verb class in Akan. Instead of saying "The sun is bright today," an Akan speaker will say "The sun brightens today."

Formal Features of Lexical Classes

The various classes have certain general meanings associated with them: nouns generally refer to entities, verbs to events, adjectives to qualities, adverbs and prepositions to circumstantials. Such notional definitions are not sufficient to identify the classes of words. Although verbs may be words that refer to actions, what expresses action more than the word *action*, which is not a verb but a noun? It is a noun because we can say *his actions* but not *he actioned*. That is, *action* is marked as a noun because it occurs with the possessive pronoun *his*, takes a plural form with -*s*, and has a noun-forming suffix in -*ion*. Formal features shared by lexical classes include inflectional suffixes (-*s*), derivational suffixes (-*ion*), function words (*his*), and position (following *his*). These terms will be discussed in the rest of this chapter and in the next, but some of the ways in which they distinguish lexical classes will be briefly indicated here.

Nouns share the following features:

1. They are inflected for plural number and/or possessive case (as in *woman, woman's, women, women's; boy, boy's, boys, boys'*).
2. They occur with noun-forming affixes, such as -*er* added to verbs (*worker*) or -*ness* added to adjectives (*happiness*).
3. They follow noun determiner function words such as *a(n), the, this, that, his, her*.

Verbs share the following features:

1. They are inflected for present tense singular, past tense, past participle, present participle (as in *sings, sang, sung, singing; walks, walked, walked, walking*).
2. They occur with verb-forming affixes such as -*ify* added to nouns (*beautify*), -*ize* added to nouns and adjectives (*idolize, regularize*), -*en* added to adjectives (*redden*), *re-* added to verbs (*react*).
3. They occur following auxiliary function words such as *can, may, will, shall* (*will go*).

Adjectives share the following features:

1. They are inflected for comparative and superlative degree (as in *prettier, prettiest*).
2. They occur with adjective-forming affixes such as -*ful* added to nouns (*beautiful*), -*able* added to verbs (*readable*).
3. They occur with intensifier or degree function words such as *very, more, most* (as in *very strange, more beautiful*).

4. They can occur in attributive position before nouns they modify or in predicative position following a verb such as *be* (*a beautiful woman; the woman is beautiful*). A useful test frame for adjectives is the following: *A _____ thing is a thing very _____.*

Adverbs share the following features:

1. A few adverbs, like adjectives, are inflected for comparative and superlative degree (*faster* in *He ran faster*).
2. Many adverbs are formed from adjectives with the adverb-forming suffix *-ly* (*beautifully*).
3. Like adjectives, they may occur with intensifier or degree words (*more swiftly, very eloquently*).
4. They can occur in final position after verbs they modify, as in the useful frame *He told the story _____* (*slowly, deliberately, quietly*).

Prepositions differ from lexical class words in that they are few in number (about 70 of them), so they can be listed and learned. They are not inflected, though they can occur with derivational suffixes such as *-ward(s)* to form adverbs (*afterward*). They can occur with specifying function words such as *straight* and *right*, and they appear before nouns that are their objects and that they relate to other words in the sentence (*straight to the heart of the matter*).

Morphemes: The Minimal Units of Meaning

> "They gave it me," Humpty Dumpty continued, "for an un-birthday present."
> "I beg your pardon?" Alice said with a puzzled air.
> "I'm not offended," said Humpty Dumpty.
> "I mean, what is an un-birthday present?"
> "A present given when it isn't your birthday, of course."
>
> Lewis Carroll, *Through the Looking-Glass*

Elizabeth in the cartoon by Lynn Johnston shown on page 44 is as aware as Humpty Dumpty that the prefix *un-* means "not," as is further shown in the following pairs of words:

A	B
desirable	undesirable
likely	unlikely
inspired	uninspired
happy	unhappy
developed	undeveloped
sophisticated	unsophisticated

Webster's Third New International Dictionary lists about 2700 adjectives beginning with *un-*.

FOR BETTER OR FOR WORSE copyright Lynn Johnston Prod. Reprinted with permission of
United Features Syndicate. All rights reserved.

If the most elemental units of meaning, the basic linguistic signs, are assumed
to be the words of a language, then it would be a coincidence that *un-* has the same
meaning in all the column B words. But this is no coincidence. The words *unde-*
sirable, unlikely, uninspired, unhappy, and the others in column B consist of at least
two meaningful units: *un + desirable, un + likely, un + inspired,* and *un + happy.*

Just as *un-* occurs with the same meaning in the words above, so does *phon* in
the following words. (You may not know the meanings of some of them, but you
will when you finish this book.)

phone	phonology	phoneme
phonetic	phonologist	phonemic
phonetics	phonological	allophone
phonetician	telephone	euphonious
phonic	telephonic	symphony

Phon is a minimal form in that it can't be divided into more elemental structures.
Ph doesn't mean anything; *pho,* though it is pronounced like *foe,* has no relation in
meaning to it; and *on* is not the preposition spelled *o-n.* In all the words in the list,
phon has the identical meaning, "pertaining to sound."

The internal structure of words is rule-governed. Thus, *uneaten, unadmired,* and
ungrammatical are words in English, but **eatenun, *admiredun,* and **grammati-*

calun (to mean "not eaten," "not admired," and "not grammatical") are not, because we form a negative meaning of a word not by **suffixing** *-un* (i.e., by adding it to the end of the word) but by **prefixing** it (i.e., by adding it to the beginning).

When Samuel Goldwyn, the pioneer moviemaker, announced "In two words: impossible," he was reflecting the common view that words are the basic meaningful elements in a language. We have already seen that this cannot be so, since some words are formed by combining a number of distinct units of meaning. The traditional term for the most elemental unit of grammatical form is **morpheme**. The word is derived from the Greek word, *morphe*, meaning "form." Linguistically speaking, then, Goldwyn should have said "In two morphemes: im-possible." *Morphology* itself consists of two morphemes, *morph + ology*. The morphemic suffix *-ology* means "science of" or "branch of knowledge concerning." Thus, the meaning of *morphology* is "the science of word forms." Knowing a language implies knowing its morphology. Like most linguistic knowledge, this is generally unconscious knowledge.

A single word may be composed of one or more morphemes:

one morpheme	boy
	desire
two morphemes	boy + ish
	desire + able
three morphemes	boy + ish + ness
	desire + able + ity
four morphemes	gentle + man + li + ness
	un + desire + able + ity
more than four	un + gentle + man + li + ness
	anti + dis + establish + ment + ari + an + ism

Some speakers will have even more morphemes for *antidisestablishmentarianism* than are shown here if they are familiar with some of the roots of the word.

A morpheme may be represented by a single sound, such as the morpheme *a* meaning "without" as in *amoral* or *asexual*, or by a single syllable, such as *child* and *-ish* in *child + ish*. A morpheme may also consist of more than one syllable: two syllables, as in *aardvark, lady, water*; three syllables, as in *Winnipeg* or *crocodile*; or four or more syllables, as in *salamander*. A morpheme — the minimal linguistic sign — is thus a grammatical unit in which there is an arbitrary union of a sound and a meaning that cannot be further analyzed. This may be too simple a definition, but it will serve our purposes for now. Every word in every language is composed of one or more morphemes.

Bound and Free Morphemes

Prefixes and Suffixes

Some morphemes, such as *boy, desire, gentle,* and *man,* can constitute words by themselves. Other morphemes, such as *-ish, -able, -ness, -ly, dis-, trans-,* and *un-,* are never words but always parts of words. Thus, *un-* is like *pre-* (*prefix, predetermine, prejudge, prearrange*), and *dis-* (*disallow, disobey, disapprove, dislike*), and *bi-* (*bipolar, bisexual, bivalved*); it occurs only before other morphemes. Such morphemes are called **prefixes**.

Prefixing is widespread in the languages of the world. For example, in Isthmus Zapotec, a language of Mexico, the plural morpheme *ka-* is a prefix:

zigi	"chin"	kazigi	"chins"
zike	"shoulder"	kazike	"shoulders"
diaga	"ear"	kadiaga	"ears"

Other morphemes occur only as **suffixes**, following other morphemes. English examples of such morphemes are *-er* (as in *singer, performer, reader*, and *beautifier*), *-ist* (as in *typist, copyist, pianist, novelist, collaborationist*, and *linguist*), and *-ly* (as in *manly, sickly*, and *friendly*), to mention a few.

These prefix and suffix morphemes have traditionally been called **bound morphemes**, because they cannot occur "unattached," as distinct from **free morphemes**, such as *man, spectacle, sick, prove*, and *allow*. Of course, in speaking we seldom use even free morphemes alone. We combine all morphemes into larger units — phrases and sentences.

Morphemes are the minimal linguistic signs. In Turkish, if you add *-ak* to a verb, you derive a noun, as in these examples:

| dur | "to stop" | dur + ak | "stopping place" |
| bat | "to sink" | bat + ak | "sinking place" or "marsh/swamp" |

In English, in order to express reciprocal action, we use the phrase *each other*, as in *understand each other, love each other*. In Turkish, one simply adds a morpheme to the verb:

| anla | "understand" | anla + s | "understand each other" |
| sev | "love" | sev + is | "love each other" |

The "reciprocal" suffix in these examples is pronounced as *s* after a vowel and as *is* after a consonant. This is similar to the process in English in which we use *a* as the indefinite article morpheme before a noun beginning with a consonant, as in *a dog*, and *an* before a noun beginning with a vowel, as in *an apple*. We will discuss the various pronunciations of morphemes in Chapter 6.

In Piro, an Arawakan language spoken in Peru, a single morpheme, *kaka*, can be added to a verb to express the meaning "cause to":

| cokoruha | "to harpoon" | cokoruha + kaka | "cause to harpoon" |
| salwa | "to visit" | salwa + kaka | "cause to visit" |

In Karok, a Native North American language spoken in the Pacific Northwest of the United States, the locative adverbial meaning "in," "on," or "at" is formed by adding *-ak* to a noun:

| ikrivaam | "house" | ikrivaamak | "in a house" |

It is accidental that both Turkish and Karok have a suffix -*ak*. Despite the similarity in form, the two meanings are different. Similarly, the reciprocal suffix -*s* in Turkish is similar in form to the English plural -*s*. Also in Karok, the suffix -*ara* has the same meaning as the English -*y*, that is, "characterized by":

> aptiik   "branch"   aptiikara   "branchy"

These examples make clear the arbitrary nature of the linguistic sign.

In Russian, the suffix -*shchik* (pronounced like the beginning of the word *she* followed by *chick*) added to a noun is similar in meaning to the English suffix -*er* in words such as *reader, teacher,* or *rider,* which when added to a verb means "one who —." The Russian suffix, however, is added to nouns and verbs, as shown in the following examples:

atom	"atom"	atomshchik	"atom-warmonger"
baraban	"drum"	barabanshchik	"drummer"
kalambur	"pun"	kalamburshchik	"punner"
beton	"concrete"	betonshchik	"concrete worker"
lom	"scrap"	lomshchik	"salvage collector"

The examples given above from different languages also illustrate "free" morphemes such as *boy* in English, *dur* in Turkish, *salwa* in Piro, and *lom* in Russian.

Infixes

Some languages also have **infixes**, morphemes that are inserted into root morphemes. Bontoc, a language spoken in the Philippines, is such a language:

Nouns/Adjectives		Verbs	
fikas	"strong"	fumikas	"to be strong"
kilad	"red"	kumilad	"to be red"
fusul	"enemy"	fumusul	"to be an enemy"

In this language, the infix -*um*- is inserted after the first consonant of the noun or adjective. Thus, a speaker of Bontoc who learns that *pusi* means "poor" would understand the meaning of *pumusi*, "to be poor," on hearing the word for the first time. Just as an English speaker who learns the verb *sneet* would know that *sneeter* is "one who sneets," a Bontoc speaker who knows that *ngumitad* means "to be dark" would know that the adjective "dark" must be *ngitad*.

English has a very limited set of infixes. A fossil infix in English is the *n* in a few words such as *stand* (cf. *stood*), *think* (*thought*), and *bring* (*brought*). English infixing was a subject of the Linguist List, a discussion group on the Internet, in November 1993 and again in July 1996. The interest in these infixes in English may be due to the fact that one can only infix obscenities as full words inserted in other words, usually into adjectives or adverbs. The most common infix in North America is the word *fuckin* and all the euphemisms for it, such as *friggin, freakin, flippin,* or *fuggin* as in *abso + fuggin + lutely* or *Winni + flippin + peg*. In Britain, a common infix is *bloody*, an obscene term in British English, and its euphemisms, such as *bloomin*. In the movie and stage musical *My Fair Lady, abso + bloomin + lutely* occurs in one of the songs sung by Eliza Doolittle.

Circumfixes

Some languages have **circumfixes**, morphemes that are attached to a root or stem morpheme both initially and finally. These are sometimes called **discontinuous morphemes**. In Chickasaw, a Muskogean language spoken in Oklahoma, the negative is formed by using both the prefix *ik-* and the suffix *-o*. The final vowel of the declarative is deleted before the negative suffix is added.

Declarative		Negative	
chokma	"he is good"	ik + chokm + o	"he isn't good"
lakna	"it is yellow"	ik + lakn + o	"it isn't yellow"
palli	"it is hot"	ik + pall + o	"it isn't hot"
tiwwi	"he opens (it)"	ik + tiww + o	"he doesn't open (it)"

An example of a more familiar "circumfixing" language is German. The past **participle** of regular verbs is formed by adding the prefix *ge-* and the suffix *-t* to the verb root. Thus, this circumfix added to the verb root *lieb,* "love," produces *geliebt,* "loved" (or "beloved," when used as an adjective).

Huckles and Ceives

> It had been a rough day, so when I walked into the party I was very chalant, despite my efforts to appear gruntled and consolate. I was furling my wieldy umbrella . . . when I saw her. . . . She was a descript person. . . . Her hair was kempt, her clothing shevelled, and she moved in a gainly way.
>
> Jack Winter, "How I Met My Wife," *The New Yorker,* July 25, 1944.

A morpheme was defined as the basic element of meaning, a phonological form that is arbitrarily united with a particular meaning and that cannot be analyzed into simpler elements. This definition has presented problems for linguistic analysis for many years, although it holds for most of the morphemes in a language. Consider words such as *cranberry, huckleberry*, and *boysenberry*. The *berry* part is no problem, but *huckle* and *boysen* occur only with *berry*, as did *cran-* until *cranapple* juice came on the market, and other morphologically complex words using *cran-* followed. The *boysen-* part of *boysenberry* was named for Boysen, who developed it as a hybrid from the blackberry and the raspberry. But few people are aware of this, and it is a bound stem morpheme that occurs only in this word. *Lukewarm* is another word with two stem morphemes, with *luke* occurring only in this word, because it is not the same morpheme as the name *Luke*.

Bound forms such as *huckle-, boysen-,* and *luke-*, require a redefinition of the concept of morpheme. Some morphemes have no meaning in isolation but acquire meaning only in combination with other specific morphemes. Thus, the morpheme *huckle-*, when joined with *berry*, has the meaning of a special kind of berry that is small, round, and purplish-blue; *luke-* when combined with *warm*, has the meaning "sort of" or "somewhat"; and so on.

Just as there are some morphemes that occur only in a single word (combined with another morpheme), there are other morphemes that occur in many words but seem to lack a constant meaning. What is the meaning of -*ceive* in *receive, perceive, conceive,* and *deceive,* or the -*mit* in *remit, permit, commit, submit, transmit,* and *admit*? Since these forms were morphemes in Latin and French before the words were borrowed in English, they are sometimes known as **etymemes** because of their etymological relevance. The meanings of such morphemes depend on the words in which they occur, on their morphological contexts. The roots may have been meaningful at one time in Latin, but they no longer are in English. In the mental lexicons of many speakers, these words would be monomorphemic, but words that appear to have a transparent structure to some speakers are opaque to others. One child, for instance, was surprised to learn that orange juice is made with oranges. Once these loan words enter the language, they may reveal a pattern by which they can be disassembled and their parts combined with others.

	-duce	-fer	-cur	-tain
re-	reduce	refer	recur	retain
con-	conduce	confer	concur	contain
in-	induce	infer	incur	*intain
de-	deduce	defer	*decur	detain

The starred "words" do not occur in English, but they could; they are at least possible words.

There are other words that seem to be composed of prefix + stem morphemes in which the stems, like the *cran-* or -*ceive,* never occur alone but always with a regular prefix. Thus, we find *inept* but no **ept, inane* but no **ane, incest* but no **cest, inert* but no **ert, disgusted* but no **gusted.*

Similarly, the stems of *upholster, downhearted,* and *outlandish* do not occur by themselves: **holster* and **hearted* (with these meanings) and *landish* (except as the maiden name of V.A. Fromkin) are not free morphemes. In addition, *downholster, uphearted,* and *inlandish,* their "opposites," are not found in any English lexicon.

To complicate things a little further, there are words such as *strawberry* in which the *straw* has no relationship to any other kind of *straw, gooseberry,* which is unrelated to *goose,* and *blackberry,* which may be blue or red. While some of these words may have historical origins, there is no present meaningful connection. The *Oxford English Dictionary* entry for the word *strawberry* states that "The reason for the name has been variously conjectured. One explanation refers the first element to Straw . . . a particle of straw or chaff, a mote, describing the appearance of the achenes scattered over the surface of the strawberry." That may be true of the word's origin, but today the *straw* in *strawberry* is not the same morpheme as that found in *strawlike* or *straw-coloured.*

The meaning of a morpheme must be constant. The morpheme -*er* means "one who does" in words such as *singer, painter, lover,* and *worker,* but the same sounds represent the "comparative" morpheme, meaning "more," in *nicer, prettier,* and *taller.* Thus, two morphemes may be pronounced identically but represent two distinct morphemes because of their difference in meaning. The same sounds may occur in another word and not represent any separate morpheme, as is shown by the final syllable in *butcher*; *-er* does not represent any morpheme, since a butcher is not one who butches. (In an earlier form of English, the word *butcher* was *bucker*, "one who dresses bucks." The *-er* in this word was then a separate morpheme.) Similarly, in *water* the *-er* is not a distinct morpheme ending; *butcher* and *water* are single morphemes or **monomorphemic** words. This follows from the concept of the morpheme as a sound–meaning unit.

Non-affix **lexical content morphemes** that cannot be analyzed into smaller parts, such as *system, boy*, or *cran-*, are called **root** morphemes. When a root morpheme is combined with affix morphemes, it forms a stem. Other affixes can be added to a stem to form a more complex stem:

root	Chomsky	*(proper) noun*
stem	Chomsky + ite	*noun + suffix*
word	Chomsky + ite + s	*noun + suffix + suffix*
root	believe	*verb*
stem	believe + able	*verb + suffix*
word	un + believe + able	*prefix + verb + suffix*
root	system	*noun*
stem	system + atic	*noun + suffix*
stem	un + system + atic	*prefix + noun + suffix*
stem	un + system + atic + al	*prefix + noun + suffix + suffix*
word	un + system + atic + al + ly	*prefix + noun + suffix + suffix + suffix*

As one adds each additional affix to a stem, a new stem and a new word are formed.

All morphemes are bound or free. Affixes (prefixes, suffixes, and infixes) are bound morphemes. Root morphemes can be bound or free:

	Free	Bound
Root	dog, cat, aardvark, corduroy, run, bottle, hot, separate, phone, museum, school . . . (and thousands more)	huckle(berry), (dis)gruntle, (un)couth, (non)chalance, (per)ceive, (in)ept, (re)mit, (in)cest, (homo)geneous . . . (and fewer than a hundred more)
Affix		(friend)ship, (lead)er, re(do), homo(geneous), hetero(geneous), trans(sex)ual, (sad)ly, (tall)ish, a(moral) . . . (and many others)

Note that there are some morpheme types not listed in this chart, such as *-ing* as in *going* or *the* or *and*.

Rules of Word Formation

"I never heard of 'Uglification,'" Alice ventured to say. "What is it?"
   The Gryphon lifted up both its paws in surprise. "Never heard of uglifying!" it exclaimed. "You know what to beautify is, I suppose?"

"Yes," said Alice doubtfully: "it means — to make — anything — prettier."

"Well, then," the Gryphon went on, "if you don't know what to uglify is, you are a simpleton."

Lewis Carroll, *Alice's Adventures in Wonderland*

When the Mock Turtle listed the different branches of arithmetic for Alice as "Ambition, Distraction, Uglification, and Derision," Alice was very confused. She wasn't really a simpleton, since *uglification* was not a common word in English until Lewis Carroll used it. There are many ways in which words enter a language. Some are discussed in Chapter 8, on language change.

Lexical Gaps

Speakers of a language may know tens of thousands of words and dictionaries may include hundreds of thousands, but no dictionary can list all **possible words** since it is possible to add to the vocabulary of a language in many ways. There are always gaps in the lexicon — words that are not in the dictionary but that can be added. Some of the gaps are due to the fact that a permissible sound sequence has no meaning attached to it (e.g., *blick, slarm,* or *krobe*). Note that the sequence of sounds must be in keeping with the constraints of the language. *Bnick* is not a "gap" because no word in English can begin with *bn*. We will discuss such constraints in Chapter 6.

Other gaps are due to the fact that possible combinations of morphemes have not been made (e.g., *ugly + ify* or *linguistic + ism*). Morphemes can be combined in this way because there are **morphological rules** in every language that determine how morphemes combine to form new words.

The Mock Turtle added *-ify* to the adjective *ugly* and formed a verb. Many verbs in English have been formed in this way: *purify, amplify, simplify, falsify*. The suffix *-ify* conjoined with nouns also forms verbs: *objectify, glorify, personify*. Notice that the Mock Turtle went even farther; he added the suffix *-cation* to *uglify* and formed a noun, *uglification*, as in *glorification, simplification, falsification*, and *purification*.

Derivational Morphology

SHOE © Tribune Media Services, Inc. All rights reserved. Reprinted with permission.

Bound morphemes such as *-ify* and *-ation* are called **derivational morphemes**. When they are added to root morphemes or stems, a word is derived. This method of word formation reflects the wonderful creativity of language.

We create new words much more frequently than we imagine. The student who wrote on his examination "Hamlet's unableness to overcome his mental undecidedness" was undoubtedly familiar with the words *inability* and *indecision* but under the pressure of the examination forgot them and created his own words based on productive derivational rules, probably influenced by the syntax of "he was unable to decide." In the cases of *inability* and *indecision*, the suffixes change the forms of the stems to which they are added and make them difficult to remember, but the stems remain unchanged with *-ness*.

In fact, hearers and readers of these neologisms readily understand them. Suppose you hear someone say "He likes to be nussed." You might ask "Is he really nussable?" even if you don't know what the verb *nuss* means. Children do this all the time. This means we must have a list of the derivational morphemes in our mental dictionaries, as well as the rules that determine how they are to be added to roots or stems to form new stems or words. We saw above that morphemes occur in a fixed order, as *un + loved* but not * *loved + un*. In addition, the order in which each new morpheme is affixed in a complex word is significant. A word is not a simple sequence of morphemes but has a **hierarchical structure**. Consider the word *unsystematically,* composed of five morphemes. The root is *system*, a noun, to which we added *-atic*, an adjective suffix, and then added the prefix *un-*, which is added to adjectives, to form the new adjective stem (or word) *unsystematic.* If we had added the prefix *un-* first, we would have derived a non-word, **unsystem*, since *un-* cannot be added to nouns.

The hierarchical structure of this word can be diagrammed as follows:

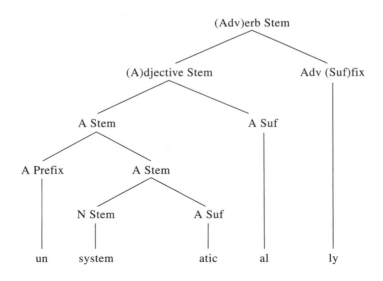

This diagram shows that the entire word — *unsystematically* — is an adverb stem composed of an adjective stem — *unsystematical* plus *-ly*, an adverbial derivational suffix. The adjective stem itself is composed of the adjective stem *unsystematic*, which is composed of the adjective prefix *un-* and the adjective stem *systematic* (composed of the noun *system* and the adjective suffix *-atic* plus the adjective suffix *-al*).

This seems to be very complicated, and it is. Morphological rules of word formation are complex. Yet every speaker of English knows them and uses them to form new words such as *uglify* or *squishable* or *linguisticism* and to understand words not heard before, as with the first time one hears the word *Chomskian*. We also unconsciously use these rules in rejecting some forms as being impossible as words in English, such as **nationism*.

When T.S. Eliot wrote in his "Love Song of J. Alfred Prufrock" that there is time for "visions and revisions," he called attention to the opposing meanings of the two words. The structure of *revision* is not *re + vision*, "a repeated vision," but *revise + ion*, "the act of revising": that is, the stem is *revise* rather than *vision*.

As the examples show, a derived word may add additional meaning to the original word (e.g., the negative meanings of words prefixed by *un-*) and may be in a different grammatical class than the underived word. When a verb is suffixed with *-able,* the result is an adjective, as in *desire + able* or *adore + able*. Or, when the suffix *-en* is added to an adjective, a verb is derived, as in *dark + en*. One may form a noun from an adjective, as in *sweet + ie*. The following table lists some other examples:

Verb to Noun	Adjective to Noun	Noun to Verb	Noun to Adjective	Verb to Adjective	Adjective to Adverb
acquitt + al	tall + ness	moral + ize	boy + ish	read + able	exact + ly
clear + ance	specific + ity	vaccin + ate	virtu + ous	creat + ive	quiet + ly
accus + ation		brand + ish	Elizabeth + an	migrat + ory	
confer + ence		haste + n	pictur + esque		
sing + er			affection + ate		
conform + ist			health + ful		
predict + ion			alcohol + ic		
free + dom			life + like		

On the other hand, not all derivational morphemes cause a change in grammatical class:

Noun to Noun	Verb to Verb	Adjective to Adjective
friend + ship	un + do	pink + ish
human + ity	re + cover	in + correct

Many prefixes fall into this category:

a + moral	mono + theism
auto + biography	re + print
ex- + wife	semi- + annual
super + human	sub + minimal

There are also suffixes of this type:

vicar + age	Vancouver + ite
kind + ly	fadd + ist
short + ish	Canad + ian
Americ + an	pun + ster

When new words enter the lexicon by the application of morphological rules, it is often the case that other complex forms will not. For example, when *Commun + ist* entered the language, other possible complex forms did not, structures such as *Commun + ite* (as in *Trotsky + ite*) or *Commun + ian* (as in *grammar + ian*). Alternative forms, however, may exist: for example, *Chomskyan* and *Chomskyist* and perhaps even *Chomskyite* (all meaning "follower of Chomsky's views of linguistics"). *Linguist* and *linguistician* are both used, but the possible word *linguite* is not. The redundancy of such alternative forms, all of which conform to the regular rules of word formation, may explain some of the accidental gaps in the lexicon. This further shows that the actual words in the language constitute only a subset of the possible words.

There are many other derivational morphemes in English and other languages, such as the suffixes meaning "diminutive," as in the words *pig + let* and *sap + ling*.

Some of the morphological rules are **productive**, meaning that they can be used freely to form new words from the list of free and bound morphemes. The suffix *-able* appears to be a morpheme that can be conjoined with any verb to derive an adjective with the meaning of the verb and the meaning of *-able*, which is something like "able to be" as in *accept + able, blam(e) + able, pass + able, change + able, breath(e) + able, adapt + able*. The meaning of *-able* has also been given as "fit for doing" or "fit for being done."

Such a rule might be stated as

(1) VERB + able → ADJECTIVE "able to be VERB-ed"
       (e.g., accept + able = "able to be accepted")

The productivity of this rule is illustrated by the fact that we find *-able* in such morphologically complex words as *un + speakabl(e) + y* and *un + come + at + able*.

We have already noted that there is a morpheme in English meaning "not" that has the form *un-* and that, when combined with adjectives such as *afraid, fit, free*, or *smooth*, forms the **antonyms**, or negatives, of these adjectives: for example, *unafraid, unfit*, and so on.

We can also add the prefix *un-* to derived words that have been formed by morphological rules:

un + believe + able
un + accept + able
un + talk + about + able
un + keep + off + able
un + speak + able

The rule that forms these words may be stated as

(2) un + ADJECTIVE → "not-ADJECTIVE"

This rule seems to account for all the examples cited. Yet we find *happy* and *unhappy*, *cowardly* and *uncowardly*, but not *sad* and **unsad* or *brave* and **unbrave*. The starred forms that follow may be merely **accidental gaps** in the lexicon. If someone refers to a person as being **unsad*, we would know that the person referred to is "not sad," and an **unbrave* person would not be brave. But, as Sandra Thompson (1975) points out, the "un-rule" may not be as productive for adjectives composed of just one morpheme as for adjectives derived from verbs.

The rule seems to be freely applicable to an adjectival form derived from a verb, as in *unenlightened, unsimplified, uncharacterized, unauthorized, undistinguished*, and so on.

However, one cannot always distinguish the meanings of the words derived from free and derivational morphemes from the morphemes themselves. Thompson (1975) has also pointed out that the *un-* forms of the following words have unpredictable meanings:

unloosen	"loosen, let loose"
unrip	"rip, undo by ripping"
undo	"reverse doing"
untread	"go back through in the same steps"
unearth	"dig up"
unfrock	"deprive (a cleric) of ecclesiastical rank"
unnerve	"fluster"

Although the words above must be listed in our mental lexicons since their meanings cannot be determined by knowing the meanings of their parts, morphological rules must also be in the grammar, revealing the relationships between words and providing the means for forming new words. Morphological rules may be more or less productive. The rule that adds an *-er* to verbs in English to produce a noun meaning "one who performs an action (once or habitually)" appears to be very productive; most English verbs accept this suffix: *lover, hunter, predictor* (notice that *-or* and *-er* have the same pronunciation), *examiner, exam-taker, analyzer*, and so forth.

Now consider the following:

sincerity	from	*sincere*
warmth	from	*warm*
moisten	from	*moist*

The suffix *-ity* is found in many other words in English, such as *chastity, scarcity*, and *curiosity*; and *-th* occurs in *health, wealth, depth, width*, and *growth*. We find *-en* in *sadden, ripen, redden, weaken*, and *deepen*. Still, the phrase **The fiercity of the lion* sounds somewhat strange, as does the sentence **I'm going to thinnen the sauce*. Someone may use the word *coolth*, but as Thompson (1975) points out, when words such as *fiercity, thinnen, fullen*, or *coolth* are used, usually it is either an error or an attempt at humour.

In such cases, a morphological rule that was once productive (as shown by the existence of related pairs such as *scarce/scarcity*) may no longer be so. Our knowledge of the related pairs, however, may permit us to use these examples in forming new words, by analogy with the existing lexical items. Such analogies often lead to the creation of new affixes, such as *aer(o)-* meaning "air" in *aerate, aerobics,* but "aviation" in *aeropolitics*; *petro-* in *petrochemical, petrodiplomat, petrodollar,* and *petropolitics,* in which the prefix relates to petroleum rather than rocks; and the new suffixes in *-holic* from *alcoholic* as in *workaholic,* or *-cast* from *broadcast* in words such as *telecast, newscast,* and *sportscast,* or *-(s)ville* as in *dullsville* (Algeo 1991).

"Pullet Surprises"

That speakers of a language know the morphemes of that language and the rules for word formation is shown as much by the errors made as by the non-deviant forms produced. Morphemes combine to form words. These words form our internal dictionaries, but given our knowledge of the morphemes of the language and the morphological rules, we can often guess the meaning of a word we do not know. Sometimes our guesses are wrong.

Amsel Greene collected errors made by her students in vocabulary-building classes and published them in a book called *Pullet Surprises* (1969). The title is taken from a sentence written by one of her high school students: "In 1957 Eugene O'Neill won a Pullet Surprise." What is most interesting about these errors is how much they reveal about the students' knowledge of English morphology. Consider the creativity of these students in the following examples:

Word	Student's Definition
gubernatorial	"to do with peanuts"
bibliography	"holy geography"
polyglot	"more than one glot"
gullible	"to do with sea birds"

The student who used the word *indefatigable* in the sentence

She tried many reducing diets, but remained indefatigable.

clearly recognized morphological structures in the spelling: *in,* meaning "not" as in *ineffective; de* meaning "off" as in *decapitate; fat,* as in *fat; able,* as in *able;* and combined meaning, "not able to take the fat off." But a still more convincing example is that of E.H. Sturtevant's grandson, who suffered from an earache and was taken to the doctor to have the ear irrigated. When he had a nosebleed, he asked if it had to be "nosigated." The same child apparently saw four planes flying overhead and was told that it was a "formation"; later, upon seeing two planes flying overhead, he claimed that it was a "twomation."

Such misidentifications of morphemes have occurred in the history of the language to produce new words and affixes. Some words ending in *s* or *z* sounds were at times mistaken for the plural forms so that a new singular was formed: for example, the originally singular form *pease* (as in *pease porridge,* "pea soup") was taken as a plural (since peas seldom come singularly), and a new singular form, *pea,* was established; so also with *cherry, asset, pry* (from *prize*). Sometimes it went the other way with the fusion of the plural ending with the root to form a new singular, as with *chintz* (and then *chintzy*), originally the plural of *chint*, and *bodice* from *bodies*. Another example is the famous *burger* series, which developed from the German *Hamburger Wurst*, like *Frankfurter Wurst* or *Wiener Wurst*, "a sausage (*Wurst*) made in Hamburg, Frankfurt, Vienna." In German, *Hamburger* was made up of the morphemes *Hamburg* (the city) and the suffix *-er*, indicating the place of origin. In English, this was interpreted as *ham* and *burger*, "a piece of the previously mentioned food in a roll and served hot," thus *beefburger, cheeseburger, pizzaburger*, and just plain *burger*. Among some speakers — especially older speakers — of Canadian English, this sandwich is known as a *hamburg* and the ground meat used in the roll as *hamburg steak*. The *Gage Canadian Dictionary* lists both of these along with *hamburgers* and *hamburger steak*, but there can be little doubt that the *-er* forms now dominate, perhaps through the pervasive influence of U.S.-based fast-food restaurant chains.

Word Coinage

As we have seen, new words may be added to the vocabulary or lexicon of a language by derivational processes. New words may also enter a language in a variety of other ways. Some are created outright to fit some purpose. Advertising has added many new words in English, such as *Kodak, nylon, Orlon*, and *Dacron*. Specific brand names such as *Xerox, Kleenex, Jell-O, Frigidaire, Brillo*, and *Vaseline* are now sometimes used as the generic names for different brands of these types of products. Notice that some of these words were created from existing words: *Kleenex* from the word *clean* and *Jell-O* from *gel*, for example. The language may still use imitation sounds to produce imitative, echoic, or onomatopoeic words such as *bebop, beep(er), bleep, blimp, burp, gack*, and *gobbledygook* (Algeo 1991). In computer speech processing, the new words *cepstrum* and *cepstral* were purposely formed by reordering the letters of *spectrum* and *spectral*. Speakers do not agree on the pronunciation of these two words. Some say "sepstrum" with an *s* sound, since the *c* precedes an *e*. Others say "kepstrum" since the *c* is pronounced as a *k* in the source word *spectrum*. Greek roots borrowed in English have also provided a means for **coining** new words. *Thermos* ("hot") plus *metron* ("measure") give us *thermometer*. From *akros* ("topmost") and *phobia* ("fear"), we get *acrophobia*, "dread of heights."

Latin, like Greek, has also provided prefixes and suffixes that are used productively with both native and non-native roots. The prefix *ex-* comes from Latin:

> ex-husband   ex-wife   ex–sister-in-law

This prefix has been turned into a word, as in *my ex*, referring particularly to an ex-spouse (probably a form of abbreviation or clipping).

The suffix *-able/-ible* discussed earlier is also Latin, borrowed via French, and can be attached to almost any English verb:

> writable   readable   answerable   movable

Compounds

> ... the Houynhnms have no Word in their Language to express any thing
> that is evil, except what they borrow from the Deformities or ill Qualities
> of the Yahoos. Thus they denote the Folly of a Servant, an Omission of a
> Child, a Stone that cuts their feet, a Continuance of foul or unseasonable
> Weather, and the like, by adding to each the Epithet of Yahoo. For instance,
> Hnhm Yahoo, Whnaholm Yahoo, Ynlhmnawihlma Yahoo, and an ill contrived
> House, Ynholmhnmrohlnw Yahoo.
>
> Jonathan Swift, *Gulliver's Travels*

New words may be formed by stringing together other words to create **compound**
words. There is almost no limit on the kinds of combinations that occur in English,
as the following list of compounds shows:

	-Adjective	**-Noun**	**-Verb**
Adjective-	bittersweet	bluenose	highborn
Noun-	headstrong	rainbow	spoonfed
Verb-	carryall	slapshot	sleepwalk

Frigidaire is a compound formed by combining the adjective *frigid* with the noun *air*.

When the two words are in the same grammatical category, the compound will
be in this category: noun + noun — *girlfriend, baby bonus, paper clip, bush pilot,
landlord, rink rat*; adjective + adjective — *icy-cold, red-hot,* and *worldly-wise*. In
many cases, when the two words fall into different categories, the class of the second or final word will be the grammatical category of the compound: noun + adjective — *headstrong, userfriendly, watertight, lifelong*; verb + noun — *pickpocket,
pinchpenny, daredevil, sawbones*. On the other hand, compounds formed with a
preposition are in the category of the non-prepositional part of the compound:
overtake, hanger-on, undertake, sundown, afterbirth, downfall, uplift.

Although two-word compounds are the most common in English, it would be difficult to state an upper limit: Consider *golden handshake, three-time loser, four-
dimensional space-time, sergeant-at-arms, mother-of-pearl, man about town, master of ceremonies*, and *daughter-in-law*.

Spelling does not tell us what sequence of words constitutes a compound;
whether a compound is spelled with a space between the two words, with a hyphen,
or with no separation at all is idiosyncratic, as shown in *blackbird, gold-tail, black-
eyed*, and *black spruce*.

Meanings of Compounds

The meaning of a compound is not always the sum of the meanings of its parts; a
blackboard may be green or white. Not everyone who wears a red coat is a *redcoat*.
The difference between the sentences *She has a red coat in her closet* and *She has
a redcoat in her closet* could be highly significant under certain circumstances.

Other compounds show that underlying the juxtaposition of words different
grammatical relations are expressed. A *boathouse* is a house for boats, but a

cathouse is not a house for cats. A *jumping bean* is a bean that jumps, a *falling star* is a "star" that falls, and a *magnifying glass* is a glass that magnifies, but a *looking glass* is not a glass that looks, nor is an *eating apple* an apple that eats; *laughing gas* does not laugh, and *running shoes* do not run.

In all these examples, the meaning of each compound includes at least to some extent the meanings of the individual parts. However, there are other compounds that do not seem to relate to the meanings of the individual parts at all. A *jack-in-a-box* is a tropical tree, and a *turncoat* is a traitor. A *highbrow* does not necessarily have a high brow, nor does a *bigwig* have a big wig, nor does an *egghead* have an egg-shaped head. A *Bluenose* is a Nova Scotian, and a *Digby chicken* is a smoke-cured herring, not a rooster or hen.

As we pointed out earlier in the discussion of the prefix *un-*, the meanings of many compounds must be learned as if they were individual simple words. Some of the meanings may be figured out. If you have never heard the word *hunchback*, it might be possible to infer the meaning, but if you have never heard the word *flatfoot* it is doubtful you would know it means "detective" or "police officer," even though the origin of the word, once you know the meaning, can be figured out.

Therefore, the words as well as the morphemes and the morphological rules must be part of our mental grammars. Dr. Seuss uses the rules of compounding when he explains that, "when tweetle beetles battle with paddles in a puddle, they call it a *tweetle beetle puddle paddle battle*" (Geisel 1965).

The pronunciation of a compound differs from the way we pronounce the sequence of two words forming a noun phrase. In a compound, the first word is usually stressed (pronounced somewhat louder and higher in pitch), and in a noun phrase the second word is stressed. Thus, we stress *red* in *redcoat* but *coat* in *red coat*.

Universality of Compounding

Other languages have rules for conjoining words to form compounds, as seen by French *cure-dent*, "toothpick"; German *Panzerkraftwagen,* "armoured car"; Russian *cetyrexetaznyi*, "four-storied"; and Spanish *tocadiscos*, "record player." In Papago, a Native North American language of Arizona and northern Mexico, the word meaning "thing" is *haʔichu*, and it combines with *doakam*, "living creatures," to form the compound *haʔichu doakam*, "animal life."

In Twi, a language of Ghana and the Ivory Coast, by combining the word meaning "son" or "child," *ɔba*, with the word meaning "chief," *ɔhene*, one derives the compound *ɔheneba*, meaning "prince." By adding the word meaning "house," *ofi*, to *ɔhene*, the word meaning "palace," *ahemfi*, is derived. The other changes that occur in the Twi compounds are due to phonological and morphological rules in the language.

In Thai, the word for "cat" is *mɛɛw*, the word for "watch" (in the sense of "to watch over") is *fâw*, and the word for "house" is *bâan*. The word for "watchcat" (like a watchdog) is the compound *mɛɛwfâwbâan* — literally, "catwatchhouse."

Compounding is therefore a common and frequent process for enlarging the vocabularies of all languages.

Acronyms

Acronyms are words derived from the initials of several words. Such words are pronounced as the spelling indicates: SARAH from *Search and Rescue and Homing*, NAFTA from *North American Free Trade Agreement*, UNESCO from *United Nations Educational, Scientific, and Cultural Organization*, and UNICEF from *United Nations International Children's Emergency Fund*. *Radar* from "*radio detecting and ranging*," *laser* from "*light amplification by stimulated emission of radiation*," and *scuba* from "*self-contained underwater breathing apparatus*" show the creative efforts of word coiners, as does *snafu*, coined by soldiers in World War II and rendered in polite circles as "*situation normal, all fouled up*." An acronym that has recently been added to the English language and that is used frequently these days is AIDS from the initials of *Acquired Immune Deficiency Syndrome*. When the string of letters is not easily pronounced as a word, the acronym is produced by sounding out each letter and consequently may be called an *initialism*, as in CFL for *Canadian Football League*, RCMP for *Royal Canadian Mounted Police* ("Mounties" or "Horsemen" as they have been called, though their horses have long been retired except for ceremonial occasions), CBC (*Canadian Broadcasting Corporation*), or UBC (*University of British Columbia*), as well as the ubiquitous GST (*Goods and Services Tax*). Another example is CARP for *Canadian Association of Retired Persons*. When the Reform Party reorganized to form a new party, it was forced to reconsider its first attempt at a name (the *Conservative Reform Alliance Party*) when its opposition gleefully pointed out the acronym that would result.

Acronyms are being added to the vocabulary daily with the proliferation of computers and the widespread use of the Internet, including MORF (*male or female*), FAQ (*frequently asked questions*), WYSIWYG (*what you see is what you get*), and POP (*post office protocol*).

Blends

FOR BETTER OR FOR WORSE copyright Lynn Johnston Prod. Reprinted with permission of United Features Syndicate. All rights reserved.

Words may be combined to produce **blends**. Blends are similar to compounds, but parts of the words combined are deleted, so they are "less than" compounds. *Smog*, from *smoke + fog; motel*, from *motor + hotel; urinalysis*, from *urine + analysis; breathalyzer*, from *breath + analyzer*; and *medicare*, from *medical + care* are examples of blends that have attained full lexical status in English. The computer term *bit*, with its pun on the word meaning "a small piece," may be seen as a blend of *b(inary dig)it*. Blending seems to have created new suffixes such as *-alyzer*, as in *eye(a)lyzer; -flation*, as in *gradeflation, oilflation*, and *taxflation*; and *-cast*, as in *telecast, newscast*, and *sportscast(er)*. The word *cranapple* may be a blend of *cranberry + apple. Broasted*, from *broiled + roasted*, is a blend that has limited acceptance in the language, as does Lewis Carroll's *chortle*, from *chuckle + snort*. Carroll is famous for both the coining and the blending of words. In *Through the Looking-Glass,* he describes the "meanings" of the made-up words in "Jabberwocky" as follows:

> . . . "Brillig" means four o'clock in the afternoon — the time when you begin broiling things for dinner. . . . "Slithy" means "lithe and slimy." . . . You see it's like a portmanteau — there are two meanings packed up into one word. . . . "Toves" are something like badgers — they're something like lizards — and they're something like corkscrews . . . also they make their nests under sun-dials — also they live on cheese. . . . To "gyre" is to go round and round like a gyroscope. To "gimble" is to make holes like a gimlet. And "the wabe" is the grass-plot round a sun-dial. . . . It's called "wabe" . . . because it goes a long way before it and a long way behind it. . . . "Mimsy" is "flimsy and miserable" (there's another portmanteau . . . for you).

Carroll's "portmanteaus" are what we have called blends, and such words can become part of the regular lexicon. Blending is even done by children; Elijah Peregrine, the grandson of a friend of one of the authors, when less than 3 years old formed the word *crocogator* by blending *crocodile* and *alligator.*

Back-Formations

Copyright © 1996 by Mell Lazarus and Creators Syndicate.

Ignorance can sometimes be creative. A new word may enter the language because of an incorrect morphological analysis. For example, *peddle* was derived from *peddler* on the mistaken assumption that *-er* was the "agentive" suffix. Such words are called **back-formations**. The verbs *hawk, stoke, swindle*, and *edit* all came into the language as back-formations — of *hawker, stoker, swindler*, and *editor. Pea* was derived from a singular word, *pease*, by speakers who thought *pease* was plural. Language purists sometimes rail against back-formations and cite *enthuse* (from *enthusiasm*) and *ept* (from *inept*) as examples of language corruption; but language is not corrupt (although the speakers who use it may be), and many words have entered the language in this way.

Some word coinage, similar to the kind of wrong morphemic analysis that produces back-formations, is deliberate. The word *bikini* is from the Bikini atoll of the Marshall Islands. Because the first syllable *bi-* in other words, such as *bipolar*, means "two," some clever person, seeing the written word and ignoring differences in pronunciation, called a topless bathing suit a *monokini*. Historically, a number of new words have entered the English lexicon in this way. Based on analogy with pairs such as *act/action, exempt/exemption*, and *revise/revision*, the new words *resurrect, pre-empt*, and *televise* were formed from the existing words *resurrection, pre-emption*, and *television*.

Abbreviations

Abbreviations of longer words or phrases may also become "lexicalized"; *nark* for *narcotics agent, hydro* for *hydro-electric, telly*, the British word for *television, prof* for *professor, piano* for *pianoforte*, and *gym* for *gymnasium* are only a few examples of such "short forms" that are now used as whole words. Other examples are *ad, bike, math, gas, phone, bus*, and *van*. This process is sometimes called **clipping**.

Words from Names

The creativity of word coinage (or vocabulary addition) is also revealed by the number of words in the English vocabulary that derive from proper names of individuals or places. Thus *Bytown*, the original name of Ottawa, bore the name of Colonel By, the builder of the Rideau Canal, and *Stanfields*, long used as a synonym for underwear, were named after the manufacturers, Stanfields, Ltd., of Truro, Nova Scotia. The Canadian writer Marshall McLuhan, who discovered the principle that "the medium is the message," gave his name to *McLuhanism*, referring to his social ideas (e.g., that the effect of the introduction of the mass media is to deaden the critical faculties of individuals); hence also *McLuhanesque, McLuhanite*, and *McLuhanize*.

Willard R. Espy (1978) compiled a book of 1500 such words. They include some old favourites:

sandwich   Named for the fourth Earl of Sandwich, who put his food between
           two slices of bread so that he could eat while he gambled.

gargantuan   Named for Gargantua, the creature with a huge appetite depicted in
             a novel by Rabelais.

jumbo   After an elephant brought to the United States by P.T. Barnum.
        ("Jumbo olives" need not be as big as an elephant, however.)

Espy admits to ignorance of the Susan, an unknown servant, from whom we derived
the compound *lazy Susan*, or the Betty or Charlotte or Chuck from whom we got
brown betty, charlotte russe, and *chuckwagon*. He does point out that *denim* was
named for the material used for overalls and carpeting, which originally was
imported "de Nimes" ("from Nimes") in France, and *argyle* for the kind of socks
worn by the chiefs of Argyll of the Campbell clan in Scotland.

Grammatical Morphemes

> "... and even ... the patriotic archbishop of Canterbury found it advisable —"
> "Found what?" said the Duck.
> "Found it," the Mouse replied rather crossly; "of course you know what
> 'it' means."
> "I know what 'it' means well enough, when I find a thing," said the Duck;
> "it's generally a frog or a worm. The question is, what did the archbishop find?"
>
> Lewis Carroll, *Alice's Adventures in Wonderland*

Morphological rules for combining morphemes into words differ from the syntactic rules of a language that determine how words are combined to form sentences.
There is, however, an interesting relationship between morphology and syntax. In
the discussion of derivational morphology, we saw that certain aspects of morphology have syntactic implications in that nouns can be derived from verbs, verbs
from adjectives, adjectives from nouns, and so on. There are other ways in which
morphology is dependent on syntax.

When we combine words to form sentences, these sentences are combinations
of morphemes, but some of these morphemes, similar to *-ceive* or *-mit*, which were
shown to derive a meaning only when combined with other morphemes in a word,
derive a meaning only when combined with other morphemes in a sentence. For
example, what is the meaning of *it* in the sentence ***It's** hot in July* or in *The arch-
bishop found **it** advisable*? What is the meaning of *to* in *He wanted her **to** go*? *To*
has a grammatical meaning as an infinitive marker, and it is a morpheme required
by the syntactic, sentence-formation rules of the language. Similarly for *have* in
*Cows **have** walked here,* which is a grammatical marker for the present perfect,
and for the different forms of *be* in both *The baby **is** crying* and *The baby's diaper
was changed*, which function, respectively, as a progressive marker and a passive
voice marker.

Inflectional Morphemes

DENNIS THE MENACE

"LOOKS LIKE WE SPEND MOST OF OUR TIME INGING...
YOU KNOW, LIKE SLEEPING, EATING, RUNNING, CLIMBING..."

DENNIS THE MENACE® used by permission of Hank Ketcham and © by North America Syndicate.

Many languages, including English to some extent, contain bound morphemes that, like *to*, are for the most part purely grammatical markers, representing concepts such as tense, number, gender, case, and so forth.

Such "bound" **grammatical morphemes** are called **inflectional morphemes**: they never change the syntactic category of the words or morphemes to which they are attached. They are always attached to completed words. Consider the forms of the verb in the following sentences:

(a) I sail the ocean blue.
(b) He sails the ocean blue.
(c) John sailed the ocean blue.
(d) John has sailed the ocean blue.
(e) John is sailing the ocean blue.

In sentence (b), the *s* at the end of the verb is an agreement marker; it signifies that the subject of the verb is third person and singular and that the verb is in the present tense. It doesn't add any lexical meaning. The *-ed* and *-ing* endings are morphemes required by the syntactic rules of the language to signal tense or aspect.

English is no longer a highly inflected language. But we do have other inflectional endings. The plurality of many count nouns, for example, is usually marked by a plural suffix attached to the singular noun, as in *boy/boys* and *cat/cats*. At the present stage of English history, there are a total of eight bound inflectional affixes:

English Inflectional Morphemes		**Examples**
-s	third person singular present	She wait-**s** at home.
-ed	past tense	She wait-**ed** at home.
-ing	progressive	She is eat-**ing** the doughnut.
-en	past participle	Mary has eat-**en** the doughnuts.
-s	plural	She ate the doughnut-**s**.
-'s	possessive	Disa'**s** hair is short.
-er	comparative	Disa has short-**er** hair than Karin.
-est	superlative	Disa has the short-**est** hair.

Inflectional morphemes in English typically follow derivational morphemes. Thus, to the derivationally complex word *un + like + ly + hood*, one can add a plural ending to form *un + like + ly + hood + s* but not **unlikeslyhood*. However, with compounds such as those previously discussed, the situation is complicated. Thus, for many speakers, the plural of *mother-in-law* is *mothers-in-law*, whereas the possessive form is *mother-in-law's*.

Some languages are highly inflective. Finnish nouns, for example, have many different inflectional endings, as shown in the following example taken from L. Campbell (1977). Don't be concerned if you don't know what all the specific **case endings** mean.

mantere	nominative singular (singular)
mantereen	genitive (possessive) singular
manteretta	partitive singular
mantereena	essive singular
mantereeseen	illative singular
mantereita	partitive plural (plural)
mantereisiin	illative plural
mantereiden	genitive plural

Exceptions and Suppletions

The regular rule that forms plurals from singular nouns does not apply to words such as *child/children, man/men, sheep/sheep, criterion/criteria*. These words are exceptions to the English inflectional rule of plural formation. Similarly, verbs such as *sing/sang* or *bring/brought* are exceptions to the regular past tense rule in English. When, as children, we are acquiring (or constructing) the grammar, we have to learn specifically that the plural of *man* is *men* and that the past of *go* is *went*. For this reason, we often hear children say *mans* and *goed*; they first learn the regular rules, and, until they learn the exceptions to these rules, they apply them generally to all the nouns and verbs. These children's errors, in fact, support our position that the regular rules exist.

Some of the irregular forms must be listed separately in our mental lexicons, as **suppletive forms**. That is, one cannot use the regular rules of inflectional morphology to add affixes to words that are exceptions. One cannot form the past tense of *bring* by adding *-ed* (**bringed*); one must substitute another word (*brought*) for the inflected form. It is possible that for regular words only the singular forms are listed since we can use the inflectional rules to form plurals. But this cannot be so with exceptions. When a new word enters the language, it is the regular inflectional rules that apply. The plural of *Bic* is *Bics*, not **Bicken*.

The past tense of the verb *hit*, as in the sentence *Yesterday John hit the roof*, and the plural of the noun *sheep*, as in *The sheep are in the meadow*, show that some morphemes seem to have no phonological shape at all. We know that *hit* in the above sentence is *hit + past* because of the time adverb *yesterday*, and we know that *sheep* is the phonetic form of *sheep + plural* because of the plural verb form *are*. Thousands of years ago, Hindu grammarians suggested that some morphemes have a **zero-form**: that is, they have no phonological representation. In our view, however, because we would like to hold to the definition of a morpheme as a constant sound–meaning form, the morpheme *hit* is marked as both present and past in the dictionary, and the morpheme *sheep* is marked as both singular and plural.

Morphology and Syntax

"Curiouser and curiouser!" cried Alice (she was so much surprised, that for the moment she quite forgot how to speak good English).

Lewis Carroll, *Alice's Adventures in Wonderland*

Some grammatical relations can be expressed either inflectionally (morphologically) or syntactically (as part of the sentence structure). We can see this in the following sentences:

England's queen is Elizabeth II.	The queen of England is Elizabeth II.
He loves books.	He is a lover of books.
The planes that fly are red.	The flying planes are red.
He is hungrier than she.	He is more hungry than she.

Grammatical relations are also signalled morphologically by derivational affixes and compounding. Thus, the second sentence in the above list shows the correspondence of "He loves books" and "He is a lover of books," which uses both the function word *of* and the derivational affix *-er*. Derivation may also be seen in "He is a bibliophile" and compounding in "He is a booklover." Consider also the relations signalled in "the wheels of my car" (function word), "my car's wheels" (inflection), and "my carwheels" (compounding).

Some people form the comparative of *beastly* only by adding *-er*. *Beastlier* is often used interchangeably with *more beastly*. There are speakers who say either. We know the rule that determines when either form of the comparative can be used or when just one can be used, as pointed out by Lewis Carroll in the quotation above.

What one language signals with inflectional affixes another does with word order and another with function words. For example, in English, the sentence *Maxim defends Victor* means something different from *Victor defends Maxim*. The word order is very important. In Russian, all the following sentences mean "Maxim defends Victor": (The letter *č* is pronounced like the *ch* in the word *cheese*; the *j* is pronounced like the *y* in *yet*.)

> Maksim zasčisčajet Viktora.
> Maksim Viktora zasčisčajet.
> Viktora Maksim zasčisčajet.
> Viktora zasčisčajet Maksim.
> Zasčisčajet Maksim Viktora.
> Zasčisčajet Viktora Maksim.

The inflectional suffix -*a* added to the name *Viktor* to derive *Viktora* shows that Victor, not Maxim, is defended.

To convey the future meaning of a verb, speakers of English use the function word *will*, as in *John will come Monday*. In French, the verb is inflected for future tense. Notice the difference between "John is coming Monday," *Jean **vient** lundi*, and "John will come Monday," *Jean **viendra** lundi*. Similarly, where English uses the grammatical markers *have* and *be*, mentioned earlier, other languages use affixing to achieve the same meaning, as illustrated by Indonesian:

> dokter mem + eriksa saja   "The doctor examines me."
> saja dip + eriksa oleh dokter   "I was examined by the doctor."

In discussing derivational and compounding morphology, we noted that knowing the meaning of the distinct morphemes may not always reveal the meaning of the morphologically complex word. This problem is not true of inflectional morphology. If we know the meaning of the word *linguist*, then we also know the meaning of the plural form *linguists*; if we know the meaning of the verb *analyze*, then we know the meaning of *analyzed* and *analyzes* and *analyzing*. This reveals another difference between derivational and inflectional morphology.

The mental grammar of the language that is internalized by the language learner includes a lexicon listing all the morphemes and the derived words of the language. The morphological rules of the grammar permit speakers to use and understand the morphemes and words in forming and understanding sentences and in forming and understanding new words (see Figure 2.1).

Morphological Analysis: Identifying Morphemes

Speakers of a language can easily learn how to analyze a word of their language into its component morphemes, since their mental grammars include a mental lexicon of morphemes and the morphological rules for their combination. But suppose you

FIGURE 2.1

(English) Morphemes

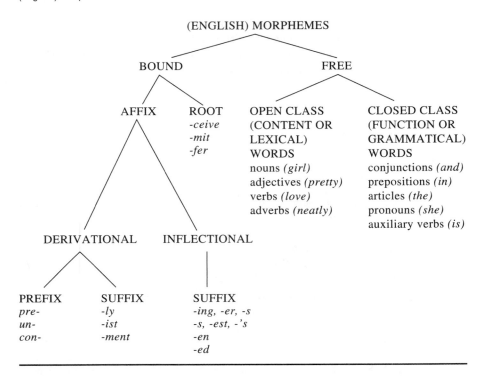

didn't know English and were a linguist from the planet Mars wishing to analyze the language. How would you find out what the morphemes of English were? How would you determine whether a word in that language had one or two or more morphemes?

The first thing to do would be to ask native speakers how they would say various words. (It would help, of course, if the speakers knew Martian so that you could ask your questions in Martian. If not, then you would have to do quite a bit of miming and gesturing and acting.) Suppose, then, you collected the following sets or **paradigms** of forms:

Adjective	Meaning
ugly	"very unattractive"
uglier	"more ugly"
ugliest	"most ugly"
pretty	"nice looking"
prettier	"more nice looking"
prettiest	"most nice looking"
tall	"large in height"
taller	"more tall"
tallest	"most tall"

To determine the morphemes in such a list, the first thing a field linguist would do is see if there are any forms that mean the same thing in different words — that is, look for recurring forms. We find them: *ugly* occurs in *ugly, uglier,* and *ugliest,* all three of which words include the meaning "very unattractive." We also find that *-er* occurs in *prettier* and *taller,* adding the meaning "more" to the adjectives to which it is attached. Similarly, *-est* adds the meaning "most." Furthermore, by asking additional questions of our English speaker, we find that *-er* and *-est* do not occur in isolation with the meanings of "more" and "most." We can therefore conclude that the following morphemes occur in English:

ugly	root morpheme	
pretty	root morpheme	
tall	root morpheme	
-er	bound morpheme	"comparative"
-est	bound morpheme	"superlative"

As we proceed further, we find other words that end with *-er* — *singer, lover, bomber, writer, teacher,* and many more words — in which the *-er* ending does not mean "comparative" but, when attached to a verb, changes it to a noun that "verbs" — *sings, loves, bombs, writes, teaches.* So we conclude that this is a different morpheme even though it is pronounced the same as the comparative. We go on and find words such as *number, umber, butter, member,* and many others in which the *-er* has no separate meaning at all — a number is not one who numbs, and a member does not memb — and therefore these words must be monomorphemic.

Once you have fully described the morphology of English, you might want to go on to describe another language. A language called Paku was written by one of the authors of this book (Fromkin) for a television series called *Land of the Lost,* originally shown on NBC in 1974 and 1975. This was a language used by the monkey people called Pakuni. Suppose you found yourself in this strange land and attempted to determine the morphemes of Paku. You would collect your data from a native Paku speaker and proceed as the Martian did with English. Consider the following data from Paku:

me	"I"	meni	"we"
ye	"you (singular)"	yeni	"you (plural)"
we	"he"	weni	"they (masculine)"
wa	"she"	wani	"they (feminine)"
abuma	"girl"	abumani	"girls"
adusa	"boy"	adusani	"boys"
abu	"child"	abuni	"children"
Paku	"one Paku"	Pakuni	"more than one Paku"

By examining these words, you find that all the plural forms end in *-ni* and that the singular forms do not. You therefore conclude that *-ni* is a separate morpheme meaning "plural," which is attached as a suffix to a noun.

These are simple examples of how one conducts a morphological analysis, but the principles remain the same for more complex languages.

Summary

Knowing a language means knowing the words of that language. When you know a word, you know both its **form** (sound) and its **meaning**; these are inseparable parts of the linguistic **sign**. The relationship between the form and the meaning is **arbitrary**. That is, by hearing the sounds (form), you cannot know the meaning of those sounds without having learned it previously. Each word is stored in our mental lexicons with information on its pronunciation (phonological representation), its meaning (semantic properties), and its syntactic class or category specification. For literate speakers, its spelling or **orthography** will also be given.

In spoken language, words are not separated by pauses (or spaces as in written language). One must know the language in order to segment the stream of speech into separate words.

Words are not the most elemental sound–meaning units; some words are structurally complex. The most elemental grammatical units in a language are **morphemes**. A morpheme is the minimal unit of linguistic meaning or grammatical function. Thus, *moralizers* is an English word composed of four morphemes: *moral + ize + er + s*.

The study of word formation and the internal structure of words is called **morphology**. Part of one's linguistic competence includes knowledge of the language's morphology — the morphemes, words, their pronunciation, their meanings, and how they are combined. Morphemes combine according to the morphological rules of the language. A word consists of one or more morphemes. **Lexical content morphemes** that cannot be analyzed into smaller parts are called **root** morphemes. When a root morpheme is combined with affix morphemes, it forms a **stem**. Other affixes can be added to a stem to form a more complex stem.

Some morphemes are **bound** in that they must be joined to other morphemes; they are always parts of words and never words by themselves. Other morphemes are **free** in that they need not be attached to other morphemes. *Free, king, serf,* and *bore* are free morphemes; *-dom,* as in *freedom, kingdom, serfdom,* and *boredom,* is a bound morpheme. **Affixes**, that is, **prefixes, suffixes, infixes,** and **circumfixes,** are bound morphemes. Prefixes occur before, suffixes after, infixes in the middle of, and circumfixes around stems.

Some morphemes, such as *huckle-* in *huckleberry* and *-ceive* in *perceive* or *receive,* have constant phonological form but meanings determined only by the words in which they occur. They are thus also bound morphemes.

Lexical content or **root** morphemes constitute the major word classes — nouns, verbs, adjectives, and adverbs. These are **open class** items because their classes are easily added to.

Morphemes may be classified as **derivational** or **inflectional**. Derivational morphological rules are rules of word formation. Derivational morphemes, when added to a root or stem, may change the syntactic word class and/or the meaning of the word: for example, adding *-ish* to the noun *boy* derives an adjective, and prefixing *un-* to *pleasant* changes the meaning by adding a negative element. Inflectional morphemes are determined by the rules of syntax. They are added to complete words, simple **monomorphemic** words or complex **polymorphemic** words (i.e., words with more than one morpheme). Inflectional morphemes never change the syntactic category of the word.

Some grammatical morphemes or **function words**, together with the bound inflectional morphemes, constitute a **closed class**; they are inserted into sentences according to the syntactic structure. The past tense morpheme, often written as *-ed*, is added as a suffix to a verb, and the future tense morpheme, *will*, is inserted in a sentence according to the syntactic rules of English.

Grammars also include ways of increasing the vocabulary, of adding new words and morphemes to the lexicon. Words can be coined outright, limited only by the coiner's imagination and the phonetic constraints of English word formation. **Compounds** are also a source of new words. Morphological rules combine two or more morphemes or words to form complex compounds, such as *lamb chop, deep-sea diver*, and *laptop*, a new word spawned by the computer industry. Frequently, the meanings of compounds cannot be predicted from the meanings of their individual morphemes.

Acronyms are words derived from the initials of several words — such as AWOL, which came into the language as the initials for "*a*way *without leave*," but the acronym is pronounced as a word. **Initialisms** are types of acronyms that are pronounced as separate letters (e.g., *MP* for *M*ember of *P*arliament). **Blends** are similar to compounds but usually combine shortened forms of two or more morphemes or words. *Brunch*, a late-morning meal, is a blend of *breakfast + lunch*. **Eponyms** (words taken from proper names, such as *john* for "toilet" or "prostitute's customer"), **back-formations**, and **abbreviations** also add to the given stock of words.

While the particular morphemes and the particular morphological rules are language-dependent, the same general processes occur in all languages.

Exercises

1. Here is how to estimate the number of words in your mental lexicon. Consult any standard dictionary.

   a. Count the number of entries on a typical page. They are usually bold-faced.

   b. Multiply the number of words per page by the number of pages in the dictionary.

   c. Pick four pages in the dictionary at random, say pages 50, 75, 125, and 303. Count the number of words on these pages.

   d. How many of these words do you know?

   e. What percentage of the total words on the four pages do you know?

f.   Multiply the words in the dictionary by the percentage you arrived at in question e. This number will tell you approximately how many English words you know.

2.   Divide these words by placing a + between their separate morphemes. (Some of the words may be *monomorphemic* and therefore indivisible.)

Example: replaces re + place + s

a.	retroactive	f.	psychology	k.	mistreatment
b.	befriended	g.	unpalatable	l.	airsickness
c.	televise	h.	holiday	m.	distraction
d.	margin	i.	grandmother	n.	saltpetre
e.	endearment	j.	morphemic		

3.   Match each expression under A with the one statement under B that characterizes it.

A

a.   noisy crow
b.   eat crow
c.   scarecrow
d.   the crow
e.   crowlike
f.   crows

B

1.   compound noun
2.   phrase consisting of adjective plus noun
3.   root morpheme plus inflectional affix
4.   root morpheme plus derivational suffix
5.   grammatical morpheme followed by lexical morpheme
6.   idiom

4.   Write the one proper description from the list under B for the italicized part of each word in A.

A

a.   terroriz*ed*
b.   un*civil*ized
c.   terror*ize*
d.   *luke*warm
e.   *im*possible

B

1.   free root
2.   bound root
3.   inflectional suffix
4.   derivational suffix
5.   inflectional prefix
6.   derivational prefix
7.   inflectional infix
8.   derivational infix

*5.   A.   Consider the following nouns in Zulu:

umfazi	"married woman"	abafazi	"married women"
umfani	"boy"	abafani	"boys"
umzali	"parent"	abazali	"parents"
umfundisi	"teacher"	abafundisi	"teachers"
umbazi	"carver"	ababazi	"carvers"
umlimi	"farmer"	abalimi	"farmers"
umdlali	"player"	abadlali	"players"
umfundi	"reader"	abafundi	"readers"

    a. What is the morpheme meaning "singular" in Zulu?

    b. What is the morpheme meaning "plural" in Zulu?

    c. List the Zulu stems and their meanings to which the singular and plural morphemes are attached.

  B. The following Zulu verbs are derived from noun stems by adding a verbal suffix.

fundisa	"to teach"	funda	"to read"
lima	"to cultivate"	baza	"to carve"

    d. Compare these to the words in section A that are related in meaning — for example, *umfundisi* ("teacher"), *abafundisi* ("teachers"), *fundisa* ("to teach"). What is the derivational suffix morpheme that specifies the category verb?

    e. What is the nominal suffix morpheme (i.e., the suffix that forms nouns)?

    f. State the morphological "noun formation rule" in Zulu.

    g. What is the stem morpheme meaning "read"?

    h. What is the stem morpheme meaning "carve"?

6. Examine the following words from Michoacan Aztec.

nokali	"my house"	mopelo	"your dog"
nokalimes	"my houses"	mopelomes	"your dogs"
mokali	"your house"	ipelo	"his dog"
ikali	"his house"	nokwahmili	"my cornfield"
kalimes	"houses"	mokwahmili	"your cornfield"
		ikwahmili	"his cornfield"

    a. The morpheme meaning "house" is

      (1) kal   (2) kali   (3) kalim   (4) ikal   (5) ka

    b. The morpheme meaning "cornfields" is

      (1) kwahmilimes   (2) nokwahmilimes   (3) nokwahmili
      (4) kwahmili   (5) ikwahmilimes

    c. The word meaning "his dogs" is

      (1) pelos   (2) ipelomes   (3) ipelos   (4) mopelo   (5) pelomes

    d. If the word meaning "friend" in this language is *mahkwa*, then the word meaning "my friends" is

      (1) momahkwa   (2) imahkwas   (3) momahkwames
      (4) momahkwaes   (5) nomahkwames

    e. The word meaning "dog" in this language is

      (1) pelo   (2) perro   (3) peli   (4) pel   (5) mopel

7. The following infinitive and past participle verb forms are found in Dutch.

Root	Infinitive	Past Participle	
wandel	wandelen	gewandeld	"walk"
duw	duwen	geduwd	"push"
zag	zagen	gezagd	"saw"
stofzuig	stofzuigen	gestofzuigd	"vacuum-clean"

With reference to the morphological processes of prefixing, suffixing, infix-ing, and circumfixing discussed in this chapter and the specific morphemes involved,

a.   State the morphological rule for forming an infinitive in Dutch.
b.   State the morphological rule for forming the Dutch past participle form.

*8. Below are some sentences in Swahili.

mtoto	amefika	"The child has arrived."
mtoto	anafika	"The child is arriving."
mtoto	atafika	"The child will arrive."
watoto	wamefika	"The children have arrived."
watoto	wanafika	"The children are arriving."
watoto	watafika	"The children will arrive."
mtu	amelala	"The man has slept."
mtu	anàlala	"The man is sleeping."
mtu	atalala	"The man will sleep."
watu	wamelala	"The men have slept."
watu	wanalala	"The men are sleeping."
watu	watalala	"The men will sleep."
kisu	kimeanguka	"The knife has fallen."
kisu	kinaanguka	"The knife is falling."
kisu	kitaanguka	"The knife will fall."
visu	vimeanguka	"The knives have fallen."
visu	vinaanguka	"The knives are falling."
visu	vitaanguka	"The knives will fall."
kikapu	kimeanguka	"The basket has fallen."
kikapu	kinaanguka	"The basket is falling."
kikapu	kitaanguka	"The basket will fall."
vikapu	vimeanguka	"The baskets have fallen."
vikapu	vinaanguka	"The baskets are falling."
vikapu	vitaanguka	"The baskets will fall."

One of the characteristics of Swahili (and Bantu languages in general) is the existence of noun classes. There are specific singular and plural prefixes that occur with the nouns in each class. These prefixes are also used for purposes of agreement between the subject–noun and the verb. In the sentences given, two of these classes are included (there are many more in the language).

a.   Identify all the morphemes you can detect, and give their meanings.

Example: -toto "child"

m-   noun prefix attached to singular nouns of Class I
a-   prefix attached to verbs when the subject is a singular noun of Class I

Be sure to look for the other noun and verb markers, including tense markers.

b.   How is the "verb" constructed? That is, what kinds of morphemes are strung together and in what order?

c.   How would you say the following in Swahili?

(1)   The child is falling.   *mtoto ana anguka*
(2)   The baskets have arrived.   *vikapu vimefika*
(3)   The man will fall.   *mtu ata anguka*

9.   One morphological process not discussed in this chapter is called **reduplication** — the formation of new words through the repetition of part or all of a word — which occurs in a number of languages. The following examples from Samoan exemplify this kind of morphological rule.

manao	"he wishes"	mananao	"they wish"
matua	"he is old"	matutua	"they are old"
malosi	"he is strong"	malolosi	"they are strong"
punou	"he bends"	punonou	"they bend"
atamaki	"he is wise"	atamamaki	"they are wise"
savali	"he travels"	pepese	"they sing"
laga	"he weaves"		

a.   What is the Samoan for the following?

(1)   they weave   *la laga*
(2)   they travel   *savavali*
(3)   he sings   *pese*

b.   Formulate a general statement (a morphological rule) that explains how to form a plural verb form from the singular verb form.   *Process of reduplication*
see quiz

10.   Below are listed some words followed by incorrect definitions. (All these errors are taken from Amsel Greene's [1969] *Pullet Surprises*.)

Word	Student's Definition
stalemate	"husband or wife no longer interested"
effusive	"able to be merged"
tenet	"a group of ten singers"
dermatology	"a study of derms"
ingenious	"not very smart"
finesse	"a female fish"

For each of these incorrect definitions, give some possible reasons why the students made the guesses they did. Where you can exemplify by reference to other words or morphemes, giving their meanings, do so.

11. Acronyms have become a part of many people's vocabularies. Often these people are unable to explain what the letters in an acronym stand for or even, sometimes, that the word is an acronym at all.

    a. List ten acronyms currently in use in Canadian English and explain the origin of each word. Do not use the ones given in the text.

    b. Invent five new acronyms (listing the words as well as the initials).

12. There are many asymmetries in English in which a root morpheme combined with a prefix constitutes a word but without the prefix is a non-word. A number of these are given in this chapter.

    a. Below is a list of such non-word roots. Add a prefix to each root to form an existing English word.

Words	Non-Words
_____	*descript
_____	*cognito
_____	*beknownst
_____	*peccable
_____	*promptu
_____	*plussed
_____	*domitable
_____	*nomer

    b. There are many more such multimorphemic words for which the root morphemes do not constitute words by themselves. How many can you think of?

Works Cited

Algeo, John, ed. 1991. *Fifty Years among the New Words: A Dictionary of Neologisms, 1941–1991*. Cambridge, UK: Cambridge University Press.

Campbell, L. 1977. "Generative Phonology vs. Finnish Phonology: Retrospect and Prospect." *Texas Linguistic Forum* 5: 21–58.

de Saussure, Ferdinand. 1969. *Course in General Linguistics*. Trans. W. Baskin. New York: McGraw-Hill.

Espy, W.R. 1978. *O Thou Improper, Thou Uncommon Noun: An Etymology of Words That Once Were Names*. New York: Clarkson N. Potter.

Geisel, T.S. (Dr. Seuss). 1965. *Fox in Socks*. New York: Random House.

Greene, Amsel. 1969. *Pullet Surprises*. Glenview, IL: Scott, Foresman.

Landau, Sidney I. 1984. *Dictionaries: The Art and Craft of Lexicography*. Cambridge, UK: Cambridge University Press.

Murray, James A.H. 1970. *The Evolution of English Lexicography.* The Romanes Lecture 1900. College Park, MD: McGrath.

Murray, James A.H., et al., eds. 1989. *Oxford English Dictionary: A New English Dictionary on Historical Principles, Founded Mainly on the Materials Collected by the Philological Society.* 1888–1933. 2nd ed. Oxford: Oxford University Press.

Sturtevant, E.H. 1947. *An Introduction to Linguistic Science.* New Haven: Yale University Press.

Thompson, S.A. 1975. "On the Issue of Productivity in the Lexikon." *Kritikon Litterrarum* 4: 332–49.

Tulloch, Sarah, comp. 1991. *The Oxford Dictionary of New Words: A Popular Guide to Words in the News.* Oxford: Oxford University Press.

Van Rooten, Luis d'Antin, ed. 1993. *Mots d'heures: Gousses, rames. The d'Antin Manuscript.* London: Grafton.

Further Reading

Anderson, Stephen R. 1992. *A-Morphous Morphology.* Cambridge, UK: Cambridge University Press.

Aronoff, Mark. 1976. *Word Formation in Generative Grammar.* Cambridge, MA: MIT Press.

Bauer, Laurie. 1983. *English Word-Formation.* Cambridge, UK: Cambridge University Press.

Hammond, Michael, and Michael Noonan, eds. 1988. *Theoretical Morphology: Approaches in Modern Linguistics.* San Diego: Academic Press.

Jensen, John T. 1990. *Morphology: Word Structure in Generative Grammar.* Amsterdam/ Philadelphia: John Benjamins Publishing.

Marchand, Hans. 1969. *The Categories and Types of Present-Day English Word-Formation.* 2nd ed. Munich: C.H. Beck'sche Verlagsbuchhandlung.

Matthews, P.H. 1976. *Morphology: An Introduction to the Theory of Word Structure.* Cambridge, UK: Cambridge University Press.

Scalise, Sergio. 1984. *Generative Morphology.* Dordrecht, Holland/Cinnaninson, U.S.: Foris Publications.

Spencer, Andrew. 1991. *Morphological Theory: An Introduction to Word Structure in Generative Grammar.* London: Basil Blackwell.

CHAPTER 3
Syntax: The Sentence Patterns of Language

The grammar of the language determines the properties of each of the sentences of the language. . . . The language is the set of sentences that are described by the grammar . . . the grammar "generates" the sentences it describes and their structural descriptions. . . . When we speak of the linguist's grammar as a "generative grammar," we mean only that it is sufficiently explicit to determine how sentences of the language are in fact characterized by the grammar.

Noam Chomsky, *Rules and Representations*

To grammar even kings bow.

J.B. Molière, *Les Femmes savantes* (1672)

"We get a lot of foreign visitors."

Knowing a language includes the ability to construct phrases and sentences out of morphemes and words. The part of the grammar that represents a speaker's knowledge of these structures and their formations is called **syntax**. The aim of this chapter is to show what syntactic structure is and what the rules that determine syntactic structures are like. Most of the examples and the specific structures will be from the syntax of English, but the principles that account for these kinds of structures are universal.

The meaning of a sentence depends to a great extent on the meaning of the words of which it is composed. But the structure of the sentence also contributes to its meaning. Word order, for example, can change the meaning. Thus,

> The dog bit the man.

is not news, but

> The man bit the dog.

is. And news is conveyed through the syntax. We might look on sentences as packets of information that serve a communicative function.

Sometimes, however, a change of word order has no effect on meaning.

> Jack Horner stuck in his thumb.
> Jack Horner stuck his thumb in.

The grammars of all languages include **rules of syntax** that reflect speakers' knowledge of these facts.

Grammatical or Ungrammatical?

The syntactic rules of a grammar also account for the fact that, even though the following sequence is made up of meaningful words, it has no meaning.

> *Bit dog man the the.

In English and in every language, every **sentence** is a sequence of words, but not every sequence of words is a sentence. Sequences of words that conform to the rules of syntax are said to be **well formed** or **grammatical**, and those that violate the syntactic rules are therefore **ill formed** or **ungrammatical**.

What Grammaticality Is Based On

In Chapter 1, we saw that speakers could distinguish strings of words as grammatical or ungrammatical depending on linguistic intuition. Here is another list of word sequences. Disregarding the sentence meanings, use *your* knowledge of English and isolate those strings that strike you as peculiar or "funny" in some way.

(1) (a) The boy found the ball.
         (b) The boy found quickly.

(c) The boy found in the house.
(d) The boy found the ball in the house.
(e) Disa slept the baby.
(f) Disa slept soundly.
(g) Zack believes Robert to be a gentleman.
(h) Zack believes to be a gentleman.
(i) Zack tries Robert to be a gentleman.
(j) Zack tries to be a gentleman.
(k) Zack wants to be a gentleman.
(l) Zack wants Robert to be a gentleman.
(m) Jack and Jill ran up the hill.
(n) Jack and Jill ran up the bill.
(o) Jack and Jill ran the hill up.
(p) Jack and Jill ran the bill up.
(q) Up the hill ran Jack and Jill.
(r) Up the bill ran Jack and Jill.

Speakers of English will normally pick out (b), (c), (e), (h), (i), (o), and (r) as strange. This shows that **grammaticality** judgements are not idiosyncratic or capricious but are determined by rules that are shared by the speakers of a language.

The syntactic rules that account for the ability to make these judgements include, in addition to rules of word order, other constraints. For example,

- The rules specify that *found* must be followed directly by an expression such as *the ball* but not by *quickly* or *in the house* as illustrated in (a)–(d).
- The verb *sleep* patterns differently than *find* in that it may be followed solely by a word such as *soundly* but not by other kinds of phrases such as *the baby* as shown in (e) and (f).
- Examples (g)–(l) show that *believe* and *try* function in opposite fashion, while *want* exhibits yet a third pattern.
- Finally, the word order rules that constrain phrases such as *run up the hill* differ from those concerning *run up the bill*, as seen in (m)–(r).

Sentences are not random strings of words. Some strings of words that we can interpret are not sentences. For example, we can understand (o) above even though we recognize it as ungrammatical. We can fix it up to make it grammatical. To be a sentence, words must conform to specific patterns determined by the syntactic rules of the language.

What Grammaticality Is Not Based On

Colorless green ideas sleep furiously. This is a very interesting sentence, because it shows that syntax can be separated from semantics — that form can be separated from meaning. The sentence doesn't seem to mean anything coherent, but it sounds like an English sentence.

> Howard Lasknik, *The Human Language: Program One*

Grammaticality is based not on what is taught in school but on the rules we acquire or construct unconsciously as children. Children acquire most of the syntactic rules of their language before they learn to read.

The ability to make grammaticality judgements does not depend on having heard the sentence before. You may never have heard or read the sentence

> Enormous crickets in pink socks danced at the prom.

but your syntactic knowledge will tell you that it is grammatical.

Grammaticality judgements do not depend on whether the sentence is meaningful or not, as shown by the following sentence:

> A verb crumpled the milk.

Although this sentence does not make much sense, it is syntactically well formed. It sounds "funny," but it differs in its "funniness" from the following string of words:

> *Milk the crumpled verb a.

You may understand ungrammatical sequences even though you know they are not well formed. To most English speakers,

> *The boy quickly in the house the ball found.

is interpretable, although these speakers recognize that the word order is irregular. On the other hand, grammatical sentences may be uninterpretable if they include nonsense strings, words with no agreed-on meaning, as shown by the first two lines of "Jabberwocky" by Lewis Carroll:

> 'Twas brillig, and the slithy toves
> Did gyre and gimble in the wabe;

Such nonsense poetry is amusing because the sentences comply with syntactic rules and sound like good English. Ungrammatical strings of nonsense words are not entertaining:

> *Toves slithy the and brillig 'twas
> wabe the in gimble and gyre did;

Grammaticality does not depend on the truth of sentences either — if it did, then lying would be impossible — on whether real objects are being discussed, or on whether something is possible or not. Untrue sentences can be grammatical, sentences discussing unicorns can be grammatical, and sentences referring to pregnant men can be grammatical.

Unconscious knowledge of the syntactic rules of grammars permits speakers to make grammaticality judgements.

What Else Do You Know about Syntax?

Reprinted with special permission of North America Syndicate.

Syntactic knowledge goes beyond being able to decide which strings are grammatical and which are not. It accounts for the double meaning, or **ambiguity**, of expressions such as the one illustrated in the cartoon above. The humour of the cartoon depends on the ambiguity of the phrase *synthetic buffalo hides*, which can mean "buffalo hides that are synthetic" or "hides of synthetic buffalo." This example illustrates that within a phrase certain words are grouped together. Sentences have structure as well as word order. The words in the phrase *synthetic buffalo hides* can be grouped in two ways. When we group them as

> synthetic (buffalo hides)

we get one meaning. When we group them as

> (synthetic buffalo) hides

we get another.

The rules of syntax allow both these groupings, and that is why the expression is ambiguous. The two structures may also be illustrated by the following diagrams:

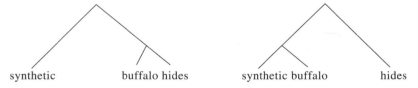

Many sentences exhibit such ambiguities, often leading to humorous results. Consider the following two sentences, which appeared in classified advertisements.

> For Sale: An antique desk suitable for lady with thick legs and large drawers.
> We will oil your sewing machine and adjust tension in your house for $10.00.

In the first advertisement, for example, the humorous reading comes from the grouping . . . (*for lady with thick legs and large drawers*) as opposed to the intended . . . (*for lady*) (*with thick legs and large drawers*), where the legs and drawers belong to the desk.

Because these ambiguities result from different structures, they are instances of **structural ambiguity**.

Contrast these sentences with

> This will make you smart.

The two interpretations of this sentence are due to the two meanings of *smart* — "clever" or "burning sensation."

Syntactic knowledge also enables us to determine the **grammatical relations** in a sentence, such as **subject** and **direct object**, and how they are to be understood. Consider the following sentences:

(1) Mary hired Bill.
(2) Bill hired Mary.
(3) Bill was hired by Mary.

In (1), Mary is the subject and is understood to be the employer who did the hiring. Bill is the direct object and is understood to be the employee. In (2), Bill is the subject, and Mary is the direct object, and (as we would expect) the meaning changes, so that we understand Bill to be Mary's employer. In (3), the grammatical relationships are the same as in (2), but we understand it to have the same meaning as (1), despite the structural differences between (1) and (3).

Syntactic rules reveal the grammatical relations between the words of a sentence and tell us when structural differences result in meaning differences and when they do not. We see that grammatical relations such as subject and direct object do not always tell us "who does what to whom," since in (1) and (2) the grammatical subject is the "who," but in (3) the subject is the "whom." These thematic roles, as opposed to grammatical relations, will be discussed in the next chapter.

Syntactic rules permit speakers to produce and understand an unlimited number of sentences never produced or heard before — another instance of linguistic creativity.

Thus, the syntactic rules in a grammar must at least account for

(1) the grammaticality of sentences,
(2) word order,
(3) structural ambiguity,
(4) grammatical relations,
(5) whether different structures have different meanings or the same meaning, and
(6) the creative aspect of language.

A major goal of linguistics is to show clearly and explicitly how syntactic rules account for this knowledge. A theory of grammar must provide a complete characterization of what speakers implicitly know about their language.

Sentence Structure

> I really do not know that anything has ever been more exciting than diagramming sentences.
>
> Gertrude Stein

Syntactic rules determine the order of words in a sentence and how the words are grouped. The grouping is hierarchical. Words from the lexicon are organized into phrases, phrases into clauses, and clauses into sentences. This organization may be analyzed from bottom to top or the other way around. A clause is a sentence, embedded or not. The sentence

> The child found the puppy, and his parents took it to a veterinarian.

is made up of two clauses that could be independent sentences but are combined into one compound sentence:

> (The child found the puppy), and (his parents took it to a veterinarian).

A clause is made up of phrases corresponding to the subject and the predicate. The subject is what the sentence is about, and the predicate is the property related to — or predicated of — the subject. The first clause may be grouped into the phrases *(the child)* and *(found the puppy)*. A further division gives *(the child) ((found) (the puppy))* and finally the individual words: *((the) (child)) ((found) ((the) (puppy)))*. It is easier to see the parts and subparts of the sentence in a **tree diagram**:

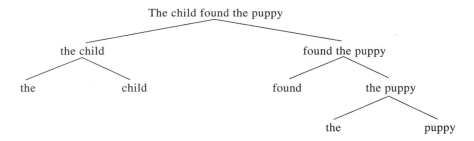

The "tree" is upside down, with its "root" being the entire sentence, *The child found the puppy*, and its "leaves" being the individual words, *the, child, found, the, puppy*. In addition to the linear order of words in a sentence, a tree diagram conveys the same information as the nested parentheses but more perspicuously. The groupings and subgroupings reflect the **hierarchical structure** of the tree.

The tree diagram shows among other things that the phrase *found the puppy* is naturally divided into two groups, *found* and *the puppy*. A different division, say *found the* and *puppy*, is unnatural in the sense that speakers of English would not use *found the* by itself or as an answer to the question "What did you do?" An answer might be *Found the puppy* but not *Found the*. In fact, *found the* cannot be an answer to any question. A word such as *found* never occurs in a single group followed only by *the*.

Other sentences with the same meaning as the original sentence can be formed:

> It was the puppy the child found.
> The puppy was found by the child.

In all such arrangements, *the puppy* remains intact. *Found the* does not remain intact, nor can the sentence be changed by moving *found the* around. All these facts show that *the puppy* is a natural structure, whereas *found the* is not.

Only one tree representation consistent with an English speaker's syntactic knowledge can be drawn for the sentence *The child found the puppy*. But the phrase *synthetic buffalo hides* has two such trees, one for each of its two meanings:

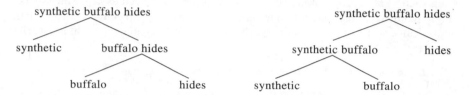

Every sentence has one or more corresponding **constituent structures** composed of hierarchically arranged parts called **constituents**. They may be graphically depicted as tree structures. Each tree corresponds to one of the possible meanings. Structural ambiguity can be explicitly accounted for by multiple tree structures.

Syntactic Categories

The grouping of constituents is not enough to understand structure. The constituents must be categorized, put into syntactic categories. Thus, a further meaning of *synthetic buffalo hides* might be "an artificial buffalo conceals itself." This has the same grouping, *(synthetic buffalo) (hides)*, as in the interpretation referring to the skins of artificial buffalo. In the first interpretation, the whole thing is a sentence (clause) in which *synthetic buffalo* is the noun phrase subject of the predicate verb phrase *hides*; the second is a noun phrase in which *hides* is the noun modified by the noun phrase *synthetic buffalo*. A more realistic example might be *Visiting professors can be boring*, where it is not clear whether it is professors who are visiting who are boring or the act of visiting certain professors that is boring (note the change of the relative clause in saying "who are boring" and "that is boring").

Each of the groupings in the tree diagram of *The child found the puppy* is a member of a large family of similar expressions. For example, *the child* belongs to a family that includes *a police officer, your neighbour, this yellow cat, he*, and countless others. Each member of this family can be substituted for *the child* without affecting the grammaticality of the sentence, although the meanings would change, of course.

A police officer found the puppy.
Your neighbour found the puppy.
This yellow cat found the puppy.
He found the puppy.

A family of expressions that can substitute for one another without loss of grammaticality is called a **syntactic category**.

The child, a police officer, and so on belong to the syntactic category **Noun Phrase (NP)**, one of several syntactic categories in English and every other language in the world. Noun Phrases may function as subject or object in a sentence, and only Noun Phrases may do so. Generally, the subject is the doer of that action and the object the person or thing affected. The subject appears to the left of the verb and the object to the right. NPs always contain some form of a noun (common noun such as *boy*, proper noun such as *John*, or pronoun such as *he*). Since *he* is a single word, you may question our calling it a *phrase*, but technically a syntactic phrase can consist of one or more words. In fact, an NP can even include a verbal complex:

> *Romeo, who was a Montague*, loved *Juliet, who was a Capulet.*

The NP subject of this sentence is *Romeo, who was a Montague*, and the object, also an NP, is *Juliet, who was a Capulet*. The whole Noun Phrase can be replaced by the noun head of the phrase (***Romeo** loved **Juliet***) or by a pronoun substitute (***He** loved **her***).

Noun Phrases are also specified by **Determiners (Det)**, function words that help to identify and mark off a limit of the NP. These words include **articles** (*the, a(n)*), demonstratives (*this, that*), possessive pronouns (*his, her, our*), possessive noun phrases (*Joe's, the man in the street's*), indefinites (*each, every, any*), and quantifiers (*one, two, three, first, second, third*).

Part of the syntactic component of a grammar is the specification of the syntactic categories in the language since this constitutes part of speakers' knowledge. That is, speakers of English know that items (a), (b), (e), (f), (g), and (i) in **(2)** are Noun Phrases even if they have never heard the term before.

(2)   (a) a bird
     (b) the red banjo
     (c) have a nice day
     (d) with a balloon
     (e) the woman who was laughing
     (f) it
     (g) John
     (h) run
     (i) the belief that the Earth is round

You can test this claim by inserting each expression into the context "_____ was lost" and "Who found _____?" Only those sentences in which NPs are inserted are grammatical because only NPs can function as subject and direct object.

Another test for Noun Phrases is the use of the **cleft sentence**. In this test, a constituent phrase is inserted into a string of the type *it is XP who/that YP*, where XP is the constituent and YP the rest of the sentence. In a cleft sentence, we cut ("cleave") one constituent (represented as XP) out of the sentence and place it in a position in which it will function as a contrasting focus of the sentence. In the sentence

> The early bird catches the worm.

we can say

> It is the early bird that catches the worm.

or

> It is the worm that the early bird catches.

There are other syntactic categories. The expression *found the puppy* is a **Verb Phrase (VP)**. Verb Phrases always contain a verb, which may be followed by other categories, such as Noun Phrases. This shows that one syntactic category may contain other syntactic categories. In **(3)**, the Verb Phrases are those that can complete the sentence "The child _____."

(3)   (a) saw a clown
(b) a bird
(c) slept
(d) smart
(e) is smart
(f) found the cake
(g) found the cake in the cupboard
(h) believed that the Earth was round

Inserting (a), (c), (e), (f), (g), and (h) will produce grammatical sentences, whereas inserting (b) or (d) would result in an ungrammatical string. Thus, (a), (c), (e), (f), (g), and (h) are Verb Phrases.

Another test for the Verb Phrase is the substitution of the pro-verb *do (so)* or *do (too)*, as in *The child saw a clown, and so did his mother*, or *. . . his mother did too*. Or, if it fits in the pseudo-cleft frame, *what YP did was XP*, in which the XP will be a Verb Phrase moved to that position to focalize it: for example, *The child saw the clown* becomes *What the child did was **see the clown***.

Other syntactic categories are **Sentence (S)**, **Adjective (Adj)**, **Noun (N)**, **Pronoun (Pro)**, **Adjective Phrase (AdjP)**, **Adverb Phrase (AdvP)**, **Preposition (P)**, **Prepositional Phrase (PP)**, **Adverb (Adv)**, **Auxiliary Verb (Aux)**, and **Verb (V)**.

The phrasal categories are based on their equivalent lexical content categories of Nouns, Verbs, Adjectives, Adverbs, and Prepositions that serve as their heads. The AdjP has an adjective as its head and may be specified by intensifiers, such as *very, rather*, or *quite*. They appear in attributive positions before nouns, which they modify — *Mary is a _____ woman (very intelligent, quite beautiful)* — or in predicative positions after copulative verbs such as *be* — *Mary is _____ (very intelligent, quite beautiful)*. The pro-adjective *so* may substitute for it: *Mary is very intelligent, and so is Max (intelligent)*.

AdvPs are headed by adverbs. Like AdjPs, they may be specified by intensifiers. They appear at the ends of sentences: *Joe told the story _____ (very quietly, rather elegantly)*. They may be replaced by the pro-adverbs *there, thus*, and *then: The teacher met the students there (downstairs) thus (calmly) then (much later)*.

PPs have prepositions as their heads. They may be specified by intensifiers such as *right (right on the mark)*. They typically designate relations in space (*in*) or time (*before*), and they take NP objects (*in the park*), but not always, as in *she ran in*. Pro-adverbial substitutes *there, thus*, and *then* may replace the PP. *The students studied there (in the park) thus (with difficulty) then (at night)*. PPs may also be moved about freely in the sentence: *In the park, the students studied with difficulty at night*.

Some of these syntactic categories should be familiar; they have traditionally been called "parts of speech." All languages have such syntactic categories; in fact, categories such as Noun, Verb, Pronoun, and Noun Phrase are universally found in the grammars of all human languages. Speakers know the syntactic categories of their language, even if they do not know the technical terms.

Phrase Structure Trees

> Who climbs the Grammar-Tree distinctly knows
> Where Noun and Verb and Participle grows.
>
> John Dryden, "The Sixth Satyr of Juvenal"

The fact that *The child found the puppy* belongs to the syntactic category of Sentence, that *the child* and *the puppy* are Noun Phrases, that *found the puppy* is a Verb Phrase, and so on can be illustrated in a tree diagram by specifying the syntactic category of each word grouping. These names are often referred to as **syntactic labels**.

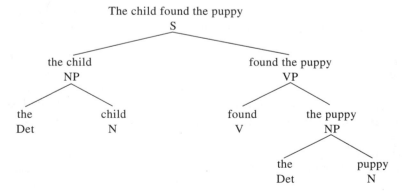

A diagram with syntactic category information provided is called a **phrase structure tree**. (It is also sometimes referred to as a **constituent structure tree**.) This tree shows that a sentence is both a linear string of words and a hierarchical structure with phrases nested in phrases.

Three aspects of speakers' syntactic knowledge of sentence structure are disclosed in phrase structure trees:

(1) the linear order of the words in the sentence,
(2) the groupings of words into syntactic categories, and
(3) the hierarchical structure of the syntactic categories (e.g., a Sentence is composed of a Noun Phrase followed by a Verb Phrase, a Verb Phrase is composed of a Verb that may be followed by a Noun Phrase, and so on).

Every sentence of English and of every human language can be represented by a phrase structure tree that explicitly reveals these properties. These trees represent the linguistic properties that are part of speakers' mental grammars.

The phrase structure tree above is correct, but it is redundant. The word *child* appears three times in the tree, *puppy* appears four times, and so on. We can streamline the tree by writing the words only once at the bottom of the diagram. Only the syntactic categories to which the words belong need to remain at the higher levels.

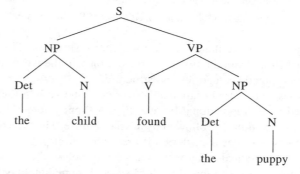

No information is lost in this simplified version. The syntactic category of each word appears immediately above that word. In this way, *the* is shown to be a Determiner, and *child* a Noun. The lowest categories in the tree, those immediately above the words, are called **lexical categories**. In Chapter 2, we discussed the fact that the syntactic category of each word is listed in our mental dictionaries. We now see how this information functions in the syntax of the language. We have not given a definition of these categories. All traditional definitions fail. In the sentence *Seeing is believing, seeing* and *believing* are nouns but are not "persons, places, or things," as a traditional definition of a noun goes. The grammar of the language and the syntactic rules define these categories.

The larger syntactic categories such as Verb Phrase are identified as consisting of all the words below that point or **node** in the tree. The VP in the above phrase structure tree consists of syntactic category nodes V and NP, and the words *found, the,* and *puppy*, which is consistent with our observation that *found the puppy* is a VP. Since *the puppy* can be traced up the tree to the node NP, this constituent is a Noun Phrase.

The phrase structure tree also states implicitly what combinations of words are not syntactic categories. For example, since there is no node above the words *found* and *the* that connects them, the two words do not constitute a syntactic category.

The phrase structure tree also shows that some syntactic categories are composed of other syntactic categories. The Sentence *The child found the puppy* consists of a Noun Phrase, *the child*, and a Verb Phrase, *found the puppy*. The Verb Phrase consists of the Verb *found* and the Noun Phrase *the puppy*. The determiner *the* and the Noun *puppy* together constitute a Noun Phrase, but individually neither is an NP.

A syntactic category includes all the categories beneath it in the tree. For example, the S in the tree above is composed of an NP followed by a VP. An S is also a Det followed by an N followed by a V followed by a Det followed by an N. The "all" is important; an S is not simply Det N V Det, as that would omit the final N that is a part of the S (i.e., *the boy found the* is not a Sentence). Every higher node is said to **dominate** all the nodes below it.

More Phrase Structure Trees

> The structure of every sentence is a lesson in logic.
>
> John Stuart Mill, *Inaugural Address at St. Andrews*

Every language contains sentences of varying phrase structure. The phrase structure tree below differs from the previous tree not only in the words that terminate it but also in its syntactic categories and structure.

This tree shows that a Verb Phrase may also consist of a Verb followed by a Noun Phrase followed by a Prepositional Phrase (PP). A Prepositional Phrase is shown to consist of a Preposition (P) followed by a Noun Phrase. This tree also illustrates that Noun Phrases may occur in three different structural positions representing three different grammatical relations: immediately below the S as the **subject**, immediately below the VP as the **direct object**, and immediately below the PP as a **prepositional object**.

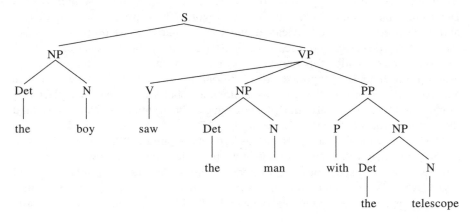

Semantically, the subject is traditionally considered to be what the sentence is about — the topic — and the doer of the action, but not always (cf. *The actor trained the monkey* and *The actor was a monkey*). The object is what is affected by the action. Grammatically, the subject appears to the left of the verb and is tied to it by an agreement of forms, so that a change in the person or number of the subject affects the form of the verb (*I am writing a letter, He is writing a letter, They are writing a letter*). In a question, the subject and the auxiliary verb are inverted (*Is he writing a letter?*). The object is found to the right of the verb; in a passive sentence, the subject and the object are reversed (*Max was struck by lightning*).

Just as tree structures reveal ambiguities, as shown earlier by phrases such as *synthetic buffalo hides*, they also account for other ambiguities, as in sentences such as *The boy saw the man with the telescope*. One meaning of this sentence — "the boy used a telescope to see the man" — is revealed by the phrase structure tree above. The key element is the position of the PP directly under the VP, where it has an adverbial function and modifies the Verb *saw*.

In its other meaning, "the boy saw a man who had a telescope in his possession," the PP *with the telescope* is positioned directly under the NP direct object, where it modifies the Noun *man*. Two different interpretations are possible because the rules of syntax permit different structuring of the same linear order of words, as revealed by the two phrase structure trees. This is made explicit in the following phrase structure tree, where the PP is part of the NP that includes *the man*.

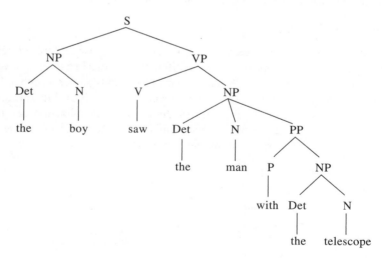

The Infinitude of Language

> So, naturalists observe, a flea
> Hath smaller fleas that on him prey;
> And these have smaller fleas still to bite 'em,
> And so proceed ad infinitum.

> Jonathan Swift, "On Poetry: A Rhapsody"

There is no longest sentence in any language, because speakers can lengthen any sentence by various means, such as adding an adjective or adding clauses. Even children know how to produce and understand very long sentences, and how to make them even longer, as illustrated by the children's rhyme about the house that Jack built.

> This is the farmer sowing the corn,
> that kept the cock that crowed in the morn,
> that waked the priest all shaven and shorn,
> that married the man all tattered and torn,
> that kissed the maiden all forlorn,
> that milked the cow with the crumpled horn,
> that tossed the dog,
> that worried the cat,
> that killed the rat,
> that ate the malt,
> that lay in the house that Jack built.

This rhyme begins with the line *This is the house that Jack built*, continues by lengthening it to *This is the malt that lay in the house that Jack built*, and so on.

You can add any of the following to the beginning of the rhyme and still have a grammatical, even longer, sentence:

> I think that . . .
> What is the name of the unicorn that noticed that . . .
> Ask someone if . . .
> Do you know whether . . .

This limitless aspect of language is also reflected in phrase structure trees. We have seen that an NP may appear in several different positions in a tree; it may come immediately under a PP, which PP may occur immediately under a higher NP, as in *the man with the telescope*. The complex (but comprehensible) Noun Phrase *The girl with the feather on the ribbon on the brim*, as shown in the phrase structure tree below, illustrates that one can repeat the number of NPs under PPs under NPs without a limit. This property of all human languages is called **recursion**.

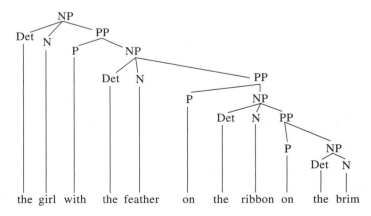

This phrase structure tree for the Noun Phrase illustrates that any syntactic category may be represented by a phrase structure tree — that is, may be the topmost node. It also illustrates the recursion of the NP within PP within NP and so on. (This property is called **recursive** because a syntactic category may *recur* in a sentence.)

The NP diagrammed above, though cumbersome, violates no rules of syntax and is grammatical. Moreover, it can be made even longer by expanding the final NP — *the brim* — by adding another PP — *of her hat* — to derive the longer phrase *the girl with the feather on the ribbon on the brim of her hat.*

The repetition or recursion of categories within categories is common in all languages. It allows speakers to use the same syntactic categories several times, with several different functions, in the same sentence. Human brain capacity is finite, able to store a finite number of categories and rules for their combination. Yet, with these finite means, an infinite set of sentences can be represented.

This linguistic property also illustrates the difference between competence and performance discussed in Chapter 1. All speakers of English have as part of their linguistic competence — their mental grammars — the ability to put NPs in PPs in NPs ad infinitum. But as the structures grow longer and longer, they become increasingly difficult to produce and understand. This could be due to short-term memory limitations, muscular fatigue, breathlessness, or any number of performance factors.

Thus, while rules give a speaker access to infinitely many sentences, no speaker utters or hears an infinite number in a lifetime; nor is any sentence of infinite length, although there is no upper limit in principle on sentence length. This property of grammars accounts for the creative aspect of language use, since it permits speakers to produce and understand sentences never spoken before.

Phrase Structure Rules

> Everyone who is master of the language he speaks ... may form new ... phrases, provided they coincide with the genius of the language.
>
> Michaelis, *Dissertation* (1769)

A phrase structure tree is a formal device for representing a speaker's knowledge. When we speak, we are not aware that we are producing sentences with such structures, but controlled experiments show that we use them in speech production and in comprehension. We don't use the tree structure diagrams per se, but we are unconsciously aware of the structures upon which these trees are based.

When we look at other phrase structure trees of English, we see certain patterns emerging. In ordinary sentences, the S is always subdivided into NP VP, the traditional subject and predicate. NPs generally contain Nouns, VPs always contain Verbs, and PPs consist of a Preposition followed by a Noun Phrase.

Of all logically possible tree structures, few actually occur, just as all word combinations do not constitute sentences in a language or even grammatical phrases. For example, a non-occurring tree structure in English is

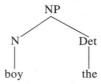

Both grammatical and ungrammatical trees must be accounted for in the grammar. Again, some kind of formal notation is required, preferably one that reveals speakers' knowledge precisely and concisely. To do this, linguists write grammars that include **phrase structure rules** that specify the constituency of syntactic categories in the language.

For example, in English a Noun Phrase (NP) can be a Determiner (Det) followed by a Noun (N). Thus, one of the several allowable NP subtrees looks like this:

The phrase structure rule that makes this explicit can be stated as

NP → Det N

This rule conveys two facts:

(1) A Noun Phrase can be a Determiner followed by a Noun.
(2) A Determiner followed by a Noun is a Noun Phrase.

The left side of the arrow is the category whose components are defined on the right side, which also shows the linear order of these components. Phrase structure rules make explicit speakers' knowledge of the order of words and the grouping of words into syntactic categories.

The phrase structure trees of the previous section show that the following phrase structure rules are part of the grammar of English.

(1) VP → V NP
(2) VP → V NP PP

Rule (1) states that a Verb Phrase can be a Verb followed by a Noun Phrase. Rule (2) states that a Verb Phrase can also be a Verb followed by a Noun Phrase followed by a Prepositional Phrase. These rules are general statements and do not refer to any specific Verb Phrase, Verb, Noun Phrase, or Prepositional Phrase.

Rules (1) and (2) can be summed up in one statement: A Verb Phrase may be a Verb followed by a Noun Phrase, which may or may not be followed by a Prepositional Phrase. By putting parentheses around the optional element, we can abbreviate rules (1) and (2) with a single rule:

VP → V NP (PP)

In fact, the NP is also optional, as shown in the following trees:

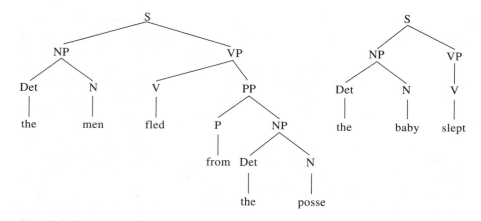

In the first case, we have a Verb Phrase consisting of a Verb plus a Prepositional Phrase, corresponding to the rule VP → V PP. In the second case, the Verb Phrase consists of a Verb alone, corresponding to the rule VP → V. All the facts about the Verb Phrase we have seen so far are revealed in a single rule:

VP → V (NP) (PP)

This rule states that a Verb Phrase may consist of a Verb followed optionally by a Noun Phrase and/or a Prepositional Phrase.

Other rules of English are

S → NP VP
PP → P NP

Growing Trees: The Relationship between Phrase Structure Rules and Phrase Structure Trees

I think that I shall never see
A poem lovely as a tree

Joyce Kilmer, "Trees"

Phrase structure trees may not be as lovely to look at as the trees Joyce Kilmer was thinking of, but if a poem is written in grammatical English its phrases and sentences can be represented by trees, and those trees can be specified by phrase structure rules.

The rules that we have discussed, repeated here, define some of the phrase structure trees of English.

S → NP VP
NP → Det N
VP → V (NP) (PP)
PP → P NP

There are several possible ways of viewing phrase structure rules. They can be regarded as tests that trees must pass to be grammatical. Each syntactic category mentioned in the tree is examined to see if the syntactic categories immediately beneath it agree with the phrase structure rules. If we were examining an NP in a tree, it would pass the test if the categories beneath it were Det and N, in that order, and fail the test otherwise, insofar as our (incomplete) set of phrase structure rules is concerned. Obviously, in a more adequate grammar of English, NPs would be specified to include many more structures.

The rules may also be viewed as a way to construct phrase structure trees that conform to the syntactic structures of the language. This is by no means suggestive of how speakers actually produce sentences. It is just another way of representing their knowledge, and it applies equally to speakers and listeners.

Conventions for generating trees have been developed. *Generating* as used here simply means "specifying." One convention is that the root of the tree, the S, occurs at the top instead of the bottom. Another convention specifies how the rules are to be applied. First, find a rule with an S on the left side of the arrow, and then put the categories on the right side below the S, as shown here:

Once started, continue by matching any syntactic category at the bottom of the partially constructed tree to a category on the left side of a rule and by expanding the tree with the categories on the right side. Proceed in this manner until only categories remain that never appear on the left-hand side of any rule, such as Det, N, and so on.

We may expand the tree started above by applying the NP rule to produce

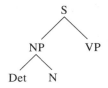

The categories at the bottom are Det, N, and VP, but only VP occurs to the left of an arrow in the set of rules. The VP rule is actually four rules abbreviated by parentheses. They are

VP → V
VP → V NP
VP → V PP
VP → V NP PP

Any one of them may be chosen to apply next; the order in which the rules appear in the grammar is irrelevant. Suppose VP → V PP is chosen to apply. Then the tree has grown to look like this:

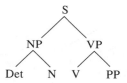

Convention dictates that we continue in this way until none of the categories at the bottom of the tree appears on the left-hand side of any rule. Thus, the PP must be expanded into a P and an NP and that NP expanded into a Det and an N. We can use a rule as many times as it can apply. In this tree, the NP rule was used twice. After we have applied all the rules that can apply, the tree looks like this:

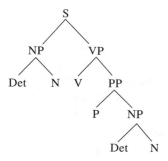

By following these conventions, we can generate only trees specified by the phrase structure rules. By implication, any tree not so specified will be ungrammatical. Whether we use the rules to generate only well-formed trees or to test the grammaticality of all possible trees is immaterial. Both methods achieve the goal of revealing syntactic knowledge. Most books on language use the rules to generate trees.

The categories that occur to the left of the arrow in a phrase structure rule are called **phrasal categories**; categories that never occur on the left side of any rule are **lexical categories**. Phrase structure trees always have lexical categories at the bottom since the rules must apply until no phrasal categories remain. The lexical categories are traditionally called "the parts of speech" and include Determiners, Nouns, Verbs, Prepositions, and so on.

The previous tree structure corresponds to a large number of sentences because each lexical category may contain many words, all listed and marked as to category in the lexicon. This is particularly true of the major, open class categories discussed in Chapter 2, such as Noun or Verb. This tree structure underlies the following sentences and millions more.

The boat sailed up the river.
A girl laughed at the monkey.
The sheepdog rolled in the mud.
The lions roared in the jungle.

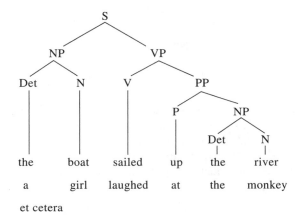

At any point during the growth of a tree, any rule may be used providing its left-side category occurs somewhere at the bottom of the tree. At the point where we chose the rule VP → V PP, we could equally well have chosen VP → V or VP → V NP PP. Doing so would have resulted in a different tree that, when the lexical categories were filled, would have been the structure for sentences such as

The boys left. (VP → V)
The wind swept the kite into the sky. (VP → V NP PP)

Since there are an infinite number of possible sentences in every language, there are limitless numbers of trees but only a finite set of phrase structure rules that specify the trees allowed by the grammar of the language.

Trees That Won't Grow

Speakers know which structures and strings of words are permitted by the syntax of their language and which are not. Such knowledge is specified implicitly by the phrase structure rules.

Since the rule S → NP VP is the only S rule in our (simplified) grammar of English, the following word sequences and their corresponding structures do not constitute English sentences:

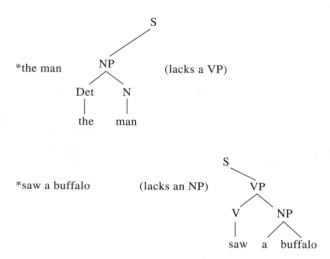

(Note that non-pertinent parts of the tree are sometimes omitted, in this case the Det and N of the NP, *a buffalo*.)

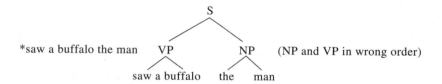

Similarly, *boy the* cannot be an NP in English because no NP rule of English syntax specifies that a Determiner can follow a Noun.

```
        NP
       /  \
      N    Det
      |     |
     boy   the
```

Rules in Other Languages

Whenever the literary German dives into a sentence that is the last you are going to see of him till he emerges on the other side of the Atlantic with his Verb in his mouth.

Mark Twain, *A Connecticut Yankee in King Arthur's Court*

Other languages have different phrase structure rules, hence different tree structures. In Swedish, the Determiner may follow the Noun in some NPs, as in *mannen* "the man" (*mann* "man" + *en* "the"). The ungrammatical tree of English is grammatical in Swedish:

There are languages that have "postpositions" that function like prepositions of English but come after the Noun Phrase instead of before it. In Japanese, *Tokyo kara* means "from Tokyo." Thus, the following tree, which does not occur in English, is found in Japanese:

```
            PP
          /    \
        NP      P
        |       |
      Tokyo   kara
```

The grammar of Japanese contains the phrase structure rule

    PP → NP P

but not the rule

    PP → P NP

Such differences between these languages and English are reflected in the phrase structure rules of the respective grammars.

In English, the Verb is always the first member of the Verb Phrase, as can be seen from the VP rule. In German, however, the Verb may occur in the final position of the Verb Phrase in some circumstances. German contains sentences such as

    Ich glaube dass Tristan Isolde liebt

that, if translated word for word, would be "I believe that Tristan Isolde loves," meaning "I believe that Tristan loves Isolde."

Despite these differences in detail, all grammars of all languages have the type of rule we are calling a phrase structure rule, which characterizes the structure of phrases, sentences, and syntactic categories of the language.

More Phrase Structure Rules

There are many sentences in English whose structures are not accounted for by the phrase structure rules given so far, including

(a) Pretty girls whispered softly.
(b) The man with the hat smiled.
(c) The teacher believes that the student knows the answer.

Sentence (a) may be represented by this phrase structure tree:

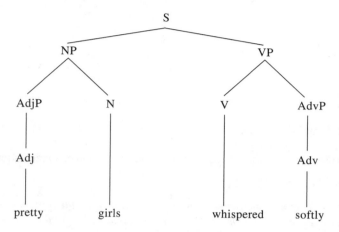

From this example, we see that a Determiner is optional in the NP. Moreover, two new lexical categories appear: Adjective (Adj) and Adverb (Adv), both optional. AdjP and AdvP have an Adjective and an Adverb as their heads, which may be preceded by Intensifiers such as *very, quite, rather, more*, and *most* and followed by PP: *The teacher was very sure of himself.* Similarly, the AdvP: *The lawyer acted quite independently of the law.*

> AdjP → (Intens) Adj (PP)
> AdvP → (Intens) Adv (PP)

All this suggests modifications to both the NP and the VP rules:

> NP → (Det) (AdjP) N
> VP → V (NP) (PP) (AdvP)

As pointed out earlier, any number of adjectives may be strung together. For simplicity, our rules will allow only one adjective and would need to be changed to account fully for English speakers' knowledge.

The addition of an optional Adverb to the VP rule allows for four more sentence types:

> The wind blew softly.
> The wind swept through the trees noisily.
> The wind rattled the windows violently.
> The wind forced the boat into the water suddenly.

The NP in sentence (b), *the man with the hat*, is similar to *the man with the telescope* seen earlier and has the following structure:

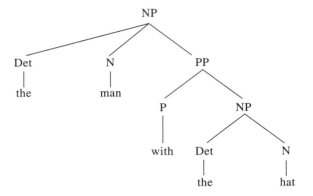

All but the final NP in the example *the girl with the feather on the ribbon on the brim of her hat* also have this structure.

The NP rule can be modified once more to include the option of a Prepositional Phrase:

NP → (Det) (AdjP) N (PP)

Sentence (c) contains another sentence: *the student knows the answer* is **embedded** in the larger sentence *The teacher believes that the student knows the answer*, which is called the **matrix sentence** or **main clause**. What should the phrase structure of this sentence be? Before we attempt to answer this question, we should look at some other data.

> That the student knows the answer is believed by the teacher.
> That the student knows the answer disturbed the teacher.

In both cases, the expression *that the student knows the answer* patterns like a Noun Phrase. Compare

> The child is believed by the teacher.
> The child disturbed the teacher.

These examples suggest that, when the word *that* is put in front of a sentence, *that* will function like an NP. The phrase structure tree for (c), then, is

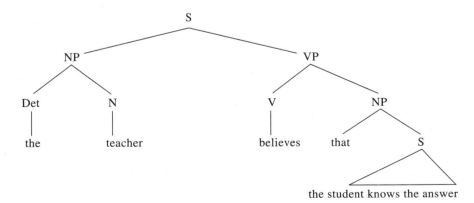

We omit the internal structure of the embedded sentence because it's not relevant. Another NP phrase structure rule is suggested:

NP → *that* S

This rule is different from previous rules in that it contains a word *(that)* rather than a category. In the next section, we'll see how words are put into phrase structure trees in general. This rule is a special case.

We now see how the ability all speakers have to embed sentences within sentences is captured. Here is an illustrative phrase structure tree:

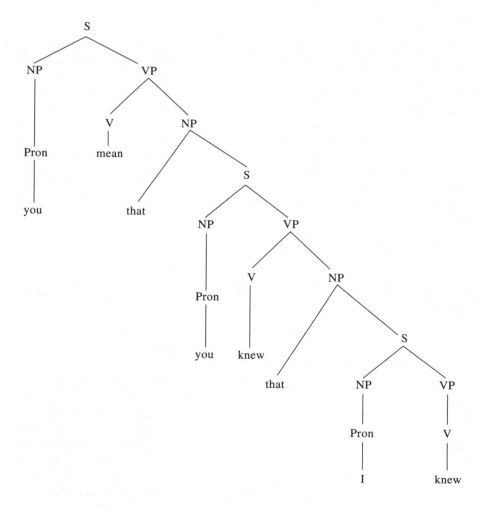

We need one final NP rule to account completely for this structure.

NP → Pronoun

Here are the phrase structure rules we have discussed so far and all we will present in this chapter.

(1) S → NP VP
(2) NP → (Det) (AdjP) N (PP)
(3) NP → *that* S
(4) NP → Pronoun
(5) VP → V (NP) (PP) (AdvP)
(6) AdjP → (Intens) Adj (PP)
(7) AdvP → (Intens) Adv (PP)
(8) PP → (Intens) P (NP)

A complete grammar of English would have many more such rules. However, even this mini-grammar can specify an infinite number of possible sentences because several categories (S, NP, VP) that appear on the left side of some rules may also appear on the right. Thus, the rules explain our observations that language is creative and that speakers with their finite memories can still produce and understand an infinite set of sentences.

There are still many sentence types of English not encompassed by these rules. Only in passing have we mentioned verbal elements such as the auxiliary verbs *have* or *may* in sentences such as *He may have left early*. Nor have we explicitly accounted for the many types of Determiners besides the Articles *the* and *a* that may precede the Noun in a Noun Phrase such as *each, several, these, many of Gershwin's*, and so on.

> Each boy found several eggs.
> These girls sang many of Gershwin's songs.

Rules (3) and (5) show that a whole sentence preceded by the word *that* may be embedded in a VP. In other data, different forms of sentences may be embedded in the VP. (Their source is beyond the scope of this introduction.)

> Joan is waiting for *you to sing* (cf. *You sing*).
> The host regrets *the PM's having left early* (cf. *The PM has left early*).
> The hostess wants *the PM to leave early* (cf. *The PM leaves early*).

Many generalizations about English are contained in these rules. For example, Noun Phrases always contain a Noun, Prepositional Phrases a Preposition, and Verb Phrases a Verb. Put more succinctly, X Phrases always contain an X, where X stands for Noun, Preposition, or Verb. The X of an X Phrase is called the **head** of that phrase. Thus, the head of a Noun Phrase is a Noun, of a Prepositional Phrase a Preposition, and so on, which is not surprising. Every phrasal category must contain at a minimum its lexical category head. It may, of course, contain other elements. A VP may or may not include an NP or a PP, but it must always contain a Verb.

The X-head may be introduced by some kind of **specifier** (Determiners with Nouns, Qualifiers with Verbs, Intensifiers with Adjectives, Adverbs, and Prepositions); it may be followed by a Complement or Object (all of them may have PP complements; Verbs and Prepositions may have NP objects); and they all may have Modifiers, such as PP modifiers of all of them and AdvPs of Adjectives and Verbs. Complements appear closer to the head, and Modifiers are farther removed. The super-rule for the X Phrase is something like

XP → (Spec) (Modifier) Head (Complement) (Modifier)

The Lexicon

We next went to the School of Languages, where three Professors sat in Consultation upon improving that of their own Country.

The first Project was to shorten Discourse by cutting Polysyllables into one, and leaving out Verbs and Participles; because in Reality all things imaginable are but Nouns.

The other was a Scheme for entirely abolishing all Words whatsoever; and this was urged as a great Advantage in Point of Health as well as Brevity. For it is plain, that every Word we speak is in some degree a Diminution of our Lungs by Corrosion.

Jonathan Swift, *Gulliver's Travels*

The learned professors of languages in Laputa proposed a scheme for abolishing all words, thinking it would be more convenient if "Men . . . [were] to carry about them such Things as were necessary to express the particular Business they are to discourse on." We doubt that this scheme could ever come to fruition, even in Laputa, not only because it would be difficult to carry around an unobservable *atom* or an abstract *loyalty*, but also because our thoughts are expressed by sentences that have structure and cannot be represented by things pulled from a sack.

Speakers of any language know thousands of words. They know how to pronounce them in all contexts, they know their meanings, and they know how to combine them in Phrases or Sentences, which means that they know their syntactic category. All of this knowledge is contained in the component of the grammar called the **lexicon**.

Together with the phrase structure rules, the lexicon provides the information needed for complete, well-formed phrase structure trees. The phrase structure rules account for the entire tree except for the words at the bottom. The words in the tree belong to the same syntactic categories that appear immediately above them. Through **lexical insertion**, words of the specified category are chosen from the lexicon and put into the tree. Only words that are specified as verbs in the lexicon are inserted under a node labelled *Verb*, and so on. Words, such as *fish*, that belong to two or more categories have separate entries in the lexicon.

Subcategorization

The lexicon contains more syntactic information than merely the lexical category of each word. If it did not, speakers of English would be unable to make the following grammaticality distinctions.

The boy found the ball.
*The boy found quickly.
*The boy found in the house.
The boy found the ball in the house.

Find is a **transitive Verb**. A transitive Verb must be followed by a Noun Phrase, its direct object. This additional specification is called **subcategorization** and is included in the lexical entry of each word.

Most words in the lexicon are subcategorized for certain contexts. Subcategorization accounts for the ungrammaticality of

*John put the milk.
*Disa slept the baby.

The Verb *put* occurs with both a Noun Phrase and a Prepositional Phrase, as in *John put the milk **in the refrigerator***. *Sleep* is an **intransitive Verb**, so it cannot be followed by an NP. This information is included as the subcategorization of each word.

Other categories besides Verbs are subcategorized. For example, within the NP, if the Determiner is lacking, only a plural Noun (or proper name) may be inserted; and, if the Determiner is *a*, then only a singular Noun may be inserted. This accounts for the following:

Puppies love warm milk.
*Puppy loves warm milk.
A puppy loves warm milk.
*A puppies love warm milk.

Subcategorization within the NP affects individual Nouns. *Belief* is subcategorized for both a PP and an S, as shown by the following two examples:

the belief in freedom of speech
the belief that freedom of speech is a basic right

The Noun *sympathy*, however, is subcategorized for a PP but not an S:

their sympathy for the victims
*their sympathy that the victims are so poor

Knowledge about subcategorization may be accounted for in the lexicon as follows:

A Fragment of the Lexicon	**Comments**
put, V, _____ NP PP	*Put* is a Verb and must be followed by both an NP and a PP within the Verb Phrase.
find, V, _____ NP	*Find* is a Verb and must be followed by an NP within the Verb Phrase.
sleep, V, _____	*Sleep* is a Verb and must not be followed by an NP within the Verb Phrase.
belief, N, _____ (PP), _____ (S)	*Belief* is a Noun and may be followed by either a PP or an S within the Noun Phrase.
sympathy, N, _____ (PP)	*Sympathy* is a Noun and may be followed by a PP within the Noun Phrase.

Just as lexical insertion ensures that Verbs are inserted under a V node in a tree, Nouns under an N node, and so on, it also ensures that, for example, intransitive Verbs such as *sleep* can appear only in trees in which the VP has no direct object. Similarly, *put* could occur only in trees in which it would be followed by an NP and a PP within the Verb Phrase, and so on. Any of these patterns may be modified by Adverbial Phrases, Prepositional Phrases, or Sentences, within the Verb Phrase or Noun Phrase, giving the circumstances of time, place, manner, instrument, et cetera. Thus, *He slept in the bathtub for three hours* has two PPs following the Verb that locate the Verb in place and time but are not necessary to the structure. One can say, simply, *He slept.*

More Lexical Differences

Different words engender different syntactic behaviour, and this aspect of a speaker's knowledge is represented in the lexicon. The verbs of English occur in a wide variety of syntactic patterns. For example, the verbs *want* and *force* appear to be similar when we consider sentences such as

> The conductor wanted the passengers to leave.
> The conductor forced the passengers to leave.

Here the verb is followed by an NP and an infinitive (i.e., the *to* form of the verb), but they differ in another syntactic context:

> The conductor wanted to leave.
> *The conductor forced to leave.

When *forced* is followed by the infinitive, the sentence is ill formed. *Try* exhibits a third pattern differing from both *want* and *force* in that it is never followed directly by an NP:

> *The conductor tried the passengers to leave.

Try is, however, similar to *want*, but not to *force*, in that it can be directly followed by an infinitive:

> The conductor tried to leave.

These different syntactic patterns of the verbs must also be specified in the lexicon, thus accounting explicitly for the knowledge speakers have about these words.

The examples given show only a single verb for each pattern, but each verb cited is representative of a class of verbs. For example, *expect*, *need*, and *wish* pattern like *want*; *allow*, *order*, and *persuade* pattern like *force*; and *condescend*, *decide*, and *manage* pattern like *try*.

Another instance of syntactically based lexical difference is found in the patterns in which *believe* and *say* appear, which, incidentally, are quite different from those of *want-*, *force-*, and *try*-class verbs:

> The teachers believe Susan is outstanding.
> The teachers say Susan is outstanding.

The teachers believe Susan to be outstanding.
*The teachers say Susan to be outstanding.

Both *believe* and *say* may be followed by a complete sentence. However, only *believe* can be followed by a "sentence" in which the verb occurs as an infinitive. As in the previous case, these patterns are representative of classes of verbs: *suppose* and *think* are like *believe; forget* and *insist* are like *say*.

A generalization emerges when the following examples are considered:

The teachers believe themselves to be outstanding.
*The teachers say themselves to be outstanding.

Believe-class verbs, but not *say*-class verbs, can be followed by a **reflexive pronoun**, a pronoun ending with *-self*. The differences in syntactic patterns are part of the lexical representation of these verbs.

The lexicon is a key component in the grammar, containing vast amounts of information on individual words.

Sentence Relatedness

> Most wonderful of all are . . . [sentences], and how they make friends one with another.
>
> O. Henry, as modified by a syntactician

Sentences may be related in various ways. For example, they may have the same phrase structure, differing only in their words, which accounts for their different meanings. We saw this earlier in sets of sentences such as *The boat sailed up the river, A girl laughed at the monkey*, et cetera.

Two sentences with different meanings may contain the same words in the same order, differing only in structure, as in *The boy saw the man with the telescope*. These are cases of structural ambiguity.

Two sentences may differ in structure, possibly with small differences in grammatical morphemes but with no difference in meaning:

The father wept silently.	The father silently wept.
The astronomer saw a quasar with a telescope.	With a telescope the astronomer saw a quasar.
Mary hired Bill.	Bill was hired by Mary.
I know that you know.	I know you know.

Two sentences may have structural differences that correspond systematically to differences in meaning.

The boy is sleeping.	Is the boy sleeping?
The boy can sleep.	Can the boy sleep?
The boy will sleep.	Will the boy sleep?
El hombre está en la casa.	¿Está el hombre en la casa?
(The man is in the house).	(Is the man in the house?)

The difference in the position of the verbal elements *is, can, will,* and *está* corresponds to whether the sentence is declarative or interrogative.

Phrase structure rules account for much syntactic knowledge, but they do not account for the fact that *Mary hired Bill* has the same meaning as *Bill was hired by Mary* but a different meaning than *Mary was hired by Bill.* Nor do they account for the systematic difference between statements and their corresponding interrogatives.

Since the grammar must account for all of a speaker's syntactic knowledge, we must look beyond phrase structure rules.

Transformational Rules

Method consists entirely in properly ordering and arranging the things to which we should pay attention.

René Descartes, *Oeuvres*, Vol. X

B.C. by permission of Johnny Hart and Creators Syndicate, Inc.

Consider the following two sentences:

(a) The father wept silently.
(b) The father silently wept.

They are represented in these two phrase structure trees:

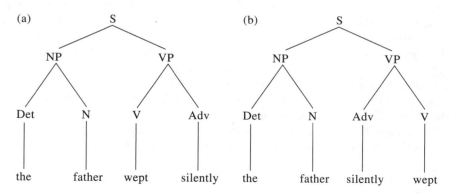

Both mean the same thing despite the position of the Adverb. The phrase structure rules place the Adverb at the end of the VP, thereby accounting for (a). How can (b) be accounted for? If we suggest a phrase structure rule with two optional Adverbs,

VP → (Adv) V (NP) (PP) (Adv)

then we are faced with the unacceptable possibility of generating ungrammatical strings such as

*The father cleverly wept bitterly.

A solution to this problem is to allow the phrase structure rules to generate the Adverb in VP final position and to have another formal device, called a **transformational rule**, move the Adverb in front of the Verb, thus deriving the structure that represents (b) from the structure that represents (a).

The basic sentences of the language, whose phrase structure trees are called **deep structures**, are specified by the phrase structure rules. Variants on those basic sentence structures are derived via transformations.

The structures of sentences that we actually speak — to which the rules of phonology are applied — are called **surface structures**. If no transformations apply, then deep structure and surface structure are the same. If transformations apply, then surface structure is the end result after all transformations have had their effects. According to some transformational theories, though, certain obligatory transformations apply to all deep structures, and thus deep and surface structures are never identical. In this introductory treatment, however, we will avoid such complexities.

In the above examples, then, the (a) tree reflects the deep structure, underlying both sentences (a) and (b). In the case of (a), the surface structure is the same as the deep structure because no transformation has been applied to it. The surface structure of (b) is represented by the (b) tree because the adverb-moving transformation has altered its deep structure.

Much syntactic knowledge not revealed by phrase structure rules is accounted for by transformations, which alter phrase structure trees by moving, adding, or deleting elements. In particular, families of structurally related sentences are revealed by virtue of having the same deep structure, with differences in surface structure created by transformational rules.

A transformation similar to the one that moves Adverbs moves Prepositional Phrases when they occur immediately under the VP. This transformation changes the deep structure of *The astronomer saw the quasar with the telescope* into the structure corresponding to *With the telescope, the astronomer saw the quasar*.

Transformations act on structures, irrespective of the words they contain. They are **structure dependent**. The transformational rule just described moves any PP as long as it is immediately under the VP. It would be responsible for *In the house, the puppy found the ball* and so on.

Further proof of the structure dependency of transformations is the fact that *With a telescope, the boy saw the man* is not ambiguous. It has only the meaning "the boy used a telescope to see the man," the meaning corresponding to the phrase structure in which the PP is immediately under the VP. The structure corresponding to the other meaning, "the boy saw a man who had a telescope," has its PP in the NP. The transformation does not apply to it because the structural requirements are not met.

Another rule moves a Particle from a position after the Verb to a position at the end of the clause. Compare the following sentences:

(1) He ran up the bill.
(2) He ran the bill up.
(3) He ran up the hill.

The verbal particle *up* and the verb *run* depend on each other for the unique meaning of the phrasal verb *run up*. We know this because *run up* has a meaning different from *run in* or *look up*. The sentences above have the same deep structure, but the surface structure of sentence (2) illustrates a **discontinuous dependency**. The verb is separated from its direct object NP. Superficially, sentence (1) resembles sentence (3), *He ran up the hill.* In this sentence, *up the hill* is a PP with *the hill* as NP object of the preposition *up* and cannot be split up. We cannot say **He ran the hill up,* but we can say *Up the hill he ran* and not **Up the bill he ran.* The VP in sentence (1) is V Particle NP, while that in sentence (3) is V PP. The structure of sentence (2) is V NP Particle.

Transformations may also delete elements. For example, the surface structure of the ambiguous sentence *George wants the job more than Martha* may be derived from two possible deep structures:

(1) George wants the job more than he wants Martha.
(2) George wants the job more than Martha wants the job.

A deletion transformation either deletes *he wants* from the structure of example (1) or *wants the job* from the structure of example (2). This is a case of **transformationally induced ambiguity**: two different deep structures with different semantic interpretations are transformed into a single surface structure.

Another transformation deletes *that* when it precedes a sentence in direct object position, but not in subject position, as illustrated by these pairs:

I know that you know.   I know you know.
That you know bothers me.   *You know bothers me.

This is a further demonstration that transformations are structure dependent.

Transformations also reveal a speaker's knowledge of the systematic relationship between statements and questions. Consider again the following sentences:

The boy is sleeping.
The boy can sleep.
The boy will sleep.

Words such as *is, can*, and *will* are in the class of **Auxiliary Verbs (Aux)**, which includes *be* and *have* as well as *may, might, would, could*, and several others. They may also be called helping verbs or auxiliary modals. The S-rule for this structure would be S → NP Aux VP. They occur in structures such as this one:

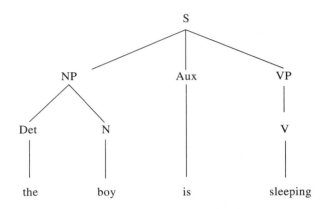

Now consider the interrogative sentences corresponding to the declarative ones just given:

Is the boy sleeping?   (Cf. The boy is sleeping.)
Can the boy sleep?   (Cf. The boy can sleep.)
Will the boy sleep?   (Cf. The boy will sleep.)

The interrogative or question sentences are related to their declarative counterparts in a simple way. In the questions, the Aux occurs at the beginning of the sentence rather than after the subject NP. This relationship can be accounted for by a transformation that moves the Aux to the front of the sentence. Phrase structure rules need only generate declarative sentences as deep structures. A transformation derives the surface structures of the corresponding interrogatives.

Consider now the following declarative–interrogative sets of sentences:

The boy who is sleeping was dreaming.
Was the boy who is sleeping dreaming?
*Is the boy who sleeping was dreaming?

The boy who can sleep will dream.
Will the boy who can sleep dream?
*Can the boy who sleep will dream?

The ungrammatical sentences show that, in forming questions, it is the Auxiliary of the topmost S, that is, the one following the entire first NP, that is placed at the front of the sentence and not simply the first Auxiliary in the sentence. This is illustrated in the following simplified phrase structure trees:

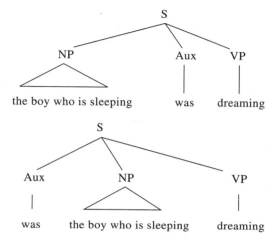

This is further evidence that syntactic categories such as Noun Phrase are basic structures in language. It is also further evidence of the structure-dependent nature of transformational rules. Transformations such as the one for forming questions must refer to structure, and not to the linear order of elements, in order to produce the correct results. This is true not only in English, for similar constraints and similar rules occur in other languages, as shown by the following sentences in Spanish (examples from Chomsky 1988).

> El hombre está en la casa.
> The man is in the house.

> ¿Está el hombre en la casa?
> Is the man in the house?

> El hombre está contento.
> The man is happy.

> ¿Está el hombre contento?
> Is the man happy?

> El hombre, que está contento, está en la casa.
> The man, who is happy, is in the house.

> ¿Está el hombre, que está contento, en la casa?
> Is the man, who is happy, in the house?

> *¿Está el hombre, que contento, está en la casa?
> *Is the man, who happy, is in the house?

More than one transformation may act on a deep structure. When they do, they do so one after the other. Consider *Is the father silently weeping?* Its deep structure is *The father is weeping silently.* The adverb-moving transformation produces the **underlying structure** *The father is silently weeping.* The question transformation acts on this structure to produce the surface structure *Is the father silently weeping*? This is illustrated in the following diagrams:

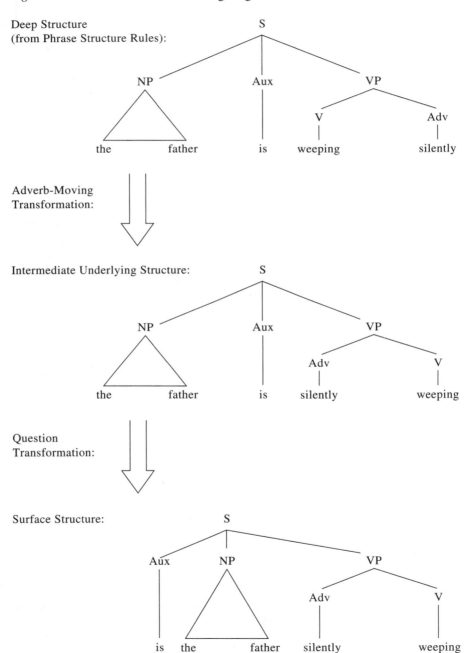

Long-Distance Relationships

Anyone who has had a friend or a spouse living in another city probably cringes at the idea of long-distance relationships. But they are indispensable to the grammar of English.

Consider first the following sentences:

> The guy seems kind of cute.
> The guys seem kind of cute.

The verb has an *s* added whenever the subject is third person singular. Such a relationship is called **agreement** or **subject–verb agreement**.

Now consider these sentences:

> The guy we met at the party next door *seems* kind of cute.
> The guys we met at the party next door *seem* kind of cute.

The verb *seem* must agree with the subject, *guy* or *guys*, and that agreement takes place over a long distance. In the examples above, the "distance" encompassed *we met at the party next door*, but there is no limit to how many words may intervene, as the following sentence illustrates:

> The guys (guy) we met at the party next door that lasted until 3 A.M. and was finally broken up by the cops who were called by the neighbours seem (seems) kind of cute.

This aspect of linguistic competence is explained by the phrase structure tree of such a sentence, which is shown below omitting much detail:

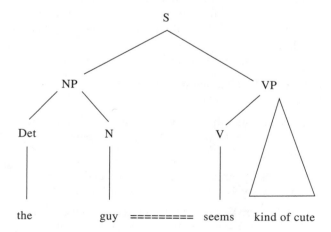

In the tree, "========" represents the intervening structure that may, in principle, be indefinitely long and complex. But speakers of English know that agreement depends on sentence structure, not on the linear order of words. Agreement is between the subject, structurally defined as the NP immediately below the S, and the main verb, structurally defined as the V in the VP immediately below the S. Other material can be ignored as far as the rule of agreement is concerned, although in actual performance, if the distance is too great, the speaker may forget what the head noun was.

"Wh-" Sentences

"Who's on first?"
"That's right!"

Bud Abbott and Lou Costello

A different long-distance relationship is illustrated by the following sentences:

(1) Helen said the prime minister wanted to hire her aide.
(2) Helen said the prime minister wanted to hire who?
(3) Who did Helen say the prime minister wanted to hire?

Either of sentences (2) and (3) might be spoken by someone who didn't hear all of the first sentence. Note, however, that the *who* that replaced *her aide* in (2) appears at the front of (3). This is evidence for a transformation that moves the **wh- word** to the front of the sentence, the same transformation that moves Aux to the front in other types of questions.

Sentence (2) is the deep structure. The fact that *who* is the direct object of the verb *hire* is explicitly revealed in the deep structure. In (3), despite the distance between *who* and *hire*, it is understood that *who* is the direct object. This is accounted for by the transformation together with the fact that (2) is the deep structure that underlies (3).

As in the case of agreement, the distance can be indefinitely long:

Who did Helen say the prime minister wanted the senator to try to convince the Commons speaker to get the MP to hire?

Unlike the agreement rule, the nature of the intervening structure makes a difference in sentences with *wh-* words, such as *who, when, what,* and *which,* as shown in the following:

Emily paid a visit to the prime minister that wants to hire who?
*Who did Emily pay a visit to the prime minister that wants to hire?

Miss Marple asked Sherlock whether Poirot had solved the crime.
Who did Miss Marple ask whether Poirot had solved the crime?
*Who did Miss Marple ask Sherlock whether had solved the crime?
*Who did Miss Marple ask Sherlock whether Poirot had solved the crime?

Sam Spade insulted the fat man's henchman.
Who did Sam Spade insult?
Whose henchman did Sam Spade insult?
*Whose did Sam Spade insult henchman?

Alice talked to the white rabbit in the afternoon.
Who talked to the white rabbit in the afternoon?
Who did Alice talk to when?
When did Alice talk to whom?
*Who when did Alice talk to?
*When to whom did Alice talk?

The constraints on the formation of *wh-* questions are rather complicated, though they are part of every English speaker's competence. If this were a book on English syntax, then the rules and limitations would have to be made explicit.

More about Sentence Structure

Normal human minds are such that . . . without the help of anybody, they will produce 1000 (sentences) they never heard spoke of . . . inventing and saying such things as they never heard from their masters, nor any mouth.

Huarte De San Juan (c. 1530–1592)

There are many more structure-dependent relationships in language than can be discussed in an introductory text. In this section, we will examine another of them. Consider the following pair of sentences:

(a) Mary hired Bill.
(b) Bill was hired by Mary.

The first of this pair is an **active sentence**; the second is **passive**. There is a systematic relationship between the structure of an active–passive pair.

(1) The subject of the passive sentence corresponds to the direct object of the active sentence.
(2) In the passive sentence, a form of the verb *to be* appears in front of the main verb, which occurs in its participle form (the form that occurs after the auxiliary verb *have* as in *She has **hired** him; I have **taken** a bath*).
(3) The subject of the active sentence appears in the passive sentence in a prepositional phrase headed by the preposition *by*, or it may be omitted altogether. Here is the phrase structure tree of (a) with the grammatical relations explicitly shown:

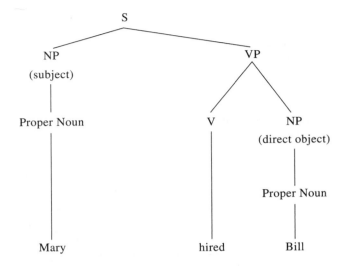

Active sentences of the form

> Subject V Direct Object

have passive counterparts of the form

> Direct Object *be* V-participle *by* Subject

where the *be* agrees with the direct object, which functions as the subject of the passive sentence. The following abbreviated trees illustrate the active and corresponding passive structures:

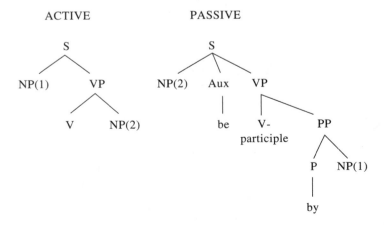

A transformation accounts for part of what English speakers know about the active–passive relationship. It applies to active sentences with the structure shown above and transforms them into their passive-structure counterparts. This shows that transformations may alter grammatical relations, change verb forms, and insert morphemes.

The active sentences are the deep structures. In deep structure, the grammatical relations of subject and direct object are interpreted semantically. Since both active and passive sentences have the same deep structure, the semantic relationships are the same in both. That is why we understand Mary as the hirer and Bill as the hired in both the active and the passive sentences.

This is a structure-dependent relationship, as all relationships involving transformations are. This may be seen by making up a nonsense sentence such as

The jabberwocky snicker-snacked the wabe.

and observing that the passive is

The wabe was snicker-snacked by the jabberwocky.

The form of *to be* that occurs in passive sentences is an Auxiliary Verb. It follows the pattern of Aux when a passive sentence is transformed into its corresponding question.

Was the wabe snicker-snacked by the jabberwocky?

These examples also illustrate that the order in which transformations occur is significant. The passive transformation must apply first, positioning the *was* for the question transformation. They could not apply in the reverse order.

Sign Language Syntax

All languages have rules of syntax similar in kind, if not in detail, to those of English, and sign languages are no exception. A signer is as capable as an oral speaker of distinguishing *dog bites man* from *man bites dog* through the order of signing.

Many languages, including English, have a transformation that moves a direct object to the beginning of the sentence to draw particular attention to it, as in the following sentence:

Many dogs my wife has rescued from the pound.

The transformation is called **topicalization** because an object to which attention is drawn generally becomes the topic of the sentence or conversation. (The deep structure underlying this sentence is *My wife has rescued many dogs from the pound.*)

In American Sign Language (ASL), a similar reordering of signs accompanied by raising the eyebrows and tilting the head upward accomplishes the same effect. The head motion and facial expressions of a signer function as markers of the special word order, much as intonation does in English or the attachment of prefixes or suffixes does in other languages.

There are constraints on topicalization similar to those on *wh-* preposing illustrated in a previous section. The following string is ungrammatical.

*Henchman, Sam Spade insulted the fat man's.

Compare it with the grammatical

> The fat man's henchman Sam Spade insulted.

Similar constraints are found in sign languages. An attempt to sign *Henchman, Sam Spade insulted the fat man's* in ASL would result in an ungrammatical sequence of signs.

In Thai, to show that an action is being done continuously, the auxiliary verb *kamlang* is inserted before the verb. Thus, *kin* means "eat," and *kamlang kin* means "is eating." In English, a form of *be* is inserted, and the main verb is changed to a gerund. In ASL, the sign for a verb such as *eat* may be articulated with a repetitive sweeping movement to achieve the same effect.

The syntax of human language is complex. It is not the aim of an introductory text to present the specific details of these complexities or even the arguments in support of some of the concepts we have presented in this chapter. Our aim, rather, is to expose the complexity of syntactic knowledge that speakers of English or any language must have.

Summary

Speakers of a language recognize the grammatical sentences of their language and know how the words in a grammatical sentence must be ordered and grouped. All speakers are capable of producing and understanding an unlimited number of sentences never before spoken or heard. They also recognize ambiguities, know when different sentences mean the same thing, and correctly perceive the grammatical relations in a sentence, such as **subject** and **direct object**. This kind of knowledge is accounted for in the grammar by the **rules of syntax**.

Sentences have structures that can be represented by **phrase structure trees** containing **syntactic categories**. Such a representation reveals the linear order of words and the constituency of each syntactic category. Syntactic categories are either **phrasal categories**, such as NP and VP, which can be decomposed into other syntactic categories, or **lexical categories**, such as Noun and Verb, which correspond to the words of the language.

A linguistic grammar is a formally stated, explicit description of the mental grammar or speaker's linguistic competence. **Phrase structure rules** characterize the basic phrase structure trees of the language, the **deep structures**, and include facts regarding syntactic constituency: a Noun Phrase may be a Determiner followed by a Noun but never (in English) a Noun followed by a Determiner.

In phrase structure rules, a category that appears on the left side of a rule may also appear on the right side. Such rules allow the same syntactic category to appear repeatedly in a phrase structure tree, which reflects a speaker's ability to produce sentences without limitations on length.

The **lexicon** represents the knowledge speakers have about the vocabulary of their language, including the syntactic category of words, what elements may occur together, expressed as **subcategorization** restrictions.

Transformational rules account for sentences whose surface structures are different but have the same meaning, such as *Mary hired Bill* and *Bill was hired by Mary*. They do this by deriving multiple surface structures from a single deep structure. Much of the meaning of a sentence is interpreted from its deep structure.

Transformational rules are also used to account for the movement of Aux or **wh-words** to the beginnings of interrogative sentences and for other systematic structural relationships that occur among the sentence structures of the language.

To capture the knowledge speakers have about the syntax of their language, the grammar requires, at a minimum, phrase structure rules, a lexicon richly endowed with speakers' knowledge about individual words, and a set of transformational rules describing the structure-dependent patterning that occurs throughout the language.

Exercises

1. Besides distinguishing grammatical from ungrammatical strings, the rules of syntax account for other kinds of linguistic knowledge, such as
   (a) when a sentence is structurally ambiguous (cf. *The boy saw the man with a telescope*),
   (b) when two sentences of different structure mean the same thing (cf. *The father wept silently* and *The father silently wept*), and
   (c) when two sentences of different structure and meaning are nonetheless structurally related, such as declarative sentences and their corresponding interrogative forms (cf. *The boy can sleep* and *Can the boy sleep?*).

   In each case (a)–(c), draw on your own linguistic knowledge of English to provide an example different from the ones in the chapter, and explain why your example illustrates the point. If you know a language other than English, provide examples in that language, if possible.

2. Consider the following sentences.

   a.   I hate war.
   b.   You know that I hate war.
   c.   He knows that you know that I hate war.

   A.   Write another sentence that includes sentence c.
   B.   What does this set of sentences reveal about the nature of language?
   C.   How is this characteristic of human language related to the difference between linguistic competence and performance? (*Hint:* Review these concepts in Chapter 1.)

3. Paraphrase each of the following sentences in two different ways to show that you understand the ambiguity involved.

Example: Smoking grass can be nauseating.
  i.   Putting grass in a pipe and smoking it can make you sick.
  ii.   Fumes from smouldering grass can make you sick.

  a.   Dick finally decided on the boat.
  b.   The professor's appointment was shocking.
  c.   The design has big squares and circles.
  d.   That sheepdog is too hairy to eat.
  e.   Could this be the invisible man's hair tonic?
  f.   The mayor is a dirty street fighter.
  g.   I cannot recommend him too highly.
  h.   Terry loves his wife, and so do I.
  i.   They said she would go yesterday.
  j.   No smoking section available.

*4. Following the patterns of the various tree examples in the text, especially in the two sections on phrase structure rules, draw phrase structure trees for the following sentences.

  a.   The puppy found the child.
  b.   The house on the hill collapsed in the wind.
  c.   A quaint house appeared.
  d.   The children put the toy in the box.

*5. Draw two phrase structure trees representing the two meanings of the sentence *The magician touched the child with the wand.* Be sure you indicate which meaning goes with which tree.

6. Write out the phrase structure rules that the following rules abbreviate. Give an example sentence illustrating each expansion. (*Hint:* Do not mix the rules — that is, VP → V Det N is not one of the rule expansions of the VP rule. There are sixteen rules altogether.)

VP → V (NP) (PP) (Adv)
NP → (Det) (Adj) N (PP)

7. In all languages, sentences can occur within sentences. For example, in exercise 2, sentence b contains sentence a, and sentence c contains sentence b. Put another way, sentence a is *embedded* in sentence b, and sentence b is embedded in sentence c. Sometimes embedded sentences appear slightly changed from their "normal" forms, but you should be able to recognize and identify the embedded sentences in the examples below. In the non-English examples, examine the original sentence, not the English translation. (The first one is done as an example.)

  a.   Yesterday I noticed <u>my accountant repairing the toilet</u>.
  b.   Becky said that Jake would play the piano.

   c. I deplore the fact that bats have wings.

   d. That Guinevere loves Lorian is known to all my friends.

   e. Who promised the teacher that Maxine wouldn't be absent?

   f. It's ridiculous that he washes his own Rolls-Royce.

   g. The woman likes the waiter to bring water when she sits down.

   h. The person who answers this question will win $100.

   i. The idea of Romeo marrying a 13-year-old is upsetting.

   j. I gave my hat to the nurse who helped me cut my hair.

   k. For your children to spend all your royalty payments on recreational drugs is a shame.

   l. Give this fork to the person I'm getting the pie for.

   m. khǎw chyâ   waǎ khruu   maa. (Thai)
       He   believe that teacher come
       "He believes the teacher is coming."

   n. Je me demande quand il partira. (French)
       I me ask   when he will leave
       "I wonder when he'll leave."

   o. Jan zei dat Piet dit boek niet heeft gelezen. (Dutch)
       Jan said that Piet this book not has read
       "Jan said that Piet has not read this book."

8. Use the rules on page 104 to create five phrase structure trees of sentences of 6, 7, 8, 9, and 10 words in length not given in the chapter. Use your own "mental lexicon" to fill in the bottoms of the trees.

9. We stated that the rules of syntax specify all and only the grammatical sentences of the language. Why is it important to say "only"? What would be wrong with a grammar that specified as grammatical sentences all of the truly grammatical ones plus a few that were not grammatical?

10. Here is a set of made-up phrase structure rules. The "initial" symbol is still S, and the "terminal symbols" (the ones that do not appear to the left of an arrow) are actual words.

   (i) S → A B C   (v) C → C *and* D
   (ii) A → *the*   (vi) D → *ran and* D
   (iii) B → *children*   (vii) D → *ran*
   (iv) C → *ran*

   A. Give three phrase structure trees that these rules characterize.

   B. How many phrase structure trees could these rules characterize? (*Hint:* Look for recursive rules.)

*11. Because languages have recursive properties, there is no limit to the potential length of sentences, and the set of sentences of any language is infinite. Give two examples (different from the ones in the text) of the following:

    a.   Noun Phrase recursion
    b.   Verb Phrase recursion
    c.   Sentence recursion

In one example, the relevant category should appear twice and in the other example at least three times. Draw one of the phrase structure trees in each case, being careful to illustrate the recursion.

12. Referring to exercise 4a–d, write down the head of each NP and VP. For example, in 4a the NP, *the puppy*, has the head *puppy*; the VP, *found the child*, has the head *found*; and the NP, *the child*, has the head *child*.

*13. In terms of subcategorization, explain why the following are ungrammatical.

    a.   *The man located.
    b.   *Jesus wept the apostles.
    c.   *Robert is hopeful of his children.
    d.   *Robert is fond that his children love animals.
    e.   *The children laughed the man.

14. We considered only transitive verbs in the chapter, ones subcategorized in the lexicon, such as *find*:

    find, V, ____ NP

There are also **ditransitive verbs** in English, ones that may be followed by two NPs, such as *give*:

    The emperor gave the vassal a castle.

Think of three other ditransitive verbs in English. Write the lexical entry for one of these verbs, following the pattern of *find* above.

15. In addition to the examples given in the chapter, write down one verb in each of the following verb classes:

    a.   *want* class:
    b.   *force* class:
    c.   *try* class:
    d.   *believe* class:
    e.   *say* class:

16. All of the *wh-* words exhibit the "long-distance" behaviour illustrated with *who* in the chapter. Invent three sentences beginning with *what, which*, and *where* in which the *wh-* word is not in its "logical" position within the sentence. Give both versions of your sentence. Here is an example with the *wh-* word *when: When could Marcy catch a flight out of here?* from *Marcy could catch a flight out of here when?*

17. There are many systematic, structure-dependent relationships among sentences, such as the one discussed in the chapter between active and passive sentences. Here is another example, based on the ditransitive verbs mentioned in exercise 14:

> The boy *wrote* his MP a letter.
> The boy *wrote* a letter to his MP.

> A philanthropist *gave* the animal rights movement $1 000 000.
> A philanthropist *gave* $1 000 000 to the animal rights movement.

a.   Describe the relationship between the first and second members of the pairs of sentences in a way similar to the way the active–passive relationship is described on pages 117–19.

b.   State why a transformation deriving one of these structures from the other is plausible.

18. State at least three differences between English and the following languages, using just the sentence(s) given. Ignore lexical differences — that is, the different vocabularies. Here is an example:

Thai: dèg   khon   níi   kamlang   kin.
      boy   *classifier*   this   *progressive*   eat
      "This boy is eating."

      mǎa   tua   nán   kin   khâaw.
      dog   *classifier*   that   eat   rice
      "That dog ate rice."

Three differences are (1) Thai has "classifiers." They have no English equivalent. (2) The demonstratives *this* and *that* follow the noun in Thai but precede the noun in English. (3) The "progressive" is expressed by a separate word in Thai. The verb does not change form. In English, the progressive is indicated by the presence of the verb *to be* and the adding of *-ing* to the verb. Thai is an SVO language.

a.   French:
    cet   homme   intelligent   comprendra   la question.
    this   man   intelligent   will understand   the question
    "This intelligent man will understand the question."

    ces   hommes   intelligents   comprendront   les questions.
    these   men   intelligent   will understand   the questions
    "These intelligent men will understand the questions."

b.   Japanese:
    watashi   ga   sakana   o   tabete   iru
    I   *subject*   fish   *object*   eat(*ing*)   am
             marker   *marker*
    "I am eating fish."

   c. Swahili:

mtoto		alivunja			kikombe	
m-	toto	a-	li-	vunja	ki-	kombe
class marker	child	he	*past*	break	*class marker*	cup

      "The child broke the cup."

watoto		wanavunja			vikombe	
wa-	toto	wa-	na-	vunja	vi-	kombe
class marker	child	they	*present*	break	*class marker*	cup

      "The children break the cups."

   d. Korean:

kɨ	sonyɔ-nɨn		wɨyu-lɨl		masi-ass-ta		
kɨ	sonyɔ-	nɨn	wɨyu-	lɨl	masi-	ass-	ta
the	boy	*subject marker*	milk	*object marker*	drink	*past*	*assertion*

      "The boy drank milk."

kɨ-nɨn		muɔs-lɨl		mɔk-ass-nya		
kɨ-	nɨn	muɔs-	lɨl	mɔk-	ass-	nya
he	*subject marker*	what	*object marker*	eat	*past*	*question*

      "What did he eat?"

   e. Tagalog:

nakita	ni	Pedro	-ng		puno	na	ang	bus
saw	*article*	Pedro	*complementizer*		full	already	*topic marker*	bus

      "Pedro saw the bus was already full."

Work Cited

Chomsky, Noam. 1988. *Language and Problems of Knowledge: The Managua Lectures.* Cambridge, MA: MIT Press.

Further Reading

Akmajian, A., R.A. Demers, and R.M. Harnish. 1979. *Linguistics: An Introduction to Language and Communication.* 2nd ed. Cambridge, MA: MIT Press.

Chomsky, Noam. 1957. *Syntactic Structures.* The Hague: Mouton.

———. 1965. *Aspects of the Theory of Syntax.* Cambridge, MA: MIT Press.

———. 1972. *Language and Mind.* Rev. ed. New York: Harcourt Brace Jovanovich.

————. 1982. *Some Concepts and Consequences of the Theory of Government and Binding.* Cambridge, MA: MIT Press.

Gazdar, Gerald, E. Klein, G. Pullum, and I. Sag. 1985. *Generalized Phrase Structure Grammar.* Cambridge, MA: Harvard University Press.

Haegeman, Liliane. 1991. *Introduction to Government and Binding Theory.* Oxford: Blackwell.

Haegeman, Liliane, and Jacqueline Guéron. 1999. *English Grammar: A General Perspective.* Oxford: Blackwell.

Horrocks, Geoffrey. 1987. *Generative Grammar.* New York: Longman.

Jackendoff, R.S. 1977. *X-Bar Syntax: A Study of Phrase Structure.* Cambridge, MA: MIT Press.

————. 1994. *Patterns in the Mind: Language and Human Nature.* New York: Basic Books.

McCawley, James D. 1988. *The Syntactic Phenomena of English.* Vols. 1 and 2. Chicago: University of Chicago Press.

Napoli, Donna Jo. 1993. *Syntax: Theory and Problems.* New York: Oxford University Press.

Newmeyer, Frederick J. 1981. *Linguistic Theory in America: The First Quarter Century of Transformational-Generative Grammar.* New York: Academic Press.

Pinker, Steven. 1994. *The Language Instinct.* New York: Harper Perennial.

Radford, Andrew. 1988. *Transformational Grammar.* New York: Cambridge University Press.

————. 1997. *Syntactic Theory and the Structure of English: A Minimalist Approach.* Cambridge, UK: Cambridge University Press.

————. 1997. *Syntax: A Minimalist Introduction.* Cambridge, UK: Cambridge University Press.

Sells, Peter. 1985. *Lectures on Contemporary Syntactic Theories: An Introduction to Government-Binding Theory, Generalized Phrase Structure Grammar, and Lexical-Functional Grammar.* Stanford: Center for the Study of Language and Information, Ventura Hall, Stanford University.

Stockwell, R.P. 1977. *Foundations of Syntactic Theory.* Englewood Cliffs, NJ: Prentice-Hall.

Stockwell, R.P., M. Bean, and D. Elliott. 1977. *Workbook for Foundations of Syntactic Theory.* Englewood Cliffs, NJ: Prentice-Hall.

Van Riemsdijk, Henk, and E. Williams. 1986. *Introduction to the Theory of Grammar.* Cambridge, MA: MIT Press.

CHAPTER 4
Semantics: The Meanings of Language

Language without meaning is meaningless.
Roman Jakobson

B.C. by permission of Johnny Hart and Creators Syndicate, Inc.

For thousands of years, philosophers have been pondering the **meaning** of *meaning*, yet speakers of a language can understand what is said to them and can produce strings of words that are meaningful to other speakers.

To understand language, we need to know the meanings of words and the morphemes that compose them. We also must know how the meanings of words combine into phrase and sentence meanings. Finally, we must interpret the meanings of utterances in the contexts in which they are made.

The study of the linguistic meanings of morphemes, words, phrases, and sentences is called **semantics**. Subfields of semantics are **lexical semantics**, which is concerned with the meanings of words and the meaning relationships among words, and **phrasal** or **sentential semantics**, which is concerned with the meanings of syntactic units larger than the word. The study of how context affects meaning — for

128

example, how the sentence *It's cold in here* comes to be interpreted as "Close the windows" in certain situations — is called **pragmatics**.

Lexical Semantics (Word Meanings)

"There's glory for you!"

"I don't know what you mean by 'glory,' " Alice said.

Humpty Dumpty smiled contemptuously. "Of course you don't — till I tell you. I meant 'there's a nice knock-down argument for you!' "

"But 'glory' doesn't mean 'a nice knock-down argument,' " Alice objected.

"When *I* use a word," Humpty Dumpty said, in rather a scornful tone, "it means just what I choose it to mean — neither more nor less."

"The question is," said Alice, "whether you *can* make words mean so many different things."

Lewis Carroll, *Through the Looking-Glass*

Learning a language includes learning the agreed-upon meanings of certain strings of sounds and learning how to combine these meaningful units into larger units that also convey meaning. The relationship between word and meaning is **arbitrary** and **conventional**. That is, there is no necessary natural connection between word and meaning (it is arbitrary), but speakers of a language agree upon the meaning of a word (it is conventional). We are not free to change the meanings of these words at will, for if we did we would be unable to communicate with anyone.

As we see from the above quotation, Humpty Dumpty certainly accepted the arbitrariness of the meaning of *glory*, but he was unwilling to accept its conventionality. Alice, on the other hand, is right. You cannot make words mean whatever you want them to mean. Of course, if you wish to redefine the meaning of each word as you use it, you are free to do so, but this would be an artificial and clumsy use of language, and most people would not wait around for very long to talk to you.

Fortunately, there are few Humpty Dumptys. All the speakers of a language share a basic vocabulary — the sounds and meanings of morphemes and words.

Dictionaries are filled with words and their meanings. So is the head of every human being who speaks a language. We are walking dictionaries. We know the meanings of thousands of words. Our knowledge of their meanings permits us to use them to express our thoughts and to understand them when heard, even though we probably seldom stop and ask ourselves "What does *boy* mean?" or "What does *walk* mean?" The meanings of words are part of linguistic knowledge and are therefore part of the grammar. Our mental storehouses of information about words and morphemes are what we have been calling the **lexicon**.

Semantic Properties

Words and morphemes have meanings. We will talk about the meanings of words, even though words may be composed of several morphemes, as noted in Chapter 2.

Suppose someone said

> The assassin was stopped before he got to Mr. Thwacklehurst.

If the word *assassin* is in your mental dictionary, then you know that it was some *person* who was prevented from *murdering* some *prominent person* named Thwacklehurst. Your knowledge of the meaning of *assassin* tells you that it was not an animal that tried to kill the man and that Thwacklehurst was not likely to be a little old man who owned a tobacco shop. In other words, your knowledge of the meaning of *assassin* includes knowing that the individual to whom that word refers is *human*, is a *murderer*, and is a killer of *prominent people*. These pieces of information, then, are some of the **semantic properties** of the word upon which speakers of the language agree. The meanings of all nouns, verbs, adjectives, and adverbs — the **content words** — and even some of the **function words** such as *with* or *over* can be at least partially specified by such properties.

The same semantic property may be part of the meanings of many different words. "Female" is a semantic property that helps to define

tigress	hen	actress	maiden
doe	mare	debutante	widow
ewe	vixen	girl	woman

The words in the last two columns are also distinguished by the semantic property "human," which is also found in

doctor   dean   professor   bachelor   parent   baby   child

The meanings of the last two of these words are also specified as "young." That is, part of the meanings of the words *baby* and *child* is that they are "human" and "young." (We will continue to indicate words by using *italics* and semantic "properties" by using double quotation marks.)

The meanings of words have other properties. The word *father* has the properties "male" and "adult," as do *uncle* and *bachelor*, but *father* also has the property "parent," which distinguishes it from the other two words.

Mare, in addition to "female" and "animal," must also denote a property of "horseness." Words have general semantic properties such as "human" or "parent," as well as more specific properties that give the word its particular meaning.

The same semantic property may occur in words of different categories. "Female" is part of the meaning of the noun *mother*, of the verb *breast-feed*, and of the adjective *pregnant*. "Cause" is a verbal property of *darken, kill,* and *uglify*:

darken	"cause to become dark"
kill	"cause to die"
uglify	"cause to become ugly"

Other semantic properties of verbs are shown in the following table:

Semantic Property	**Verbs Having It**
motion	bring, fall, plod, walk, run ...

contact	hit, kiss, touch . . .
creation	build, imagine, make . . .
sense	see, hear, feel . . .

For the most part, no two words have the same meaning (but see the discussion of synonyms on page 137). Additional semantic properties make for finer and finer distinctions in meaning. *Plod* is distinguished from *walk* by the property "slow," and *stalk* is distinguished from *plod* by a property such as "purposeful."

Evidence for Semantic Properties

Semantic properties are not directly observable. Their existence must be inferred from linguistic evidence. One source of such evidence is found in the speech errors, or "slips of the tongue," that we all produce. Consider the following unintentional word substitutions (**semantic substitutions**) that some speakers have actually spoken.

Intended Utterance	**Actual Utterance (Error)**
bridge of the nose	bridge of the neck
when my gums bled	when my tongues bled
he came too late	he came too early
Mary was young	Mary was early
the lady with the dachshund	the lady with the Volkswagen
that's a horse of another colour	that's a horse of another race
he has to pay her alimony	he has to pay her rent

These errors and thousands we and others have collected reveal that the incorrectly substituted words are not random substitutions but share some semantic properties with the intended words. *Nose* and *neck, gums* and *tongues*, are all "body parts" or "parts of the head." *Young, early*, and *late* are related to "time." *Dachshund* and *Volkswagen* are both "German" and "small." The semantic relationships between *colour* and *race* and even between *alimony* and *rent* are rather obvious. Besides the confusion in semantic properties, these errors show other influences that may indicate how the lexicon is organized in our heads. For example, the similarities in the initial sounds of *nose* and *neck*, and the vowel sounds of *gums* and *tongues* also contribute to the confusion; and the frequent collocation or co-occurrence (words found together) of *horse* and *race* and of *pay* and *rent* influences the mistaken choice of words in the last two examples.

The semantic properties that describe the linguistic meaning of a word should not be confused with other non-linguistic properties, such as physical properties. Scientists know that water is composed of hydrogen and oxygen, but such knowledge is not part of a word's meaning. We know that water is an essential ingredient of lemonade or a bath. We need not know any of these things, though, to know what the word *water* means and to be able to use and understand this word in a sentence. Scientifically, perhaps, a whale is a kind of mammal, but most people think of it as a kind of fish since it lives in water. In German, it is even called a *Wahlfisch*. Apparently we consider certain features more important than others in identifying entities.

Semantic Properties and the Lexicon

The lexicon is the part of the grammar that contains the knowledge speakers have about individual words and morphemes, including semantic properties. Words that share a semantic property are said to be in a semantic class, such as that of "female" words. Semantic classes may intersect, such as the class of words with the properties "female" and "young." The words *girl* and *filly* would be members of this class. In some cases, the presence of one semantic property can be inferred from the presence or absence of another. For example, words with the property "human" also have the property "animate."

One way of expressing these facts about semantic properties is through the use of **semantic features**. Semantic features are a formal or notational device for expressing the presence or absence of semantic properties by pluses and minuses. For example, the lexical entries for words such as *father, girl, woman, mare*, and *stalk* would appear as follows (with other information omitted):

father	**girl**	**woman**	**mare**	**stalk**
+male	+female	+female	+female	+motion
+human	+human	+human	–human	+slow
+parent	+young	–young	–young	+purposeful
. . .	. . .	. . .	+horseness	. . .
			. . .	

Intersecting classes share the same features; members of the class of words referring to human females are marked "plus" for the features "human" and "female." Some features need not be specifically mentioned. For example, if a word is [+human], then it is automatically [+animate]. This generalization can be expressed as a **redundancy rule**, which is part of the lexicon.

> A word that is [+human] is [+animate].

This rule specifies that [+animate] need not be specified in the lexical entries for *father, girl, professor*, and so on, since it can be inferred from the feature [+human].

Another difference between nouns may be captured by the use of the feature [+/– count]. Nouns that can be enumerated — *one potato, two potatoes* — are called **count nouns**. They can be preceded by the indefinite article *a* in the singular or by the quantifier *many* but not by *much* with plural forms. Nouns such as *rice, water*, and *milk*, which cannot be enumerated or preceded by *a* or *many* but can by *much* or by nothing at all, are called **non-count** or **mass nouns**:

I have a dog.	*I have a rice.
I have two dogs.	*I have two rice(s).
I have many dogs.	*I have many rice(s).
*I have much dog(s).	I have much rice.
*I like dog.	I like rice.

They may be distinguished in the lexicon by one feature:

dog	potato	rice	water	milk
+count	+count	−count	−count	−count

Count nouns may be either abstract (e.g., *idea*) or concrete (e.g., *girl*), as may mass nouns (e.g., *information* or *soup*). We cannot speak of "a bravery" or "braveries," nor do we generally speak of "two soups," though we do informally use such an expression instead of "two cups of soup." In so doing, we are deliberately treating a mass noun as if it were a count noun. Other mass nouns are more resistant to such use; few speakers of English would talk about "a furniture."

Some semantic redundancy rules infer "negative" properties. For example, if something is "human," then it is not "abstract"; an activity that is "slow" is not "fast." Thus, we can state the following two redundancy rules:

A word that is [+human] is [−abstract].
A word that is [+slow] is [−fast].

Thus, without further specification in the lexicon, *woman* is [−abstract], and the verb *crawl*, which is [+slow], is also [−fast] by the second redundancy rule.

More Semantic Relationships

GARFIELD copyright 1990 PAWS, Inc. Reprinted with permission of Universal Press Syndicate. All rights reserved.

Our linguistic knowledge about words, their semantic properties, and the relationships among them is illustrated by the Garfield cartoon, which shows that "small" is a semantic property of *morsel* but not of *glob*.

Consider the following knowledge about words that speakers of English have:

If something *swims*, then it is in a liquid.
If something is *splashed*, then it is a liquid.

If you say you saw a bug swimming in a container of *goop*, anyone who understands English would agree that *goop* is surely a liquid — that is, it has the semantic feature [+liquid]. Even without knowing what *goop* refers to, you know you can talk about pouring goop, drinking goop, or plugging a hole where goop is leaking out and forming droplets. The words *pour, drink, leak,* and *droplet* are all used with items relating to the property "liquid."

Similarly, we would know that *sawing goop in half, melting goop*, or *bending goop* are semantically ill-formed expressions because none of these activities applies sensibly to objects that are [+liquid].

In some languages, the fact that certain verbs can occur appropriately with certain nouns is reflected in the verb morphology. For example, in the Native North American language Navajo, there are different verb forms for objects with different semantic properties. The verbal suffix *-léh* is used with words with semantic features [+long] and [+flexible], such as *rope*, whereas the verbal suffix *-túh* is used for words such as *spear*, which is [+long] and [–flexible].

Homonyms and Ambiguity

> "Mine is a long and sad tale!" said the Mouse, turning to Alice and sighing.
>
> "It is a long tail, certainly," said Alice, looking with wonder at the Mouse's tail, "but why do you call it sad?"
>
> Lewis Carroll, *Alice's Adventures in Wonderland*

THE BORN LOSER reprinted by permission of Newspaper Enterprise Association, Inc.

Knowing a word means knowing both its sounds (pronunciation) and its meaning. Both are crucial in determining whether two words are the same or different. If two words differ in pronunciation but have the same meaning, such as *chesterfield* and *couch*, they are different words. Likewise, two words with identical pronunciation but significantly different meanings, such as *tale* and *tail*, are also considered different words, as indicated by the difference in spelling. But even if the spelling and pronunciation are identical and the meaning is different, the words are different. *Bat* the flying rodent and *bat* for hitting baseballs are different words because they have different meanings even though they are pronounced and spelled identically.

Words such as the two *bats* are called **homonyms**. Homonyms are words that have the same form, written or spoken, but differ in meaning. If the different words are pronounced the same, whether or not they are written the same, they are called **homophones**. *To, too*, and *two* are homophones because they are pronounced the same, despite their spelling differences.

Different words that are spelled the same, whether or not they are pronounced the same, are called **homographs**. Of course, if they are pronounced the same, they are also homophones. Thus, *pen* the writing instrument and *pen* the cage are both homographs and homophones. *Lead* the verb and *lead* the metal are homographs but not homophones. *Tail* and *tale* are homophones but not homographs.

Both homophones and homographs are types of homonyms. Complete homonymy occurs when both the spelling and the pronunciation are the same but the meaning differs (*pen, bat*). Partial homonymy (called **heteronyms**) occurs where there is an identity of form in one medium only (i.e., speech or writing). Examples would be homophones that are spelled differently (*tail/tale*) or homographs that are pronounced differently, such as *dove* the bird and *dove* the past tense of *dive*, as well as *bass, bow, lead, wind*, and well over a hundred others.

We can summarize these relations among different words — that is, words different in concept and historical origin.

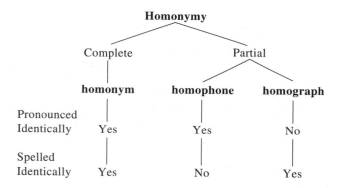

When a word has multiple meanings that are related conceptually or historically, it is said to be **polysemous** (polly-seamus). It is difficult to determine whether a word with several different meanings should be treated as one word (polysemous) or as several words that happen to look or sound the same (homonyms). *Bear* is polysemous, with meanings "to tolerate," "to carry," and "to support," among others found in the dictionary. *Bear* is also a homonym. Homonyms generally have separate dictionary entries, often marked with superscripts to indicate differences. One *bear* is the polysemous verb just mentioned. The other *bear* refers to the animal. It, too, is polysemous, with other meanings such as "a falling stock market." *Bare*, which is pronounced the same as *bear*, is a third homophone (heteronym).

Homonyms and polysemous words can create ambiguities. A sentence is ambiguous if it can be understood or interpreted in more than one way. The sentence *I'll meet you by the bank* may mean "I'll meet you by the financial institution" or "I'll meet you by the riverside." Sometimes additional context can help to disambiguate the sentence:

> I'll meet you by the bank, in front of the automated teller machine.
> I'll meet you by the bank. We can go skinny-dipping.

Homophones are good candidates for humour as well as for confusion.

"How is bread made?"

"I know *that*!" Alice cried eagerly.

"You take some flour —"

"Where do you pick the flower?" the White Queen asked. "In a garden, or in the hedges?"

"Well, it isn't *picked* at all," Alice explained; "it's *ground* —"

"How many acres of ground?" said the White Queen.

Lewis Carroll, *Through the Looking-Glass*

The humour of this passage is due to the two sets of homophones: *flower* and *flour* and the two meanings of *ground*. Alice means *ground* as the past tense of *grind*, whereas the White Queen is interpreting *ground* to mean "earth." Another example is the witty couplet by Hilaire Belloc:

When I am dead, I hope it may be said,

"His sins were scarlet, but his books were read."

Hilaire Belloc, from *Complete Verse*, Random House UK Ltd. By permission of Peters, Fraser & Dunlop on behalf of the Estate of Hilaire Belloc.

The humour here, of course, depends on the pronunciation of *read* (past tense verb) with its homonym *red* and the linking of both words with *books* and *scarlet*.

A somewhat different instance of homonyms occurs with *have* and *be*. In the following sentences, both are verbs:

(1) Robert *has* a dog named Cecelia.
(2) Dogs *are* intelligent animals.

Both also occur as auxiliaries. In addition, the auxiliary *be* has two homonyms, one that occurs with *-ing* forms and one that indicates the passive voice:

(3) Cecelia *has* seen ten squirrels today.
(4) They *are* running fast.
(5) The women *were* given gifts by Senator Snort.

Ambiguity may also result from the use of these homonyms, as in

(6) They are moving sidewalks.

When *are* is understood as a verb (called a **copula** when used in this way), *moving* is a participle modifying *sidewalks*. The overall meaning is something like "those things are sidewalks that move." If *are* is an auxiliary, then the meaning is "those workers are relocating the sidewalks."

Synonyms and Paraphrases

Does he wear a turban, a fez or a hat?

Does he sleep on a mattress, a bed or a mat, or a Cot,

The Akond of Swat?
Can he write a letter concisely clear,
Without a speck or a smudge or smear or Blot,
The Akond of Swat?

Edward Lear, "The Akond of Swat"

There are not only words that sound the same but have different meanings; there are also words that sound different but have the same or nearly the same meaning. Such words are called **synonyms**. For example, the famous "parrot" sketch in which John Cleese insists that

> This parrot is no more. It has ceased to be. It's expired and gone to meet its maker. This is a late parrot. It's a stiff. Bereft of life, it rests in peace. If you hadn't nailed it to the perch, it would be pushing up the daisies. It's rung down the curtain and joined the choir invisible. This is an ex-parrot.

Monty Python

There are dictionaries of synonyms that contain hundreds of entries, such as

apathetic/phlegmatic/passive/sluggish/indifferent
pedigree/ancestry/genealogy/descent/lineage

It has been said that there are no perfect synonyms — that is, no two words ever have *exactly* the same meaning. Still, the following pairs of sentences have very similar meanings.

(1) He's sitting on the chesterfield. / He's sitting on the sofa. / He's sitting on the couch.
(2) I'll be happy to come. / I'll be glad to come.

Some individuals may always use *chesterfield* or *sofa* instead of *couch*, but if they know the three words they will understand the sentences and interpret them to mean the same thing. The degree of semantic similarity between words depends to a great extent on the number of semantic properties they share. *Chesterfield, sofa*, and *couch* refer to the same type of object and share most, if not all, of their semantic properties. However, there is always some context in which one could appear and not the other. For example, a patient might lie on a psychiatrist's couch rather than on a psychiatrist's chesterfield or sofa, and even in Canada we have *couch potatoes* rather than *chesterfield potatoes*.

A polysemous word may share one of its meanings with another word, a kind of partial synonymy. For example, *mature* and *ripe* are polysemous words that are synonyms when applied to fruit but not when applied to animals. *Deep* and *profound* are another such pair. Both may apply to thought, but only *deep* applies to water.

Sometimes words that are ordinarily opposites can mean the same thing in certain contexts; thus, a *good* scare is the same as a *bad* scare. Similarly, a word with a positive meaning in one form, such as the adjective *perfect*, when used adverbially, undergoes a "weakening" effect, so that *a perfectly good bicycle* is neither perfect nor always good. *Perfectly good* means something more like "adequate."

When synonyms occur in otherwise identical sentences, the sentences will be paraphrases. Sentences are **paraphrases** if they have the same meaning (except possibly for minor differences in emphasis). Consider *She forgot her handbag* and *She forgot her purse*. This use of synonyms may create **lexical paraphrase**, just as the use of homonyms may create lexical ambiguity.

Sentences may also be paraphrases because of *structural differences* that are not essential to their meaning, as in the following sentences:

The girl kissed the boy. / The boy was kissed by the girl.

Although there may be a difference in emphasis in these two sentences — in the second the emphasis is on what happened to the boy, whereas in the first the emphasis is on what the girl did — the meaning relations between the verb *kiss* and the two noun phrases are the same in both cases, and on this basis the two sentences are paraphrases of each other.

Antonyms

> As a rule, man is a fool;
> When it's hot, he wants it cool;
> When it's cool, he wants it hot;
> Always wanting what is not.
>
> Anonymous

The meaning of a word may be partially defined by saying what it is not. *Male* means *not female*. *Dead* means *not alive*. Words that are opposite in meaning are often called **antonyms**. Ironically, the basic property of two words that are antonyms is that they share all but one semantic property. *Beautiful* and *tall* are not antonyms; *beautiful* and *ugly*, or *tall* and *short*, are. The property they do not share is present in the one and absent in the other.

There are several kinds of antonymy. There are **complementary pairs**:

alive/dead   present/absent   awake/asleep

They are complementary in that *not alive = dead, not dead = alive*, and so on.
There are **gradable pairs** of antonyms:

big/small   hot/cold   fast/slow   happy/sad

With gradable pairs, the negative of one word is not synonymous with the other. For example, someone who is *not happy* is not necessarily *sad*. It is also true of gradable antonyms that more of one is less of another. More bigness is less smallness, wider is less narrow, and taller is less short. Gradable antonyms are often found among sets of words that partition a continuum:

tiny–small–medium–large–huge–gargantuan
euphoric–elated–happy–so-so–sad–gloomy–despondent

Another characteristic of many pairs of gradable antonyms is that one is **marked** and the other **unmarked**. The unmarked member is the one used in questions of degree. We ask, "How *high* is it?" (not "How low is it?") or "How *tall* is she?" We answer "Three hundred metres high" or "Five feet tall" but never "Five feet short," except humorously. *High* and *tall* are the unmarked members of *high/low* and *tall/short*. Notice that the meanings of these adjectives and other similar ones are relative. The words themselves provide no information about absolute size. Because of our knowledge of the language, and of things in the world, this relativity normally causes no confusion. Thus, we know that *a small elephant* is much bigger than *a large mouse*.

Another kind of "opposite" involves pairs such as

give/receive   buy/sell   teacher/pupil

They are called **relational opposites**, and they display symmetry in their meaning. If X *gives* Y to Z, then Z *receives* Y from X. If X is Y's *teacher*, then Y is X's *pupil*. Pairs of words ending in *-er* and *-ee* are usually relational opposites. If Mary is Bill's *employer*, then Bill is Mary's *employee*.

Comparative forms of gradable pairs of adjectives often form relational pairs. Thus, if Sally is *taller* than Alfred, then Alfred is *shorter* than Sally. If a Cadillac is *more expensive* than a Ford, then a Ford is *cheaper* than a Cadillac.

If meanings of words were indissoluble wholes, then there would be no way to make the interpretations that we do. We know that *big* and *red* are not opposites because they have too few semantic properties in common. They are both adjectives, but *big* is of the semantic class involving size, whereas *red* is a colour. On the other hand, *buy* and *sell* are relational opposites because both contain the semantic property "transfer of goods or services," and they differ only in one property, "direction of transfer."

Semantic redundancy rules such as those discussed above can reveal knowledge about antonyms:

A word that is [+married] is [−single].
A word that is [+single] is [−married].

These rules show that any word that bears the semantic property "married," such as *wife*, is understood to lack the semantic property "single"; conversely, any word that bears the semantic property "single," such as *bachelor*, will not have the property "married."

Formation of Antonyms

In English, there are a number of ways to form antonyms. You can add the prefix *un-*

likely/unlikely   able/unable   fortunate/unfortunate

or you can add *non-*

entity/nonentity   conformist/nonconformist

or you can add *in-*

tolerant/intolerant   discreet/indiscreet   decent/indecent

Other prefixes may also be used to form negative words morphologically: *il-*, as in *illegal; mis-*, as in *misbehave; dis-*, as in *displease*. The suffix *-less*, as in *toothless*, also negates the meaning of a stem morpheme.

There are words with many semantic properties in common that are neither synonyms nor near synonyms. Speakers of English know that the words *red, white*, and *blue* are "colour" words indicating a class to which they all belong. Similarly, *lion, tiger, leopard*, and *lynx* have the feature [+feline]. Such sets of words are called **hyponyms**. The relationship of **hyponymy** is between the more general term (the **superordinate** or **hypernym**), such as *colour*, and the more specific instances of it, such as *red* or *white*. Thus, *red* is a hyponym of *colour*, and *lion* is a hyponym of *feline*; equivalently, *colour* has the hyponym *red*, and *feline* has the hyponym *lion*.

Words such as *man* and *boy* may be considered as hyponyms of *human*. You can say *A man is a human* but not *A human is a man* (the person might be a woman, a girl, or a boy, which are all co-hyponyms of *man*). Hyponymy is thus a "kind of" relationship. (A man is a *kind* of human; red is a *kind* of colour.)

Sometimes there is no single word in the language that encompasses a set of hyponyms. *Clarinet, guitar, horn, marimba, piano, trumpet*, and *violin* are hyponyms because they are "musical instruments," but there isn't a single word meaning "musical instrument" that has these words as its hyponyms.

Because we know the semantic properties of words, we know when two words are antonyms, synonyms, hyponyms, or homonyms or are unrelated in meaning.

Metonyms and Meronyms

A **metonym** is a word used in place of another word or expression to convey the same meaning. The use of *brass* to refer to military officers and the use of *Ottawa* to indicate the federal government are examples of metonymy. *Crown* is a metonym for the monarchy or for an agent of the monarchy, such as the prosecutor in a criminal trial.

A related term is **meronym**. This is a part-to-whole relationship in which the meronym is "part of" a larger entity. *Leaf, branch*, and *root* are meronyms or parts of *tree*, but unlike metonyms they do not represent "tree."

Retronyms

Day baseball, silent movie, surface mail, and *whole milk* are all expressions that once were redundant. In the past, all baseball games were played in daylight, all movies were silent, air and electronic mail didn't exist, and low-fat and skim milk were not yet available. **Retronym** is the term reserved for these expressions, but strictly speaking it applies not to the individual words themselves but to the combinations.

Names

> "My name is Alice ..."
>
> "It's a stupid name enough!" Humpty Dumpty interrupted impatiently. "What does it mean?"
>
> "Must a name mean something?" Alice asked doubtfully.
>
> "Of course it must," Humpty Dumpty said with a short laugh. "My name means the shape I am — and a good handsome shape it is, too. With a name like yours, you might be any shape, almost."
>
> Lewis Carroll, *Through the Looking-Glass*

> I was Joan Foster, there was no doubt about that; people called me by that name and I had authentic documents to prove it. But I was also Louisa K. Delacourt.
>
> Margaret Atwood, *Lady Oracle*

"What's in a name?" is a question that has occupied philosophers of language for centuries. Plato was concerned with whether names were "natural," though the question did not bother Adam when he named the animals; Humpty Dumpty thinks his name means his shape, and in part it does.

Usually, when we think of names, we think of names of people or places, which are **proper names**. Proper names are different from most words in the language in that they refer to a specific object or entity but usually have little meaning or sense beyond a power of referral. Of course, if a word with sense, such as *lake*, is incorporated into a proper name such as *Lake Louise*, then the proper noun has the semantic properties of *lake*. Caution is needed, though, since a restaurant named *Lake Louise* would not have any lakelike meaning.

The meaning of a word such as *dog* or *sincerity* imparts a sense that permits you to recognize specific instances of that class of entities or even to have an abstract vision of what is meant, but you cannot pet *dog* or doubt *sincerity*. You can only pet a specific dog, Fido, or doubt a specific instance of sincerity, such as a political promise. Nothing in the world corresponds to *dog* the way *Paris* refers to the city of Paris.

Within their contexts, proper names refer to unique objects or entities. The objects may be extant, such as those designated by

Disa Karin Viktoria Lubker
Hudson Bay
the Stanley Cup

or extinct, such as

Socrates
Troy

or even fictional, such as

Sherlock Holmes
Sara Binks
Oz

Proper names are **definite**, which means they refer to a unique object insofar as the speaker and the listener are concerned. If I say

Mary Smith is coming to dinner.

my spouse understands Mary Smith to refer to our friend Mary Smith, not to one of the dozens of Mary Smiths in the phone book.

Because they are inherently definite, proper names in English are not in general preceded by *the*:

*the John Smith
*the Alberta

There are exceptions, such as the names of rivers, ships, and erected structures

the St. Lawrence
the Skydome
the *Bluenose*
the Eiffel Tower
the CN Tower

and there are special cases such as *the John Smiths* to refer to the family of John Smith. Also, for the sake of clarity or literary effect, it is possible to precede a proper name by an article if the resulting noun phrase is followed by a modifying expression such as a prepositional phrase or a sentence:

The Paris of the 1920s . . .
The Toronto that everyone loves to hate . . .

In some languages, such as Greek and Hungarian, articles normally occur before proper names. Thus, we find in Greek

O Spiros agapai tin Sophia.

which is literally "The Spiro loves the Sophie," where *O* is the masculine nominative form of the definite article and *tin* the feminine accusative form. This indicates that some of the restrictions we observed are particular to English and may be due to syntactic rather than semantic rules of language.

Proper names cannot usually be pluralized, though they can be plural, such as *the Great Lakes* or *the Pleiades*. There are exceptions, such as *the John Smiths* already mentioned or expressions such as *the linguistics department has three Bobs*, meaning three people named Bob, but they are special locutions used in particular circumstances. Because proper names generally refer to unique objects, it is not surprising that they occur mainly in the singular.

For the same reason, proper names cannot in general be preceded by adjectives. Many adjectives have the semantic effect of **narrowing** the field of reference, so that the noun phrase *a red house* is a more specific description than simply *a house*; but what proper names refer to is already completely narrowed down, so modification by adjectives seems peculiar. Again, as in all these cases, extenuating circumstances give rise to exceptions. Language is nothing if not flexible, and we find expressions such as *young John* used to distinguish between two people named John. We also find adjectives applied to emphasize some quality of the object referred to, such as *the wicked Borgias* or *the brilliant Professor Einstein*.

Names may be coined or drawn from the stock of names that the language provides, but once a proper name has been coined it cannot be pluralized or preceded by *the* or any adjective (except in cases like those cited above), and it will be used to refer uniquely, for these rules are among the many rules already in the grammar, and speakers know they apply to all proper names, even new ones.

Phrase and Sentence Meaning

"Then you should say what you mean," the March Hare went on.

"I do," Alice hastily replied, "at least — I mean what I say — that's the same thing, you know."

"Not the same thing a bit!" said the Hatter. "You might just as well say that 'I see what I eat' is the same thing as 'I eat what I see'!"

"You might just as well say," added the March Hare, "that 'I like what I get' is the same thing as 'I get what I like'!"

"You might just as well say," added the Dormouse . . . "that 'I breathe when I sleep' is the same thing as 'I sleep when I breathe'!"

"It *is* the same thing with you," said the Hatter.

Lewis Carroll, *Alice's Adventures in Wonderland*

Words and morphemes are the smallest meaningful units in language. We have been studying their meaning relationships and semantic properties as lexical semantics. For the most part, however, we communicate in phrases and sentences. The meaning of a phrase depends on both the meaning of its words and how those words are combined structurally. Some of the semantic relationships we observed between words are also found between sentences. While words may be synonyms, two sentences may be paraphrases because they contain synonymous words or because of structural differences that do not affect meaning:

> They ran the bill up.
> They ran up the bill.

Similarly, words may be homonyms, hence ambiguous when spoken; sentences may also be ambiguous because they contain homonyms, as in *I need to buy a pen for Shelby*, or because of their structures, as in the sentence from Chapter 3, *The boy saw the man with the telescope*.

Words have antonyms, and sentences can be negated. Thus, the opposite of *He is alive* is both *He is dead*, using an antonym, and *He is not alive*, using negation.

Words are used for naming purposes, and sentences can be used that way as well. Both words and sentences can be used to refer to, or point out, objects, and both may have further meaning beyond this referring capability, as we will see in a later section.

The study of how word meanings combine into phrase and sentence meanings, and the meaning relationships among these larger units, is called **phrasal** or **sentential semantics** to distinguish it from lexical semantics.

Phrasal Meaning

> . . . I placed all my words with their interpretations in alphabetical order. And thus in a few days, by the help of a very faithful memory, I got some insight into their language.
>
> Jonathan Swift, *Gulliver's Travels*

Although it is widely believed that learning a language is merely learning the words of that language and what they mean — a myth apparently accepted by Gulliver — there is more to it than that, as you know if you have ever tried to learn a foreign language. We comprehend sentences because we know the meanings of individual words and because we know the rules for combining their meanings.

Noun-Centred Meaning

We know the meanings of *red* and *balloon*. The semantic rule to interpret the combination *red balloon* adds the property "redness" to the properties of *balloon*. The phrase *the red balloon*, because of the presence of the definite article *the*, means "a particular instance of redness and balloonness." A semantic rule for the interpretation of *the* accounts for this.

The phrase *large balloon* would be interpreted by a different semantic rule, because part of the meaning of *large* is that it is a relative concept. *Large balloon* means "large for a balloon." What is large for a balloon may be small for a house and gargantuan for a cockroach, yet we correctly comprehend the meanings of *large balloon, large house*, and *large cockroach*.

The semantic rules for adjective–noun combinations are complex. A *good friend* is a kind of friend, just as a *red brick* is a kind of brick. But a *false friend* is not any kind of friend at all. The semantic properties of "friendness" are cancelled out by the adjective *false*. Thus, semantic rules for noun phrases containing *good* and *false* are quite different. A third kind of rule governs adjectives such as *alleged*; the meaning of *alleged murderer* is someone accused of murder, but the semantic rules in this case do not tell us whether an alleged murderer is or is not a murderer.

Exemplars of Class of Adjective (Adj)	**Truth of "An Adj X is an X"** (e.g., A *red ball* is a *ball*.)
good, red, large, etc.	true
false, counterfeit, phony, etc.	false
alleged, purported, putative, etc.	undetermined

There are many more rules involved in the semantics of noun phrases. Because noun phrases may contain prepositional phrases, semantic rules are needed for expressions such as *the house with the white fence*. We have seen how the rules account for *the house* and *the white fence*. The semantic rule for prepositions indicates that two objects stand in a relationship determined by the meaning of the particular preposition. For *with*, that relationship is "accompanies" or "is part of." A preposition such as *on* means a certain spatial relationship, and so on for other prepositions.

The syntactic notion of *head* plays a significant role in semantic rules; in the structure of a phrase, its head determines the phrase's principal meaning. The head of a noun phrase will be the noun, the head of a verb phrase the verb, and so on. Since *brick* is the head of the noun phrase *the red brick*, the meaning of *a red brick* is a kind of brick. On the other hand, *red* is the head of the expression *brick red*, and the meaning of *brick red* is a certain kind of red.

Meanings build on meanings. Noun phrases are combinations of meanings of nouns, adjectives, articles, and even sentences. (The noun phrase *the fact he knew too much* is a combination of *the, fact*, and the sentence *he knew too much*.) In turn, sentences are combinations of noun phrases, verb phrases, and so on. All these combinations make sense because the semantic rules of grammar, like rules of phonology or syntax, operate systematically and predictably to incorporate the meanings of the phrasal components into the meaning of the phrase.

Verb-Centred Meaning

In all languages, the verb plays a central role in sentence structure and meaning. In English, the verb determines the number of objects and limits the semantic properties of both the subject and its objects. For example, *find* requires an animate subject and is subcategorized for one object. In formal, written English, the presence of a verb is essential for a complete sentence.

Languages of the world may be classified according to whether the verb occurs initially, medially, or finally in their basic sentences.

Thematic Roles

The noun phrase subject of a sentence and the constituents of the verb phrase are semantically related in various ways to the verb. The relations depend on the meaning of the particular verb. For example, the NP *the boy* in *The boy found a red brick* is called the **agent** or "doer" of the action of finding. The NP *a red brick* is the **theme** and undergoes the action. (The boldfaced words are technical terms of semantic theory.) Part of the meaning of *find* is that its subject is an agent and its direct object is a theme.

The noun phrases within a verb phrase whose head is *put* have the relation of theme and **goal**. In the verb phrase *put the red brick on the wall, the red brick* is the theme, and *on the wall* is the goal. The entire phrase is interpreted to mean that the theme of *put* changes its position to the goal. The subject of *put* is also an agent, so that, in *The boy put the red brick on the wall*, the boy performs the action. The knowledge speakers have about *find* and *put* is revealed in their lexical entries:

> find, V _____ NP (agent, theme)
> put, V _____ NP, PP (agent, theme, goal)

The thematic roles are contained in parentheses. The first one states that the subject is an agent.

The remaining thematic roles belong to the categories for which the verb is subcategorized. The direct object of both *find* and *put* will be a theme. The prepositional phrase for which *put* subcategorizes will be a goal.

The semantic relationships we have called theme, agent, and goal are among the **thematic roles** of the verb. Other thematic roles are **location**, where the action occurs; **source**, where the action originates; **instrument**, an object used to accomplish the action; **experiencer**, one receiving sensory input; **causative**, a natural force that brings about a change; and **possessor**, one who owns or has something. (Note that this list is not complete.) These thematic roles may be summed up as follows:

Thematic Role	Description	Example
Agent	the one who performs an action	*Joyce* ran.
Theme	the one or thing that undergoes an action	Mary called *Bill*.
Location	the place where an action occurs	It rains *in Spain*.
Goal	the place to which an action is directed	Put the cat *in the porch*.
Source	the place from which an action originates	He flew from *Winnipeg* to Regina.
Instrument	the means by which an action is performed	Jo cuts hair *with a razor*.
Experiencer	one who perceives something	*Helen* heard Robert playing the piano.
Causative	a natural force that causes a change	*The wind* damaged the roof.
Possessor	one who has something	The tail of *the dog* got caught in the door.

Our knowledge of verbs includes their syntactic category, how they are subcategorized, and the thematic roles that their NP subject and object(s) have, and this knowledge is explicitly represented in the lexicon.

Thematic roles are the same in sentences that are paraphrases. In both these sentences,

> The dog bit the man.
> The man was bitten by the dog.

the dog is the agent, and *the man* is the theme.

Thematic roles may remain the same in sentences that are not paraphrases, as in the following examples:

> The boy opened the door with the key.
> The key opened the door.
> The door opened.

In all three sentences, *the door* is the theme, the thing that gets opened. In the first two sentences, *the key*, despite its different structural positions, retains the thematic role of instrument. The three examples illustrate the fact that English allows many different thematic roles to be the subject of the sentence (S) — that is, the first NP under the S. These sentences have as subjects an agent (*the boy*), an instrument (*the key*), and a theme (*the door*).

The sentences below illustrate other kinds of subjects:

> This hotel forbids dogs.
> It seems that Samson has lost his strength.

In the first example, *this hotel* has the thematic role of location. In the second, the subject *it* is semantically empty and lacks a thematic role entirely.

Thematic Roles in Other Languages

Contrast English with German. German is much stingier about which thematic roles can be subjects. For example, to express the idea "This hotel forbids dogs," a German speaker would have to say

> In diesem Hotel sind Hunde verboten.

Literally, this means "In this hotel are dogs forbidden." German does not permit the thematic role of location to occur as a subject; it must be expressed as a prepositional phrase. If we translated the English sentence word for word into German, then the results would be ungrammatical in German:

> *Dieses Hotel verbietet Hunde.

Differences such as these between English and German show that learning a foreign language is not a matter of simple word-for-word translation. You must learn the grammar, and that includes learning the syntax and semantics and how the two interact.

In many languages, thematic roles are reflected in the **case** assumed by the noun. The *case*, or **grammatical case**, of a noun is the particular morphological shape that it takes. English does not have an extensive case system, but the possessive form of a noun, as in *the boy's red brick*, is called the genitive or possessive case.

In languages such as Finnish, the noun assumes a morphological shape according to its thematic role in the sentence. For example, in Finnish *koulu-* is the root meaning "school," and *-sta* is a case ending that means "directional source." Thus, *koulusta* means "from the school." Similarly, *kouluun* (*koulu + un*) means "to the school."

Some of the information carried by grammatical case in languages such as Finnish is borne by prepositions in English. Thus, *from* and *to* often indicate the thematic roles of source and goal. Instrument is marked by *with*, location by prepositions such as *on* and *in*, possessor by *of*, and agent, experiencer, and causative with *by* in passive sentences. The role of theme is generally unaccompanied by a preposition, as its most common syntactic function is direct object. Agent is also unaccompanied by a preposition when it is the structural subject of the sentence. What we are calling thematic roles in this section has sometimes been studied as **case theory**.

In German, case distinctions appear on articles as well as on nouns and adjectives. Thus, in

> Sie liebt den Mann.

"She loves the man," the article *den* is in the accusative case. In the nominative case, it would be *der*. Languages with a rich system of case are often more constraining as to which thematic roles can occur in the subject position. German, as we saw above, is one such language.

The Theta-Criterion

A universal principle has been proposed called the **theta-criterion**, which states in part that a particular thematic role may occur only once in a sentence. Thus, sentences such as

> *The boy opened the door with the key with a lock-pick.

are semantically anomalous because two noun phrases bear the thematic role of instrument.

In English, the thematic role of possessor is indicated in two ways syntactically: either as *the boy's red hat* or as *the red hat of the boy*. However, *the boy's red hat of Bill* is semantically anomalous according to the theta-criterion because both *the boy* and *Bill* have the thematic role of possessor.

Irrespective of how we label the semantic relations that exist between verbs and noun phrases, they are part of every speaker's linguistic competence and account for much of the meaning in language.

Semantics and Syntax

Syntax is concerned with how words are combined to form phrases and sentences; semantics is concerned with what these combinations mean. The theta-criterion, discussed in the previous section, is an instance in which semantics and syntax interact: the semantic constraint that no thematic role may occur more than once has the effect of restricting the NPs and PPs that may follow the Verb in a Verb Phrase.

Words versus Phrases

We have seen throughout this chapter and the previous one that the same meaning may be expressed syntactically in more than one way — the phenomenon of paraphrase. The semantic property of possession may be expressed by the genitive case such as *England's king* or by an "of" construct such as *the king of England*. Paraphrases result when the same meaning — the same truth condition — is expressed in different syntactic structures.

A similar situation arises with certain semantic concepts such as "ability," "permission," or "obligation." They may be expressed syntactically by means of "auxiliary" or "helping" verbs:

> He *can* go.
> He *may* go.
> He *must* go.

They may also be expressed phrasally, without the auxiliaries:

> He is *able* to go. / He has the *ability* to go.
> He is *permitted* to go. / He has *permission* to go.
> He is *obliged* to go. / He has an *obligation* to go.

It is often possible to substitute a phrase for a word without affecting the sense of the sentence:

> John saw Mary.
> John perceived Mary using his eyes.

> The professor lectured the class.
> The professor delivered a lecture to the class.

When Passives Do Not Work

Active–passive pairs constitute another common type of paraphrase:

> The child found the puppy.
> The puppy was found by the child.

This relationship between actives and passives is based on syntactic structure as discussed in Chapter 3. However, some active sentences do not have a well-formed passive counterpart. For example,

> John resembles Bill.
> The book cost ten dollars.

cannot undergo a passive transformation to give

> *Bill was resembled by John.
> *Ten dollars was cost by the book.

Semantically, when the subject of an active sentence is in a state described by the verb and direct object, there is no passive paraphrase. Since *John* is in a state of resembling Bill — John doesn't do anything — the sentence cannot produce a passive counterpart. This shows how the semantics of verbal relationships may affect syntactic relationships.

Passives are usually paraphrases of their active counterparts, but there are exceptions when "quantifiers" (e.g., *every, each, some, two, many, several, few*) get involved. Consider

> Every person in this room speaks two languages.
> Two languages are spoken by every person in this room.

These two sentences do not have the same truth conditions. Suppose there are three people in the room, Tom, Dick, and Mary. Tom speaks English and Russian, Dick speaks French and Italian, and Mary speaks Chinese and Thai. Then the first sentence is true. The second, however, is false because there are no two languages that everyone speaks.

Pronouns and Coreferentiality

Another example of how syntax and semantics interact has to do with **reflexive pronouns**, such as *herself* or *themselves*. The meaning of a reflexive pronoun always refers back to some **antecedent**. In *Jane bit herself, herself* refers to Jane. Syntactically, reflexive pronouns and their antecedents must occur under the same S in the phrase structure tree. Compare the phrase structure tree of *Jane bit herself* with the phrase structure tree of **Jane said that herself slept*:

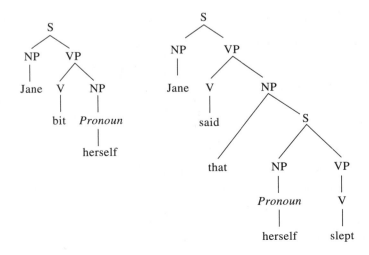

In the second tree, *Jane* is in the topmost S, but *herself* is in a different, embedded S. Syntactic and semantic rules do not allow the pronoun to be reflexive. The interaction between the rules tells us that in *Jane bit her* the pronoun *her* cannot refer to Jane; it must refer to some other person.

Sentence structure also plays a role in determining when a pronoun and a noun phrase in different clauses are **coreferential** — that is, refer to the same object. For example, in

> John believes that he is a genius.

the pronoun *he* can be interpreted as John or as some person other than John. However, in

> He believes that John is a genius.

the coreferential interpretation is impossible. *John* and *he* cannot refer to the same person. It appears that a pronoun antecedent cannot occur to the left of the noun phrase if the two refer to the same person. However, the rule is not that simple. In the sentence

> The fact that he is considered a genius bothers John.

he and *John* can be interpreted as coreferential. A somewhat complicated semantic rule that refers to sentence structure is at work here. A precise statement of this rule goes beyond the scope of this introductory text. The point is that syntax and semantics interrelate in complex ways.

We have knowledge of syntactic rules, of semantic rules, and of how these rules interact. The fact that we have this knowledge is demonstrated by our ability to make judgements of grammaticality, recognize ambiguities and paraphrases, and know what the antecedents of pronouns are.

Sentential Meaning

The meaning of a sentence is built, in part, from the meanings of noun phrases and verb phrases. Adverbs may add to or qualify the meaning. *The boy found the ball yesterday* specifies a time component to the meaning of the boy's finding the ball. Adverbs such as *quickly, fortunately, often,* et cetera would affect the meaning in other ways.

Like noun phrases, sentences have sense, which is usually what we are referring to when we talk about the meaning of a sentence. Some linguists would also say that certain sentences have reference, namely ones that can be true or false. Their reference, or extension, is *true* if the sentence is true and *false* if the sentence is false.

The "Truth" of Sentences

... Having Occasion to talk of Lying and false Representation, it was with much Difficulty that he comprehended what I meant.... For he argued thus: That the Use of Speech was to make us understand one another and to receive

Information of Facts; now if any one said the Thing which was not, these Ends
were defeated; because I cannot properly be said to understand him. . . . And
these were all the Notions he had concerning that Faculty of Lying, so perfectly
well understood, and so universally practiced among human Creatures.

Jonathan Swift, *Gulliver's Travels*

We have seen how sentence meaning is partially based on the meanings of its
words and phrases. Knowing the meaning of a declarative sentence means knowing under what circumstances that sentence would be true. Those "circumstances"
are called the **truth conditions** of the sentence.

In the world as we know it, the sentence

The Canadian Constitution was patriated in 1982.

is true, and the sentence

The Constitution was patriated in 1992.

is false. We know the meanings of both sentences equally well, and knowing their
meanings means knowing their truth conditions. We compare their truth conditions
with "the real world" or historical facts, and we can thus say which one is true and
which one false.

We can, however, understand well-formed sentences of our language without
knowing their truth values. Knowing the truth conditions is not the same as knowing the actual facts. Rather, the truth conditions permit us to examine the world and
learn the actual facts. If we did not know the linguistic meaning — if the sentence
were in an unknown language — then we could never determine its truth, even if
we had memorized an encyclopedia. We may not know the truth of

The Mecklenburg Charter was signed in 1770.

but if we know its meaning we know in principle how to discover its truth, even if
we do not have the means to do so. For example, consider the sentence

The moon is made of green cheese.

We knew before space travel that going to the moon would test the truth of the
sentence.

Now consider this sentence:

Rufus believes that the Constitution was patriated in 1992.

This sentence is true if some individual named Rufus does believe the statement,
and it is false if he does not. Those are its truth conditions.

It does not matter that a subpart of the sentence is false. An entire sentence may
be true even if one or more of its parts are false and vice versa. Truth is determined
by the semantic rules that permit us to combine the subparts of a sentence and still
know under what conditions the sentence is true or false.

Sentences and Truth Conditions

Linguists distinguish two types of truthful sentences. One set of sentences is linguistically true — that is, a sentence is necessarily true because of the definitions of the words used in the sentence. Thus, *A widow is a person whose husband is no longer alive* is said to be analytically true because the word *widow* implies that we are speaking of a woman (a man is a *widower*). The woman was at one time married (hence had a husband), her husband is no longer living, and, finally, she has not remarried. Should all of these conditions not be met, the sentence will be untrue because of the way speakers of English understand the word *widow*. **Analytic** sentences are thus "true by definition."

The truth of the second type of truthful sentence depends on its agreement with the world as we know it. The truth of a sentence such as *The widow's husband died last year* can be determined only if we know something of last year's events. Our understanding of the truth of such sentences depends on our knowing something of the events and conditions in the world. In this case, we may have to speak with our neighbours or consult the public records. Such sentences are known as **synthetic** and, unlike analytic sentences, require more than linguistic knowledge.

A sentence such as *A unicorn is a single-horned beast* may be considered analytically true because, as the name itself tells us, this creature has but one horn; so, too, a *triangle*, by its very name, must be a three-sided figure. The difference between a unicorn and a triangle, however, rests in the fact that most people encounter triangles but never a unicorn. Certainly, a sentence such as *Unicorns live in the Winnipeg Zoo* can easily be checked and will confirm that unicorns, along with dragons and fairies, exist only in art or fantasy.

The opposite of analytic sentences is **contradictory** sentences, which are necessarily false because of the meanings of the words themselves. If we were to hear that *A widow's husband was alive and well in Calgary*, then we would conclude that this "widow" was no *widow* at all. Sentences calling attention to the fourth side of a triangle or to *colourless green ideas* are clearly contradictory and necessarily false.

Knowing a language includes knowing the semantic rules for combining meanings and the conditions under which sentences are true or false.

Entailment

Sometimes knowing the truth of one sentence **entails** or necessarily implies the truth of another sentence. For example, if we know it is true that

> Corday assassinated Marat.

then we know it is true that

> Marat is dead.

It is logically impossible for the former to be true and the latter false. The sentence *The brick is red* entails *The brick is not white*, *Mortimer is a bachelor* entails

Mortimer is male, and so on. These entailments are part of the semantic rules we have been discussing. Much of what we know about the world comes about from knowing the entailments of true sentences.

Contradiction

Contradiction is negative entailment — that is, where the truth of one sentence necessarily implies the falseness of another sentence. For example,

> Elizabeth II is the queen of Canada.
> Elizabeth II is a man.

If the first sentence is true, then the second is necessarily false. A pair of sentences such as

> Scott is a baby.
> Scott is an adult.

generally involves contradiction — though, of course, it is possible that Scott is an adult but that we object to his behaviour.

Sense and Reference

> It is natural . . . to think of there being connected with a sign . . . besides . . . the reference of the sign, also what I should like to call the sense of the sign. . . .
>
> Gottlob Frege, *On Sense and Reference*

Just as knowing the meaning of a declarative sentence means knowing how to determine its truth value, knowing the meanings of certain noun phrases means knowing how to discover what objects the noun phrases refer to. For example, in the sentence

> The boy put the red brick on the wall.

knowing the meaning of *the red brick* enables us to identify the object being referred to. As with the truth of sentences, we need only know, in principle, how to identify the object; a blindfolded person would comprehend the meaning.

The object "pointed to" in such a noun phrase is called its **referent**, and the noun phrase is said to have **reference**.

For many noun phrases, there is more to meaning than just reference. For example, *the red brick* and *the first brick from the right* may refer to the same object — that is, they may be **coreferential**. Nevertheless, we would be reluctant to say that the two expressions have the same meaning because they have the same reference. There is some additional meaning to these expressions, often termed **sense**. Thus, noun phrases may have sense and reference, which together comprise the meaning. Knowing the sense of a noun phrase allows us to identify its referent. Sometimes the term **extension** is used for *reference* and **intension** for *sense*. Another example of sense and reference might be the relations between *the prime minister of Canada, the leader of the Liberal party*, and *Jean Chrétien*. In 2000, these all referred to the same person — they all had the same reference — but the sense of each is different, so that one might know what the prime minister of Canada was but not who it was. Several years ago, the prime minister of Canada and the leader of the Liberal party was Pierre Trudeau, and later the prime minister of Canada was the leader of the Progressive Conservatives, Joe Clark, then Brian Mulroney, and then Kim Campbell. And the prime minister of Great Britain is someone else.

Certain proper names appear to have only reference. Thus, a name such as Kelly Jones points out a certain person, its referent, but seems to have little meaning beyond that. Nonetheless, some proper names do seem to have meaning over and above their ability to refer. Humpty Dumpty suggested that his name means "a good round shape." Certainly, the name *Sue* has the semantic property "female," as evinced by the humour in "A Boy Named Sue," a song sung by Johnny Cash. *The Pacific Ocean* has the semantic properties of "ocean," and even names such as *Fido* and *Bossie* are associated with dogs and cows, respectively.

Sometimes two different proper names have the same referent, such as Superman and Clark Kent, Dr. Jekyll and Mr. Hyde, or Samuel Clemens and Mark Twain. It is a hotly debated question in the philosophy of language whether two such expressions have the same meaning or differ in sense.

While some proper nouns appear to have reference but no sense, other noun phrases have sense but no reference. If not, then we would be unable to understand sentences such as

> The present king of France is bald.
> By the year 3000, our descendants will have left Earth.

Speakers of English can understand these sentences even though France now has no king and our descendants of a millennium from now do not exist.

When Rules Are Broken

> For all a rhetorician's rules
> Teach nothing but to name his tools.
>
> Samuel Butler, *Hudibras*

The rules of language are not laws of nature. Only by a "miracle" can the laws of nature be broken, but the rules of language are broken every day by everybody. This lawlessness is not human perversity but another way in which language is put to use.

There are three kinds of rule violation we will discuss: **anomaly**, a violation of semantic rules to create "nonsense"; **metaphor**, or non-literal meaning; and **idioms**, in which the meaning of an expression may be unrelated to the meaning of its parts.

Anomaly: No Sense and Nonsense

> Don't tell me of a man's being able to talk sense; everyone can talk sense. Can he talk nonsense?
>
> William Pitt

If in a conversation someone said to you

My brother is an only child.

you might think that he was making a joke or that he did not know the meanings of the words he was using. You would know that the sentence was strange or **anomalous**, yet it is certainly an English sentence. It conforms to all the grammatical rules of the language. It is strange because it represents a contradiction; the meaning of *brother* includes the fact that the individual referred to is a male human who has at least one sibling.

The sentence

That bachelor is pregnant.

is anomalous for similar reasons; the word *bachelor* contains the semantic property "male," whereas the word *pregnant* has the semantic property "female." Through a semantic redundancy rule, *pregnant* will also be marked [–male]. The anomaly arises from trying to equate something that is [+male] with something that is [–male].

The semantic properties of words determine what other words they can be combined with. One sentence used by linguists to illustrate this fact is Noam Chomsky's (1957) famous sentence

Colourless green ideas sleep furiously.

The sentence seems to obey all the syntactic rules of English. The subject is *colourless green ideas*, and the predicate is *sleep furiously*. It has the same syntactic structure as the sentence

Dark green leaves rustle furiously.

but there is obviously something wrong *semantically* with the sentence. The meaning of *colourless* includes the semantic property "without colour," but it is combined with the adjective *green*, which has the property "green in colour." How can something be both "without colour" and "green in colour" simultaneously? Other such semantic violations also occur in the sentence.

There are other sentences that sound like English sentences but make no sense because they include words that have no meaning; they are **uninterpretable**. We can only interpret them if we dream up some meaning for each "no-sense" word. Lewis Carroll's "Jabberwocky" (from *Through the Looking-Glass*) is probably the most famous poem in which most of the content words have no meaning — they do not exist in the lexicon of the grammar. Still, all the sentences "sound" as if they should be or could be English sentences:

'Twas brillig, and the slithy toves
   Did gyre and gimble in the wabe;
All mimsy were the borogoves,
   And the mome raths outgrabe.
. . .

He took his vorpal sword in hand:
   Long time the manxome foe he sought —
So rested he by the Tumtum tree,
   And stood awhile in thought.

Without knowing what *vorpal* means, we nevertheless know that

He took his vorpal sword in hand.

means the same thing as

He took his sword, which was vorpal, in hand.
It was in his hand that he took his vorpal sword.

Knowing the language, and assuming that *vorpal* means the same thing in the three sentences (because the same sounds are used), we can decide that the sense or truth conditions of the three sentences are identical. In other words, we are able to decide that two things mean the same thing even though we do not know what either one means. We decide by assuming that the semantic properties of *vorpal* are the same whenever it is used.

We now see why Alice commented, when she had read "Jabberwocky,"

"It seems very pretty, but it's *rather* hard to understand!" (You see she didn't like to confess, even to herself, that she couldn't make it out at all.) "Somehow it seems to fill my head with ideas — only I don't exactly know what they are!"

The semantic properties of words show up in other ways in sentence construction. For example, if the meaning of a word includes the semantic property "human" in English, then we can replace it with one sort of pronoun but not another. This semantic feature determines that we call a boy *he* and a table *it*, not vice versa.

According to Mark Twain, Eve had such knowledge in her grammar, for she writes in her diary that,

If this reptile is a man, it ain't an *it*, is it? That wouldn't be grammatical, would it? I think it would be *he*. In that case one would parse it thus: nominative *he*; dative, *him*; possessive, *his'n*.

Semantic violations in poetry may form strange but interesting aesthetic images, as in Dylan Thomas's phrase *a grief ago*. *Ago* is ordinarily used with words specified by some temporal semantic feature:

a week ago		*a table ago
an hour ago	but not	*a dream ago
a month ago		*a mother ago
a century ago		

When Thomas used the word *grief* with *ago*, he was adding a durational feature to *grief* for poetic effect.

In the poetry of e.e. cummings, there are phrases such as

> the six subjunctive crumbs twitch
> a man . . . wearing a round jeer for a hat
> children building this rainman out of snow

Although all of these phrases violate some semantic rules, we can understand them; it is the breaking of the rules that creates the imagery desired. The ability to understand these phrases and at the same time recognize their anomalous or deviant nature demonstrates knowledge of the semantic system and semantic properties of the language.

Metaphor

> Our doubts are traitors.
>
> William Shakespeare

> Walls have ears.
>
> Cervantes

> The night has a thousand eyes
> and the day but one.
>
> Frances William Bourdillon

Sometimes the breaking of semantic rules can be used to convey a particular idea. *Walls have ears* is certainly anomalous, but it can be interpreted as meaning "You can be overheard even when you think nobody is listening." In some sense, the sentence is ambiguous, but the literal meaning is so unlikely that listeners stretch their imaginations for another interpretation. That "stretching" is based on semantic properties that are inferred or that provide some kind of resemblance. Such nonliteral interpretations of sentences are called **metaphors**.

The literal meaning of a sentence such as

> My new car is a lemon.

is anomalous. We could, if driven to the wall (another metaphor), provide some literal interpretation that is plausible if given sufficient context. For example, the *new car* may be a miniature toy carved out of a piece of citrus fruit. The more common meaning, however, would be metaphorical and interpreted as referring to a newly purchased automobile that breaks down and requires constant repairs. The imagination stretching in this case may relate to the semantic property "tastes sour" that *lemon* possesses.

Metaphors are not necessarily anomalous when taken literally. The literal meaning of the sentence

> Dr. Jekyll is a butcher.

is that a physician named Jekyll also works as a retailer of meats or a slaughterer of animals used for food. The metaphorical meaning is that the doctor named Jekyll is harmful, possibly murderous, and apt to operate unnecessarily.

Similarly, the sentence

> John is a snake in the grass.

can be interpreted literally to refer to a pet snake named John on the lawn. Metaphorically, the sentence has nothing to do with a scaly, limbless reptile. On the other hand, Emily Dickinson's "narrow fellow in the grass" describes a real snake as human.

To interpret metaphors, we need to understand both the literal meanings and facts about the world. To understand the metaphor

> Time is money.

it is necessary to know that in our society we are often paid according to the number of hours or days worked. To recognize that the sentence

> Jack is a pussycat.

has a different meaning from

> Jack is a tiger.

requires knowledge that the metaphorical meaning of each sentence does not depend on the semantic property "feline." Rather, other semantic properties of these two words provide grounds for the metaphor.

Metaphorical use of language is language creativity at its highest. Nevertheless, the basis of metaphorical use is the ordinary linguistic knowledge about words, their semantic properties, and their combining powers that all speakers possess.

In *Metaphors We Live By*, G. Lakoff and M. Johnson (1980) show how pervasive the metaphor is in ordinary speech and how it structures thought and experience. For instance, the *Argument is war* metaphor may be seen in sentences such as

> Your claims are indefensible.
> She attacked every weak point in my argument.
> I demolished his argument.

Our attitudes toward arguments might be quite different if the prevailing metaphor were *Argument is dance.*

Idioms

Knowing a language includes knowing the morphemes, simple words, compound words, and their meanings. In addition, it means knowing fixed phrases, consisting of more than one word, with meanings that cannot be inferred from the meanings of the individual words. The usual semantic rules for combining meanings do not

apply. Such expressions are called **idioms**. All languages contain many idiomatic phrases, as in these English examples:

> sell down the river
> haul over the coals
> eat my hat
> let their hair down
> put his foot in his mouth
> throw her weight around
> snap out of it
> cut it out
> hit it off
> get it off
> bite your tongue
> give a piece of your mind

Idioms are similar in structure to ordinary phrases except that they tend to be frozen in form and do not readily enter into other combinations or allow the word order to change. Thus,

(1) She put her foot in her mouth.

has the same structure as

(2) She put her bracelet in her drawer.

However, whereas

The drawer in which she put her bracelet was hers.
Her bracelet was put in her drawer.

are sentences related to sentence (2),

The mouth in which she put her foot was hers.
Her foot was put in her mouth.

do not have the idiomatic sense of sentence (1).

On the other hand, the words of some idioms can be moved without affecting the idiomatic sense:

The RCMP kept tabs on radicals.
Tabs were kept on radicals by the RCMP.
Radicals were kept tabs on by the RCMP.

Idioms can break the rules on combining semantic properties. The object of *eat* must usually be something with the semantic property "edible," but in

He ate his hat.
Eat your heart out.

this restriction is violated.

Idioms, grammatically as well as semantically, have special characteristics. They must be entered into the lexicon or mental dictionary as single "items," with their meanings specified, and speakers must learn the special restrictions on their use in sentences.

Many idioms may have originated as metaphorical expressions that "took hold" in the language and became frozen in form and meaning.

Pragmatics

Pragmatics is concerned with the interpretation of linguistic meaning in context. Two kinds of context are relevant. The first is **linguistic context** — the discourse that precedes the phrase or sentence to be interpreted. Taken by itself, the sentence

Amazingly, he already loves her.

is essentially uninterpretable. The linguistic meaning is that something male and animate has arrived at a state of loving something female and animate, and the speaker finds something astonishing about it. There are no referents for *he* and *her*, and the reason for *amazingly* is vague. But if the sentence preceding it were *John met Mary yesterday*, its interpretation would be clearer.

John met Mary yesterday.
Amazingly, he already loves her.

The discourse suggests the second kind of context — **situational**, or knowledge of the world. To interpret the sentences fully, the listener must know the real-world references of John and Mary. Moreover, the interpretation of *amazingly* is made clear by the general belief that a person ordinarily needs more than a day to complete the act — the completion indicated by *already* — of falling in love.

Even innocent-sounding sentences, such as

> John believes he is a genius.

are ambiguous, for it is unclear in the absence of situational context whether *he* is coreferential with *John* or refers to some other person.

Situational context includes speaker, hearer, and any third parties present, along with their beliefs and their beliefs about what the others believe. It includes what has been previously uttered, the physical environment, the topic of conversation, the time of day, and other circumstances surrounding the participants in the discourse. Almost any imaginable extra-linguistic factor may, under appropriate circumstances, influence how language is interpreted.

Pragmatics is also about language use. It tells us that calling someone a *son of a bitch* is not a zoological opinion but an insult. It tells us that when a street person asks *Do you have any spare change?* it is not a fiduciary inquiry but a request for money. It tells us that, when a justice of the peace says, in the appropriate setting, *I now pronounce you husband and wife*, an act of marrying was performed.

Because pragmatics is concerned with the interpretation and use of language in context, it may be considered part of what we call **linguistic performance**.

Linguistic Context: Discourse

> Put your discourse into some frame, and start not so wildly from my affair.
>
> William Shakespeare, *Hamlet*

Linguistic knowledge accounts for speakers' ability to combine phonemes into morphemes, morphemes into words, and words into sentences. Knowing a language also permits combining sentences together to express complex thoughts and ideas. These larger linguistic units are called **discourse**.

The study of discourse, or **discourse analysis**, involves many aspects of linguistic performance as well as **linguistic competence**. Discourse analysis involves questions of style, appropriateness, cohesiveness, rhetorical force, topic/subtopic structure, differences between written and spoken discourse, and the like.

Our immediate concern in the following discussion is merely to point to a few aspects of discourse that bear on the interpretation of linguistic meaning.

Pronouns

Pronouns may be used in place of noun phrases or may be used to refer to an entity presumably known to the discourse participants. When that presumption fails, miscommunication may result.

Pronominalization occurs both in sentences and across the sentences of a discourse. Within a sentence, the structure limits the choice of pronoun. We saw previously that a reflexive pronoun must be used if both it and its antecedent are in the same S in the phrase structure tree. Likewise, we saw that sentence structure also dictates whether a pronoun and a noun phrase can be interpreted as coreferential.

In a discourse, prior linguistic context plays a primary role in pronoun interpretation. Consider the following discourse:

> It seems that the man loves the woman.
> Many people think he loves her.

In the most "natural" interpretation, *her* is "the woman" referred to in the first sentence, whoever she happens to be. But it is also possible for *her* to refer to a different person, a person identified contextually, say with a gesture. In such a case, *her* would be spoken with added emphasis:

> Many people think he loves *her*!

Similarly, *he* would be taken as coreferential with *the man*, but that interpretation is not necessarily the case. Intonation and emphasis would provide clues on how the pronoun is to be taken.

As far as syntactic rules are concerned, pronouns are noun phrases and may occur anywhere that a noun phrase may occur. Semantic rules of varying complexity establish whether a pronoun and some other noun phrase in the discourse can be interpreted as coreferential. A minimum condition of coreferentiality is that the pronoun and its antecedent have the same semantic feature values for the semantic properties of number and gender. In an attempt to avoid gender-specific language, many people violate this condition by the use of the plural *they* in sentences such as *Anyone may come if they like*.

When semantic rules and contextual interpretation determine that a pronoun is coreferential with a noun phrase, we say that the pronoun is **bound** to that noun phrase antecedent. If *her* in the previous example refers to "the woman," then it would be a bound pronoun. When a pronoun refers to some object not explicitly mentioned in the discourse, it is said to be **free** or **unbound**. The reference of a free pronoun must ultimately be determined by the situational context. First and second person non-reflexive pronouns are bound to the speaker and hearer respectively. Reflexive pronouns, sometimes called **anaphors**, are always bound. They require an antecedent in the sentence.

In the preceding example, semantic rules permit *her* either to be bound to *the woman* or to be a free pronoun, referring to some person not explicitly mentioned. The ultimate interpretation is context-dependent.

Anaphora

Referring to the discourse in the previous section, it would not, strictly speaking, be ungrammatical if it went this way:

> It seems that the man loves the woman.
> Many people think the man loves the woman.

However, most people would find such a discourse stilted and would prefer to use the pronouns *he* and *her: Many people think he loves her*. Often the use of pronouns is a stylistic decision, and stylistics is a part of pragmatics.

The process of replacing a longer expression by a pronoun or another kind of "pro-form" is called **anaphora**. Some examples of anaphora in English are

> Jan saw *the boy with the telescope.*
> Dan also saw <u>him</u> (= *the boy with the telescope*). (pronoun)

(Technically, what we call *pronouns* are "pro-noun phrases" in that they are *anaphors* that replace entire noun phrases.)

> *Emily hugged* Cassidy, as <u>did</u> (= hugged Cassidy) Zachary. (pro-verb phrase)
> *I am sick, which (= I am sick* or *my being sick) depresses me.* (pro-sentence)

This last example shows how sentences may function as noun phrases under anaphora. The pro-form *which* is a noun phrase since it is the subject of *which depresses me.* That is one of the reasons that embedded sentences were shown in a previous chapter as immediately dominated by the node NP.

Missing Parts

The process of anaphora replaces whole phrases with pro-forms. Sometimes in discourse, or even within sentences, entire phrases may be omitted and not replaced by a pro-form but still understood because of context. Such utterances taken in isolation appear to violate the rules of syntax, as in the sentence *My uncle has too*, but in the following discourse it is perfectly acceptable:

> First speaker: My aunt has been dieting strenuously.
> Second speaker: My uncle has too.

The second speaker can be understood to mean "My uncle has been dieting strenuously." The missing part of the verb phrase is understood from previous discourse.

Entire sentences may be "filled in" this way:

> First speaker: My aunt has been dieting strenuously, and she has lost a good
>   deal of weight.
> Second speaker: My mother has too.

The second speaker can be understood to have meant "My mother has been dieting strenuously, and she has lost a good deal of weight." Rules of discourse provide not only the missing parts of the verb phrase but also the entire second sentence meaning.

A process called **gapping** occurs when a repeated verb is omitted in similar contexts. Thus, in the following example, Bill is understood to have *washed* the cherries:

> Jill washed the grapes and Bill the cherries.

In a similar process, called **sluicing**, what follows a *wh-* word in an embedded sentence is omitted but understood:

Your ex-husband is dancing with someone, but I don't know who.
My cat ate something, and I wish I knew what.
She said she was coming over, but she didn't say when.

Missing from the end of the first sentence is *he is dancing with*, missing from the second sentence is *she ate*, and missing from the third sentence is *she was coming over*.

The Articles *the* and *a*

PEANUTS reprinted by permission of UFS, Inc.

There are discourse rules that apply regularly, such as those that determine the occurrence of the **articles** *the* and *a*. The article *the* is used to indicate that the referent of a noun phrase is agreed upon by speaker and listener. If someone says

I saw the dog.

then it is assumed that a certain dog is being discussed. No such assumption accompanies

I saw a dog.

which is more of a description of what was seen than a reference to a particular animal. Nevertheless, there are occasions when the indefinite article may have a specific reference, as seen in the following responses to the statement "I am looking for a dog":

I hope you find one. (indefinite non-specific)
I hope you find it. (indefinite specific)

Often a discourse will begin with the use of indefinite articles, and, once everyone agrees on the referents, definite articles start to appear. A short example illustrates this transition:

I saw *a* boy and *a* girl holding hands and kissing.
Oh, it sounds lovely.
Yes, *the* boy was quite tall and handsome, and he seemed to like *the* girl a lot.

These examples show that some rules of discourse are similar to grammatical rules in that a violation produces unacceptable results. If the final sentence of this discourse were

Yes, a boy was quite tall and handsome, and he seemed to like a girl a lot.

most speakers would find it unacceptable.

Situational Context

> Depending on inflection, [the French] *ah bon* can express shock, disbelief,
> indifference, irritation, or joy.
>
> Peter Mayle, *Toujours Provence*

Much discourse is telegraphic in nature. Verb phrases are not specifically mentioned, entire clauses are left out, direct objects disappear, pronouns abound. Yet people still understand one another, partly because rules of grammar and rules of discourse combine with contextual knowledge to fill in gaps and make the discourse cohere. Much of the contextual knowledge is knowledge of who is speaking, who is listening, what objects are being discussed, and general facts about the world we live in, called **situational context**.

Often what we say is not literally what we mean. When we ask at the dinner table if someone can "pass the salt," we are not querying his ability to do so; if someone says "You're standing on my foot," she is not making idle conversation. She is asking you to stand somewhere else. We say "It's cold in here" to mean "Shut the window," "Turn up the heat," "Let's leave," or a dozen other things that depend on the real-world situation at the time of speaking.

In the following sections, we will look briefly (and incompletely) at a few of the ways that real-world context influences and interacts with meaning.

Maxims of Conversation

> Though this be madness, yet there is method in't.
>
> William Shakespeare, *Hamlet*

Speakers recognize when a series of sentences hangs together or when it is disjointed. The discourse below, which gave rise to Polonius's remark quoted at the head of this section, does not seem quite right — it is not **coherent**.

POLONIUS: What do you read, my lord?

HAMLET: Words, words, words.

POLONIUS: What is the matter, my lord?

HAMLET: Between who?

POLONIUS: I mean, the matter that you read, my lord.

HAMLET: Slanders, sir: for the satirical rogue says here that old men have grey beards, that their faces are wrinkled, their eyes purging thick amber and plum-tree gum, and that they have a plentiful lack of wit, together with most weak hams: all of which, sir, though I most powerfully and potently believe, yet I hold it not honesty to have it thus set down;

for yourself, sir, should grow old as I am, if like a crab you could go backward.

Hamlet, who is feigning insanity, refuses to answer Polonius's questions "in good faith." He has violated certain conversational conventions or **maxims of conversation** first discussed by H. Paul Grice in 1967. One such maxim — the **maxim of quantity** — states that a speaker's contribution to the discourse should be as informative as is required — neither more nor less. Hamlet has violated this maxim. In answering "Words, words, words" to the question of what is being read, he is providing too little information. His final remark goes to the other extreme in providing more information than required.

He also violates the **maxim of relevance**, when he "misinterprets" the question about the reading matter as a matter between two individuals.

The "run-on" nature of Hamlet's final remark, a violation of the **maxim of manner**, is another source of incoherence. This effect is increased in the final sentence by the somewhat bizarre choice of phrasing to compare growing younger with walking backward, a violation of the **maxim of quality**, which requires sincerity and truthfulness.

The four conversational maxims, parts of the broad **Cooperative Principle**, may be summarized as follows:

Name of Maxim	Description of Maxim
Quantity	Say neither more nor less than the discourse requires.
Relevance	Be relevant.
Manner	Be brief and orderly; avoid ambiguity and obscurity.
Quality	Do not lie; do not make unsupported claims.

Unless, like Hamlet, we are being deliberately uncooperative, we adhere to these maxims as well as to other conversational principles such as **turn-taking** (i.e., knowing when it is our time to speak and when to listen). And we assume that others will adhere to them as well. Bereft of context, if one man says (truthfully) to another *I have never slept with your wife*, that would be grounds for provocation because the topic of conversation should be unnecessary, a violation of the maxim of quantity.

Asking an able-bodied person at the dinner table *Can you pass the salt?*, if answered literally, would force the responder into stating the obvious, a violation of the maxim of quantity. To avoid this, the person asked seeks a reason for the question and deduces that the asker would like to have the salt.

The maxim of relevance explains how saying *It's cold in here* to a person standing by an open window might be interpreted as a request to close it, else why make the remark to that particular person in the first place?

Conversational conventions such as these allow the various sentence meanings to be sensibly connected into discourse meaning and integrated with context, much as rules of sentence grammar allow word meanings to be sensibly (and grammatically) connected into sentence meaning.

Speech Acts

PEANUTS reprinted by permission of UFS, Inc.

We can use language to do things: make promises, lay bets, issue warnings, christen boats, place names in nomination, offer congratulations, or swear testimony. The theory of **speech acts** describes how this is done. By saying *I warn you that there is a sheepdog in the closet*, we not only say something but also *warn* someone. Verbs such as *bet, promise, warn,* and so on are **performative verbs**. Using them in a sentence does something extra to the statement.

There are hundreds of performative verbs in every language. The following sentences illustrate their usage:

> I *bet* you five dollars the Rough Riders win.
> I *challenge* you to a match.
> I *dare* you to step over this line.
> I *fine* you $100 for speeding.
> I *move* that we adjourn.
> I *nominate* Batman for mayor of Gotham City.
> I *promise* to improve.
> I *resign*!

In all these sentences, the speaker is the subject (i.e., the sentences are in the "first person") who, by uttering the sentence, is accomplishing some additional action, such as daring, nominating, or resigning. Also, all these sentences are affirmative, declarative, and in the present tense. They are typical **performative sentences**.

An informal test to see whether a sentence contains a performative verb is to begin it with the words *I hereby. . . .* Only performative sentences sound right when begun this way. Compare *I hereby apologize to you* with the somewhat strange *I hereby know you.* The first is generally taken as an act of apologizing. In all the examples given, insertion of *hereby* would be acceptable. As the cartoon at the beginning of this section shows, Snoopy is aware that he is uttering a performative with his use of *hereby*, but he seems unaware that *despise* is a non-performative verb.

Actually, every utterance is some kind of speech act. Even when there is no explicit performative verb, as in *It is raining*, we recognize an implicit performance of *stating*. On the other hand, *Is it raining?* is a performance of *questioning*, just as *Leave!* is a performance of *ordering*. In all these instances, we could use, if we chose, an actual performative verb: ***I state*** *that it is raining;* ***I ask*** *if it is raining;* ***I order*** *you to leave.*

In studying speech acts, we are acutely aware of the importance of the *context of the utterance*. In some circumstances, *There is a sheepdog in the closet* is a warning, but the same sentence may be a promise or even a mere statement of fact, depending on circumstances. We call this purpose — a warning, a promise, a threat, or whatever — the **illocutionary force** of a speech act. The way a sentence is taken — its effect — is its *perlocutionary force*. Thus, *There is a sheepdog in the closet* might be intended as a warning but taken as a simple statement of fact.

Speech act theory aims to tell us when we appear to ask questions but are really giving orders or when we say one thing with special (sarcastic) intonation and mean the opposite. Thus, at a dinner table, the question *Can you pass the salt?* means the order *Pass the salt!* It is not a request for information, and *Yes* is an inappropriate response.

Because the illocutionary force of a speech act depends on the context of the utterance, speech act theory is a part of pragmatics.

Presuppositions

> You mentioned your name as if I should recognize it, but beyond the obvious facts that you are a bachelor, a solicitor, a Freemason, and an asthmatic, I know nothing whatever about you.
>
> Sir Arthur Conan Doyle, "The Norwood Builder," *The Memoirs of Sherlock Holmes*

Speakers often make implicit assumptions about the real world, and the sense of an utterance may depend on those assumptions. The **presuppositions** of an utterance are those assumptions, the truth of which is required in order that the utterance be appropriate. Consider the following sentences:

(1) Have you stopped hugging your sheepdog?
(2) Who bought the badminton set?
(3) John doesn't write poems anymore.
(4) The present king of France is bald.
(5) Would you like another beer?

In sentence (1), the speaker has *presupposed* that the listener has at some past time hugged his sheepdog. In (2), there is the presupposition that someone has already bought a badminton set, and in (3) it is assumed that John once wrote poetry.

We have already run across the somewhat odd (4), which we decided we could understand even though France does not currently have a king. The use of the definite article *the* usually presupposes an existing referent. When presuppositions are inconsistent with the actual state of the world, the utterance is felt to be strange, unless a fictional setting is agreed upon by the conversants, as in a play.

Sentence (5) presupposes or implies that you have already had at least one beer. Part of the meaning of the word *another* includes this presupposition. The Mad Hatter in *Alice's Adventures in Wonderland* appears not to understand presuppositions:

> "Take some more tea," the March Hare said to Alice, very earnestly.
> "I've had nothing yet," Alice replied in an offended tone, "so I can't take more."
> "You mean you can't take *less*," said the Hatter. "It's very easy to take *more* than nothing."

The humour in this passage comes from the meaning of the word *more*, which presupposes some earlier amount.

These phenomena may also be described as **implication**. Part of the meaning of *more* implies that there has already been something. The definite article *the*, in these terms, entails or implies the existence of the referent within the current context.

Presuppositions can be used to communicate information indirectly. If someone says *My brother is rich*, we assume that person has a brother, even though that fact is not explicitly stated. Much of the information that is exchanged in a conversation or discourse is of this kind. Often, after a conversation has ended, we will realize that some fact was imparted to us that was not specifically mentioned. That fact is often a presupposition.

The use of language in a courtroom is restricted so that presuppositions cannot influence the court or jury. The famous type of question *Have you stopped beating your wife?* is disallowed in court, because accepting the validity of the question means accepting its presuppositions; the question contains an inevitable conclusion. Unfortunately, questions and comments are not usually as transparent as this above example, and we must be especially alert to underlying presuppositions that may encourage prejudice and bigotry. Presuppositions are so much a part of natural discourse that they become second nature and we do not think of them, any more than we are directly aware of the many other rules and maxims that govern language and its use in context.

Deixis

In all languages, there are many words and expressions whose reference relies entirely on the situational context of the utterance and can only be understood in light of these circumstances. This aspect of pragmatics is called **deixis** (pronounced "dike-sis") or **indexicality**, both of which derive from classical Greek and Latin, in which they referred to pointing or indicating. First and second person pronouns such as

> my   mine   you   your   yours   we   ours   us

are always deictic because they are free pronouns and their reference is entirely dependent on context. You must know who the speaker and listener are in order to interpret them.

Third person pronouns are deictic if they are *free*. If they are *bound*, then their reference is known from the linguistic context. One peculiar exception is the "pronoun" *it* when used in sentences such as

> It appears as though sheepdogs are the missing link.
> The patriotic archbishop of Canterbury found it advisable. . . .

DENNIS THE MENACE® used by permission of Hank Ketcham and © by North America Syndicate.

In these cases, the *it* does not function as a true pronoun by referring to some entity. Rather, *it* is a grammatical morpheme, a place-holder as it were, required to satisfy the English rules of syntax.

Expressions such as

> this person
> that man
> these women
> those children

are deictic, for they require pragmatic information in order for the listener to make a referential connection and understand what is meant. The above examples illustrate **person deixis**. They also show that the use of **demonstratives** such as *this* and *that* is deictic.

There is also **time deixis** and **place deixis**. The following examples are all deictic expressions of time:

now	then	tomorrow
this time	that time	seven days ago
two weeks from now	last week	next April

In order to understand what specific times such expressions refer to, we need to know when the utterance was said. Clearly, *next week* has a different reference when uttered today rather than a month from today. If you found an advertising leaflet on the street that said "BIG SALE NEXT WEEK" with no date given, you would not know whether the sale had already taken place.

Expressions of place deixis require contextual information about the place of the utterance, as shown by the following examples:

here	there	this place
that place	this ranch	those towers over there
this city	these parks	yonder mountains

In addition to space and time, deixis may involve **social and occupational** relationships. The meaning of a word such as *teacher* or *doctor* in sentences such as *Teacher told us to read the chapter* and *Doctor insists that you take the medicine* depends on who is speaking. Although Denis the Menace and the bewildered caller in the above cartoon both use the same word, *mother*, they have very different notions of who is being referred to. The cartoon indicates what can happen if deictic expressions are misinterpreted.

Directional terms such as

before/behind	left/right	front/back

are deictic insofar as you need to know which way the speaker is facing. In Japanese, the verb *kuru*, "come," can be used only for motion toward the place of utterance. A Japanese speaker cannot call up a friend and ask

May I *kuru* to your house?

as you might, in English, ask "May I come to your house?" The correct verb is *iku*, "go," which indicates motion away from the place of utterance. These verbs thus have a deictic aspect to their meaning.

Deixis abounds in language use and marks one of the boundaries of semantics and pragmatics. The pronoun *I* certainly has a meaning independent of context — its semantic meaning, which is "the speaker" — but context is necessary to know who the speaker is, hence what "I" refers to.

Summary

Knowing a language is knowing how to produce and understand sentences with particular meanings. The study of linguistic meaning is called **semantics**. **Lexical semantics** is concerned with the meanings of morphemes and words; **phrasal semantics** is concerned with phrases and sentences. The study of how context affects meaning is called **pragmatics**.

The meanings of morphemes and words are defined in part by their **semantic properties**, whose presence or absence is indicated by use of **semantic features**. Relationships between semantic properties, such as that "human" implies "animate," can be expressed through **redundancy rules**.

When two words have the same sounds but different meanings, they are **homonyms** (e.g., *bear* and *bare*). The use of homonyms may result in **lexical ambiguity**, which occurs when an utterance has more than one meaning. (**Structural ambiguity**, as in *synthetic buffalo hides*, is due to sentence structure.) **Heteronyms** are words spelled the same but pronounced differently or pronounced the same and spelled differently. They also have different meanings, such as *sow*, a female pig, and *sow*, meaning to scatter seeds, or *I* and *eye*. **Homographs** are words spelled the same, possibly pronounced the same, and having different meanings, such as *trunk* of an elephant and *trunk* for storing clothes.

When two words have the same meaning but different sounds, they are **synonyms** (e.g., *chesterfield* and *couch*). The use of synonyms may result in **paraphrase**, which occurs when two different utterances have the same meaning. Paraphrase may also arise when sentences differ structurally in ways that do not affect meaning, as in *Hail, Richard, England's king / Hail, Richard, king of England*.

When a word has differing meanings that are conceptually and historically related, it is said to be **polysemous**. For example, *good* means "well behaved" in *good child* and "sound" in *good investment*. Polysemous words may be partially synonymous in that they share one or more of their meanings with other words.

Two words that are "opposite" in meaning are **antonyms**. Antonyms have the same semantic properties except for the one that accounts for their oppositeness. There are antonymous pairs that are **complementary** (*alive/dead*), **gradable** (*hot/cold*), and **relational opposites** (*buy/sell, employer/employee*).

When the meaning of one word is included in that of a more general word, it is a **hyponym** of the general word, and the general word is the **superordinate** or **hypernym** (e.g., *dog* and *animal*).

Hyponyms are words, such as *red* and *white*, that share a feature indicating that they all belong to the same class; **metonyms** are "substitute" words, such as *Ottawa* for the federal government; **meronyms** are parts of a thing, such as *root, trunk*, or *branch* of a *tree*; and **retronyms** are expressions such as *broadcast television* that once were redundant but now make necessary distinctions due to changes in the world — in this case, the advent of cable television.

Proper names are special morphemes used to designate particular objects uniquely — that is, they are **definite**. Proper names cannot ordinarily be preceded by an article or an adjective, or be pluralized, in English.

Languages have rules for combining the meanings of parts into the meaning of the whole. For example, *red balloon* has the semantic properties of *balloon* combined with the semantic property of *red* in an additive manner. Such combinations are not always additive. The phrase *counterfeit dollar* does not simply have the semantic properties of *dollar* plus something else.

In building larger meanings from smaller meanings, the semantic rules interact with the syntactic rules of the language. For example, if a noun phrase and a non-reflexive pronoun occur within the same S, then semantic rules cannot interpret them to be **coreferential** — that is, having the same referent. Thus, in *Mary bit her*, the *her* refers to someone other than Mary.

Words, phrases, and sentences generally have **sense**, which is part of their meaning. By knowing the sense of an expression, you can determine its **reference**, if any — namely, what it points to in the world. Some meaningful expressions (e.g., *the* *present king of France*) have sense but no reference, while others, such as proper nouns, often have reference but no sense. The sense of a declarative sentence is its **truth conditions,** the aspect of meaning that allows you to determine whether the sentence is *true* or *false*. The reference of a declarative sentence, when it has one, is its truth value, either true or false. Two sentences are **paraphrases** if they have the same truth conditions.

There are two kinds of truthful sentences: **analytic** and **synthetic.** The first type is a sentence such as *A widow is a woman whose husband is no longer living.* In other words, given the meanings of the words, the statement must of necessity be true. Synthetic sentences, however, draw on our understanding of the world, as in *Jan is a widow,* for which we need extra-linguistic information to determine the truth of the statement. **Contradictory** statements are "by definition" false because of the language itself. References to a triangle's fourth side, for example, or to a bachelor as a married man are contradictory because of the meanings of *triangle* and *bachelor.*

The meaning of a sentence is determined in part by the **thematic roles** of the noun phrases in relation to the verb. These semantic relationships indicate who, to whom, toward what, from which, with what, and so on.

Sentences are **anomalous** when they deviate from certain semantic rules. *The six subjunctive crumbs twitched* and *The stone ran* are anomalous. Other sentences are **uninterpretable** because they contain nonsense words, such as *An orkish sluck blecked nokishly.*

Many sentences have both a literal and a non-literal or **metaphorical** interpretation. *He's out in left field* may be a literal description of a baseball player or a metaphorical description of someone mentally deranged.

Idioms are phrases whose meaning is *not* the combination of the meanings of the individual words (e.g., *put her foot in her mouth*). Idioms often violate co-occurrence restrictions of semantic properties.

The general study of how context affects linguistic interpretation is **pragmatics.** Context may be *linguistic* — what was previously spoken or written — or *knowledge of the world,* what we have called **situational context.**

Discourse consists of several sentences, including exchanges between speakers. Pragmatics is important when interpreting discourse, as when determining whether a pronoun in one sentence has the same referent as a noun phrase in another sentence.

Anaphora is the general term for replacing phrases with pro-forms, including *pro-nouns,* which are actually *pro-noun phrases, pro-verbs,* and *pro-sentences.* Linguistic context often reveals when a missing part can be understood from something previously said, such as "will wash" in *Jan will wash grapes and Jon _____ cherries.*

Well-structured discourse follows certain rules and **maxims,** such as "be relevant," that make the discourse coherent. There are also grammatical rules that affect discourse, such as those that determine when to use the definite article *the.*

Pragmatics includes **speech acts, presuppositions,** and **deixis.** Speech act theory is the study of what an utterance does beyond just saying something. The effect of what is done is called the **illocutionary force** of the utterance. For example, use of a **performative verb** such as *bequeath* may be an act of bequeathing, which may even have legal status.

Presuppositions are implicit assumptions that accompany certain utterances. *Have you stopped hugging Sue?* carries with it the presupposition that at one time you hugged Sue.

Deictic terms such as *you, there*, and *now* require knowledge of the circumstances (the person, place, or time) of the utterance to be interpreted referentially.

Exercises

1. For each group of words given below, state what semantic property or properties are shared by the (i) words and the (ii) words, and what semantic property or properties differentiate the classes of (i) words and (ii) words.

    Example: (i) widow, mother, sister, aunt, seamstress
    (ii) widower, father, brother, uncle, tailor
    The (i) and (ii) words are "human."
    The (i) words are "female," and the (ii) words are "male."

    a.   (i) bachelor, man, son, paperboy, pope, chief
         (ii) bull, rooster, drake, ram
    b.   (i) table, stone, pencil, cup, house, ship, car
         (ii) milk, alcohol, rice, soup, mud
    c.   (i) book, temple, mountain, road, tractor
         (ii) idea, love, charity, sincerity, bravery, fear
    d.   (i) pine, elm, ash, weeping willow, sycamore
         (ii) rose, dandelion, aster, tulip, daisy
    e.   (i) book, letter, encyclopedia, novel, notebook, dictionary
         (ii) typewriter, pencil, ballpoint, crayon, quill, charcoal, chalk
    f.   (i) walk, run, skip, jump, hop, swim
         (ii) fly, skate, ski, ride, cycle, canoe, hang-glide
    g.   (i) ask, tell, say, talk, converse
         (ii) shout, whisper, mutter, drawl, holler
    h.   (i) alleged, counterfeit, false, putative, accused
         (ii) red, large, cheerful, pretty, stupid
         (*Hint*: Is an alleged murderer always a murderer?)

2. Explain the semantic ambiguity of the following sentences by providing two sentences that paraphrase the two meanings. Example: *She can't bear children* can mean either *She can't give birth to children* or *She can't tolerate children*.

    a.   He waited by the bank.
    b.   Is he really that kind?
    c.   The proprietor of the fish store was the sole owner.

d. The long drill was boring.

e. When he got the clear title to the land, it was a good deed.

f. It takes a good ruler to make a straight line.

g. He saw that gasoline can explode.

*3. There are several kinds of antonymy. Which of the pairs in columns A and B are complementary, gradable, or relational opposites?

A	B
good	bad
expensive	cheap
parent	offspring
beautiful	ugly
false	true
lessor	lessee
pass	fail
hot	cold
legal	illegal
larger	smaller
poor	rich
fast	slow
asleep	awake
husband	wife
rude	polite

*4. The following sentences consist of a verb, its noun phrase subject, and various objects. Identify the thematic relation of each noun phrase, indicating whether it is *agent, theme, location, instrument, source, goal, experiencer, causative*, or *possessor*.

$$a \qquad\qquad t \qquad\qquad s \qquad\qquad i$$

Example: The boy took the books from the cupboard with a handcart.

a. Mary found a ball in the house.

b. The children ran from the playground to the wading pool.

c. One of the men unlocked all the doors with a paper clip.

d. John melted the ice with a blowtorch.

e. The sun melted the ice.

f. The ice melted.

g. The farmer loaded hay onto the truck.

h. The farmer loaded the hay with a pitchfork.

i. The hay was loaded on the truck by the farmer.

5. It is often the case that the subject of the sentence has the thematic role of agent, as can be seen in the previous exercise. With verbs such as *receive*, however, the subject is not the agent. Think of five other verbs in which the subject is clearly not the agent. Can you identify the actual thematic role of the subject

in your examples? For example, we would surmise that the subject of *receive* has the thematic role of goal.

*6. Some linguists and philosophers distinguish between two kinds of truthful statements: one follows from the definition or meaning of a word; the other simply happens to be true in the world as we know it. Thus, *Kings are monarchs* is true because the word *king* has the semantic property "monarch" as part of its meaning, but *Kings are rich* is circumstantially true. We can imagine a poor king, but a king who is not a monarch is not truly a king. Sentences such as *Kings are monarchs* are said to be **analytic**, true by virtue of meaning alone. Examine the following sentences to determine which are analytic and which are not.

  a.   Queens are monarchs.
  b.   Queens are female.
  c.   Queens are mothers.
  d.   Dogs are four-legged.
  e.   Dogs are animals.
  f.   Cats are felines.
  g.   Cats are stupid.
  h.   Audrey MacLaughlin is Audrey MacLaughlin.
  i.   Audrey MacLaughlin was the first woman to lead a federal political party in Canada.
  j.   Uncles are male.

7. The opposite of *analytic* (see previous exercise) is **contradictory**. A sentence that is false due to the meaning of its words alone is contradictory. *Kings are female* is an example. Which of the following sentences are contradictory?

  a.   My aunt is a man.
  b.   Witches are wicked.
  c.   My brother is an only child.
  d.   The evening star isn't the morning star.
  e.   The evening star isn't the evening star.
  f.   Babies are adults.
  g.   Babies can lift one tonne.
  h.   Puppies are human.
  i.   My bachelor friends are all married.
  j.   My bachelor friends are all lonely.

8. In sports and games, many expressions are "performative." By shouting *"You're out!"* the first-base umpire performs an act. Think of a half-dozen or so similar examples and explicate their use.

9. A criterion of a "performance sentence" is whether you can begin it with *I hereby*. Notice that if you say sentence a aloud it sounds like a genuine

apology, but to say sentence b aloud sounds odd because you cannot perform an act of knowing.

a.   I hereby apologize to you.
b.   I hereby know you.

Test whether the following sentences are performance sentences by inserting *hereby* and seeing whether they sound "right."

c.   I testify that she met the agent.
d.   I know that she met the agent.
e.   I suppose the Expos will win.
f.   He bet her $2500 that the Liberals would win.
g.   I dismiss the class.
h.   I teach the class.
i.   We promise to leave early.
j.   I owe Revenue Canada $1 000 000.
k.   I bequeath $1 000 000 to Revenue Canada.
l.   I swore I didn't do it.
m.   I swear I didn't do it.

*10. The following sentences make certain presuppositions. What are they? (The first one has been done for you.)

a.   The police ordered the minors to stop drinking.
     Presupposition: <u>The minors were drinking.</u>
b.   Please take me out to the ball game again.
c.   Valerie regretted not receiving a new T-bird for Labour Day.
d.   That her pet turtle ran away made Emily very sad.
e.   The administration forgot that the professors support the students.
     (Cf. *The administration believes that the professors support the students*, in which there is no such presupposition.)
f.   It is strange that Canada entered World War II in 1939.
g.   Isn't it strange that Canada entered World War II in 1939?
h.   Disa wants more popcorn.
i.   Why don't pigs have wings?
j.   Who discovered America in 1492?

11. A.   Consider the following "facts" and then answer the questions.

         Roses are red, and bralkions are too.
         Booth shot Lincoln and Czolgosz, McKinley.
         Casca stabbed Caesar, and so did Cinna.
         Frodo was exhausted, as was Sam.

         a.   What colour are bralkions?
         b.   What did Czolgosz do to McKinley?

    c.   What did Cinna do to Caesar?

    d.   What state was Sam in?

B. Now consider these facts and explain how it is that you are able to determine the truth of each statement in a through e.

Black Beauty was a stallion.
Mary is a widow.
John remembered to send Mary a birthday card.
John didn't remember to send Jane a birthday card.
Flipper is walking.

    a.   Black Beauty was male?

    b.   Mary was never married?

    c.   John sent Mary a card?

    d.   John sent Jane a card?

    e.   Flipper has legs?

Part A illustrates your ability to interpret meanings when syntactic rules have deleted parts of the sentence. Part B illustrates your knowledge of semantic features and presuppositions.

12. Examine the following sentences for any deictic expressions they may contain. (*Hint:* Proper names and noun phrases containing *the* are not considered deictic expressions. Also, all sentences do not include such expressions.)

    a.   I saw her standing there.

    b.   Dogs are animals.

    c.   Yesterday, all my troubles seemed so far away.

    d.   The name of this rock band is The Beatles.

    e.   The Canadian Constitution was patriated in 1982.

    f.   The Canadian Constitution was patriated last year.

    g.   Copper conducts electricity.

    h.   The treasure chest is on the right.

    i.   These are the times that try men's souls.

    j.   There is a tide in the affairs of men which taken at the flood leads on to fortune.

*13. State for each pronoun in the following sentences whether it is free, bound, or either bound or free. Consider each sentence independently.

    Example: John finds himself in love with her.
            himself — bound; her — free
    Example: John said that he loved her.
            he — bound or free; her — free

    a.   Louise said to herself in the mirror: "I'm so ugly."

    b.   The fact that he considers her pretty pleases Maria.

c. Whenever I see you, I think of her.
d. John discovered that a picture of himself was hanging in the post office, and that fact bugged him, but it pleased her.
e. It seems that she and he will never stop arguing with them.
f. Persons are prohibited from picking flowers from any but their own graves. (on a sign in a cemetery)

14. The following sentences may be either lexically or structurally ambiguous or both. Provide paraphrases showing you comprehend all the meanings.

> Example: I saw him walking by the bank.
> Meaning 1: I saw him, and he was walking by the riverbank.
> Meaning 2: I saw him, and he was walking by the financial institution.
> Meaning 3: I was walking by the riverbank when I saw him.
> Meaning 4: I was walking by the financial institution when I saw him.

a. We laughed at the colourful ball.
b. He was knocked over by the punch.
c. The police were urged to stop drinking by the fifth.
d. I said I would file it on Thursday.
e. I cannot recommend visiting professors too highly.
f. The licence fee for pets owned by senior citizens who have not been altered is $1.50. (actual notice)
g. What looks better on a handsome man than a tux? Nothing! (attributed to Mae West)

Works Cited

Chomsky, Noam. 1957. *Syntactic Structures*. The Hague: Mouton.
Grice, H.P. 1971. "Utterer's Meaning." In J.R. Searle, ed. Oxford: Oxford University Press.
———. 1975. "Logic and Conversation." In P. Cole and J. Morgan, eds. *Syntax and Semantics* 3: 41–58. New York: Academic Press.
Lakoff, G., and M. Johnson. 1980. *Metaphors We Live By*. Chicago: University of Chicago Press.

Further Reading

Austin, J.L. 1962. *How to Do Things with Words*. Cambridge, MA: Harvard University Press.
Brown, G., and G. Yule. 1983. *Discourse Analysis*. Cambridge, UK: Cambridge University Press.
Chierchia, Gennaro, and Sally McConnell-Ginet. 1990. *Meaning and Grammar: An Introduction to Syntax*. Cambridge, MA: MIT Press.
Davidson, D., and G. Harman, eds. 1972. *Semantics of Natural Languages*. Dordrecht, The Netherlands: Reidel.

Fraser, B. 1995. *An Introduction to Pragmatics*. Oxford: Blackwell.

Green, Georgia M. 1989. *Pragmatics and Natural Language Understanding*. Hillsdale, NJ: Lawrence Erlbaum Associates.

Grice, H.P. 1975. "Logic and Conversation." In P. Cole and J. Morgan, eds., *Syntax and Semantics* 3: 41–58. New York: Academic Press.

Hawkins, John A. 1985. *A Comparative Typology of English and German*. Austin: University of Texas Press.

Hurford, J.R., and B. Heasley. 1983. *Semantics: A Coursebook*. Cambridge, UK: Cambridge University Press.

Jackendoff, Ray. 1983. *Semantics and Cognition*. Cambridge, MA: MIT Press.

———. 1993. *Patterns in the Mind*. New York: HarperCollins.

Katz, J. 1972. *Semantic Theory*. New York: Harper & Row.

Lakoff, G. 1987. *Women, Fire, and Dangerous Things: What Categories Reveal about the Mind*. Chicago: University of Chicago Press.

Larson, R., and G. Segal. 1995. *Knowledge of Meaning*. Cambridge, MA: MIT Press.

Levinson, S.C. 1983. *Pragmatics*. Cambridge, UK: Cambridge University Press.

Lyons, J. 1977. *Semantics*. Cambridge, UK: Cambridge University Press.

Mey, J.L. 1993. *Pragmatics: An Introduction*. Oxford: Blackwell.

Palmer, F.R. 1994. *Grammatical Roles and Relations*. Cambridge, UK: Cambridge University Press.

Parsons, Terence. 1994. *Events in the Semantics of English: A Study in Subatomic Semantics*. Cambridge, MA: MIT Press.

Searle, John R. 1969. *Speech Acts: An Essay in the Philosophy of Language*. Cambridge, UK: Cambridge University Press.

Sperber, D., and D. Wilson. 1986. *Relevance: Communication and Cognition*. Oxford: Blackwell.

CHAPTER 5
Phonetics: The Sounds of Language

The sounds of speech are all around us. We use them, we hear them, we enjoy and suffer from them, and in general we know remarkably little about them. Not from lack of interest or percipience, since we are in many ways fascinated by the sounds that we and others utter and immensely skilful at discriminating and interpreting them, but rather from the inherent difficulty of coming to grips with anything so transient.

J.D. O'Connor, *Phonetics* (1973)

Phonetics is concerned with describing the speech sounds that occur in the languages of the world. We want to know what these sounds are, how they fall into patterns, and how they change in different circumstances. . . . The first job of a phonetician is . . . to try to find out what people are doing when they are talking and when they are listening to speech.

Peter Ladefoged, *A Course in Phonetics*, 2nd Edition (1982)

Many people, when asked about language, think first of the written form because they recall most vividly those years in school when, under the guidance of a teacher, they mastered the fundamentals of reading and writing. Few, if any of us, can recall the earlier years in which we mastered the sound system of our mother tongue.

Language may manifest itself in many ways apart from the written system learned in school; it may be encoded electronically or appear in the signing system employed by the hearing impaired. For most people, however, language was first realized through sounds that are created and manipulated by the lungs and thorax and in the oral and nasal passages.

As J.D. O'Connor reminds us, these "sounds of speech are all around us." From our first waking moment to the moment we surrender our consciousness, most of us are submerged in the sounds of speech as we talk with family, friends, acquaintances, and strangers or listen to the talk on radio or television. While we display great skill in producing and interpreting speech sounds, we also, as O'Connor remarks, consciously know little about those sounds.

We might ask why, if we are able to employ the sounds of our language with such skill, we need to learn any more about them. A first, more philosophical, response might be that, as language is arguably the most defining of all human actions, understanding any aspect of language is part of our continual attempt to understand what it means to be human. Most of us learn our "mother tongue" by first discriminating speech sounds from all the noise that surrounds us and then attempting to replicate those sounds and the patterns we hear in them. The fact that we learn language in this manner has been seen as one cause of constant change in every living language; as children attempt to replicate the sounds of their parents, they do so imperfectly, and this leads to changes, each of which may seem minute in itself but which may become significant over time.

But the physical nature of sounds is not only of historical interest, because the fact that language most commonly manifests itself in sounds produced by the human vocal apparatus helps to explain many things that we hear in everyday speech. It is not unusual, for example, in informal conversation to hear the word *something* pronounced with an intrusive *p* in it (as in *sumpthing*); this is the result of slight incoordination in moving between the *m* and the *th* sounds. If we are to understand why and how this occurs, we must first understand something about the sounds themselves and the qualities they share. It is the purpose of this chapter to make us more aware of speech sounds, in particular the sounds of English.

Knowledge of a language includes knowledge of the morphemes, words, phrases, and sentences, but it also includes knowing what sounds are in the language and how they may be "strung" together to form meaningful units. Although the sounds of French or Xhosa or Quechua are uninterpretable to someone who does not speak those languages, and although there may be some sounds in one language that are not in another, the sounds of all the languages of the world together constitute a limited set. This chapter will discuss these speech sounds, how they are produced, and how they may be characterized.

Sound Segments

The study of speech sounds is called **phonetics**. To describe these sounds, it is necessary to know what an individual sound is and how each sound differs from all others.

This is not as easy as it may seem. A speaker of English knows that there are three sounds in the word *cat*, the initial sound represented by the letter *c*, the second sound by *a*, and the final sound by *t*. Yet physically the word is just one continuous sound. You can **segment** the one sound into parts because you know English. The ability to analyze a word into its individual sounds does not depend on knowledge of how the word is spelled. Both *not* and *knot* have three sounds even though the first sound in *knot* is represented by the two letters *kn*. The printed word *psycho* has six letters that represent only four sounds — *ps, y, ch, o.*

It is difficult, if not impossible, to segment the sounds of a throat being cleared into a sequence of discrete units because these sounds are not the sounds of any morpheme in any human language. This difficulty does not arise because clearing the throat is a single continuous sound; in ordinary speech, we do not normally produce one sound followed by another and finally by a third sound in, for example, the word *cat*. We move our organs of speech continuously and produce a continuous signal.

HERMAN®

by Jim Unger

5-30   © 1978 Jim Unger

"Keep out! Keep out! K-E-E-P O-U-T."

Although the sounds we produce and hear and comprehend during speech are continuous, everyone throughout history who has attempted to analyze language has recognized that speech utterances can be segmented into individual units. According to an ancient Hindu myth, the god Indra, in response to an appeal made by the other gods, attempted for the first time to segment speech into its separate elements. After he accomplished this feat, according to the myth, the sounds could be regarded as language. Indra thus may have been the first phonetician.

Speakers of English can, despite the Herman cartoon, separate *keep out* into two words because they know the language. We do not, however, pause between words even though we sometimes have that illusion. Children learning a language reveal this problem. A two-year-old child going down a flight of stairs, when told to *hold on*, replied *I'm holding don*, not knowing where the break between the words occurred. In the course of history, the errors in deciding where a boundary falls between two words can change the forms of words. At an earlier stage of English, the words *apron* and *adder* were *napron* and *nadder*; they were misperceived in the phrases *a napron* and *a nadder* as *an apron* and *an adder* by so many speakers that they lost their initial *n*.

The lack of breaks between words and individual sounds often makes us think that speakers of foreign languages run their words together, not realizing that we do so also. X-ray motion pictures of someone speaking make this lack of breaks in the speech chain clear. One can see the tongue, jaw, and lips in continuous motion while the "individual sounds" are being produced.

Yet, if you know a language, you have no difficulty segmenting the continuous sounds. In this way, speech is similar to music. A person who has not studied music cannot write the sequence of individual notes combined by a violinist into one changing continuous sound. A trained musician, however, finds it a simple task. Every human speaker, without special training, can segment a speech signal. Just as one cannot analyze a musical passage without musical knowledge, so also linguistic knowledge is required to segment speech into pieces.

Identity of Speech Sounds

FOR BETTER OR FOR WORSE copyright Lynn Johnston Prod. Reprinted with permission of United Features Syndicate. All rights reserved.

It is amazing, given the continuity of speech, that we are able to understand which words are put together to form an utterance. This achievement is even more surprising because no two speakers ever say "the same thing." The speech signal produced when one speaker says *cat* will not be exactly the same as the signal produced by another speaker's *cat* or even the repetition of the word by the same speaker. Yet speakers understand each other because they know the same language.

Our knowledge of a language determines when we judge physically different sounds to be the same; we know which aspects or properties of the signal are linguistically important and which are not. For example, if someone coughs in the middle of saying "How (cough) are you?" a listener will interpret this simply as "How are you?" Men's voices are usually lower in overall pitch than women's, and some people speak more slowly than others, but differences in pitch or tempo are not linguistically significant.

Our linguistic knowledge, our mental grammar, makes it possible to ignore nonlinguistic differences in speech. Furthermore, we are capable of making many sounds that we know intuitively are not speech sounds in our language. Many

English speakers can make a clicking sound that writers sometimes represent as *tsk tsk tsk*. But these sounds are not part of the English sound system. They never occur as part of the words of the sentences we produce. It is, in fact, difficult for many English speakers to combine this clicking sound with other sounds. Yet clicks are speech sounds in Xhosa, Zulu, Sotho, and Khoikhoi — languages spoken in southern Africa — just like the *k* or *t* in English. Speakers of those languages have no difficulty producing them as parts of words. The word *Xhosa* begins with one of these clicks. Thus, *tsk* is a speech sound in Xhosa but not in English. The sound represented by the letters *th* in the word *think* is a speech sound in English but not in French. The sound produced with a closed mouth when we are trying to clear a tickle in the throat is not a speech sound in any language, nor is the sound produced when we sneeze.

The science of phonetics attempts to describe all the sounds used in human language — sounds that constitute a subset of the totality of sounds that humans are capable of producing.

The way we use our linguistic knowledge to produce meaningful utterances is complicated. It can be viewed as a chain of events starting with an idea or message in the mind of the speaker and ending with a similar message in the brain of the hearer. The message is put into a form that is dictated by the language we are speaking. It must then be transmitted by nerve signals to the organs of speech articulation, which produce the different physical sounds.

Speech sounds can be described at any stage in this chain of events. The study of the physical properties of the sounds themselves is called **acoustic phonetics**, and the study of the way listeners perceive these sounds is called **auditory phonetics**. **Articulatory phonetics** — the study of how the vocal tract produces the sounds of language — is the primary concern of this chapter.

Spelling and Speech

The one-l lama,
He's a priest.
The two-l llama,
He's a beast.

And I will bet
A silk pajama
There isn't any
Three-l lllama.

Ogden Nash, "The Lama," from *Verses from 1929 On*, by Ogden Nash. Copyright 1931 by Ogden Nash. Copyright © renewed 1985 by Frances Nash, Isabel Nash Eberstadt, and Linnell Nash Smith. By permission of Curtis Brown, Ltd.

Beware of heard, a dreadful word
That looks like beard and sounds like bird.
And dead: it's said like bed, not bead;

For goodness' sake, don't call it deed!
Watch out for meat and great and threat.
(They rhyme with suite and straight and debt.)
A moth is not a moth in mother,
Nor both in bother, broth in brother.

Richard Krogh

Alphabetic spelling represents the pronunciations of words. Frequently, the sounds of the words in a language are unsystematically represented by **orthography** — that is, by spelling — and it can become confusing to refer to the sounds as they are spelled in English words. Suppose, for example, all Earthlings were destroyed by some horrible catastrophe, and years later Martian astronauts exploring Earth discovered some fragments of English writing that included the following sentence:

Did he believe that Caesar could see the people seize the seas?

How would a Martian linguist decide that *e, ie, ae, ee, eo, ei*, and *ea* all represent the same sound? To add to the confusion, this sentence might crop up later:

The silly amoeba stole the key to the machine.

English speakers learn how to pronounce these words when learning to read and write and know that *y, oe, ey*, and *i* also represent the same sound as the boldface letters in the first sentence.

The Phonetic Alphabet

The English have no respect for their language, and will not teach their children to speak it. They cannot spell it because they have nothing to spell it with but an old foreign alphabet of which only the consonants — and not all of them — have any agreed speech value.

George Bernard Shaw, Preface, *Pygmalion*

The discrepancy between spelling and sound gave rise to a movement of "spelling reformers" called **orthoepists**. They wanted to revise the alphabet so that one letter would correspond to one sound and one sound to one letter, thus simplifying spelling. This is a **phonetic alphabet**.

George Bernard Shaw followed in the footsteps of three centuries of spelling reformers in England. In typical Shavian manner, he pointed out that we could use the English spelling system to spell *fish* as *ghoti* — the *gh* like the sound in *enough*, the *o* like the sound in *women*, and the *ti* like the sound in *nation*. Shaw was so concerned about English spelling that he included a provision in his will for a new "Proposed English Alphabet" to be administered by a "Public Trustee" who would have the duty of seeking and publishing a more efficient alphabet. This alphabet was to have at least 40 letters to enable "the said language to be written without indicating single sounds by groups of letters or by diacritical marks." After Shaw's death in 1950, 450 designs for such an alphabet were submitted from all parts of the globe. Four alphabets were judged to be equally good, and the £500 sterling prize was divided among their designers, who collaborated to produce the alphabet designated in Shaw's will. Shaw also stipulated in his will that his play *Androcles and the Lion* be published in the new alphabet, with "the original Doctor Johnson's lettering opposite the transliteration page by page and a glossary of the two alphabets." This version of the play was published in 1962.

It is easy to understand why spelling reformers believe there is a need for a phonetic alphabet. Different letters may represent a single sound, as is shown in the following instances:

> to   too   two   through   threw   clue   shoe

A single letter may represent different sounds:

> dame   dad   father   village   many

A combination of letters may represent a single sound:

shoot	character	Thomas	physics
either	deal	rough	nation
coat	glacial	theatre	plain

Some letters have no sound at all in certain words:

mnemonic	whole	resign	ghost
pterodactyl	write	hole	corps
psychology	sword	debt	gnaw
bough	lamb	island	knot

Some sounds are not represented in the spelling. In many words, the letter *u* represents a *y* sound followed by a *u* sound:

cute	(cf. coot)
futile	(cf. rule)
utility	(cf. Uzbek)

One letter may represent two sounds; the final *x* in *Xerox* represents a *k* followed by an *s*.

Whether we support or oppose spelling reform, it is clear that we cannot depend on the spellings of words to describe the sounds of English. The alphabets designed to fulfil Shaw's will were not the first phonetic alphabets. One of the earliest was produced by Robert Robinson in 1617. In Shaw's lifetime, the phonetician Henry Sweet, the prototype for Shaw's own Henry Higgins in the play *Pygmalion* (and in the film version, *My Fair Lady*), produced a phonetic alphabet.

In 1888, the interest in the scientific description of speech sounds led the **International Phonetic Association (IPA)** to develop a phonetic alphabet that could be used to symbolize the sounds found in all languages. Since many languages use a Roman alphabet like that used in the English writing system, the IPA phonetic symbols were based on the Roman letters. These phonetic symbols have a consistent value — unlike ordinary letters, which may or may not represent the same sounds in the same or different languages.

The original IPA phonetic alphabet was the primary one used all over the world, by phoneticians, language teachers, speech pathologists, linguists, and anyone wishing to symbolize the "spoken word," until 1989, when, from August 18 to 21, approximately 120 members of the association met in Kiel, West Germany, to work on revisions. The symbols used in this text are those from the revised IPA alphabet unless otherwise noted.

Even if we could specify all the details of different pronunciations, we would not want to. A basic fact of speech is that no two utterances are exactly the same. The *Good morning*s said twice in succession on the same day by the same speaker will not be physically identical, and the *Good morning* of a second speaker will differ from those of the first speaker. Yet all these *Good morning*s are considered by speakers of English to be repetitions of the same utterance.

Some differences in the sounds of an utterance are important when one is trying to comprehend what is being said, and other differences can be ignored. Even though we never produce or hear exactly the same utterance twice, speakers know when two utterances are *linguistically* the same or different. Some properties of the sounds are therefore more important linguistically than others.

A phonetic alphabet should include enough symbols to represent the "crucial" linguistic differences. At the same time, it should not, and cannot, include non-crucial differences, since such differences are infinitely varied.

A list of phonetic symbols that can be used to represent speech sounds of English is given in Table 5.1. The symbols omit many details about the sounds and how they are produced in different words and in different places in words. These symbols are meant to be used by persons knowing English. These are not all the phonetic symbols needed for English sounds; when we discuss the sounds in more detail later in the chapter we will add appropriate symbols.

The symbol [ə] is called a schwa. It will be used in this book only to represent unstressed vowels. (There is great variation in the way speakers of English produce

TABLE 5.1
A Phonetic Alphabet for English Pronunciation

Consonants						Vowels			
p	pill	t	till	k	kill	i	beet	ɪ	bit
b	bill	d	dill	g	gill	e	bait	ɛ	bet
m	mill	n	nil	ŋ	ring	u	boot	ʊ	foot
f	feel	s	seal	h	heal	o	boat	ɔ	bore
v	veal	z	zeal	l	leaf	æ	bat		
θ	thigh	č	chill	r	reef	ʌ	butt	ɑ	pot/bar
ð	thy	ǰ	Jill	j	you			ə	sofa
š	shill	ʍ	which	w	witch	aj	bide	aw/æw	vowed
ž	azure					ɔj	boy		

this unstressed vowel, but it is phonetically similar to the wedge symbol [ʌ], which will be used only in stressed syllables.)

Speakers of some English dialects pronounce the words *which* and *witch* identically, in which case the initial sound of both words is symbolized by *w* in the chart. Other speakers of English pronounce *bought* and *pot* with the same vowel; and still others pronounce them with the vowel sounds in *bore* and *bar*, respectively. We have thus listed both words in the chart of symbols. Similarly, some speakers — notably, speakers of Canadian English — distinguish the diphthong in *bite* and *bide* as [bʌjt] and [bajd]. Unfortunately, it is not possible in an introductory text to include all of the phonetic symbols required to represent each English dialect. We apologize if a vowel sound in your dialect is not included in the table.

Some of the symbols in Table 5.1 are those traditionally used by linguists in North America in place of IPA symbols; others are listed below:

North America	IPA
š	ʃ
ž	ʒ
č	tʃ
ǰ	dʒ
ᴜ	ʊ

Using these symbols, we can now unambiguously represent the pronunciations of words. For example, words spelled with *ou* may have different pronunciations. To distinguish between the symbols representing sounds and the alphabet letters, we put the phonetic symbols between brackets:

Spelling	Pronunciation
though	[ðo]
thought	[θɑt]
rough	[rʌf]
bough	[baw]
through	[θru]
would	[wᴜd]

Only in *rough* do the letters *gh* represent any sound — that is, the sound [f]; *ou* represents six different sounds, and *th* represents two different sounds. The *l* in *would*, like the *gh* in all but one of the words above, is not pronounced at all.

We will continue to use square brackets around the phonetic transcription to distinguish it from ordinary spelling.

Articulatory Phonetics

The principles of pronunciation are those general laws of articulation that determine the character, and fix the boundaries of every language; as in every system of speaking, however irregular, the organs must necessarily fall into some common mode of enunciation or the purpose of Providence in the gift of speech would be absolutely defeated. These laws, like every other object of philosophical inquiry, are only to be traced by an attentive observation and enumeration of particulars. . . .

John Walker (1823)

All speech sounds are produced by the upper respiratory tract. To understand the nature of language, it is necessary to understand the nature of these sounds and how they are produced. Articulatory phonetics attempts to provide a framework to do so.

Airstream Mechanisms

The production of any speech sound (or any sound at all) involves the movement of air. Most speech sounds are produced by pushing lung air through the opening between the vocal cords — this opening is called the **glottis** and is located in the **larynx** (popularly known as "the voice box") — through the **pharynx**, and out of the **oral cavity** through the mouth and sometimes through the nose. Since lung air is used, these sounds are called **pulmonic** sounds; since the air is pushed *out*, they are called **egressive**. The majority of sounds used in the languages of the world are thus produced by a pulmonic **egressive airstream mechanism**. All the sounds of English are produced in this manner.

Other **airstream mechanisms** are used in other languages to produce sounds called **ejectives, implosives**, and **clicks**. Instead of lung air, the body of air in the mouth may be moved. When this air is sucked in instead of pushed out, **ingressive** sounds, such as implosives and clicks, are produced. When the air in the mouth is pushed out, ejectives are produced; they are therefore also **egressive sounds**. Implosives and ejectives are produced by a **glottalic airstream mechanism**, while clicks are produced by a **velaric airstream mechanism**.

Ejectives are found in many Native North American and African languages as well as languages spoken in the Caucasus, the region between the Black and Caspian seas. Implosives also occur in the languages of the North American Natives and throughout Africa, India, and Pakistan. Clicks occur in the Southern Bantu languages such as Xhosa and Zulu and in the languages spoken by the Bushmen and Khoikhoi. A detailed description of these different airstream mechanisms goes beyond the requirements of an introductory text. They are mentioned to show that sounds can be classified according to the airstream mechanism used to produce them. In the rest of this chapter, we will discuss only sounds produced by a pulmonic egressive airstream mechanism.

Consonants

The sounds of all languages fall into two major natural classes, **consonants** and **vowels**, often referred to by the cover symbols **C** and **V**. **Consonantal** sounds are produced with some restriction or closure in the vocal tract as the air from the lungs is pushed through the glottis and out of the mouth.

Places of Articulation

Different consonantal sounds result when we change the shape of the oral cavity by moving the lips and tongue, the **articulators**, and change the **place of articulation** in the oral cavity. The major consonantal place features are given below. As you can see from Figure 5.1, the places of articulation are in the upper part of the mouth (upper lip, upper teeth, alveolar ridge, palate, and velum, and the apex, front, back, or dorsal areas of the tongue). Sounds may be described by the articulator used and the place of articulation (e.g., apico-alveolar, fronto-palatal, dorso-velar), but normally naming the place of articulation is sufficient. As you read the description of each class of sounds, pronounce the sounds and try to feel which articulators are moving and where they are moving to.

Bilabials: [p], [b], [m]

When we produce a **[p]**, **[b]**, or **[m]**, we articulate by bringing both lips together. These sounds are therefore called **bilabials**.

Labiodentals: [f], [v]

We also use our lips to form **[f]** and **[v]**, as in *fine* [fajn] and *vine* [vajn]. We articulate these sounds by touching the bottom lip to the upper teeth, **labio** referring to the lips and **dental** to the teeth — hence, **labiodentals**.

Interdentals: [θ], [ð]

Both [θ] and [ð] are represented orthographically by the *th* in the words *thin* [θɪn], *ether* [iθər], *then* [ðɛn], and *either* [iðər] (or, as some pronounce the last word, [ajðər]). To articulate these "between the teeth" sounds in English (**interdentals**), we commonly insert the tip of the tongue between the upper and lower teeth. On the other hand, some speakers of English produce [θ] and [ð] by placing the tongue against the back of the upper teeth. Still another method of articulation is employed in Danish, in which it is common to place the tongue against the lower teeth, raising the front of the tongue to produce [ð] (but not [θ], a sound not employed in that language).

Alveolars: [t], [d], [n], [s], [z], [l], [r]

Alveolar sounds are articulated by raising the front part of the tongue to the **alveolar ridge** (see Figure 5.1). The first sounds of *do* [du], *new* [nu], *two* [tu], *Sue* [su], and *zoo* [zu] are all alveolar sounds. You will feel your tongue touch — or almost touch — the bony tooth ridge as you produce these sounds.

To produce the **lateral [l]**, the tongue is raised to the alveolar ridge with the sides of the tongue down, permitting the air to escape laterally over the sides of the tongue.

The sound **[r]** is produced in a variety of ways. Many speakers of English produce *r* by curling the tip of the tongue back behind the alveolar ridge. Such sounds are described as **retroflex**.

FIGURE 5.1

The vocal tract: Places of articulation.

1. bilabial   2. labiodental   3. interdental   4. alveolar   5. (alveo) palatal   6. velar
7. uvular   8. glottal

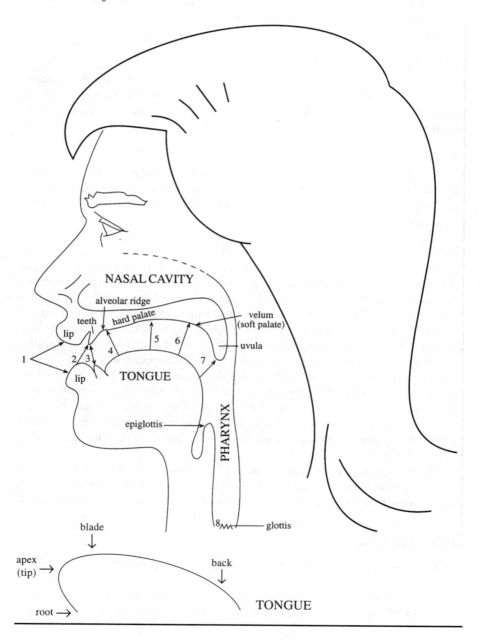

Alveopalatals: [š], [ž], [č], [ǰ]

To produce the sounds in the middle of the words *mesher* [mɛšər] and *measure* [mɛžər], the front part of the tongue is raised to a point on the hard palate just behind the alveolar ridge. These **alveopalatal** sounds, along with [č] and [ǰ], the sounds that begin and end the words *church* and *judge*, are sometimes referred to as **palatals**.

Velars: [k], [g], [ŋ]

Another class of sounds is produced by raising the back of the tongue to the soft palate or velum. The initial and final sounds of the words *kick* [kɪk] and *gig* [gɪg], and the final sounds of the words *back* [bæk], *bag* [bæg], and *bang* [bæŋ], are thus called **velar** sounds.

Uvulars: [R], [q], [G]

Uvular sounds are produced by raising the back of the tongue to the uvula. The *r* in French is uvular and is symbolized by **[R]**. Uvular sounds are also found in other languages. Arabic, for example, has two uvular sounds symbolized as **[q]** and **[G]**. Uvular sounds do not occur in English.

Glottals: [ʔ], [h]

The **[h]** sound that starts words such as *hat* [hæt], *who* [hu], and *hair* [her] is a **glottal** sound. The glottis is open; no other modification of the airstream mechanisms occurs in the mouth. The tongue and lips are usually in the position for the production of the following vowel as the airstream passes through the open glottis.

If the air is stopped completely at the glottis by tightly closed vocal cords, then the sound produced is a **glottal stop**. This is the sound sometimes used instead of [t] in *button* and *Latin*. It may also occur in colloquial speech at the end of words such as *don't*, *won't*, or *can't*. In Scots English, some other British dialects, and one American dialect, it regularly replaces the "tt" sound in words such as *bottle* or *glottal*. If you say "ah-ah-ah-ah-" with one "ah" right after another, but do not sustain the vowel sound, you will be producing glottal stops between the vowels. The IPA symbol for a glottal stop looks something like a question mark without the dot on the bottom [ʔ].

Table 5.2 summarizes the classification of the consonants of English according to place of articulation. The glottal stop is not included in this table since it is used only by some speakers in some words. The uvular sounds do not occur in English.

Manners of Articulation

We have described a number of classes of consonants according to their places of articulation, yet we are unable to distinguish the sounds in each class from one another. What distinguishes [p] from [b] or [b] from [m]? All are bilabial sounds. What is the difference between [t], [d], and [n], all alveolar sounds?

TABLE 5.2
Place of Articulation of English Consonants

Bilabial:	p	b	m				
Labiodental:	f	v					
Interdental:	θ	ð					
Alveolar:	t	d	n	s	z	l	r
Alveopalatal:	š	ž	č	ǰ			
Velar:	k	g	ŋ				
Glottal:	h						

Speech sounds are also differentiated by the way the airstream is affected as it travels from the lungs up and out through the mouth and nose. Such features or phonetic properties have traditionally been referred to as **manners of articulation** or simply as manner features.

Voiced and Voiceless Sounds

If the vocal cords are apart when the airstream is pushed from the lungs, then the air passes freely into the **supraglottal cavities** (those parts of the vocal tract above the glottis). The sounds produced in this way are **voiceless sounds**; for example, [p], [t], [k], and [s] in the words *seep* [sip], *seat* [sit], and *seek* [sik] are voiceless.

If the vocal cords are together, then the airstream forces its way through and causes them to vibrate. Sounds such as [b], [d], [g], and [z] in words such as *cob* [kɑb], *cod* [kɑd], *cog* [kɑg], and *daze* [dez] are **voiced sounds**. If you put a finger in each ear and say "z-z-z-z-z-," you will feel the vibrations of the vocal cords. If you now say "s-s-s-s-s-," you will not feel these vibrations (although you might hear a hissing sound in your mouth). When you whisper, you are making all the speech sounds voiceless.

The voiced/voiceless distinction is an important one in English. It is this phonetic feature or property that distinguishes between word pairs such as the following:

rope/robe	fate/fade	rack/rag	wreath/wreathe
[rop]/[rob]	[fet]/[fed]	[ræk]/[ræg]	[riθ]/[rið]

The first word of each pair ends with a voiceless sound and the second word with a voiced sound. All other aspects of the sounds of these words are identical; the position of the lips and tongue is the same in each of the paired words.

The voiced/voiceless distinction is also shown in the following pairs; the first word begins with a voiceless sound and the second with a voiced sound:

fine/vine	seal/zeal	choke/joke
[fajn]/[vajn]	[sil]/[zil]	[čok]/[ǰok]

The initial sounds of the first words of the following pairs are also voiceless, and for many speakers of English the second words begin with voiced sounds. (We will discuss other differences between the initial [p] and [b] sounds below; the phonetic transcriptions of many of these words have been simplified to help the reader grasp basic concepts and may include other details in subsequent sections.)

peat/beat   tune/dune   cane/gain
[pit]/[bit]   [tun]/[dun]   [ken]/[gen]

Aspirated and Unaspirated Sounds

In our discussion of the voiceless bilabial stop [p], we did not distinguish the initial sound in the word *pit* from the second sound in the word *spit*. There is, however, a phonetic difference in these two voiceless stops. During the production of voiceless sounds, the glottis is open, and air passes freely through the opening between the vocal cords. When a voiceless sound is followed by a voiced sound such as a vowel, the vocal cords must close in order to permit them to vibrate.

Voiceless sounds fall into two classes depending on the "timing" of the vocal cord closure. In English, when we pronounce the word *pit*, there is a brief period of voicelessness immediately after the *p* sound is released. That is, after the lips come apart, the vocal cords remain open for a very short time. Such sounds are called **aspirated** because an extra puff of air is produced.

When we pronounce the *p* in *spit*, however, the vocal cords start vibrating as soon as the lips are opened. Such sounds are called **unaspirated**. The *t* in *tick* and the *k* in *kin* are also aspirated voiceless stops, while the *t* in *stick* and the *k* in *skin* are unaspirated. If you hold a strip of paper in front of your lips and say *pit*, a puff of air (the aspiration) will push the paper. The paper will not move when you say *spit*.

When a fully voiced [b], or any voiced stop, is produced, the vocal cords vibrate throughout the articulation. In English, voiced stops may not be fully voiced. Figure 5.2 shows in diagrammatic from the timing of the articulators (in this case the lips) in relation to the state of the vocal cords. Notice that, in the production of the voiced [b], the vocal cords are vibrating throughout the closure of the lips and continue to vibrate for the vowel production after the lips are opened. Most English speakers do not voice initial [b] to the full extent. Because we heavily aspirate an initial [p], there is no difficulty in distinguishing these two sounds. In the unaspirated *p* in *spin*, the vocal cords are open during the lip closure and come together and start vibrating as soon as the lips open. In the production of the aspirated *p* in *pin*, the vocal cords remain apart for a brief period after the lip closure is released. These remarks apply to all English stops.

Aspirated stops may be indicated by following the phonetic symbol with a raised ^{h}:

pate [p^{h}et]   spate [spet]
tale [t^{h}el]   stale [stel]
kale [k^{h}el]   scale [skel]

Nasal and Oral Sounds

The voiced/voiceless distinction differentiates the bilabial [b] from [p], but [m] is also voiced. What, then, distinguishes [m] from [b]? Perhaps the first thing to

FIGURE 5.2

Timing of articulators and vocal cord vibration for voiced, voiceless unaspirated, and voiceless aspirated stops.

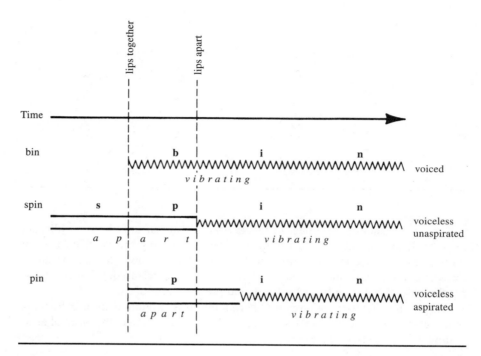

notice is that when you produce [m] air escapes not only through the mouth (when the lips are opened) but through the nose as well. [m], in other words, is a nasal sound.

In Figure 5.1, the roof of the mouth is divided into the **palate** and the soft palate (or **velum**). The palate is the hard bony structure we can feel at the front of the mouth. As we move back toward the throat, we encounter the velum, where the flesh becomes soft and movable. Hanging from the end of the velum is the uvula. When the velum is raised all the way to touch the back of the throat, the passage through the nose is cut off, and air can escape only through the mouth.

Sounds such as [p] and [b], produced with the velum up, blocking the air from escaping through the nose, are called **oral sounds**. When the velum is lowered, air escapes through the nose as well as the mouth, producing **nasal sounds**. [m], [n], and [ŋ] are the nasal consonants of English. Figure 5.3 shows the position of the lips and the velum when [m], [b], and [p] are articulated. [p], like [b] and [m], is produced by stopping the air flow at the lips. It differs from both [b] and [m] by being voiceless; it differs from [m] in being oral.

FIGURE 5.3

Position of lips and velum for [m] (lips together, velum down) and [b] or [p] (lips together, velum up).

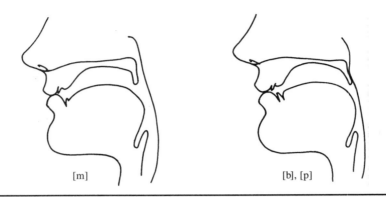

[m]   [b], [p]

The same nasal/oral difference occurs in *beet* [bit] and *meat* [mit], *dear* [dir] and *near* [nir]; in [b] and [d], the velum is raised, preventing the air from flowing through the nose, whereas in [m] and [n] the velum is down, letting the air go through both the nose and the mouth when the closure is released. [m], [n], and [ŋ] are therefore nasal sounds, and [b], [d], and [g] are oral sounds.

The **phonetic features** or properties permit the classification of all speech sounds into four classes: voiced, voiceless, nasal, and oral, in addition to the place of articulation classes discussed earlier.

Stops: [p], [b], [m], [t], [d], [n], [k], [g], [ŋ], [č], [ǰ], [ʔ]

We witness ever finer distinctions of speech sounds as we attempt to define how it is that one sound differs from another. We might note that [t] is a voiceless, alveolar, oral sound, but then [s] is also a voiceless, alveolar, oral sound — yet it is quite different. What distinguishes these two sounds?

The airstream, after entering the oral cavity, may be stopped completely, may be partially obstructed, or may flow freely out of the mouth. Sounds that are stopped completely in the oral cavity for a brief period, such as [t], are, not surprisingly, called **stops**. In the production of the nasal stops [n], [m], and [ŋ], although air flows freely through the nose, it is blocked completely in the mouth; consequently, nasal consonants are stops. The initial and final sounds in the following words are stops in English: *top, bomb, dude, dune, boot, tack, nag, bang.*

Non-nasal or oral stops are also called **plosives** because the air that is blocked in the mouth "explodes" when the closure is released. This explosion does not occur with nasal stops because the air escapes through the nose.

[p], **[b]**, and **[m]** are bilabial stops, with the airstream stopped at the mouth by the complete closure of the lips.

[t], [d], and [n] are alveolar stops; the airstream is stopped by the tongue, which makes a complete closure at the alveolar ridge.

[k], [g], and [ŋ] are velar stops with complete closure at the velum.

[č] and [ǰ] are alveopalatal or palatal affricates with complete stop closure. They will be discussed below.

[ʔ] is a glottal stop; though there is no stoppage of air in the oral cavity, air is completely stopped at the glottis.

In Quechua, a major language spoken in Bolivia and Peru, one also finds **uvular** stops that are produced when the back of the tongue is raised and moved backward to form a complete closure with the uvula. The letter *q* in words in this language, as in the name of the language, usually represents a uvular stop, which may be voiced or voiceless.

All speech sounds are in the class of either continuants or stops (non-continuants), which of course intersect with other classes. Table 5.3 shows the classification of some of the sounds in English according to the place of articulation features and the manner features discussed so far.

Fricatives: [s], [z], [f], [v], [θ], [ð], [š], [ž], [h]

In the production of some sounds, the airstream is not completely stopped but is obstructed from flowing freely. If you put your hand in front of your mouth and produce an [s], [z], [f], [v], [θ], [ð], [š], [ž], or [h] sound, you will feel the air coming out of your mouth. The passage in the mouth through which the air must pass, however, is very narrow, causing friction or turbulence. Such sounds are called **fricatives**. (They are also sometimes referred to as **spirants**, from the Latin word *spirare*, "to blow.")

In the production of the labiodental fricatives [f] and [v], the friction is created at the lips, where a narrow passage permits the air to escape.

[s] and [z] are alveolar fricatives with the friction created at the alveolar ridge.

The palatal or alveopalatal fricatives, [š] and [ž], such as those in *mesher* [mɛšər] and *measure* [mɛžər], are produced with friction created as the air passes through the narrow opening behind the alveolar ridge. In English, the voiced palatal fricative never begins words (except words borrowed from the French, such as *genre* or *gendarme*, which some English speakers produce with a French pronunciation). The

TABLE 5.3

Classes of Speech Sounds

	Oral			Nasal		
Voiced	b	d	g	m	n	ŋ
Voiceless	p	t	k	*		

*Nasal consonants in English are usually voiced. Both voiced and voiceless nasal sounds occur in other languages.

voiceless palatal sound begins the words *shoe* [šu] and *sure* [šur] and ends the words *rush* [rʌš] and *push* [puš].

The **[h]** occurring at the beginning of words such as *high* and *happy* is classified as a *voiceless glottal fricative*. However, [h] differs from "true" consonants in that there is no obstruction in the oral cavity. It also differs from vowels that are articulated by moving the tongue. When it is both preceded and followed by a vowel, it is often voiced in English, as in *ahead* and *cohabit*.

In the production of the interdental fricatives [θ] and [ð], represented by *th* in *thin* and *then*, the friction occurs at the opening between the tongue and the teeth.

Most dialects of modern English do not include velar fricatives, although they occurred in an earlier stage of English in words such as *right, knight, enough*, and *through*, where the *gh* occurs in the spelling. If you raise the back of the tongue as if you were about to produce a [g] or [k], but stop just short of touching the velum, you will produce a velar fricative. The *ch* ending in the German pronunciation of the composer's name *Bach* is a velar fricative. Some speakers of modern English substitute a voiceless velar fricative in words such as *bucket* and a voiced velar fricative in words such as *wagon* for the velar stops that occur for other speakers in those words. **[x]** is the IPA symbol for the voiceless velar fricative and **[ɣ]** for the voiced velar fricative.

In some languages of the world, such as French, *uvular fricatives* occur as the sound represented by *r* in French words such as *rouge*, "red," or *rose*, "pink." In Arabic, *pharyngeal fricatives* are produced by pulling the tongue root toward the back wall of the pharynx. It is difficult to pull the tongue back far enough to make a complete pharyngeal stop closure, but both voiced and voiceless pharyngeal fricatives can be produced and can be distinguished from velar fricatives.

Affricates: [č], [ǰ]

Some sounds are produced by a stop closure followed immediately by a slow release of the closure characteristic of a fricative. These sounds are called **affricates**. The sounds that begin and end the words *church* and *judge* are voiceless and voiced affricates, respectively. Phonetically, an affricate is a sequence of a stop plus a fricative. Thus, the *ch* in *church* is the same as the sound combination [t] + [š] as shown by observing that in fast speech *white shoes* and *why choose* may be pronounced identically. The voiceless and voiced affricates may be symbolized as [tš] (IPA [tʃ]) and [dž] (IPA [dʒ]), respectively. In the North American tradition, [č] and [ǰ] are the more commonly used symbols for these sounds and the ones used in this book.

Because the air is stopped completely during the initial articulation of an affricate, these sounds are classified as stops.

Liquids: [l], [r]

In the production of the sounds **[l]** and **[r]**, there is some obstruction of the airstream in the mouth but not enough to cause any real constriction or friction. These sounds are called **liquids**. If, as described earlier, the tongue is raised to the alveolar ridge but the sides are down so that air can escape laterally over the sides, then a lateral liquid [l] is produced.

The *r* sounds found in dialects of English as well as in other languages differ somewhat from each other. We are using the symbol [r] for this whole class of sounds. In some languages, the *r* may be a **trill**, produced by the tip of the tongue vibrating against the roof of the mouth. A trilled [r] occurs in Scots English and in many languages, such as Spanish. In addition, uvular trills occur, produced by vibrating the uvula. Some French speakers use uvular trills in the pronunciation of *r*; others use uvular fricatives.

In other dialects and languages, the *r* is produced by a single **tap** or **flap** of the tongue against the alveolar ridge. Some speakers of British English pronounce the *r* in the word *very* with this flap. It sounds like a "very fast" *d*. Most American and Canadian speakers produce a flap instead of a [t] or a [d] in words such as *writer* or *rider, latter* or *ladder*. As a test of whether you use a flap in this position, you might try saying the following sentence to a friend: "The painter left the ladder outside the barn and the paint inside." Then ask, "Where was the latter?" If the answer is "Outside," then you can be pretty sure you use a flap. North American linguists often use the upper case [D] to represent the sound.

In English, [l] and [r] are regularly voiced. When they follow voiceless sounds, as in *please* and *price*, they may be automatically devoiced. Many languages, such as Welsh, have a voiceless *l*; the name *Lloyd* in that language starts with such a voiceless consonant.

Some languages may lack liquids entirely or have only one. The Cantonese dialect of Chinese has the liquid, [l]. Some English words are difficult for Cantonese speakers to pronounce, and they may substitute an [l] for an [r] when speaking English. The acoustic similarity of these sounds disposes speakers of languages with only one liquid to use that liquid as a substitute when speaking other languages for the sound that their own language lacks. This physical similarity is why they are grouped together in one class and why they function as a single class of sounds in certain circumstances.

In English, the only two consonants that occur after an initial [k], [g], [p], or [b] are the liquids [l] and [r]. Thus, we have *crate* [kret], *clock* [klɑk], *plate* [plet], *prate* [pret], *bleak* [blik], *break* [brek], but no word starting with [ps], [bt], [pk], and so on. (Notice that in words such as *psychology* or *pterodactyl* the *p* is not pronounced. Similarly, in *knight* or *knot* the *k* is not pronounced, although at an earlier stage in English it was.)

Glides: [j], [w]

The sounds **[j]** and **[w]**, the initial sounds of *you* [ju] and *woo* [wu], are produced with little or no obstruction of the airstream in the mouth. When occurring in a word, they must always be either preceded or followed directly by a vowel. In articulating [j] or [w], the tongue moves rapidly in gliding fashion either toward or away from a neighbouring vowel, hence the term **glide**. Glides are transitional sounds that are sometimes called **semivowels**.

[j] is a *palatal glide*; the blade of the tongue is raised toward the hard palate in a position almost identical to that in producing the vowel sound [i] in the word *beat* [bit]. In pronouncing *you* [ju], the tongue moves rapidly from the [j] to the [u] vowel.

The glide [w] is produced by both raising the back of the tongue toward the velum and simultaneously rounding the lips. It is thus a *labiovelar* glide or a rounded velar glide. In the dialect of English in which speakers have different pronunciations for the words *which* and *witch*, the velar glide in the first word is voiceless [ʍ] (an "upside down" *w*), and in the second word it is voiced [w]. The position of the tongue and the lips for [w] is similar to that for producing the vowel sound in *lute* [lut], but the [w] is a glide because the tongue moves quickly to the following vowel.

Phonetic Symbols for North American English Consonants

The place and manner properties of speech sounds make it possible to distinguish each consonant sound from all others that occur in American English. Table 5.4 lists the consonants by their phonetic features. The rows stand for manner of articulation and the columns for place of articulation. Symbols for aspirated stops and the glottal stop are not included since this is a minimal list of symbols by which all morphemes and words can be distinguished. Thus, the symbol [p] for the voiceless bilabial stop is sufficient to differentiate the word *peat* [pit] from the voiced bilabial stop symbol [b] in *beat* [bit]. If a more detailed **phonetic transcription** of these

TABLE 5.4

Minimal Set of Phonetic Symbols for North American English Consonants

Manner of Articulation	Bilabial	Labiodental	Interdental	Alveolar	Palatal	Velar	Glottal
Stop (oral)							
voiceless	p			t		k	
voiced	b			d		g	
Nasal (stop)	m			n		ŋ	
Fricative							
voiceless		f	θ	s	š		h[1]
voiced		v	ð	z	ž		
Affricate							
voiceless					č		
voiced					ǰ		
Glide							
voiceless	ʍ					ʍ	
voiced	w[2]				j	w[2]	
Liquid				l r			

1. [h] is sometimes classified with the glides because in many languages it combines with other sounds the way that glides do.
2. [w] is classified as both a bilabial because it is produced with both lips rounded and as a velar because the back of the tongue is raised toward the velum.

words (sometimes referred to as a **narrow** phonetic transcription) is desired, then the symbol [pʰ] can be used, as in [pʰit].

Vowels

> HIGGINS: Tired of listening to sounds?
> PICKERING: Yes. It's a fearful strain. I rather fancied myself because I can pro-
> nounce twenty-four distinct vowel sounds, but your hundred and thirty
> beat me. I can't hear a bit of difference between most of them.
> HIGGINS: Oh, that comes with practice. You hear no difference at first, but you
> keep on listening and presently you find they're all as different as A
> from B.
>
> George Bernard Shaw, *Pygmalion*

The quality of vowels is determined by the particular configuration of the vocal tract. Different parts of the tongue may be raised or lowered. The lips may be spread or pursed. The passage through which the air travels, however, is never so narrow as to obstruct the free flow of the airstream.

Vowel sounds carry pitch and loudness; you can sing vowels. They may be long or short. Vowels can "stand alone" — they can be produced without any consonants before or after them. You can say the vowels of *beat* [bit], *bit* [bɪt], or *boot* [but], for example, without the initial [b] or the final [t].

There have been many different schemes for describing vowel sounds. They may be described by articulatory features, as in classifying consonants. Many beginning students of phonetics find this method more difficult to apply to vowel articulations than to consonant articulations. In producing a [t], you can feel your tongue touch the alveolar ridge. When you make a [p], you can feel your two lips come together, or you can watch the lips move in a mirror. Because vowels are produced without any artic-ulators touching or even coming close together, it is often difficult to figure out just what is happening. One of the authors of this book, at the beginning of her graduate work, almost gave up the idea of becoming a linguist because she could not under-stand what was meant by "front," "back," "high," and "low" vowels. These terms do have meaning, though. If you watch an X-ray movie of someone talking, you can see why vowels have traditionally been classified according to three questions.

1. How high is the tongue?
2. What part of the tongue is involved — that is, what part is raised or lowered?
3. What is the position of the lips?

Tongue Position

The three diagrams in Figure 5.4 show that the tongue in the production of the vow-els in the words *he* [hi] and *who* [hu] is very high in the mouth; in [hi] it is the blade of the tongue that is raised, and in [hu] it is the back part of the tongue that is raised. (Prolong the vowels of these words and try to feel your tongue rise.)

FIGURE 5.4

Position of the tongue in producing the vowels in *he, who,* and *hah.*

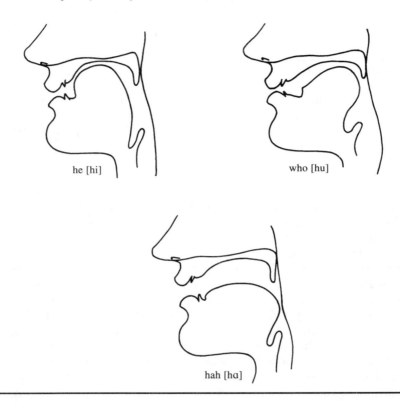

Tongue position may also be accompanied by jaw height and mouth opening. **High vowels** may be accompanied by raised jaw and close (but not closed) mouth, so that high vowels are also called close vowels. With **low vowels**, the jaw is lowered, and the mouth is open, hence they are also called open vowels.

To produce the vowel sound of *hah* [hɑ], the back of the tongue is lowered, as is the jaw, and the mouth is open. (The reason a doctor examining your throat may ask you to say "ah" is that the tongue is low and easy to see over.) This vowel is therefore a low, back vowel.

The vowels [ɪ] and [ʊ] in the words *hit* [hɪt] and *put* [pʊt] are similar to those in *he* [hi] and *who* [hu], with slightly lowered tongue positions.

The vowel [æ] in *hat* [hæt] is produced with the front part of the tongue lowered, similar to the low vowel [ɑ] but with the front rather than the back part of the tongue lowered.

The vowels [e] and [o] in *bait* [bet] and *boat* [bot] are **mid vowels**, produced by raising the tongue to a position midway between the high and low vowels discussed above. [ɛ] and [ɔ] in the words *bet* [bɛt] and *bore* [bɔr] are also mid vowels, produced with a slightly lower tongue position than [e] and [o].

To produce the vowel [ʌ] in the word *butt* [bʌt] or the *schwa* vowel [ə] that occurs in the second syllable of the word *sofa* [sofə] or *Rosa* [rozə], the tongue is neither high nor low, neither front nor back. These are mid, central vowels, as shown in Figure 5.5. The vowels on the chart show the part of the tongue from front to back on the horizontal axis that is involved in the articulation of the vowel and the height of the tongue on the vertical axis.

Lip Rounding

Vowels also differ as to whether the lips are rounded. The vowels [u], [ʊ], [o], and [ɔ] in *boot, put, boat,* and *bore* are **rounded vowels** produced with the lips pursed, or rounded, and with the back of the tongue at decreasing heights. The low vowel [ɑ] in the words *bar, bah,* and *aha* is the only English **back vowel** that occurs without lip rounding.

All non-back vowels in English are also unrounded. This is not true of all languages. French and Swedish, for example, have both front- and back-rounded vowels. In English, a high back-unrounded vowel does not occur, but in Mandarin Chinese, in Japanese, in the Cameroonian language Feʔfeʔ, and in many other languages this vowel is part of the phonetic inventory of sounds. There is a Chinese word meaning "four" with an initial [s] followed by a vowel similar to the one in *boot* but with non-rounded spread lips. This Chinese word is distinguished from the word meaning "speed," pronounced like the English word *sue* with a high back-rounded vowel.

Some of these pronunciations may differ from yours. For example, most speakers of Canadian English (and some speakers of American English) pronounce the

FIGURE 5.5

Classification of North American English vowels.

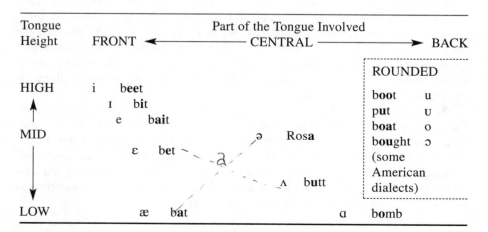

words *cot* and *caught* identically, while speakers of other dialects will differentiate the two words. There are English dialects in which an *r* sound is not pronounced unless it occurs before a vowel. The **inventory of sounds** in this book reflects an attempt to provide at least the major symbols that can be used to describe the dialects of North American English. We are aware that this inventory will not necessarily reflect those of speakers of other dialects.

Diphthongs

Many languages, including English, have vowels called **diphthongs** that can also be described as a sequence of two sounds, vowel + glide. The vowels we have studied so far are all simple vowels called **monophthongs**. The vowel sounds in the words *bide* [bajd] and *rye* [raj] are produced with the low **lax vowel** sound [a] followed by the [j] glide. [a] is formed in the central area, between the front [æ] of *bat* and the back [ɑ] of *father*. The vowels in *bowed* (i.e., "bent") [bawd], *brow* [braw], and *hour* [awr] are produced by some speakers of English with a similar [a] sound followed by the glide [w]. Some speakers of English produce this diphthong as [æw], with the front low-unrounded vowel instead of the back vowel. As we shall see in Chapter 7, most Canadians (and some speakers of American dialects) raise the low back vowel [a] to the mid central-unrounded vowel [ʌ] before the glides [j] and [w] in words such as *rice* and *house*, when the diphthong is followed by a voiceless consonant. The third diphthong that occurs in English is the vowel sound in *boy* [bɔj] and *soil* [sɔjl], which is the vowel that occurs in *bore* (without the [r]) followed by the palatal glide [j], [ɔj]. Some speakers of broad Newfoundland English use the vowel [ʌ] in this diphthong ([ʌj]), thus pronouncing *boy* and *buy* the same.

Nasalization of Vowels

Vowels, like consonants, can be produced with a raised velum that prevents the air from escaping through the nose or with a lowered velum that permits air to pass through the **nasal passages**. When the nasal passages are blocked, *oral* vowels are produced; when the nasal passages are open, *nasalized* vowels are produced. In English, nasalized vowels occur before nasal consonants in the same syllable, and oral vowels occur before oral consonants. In fast colloquial speech, some speakers drop the nasal consonant when it occurs before voiceless stops, as in *hint* or *camp*, leaving just the nasalized vowel, but the words originate with nasal consonants.

The words *bean, bin, bane, Ben, ban, boon, bun, bone, beam, bam, boom, bing, bang*, and *bong* are examples of words that contain nasalized vowels. To show the nasalization of a vowel in a phonetic transcription, a **diacritic** mark such as a "tilde" [˜] is placed over the vowel, as in *bean* [bĩn] and *bone* [bõn]. Because nasalized vowels in English predictably appear before nasal consonants, it is generally unnecessary to show the diacritic unless a more detailed transcription — sometimes referred to as a **narrow transcription** — is required.

In languages such as French, Polish, and Portuguese, nasalized vowels may occur when no nasal consonant is adjacent. In French, for example, the word meaning "year" is *an* [ã], and the word for "sound" is *son* [sõ]. The *n* in the spelling is not pronounced but indicates in these words that the vowels are nasalized.

Long and Short (Tense and Lax Vowels)

Figure 5.5 shows that the vowel [i] is produced with a slightly higher tongue position than [ɪ]. This is also true for [e] and [ɛ], [u] and [ʊ], and [o] and [ɔ]. These pairs of vowels are also distinguished by **length**, with the vowel in the first word of the following pairs longer in duration than the vowel in the second word. *Long* vowels in English are also produced with greater tension of the tongue muscles than their *short* counterparts and are therefore also referred to as **tense vowels**. We will use the long/short distinction when referring to them in this book.

Long (Tense)		Short (Lax)	
i	beat	ɪ	bit
e	bait	ɛ	bet
u	boot	ʊ	put
o	boat	ɔ	bought

Long tense vowels are sometimes diphthongized by some speakers of English; in such cases, tense front vowels are followed by a short [j] glide, producing [iʲ] and [eʲ], while tense back vowels conclude with a short [w] glide, [uʷ], and [oʷ].

In some languages, there are vowels and/or consonants that differ phonetically from each other only by duration. That is, neither height of the tongue nor tenseness distinguishes the vowel from its counterpart in pairs of words that contrast in meaning. It is customary to transcribe this difference either by doubling the symbol or by using a diacritic "colon" after the segment — for example, [aa] or [a:], [bb] or [b:]. Long or doubled segments may be referred to as **geminate**. Since English long tense vowels not only differ in length from their short lax counterparts but differ qualitatively in tongue height, we use different symbols to distinguish them.

Major Classes

A speech sound may be viewed as a bundle of features such as those we have been examining. Thus, [s] may be described as an alveolar, voiceless, oral fricative. But this and the other classes of sound outlined above also combine to form larger and more general classes that are important in the patterning of sounds in the world's languages, for there are more features that can be ascribed to sounds such as [s].

Non-Continuants and Continuants

Stop sounds are called **non-continuants** because they are produced with total obstruction of the airstream and can be distinguished from all other speech sounds, which are defined as **continuants** because the stream of air flows continuously out of the mouth. Hence, nasal stops are non-continuants.

Obstruents and Sonorants

The non-nasal stops, the fricatives, and the affricates form a major class of sounds called **obstruents**. Because the airstream cannot escape through the nose, it is either fully obstructed in its passage through the vocal tract, as in non-nasal stops and affricates, or partially obstructed in the production of fricatives.

Obstruents are distinguished from the major class of sounds called **sonorants**, which are produced with relatively free airflow through either the mouth or the nose and thus have greater acoustic energy than their obstruent counterparts. Nasal stops are sonorant because, although the air is blocked in the mouth, it continues to resonate and move through the nose. Vowels, the liquids [l] and [r], and the glides [w] and [j] are sonorants because the air resonates without being stopped.

Fricatives are continuant obstruents because, although the air is not completely stopped in its passage through the oral cavity, it is obstructed, causing friction.

Non-nasal stops and affricates are non-continuant obstruents; there is complete blockage of the air during the production of these sounds. The closure of a stop is released abruptly as opposed to the closure of an affricate, which is released gradually, causing friction.

Consonants and Vowels

The sounds of all human languages fall into two major natural classes: consonants and vowels. Consonants include a number of subclasses: stops (including affricates and nasals), fricatives, liquids, and glides. The class of vowels includes oral, nasal, front, central, back, high, mid, and low vowels.

Nasals and liquids, for the reasons given above, are sonorants, yet they resemble the obstruents in that the oral cavity is constricted during their articulation. Obstruents, liquids, and nasals form a natural class of consonantal sounds that differ phonetically from the vocalic (or non-consonantal) class of vowels and glides.

Labials: [p], [b], [m], [f], [v]

The class of **labial** consonants includes the class of bilabial sounds — [p], [b], [m] — as well as the labiodentals — [f] and [v]. Bilabial and labial sounds are those articulated with the involvement of the lips.

Coronals: [d], [t], [n], [s], [z], [l], [r], [š], [ž], [č], [ǰ]

Coronals include the alveolars — [d], [t], [n], [s], [z], [l], [r] — the palatals — [š], [ž] — and the affricates — [č], [ǰ] — which are all sounds articulated by raising the tongue blade toward the alveolar ridge or the hard palate.

Anteriors: [p], [b], [m], [t], [d], [n], [f], [v], [s], [z], [θ], [ð], [l], [r]

Anterior sounds are consonants produced in the front part of the mouth in front of the **palato-alveolar** area. They include bilabials, labiodentals, alveolars, and alveopalatals.

Sibilants: [s], [z], [š], [ž], [č], [ǰ]

Another class of consonantal sounds is characterized by an acoustic, rather than an articulatory, property of its members. The friction created in the production of the fricatives in the words *sit* [sɪt], *zip* [zɪp], *shoe* [šu], and *measure* [mɛžər] and the affricates in the words *church* [čʌrč] and *judge* [ǰʌǰ] causes a "hissing" sound. These sounds are in a class of **sibilants**.

Thus, we see that a phonological segment may be a member of a number of classes; for example, [s] can be categorized as belonging to the following classes: continuant, obstruent, consonant, alveolar, coronal, and sibilant.

Syllables and Syllabic Sounds

The discrete sounds of a language group together to form larger units, the **syllables** of the language. Speakers of English, for example, recognize that the individual sounds of words such as *carnival* and *unhelpful* form three syllables: *car ni val* and *un help ful*. Even if they don't know the precise meaning of *a syllable* — and even linguists have found it difficult to provide a precise definition of the word — speakers still recognize these groupings in each word.

Syllables may be said to be built around peaks of sonorance — that is, they form, or centre on, a sound that is heard as the loudest in the syllable. Since vowels tend to have more prominence than consonants, they usually form the **nucleus** of the syllable, with the possibility of consonants preceding (called the **onset**) and/or following (the **coda**) the vowels. The nucleus + the coda constitute the subsyllabic unit called a **rhyme**. A vowel alone may constitute the syllable and be both nucleus and rhyme, as in the indefinite article *a*; it may be more complex, as in the following examples:

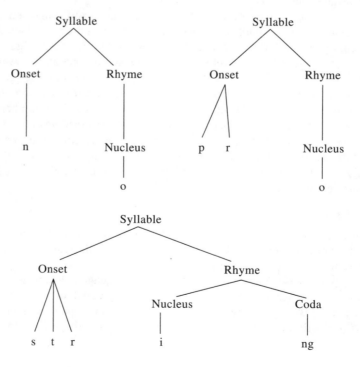

The common pronunciation of the second syllable of *apple* suggests that some consonants can form the nucleus of a syllable. The [l] in this word is clearly a syllable without a vowel to form the nucleus. In fact, we can say that liquids and nasals, along with vowels, can be **syllabic** — that is, act as the nucleus of a syllable — as in the words *Rachel* [rečļ], *friar* [frajr̩], *rhythm* [rɪðm̩], and *listen* [lɪsn̩] (the diacritic under the [l], [r], [m], and [n] shows that these sounds are syllabic). Some transcriptions, however, place a schwa [ə] before the syllabic liquid or nasal to indicate that these are separate syllables, and, to simplify matters, we will follow this practice.

Syllables and morphemes are not the same thing, we should observe, even though at times they may seem to be identical. Thus, the syllables and morphemes of *unhelpful* are the same, but that is not the case with *automobile*, which consists of only two morphemes (*auto* + *mobile*) but has four syllables.

Prosodic Suprasegmental Features

Speech sounds that are identical in their place or manner features may differ in duration (length), pitch, or loudness. A vowel can be lengthened by prolonging it. A consonant is made long by maintaining the closure or obstruction for a longer period of time.

When we speak, we also change the **pitch** of our voices. The pitch produced depends on how fast the vocal cords vibrate; the faster they vibrate, the higher the pitch. In physical or acoustic terms, pitch is referred to as the **fundamental frequency** of the sound signal.

We are also able to change the loudness of the sounds and sound sequences. In many languages, some syllables or vowels are produced more loudly with a simultaneous change in pitch (usually higher) and longer duration than other vowels in the word or sentence. They are referred to as **stressed** or **accented** vowels or syllables. For example, the first syllable of *digest*, the noun meaning "summation of articles" or a "journal," is stressed, while in *digest*, the verb meaning "to absorb food," the second syllable is stressed. Stress can be marked in a number of ways — for example, by putting an "accent" mark over the stressed vowel.

In Chapter 6, we will further discuss features such as **length**, pitch, and the complex feature **stress** and how they are used in various languages to distinguish the meanings of words and sentences. Such features are often referred to as **prosodic** or **suprasegmental features**.

Tone and Intonation

Speakers of all languages vary the pitch of their voices when they talk; the pitch produced depends on how fast the vocal cords vibrate — the faster they vibrate, the higher the pitch.

The way pitch is used linguistically differs from language to language. In English, it doesn't much matter whether you say *cat* with a high pitch or a low pitch. It will still mean "cat." But if you say [ba] with a high pitch in Nupe (a language spoken in Nigeria), it will mean "to be sour," whereas if you say [ba] with a low pitch, it will mean "to count." Languages that use the pitch of individual vowels or sylla-bles to contrast meanings of words are called **tone** languages.

The majority of the languages in the world are tone languages. There are more than 1000 tone languages in Africa alone; many languages of Asia, such as Chinese, Thai, and Burmese, are tone languages, as are many Native North American languages.

Thai is a language that has contrasting pitches or tones. The same string of seg-mental sounds represented by [naa] will mean different things if one says the sounds with a low pitch, a mid pitch, a high pitch, a falling pitch from high to low, or a rising pitch from low to high. Thai therefore has five linguistic tones:

[naa]	[___]	low tone	"a nickname"
[naa]	[—]	mid tone	"rice paddy"
[naa]	[⎯]	high tone	"young maternal uncle or aunt"
[naa]	[⌐\]	falling tone	"face"
[naa]	[_/]	rising tone	"thick"

Diacritics are used to represent distinctive tones in the phonetic transcriptions:

[ˋ]	L	low tone	
[ˉ]	M	mid tone	
[ˊ]	H	high tone	
[ˆ]	HL	falling tone	(high to low)
[ˇ]	LH	rising tone	(low to high)

We can use these diacritics placed above the vowels to represent the tonal con-trasts in any language in which the pitch of the vowel is important in conveying meaning, as illustrated by the three contrastive tones in Nupe:

| [bá] | "be sour" | [bā] | "cut" | [bà] | "count" |
| H | | M | | L | |

Akan, sometimes called Twi, the major language of Ghana, has two tones, which are shown in the contrasting two-syllable words:

dù à   [_]   "tail"   dù á   [_⎻]   "tree"

L L   L H

kɔ tɔ́   [_⎻]   "go buy"   kɔ́ tɔ   [⎻_]   "crab"

L H   H L

In some tone languages, the pitch of each tone is level; in others, the direction of the pitch (whether it glides from high to low or from low to high) is important. Tones that "glide" are called **contour tones**; tones that do not are called **level** or **register tones**. The contour tones of Thai are represented by using a high tone followed by a low tone for a falling glide and a low followed by a high for a rising tone.

In a tone language, it is not the absolute pitch of the syllables that is important but the relations among the pitches of different syllables. After all, some individual speakers have high-pitched voices, others low-pitched, and others medium-pitched.

In many tone languages, we find a falling-off of the pitch, a continued downdrifting of the tones.

In the following sentence in Twi, the relative pitch rather than the absolute pitch is important:

"Kofi searches for a little food for his friend's child."

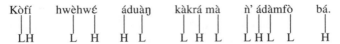

The actual pitches of these syllables would be rather different from each other, as shown below (the higher the number, the higher the pitch):

7		fí							
6				hwɛ́	á				
5	Kò						krá		
4			hwè						á
3					duàŋ	kà			bá
2							mà ǹ'		
1									dàmfò

The lowering of the pitch is called **downdrift**. In languages with downdrift — and many tone languages in Africa are downdrift languages — a high tone that occurs after a low tone, or a low tone after a high tone, is lower in pitch than the preceding similarly marked tone. Notice that the first high tone in the sentence is given the pitch value 7. The next high tone (which occurs after an intervening low tone) is 6: that is, it is lower in pitch than the first high tone.

This example shows that in analyzing tones, just as in analyzing segments, all the physical properties need not be considered; only essential features are important in language — in this case, whether the tone is "high" or "low" in relation to the other pitches but not the specific pitch of that tone.

Languages that are not tone languages, such as English, are called **intonation** languages. The pitch contour of the utterance varies, but in an intonation language, as opposed to a tone language, pitch is not used to distinguish words from each other.

Diacritics

In the sections on vowel nasalization, prosodic features, and tone, we presented a number of **diacritic** marks that can be used to modify the basic phonetic symbols.

A [~] over the vowel was used to mark vowel nasalization, the doubling of a symbol or a [:] after the symbol to show length, an acute accent to show stress, and various accent marks to show tones.

Other diacritics provide additional ways of showing phonetic differences between speech sounds.

To differentiate a voiceless lateral liquid such as the sound written *ll* in *Lloyd* as spoken in Welsh, the symbol [̥] is placed under the segmental symbol. Thus, in Welsh the name is pronounced [l̥ɔjd], and in English it is pronounced [lɔjd].

Cover symbols are used when a class of sounds is referred to. A capital C is often used to represent the class of consonants, V for the class of vowels, G for glides, and L for liquids. A syllabic consonant or a syllabic liquid may also be specified as C̩ or L̩. And a rounded consonant, which often occurs before a rounded vowel, can be specified by a superscript small [ʷ].

We can summarize these diacritics and additional symbols as follows:

C = consonant	C: = long C	Cʷ = rounded C
V = vowel	V: = long V	Ṽ = nasalized
L = liquid	L̥ = voiceless	L̩ = syllabic
G = glide	V́ = stressed V	

Tones:

V́ = high	V̀ = low	V̄ = mid
V̌ = rising	V̂ = falling	

Phonetic Symbols and Spelling Correspondences

Table 5.5 shows the sound–spelling correspondences for North American English consonants and vowels. Note that all possible spellings are not given; these, however, should provide enough examples to help students pair sounds and English orthography.

The symbols given in the list are not sufficient to represent the pronunciation of words in all languages. The symbol [**x**], for example, is needed for the voiceless velar fricative in the German word *Bach*, and [**ʁ**] is needed for the French voiced uvular fricative. English does not have rounded front vowels, but languages such as French and Swedish do, and English once did. French front rounded vowels can be symbolized as follows:

[y] as in *tu* [ty] "you" (singular)	The tongue position is like that for [i], but the lips are rounded.
[ø] as in *bleu* [blø] "blue"	The tongue position is like that for [e], but the lips are rounded.
[œ] as in *heure* "hour"	The tongue position is like that in [ɛ], but the lips are rounded.

TABLE 5.5
Phonetic Symbol/English Spelling Correspondences

CONSONANTS	
Symbol	**Examples**
p	*sp*it ti*p* a*pp*le am*p*le
pʰ	*p*it *p*rick *p*laque a*pp*ear
b	*b*it ta*b* *b*rat *b*u*bb*le
m	*m*itt ta*m* s*m*ack E*mm*y ca*m*p co*mb*
t	s*t*ick pi*t* kiss*e*d wri*t*e
tʰ	*t*ick in*t*end *pt*erodactyl a*tt*ack
d	*D*ick ca*d* *d*rip love*d* ri*d*e
n	*n*ick ki*n* s*n*ow m*n*emonic g*n*ostic p*n*eumatic k*n*ow
k	s*k*in sti*ck* s*c*at criti*que* ex*c*eed
kʰ	*c*url *k*in *ch*aracter *c*ritic me*ch*anic *c*lose
g	*g*irl bur*g* lon*g*er Pittsbur*gh*
ŋ	si*ng* thi*n*k fi*n*ger
f	*f*at *ph*iloso*ph*y *f*lat *ph*logiston co*ff*ee ree*f* cou*gh*
v	*v*at do*v*e gra*v*el
s	*s*ip *s*kip *ps*ychology pa*ss* pat*s* democra*c*y *sc*issors fa*s*ten de*c*eive de*s*cent
z	*z*ip ja*zz* ra*z*or pad*s* kisse*s* *X*erox de*s*ign la*z*y sci*ss*or*s* mai*z*e
θ	*th*igh *th*rough wra*th* e*th*er Ma*tth*ew
ð	*th*y *th*eir wea*th*er la*th*e ei*th*er
š	*sh*oe mu*sh* mi*ss*ion na*t*ion fi*sh* gla*ci*al *s*ure
ž	mea*s*ure vi*s*ion a*z*ure ca*s*ual deci*s*ion rou*ge* (for those who do not pronounce this word with the final sound of *judge*)
č	*ch*oke ma*tch* fea*t*ure ri*ch* righ*te*ous
ǰ	ju*dge* mi*d*get *G*eorge ma*g*istrate resi*d*ual
l	*l*eaf fee*l* ca*ll* fe*l*t co*ll*ar sing*le*
r	*r*eef fea*r* Pa*r*is singe*r*
j	*y*ou *y*es feu*d* *u*se
w	*w*itch s*w*im q*u*een
ʌ	*wh*ich *wh*ere *wh*ale (for speakers who pronounce *which* differently from *witch*)
h	*h*at w*h*o w*h*ole re*h*ash
ʔ	bo*tt*le bu*tt*on glo*tt*al (for some speakers)

(Continued)

TABLE 5.5 *(Continued)*

VOWELS

Symbol	Examples
i	b**ee**t b**ea**t b**e** rec**ei**ve k**ey** bel**ie**ve am**oe**ba p**eo**ple C**ae**sar Vas**e**line ser**e**ne
ɪ	b**i**t cons**i**st **i**njury b**i**n
e	b**a**te b**ai**t r**ay** gr**ea**t **ei**ght g**au**ge r**ei**gn th**ey**
ɛ	b**e**t ser**e**nity s**ay**s g**ue**st d**ea**d s**ai**d
æ	p**a**n **a**ct l**au**gh c**o**mrade
u	b**oo**t l**u**te wh**o** s**e**wer thr**ough** t**o** t**oo** tw**o** m**o**ve L**ou**
ʊ	p**u**t f**oo**t b**u**tcher c**oul**d
ʌ	c**u**t t**ou**gh am**o**ng **o**ven d**oe**s c**o**ver fl**oo**d
o	c**oa**t g**o** b**eau** gr**ow** th**ough** t**oe** **ow**n **o**ver
ɔ	c**au**ght st**a**lk s**aw** b**a**ll **awe** (in some — especially American — dialects)
ɑ	c**o**t c**au**ght f**a**ther s**aw** mel**o**dic (in Canadian English)
ə	sof**a** **a**lone symph**o**ny s**u**ppose mel**o**dy tedi**ou**s th**e** **A**meric**a**
aj	b**y** d**ie** d**ye** St**ei**n **ai**sle ch**oi**r l**i**ar **i**sland s**i**gn
aw, æw	br**ow**n c**ow**ard
ɔj	b**oy** d**oi**ly

glides (handwritten, left margin bracketing aj, aw/æw, ɔj)

Summary

The science of speech sounds is called **phonetics**. It aims to provide the set of features or properties that can be used to describe and distinguish all the sounds used in human language.

When we speak, we produce continuous stretches of sound that are the physical representations of strings of discrete linguistic segments. Knowledge of a language permits us to segment the continuous sound into linguistic units — words, morphemes, and sounds.

The discrepancy between spelling and sounds in English and other languages motivated the development of **phonetic alphabets** in which one letter corresponds to one sound. The major phonetic alphabet in use is that of the **International Phonetic Association (IPA)**, which includes modified Roman letters and **diacritics** by means of which the sounds of all human languages can be represented. To distinguish between the **orthography**, or spelling, of words and their pronunciations, **phonetic transcriptions** may be put between square brackets, as in [fonetɪk] for *phonetic*.

All English speech sounds are produced by the movement of lung air through the vocal tract — through the **glottis** or vocal cords, up the pharynx, through the oral cavity, and out of the mouth and sometimes through the nose. All human speech sounds fall into classes according to their phonetic properties or features — that is, according to how they are produced.

All speech sounds are either **consonants** or **vowels**, and all consonants are either **obstruents** or **sonorants**. Consonants are produced with some obstruction of the airstream in the **supraglottal** cavities. Consonants are distinguished according to where they are articulated in the vocal tract, their **place of articulation**, including **bilabial, labiodental, alveolar, palatal, velar, uvular**, and **glottal**.

Speech sounds are also classified according to their **manner of articulation**. They may be **voiced** or **voiceless, oral** or **nasal**; they may be **stops, fricatives, liquids, glides**, or **vowels**. During the production of voiced sounds, the vocal cords or glottis are together and vibrating, whereas in voiceless sounds the glottis is open and non-vibrating. Voiceless sounds may also be **aspirated** or **unaspirated**. In the production of aspirated sounds, the vocal cords remain apart for a brief time after the stop closure is released, thus producing a puff of air at the time of the release.

Vowels form the nuclei of syllables. They differ according to the position of the tongue and lips: high, mid, or low tongue; **front**, mid, or **back** of the tongue; **rounded** or **unrounded** lips. The vowels in English may be **tense** (long) or **lax** (short). Tense vowels are slightly longer in duration than lax vowels. Vowels may also be **stressed** (longer, higher in pitch, and louder) or unstressed. Syllables are built around peaks of sonorants — the nucleus. Consonants may precede (the onset) or follow the nucleus (the rhyme). The rhyme may consist of the nucleus and coda. Liquids and nasal consonants may also act as the nucleus of a syllable as in the word *apple*.

In many languages, the pitch of the vowel or syllable is linguistically significant; for example, two words may contrast in meaning if one is produced with a high pitch and another with a low pitch. Such languages are called **tone** languages as opposed to **intonation** languages, in which pitch is never used to contrast words. In intonation languages, however, the rise and fall of pitch may contrast meanings of sentences. In English, the statement *Mary is a teacher* will end with a fall in pitch, but as a question — *Mary is a teacher?* — the pitch will rise.

In some languages, long vowels or consonants contrast with their shorter counterparts. When they are symbolized by doubling, as in [aa] or [tt], they may be called **geminates**.

Length, pitch, and **loudness** are **prosodic** or **suprasegmental** features. Diacritics to specify properties such as **nasalization, length, stress**, or **tone** may be combined with the phonetic symbols for more detailed phonetic transcriptions.

By means of these phonetic features, all speech sounds of all languages can be described.

Exercises

*1. Write the phonetic symbol for the first sound in each of the following words, according to the way you pronounce it.

Examples: ooze [u]   psycho [s]

a. judge   e. pneumonia   i. civic
b. Thomas   f. thought   j. usury
c. though   g. contact
d. easy   h. phone

*2. Write the phonetic symbol for the *last* sound in each of the following words.

a. fleece   e. watch   i. bleached
b. neigh   f. cow   j. rags
c. long   g. rough
d. health   h. cheese

*3. Write the following words in phonetic transcription according to your pronunciation.

Examples: knot [nɑt]   delightful [dilajtfəl] or [dəlajtfəl]

a. physics   d. coat   g. tease
b. merry   e. yellow   h. heath
c. weather   f. marry

*4. Below is a phonetic transcription of one of the verses in the poem "The Walrus and the Carpenter" by Lewis Carroll. The speaker who transcribed it may not have exactly the same pronunciation as you; there are many alternative correct versions. However, there is one major error in each line that is an impossible pronunciation for any North American English speaker. The error may consist of an extra symbol, a missing symbol, or a wrong symbol in the word. Note that the phonetic transcription that is given is a narrow transcription; aspiration is marked, as is the nasalization of vowels. This is to illustrate a detailed transcription. However, none of the errors involves aspiration or nasalization of vowels.

Write the word in which the error occurs in the *correct* phonetic transcription.

Corrected Word

a. ðə tʰãjm hæz cʌ̃m   [kʰʌ̃m]
b. ðə wɔlrəs sed
c. tʰu tʰɑlk əv mẽni θĩŋz
d. əv šuz ãnd šɪps
e. ænd silĩŋ wæx
f. əv kʰæbəgəz ænd kʰĩŋz
g. ænd waj ðə si ɪs bɔjlĩŋ hɑt
h. ænd wɛθər pʰɪgz hæv wĩŋz

5. Write the symbol that corresponds to each of the following phonetic descriptions; then give an English word that contains this sound.

Example: voiced alveolar stop   [d]   *dog*

a. voiceless bilabial unaspirated stop
b. low front vowel
c. lateral liquid
d. velar nasal
e. voiced interdental fricative
f. voiceless affricate
g. palatal glide
h. mid lax front vowel
i. high back tense vowel
j. voiceless aspirated alveolar stop

*6. In each of the following pairs of words, the boldfaced sounds differ by one or more phonetic properties (features). State both the differences and what properties they have in common.

> Example: phone–phonic
>
> The *o* in *phone* is mid, tense, round.
> The *o* in *phonic* is low, unround.
> Both are back vowels.

a. **bath–bathe**
b. **reduce–reduction**
c. **cool–cold**
d. **wife–wives**
e. **cats–dogs**
f. **impolite–indecent**

*7. Write a phonetic transcription of the italicized words in the following stanzas from a poem by Richard Krogh.

> I take it you already *know*
> Of *tough* and *bough* and *cough* and *dough*?
> Some may stumble, but not *you*,
> On *hiccough, thorough, slough* and *through*?
> So now you are ready, perhaps,
> To learn of less familiar traps?
> Beware of *heard*, a dreadful *word*
> That looks like *beard* and sounds like *bird*.
> And *dead*; it's *said* like *bed*, not *bead*;
> For goodness' sake, don't call it *deed*!
> Watch out for *meat* and *great* and *threat*.
> (They rhyme with *suite* and *straight* and *debt*.)
> A *moth* is not a moth in *mother*,
> Nor *both* in *bother*, *broth* in *brother*.

*8. For each group of sounds listed below, state the phonetic feature or features that they all share.

> Example: [p] [b] [m]   Shared features: labial, stop, consonant

a. [g] [p] [t] [d] [k] [b]
b. [u] [ʊ] [o] [ɔ]
c. [i] [ɪ] [e] [ɛ] [æ]
d. [t] [s] [š] [p] [k] [č] [f] [h]
e. [v] [z] [ž] [j] [ŋ] [g] [d] [b] [l] [r] [w] [ǰ]
f. [t] [d] [s] [š] [n] [č] [ǰ]

9. Match the sounds under column A with one or more phonetic properties from column B as illustrated in the first one.

A	B
[u] 5, 8	1. velar
[θ]	2. nasal
[s]	3. coronal
[b]	4. stop
[l]	5. rounded
[t]	6. interdental
[a]	7. voiceless
[m]	8. back
	9. liquid
	10. labial

10. Write the following sentences in regular English spelling.

   a. fõnɛtɪks ɪz ðə stʌdi ʌv spič sawndz

   b. ɑl lǽŋgwɪǰəz juz sawndz produst baj ðə ʌpər rɛspərətɔri sɪstəm

   c. ĩn wʌn dajələkt ʌv ɪŋglɪš kɑt ðə nawn ǽnd kɔt ðə vʌrb ar pronawnst ðə sẽm

   d. sʌm pipəl θɪŋk fõnɛtɪks ɪz vɛri ĩntərɛstĩŋ

*11. What phonetic property or feature distinguishes the sets of sounds in column A from those in column B?

A		B	
a.	[i] [ɪ]	a.	[u] [ʊ]
b.	[p] [t] [k] [s] [f]	b.	[b] [d] [g] [z] [v]
c.	[p] [b] [m]	c.	[t] [d] [n] [k] [g] [ŋ]
d.	[i] [ɪ] [u] [ʊ]	d.	[e] [ɛ] [o] [ɔ] [æ] [a]
e.	[f] [v] [s] [z] [š] [ž]	e.	[č] [ǰ]
f.	[i] [ɪ] [e] [ɛ] [æ]	f.	[u] [ʊ] [o] [ɔ] [a]

Work Cited

Walker, John. 1823. *A Critical Pronouncing Dictionary and Expositor of the English Language.* 26th ed. London: A. Wilson.

Further Reading

Abercrombie, David. 1967. *Elements of General Phonetics.* Chicago: Aldine.

Catford, J.C. 1977. *Fundamental Problems in Phonetics.* Bloomington: Indiana University Press.

Clark, John, and Colin Yallop. 1990. *An Introduction to Phonetics and Phonology.* Oxford: Blackwell.

Crystal, David. 1985. *A Dictionary of Linguistics and Phonetics.* Oxford: Blackwell.

International Phonetic Association. 1989. *Principles of the International Phonetic Association.* Rev. ed. London: IPA.

Ladefoged, Peter. 1993. *A Course in Phonetics.* 3rd ed. Fort Worth: Harcourt Brace Jovanovich.

Ladefoged, Peter, and Ian Maddieson. 1996. *The Sounds of the World's Languages.* Oxford: Blackwell.

MacKay, Ian R.A. 1987. *Phonetics: The Science of Speech Production.* 2nd ed. Boston: Little Brown.

Pullum, Geoffrey K., and William A. Ladusaw. 1986. *Phonetic Symbol Guide.* Chicago: University of Chicago Press.

CHAPTER 6
Phonology: The Sound Patterns of Language

Speech is human, silence is divine, yet also brutish and dead; therefore we must learn both arts.

Thomas Carlyle (1795–1881)

From the Arctic Circle to the Cape of Good Hope, people speak to each other. The totality of the sounds they produce constitutes the universal set of human speech sounds. The same relatively small set of phonetic properties or features characterizes all these sounds; the same classes of these sounds are utilized in all spoken languages, and the same kinds of regular patterns of speech sounds occur all over the world. When you learn a language, you learn which speech sounds occur in your language and how they pattern.

Phonology is concerned with this kind of linguistic knowledge. Phonetics is a part of phonology and provides the means for describing speech sounds; phonology is concerned with the ways in which these speech sounds form systems and patterns in human language. Phonology, like grammar, is used in two ways — as the mental representation of linguistic knowledge and as the description of this knowledge. Thus, the word *phonology* refers either to the representation of the sounds and sound patterns in a speaker's grammar or to the study of the sound patterns in a language or in human language in general.

Phonological knowledge permits a speaker to produce sounds that form meaningful utterances, to recognize a foreign "accent," to make up new words, to add the appropriate phonetic segments to form plurals and past tenses, to produce aspirated and unaspirated voiceless stops in the appropriate context, to know what is or is not a sound in one's language, and to know that different phonetic strings may represent the same morpheme.

Phonemes: The Phonological Units of Language

In the physical world the naive speaker and hearer actualize and are sensitive to sounds, but what they feel themselves to be pronouncing and hearing are "phonemes."

Edward Sapir (1933)

Phonological knowledge goes beyond the ability to produce all the phonetically different sounds of a language. It includes this ability, of course. A speaker of English can produce the sound [θ] and knows that this sound occurs in English, in words such as *thin* [θĩn], *ether* [iðər], and *bath* [bæθ]. English speakers may or may not be able to produce a "click" or a velar fricative, but even if they can they know that such sounds are not part of the phonetic inventory of English. Many speakers are unable to produce such "foreign" sounds.

A speaker of English also knows that [ð], the voiced counterpart of [θ], is a sound of English, occurring in words such as *either* [iðər], *then* [ðẽn], and *bathe* [beð]. French speakers similarly know that [θ] and [ð] are not part of the phonetic inventory of French and often find it difficult to pronounce words such as *this* [ðɪs] and *that* [ðæt], pronouncing them as if they were spelled *zis* and *zat* or *dis* and *dat*.

Sounds that Contrast

Knowing the sounds (the phonetic units) of a language is only a small part of phonological knowledge.

In earlier chapters, we discussed speakers' knowledge of the arbitrary sound–meaning units that comprise their vocabulary, the morphemes and words in their mental lexicons. We saw that knowing a word means knowing both its form (its sounds) and its meaning. Most of the words in a language differ in both form and meaning, sometimes by just one sound. The importance of phonology is shown by the fact that one can change one word into another simply by changing one sound.

Consider the forms and meanings of the following English words:

sip	fine	chunk
zip	vine	junk

Each word differs from the other words in both form and meaning. The difference between *sip* and *zip* is "signalled" by the fact that the initial sound of the first word is *s* [s] and the initial sound of the second word is *z* [z]. The forms of the two words — that is, their sounds — are identical except for the initial consonants. [s] and [z] can therefore distinguish or **contrast** words. They are **distinctive** sounds in English. Such distinctive sounds are called **phonemes**.

We see from the contrast between *fine* and *vine* and between *chunk* and *junk* that [f], [v], [č], and [ǰ] must also be phonemes in English for the same reason — because substituting a [v] for [f] or a [č] for [ǰ] produces a different word, a different form with a different meaning.

Minimal Pairs

The "B.C." cartoon on the facing page illustrates the fact that [ɪ] and [i] in the pair *crick* and *creek* and [ʊ] and [o] in the pair *crook* and *croak* are phonemes. The substitution of one for the other makes a different word. The phonological difference between the two words in each pair is minimal because they are identical in form

B.C. by permission of Johnny Hart and Creators Syndicate, Inc.

except for one sound segment that occurs in the same place in the string. For this reason, such pairs of words are referred to as **minimal pairs**. These four words, together with *crake* (a short-billed bird), *crack*, and *crock*, constitute a **minimal set**.

All the words in the set differ by just one sound, and they all differ in meaning. The vowels that contrast these meanings are thus in the class of vowel phonemes in English.

For some speakers, *crick* and *creek* are pronounced identically, another example of regional dialect differences, but most speakers of this dialect still contrast the vowels in *beat* and *bit*, so these high front vowels are contrastive, and therefore phonemes, in their dialect.

The distinct sounds that occur in a minimal pair or a minimal set are phonemes since they contrast meanings. *Sip* and *zip*, *fine* and *vine*, and *chunk* and *junk* are minimal pairs in English; [s], [z], [f], [v], [č], and [ǰ] are phonemes in English.

Seed [sid] and *soup* [sup] are not a minimal pair because they differ in two sounds, the vowels and the final consonants. It is thus not evident which difference in sound makes for the differences in meaning. *Bat* [bæt] and *tad* [tæd] do not constitute a minimal pair because, although only one sound differs in the two words, the [b] occurs initially and the [d] occurs finally. However, [i] and [u] do contrast in the minimal pair *seep* [sip] and *soup* [sup], [d] and [p] contrast in *deed* [did] and *deep* [dip], and [b] and [d] contrast in the following minimal pairs:

bead	[bid]	deed	[did]
bowl	[bol]	dole	[dol]
rube	[rub]	rude	[rud]
lobe	[lob]	load	[lod]

Substituting a [d] for a [b] changes both the phonetic form and its meaning. [b] and [d] also contrast with [g], as is shown by the following:

bill/dill/gill   rib/rid/rig

Therefore, [b], [d], and [g] are all phonemes in English, and *bill, dill*, and *gill* constitute a minimal set. We have many minimal sets in English, so it is relatively easy to determine what the English phonemes are. The words in the following minimal set differ only in their vowels; each vowel thus represents a distinct phoneme:

beat	[bit]	[i]	boot	[but]	[u]
bit	[bɪt]	[ɪ]	but	[bʌt]	[ʌ]
bait	[bet]	[e]	boat	[bot]	[o]
bet	[bɛt]	[ɛ]	bought	[bɔt]	[ɔ] (in many American dialects)
bat	[bæt]	[æ]	bot	[bɑt]	[ɑ]

Not all these words are part of a minimal pair set for all speakers. Most speakers of Canadian English, for instance, would not distinguish between *bought* and *bot*, pronouncing both [bɑt] even if they knew that a *bot* was the larva of a botfly or a clipped form of *robot*. The two vowel sounds do not contrast in this dialect, where *cot* and *caught* are the same, though they might contrast in another.

Also, [ʊ] and [ɔj], which are not part of the minimal set listed above, are phonemes of English. They contrast meanings in other minimal pairs, such as *book* [bʊk] and *beak* [bik], *look* [lʊk] and *leak* [lik], *boy* [bɔj] and *buy* [baj], or *soil* [sɔjl] and *sail* [sel]. The diphthongs [ɔj], [aj], and [aw] are considered to be single vowel sounds even though each includes an off-glide because, in English, they function like the monophthongal vowels, as is further illustrated by the following minimal set including all three diphthongs:

| bile | bowel | boil |
| [bajl] | [bawl] | [bɔjl] |

In broad Newfoundland English, the two diphthongs [aj] and [ɔj] are not distinguished in any set, and both are pronounced as [aj], so that *boil* and *bile* are pronounced the same. In this dialect, then, there is no phonemic contrast between these two diphthongs.

In some languages, particularly with relatively long words of many syllables, it is not as easy to find minimal sets or even minimal pairs to illustrate the contrasting sounds, the phonemes of these languages. Even in English, which has many **monosyllabic** words (words of one syllable) and hundreds of minimal pairs, there are very few minimal pairs in which the phonemes [θ] and [ð] contrast. In a computer search, only one pair was found in which they contrast initially, one in which they contrast medially, and four in which they contrast finally. All four pairs in which they contrast finally are noun–verb pairs, the result of historical sound change that will be discussed in a later chapter.

[θ]	[ð]
thigh	**thy**
ether	either
mouth (noun)	mouth (verb)
teeth	teethe
loath	loathe
wreath	wreathe
sheath	sheathe

Some speakers do not exhibit minimal pairs with *ether/either* since they pronounce the latter as [ajðər]. But even if the above pairs did not occur, [θ] and [ð] can be analyzed as distinct phonemes. Each contrasts with other sounds in the language as, for example, *thick* [θɪk]/*sick* [sɪk] and *though* [ðo]/*dough* [do]. Note also that one cannot substitute the voiced and voiceless interdental fricatives in the words in which they do occur without producing nonsense forms; for example, if we substitute the voiced [ð] for the voiceless [θ] in *thick*, we get [ðɪk], which has no meaning, showing that the phonemes that represent its form and its meaning are inseparable. You cannot pronounce the word any way you like, substituting other sounds for the phonemes in the word.

Free Variation

Some words in English are pronounced differently by different speakers. For example, some speakers pronounce the word *economics* with an initial [i] and others with an initial [ε]. In this word, [i] and [ε] are said to be in **free variation**. However, we cannot substitute [i] and [ε] for each other in all words. *Did you beat the drum?* does not mean the same thing as *Did you bet the drum?* An old song of the 1930s was based on the notion of free variation:

> You say [iðər] and I say [ajðər],
> You say [niðər] and I say [najðər],
> [iðər] [ajðər] [niðər] [najðər],
> Let's call the whole thing off.

The difference however, is often one of dialect, for, as the Irish speaker said when asked which was the correct pronunciation, [iðər] or [ajðər], "It's [neðər]."

Phonemes, Phones, and Allophones

You may be wondering why we have included a second chapter on phonological units. The entire previous chapter discussed these sounds. But as noted earlier in discussing morphology, syntax, and semantics, linguistic knowledge is more complex than it appears to one who knows a language. Since the knowledge is unconscious, we are unaware of many of the complexities.

Phonemes are not physical sounds. They are abstract mental representations of the phonological units of a language, the units used to represent the forms of words in our mental lexicons. These phonemic representations of words, together with the phonological rules of the language, determine the phonetic units that represent their pronunciation.

If phonemes are not the actual sounds, what are they? We can illustrate the difference between a phoneme and a phonetic segment, called a **phone**, by referring to the difference between oral and nasalized vowels in English. In Chapter 5, we noted that both oral and nasalized vowels occur *phonetically* in English.

bean	[bĩn]	bead	[bid]
roam	[rõm]	robe	[rob]

Nasalized vowels occur in English syllables only before nasal consonants. If one substituted an oral vowel for the nasal vowels in *bean* and *roam*, the meanings of the two words would not be changed. Try to say these words keeping your velum up until your tongue makes the stop closure of the [n] or your lips come together for the [m]. It will not be easy, because in English we automatically lower the velum when producing vowels before nasals in the same syllable. Now try to pronounce *bead* and *robe* with a nasal vowel. [bĩd] would still be understood as *bead*, although your pronunciation would probably sound very nasal. In other words, nasal and oral vowels *do not* **contrast**. There is just one set of vowel phonemes in English even though there are two sets of vowel phones: oral vowels and nasal vowels.

There is a general principle or rule in the phonology of English that tells us when nasalized vowels occur — always before nasal consonants, never before oral consonants. The oral vowels in English differ phonemically from each other, whereas the differences between the oral vowels and their nasal counterparts do not. This is because there is no principle or rule to predict when, for example, [i] occurs instead of [e] or [u] or [ɑ] or any of the other vowel phonemes. We must learn that [i] occurs in *beat* and [e] in *bait*. We do not have to learn that the nasalized version of [i] occurs in *beam* [bĩm] or *bean* [bĩn] or that the nasalized [ũ] occurs in *boom* [bũm] or *boon* [bũn]. Rather, we generalize from the occurrences of oral and nasal vowels in English, and we form a mental rule which nasalizes all vowels before nasal consonants.

The rule, or general principle, that predicts when a vowel phoneme will be realized as an oral vowel phone and when the same vowel phoneme will be a nasalized phone is exemplified in the sets of words and non-words in Table 6.1.

As the words in Table 6.1 illustrate, in English oral vowels occur in final position and before non-nasal consonants; nasalized vowels occur only before nasal consonants. More specifically, nasal vowels occur before nasal consonants that follow and are in the same syllable. For most speakers, the [o] vowel in the word *roman* [ro-mə̃n] is not nasalized since it occurs before a syllable break symbolized as -, but the [ə̃] is because the vowel and the [n] are in the same syllable. The "non-words" show us that nasalized vowels do not occur finally or before non-nasal consonants. Therefore, oral vowels and their nasalized counterparts never contrast.

Most speakers of English are unaware that the vowels in *bead* and *bean* are different sounds; they are aware of phonemes but not of the physical sounds (phones) that they produce and hear.

Since nasalized vowels do occur phonetically but not phonemically, we can conclude that there is no one-to-one correspondence between phonetic segments and

TABLE 6.1

Nasal and Oral Vowels: Words and Non-Words

Words						Non-Words		
bee	[bi]	bead	[bid]	bean	[bĩn]	*[bĩ]	[bĩd]	*[bin]
lay	[le]	lace	[les]	lame	[lẽm]	*[lẽ]	*[lẽs]	*[lem]
baa	[bæ]	bad	[bæd]	bang	[bæ̃ŋ]	*[bæ̃]	*[bæ̃d]	*[bæŋ]

phonemes in a language. One phoneme may be realized phonetically (i.e., pronounced) as more than one phone — phonetic segment. A phoneme may also be represented by only one phone.

The different phones that are the realizations of a phoneme are called the **allophones** of that phoneme. An allophone is therefore a predictable phonetic variant of a phoneme. In English, each vowel phoneme has both an oral and a nasalized allophone. The choice of the allophone is not random or haphazard; it is rule-governed. No one is explicitly taught these rules. They are learned subconsciously when the native language is acquired. Language acquisition, to a certain extent, is rule construction.

To distinguish between a phoneme and its allophones (the phonetic segments or phones that symbolize the way the phoneme is pronounced in different contexts), we will use slashes / / to enclose phonemes and continue to use square brackets [ ] for allophones or phones; for example, [i] and [ĩ] are allophones of the phoneme /i/, [ɪ] and [ĩ] are allophones of the phoneme /ɪ/, and so on. Thus, we will represent *bead* and *bean* phonemically as /bid/ and /bin/. The rule for the distribution of oral and nasal vowels in English shows that phonetically these words will be pronounced as [bid] and [bĩn], respectively. Words are stored in our mental dictionaries in their phonemic forms. We refer to them as **phonemic transcriptions**. The pronunciations of these words are given in **phonetic transcriptions**, between square brackets.

In Chapter 5, we mentioned another example of allophones of a single phoneme. We noted that some speakers of English substitute a glottal stop for the [t] at the end of a word such as *don't* or *can't* or in the middle of a word such as *bottle* or *button*. The substitution of the glottal stop does not change the meanings of any words; [dõnt] and [dõnʔ] do not contrast in meaning, nor do [batəl] or [baʔəl]. [ræbəl] and [ræʔəl] do contrast, as the pronunciations of *rabble* and *rattle*, but note that [rætəl] with a [t] or [ræɾəl] with the flapped [ɾ] or [ræʔəl] with a glottal stop are all possible pronunciations of the word *rattle*. [t], [ɾ], and [ʔ] do not contrast; they are all allophones of the phoneme /t/.

The function of phonemes is to contrast meanings. Phonemes in themselves have no meaning, but when combined with other phonemes they constitute the forms by which meanings of words and morphemes are expressed.

Complementary Distribution

Minimal pairs illustrate that some speech sounds are contrastive in a language, and these sounds represent the set of phonemes. We also saw that some sounds are not distinct; they do not contrast meanings. [t] and [ʔ] were cited as examples of sounds that do not contrast. The substitution of one for the other does not create a minimal pair.

Oral and nasal vowels in English are also non-distinct sounds. Unlike the [t], [ʔ], and [ɾ], the allophones of /t/, the oral and nasal allophones of each vowel phoneme never occur in the same phonological context. This was illustrated in Table 6.1. They complement each other and are said to be in **complementary distribution**. This is further shown in Table 6.2.

TABLE 6.2
Distribution of Oral and Nasal Vowels in English Syllables

	In Final Position	Before Nasal Consonants	Before Oral Consonants
Oral Vowels	Yes	No	Yes
Nasal Vowels	No	Yes	No

When oral vowels occur, nasal vowels do not occur, and vice versa. It is in this sense that the phones are said to complement each other or to be in complementary distribution.

The concept of complementary distribution is illustrated by Clark Kent and Superman, who represent in different forms only one person. When Kent is present, Superman is not; when Superman is present, Kent is not. Kent and Superman are therefore in complementary distribution, just as [i] and [ĩ] are in complementary distribution. Of course, there is a difference between their "distribution" and the two allophones of the phoneme /i/ since Kent and Superman can occur in the same environment (e.g., talking to Lois Lane), whereas [i] and [ĩ] never occur in the same environment or under the same conditions. Kent and Superman are thus more similar to the allophones of /t/ — [t] and [ʔ] — which do occur in the same environment. The important point is that the concept of two physical manifestations of a single abstract unit is true of both Kent and Superman and of [i] and [ĩ].

Not all sounds that are in complementary distribution in one dialect of English appear in complementary distribution in another. Unlike most other dialects of Canadian or American English, [ɪ] and [ɛ] are in complementary distribution in some parts of Newfoundland, away from the Avalon Peninsula. [ɪ] occurs everywhere except before [r], where [ɛ] occurs. Thus, *bit* and *bet* are both pronounced as *bit* ([bɪt]), while *beer* and *bear* are pronounced as *bear* ([bɛr]). Both vowels are thus allophones of one phoneme in this dialect (Wells 1982).

When sounds are in complementary distribution, they do not contrast with each other. The replacement of one sound with the other will not change the meaning of the word, although it might not sound like typical English pronunciation. Given these facts about the patterning of sounds in a language, a phoneme can be defined as a set of phonetically similar sounds that are in complementary distribution with each other and do not contrast. A set can, of course, consist of only one member. Some phonemes are represented by only one sound, one allophone. When there is more than one allophone in the set, the phones must have **phonetic similarity** — that is, they must share most of the same phonetic features. In English, the velar nasal [ŋ] and the glottal fricative [h] are in complementary distribution; [ŋ] is not found word initially, and [h] does not occur word finally. But they share very few phonetic features; [ŋ] is a voiced velar nasal stop; [h] is a voiceless glottal fricative. Therefore, they are not allophones of the same phoneme; /ŋ/ and /h/ are allophones of different phonemes.

We mentioned that speakers of a language perceive the different sounds of a single phoneme as being one sound. Two sounds that are not phonetically similar would not be thus perceived. Furthermore, it would be difficult for children to classify such sounds together as representing one phoneme. The phonetic similarity criterion reflects the ways in which allophones function together and the kinds of generalization that children can make in acquiring the phonological contrasts of the language.

Distinctive Features

We generally are not aware of the phonetic properties or features that distinguish the phonemes of our language. Phonetics provides the means to describe these sounds, showing how they differ; phonology tells us which sounds function as phonemes to contrast the meanings of words.

In order for two phonetic forms to differ and to contrast meanings, there must be some phonetic difference between the substituted sounds. The minimal pairs *seal* [sil] and *zeal* [zil] show that [s] and [z] represent two contrasting phonemes in English. They cannot be allophones of one phoneme since we cannot replace the [s] with the [z] without changing the meaning of the word. Furthermore, they are not in complementary distribution; both occur word initially before the vowel [i]. They therefore are phones that function as allophones of the phonemes /s/ and /z/. From the discussion of phonetics in Chapter 5, we know that the only difference between [s] and [z] is a voicing difference; [s] is voiceless and [z] is voiced. It is this phonetic feature that distinguishes the two words. Voicing thus plays a special role in English (and in many other languages). It also distinguishes *feel* and *veal* [f]/[v] and *cap* and *cab* [p]/[b]. When a feature distinguishes one phoneme from another, it is a **distinctive feature** (or a phonemic feature). When two words are exactly alike phonetically except for one feature, the phonetic difference is **distinctive** since this difference alone accounts for the contrast or difference in meaning.

Feature Values

One can think of voicing and voicelessness as the presence or absence of a single **feature**, voicing. Thus, a single feature can be thought of as having two values, plus (+), which signifies its presence, and minus (−), which signifies its absence. /b/ is therefore [+voiced] and /p/ is [−voiced]. We could have called this feature "voiceless" and specified /b/ as [−voiceless] and /p/ as [+voiceless]. We will, however, refer to these features by their traditional designations.

The presence or absence of nasality can similarly be designated as [+nasal] or [−nasal], with [m] being [+nasal] and [b] or [p] being [−nasal]. A [−nasal] sound is equivalent to an oral sound.

The phonetic and phonemic symbols are **cover symbols** for a set or bundle of distinctive features, a shorthand method of specifying the phonetic properties of the segment. Phones and phonemes are not indissoluble units; they are similar to molecules, which are composed of atoms. Phones and phonemes are composed of phonetic features. A more explicit transcription of /p/, /b/, and /m/ may thus be given as

	p	b	m
Stop	+	+	+
Labial	+	+	+
Voiced	−	+	+
Nasal	−	−	+

Aspiration is not listed as a feature in the above phonemic specification of these units because it is non-distinctive, and it is not necessary to include both [p] and [pʰ] as phonemes. In a phonetic transcription, however, the aspiration would be specified where it occurs. This will be discussed below.

A phonetic feature is distinctive when the + value of that feature found in certain words contrasts with the − value of that feature in other words. Each phoneme must be distinguished from all other phonemes in a language by at least one feature value distinction.

Since the phonemes /b/, /d/, and /g/ contrast by virtue of their place of articulation features — labial, alveolar, and velar — these place features are also distinctive in English. Since uvular sounds do not occur in English, the place feature *uvular* is non-distinctive. The distinctive features of the voiced stops in English are shown in the following **feature matrix**:

	b	m	d	n	g	ŋ
Stop	+	+	+	+	+	+
Voiced	+	+	+	+	+	+
Labial	+	+	−	−	−	−
Alveolar	−	−	+	+	−	−
Velar	−	−	−	−	+	+
Nasal	−	+	−	+	−	+

Each of the phonemes in the above chart differs from all the other phonemes by at least one distinctive feature.

The following minimal pairs further describe some of the distinctive features in the phonological system of English.

> **bat**   [bæt]   **mat**   [mæt]   The difference between *bat* and *mat* is due only to the difference in nasality between [b] and [m]. [b] and [m] are identical in all features except for the fact that [b] is oral or [−nasal] and [m] is nasal or [+nasal]. Therefore, nasality or [±nasal]* is a distinctive feature of English consonants.

*The symbol ± before a feature should be read as "plus or minus" that feature, showing that it is a **binary-valued** feature.

rack	**[ræk]**	**rock**	**[rɑk]**	The two words are distinguished only because [æ] is a front vowel and [ɑ] is a back vowel. They are both low, unrounded vowels. [±back] is therefore a distinctive feature of English vowels.
said	**[sɛd]**	**zed**	**[zɛd]**	The difference is due to the voicelessness of the [s] in contrast to the voicing of the [z]. Therefore, voicing ([±voiced]) is a distinctive feature of English consonants.

Predictability of Redundant Non-Distinctive Features

We saw above that nasality is a distinctive feature of English consonants. Given the arbitrary relationship between form and meaning, there is no way to predict that the word *mean* begins with a nasal bilabial stop [m] and that the word *bean* begins with an oral bilabial stop [b]. You learn this when you learn the words. We also saw that nasality is not a distinctive feature for English vowels; the nasality feature value of the vowels in *bean*, *mean*, *comb*, and *sing* is predictable since they occur before syllable-/word-final nasal consonants. When a feature value is predictable by rule, it is a **redundant** feature. Thus, nasality is a redundant feature for English vowels but a non-redundant (distinctive or phonemic) feature for English consonants.

This is not the case in all languages. In French, nasality is a distinctive feature for both vowels and consonants: *gars* pronounced [ga], "lad," contrasts with *gant* [gã], which means "glove," and *bal* [bal], "dance" contrasts with *mal* [mal], "evil/pain." In Chapter 5, other examples of French nasalized vowels are presented. Thus, French has both oral and nasal consonant and vowel phonemes; English has oral and nasal consonant phonemes but only oral vowel phonemes. Both languages, however, have oral and nasal consonant and vowel phones.

In the Ghanaian language Akan (or Twi), nasalized and oral vowels occur both phonetically and phonemically; nasalization is a distinctive feature for vowels in Akan, as the following examples illustrate:

[ka]	"bite"	[kã]	"speak"
[fi]	"come from"	[fĩ]	"dirty"
[tu]	"pull"	[tũ]	"hole/den"
[nsa]	"hand"	[nsã]	"liquor"
[či]	"hate"	[čĩ]	"squeeze"
[pam]	"sew"	[pãm]	"confederate"

These examples show that vowel nasalization is not predictable in Akan. As shown by the last minimal pair — [pam]/[pãm] — there is no rule that nasalizes vowels before nasal consonants. We also find word-final oral vowels contrasting with word-final nasalized vowels (after identical initial consonants). The change of form — the substitution of nasalized for oral vowels or vice versa — changes the meaning. Both oral and nasal vowel phonemes must therefore exist in Akan.

Note that two languages may have the same phonetic segments (phones) but two different phonemic systems. Both oral and nasalized vowels exist in English and

Akan phonetically; English has no nasalized vowel phonemes, but Akan does. The same phonetic segments function differently in the two languages. Nasalization of vowels in English is redundant and non-distinctive; nasalization of vowels in Akan is non-redundant and distinctive.

Another non-distinctive feature in English is aspiration. In the previous chapter, we pointed out that in English both aspirated and unaspirated voiceless stops occur. The voiceless aspirated stops [pʰ], [tʰ], [kʰ] and the voiceless unaspirated stops [p], [t], [k] are in complementary distribution in English, as shown in the following chart:

Syllable Initial before a Stressed Vowel			After a Syllable-Initial /s/			*Non-Word		
[pʰ]	[tʰ]	[kʰ]	[p]	[t]	[k]			
pill	*till*	*kill*	*spill*	*still*	*skill*	*[pɪl]	*[tɪl]	*[kɪl]
[pʰɪl]	[tʰɪl]	[kʰɪl]	[spɪl]	[stɪl]	[skɪl]	*[spʰɪl]	*[tʰɪl]	*[skʰɪl]
par	*tar*	*car*	*spar*	*star*	*scar*	*[par]	*[stʰar]	*[kar]
[pʰar]	[tʰar]	[kʰar]	[spar]	[star]	[skar]	*[spʰar]	*[tʰar]	*[skʰar]

Where the unaspirated stops occur, the aspirated do not and vice versa. In addition, although they do not contrast, the one set does not occur where the other set does, as shown in the non-words. One can say *spit* with an aspirated [pʰ], as [spʰɪt], and it would be understood as *spit*, but your listeners would probably think you were spitting out your words. Given this distribution, we see that aspiration is a redundant, non-distinctive feature in English; aspiration is predictable, occurring as a feature of voiceless stops in the specified phonemic environments.

This is the reason speakers of English (if they are not analyzing the sounds as linguists or phoneticians) usually consider the [pʰ] in *pill* and the [p] in *spill* to be the "same" sound, just as they consider the [i] and [ĩ] that represent the phoneme /i/ in *bead* and *bean* to be the "same." They do so because the difference between them, in this case the feature *aspiration*, is **predictable, redundant, non-distinctive**, and **non-phonemic** (all equivalent terms). This distribution of aspirated and unaspirated voiceless stops is a fact about English phonology. There are two *p* sounds (or phones) in English but only one *p* phoneme. (This is also true of /t/ and /k/.) This illustrates why we referred to the phoneme as an abstract unit. We do not utter phonemes; we produce phones. /p/ is a phoneme in English that is realized phonetically (pronounced) as either [p] or [pʰ]. [p] or [pʰ] are allophones of the phoneme /p/. The notion of abstractness is not unique to phonology. We have many abstract mental concepts. The number 3 is not represented in our cognitive arithmetic system as three physical objects. It represents three of anything — dogs, pencils, continents, jelly beans, linguists, phonemes, dreams, ideas. It is thus even more abstract than the phonemes of a language that are represented by specific physical objects. Children know that 3 can be three of anything; they also know that /p/ can be [p] and [pʰ].

Unpredictability of Phonemic Features

We saw above that the same phones (phonetic segments) can occur in two languages but pattern differently because the phonemic system, the phonology of the languages, is different. English, French, and Akan have oral and nasal vowel phones; in English, oral and nasal vowels are allophones of one phoneme, whereas in French and Akan they represent distinct phonemes.

Aspiration of voiceless stops further illustrates the asymmetry of the phonological systems of different languages. Both aspirated and unaspirated voiceless stops occur in English and Thai (the major language spoken in Thailand), but they function differently in the two languages. Aspiration in English is not a phonemic or distinctive feature, because its presence or absence is predictable. In Thai, however, it is not predictable, as the following examples show:

Voiceless Unaspirated		Voiceless Aspirated	
[paa]	"forest"	[pʰaa]	"to split"
[tam]	"to pound"	[tʰam]	"to do"
[kat]	"to bite"	[kʰat]	"to interrupt"

The voiceless unaspirated and the voiceless aspirated stops in Thai are not in complementary distribution. They occur in the same positions in the minimal pairs above; they contrast and are therefore phonemes in Thai. In both English and Thai, the phones [p], [t], [k], [pʰ], [tʰ], and [kʰ] occur. In English, they represent the phonemes /p/, /t/, and /k/; in Thai, they represent the phonemes /p/, /t/, /k/, /pʰ/, /tʰ/, and /kʰ/. Aspiration is a distinctive feature in Thai; it is a non-distinctive redundant feature in English.

The phonetic facts alone do not reveal what is distinctive or phonemic.

> **The phonetic representation of utterances shows what speakers know about the pronunciation of utterances; the phonemic representation of utterances shows what the speakers know about the abstract underlying phonology.**

That *pot/pat* and *spot/spat* are transcribed with an identical /p/ reveals the fact that English speakers consider the [pʰ] in *pot* [pʰɑt] and the [p] in *spot* [spɑt] to be phonetic manifestations of the same phoneme /p/. What distinguishes these words for an English speaker is the presence or absence of /s/, not of aspiration.

In learning a language, a child learns which features are distinctive in that language and which are not. One phonetic feature may be distinctive for one class of sounds but predictable or non-distinctive for another class of sounds (e.g., the feature nasality in English).

In Chapter 5, we pointed out that in English the tense vowels /i/, /e/, /u/, and /o/ are also higher (articulated with a higher tongue position) and longer in duration than their lax vowel counterparts /ɪ/, /ɛ/, /ʊ/, and /ɔ/. The distinction between the tense and lax vowels can be shown simply by using the feature tense/lax or [±tense]. Using this specification, the small difference in tongue height between the tense and lax vowels is non-distinctive, as is the length difference. In the low vowels, [æ] and [a] are lax vowels ([−tense]) and [ɑ] is [+tense]. Since [a] and [ɑ] are both [+back], tenseness may also distinguish between them. However, since [a] and [ɑ] do not contrast phonemically, they may be taken as allophones of the phoneme /a/ in contrast to /æ/. The tense vowel phonemes in English would then include /i/, /e/, /u/, /o/, /a/ and the lax vowels /ɪ/, /ɛ/, /ʊ/, /ɔ/, /æ/.

Vowel length is predictable in English: vowels are longest in word-final position (*bee*), longer before voiced sounds than voiceless sounds (*bead* vs. *beat*), and longer before continuants than stops (*beef* vs. *beet*).

In other languages, long and short vowels are identical except for length. Thus, length can be a non-predictable distinctive feature. Vowel length is phonemic in Danish, Finnish, Arabic, and Korean. Consider the following "minimal pairs" in Korean:

il	"day"	i:l	"word"
seda	"to count"	se:da	"strong"
kul	"oyster"	ku:l	"tunnel"

Vowel length is also phonemic in Japanese:

biru	"building"	bi:ru	"beer"
tsuji	a proper name	tsu:ji	"moving one's bowels"

When teaching at a university in Japan, one of the authors of this book inadvertently pronounced Ms. Tsuji's name as Tsu:ji-san. (The *-san* is a suffix used to show respect.) The effect of this error quickly taught him to understand the phonemic nature of vowel length in Japanese.

Consonant length is also contrastive in Japanese. A consonant may be lengthened by prolonging the closure: a long *t* [t:] or [tt] can be produced by holding the tongue against the alveolar ridge twice as long as for a short *t* [t]. The following minimal pairs illustrate that length is a phonemic feature for Japanese consonants:

šite	"doing"	šitte	"knowing"
saki	"ahead"	sakki	"before"

Luganda, an African language, also contrasts long and short consonants; /kkula/ means "treasure" and /kula/ means "grow up." (In both words, the first vowel is produced with a high pitch and the second with a low pitch.)

The Italian word for "grandfather" is *nonno* /nonno/, contrasting with the word for "ninth," which is *nono* /nono/.

In English, consonants may be pronounced long if they occur across word boundaries. Many English speakers will produce a longer closure of the /t/ in *white tie* than in *why tie?* In such cases, the [t:] is in free variation with a short [t]. Length is not a distinctive feature for English consonants.

The phonemic contrast between long and short consonants and vowels can be symbolized by the colon — /t:/ or /a:/ — or by doubling the segment — /tt/ or /aa/. Such long segments are sometimes referred to as **geminates**. Since phonemic symbols are simply cover symbols for a number of distinctive feature values, it does not matter which symbol one uses. This can be shown by specifying the features that distinguish between /nonno/ or /non:o/ and /nono/; the /nn/ or /n:/ is marked as [+long] and the /n/ as [–long], whichever symbol is used for length, as long as one is consistent.

Sometimes the choice of symbol is determined by practicality. Both print-*a* [a] and script-*a* [ɑ] are low back vowels differing in tenseness, [a] being [–tense] and [ɑ] being [+tense]. They do not contrast with each other in context, [a] appearing before glides to form diphthongs and [ɑ] elsewhere. Most North American linguists use one or the other of these characters to represent the phoneme, since they do not contrast phonemically, only phonetically, in most dialects. Since it does not matter which symbol is used, most use print-*a* because it is the character used on typewriters and computer keyboards, so it is conveniently taken as the phonemic symbol for the low back vowel with the phonetic variants [a] and [ɑ].

More on Redundancies

The value of some features of a single phoneme is predictable or redundant due to the specification of the other features of that segment. That is, given the presence of certain feature values, one can predict the value of other features in that segment.

In English, all front vowels are predictably non-round, and the non-low back vowels are predictably round. Unlike in French, there are no rounded front vowels in English. We can thus say that if a vowel in English is specified as [–back] it is also redundantly, predictably [–round], and the feature value for round is absent from the representation. A "blank" would occupy its place, indicating that the value of that feature is predictable by a phonological rule of the language. Similarly for vowels specified as [–back, –low], which are predictably [–round]. The feature [±low] seems to distinguish [ɑ], which is [+back, +low, –rounded], and [ɔ], which is [+back, –low, +rounded]. Many dialects of English do not distinguish these two sounds phonemically. Some, including Canadian English, have only [ɑ] in words such as *cot* and *caught*, phonemically /kat/, and others have only [ɔ], phonemically /kɔt/.

Similarly, in English all nasal consonant phonemes are predictably voiced. Thus, voicing is non-distinctive for nasal consonants and need not be specified in marking the value of the voicing feature for this set of phonemes. Phonetically in English, the nasal phonemes may be voiceless (indicated by the small ring under the symbol) when they occur after a syllable-initial /s/, as in *snoop*, which phonemically is /snup/ and phonetically may be [sn̥up]. The voicelessness is predictable from the context.

This can be accounted for at the phonemic level by the following:

Redundancy Rule: If a phoneme is [+nasal], then it is also [+voiced].

In Burmese, however, we find the following minimal pairs:

/ma/	[ma]	"health"	/m̥a/	[m̥a]	"order"
/na/	[na]	"pain"	/n̥a/	[n̥a]	"nostril"

The fact that some nasal phonemes are [+voiced] and others [−voiced] must be specified in Burmese; the English redundancy rule does not occur in the grammar of Burmese. We can illustrate this phonological difference between English and Burmese in the following phonemic distinctive feature matrices:

	Burmese:	**/m/**	**/m̥/**	**English:**	**/m/**
Nasal		+	+		+
Labial		+	+		+
Voicing		+	−		

Note that the value for the voicing feature is left blank for the English phoneme /m/ since the [+] value for this feature is specified by the redundancy rule given above.

As noted earlier, the value of some features in a segment is predictable because of the segments that precede or follow that segment; the phonological context determines the value of the feature rather than the presence of other feature values in that segment. Aspiration cannot be predicted in isolation but only when a voiceless stop occurs in a word, since the presence or absence of the feature depends on where the voiceless stop occurs and what precedes or follows it. It is determined by its **phonemic environment**. Similarly, the oral or nasal quality of a vowel depends on its environment. If it is followed by a nasal consonant, then it is predictably [+nasal].

For certain classes of sounds, the values of some features are universally implied for all languages. Thus, all oral stops — [−continuant] segments — are universally and predictably [−syllabic], regardless of their phonemic context.

Syllable Structure

Words are composed of one or more syllables. A **syllable** is a phonological unit that is composed of one or more phonemes. Every syllable has a **nucleus**, usually a vowel (but it may be a syllabic liquid or nasal). The nucleus may be preceded by one or more phonemes, called the syllable **onset**, and followed by one or more segments, called the syllable **coda**. At an early age, children learn that certain words rhyme. In rhyming words, the nucleus and the coda of the final syllable are identical, as in the following jingle:

> Jack and **Jill**
> Went up the **hill**
> To fetch a pail of water.
> Jack fell **down**
> And broke his cr**own**
> And Jill came tumbling after.

For this reason, the nucleus + coda constitute the subsyllabic unit called a **rhyme**. A syllable thus has a **hierarchical** structure. Using the Greek letter *sigma* (σ) as the symbol for the phonological unit *syllable*, we can show the hierarchical structure of the monosyllabic word *splints*:

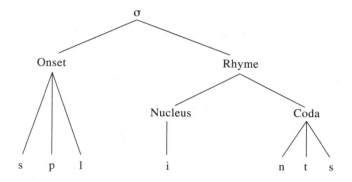

Sequential Constraints

Suppose you were given four cards, each of which had a different phoneme of English printed on it:

| k | | b | | l | | ɪ |

If you were asked to arrange these cards to form all the "possible" words that these four phonemes could form, you might order them as follows:

```
b    l    ɪ    k
k    l    ɪ    b
b    ɪ    l    k
k    ɪ    l    b
```

These arrangements are the only permissible ones for these phonemes in English. */lbkɪ/, */ɪlbk/, */bkɪl/, and */ɪlkb/ are not possible words in the language. Although /blɪk/ and /klɪb/ are not existing words (you will not find them in a dictionary), if you heard someone say

"I just bought a beautiful new *blick*."

you might ask "What's a 'blick'?" If you heard someone say

"I just bought a beautiful new *bkli*."

you would probably reply "What did you say?"

Your knowledge of English "tells" you that certain strings of phonemes are permissible and that others are not. After a consonant such as /b/, /g/, /k/, or /p/, another stop consonant is not permitted by the rules of the grammar. If a word begins with an /l/ or an /r/, every speaker "knows" that the next segment must be a vowel. That is why */lbɪk/ does not sound like an English word. It violates the restrictions on the sequencing of phonemes.

Other such constraints exist in English. If the initial sounds of *chill* or *Jill* begin a word, then the next sound must be a vowel. /čat/ or /čon/ or /čæk/ are possible words in English, as are /ǰæl/ or /ǰot/ or /ǰalɪk/, but */člit/ and */ǰpurz/ are not. No more than three sequential consonants can occur at the beginning of a word, and these three are restricted to /s/ + /p, t, k/ + /l, r, w, j/. There are even restrictions if this condition is met. For example, /stl/ is not a permitted sequence, so *stlick* is not a possible word in English, but *strick* is.

Other languages have different sequential restrictions. In Polish, *zl* is a permissible combination, as in *zloty*, a unit of currency.

The constraints on sequences of segments are called **phonotactic** constraints or simply the phonotactics of the language. If we examine the phonotactics of English, we find that word phonotactics are in fact based on syllable phonotactics. That is, only the clusters that can begin a syllable can begin a word, and only a cluster that can end a syllable can end a word. Medially in a multisyllabic word, the clusters consist of syllable-final + syllable-initial sequences. Words such as *instruct* /ɪnstrʌkt/, with the medial cluster /nstr/, or *explicit* /ɛksplɪsɪt/, with the medial cluster /kspl/, can be divided into well-formed syllables /ɪn $ strʌkt/ and /ɛk $ splɪs $ ɪt/ (using $ to symbolize a syllable boundary). We, as speakers of English, know that "constluct" is not a possible word because the second syllable starts with a non-permissible sequence /stl/ or /tl/. Syllables, then, are important phonological units.

In Asante Twi, a word may end only in a vowel or a nasal consonant. /pik/ is not a possible Twi word, because it breaks the sequential rules of the language, and /mba/ ("not come" in Twi) is not a possible word in English for similar reasons, although it is a word in Twi.

All languages have constraints on the permitted sequences of phonemes, though different languages have different constraints. Just as spoken language has sequences of sounds that are not permitted in the language, so, too, sign languages have forbidden combinations of features. They differ from one sign language to another, just as the constraints on sounds and sound sequences differ from one spoken language to another. A permissible sign in a Chinese sign language may not be a permissible sign in ASL and vice versa. Children learn these constraints when they learn the spoken or signed language, just as they learn what the phonemes are and how they are related to phonetic segments.

Lexical Gaps

Although *bot* [bɑt] and *crake* [krek] are not words for some speakers, and [bʊt] (to rhyme with *put*), *crack* [krɛk], *cruke* [kruk], cruk [krʌk], and *crike* [krajk] are not now words in English, they are "possible words." That is, they are strings of sounds, all of which represent phonemes, in sequences that are permissible in English in that they obey the phonotactic constraints of the language. We might say that they are **nonsense words** (permissible forms with no meanings) or possible words.

Madison Avenue advertisers constantly use possible but non-occurring words for the names of new products. We would hardly expect a new product to come on the market with the name [xik], because [x] (the voiceless velar fricative) is not a phoneme in English. Nor would a new soap be called *Zhleet* [žlit], because in English the voiced palatal fricative [ž] cannot occur initially before a liquid. Possible but non-occurring words such as *Bic* [bɪk], before it was coined as a brand name, are **accidental gaps** in the vocabulary. An accidental gap is a form that conforms to all the phonological rules of the language but has no meaning. An occurring word is a combination of both a permitted form and a meaning.

Natural Classes

Suppose you were writing a grammar of English and wished to include all the generalities that children acquire about the set of phonemes and their allophones. One way of showing what speakers of the language know about the predictable aspects of speech is to include these generalities as **phonological rules** in the phonological component of the grammar. These are not the rules that someone teaches you in school or that you must obey because someone insists on it; they are rules that are known unconsciously and that express the phonological regularities of the language.

In English phonology, such rules determine the conditions under which vowels are nasalized or voiceless stops are aspirated. They are general rules, applying not to a single sound but to classes of sounds. They also apply to all the words in the vocabulary of the language, and they even apply to nonsense words that are not in the language but could enter it (e.g., *sint, peeg,* and *sparg,* which would be /sɪnt/, /pig/, and /sparg/ phonemically and [sĩnt], [pʰig], and [sparg] phonetically).

There are also less general rules found in all languages, and there may be exceptions to these general rules. But what is of greater interest is that, the more we examine the phonologies of the many thousands of languages of the world, the more we find similar phonological rules that apply to the same broad classes of sounds, such as the ones we have mentioned — nasals, voiceless stops, alveolars, labials, and so on.

For example, many languages of the world include the rule that nasalizes vowels before nasal consonants. One need not include a list of the individual sounds to which the rule applies or the sounds that result from its application. We stated the rule above as

Nasalize a vowel when it is followed by a nasal consonant in the same syllable.

This rule will apply to all vowel phonemes when they occur in a context before any segment marked [+nasal] and will add the feature [+nasal] to the feature matrix of the vowels.

Another rule that occurs frequently in the world's languages changes the place of articulation of nasal consonants to the place of articulation of a following consonant. Thus, an /n/ will become an [m] before a /p/ or /b/ and will become a velar [ŋ] before a /k/ or /g/. When two sequential segments agree in their place of artic-ulation, they are called **homorganic consonants**. This homorganic nasal rule occurs in Akan as well as in English and many other languages.

Many languages have rules that refer to [+voiced] and [–voiced] sounds. Note that the aspiration rule in English applies to the class of voiceless stops. As in the vowel nasality rule, we did not list the individual segments in the rule since it applies to all the voiceless stops /p/, /t/, and /k/, as well as /č/.

That we find such similar rules that apply to the same classes of sounds across languages is not surprising since such rules often have phonetic explanations and these classes of sounds are defined by phonetic features. For this reason, such classes are called **natural classes** of speech sounds.

> **A natural class is a group of sounds that share one or more distinctive features.**

Children find it easier to learn a rule (or construct it) that applies to a natural class of sounds; they do not have to remember the individual sounds, simply the features that these sounds share.

This fact about phonological rules and natural classes illustrates why individual phonemic segments are better regarded as combinations or complexes of features than as indissoluble whole segments. If such segments are not specified as feature matri-ces, then the similarities among /p/, /t/, and /k/ or /m/, /n/, and /ŋ/ would not be revealed. It should be just as easy for a child to learn a rule such as

> **(a) Nasalize vowels before /p/, /i/, or /z/.**

as to learn a rule such as

> **(b) Nasalize vowels before /m/, /n/, or /ŋ/.**

Rule (a) has no phonetic explanation, whereas rule (b) does. It is easier to lower the velum to produce a nasalized vowel in anticipation of a following nasal conso-nant than to prevent the velum from lowering before the consonant closure.

A natural class is a set of phonemes that can be defined by fewer features than any of its members. The class that includes the phonemes /p, t, k, b, d, g, m, n, ŋ, č, ǰ/ can be defined by specifying one feature, [–continuant]. The phoneme /p/ requires three feature specifications, as do the other phonemes in this set.

A class of sounds that can be defined by fewer features than another class of sounds is clearly more general. Thus, the class of [–continuant, –nasal] sounds is in some sense more natural than the class that includes all the non-nasal stops except /p/. The only way to refer to such a class is to list all the segments in that class. Try to do this with feature notation; you will see why such a class is far from natural.

This does not mean that no language has a rule that applies to a single sound or even to a class of stops excluding /p/. One does find complex rules in languages, including rules that apply to an individual member of a class, but rules pertaining to natural classes occur more frequently than other types of rules, and an explana-tion is provided for this fact by reference to phonetic properties.

A phonological segment may be a member of a number of classes; for example, /s/ is a member of the class of [+obstruent]s, [+consonantal]s, [+alveolar]s, [+coronal]s, [–stop]s, [+continuant]s, [+sibilant]s, and so on.

The major classes discussed in Chapter 5 are all natural classes referred to in phonological rules of all languages. They can also be specified by + and – feature values:

> [+CONSONANTAL] = consonants
> [–CONSONANTAL] = vowels

> [+SONORANT] = nasals, liquids, glides, vowels
> [–SONORANT] = stops and fricatives (OBSTRUENTS)

> [+SYLLABIC) = vowels, some liquids and nasals
> [–SYLLABIC) = consonants, glides, some liquids and nasals

All speech sounds can thus be specified as shown in Table 6.3.

Feature Specifications for North American English Consonants and Vowels

Using the phonetic properties or features provided in Chapter 5 and the additional features in this chapter, we can provide feature matrices for all the phonemes in English using the + or – value for each feature. One can then easily identify the members of each class of phonemes by selecting all the segments marked + or – for a single feature. Thus, the class of high vowels, /i, ɪ, u, ʊ/, are marked [+high] in the vowel feature chart of Table 6.4; the class of stops, /p, b, m, t, d, n, k, g, ŋ, č, ǰ/, are the phonemes marked [–continuant] on the consonant chart in Table 6.5.

The feature [±mid] is not required to distinguish each vowel. The vowels marked [+mid] are already distinguished from high and low vowels by being specified as [–high], [–low]. The stressed central vowels [a] and [ʌ] are sometimes specified as back vowels; if this were done, then the feature [±front] would not be necessary. We have included the features [mid] and [central] to show more clearly the

TABLE 6.3
Feature Specification of Major Natural Classes of Sounds

	Obstruents O	Nasals N	Liquids L	Glides G	Vowels V
Features					
Consonantal	+	+	+	–	–
Sonorant	–	+	+	+	+
Syllabic	–	+ / –	+ / –	–	+
Nasal	–	+	–	–	–

TABLE 6.4
Specification of Phonemic Features of North American Stressed Vowels

Features	i	ɪ	e	ɛ	æ	u	ʊ	o	ɔ	a	ɑ	ʌ
High	+	+	−	−	−	+	+	−	−	−	−	−
Mid	−	−	+	+	−	−	−	+	+	−	−	+
Low	−	−	−	−	+	−	−	−	−	+	+	−
Back	−	−	−	−	−	+	+	+	+	+	+	+
Central	−	−	−	−	−	−	−	−	−	+	−	+
Rounded	−	−	−	−	−	+	+	+	+	−	−	−
Tense/Long	+	−	+	−	−	+	−	+	−	−	+	−

phonetic quality of the vowel phonemes. Table 6.4 also distinguishes between the phones [a], [ɑ], and [ɔ], where they are phonetically but not phonemically distinct. Canadian English would include them as allophones of /a/.

More on Prosodic Phonology

Intonation

B.C. by permission of Johnny Hart and Creators Syndicate, Inc.

In Chapter 5, we discussed the use of pitch as a phonetic feature in reference to tone languages and intonation languages. In this chapter, we have discussed the use of phonetic features to distinguish meaning. We can now see that pitch can be a phonemic feature in languages such as Chinese, Thai, and Akan. Such relative pitches are referred to phonologically as contrasting **tones**. We also pointed out that there are languages that are not tone languages, such as English. Pitch may still play an important role in these languages. It is the **pitch contour** or **intonation** of the phrase or sentence that is important.

In English, syntactic differences may be shown by different intonation contours. We say *John is going* as a statement with a falling pitch but as a question with a rising pitch.

TABLE 6.5
Phonemic Features of North American Consonants

Features	p	b	m	t	d	n	k	g	ŋ	f	v	θ	ð	s	z	š	ž	č	ǰ	l	r	j	w	h
Consonantal	+	+	+	+	+	+	+	+	+	+	+	+	+	+	+	+	+	+	+	+	+	−	−	+
Sonorant	−	−	+	−	−	+	−	−	+	−	−	−	−	−	−	−	−	−	−	+	+	+	+	−
Syllabic	−	−	−/+	−	−	−/+	−	−	−/+	−	−	−	−	−	−	−	−	−	−	−/+	−/+	−	−	−
Nasal	−	−	+	−	−	+	−	−	+	−	−	−	−	−	−	−	−	−	−	−	−	−	−	−
Voiced	−	+	+	−	+	+	−	+	+	−	+	−	+	−	+	−	+	−	+	+	+	+	+	−
Continuant	−	−	−	−	−	−	−	−	−	+	+	+	+	+	+	+	+	−	−	+	+	+	+	+
Labial	+	+	+	−	−	−	−	−	−	+	+	−	−	−	−	−	−	−	−	−	−	−	+	−
Alveolar	−	−	−	+	+	+	−	−	−	−	−	−	−	+	+	−	−	−	−	+	+	−	−	−
Palatal	−	−	−	−	−	−	−	−	−	−	−	−	−	−	−	+	+	+	+	−	−	+	−	−
Velar	−	−	−	−	−	−	+	+	+	−	−	−	−	−	−	−	−	−	−	−	−	−	+	−
Coronal	−	−	−	+	+	+	−	−	−	−	−	+	+	+	+	+	+	+	+	+	+	+	−	−
Sibilant	−	−	−	−	−	−	−	−	−	−	−	−	−	+	+	+	+	+	+	−	−	−	−	−
Lateral	−	−	−	−	−	−	−	−	−	−	−	−	−	−	−	−	−	−	−	+	−	−	−	−
Anterior	+	+	+	+	+	+	−	−	−	+	+	+	+	+	+	−	−	−	−	+	+	−	−	−

Note: The [+voicing] feature value is redundant for English nasals, liquids, and glides (except for /h/) and could have been left blank for this reason. The feature specifications for [±coronal] and [±sibilant] are also redundant. These redundant, predictable feature specifications are provided simply to illustrate the segments in these natural classes. Note that we have not included the allophones [pʰ, tʰ, kʰ], since the aspiration is predictable at the beginning of syllables and these phones are not distinct phonemes in English.

A sentence that is ambiguous when written may be unambiguous when spoken:

(a) Tristram left directions for Isolde to follow.

If Tristram wanted Isolde to follow him, then the sentence would be pronounced with the rise in pitch on the first syllable of *follow*, followed by a fall in pitch, as in (b):

(b) <u>Tristram left directions for Isolde to</u>|follow.\\

The sentence can also mean that Tristram left a set of directions he wanted Isolde to use. If this is the intention, then the highest pitch comes on the second syllable of *directions*, as in (c):

(c) <u>Tristram left di</u>|rections|for Isolde to follow.

The way we have indicated pitch is of course highly oversimplified. Before the big rise in pitch, the voice does not remain on the same monotone low pitch. These pitch diagrams merely indicate when there is a special change in pitch.

Thus, pitch plays an important role in both tone languages and intonation languages but in different ways.

Word Stress

In English and many other languages, one or more of the syllables in each content word (words other than the "little words" *to, the, a, of,* and so on) are stressed. The stressed syllable is marked by an acute mark (´) in the following examples:

pérvert	(noun)	as in	My neighbour is a pervert.
pervért	(verb)	as in	Don't pervert the idea.
súbject	(noun)	as in	Let's change the subject.
subjéct	(verb)	as in	He'll subject us to criticism.

These minimal pairs show that stress is contrastive in English; it distinguishes between nouns and verbs.

In some words, more than one vowel is stressed, but if so then one of these stressed vowels receives greater stress than the others. We have indicated the most highly stressed vowel by an acute accent over the vowel (we say this vowel receives the **accent**, or *primary* **stress**, or *main* stress); the other stressed vowels are indicated by marking a grave accent (`) over the vowels (these vowels receive secondary stress):

rèsignátion	lìnguístics	sỳstemátic
fùndaméntal	ìntrodúctory	rèvolútion

Generally, speakers of a language know which syllable receives primary stress or accent, which receives secondary stress, and which syllables are not stressed at all; it is part of their knowledge of the language.

The stress pattern of a word may differ from dialect to dialect. For example, in most varieties of North American English, the word *láboratòry* has two stressed syllables; in one dialect of British English, it receives only one stress [ləbˈɔrətri].

Because the vowel qualities in English are closely related to whether they are stressed or not, the British vowels differ from the North American vowels in this word; in fact, in the British version, one vowel "drops out" completely because it is not stressed.

Just as stressed syllables in poetry reveal the metrical structure of the verse, so too phonological stress patterns relate to the metrical structure of a language.

There are a number of ways used to represent stress. Above we used grave and acute accent marks. We can also specify which syllable in the word is stressed by marking the syllable **s** if strongly stressed, **w** if weakly stressed, and leaving it unmarked if unstressed:

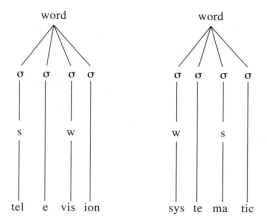

Stress is also sometimes shown by placing a 1 over the primary stressed syllable, placing a 2 over the secondary stressed syllable, and leaving the unstressed vowels unmarked:

2	1	2	1	1	2
fundamental		introductory		secondary	

Stress is a property of a syllable rather than a segment, so it is a prosodic or suprasegmental feature. Tone may also be a property of a syllable rather than a single vowel; it too, then, would be a suprasegmental feature.

To produce a stressed syllable, one may change the pitch (usually by raising it), make the syllable louder, or make it longer. We often use all three of these phonetic features to stress a syllable.

Sentence and Phrase Stress

When words are combined into phrases and sentences, one of the syllables receives greater stress than all others. That is, just as there is only one primary stress in a word spoken in isolation (e.g., in a list), so too only one of the vowels in a phrase (or sentence) receives primary stress or accent; all the other stressed vowels are "reduced"

© Howie Schneider.

to secondary stress. A syllable that receives the main stress when the word is not in a phrase may have only secondary stress in a phrase:

1	1	1	2		
tight + rope → tightrope					("a rope for acrobatics")
1	1	2	1		
tight + rope → tight rope					("a rope drawn taut")
1	1	1	2		
hot + dog → hotdog					("frankfurter")
1	1	2	1		
hot + dog → hot dog					("an overheated dog")
1	1	1	2		
red + coat → redcoat					("a British soldier")
1	1	2	1		
red + coat → red coat					("a coat that is red")
1	1	1	2		
red + chamber → Red Chamber					("the Canadian Senate")
1	1	2	1		
red + chamber → red chamber					("a room painted red")

In English, we place primary stress on an adjective followed by a noun when the two words are combined in a compound noun (usually, but not always, written as one word), but we place the stress on the noun when the words are not joined in this way. The differences between the pairs above are therefore predictable:

Compound Noun	**Adjective + Noun**
tightrope	tight rope
hotdog	hot dog
redcoat	red coat
Red Chamber	red chamber

These minimal pairs show that stress may be predictable if phonological rules include non-phonological information — that is, the phonology is not independent of the rest of the grammar. The stress differences between the noun and the verb pairs (*subject* as noun and verb) discussed in the previous section are also predictable from the word category.

The differences in the English sentences we used to illustrate intonation contours may also be described by referring to the word on which the main stress is placed. The main stress, we might notice, tends to fall on the same word that experiences a rise in pitch:

(a) Tristram left directions for Isolde to follow.

(b) Tristram left directions for Isolde to follow.

In sentence (a), the primary stress is on the word *follow*, and in (b) the primary stress is on *directions*.

The Rules of Phonology

No rule is so general which admits not some exception.
Robert Burton, *The Anatomy of Melancholy*

But that to come
Shall all be done by the rule.
William Shakespeare, *Antony and Cleopatra*

The relationship between the phonemic representations that are stored in one's mental lexicon and the phonetic representations that reflect the pronunciation of these words is rule-governed. These phonological rules relate the minimally specified phonemic representation to the phonetic representation and are part of a speaker's knowledge of the language. The phonemic representations are minimally specified in the mental grammar because some features or feature values are predictable. The **underspecification** reveals the redundancy of such features, a fact about the knowledge speakers have of the phonology.

The phonemic representation, then, should include only the non-predictable distinctive features of the string of phonemes that represent the words. The phonetic representation derived by applying these rules includes all the linguistically relevant phonetic aspects of the sounds. It does not include all the physical properties of the sounds of an utterance, because the physical signal may vary in many ways that have little to do with the phonological system. The absolute pitch of the sounds, the rate of speech, or its loudness are not linguistically significant. The phonetic transcription is therefore also an abstraction from the physical signal; it includes the non-variant phonetic aspects of the utterances, those features that remain relatively the same from speaker to speaker and from one time to another.

Although the specific rules of phonology differ from language to language, the kinds of rules, what they do, and the natural classes they refer to are the same cross-linguistically.

Assimilation Rules

We have seen that nasalization of vowels in English is non-phonemic because it is predictable by rule. The vowel nasalization rule is an **assimilation rule**; it assimilates one segment to another by "copying" or "spreading" a feature of a sequential phoneme on to its neighbouring segment, thus making the two phones more similar. Assimilation rules are, for the most part, caused by articulatory or physiological processes. There is a tendency when we speak to increase the **ease of articulation** — that is, to make it easier to move the articulators. We noted above that it is easier to lower the velum while a vowel is being pronounced before a nasal stop closure than to wait for the articulators to come together. We can state the vowel nasalization rule as

Nasalize vowels and diphthongs before nasals (within the same syllable).

This rule specifies the class of sounds affected by the rule:

vowels and diphthongs

It states what phonetic change will occur by applying the rule

Change phonemic oral vowels to phonetic nasal vowels.

And it specifies when the rule applies, the context or phonemic **environment**:

before nasals within the same syllable

All three kinds of intonation segments affected, phonemic environment, phonetic change — must be included in the statement of a phonological rule, or it would not explicitly state the regularities that constitute speakers' phonological knowledge.

Phonologists often use a shorthand notation to write rules, similar to the way scientists and mathematicians use symbols. Every physicist knows that $E = mc^2$ means "Energy equals mass times the square of the velocity of light." We can also use such notations to state the nasalization rule as

V → [+nasal]/_____[+nasal](C) \$

Similar to the way we use "=" instead of "equals" in mathematical equations and formulas, we will use an arrow "→" instead of "becomes" or "is" or "is changed to" to represent the change that the rule specifies. The segment to the left of the arrow is changed to whatever is on the right of the arrow in the specified environment. The rule applies if the nasal is the final consonant in the syllable or if it is followed by another consonant, as in *dam* [dæ̃m] and *damp* [dæ̃mp]. The optional final consonant is thus put in parentheses, which means that the segment may or may not be present in the environment.

What occurs on the left side of the arrow fulfils the first requirement for a rule: it specifies the class of sounds affected by the rule. What occurs on the right side of the arrow specifies the change that occurs, thus fulfilling the second requirement of a phonological rule.

To fulfil the third requirement of a rule — the phonological environment or context where the rule will apply — we can formalize the notion of "environment" or "in the environment" and the notions of "before" and "after," since it is also important to specify whether the vowels to be nasalized occur before or after a nasal. In this case, the [+nasal] segment in the context is followed by the syllable boundary symbol $ to show that the rule applies only if the nasal segment is in the same syllable. In some languages, nasalization occurs after rather than before nasal segments. We will use the following notations:

| / | is used to mean "in the environment of." |
| _____ | is placed before or after the relevant segment(s) that determine the change. |

The nasalization rule given in formal notation on the preceding page can be stated in words:

> **A vowel becomes or is nasalized in the environment before a nasal segment in the same syllable.**

Any rule written in formal notation can also be stated in words. The use of notation is, as stated above, a shorthand way of presenting the information. It also often reveals the function of the rule more explicitly. It is easy to see in the formal statement that this is an assimilation rule since the change to [+nasal] occurs before [+nasal] segments.

Assimilation rules in languages reflect what phoneticians often call **coarticulation** — the spreading of phonetic features either in anticipation of sounds or in the perseveration of articulatory processes. This "sloppiness" tendency may become regularized as rules of the language.

The following example illustrates how the English vowel nasalization rule applies to the phonemic representation of words and shows the assimilatory nature of the rule — that is, the feature value of the vowel in the phonemic representation changes from [−nasal] to [+nasal]:

	"Bob"			"Bomb"		
Phonemic representation	/b	a	b/	/b	a	m/
Nasality: phonemic feature value	−	−	−	−	−	+
Apply nasal rule	NA*				↓	
Nasality: phonetic feature value	−	−	−	−	+	+
Phonetic representation	[b	ɑ	b]	[b	ɑ̃	m]

*NA = "not applicable."

There are many other examples of assimilation rules in English and other languages. There is an optional ("**free variation**") rule in English that, particularly in fast speech, devoices the nasals and liquids in words such as *snow* /sno/ [sn̥o], *slow* /slo/ [sl̥o], *smart* /smart/ [sm̥art], *probe* /prob/ [pʰr̥ob], and so on. The feature

[–voiced] of the /s/ or /p/ carries over onto the following segment. Because voiceless nasals and liquids do not occur phonemically — do not contrast with voiced sonorants — the vocal cords need not react quickly. The devoicing will not change the meanings of the words; [slɑt] and [sl̥ɑt] both mean "slot."

Vowels may also become devoiced or voiceless in a voiceless environment. In Japanese, high vowels are devoiced when preceded and followed by voiceless obstruents; in words such as *sukiyaki*, the /u/ becomes [u̥]. This assimilation rule can be stated as follows:

$$\begin{bmatrix} \text{–consonantal} \\ \text{+syllabic} \end{bmatrix} \rightarrow [\text{–voiced}] / \begin{bmatrix} \text{–sonorant} \\ \text{–voiced} \end{bmatrix} \underline{\hspace{2em}} \begin{bmatrix} \text{–sonorant} \\ \text{–voiced} \end{bmatrix}$$

This rule states that any Japanese vowel (a segment that is non-consonantal and syllabic) becomes devoiced ([–voiced]) in the environment of, or when it occurs (/) between, voiceless obstruents. The rule applies most often to high vowels but may apply to other vowels as well. Notice that the dash occurs not immediately after the slash or at the end of the rule but between the segment matrices represented as [–sonorant, –voiced].

This rule includes the three kinds of information required:

(a)   the class of sounds affected: vowels ($\begin{bmatrix} \text{–consonantal} \\ \text{+syllabic} \end{bmatrix}$)

(b)   the phonemic environment: between two voiceless obstruents

($\begin{bmatrix} \text{–sonorant} \\ \text{–voiced} \end{bmatrix} \underline{\hspace{2em}} \begin{bmatrix} \text{–sonorant} \\ \text{–voiced} \end{bmatrix}$)

(c)   The phonetic change: devoicing $\begin{bmatrix} \text{–consonantal} \\ \text{+syllabic} \\ \text{+voiced} \end{bmatrix}$ becomes $\begin{bmatrix} \text{–consonantal} \\ \text{+syllabic} \\ \text{–voiced} \end{bmatrix}$

The rule does not specify the class of segments to the left of the arrow as [+voiced] because phonemically all vowels in Japanese are voiced. It therefore simply has to include the change on the right side of the arrow.

We can illustrate the application of this rule in Japanese as we did with the vowel nasalization rule in English:

	"Sukiyaki"							
Phonemic representation	/s	u	k	i	j	a	k	i/
Voicing: phonemic feature value	–	+	–	+	+	+	–	+
Apply devoicing rule		↓						
Voicing: phonetic feature value	–	–	–	+	+	+	–	+
Phonetic representation	[s	u̥	k	i	j	a	k	i]

Feature-Changing Rules

The English vowel nasalization and devoicing rules and the Japanese devoicing rule change feature specifications. That is, in English the [–nasal] value of phonemic vowels is changed to [+nasal] phonetically through a spreading process when the vowels occur before nasals. Vowels in Japanese are phonemically voiced, and the rule changes vowels that occur in the specified environment into phonetically voiceless segments.

The rules we have discussed are phonetically plausible, as are other assimilation rules, and can be explained by natural phonetic processes. This fact does not mean that all these rules have to occur in all languages. In fact, if they always occurred, then they would not have to be learned at all; they would apply automatically and universally and therefore would not have to be included in the grammar of any particular language. They are not, however, universal.

There is a nasal assimilation rule in Akan that nasalizes voiced stops when they follow nasal consonants:

| /ɔ bá/ | [ɔbá] | "he comes" | /ɔ ḿ bá/ | [ɔmmá] | "he doesn't come" |
| *he come* | | | *he not come* | | |

The /b/ of the verb "come" becomes an [m] when it follows the negative /m/.

This assimilation rule also has a phonetic explanation; the velum is lowered to produce the nasal consonant and remains down during the following stop. Although it is a phonetically "natural" assimilation rule, it does not occur in the grammar of English; the word *amber*, for example, shows an [m] followed by a [b]. A child learning Akan must learn this rule, just as a child learning English learns to nasalize all vowels before nasal consonants, a rule that does not occur in the grammar of Akan.

Assimilation rules such as the ones we have discussed in English, Japanese, and Akan often have the function of changing the value of phonemic features. They are **feature-changing** or **feature-spreading rules**. Although nasality is non-distinctive for vowels in English, it is a distinctive feature for consonants, and the nasalization rule therefore changes a feature value.

The Akan rule is a feature-changing rule that states that [m] is an allophone of /b/ as well as an allophone of /m/:

There is no one-to-one relationship between phonemes and their allophones.

This fact can be illustrated in another way:

| Akan Phonemes | /b/ | /m/ |
| Akan Phones | [b] | [m] |

We will provide more examples of this one-to-many or many-to-one mapping between phonemes and allophones below.

Dissimilation Rules

It is understandable why assimilation rules are found in so many languages. As pointed out, they permit greater ease of articulation. It might seem strange, then, to learn that one also finds **dissimilation rules** in languages, rules in which a segment becomes *less* similar to another segment rather than more similar. But such rules do exist. They also have a "natural" explanation, often from the point of view of the hearer rather than the speaker. That is, in listening to speech, if sounds are too similar, we may miss the contrast.

A "classic" example of dissimilation occurred in Latin, and the results of this process show up in modern-day English. There was a derivational suffix *-alis* in Latin that was added to nouns to form adjectives. When the suffix was added to a noun that contained the liquid /l/, the suffix was changed to *-aris* — that is, the liquid /l/ was changed to the liquid /r/. These words came into English as adjectives ending in *-al* or, in their dissimilated forms, in *-ar,* as shown in the following examples:

-al	**-ar**
anecdot-al	angul-ar
annu-al	annul-ar
ment-al	column-ar
pen-al	perpendicul-ar
spiritu-al	simil-ar
ven-al	vel-ar

As *columnar* illustrates, the /l/ need not be the consonant directly preceding the dissimilated segment.

Dissimilation rules are quite rare, but they do occur, as shown by the examples above. The African language Kikuyu also has a dissimilation rule in which a prefix added to a verb begins with a velar fricative if the verb begins with a stop but with a velar stop if the verb begins with a continuant.

Feature Addition Rules

Some phonological rules are neither assimilation nor dissimilation rules. The aspiration rule in English, which aspirates a voiceless stop at the beginning of a syllable, simply adds a non-distinctive feature. As we did in the nasalization rule earlier, we can use the symbol $ to represent a syllable boundary. Generally, aspiration occurs only if the following vowel is stressed. The /p/ in *pit* and *repeat* is aspirated, but the /p/ in *in $ spect* or *com $ pass* is usually unaspirated (although if aspirated it will not change meaning since aspiration is non-phonemic). Using the feature [+stress] to indicate a stressed syllable and to symbolize stressed vowels, the aspiration rule may be stated as follows:

$$\begin{bmatrix} -\text{continuant} \\ -\text{voiced} \end{bmatrix} \rightarrow [+\text{aspirated}] \,/\, \$ \rule{1cm}{0.4pt} \begin{bmatrix} -\text{consonantal} \\ +\text{stress} \end{bmatrix}$$

Voiceless stops ([–continuant, –voiced] segments) become (are) aspirated when they occur syllable initially before stressed vowels (/$___ V́).

Aspiration is neither present nor absent in any phonemic feature matrices in English. Assimilation rules do not add new features but change phonemic feature values, whereas the aspiration rule adds a new feature not present in phonemic matrices.

Remember that /p/ and /b/ (and all such symbols) are simply cover symbols that do not reveal the phonemic distinctions. In the phonemic and phonetic feature matrices, these differences are made explicit, as shown in the following phonemic matrices:

	/p/	/b/	
Consonantal	+	+	
Continuant	−	−	
Labial	+	+	
Voiced	−	+	← distinctive difference

The non-distinctive feature "aspiration" is not included in these phonemic representations because aspiration is predictable.

Segment Deletion and Addition Rules

In addition to assimilation and dissimilation (feature-changing) and feature-addition rules, **phonological rules** can delete or add entire phonemic segments. In French, for example, as demonstrated by Sanford Schane (1968), word-final consonants are deleted when the following word begins with a consonant (oral, nasal, or liquid), but they are retained when the following word begins with a vowel or a glide, as illustrated in Table 6.6.

TABLE 6.6
Distribution of Word-Final Consonants in French

Before a consonant:	/pətit tablo/	[pəti tablo]	"small picture"
	/noz tablo/	[no tablo]	"our pictures"
Before a liquid:	/pətit livr/	[pəti livr]	"small book"
	/noz livr/	[no livr]	"our books"
Before a nasal:	/pətit navet/	[pəti navɛ]	"small turnip"
	/noz navets/	[no navɛ]	"our turnips"
Before a vowel:	/pətit ami/	[pətit ami]	"small friend"
	/noz amis/	[noz ami]	"our friends"
Before a glide:	/pətit wazo/	[pətit wazo]	"small bird"
	/noz wazo/	[noz wazo]	"our birds"

Sanford Schane, *French Phonology and Morphology* (Cambridge, MA: MIT Press, 1968). By permission of The MIT Press.

Table 6.6 represents a general rule in French applying to all word-final consonants. We distinguished these five classes of sounds by the features *consonantal, sonorant, syllabic,* and *nasal.* We noted that oral and nasal consonants and liquids were specified as [+consonantal] and vowels and glides as [–consonantal]. We can now see why such "super classes" or "cover features" are important. Using the symbol Ø to represent the "null" unit (or zero) and # as "word boundary," we can state the French rule simply as

[+consonantal] → Ø/ _____ ## **[+consonantal]**

This rule can be "translated" into words as

A consonantal segment (obstruent, liquid, or nasal) is deleted or becomes null (→Ø) in the environment (/) at the end of a word (_____ #) that is followed by a word beginning with an obstruent or liquid or nasal (# [+consonantal]).

or simply as

Delete a consonant before a word beginning with a consonant.

In Schane's complete analysis, many words that are pronounced with a final consonant actually have a vowel as their word-final segment in phonemic representation. The vowel prevents the rule of word-final consonant deletion from applying. The vowel itself is deleted by another, later rule. Given this rule in the grammar of French, *petit* would be phonemically /pətit/. It need not be additionally represented as /pəti/, because the rule determines the phonetic shape of the word.

Deletion rules also show up as optional rules in fast speech or casual speech in English. They result, for example, in the common contractions changing *he is* [hi ɪz] to *he's* [hiz] or *I will* [aj wɪl] to *I'll* [ajl]. In ordinary speech, most of us also "delete" the unstressed vowels that are shown in bold type in words such as the following:

myst**e**ry   gen**e**ral   mem**o**ry   fun**e**ral   vig**o**rous   Barb**a**ra

These words in casual speech sound as if they were written

mystry   genral   memry   funral   vigrous   Barbra

Phonological rules, therefore, can be either optional or obligatory.

Phonological rules may also insert consonants or vowels, which is called **epenthesis**. In some cases, epenthesis occurs to "fix up" non-permitted sequences. In English morphemes, nasal/non-nasal **consonant clusters** must be homorganic, both labial, both alveolar, or both velar. We find /m/ before /p/ and /b/ as in *ample* and *amble*; /n/ before /t/ and /d/ in *gentle* and *gender*; and /ŋ/ before /k/ and /g/ in *ankle* and *angle*. (You may not realize that the nasal in the last two words has a velar articulation because the spelling can obscure this fact. If you pronounce these words carefully, you will see that the back of your tongue touches the velum in the articulation of both the *n* and the *k*.) /m/ before /t, d, k, g/ does not occur morpheme internally, nor does /n/ before /p, b, k, g/ or /ŋ/ before /p, b, t, d/. Because of this sequential constraint, many speakers pronounce the name *Fromkin* with an epenthetic [p], as if it were written *Frompkin*. She also receives letters addressed in this way.

The same process of epenthesis occurred in the history of English. The earlier form of the word *empty* had no *p*. Similarly, a /d/ was inserted in the word *ganra* to give us the modern *gander* and a /d/ at the end of *soun* to produce *sound*.

In the history of Spanish, many words that now start with an *e* followed by an [s] followed by another consonant came from Latin words that were not vowel initial. For example, the Spanish word *escribir*, "to write," was *scribere* in Latin (the *sc* representing /sk/), and the Spanish word for "school," *escuela*, comes from the Latin word *schola* through epenthesis. Similarly, the French *étoile* derived from the Latin *stella*.

Movement (Metathesis) Rules

Phonological rules may also move phonemes from one place in the string to another. Such rules are called **metathesis** rules. They are less common, but they do exist. In some dialects of English, for example, the word *ask* is pronounced [æks], but the word *asking* is pronounced [æskɪn] or [æskɪŋ]. In these dialects, a metathesis rule "switches" the /s/ and /k/ in certain contexts. In Old English, the verb was *aksian*, with the /k/ preceding the /s/. A historical metathesis rule switched these two consonants, producing *ask* in most dialects of English. Children's speech shows many cases of metathesis (which are later corrected as the child approaches the adult grammar): *aminal* [æmənəl] for *animal* and *pusketti* [pʰəskɛti] for *spaghetti* are common children's pronunciations.

In Hebrew, there is a metathesis rule that reverses a pronoun-final consonant with the first consonant of the following verb if the verb starts with a sibilant. These reversals are in "reflexive" verb forms, as shown in the following examples:

Non–Sibilant-Initial Verbs		Sibilant-Initial Verbs	
kabel	"to accept"	tsadek	"to justify"
lehit-kabel	"to be accepted"	lehits-tadek	"to apologize"
		(*not* *lehit-tsadek)	
pater	"to fire"	šameš	"to use for"
lehit-pater	"to resign"	lehiš-tameš	"to use"
		(*not* *lehit-šameš)	
bayeš	"to shame"	sader	"to arrange"
lehit-bayeš	"to be shamed"	lehis-tader	"to arrange oneself"
		(*not* *lehit-sader)	

We see, then, that phonological rules have a number of different functions, among which are the following:

(1) **Change feature values** (vowel nasalization rule in English).
(2) **Add new features** (aspiration in English).
(3) **Delete segments** (final consonant deletion in French).
(4) **Add segments** (vowel insertion in Spanish).
(5) **Reorder segments** (metathesis rule in Hebrew).

These rules, when applied to the phonemic representations of words and phrases, result in phonetic forms that differ from the phonemic forms. If such differences were unpredictable, we would find it difficult to explain how we can understand what we hear or how we produce utterances that represent the meanings we wish to convey. The more we look at languages, however, the more we see that many aspects of the phonetic forms of utterances that appear at first to be irregular and unpredictable are actually rule-governed. We learn, or construct, these rules when we are learning the language as children. The rules represent "patterns" or general principles.

From One to Many and from Many to One

The discussion on how phonemic representations of utterances are realized phonetically included an example from the African Ghanaian language Akan to show that the relationship between a phoneme and its allophonic realization may be complex. The same phone may be an allophone of two or more phonemes, as [m] was shown to be an allophone of both /b/ and /m/ in Akan.

We can also illustrate this complex mapping relationship in English. Consider the boldfaced vowels in the following pairs of words:

	A		**B**	
/i/	compete	[i]	competition	[ə]
/ɪ/	medicinal	[ɪ]	medicine	[ə]
/e/	maintain	[e]	maintenance	[ə]
/ɛ/	telegraph	[ɛ]	telegraphy	[ə]
/æ/	analysis	[æ]	analytic	[ə]
/a/	solid	[ɑ]	solidity	[ə]
/o/	phone	[o]	phonetic	[ə]
/u/	Talmudic	[u]	Talmud	[ə]

In column A, all the boldfaced vowels are stressed vowels with a variety of different vowel phones; in column B, all the boldfaced unstressed vowels are pronounced [ə]. How can one explain the fact that the same root morphemes that occur in both words of the pairs have different pronunciations?

In the chapter on morphology, we defined a morpheme as a sound–meaning unit. Changing either would make a different morpheme. It doesn't seem plausible (nor is it necessary) for speakers of English to represent these root morphemes with distinct phonemic forms if there is some general rule that relates the stressed vowels in column A to the unstressed schwa vowel [ə] in column B.

Speakers of English know (unconsciously of course) that one can derive one word from another by the addition of derivational morphemes. This is illustrated above by adding -ition and -ance to verb roots to form nouns or -al and -ic to nouns to form adjectives. In English, the syllable that is stressed depends to a great extent on the phonemic structure of the word, the number of syllables, and so on. In a number of cases, the addition of derivational suffixes changes the stress pattern of the word, and the vowel that was stressed in the root morpheme becomes unstressed in the derived form. (The stress rules are rather complex and will not be detailed in this introductory text.) When a vowel is unstressed in English, it is pronounced as [ə], which is a **reduced vowel**.

All the root morphemes of column A are represented phonemically by their value when stressed. A simple rule predicts that their vowels are changed to [ə] when unstressed. We can conclude, then, that [ə] is an allophone of all English vowel phonemes. The rule to derive the schwa can be stated simply as

Change a vowel to an [ə] when it is unstressed.

This rule is oversimplified, because when an unstressed vowel occurs as the final segment of some words it retains its full vowel quality, as shown in words such as *confetti, motto,* and *democracy.* In some dialects, all unstressed vowels, including final vowels, are reduced.

The rule that "reduces" unstressed vowels to schwas is another example of a rule that changes feature values.

In a phonological description of a language that we do not know, it is not always possible to determine from the phonetic transcription what the phonemic representation is. However, given the phonemic representation and the phonological rules, we can always derive the correct phonetic transcription. Of course, in our mental grammars, this derivation is no problem, because the words are listed phonemically and because we know the rules of the language.

Another example will illustrate this aspect of phonology. In English, /t/ and /d/ are both phonemes, as is illustrated by the minimal pairs *tie/die* and *bat/bad*. When /t/ or /d/ occurs between a stressed and an unstressed vowel, they both become a flap [D]. The IPA symbol for the flap is [ɾ]. For many speakers of English, *writer* and *rider* are pronounced identically as [rajDər], yet these speakers know that *writer* has a phonemic /t/ because of *write* /rajt/, whereas *rider* has a phonemic /d/ because of *ride* /rajd/. Canadians almost always distinguish between *writer* and *rider* on the basis of the diphthong. The "flap rule" may be stated informally:

An alveolar stop becomes a voiced flap when preceded by a stressed vowel and followed by an unstressed vowel.

The application of this rule is illustrated as follows:

Phonemic representation	write	writer	ride	rider
	/rajt/	/rajt + ər/	/rajd/	/rajd + ər/
		↓		↓
Apply rule	NA*	D	NA	D
		↓		↓
Phonetic representation		[rʌjDar]		[rajDar]

*NA = "not applicable."

The underlying distinction between /t/ and /d/ in these two words is evident in the way they are treated in many varieties of Canadian English, in which the allophone of /aj/ before [t] is [ʌj] and that before [d] is [aj]. When the medial stop became the flap [D], the diphthong [ʌj] remained, thus contrasting *writer* as [rʌjDər] as opposed to *rider* as [rajDər]. Now the contrast between the consonant phonemes /t/ and /d/ is indicated by the distinction between the vowel allophones, a paradox first pointed out by Martin Joos (1942) and labelled "Canadian raising" by J. Chambers (1973). For further discussion of this feature of Canadian English, see Chapter 7.

We are omitting other phonetic details that are also determined by phonological rules, such as the fact that in *ride* the vowel is slightly longer than in *write* because it is followed by a voiced [d], which is a phonetic rule in many languages. We are using the example only to illustrate the fact that two distinct phonemes may be realized phonetically by the same phone.

Such cases show that we cannot arrive at a phonological analysis by simply inspecting the phonetic representation of utterances. If we just looked for minimal pairs as the only evidence for phonology, we would have to conclude that [D] is a phoneme in English because it contrasts phonetically with other phonetic units: *riper* [rʌjpər], *rhymer* [rãjmər], *riser* [rajzər], and so forth. Grammars are much more complex than this pairing shows. The fact that *write* and *ride* change their phonetic forms when suffixes are added shows that there is an intricate mapping between phonemic representations of words and phonetic pronunciations.

Notice that in the cases of the "schwa rule" and the "flap rule" the allophones derived from the different phonemes by rule are different in features from all other phonemes in the language. That is, there is no [D] phoneme, but there is a [D] phone. This was also true of aspirated voiceless stops and nasalized vowels. The set of phones is larger than the set of phonemes.

The English "flap rule" also illustrates an important phonological process called **neutralization**; the voicing contrast between /t/ and /d/ is **neutralized** in the specified environment. That is, /t/ never contrasts with /d/ in the environment between a stressed and an unstressed vowel.

Similar rules showing there is no one-to-one relation between phonemes and phones are found in other languages. In both Russian and German, when voiced obstruents occur at the end of a word or syllable, they become voiceless. Both voiced and voiceless obstruents do occur in German as phonemes, as is shown by the following minimal pair:

      tier   [ti:r]   "animal"   dir   [di:r]   "to you"

At the end of a word, however, only [t] occurs; the words meaning "bundle," *Bund* /bʊnd/, and "colourful," *bunt* /bʊnt/, are phonetically identical and pronounced [bũnt].

The German devoicing rule, like the vowel reduction rule in English and the homorganic nasal rule, changes the specifications of features. In German, the phonemic representation of the final stop in *Bund* is /d/, specified as [+voiced]; it is changed by rule to [–voiced] to derive the phonetic [t] in word-final position.

This rule in German further illustrates that we cannot decide what the phonemic representation of a word is, given only the phonetic form; [bũnt] can be derived from either /bʊnd/ or /bʊnt/. However, given the phonemic representations and the rules of the language, the phonetic forms are automatically derived.

The Function of Phonological Rules

The function of the phonological rules in a grammar is to provide the phonetic information necessary for the pronunciation of utterances. We can illustrate this point in the following way:

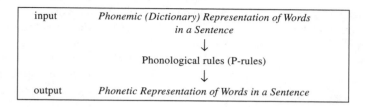

input	*Phonemic (Dictionary) Representation of Words in a Sentence*
	↓
	Phonological rules (P-rules)
	↓
output	*Phonetic Representation of Words in a Sentence*

The input to the P-rules is the phonemic representation; the P-rules apply to or operate on the phonemic strings and produce as output the phonetic representation.

The application of rules in this way is called a **derivation**. We have given a number of examples of derivations, which show how phonemically oral vowels become nasalized, how phonemically unaspirated voiceless stops become aspirated, how contrastive voiced and voiceless alveolar stops in English merge to become flaps, and how German voiced obstruents are devoiced. A derivation is thus an explicit way of showing both the effects of a phonological rule and the function of phonological rules (P-rules) in a grammar.

All the examples of derivations we have considered so far show the applications of just one phonological rule. It must be the case, however, that more than one rule may apply to a word. For example, the word *tempest* is phonemically /tɛmpɛst/ (as shown by the pronunciation of *tempestuous* [tʰɛ̃mpʰɛsčuəs]) but phonetically [tʰɛ̃mpəst]. Three rules apply to it: the aspiration rule, the vowel nasalization rule, and the schwa rule. We can derive the phonetic form from the phonemic representation as follows:

Underlying phonemic representation	/	t	ɛ	m	p	ɛ	s	t	/	
Aspiration rule		tʰ								
Nasalization rule			ɛ̃							
Schwa rule						ə				
Surface phonetic representation	[	tʰ	ɛ̃	m	p	ə	s	t	]	

We are using phonetic symbols instead of matrices in which the feature values are changed. These derivatives are equivalent, however, as long as we understand that a phonetic symbol is a *cover term* representing a matrix with all distinctive features marked either + or − (unless, of course, the feature is non-distinctive, such as the nasality value for phonemic vowels in English).

Slips of the Tongue: Evidence for Phonological Rules

"Slips of the tongue" or "speech errors" in which we deviate in some way from the intended utterance show phonological rules in action. Some of these slips are called **spoonerisms**, after William Archibald Spooner, a distinguished head of an Oxford college in the early 1900s, who is reported to have referred to Queen Victoria as "that queer old dean" instead of "that dear old queen" and berated his class of students by saying "You have hissed my mystery lecture" instead of the intended "You have missed my history lecture" and "You have tasted the whole worm" instead of "You have wasted the whole term." We all make speech errors, however, and they tell us interesting things about language and its use. Consider the following speech errors:

	Intended Utterance	**Actual Utterance**
(1)	gone to seed	god to seen
	[gãn tə sid]	[gɑd tə sĩn]
(2)	stick in the mud	smuck in the tid
	[stɪk ĩn ðə mʌd]	[smʌk ĩn ðə tʰɪd]
(3)	speech production	preach seduction
	[spič pʰrədʌkšə̃n]	[pʰrič sədʌkšə̃n]

In the first example, the final consonants of the first and third words were reversed. Notice that the reversal of the consonants also changed the nasality of the vowels. The vowel [ã] in the intended utterance is replaced by [ɑː]; in the actual utterance, the nasalization was "lost," because the vowel no longer occurred before a nasal consonant. The vowel in the third word, which was the non-nasal [i] in the intended utterance, became [ĩ] in the error, because it was followed by /n/. The nasalization rule applied.

In the other two errors, we see the application of the aspiration rule. In the intended *stick*, the /t/ would have been realized as unaspirated because it is not syllable initial; when it was switched with the /m/ in *mud*, it was pronounced as the aspirated [tʰ], because it occurred initially. The third example also illustrates the application of the aspiration rule in performance.

The Pronunciation of Morphemes

We noted that a single morpheme may have different pronunciations — that is, different phonetic forms — in different contexts. Thus, *write* /rajt/ is pronounced [rajt] but is pronounced [rʌjDr̩] in Canadian English and [rajDr̩] in most other North American dialects when the suffix *-er* is added.

We also saw that in French a morpheme such as /noz/, meaning "our," is pronounced [no] before words beginning with [+consonantal] sounds and as [noz] before word-initial [–consonantal] sounds.

Furthermore, in English, **underlying** phonemic vowels "reduce" to schwa [ə] when they are unstressed. The particular phonetic forms of some morphemes are determined by regular phonological rules that refer only to the phonemic context, as is true of the alternative vowel forms of the following sets:

m[ɛ]l[ə]dy	h[ɑ]rm[ə]ny	s[ɪ]mph[ə]ny
m[ə]l[o]dious	h[ɑ]rm[o]nious	s[ɪ]mph[o]nious
m[ə]l[ɑ]dic	h[ɑ]rm[ɑ]nic	s[ɪ]mph[ɑ]nic

The vowel rules that determine these pronunciations are rather complicated and beyond the scope of this text. The examples are presented simply to show that the morphemes in "melody," "harmony," and "symphony" vary phonetically in these words.

Another example of a morpheme in English with different phonetic forms is the plural morpheme. In column A, all the nouns end in voiced non-sibilant sounds, and to form their plurals you add the voiced [z]. All the words in column B end in voiceless non-sibilant sounds, and you add a voiceless [s]. The words in column C end in both voiced and voiceless sibilants, which form their plurals with the insertion of a schwa followed by [z]. This is another example of an epenthesis rule. The nouns in column D are irregular, and the plural forms must be memorized:

A	**B**	**C**	**D**
cab	cap	bus	child
cad	cat	bush	ox
bag	back	buzz	mouse
love	cuff	garage	sheep
lathe	faith	match	criterion
cam		badge	
can			
bang			
call			
bar			
spa			
boy			
add [z]	**add [s]**	**add [əz]**	

Children do not have to learn the plural rule by memorizing the individual sounds that require the [z] or [s] or [əz] plural ending, because these sounds form natural classes. A grammar that included lists of these sounds would not reveal the regularities in the language or what a speaker knows about the regular plural formation rule.

The regular plural rule does not work for a word such as *child*, which in the plural is *children*, or for *ox*, which becomes *oxen*, or for *sheep*, which is unchanged phonologically in the plural. *Child, ox*, and *sheep* are exceptions to the regular rule. We learn these exceptional plurals when learning the language, often after we have constructed or discovered the regular rule, which occurs at a very early age. The late Harry Hoijer, a well-known anthropological linguist, used to play a game with his two-year-old daughter. He would say a noun, and she would give him the plural form if he said the singular and the singular if she heard the plural. One day he said *ox* [ɑks], and she responded [ɑk], apparently not knowing the word and thinking that the [s] at the end must be the plural suffix. Children also often "regularize" exceptional forms, saying *mouses* and *sheeps*.

If the grammar represented each unexceptional or regular word in its singular and plural forms — for example, *cat* /kæt/, *cats* /kæts/; *cap* /kæp/, *caps* /kæps/; and so on — it would imply that the plurals of *cat* and *cap* were as irregular as the plurals of *child* and *ox*. Of course, they are not. If a new toy appeared on the market called a *glick* /glɪk/, a young child who wanted two of them would ask for two *glicks* /glɪks/ and not two *glicken*, even if the child had never heard the word *glicks*. The child knows the regular rule to form plurals. An experiment conducted by the linguist Jean Berko Gleason showed that very young children can apply this rule to words they have never heard. A grammar that describes such knowledge (the internalized mental grammar) must then include the general rule.

This rule, which determines the phonetic representation or pronunciation of the plural morpheme, is somewhat different from some of the other phonological rules we have discussed. The "aspiration rule" in English applies to a word whenever the phonological description is met; it is not the case, for example, that a /t/ is aspirated only if it is part of a particular morpheme or only in nouns or adjectives. The "flap rule," which changes the phonetic forms of the morphemes *write* and *ride* when a suffix is added, is also completely automatic, depending solely on the phonological environment. The plural rule, however, applies only to the inflectional plural morpheme. To see that it is not "purely" phonological in nature, consider the following words:

race	[res]	ray	[re]	ray + pl.	[rez]	*[res]
sauce	[sɑs]	saw	[sɑ]	saw + pl.	[sɑz]	*[sɑs]
rice	[rajs]	rye	[raj]	rye + pl.	[rajz]	*[rajs]

The examples show that the [z] in the plural is not determined by the phonological context, because in an identical context an [s] occurs. It applies only to certain morphemes.

Morphophonemics

THE BORN LOSER reprinted by permission of Newspaper Enterprise Association, Inc.

The rule that determines the phonetic form of the plural morpheme is a **morphophonemic rule**, because its application is determined by both the morphology and the phonology. When a morpheme has alternative phonetic forms, these forms are called **allomorphs** by some linguists. [z], [s], and [əz] would be allomorphs of the regular plural morpheme and would be determined by rule.

To show how such a rule may be applied, assume that the regular, productive, plural morpheme has the phonological form /z/, with the meaning "plural." The regular "plural rule" can be stated in a simple way:

(a) Insert an [ə] before the plural ending when a regular noun ends in a sibilant —
/s/, /z/, /š/, /ž/, /č/, or /ǰ/.

(b) Change the voiced /z/ to voiceless [s] when it is preceded by a voiceless sound.

If neither (a) nor (b) applies, then /z/ will be realized as [z]; no segments will be added, and no features will be changed.

	bus + pl.	*butt* + pl.	*bug* + pl.
Phonemic Representation	/bʌs + z/ ↓	/bʌt + z/ ↓	/bʌg + z/
apply rule (a)	ə	NA*↓	NA
apply rule (b)	NA	s	NA
Phonetic Representation	[bʌsəz]	[bʌts]	[bʌgz]

*NA = "not applicable."

The plural formation rule will derive the phonetic forms of plurals for all regular nouns (remember, this plural is /z/).

As we have formulated these rules, (a) must be applied before (b). If we applied the two parts of the rule in reverse order, then we would derive incorrect phonetic forms:

Phonemic Representation	/bʌs + z/ ↓
apply rule (b)	↓ s
apply rule (a)	ə
Phonetic Representation	*[bʌsəs]

An examination of the rule for the formation of the past tense of verbs in English shows some interesting parallels with the plural formation of nouns.

A	**B**	**C**	**D**
grab	reap	state	be
hug	peak	raid	run
seethe	unearth		sing
love	huff		have
buzz	kiss		go
rouge	wish		hit
judge	pitch		
fan			
ram			
long			
kill			
care			
tie			
bow			
hoe			
add [d]	**add [t]**	**add [əd]**	

The productive regular past tense morpheme in English is /d/ phonemically but [d] (column A), [t] (column B), or [əd] (column C) phonetically, again depending on the final phoneme of the verb to which it is attached. D-column verbs are exceptions.

The past tense rule in English, like the plural formation rule, must include morphological information. Notice that after a vowel or diphthong the form of the past tense is always [d], even though no phonological rule would be violated if a [t] were added, as shown by the words *tight, bout,* and *rote.* When the word is a verb, and when the final alveolar represents the past tense morpheme, however, it must be a voiced [d] and not a voiceless [t]. For this reason, /d/ is taken as the normal, unmarked representation of the past tense morpheme. It is the default value of the past tense morpheme — what the morpheme is realized as when it is not realized as something else — that is, [t] or [əd]. For similar reasons, /z/ is taken as the normal, unmarked representation of the plural morpheme of nouns. Both [s] and [z] can occur after vowels and diphthongs, as in *ice/eyes* and *race/raze.* When the word is a noun, and when the final alveolar sibilant represents the plural morpheme, it must be a voiced [z] and not a voiceless [s].

There is a plausible explanation for why an [ə] is inserted in the past tense of regular verbs ending with alveolar stops (and in nouns ending with sibilants). Because we do not contrast long and short consonants in English, it is difficult for English speakers to perceive a difference in consonantal length. If we added a [z] to *squeeze,* then we would get [skwizz], which would be hard for English speakers to distinguish from [skwiz]; similarly, if we added a [d] to *load,* then it would be [lodd] phonetically in the past and [lod] in the present, which would also be difficult to perceive.

More Sequential Constraints

Some of the sequential constraints on phonemes that were discussed previously may show up as morphophonemic rules. The English homorganic nasal constraint applies between some morphemes as well as within a morpheme. The negative prefix *in-*, which, like *un-*, means "not," has three allomorphs:

[ĭn]	before vowels:	inexcusable, inattentive, inorganic
	and alveolars:	intolerable, indefinable, insurmountable
[ĭm]	before labials:	impossible, imbalance
[ĭŋ]	before velars:	incomplete, inglorious

The pronunciation of this morpheme is often revealed by the spelling as *im-* when it is prefixed to morphemes beginning with /p/ or /b/. Because we have no letter "ŋ" in our alphabet (although it exists in alphabets used in other languages), the velar [ŋ] is written as *n* in words such as *incomplete.* You may not realize that you pronounce the *n* in *inconceivable, inglorious, incongruous,* and other such words as [ŋ] because your homorganic nasal rule is as unconscious as other rules in your grammar. It is the job of linguists and phoneticians to bring such rules to consciousness or to reveal them as part of the grammar. If you say these words in normal tempo without pausing after the *in-*, you should feel the back of your tongue rise to touch the velum.

In Akan, the negative morpheme also has three nasal allomorphs: [m] before /p/, [n] before /t/, and [ŋ] before /k/, as is shown in the following cases:

mɪ pɛ	"I like"	mɪ mpɛ	"I don't like"
mɪ tɪ	"I speak"	mɪ ntɪ	"I don't speak"
mɪ kɔ	"I go"	mɪ ŋkɔ	"I don't go"

We see, then, that one morpheme may have different phonetic forms or allomorphs. We have also seen that more than one morpheme may occur in the language with the same meaning but in different forms — such as *in-, un-,* and *not* (all meaning "not"). It is not possible to predict which of these forms will occur, so they are separate, synonymous morphemes. It is only when the phonetic form is predictable by general rule that we find different phonetic forms of a single morpheme.

The nasal homorganic rule is a **feature-changing rule**. It can be stated simply as

> **Change the place of articulation of a nasal consonant so that it agrees with the place feature value of a following consonant.**

In other words, nasal consonants agree in place of articulation with a following consonant.

Given this rule, we can represent this *in-* negative prefix morpheme by the phonemic representation /ɪn/. Before vowels and before morphemes beginning with /t/ or /d/, the homorganic nasal rule will change nothing since the rule is not violated. The morpheme will be represented by the allomorph [ɪ̃n] (after the vowel nasalization rule applies), as in the words *indecision, interminable,* and *inoperative.* Before a morpheme beginning with a labial consonant /b/ or /p/, the alveolar feature of /n/ will be changed by the rule to agree with the place of articulation of the labials, as in *impossible* and *impertinent.* Similarly, this feature-changing rule will assimilate the /n/ in /ɪn-/ to a velar nasal before morphemes beginning with /k/ or /g/ in words such as *incoherent.*

Deriving all forms of the morpheme from /ɪn-/ is the simplest way of revealing this morphological/phonological knowledge. One could represent the morpheme as /ɪm-/ or /ɪŋ/ instead. But the rule would then have to be complicated:

> **Change the place of articulation of a nasal consonant so that it agrees with the place feature value of a following consonant, and change the nasal consonant to [n] before a vowel.**

This will derive the correct forms of the morpheme but in a more complex fashion than is needed. Rule statements should be as simple and elegant as possible. This principle, known as *Occam's razor,* applies not just in phonology but also in all science. In essence, the simpler the rule, the more general the explanation.

Thus, when two allophones can be derived from one phoneme, one selects as the underlying segment the allophone that makes the rules and the phonetic feature matrices as simple as possible. For example, deriving the unaspirated and aspirated voiceless stops in English from an underlying /p/ makes aspiration redundant and unnecessary as a phonetic feature value. If /pʰ/ were the phoneme, then the phonetic features would be more complex.

In some cases, different phonetic forms of the same morpheme may be derived by segment deletion rules, as in the following examples:

A		**B**	
sign	[sajn]	signature	[sɪgnəčər]
design	[dəzajn]	designation	[dɛzɪgnešən]
paradigm	[pʰærədajm]	paradigmatic	[pʰærədɪgmæDək]

In none of the words in column A is there a phonetic [g], but in each corresponding word in column B a [g] occurs. Our knowledge of English phonology accounts for these phonetic differences. The "[g]–no [g]" alternation is regular, and we apply it to words that we have never heard before. Suppose someone says

He was a salignant [səlɪgnənt] man.

Even if you do not know what the word means, you might ask (perhaps to hide your ignorance)

Why, did he salign [səlajn] somebody?

It is highly doubtful that a speaker of English would pronounce the verb form with the *-ant* dropped as [səlɪgn], because the phonological rules of English would delete the /g/ when it occurred in this context. This rule might be stated as

Delete a /g/ when it occurs before a final nasal consonant.

The /g/ may be deleted under other circumstances as well, as indicated by its absence in *signing* and *signer*. The rule is even more general, as evidenced by the pairs *gnostic* [nostɪk] and *agnostic* [ægnɑstɪk] and the words *cognition, recognition, agnosia*, and others, all of which contain the same morpheme related to knowledge. The rule can be stated as

Delete a /g/ when it occurs word initially before a nasal consonant or before a word-final nasal.

Given this rule, the phonemic representation of the stems in *sign/signature, design/designation, resign/resignation, repugn/repugnant, phlegm/phlegmatic, paradigm/paradigmatic, diaphragm/diaphragmatic, gnosis, agnosia, agnostic,* and *recognition* will include a phonemic /g/ that will be deleted by the regular rule if a suffix is not added. By stating the class of sounds that follow the /g/ (nasal consonants) rather than any specific nasal consonant, the rule deletes the /g/ before both /m/ and /n/.

An alternative analysis is to present the root morpheme *sign* as /sajn/. No /g/ would have to be deleted to derive the verb, but to derive the noun *signature* an insertion rule would be required, and all the words that have a [g] in the derived words and no [g] in the roots would have to be listed. By representing the root morphemes with a phonemic /g/, the regular, automatic, non-exceptional rule of /g/ deletion stated above derives the correct forms and reveals this phonotactic constraint in the language.

The phonological rules that delete whole segments, add segments and features, and change features also account for the various phonetic forms of some morphemes. This point can be further illustrated by the following words:

A			**B**		
bomb	/bamb/	[bãm]	bombardier	/bambədir/	[bãmbədir]
iamb	/ajæmb/	[ajæ̃m]	iambic	/ajæmbɪk/	[ajæ̃mbək]
crumb	/krʌmb/	[kʰrʌ̃m]	crumble	/krʌmbl/	[kʰrʌ̃mbəl]

A speaker of English knows when to pronounce a /b/ and when not to. The relationship between the pronunciation of the column A words and their column B counterparts is regular and can be accounted for by the following rule:

Delete a word-final /b/ when it occurs after an /m/.

Notice that the underlying phonemic representation of the A and B stems is the same.

Phonemic Representation	/bamb/	/bamb + adir/	/bʌlb/
	↓		
apply /b/ deletion rule	Ø	*NA↓	NA
unstressed vowel rule	↓NA	↓ ə	NA
nasalization rule	ã	ã	NA
Phonetic Representation	[bãm]	[bãmbədir]	[bʌlb]

*NA = "not applicable."

The rules that delete the segments are general phonological rules, but their application to phonemic representations results in deriving different phonetic forms of the same morpheme.

Phonological Analysis: Discovering Phonemes

No one has to teach us, as children, how to discover the phonemes of our language. We do it unconsciously and at an early age know what they are. Before reading this book, or learning anything about phonology, you knew an *l* sound was part of the English sound system, a phoneme in English, because it contrasts words such as *leaf* and *reef*. But you probably did not know that the *l* in *leaf* and the one in *feel* are two different sounds. There is only one /l/ phoneme in English but more than one *l* phone. The /l/ that occurs before back vowels and at the end of words is produced not only as a lateral but also with the back of the tongue raised toward the velum, and it is therefore a *velarized l*. (Without more training in phonetics, you may not hear the difference; try to sense the difference in your tongue position when you say *leaf, lint, lay*, and *let* as opposed to *lude, load, lot, deal, dill, dell*, and *doll*.)

The linguist from Mars, referred to in Chapter 2, who is trying to write a grammar of English, would have to decide whether the two *l* sounds observed in English words represent separate phonemes or are allophones of a single phoneme. How can this be done? How would any phonologist determine what the phonological system of a language is?

To do a phonemic analysis, we must transcribe the words to be analyzed in great phonetic detail since we don't know in advance which phonetic features are distinctive and which are not.

Consider the following Finnish words:

1.	[kudot] "failures"	5.	[madon] "of a worm"
2.	[kate] "cover"	6.	[maton] "of a rug"
3.	[katot] "roofs"	7.	[ratas] "wheel"
4.	[kade] "envious"	8.	[radon] "of a track"

Given these words, do the voiceless/voiced alveolar stops [t] and [d] represent different phonemes, or are they allophones of the same phone?

Here are a few hints as to how a phonologist might proceed:

(1) Check to see if there are any minimal pairs.
(2) 2 and 4 are minimal pairs: [kate] "cover" and [kade] "envious"; 5 and 6 are minimal pairs: [madon] "of a worm" and [maton] "of a rug."
(3) [t] and [d] in Finnish thus represent the distinct phonemes /t/ and /d/.

That was an easy problem. Now consider the data from Greek, concentrating on the following sounds, three of which do not occur in English:

[x]   voiceless velar fricative
[k]   voiceless velar stop
[c]   voiceless palatal stop
[ç]   voiceless palatal fricative

1.	[kano] "do"	9.	[çeri] "hand"
2.	[xano] "lose"	10.	[kori] "daughter"
3.	[çino] "pour"	11.	[xori] "dances"
4.	[cino] "move"	12.	[xrima] "money"
5.	[kali] "charms"	13.	[krima] "shame"
6.	[xali] "plaight"	14.	[xufta] "handful"
7.	[çeli] "eel"	15.	[kufeta] "bonbons"
8.	[ceri] "candle"	16.	[oçi] "no"

To determine the status of [x], [k], [c], and [ç], you should answer the following questions.

(1) Are there any minimal pairs in which these sounds contrast?
(2) Are the sounds in complementary distribution?
(3) If non-contrasting phones are found, what are the phonemes and their allophones?
(4) What are the phonological rules by which the allophones can be derived?

The answers to these four questions follow:

(1) By analyzing the data, we find that [k] and [x] contrast in a number of minimal pairs, for example, in [kano] and [xano]. [k] and [x] are therefore distinctive. [ç] and [c] also contrast in [çino] and [cino] and are therefore distinctive. But what about the velar fricative [x] and the palatal fricative [ç]? And the velar stop [k] and the palatal stop [c]?

We can find no minimal pairs that would conclusively show that these represent separate phonemes.

(2) We now proceed to answer the second question: Are these phones in complementary distribution?

One way to see if sounds are in complementary distribution is to list each phone with the environment in which it is found:

	before [a]	before [i]	before [e]	before [o]	before [u]	before [r]
[k]	yes	no	no	yes	yes	yes
[x]	yes	no	no	yes	yes	yes
[c]	no	yes	yes	no	no	no
[ç]	no	yes	yes	no	no	no

We see that [k] and [x] are not in complementary distribution; they both occur before back vowels. Nor are [c] and [ç] in complementary distribution. They both occur before front vowels. But the stops [k] and [c] are in complementary distribution; [k] occurs before back vowels and [r] and never before front vowels. [c] occurs only before front vowels and never before back vowels or [r]. Similarly, [x] and [ç] are in complementary distribution for the same reason. We therefore conclude that [k] and [c] are allophones of one phoneme and that the fricatives [x] and [ç] are allophones of one phoneme. The pairs of allophones also fulfil the criterion of phonetic similarity. The first two are [–anterior] stops; the second two are [–anterior] fricatives.

(3) Which phones should we select to represent these two phonemes? When two allophones can be derived from one phoneme, one selects as the underlying segment the allophone that makes the rules and the phonemic feature complexes as simple as possible, as we illustrated with the English unaspirated and aspirated voiceless stops.

For the velar and palatal stops and fricatives in Greek, the rules appear to be equal in simplicity. In addition to adhering to the simplicity criterion, phonologists attempt to state rules that have natural phonetic explanations. Often these rules turn out to be the simplest solutions. In many languages, velar sounds become palatal before front vowels. This is an assimilation rule; palatal sounds are produced toward the front of the mouth, as are front vowels. Thus, we select /k/ as a phoneme with the allophones [k] and [c] and /x/ as a phoneme with the allophones [x] and [ç].

(4) We can now state the rule by which the palatals can be derived from the velars:

Palatalize velar consonants before front vowels.

Using feature notation, we can state the rule as

[+velar] → [+palatal] /___ [−backl]

Since only consonants are marked for the feature [velar] and only vowels for the feature [back], it is not necessary to include the feature [consonantal] or [syllabic] in the rule or any other features that are not required to define the segments to which the rule applies, the change that occurs, or the segments in the environment in which the rule applies. The simplicity criterion constrains us to state the rule as simply as we can.

Summary

Part of one's knowledge of a language is knowledge of the **phonology** or sound system of that language — the inventory of **phones**, the phonetic segments that occur in the language, and the ways in which they pattern. It is this patterning that determines the inventory of **phonemes** — the segments that differentiate words.

Phonetic segments are enclosed in square brackets, [ ], and phonemes are enclosed between slashes, / /. When phones occur in **complementary distribution**, they are **allophones** — predictable phonetic variants — of phonemes. For example, in English aspirated voiceless stops, such as the initial sounds in the words *pill, till,* and *kill* are in complementary distribution (never occur in the same phonological environment) as the unaspirated voiceless stops following the *s* /s/ in *spill, still,* and *skill*; thus, the aspirated *p, t,* and *k* ([pʰ], [tʰ], [kʰ]) and the unaspirated [p], [t], and [k] are allophones of the phonemes /p/, /t/, and /k/, respectively. On the other hand, phones that occur in the same environment and that differentiate words, such as the [b] and [m] in *boat* [bot] and *moat* [mot], represent two distinct phonemes, /b/ and /m/.

Some phones may be allophones of more than one phoneme. There is no one-to-one correspondence between the phonemes of a language and their allophones. In English, for example, stressed vowels become unstressed according to regular rules and ultimately reduce to schwa [ə], which is an allophone of each English vowel.

Phonological segments — phonemes and phones — are composed of **phonetic features** such as **voiced, nasal, labial**, and **continuant**, whose presence or absence is indicated by + or − signs. They distinguish one segment from another. When a phonetic feature causes a word contrast, as **nasal** does in *boat* and *moat*, it is a **distinctive feature**. Thus, in English the binary-valued feature [±nasal] is a distinctive feature, whereas [±aspiration] is not.

When two words (different forms with different meanings) are distinguished by a single phone occurring in the same position, they constitute a **minimal pair**. Some pairs, such as *boat* and *moat*, contrast by means of a single distinctive feature —

in this case, [±nasal], where /b/ is [–nasal] and /m/ is [+nasal]. Other minimal pairs may show sounds contrasting in more than one feature — for example, *dip* versus *sip*, where /d/, a voiced alveolar stop, is [+voiced, –continuant], and /s/, a voiceless alveolar fricative, is [–voiced, + continuant]. Minimal pairs and sets also occur in sign languages: signs may contrast by hand configuration, place of articulation, or movement.

Some sounds differ phonetically but are non-phonemic because they are in **free variation**, which means that either sound may occur in the identical environment without changing the meaning of the word. The glottal stop [ʔ] in English is in free variation with the [t] in words such as *don't* or *bottle* and is therefore not a phoneme in English.

Phonetic features that are **predictable** are non-distinctive and **redundant**. The nasality of vowels in English is a redundant feature since all vowels are nasalized before nasal consonants. One can thus predict the + or – value of this feature in vowels. A feature may therefore be distinctive in one class of sounds and non-distinctive in another. Nasality is distinctive for English consonants and non-distinctive predictable for English vowels.

Phonetic features that are non-distinctive in one language may be distinctive in another. Aspiration is distinctive in Thai and non-distinctive in English; both aspirated voiceless stops and unaspirated voiceless stops are phonemes in Thai.

The phonology of a language also includes constraints on the sequences of phonemes in the language, as exemplified by the fact that in English two stop consonants may not occur together at the beginning of a word; similarly, the final sound of the word *sing*, the velar nasal, never occurs word initially. These sequential constraints determine what are *possible* but non-occurring words in a language and what phonetic strings are "impossible" or "illegal." For example, *blick* [blɪk] is not now an English word, but it could become one, whereas *kbli* [kbli] or *ngos* [ŋos] could not. These possible but non-occurring words constitute **accidental gaps**.

Words in some languages may also be phonemically distinguished by **prosodic** or **suprasegmental features**, such as **pitch, stress**, and segment duration or **length**. Languages in which syllables or words are contrasted by pitch are called **tone** languages. **Intonation** languages may use pitch variations to distinguish meanings of phrases and sentences.

In English, words and phrases may be differentiated by **stress**, as in the contrast between the noun *pérvert*, in which the first syllable is stressed, and the verb *pervért*, in which the final syllable is stressed. In the compound noun *hótdog* versus the adjective + noun phrase *hot dóg*, the former is stressed on *hot*, the latter on *dog*.

Vowel **length** and consonant **length** may be phonemic features. Both are contrastive in Japanese, Finnish, Italian, and many other languages.

The relationship between the **phonemic representation** of words and sentences and the **phonetic representation** (the pronunciation of these words and sentences) is determined by general **phonological rules**.

Phonological rules in a grammar apply to phonemic strings and alter them in various ways to derive their phonetic pronunciation:

1. They may be **assimilation rules** that change feature values of segments, thus spreading phonetic properties. The rule that nasalizes vowels in English before nasal consonants is such a rule.
2. They may be **dissimilation rules** that change feature values to make two phonemes in a string more dissimilar, as in the Latin liquid rule.
3. They may *add* non-distinctive features that are predictable from the context. The rule that aspirates voiceless stops at the beginning of words and syllables in English is such a rule.
4. They may *insert* segments that are not present in the phonemic string. Insertion is also called **epenthesis**. The rule in Spanish that inserts an [e] before word-initial /s/ consonant clusters is an example of an addition or insertion rule.
5. They may *delete* phonemic segments in certain contexts. Contraction rules in English are **deletion** rules.
6. They may *transpose* or move segments in a string. These **metathesis** rules occur in many languages, including Hebrew. The rule in certain North American dialects that changes an /sk/ to [ks] in final position is also a metathesis rule.

Phonological rules often refer to entire classes of sounds rather than to individual sounds. These are **natural classes**, characterized by the phonetic features that pertain to all the members of each class, such as voiced sounds, or, using +'s and −'s, the class specified as [+voiced]. A natural class can be defined by fewer features than are required to distinguish a member of that class. Natural classes reflect the ways in which we articulate sounds or, in some cases, the acoustic characteristics of sounds. Such classes, therefore, do not have to be learned in the same way as groups of sounds that are not phonetically similar. Natural classes provide explanations for the occurrence of many phonological rules.

In the writing of rules, linguists use formal notations, which often reveal linguistic generalizations of phonological processes.

A morpheme may have different phonetic representations, which are determined by the **morphophonemic** and phonological rules of the language. Thus, the regular plural morpheme is phonetically [z] or [s] or [əz], depending on the final phoneme of the noun to which it is attached.

There is a methodology that linguists (or students of linguistics) can use to discover the phonemes of a language, such as looking for minimal pairs and complementary distribution. The allophone of a phoneme that results in the simplest statement of the rules of distribution is selected as the underlying phoneme from which the phonetic allophones are derived via phonological rules.

The phonological and morphophonemic rules in a language show that the phonemic shape of a word or phrase is not identical to its phonetic form. The phonemes are not actual phonetic sounds but abstract mental constructs that are realized as sounds by the operation of rules such as those described above. No one is taught these rules, yet everyone knows them subconsciously.

Exercises

All the data in languages other than English are given in phonetic transcription without square brackets unless otherwise stated. The phonetic transcriptions of English words are given within square brackets.

*1. Consider the distribution of [r] and [l] in Korean in the following words:

rupi	"ruby"	mul	"water"
kiri	"road"	pal	"big"
saram	"person"	səul	"Seoul"
irɯmi*	"name"	ilkop	"seven"
ratio	"radio"	ipalsa	"barber"

Are [r] and [l] allophones of one or two phonemes?

   a.   Do they occur in any minimal pairs?
   b.   Are they in complementary distribution?
   c.   In what environments does each occur?
   d.   If you conclude that they are allophones of one phoneme, state the rule that can derive the phonetic allophonic forms.

*2. In Southern Kongo, a Bantu language spoken in Angola, the non-palatal segments [t, s, z] are in complementary distribution with their palatal counterparts [č, š, ž], as shown in the following words:

tobola	"to bore a hole"	čina	"to cut"
tanu	"five"	čiba	"banana"
kesoka	"to be cut"	nkoši	"lion"
kasu	"emaciation"	nselele	"termite"
kunezulu	"heaven"	ažimola	"alms"
nzwetu	"our"	lolonži	"to wash house"
zevo	"then"	zenga	"to cut"
žima	"to stretch"		

   a.   State the distribution of each pair of segments given below. (Assume that the non-occurrence of [t] before [e] is an **accidental gap**.)

       Example: [t]–[č]: [t] occurs before the back vowels [o, a, u]; [č] occurs before [i].
       [s]–[š]
       [z]–[ž]

   b.   Using the criteria of simplicity and naturalness discussed in the chapter, state which phones should be used as the basic phoneme for each pair of non-palatal and palatal segments in Southern Kongo.

*[ɯ] is a high back unrounded vowel. It does not affect your analysis in this problem.

c. Using the rules stated in the chapter as examples (phonological rules for Southern Kongo were not given), state in your own words the *one* phonological rule that will derive all the phonetic segments from the phonemes. Do not state a separate rule for each phoneme; state only a general rule for all three phonemes you listed in b.

3. Pairs such as *top* and *chop*, *dunk* and *junk*, and *so* and *show* reveal that /t/ and /č/, /d/ and /ǰ/, and /s/ and /š/ are distinct phonemes in English. Although it is difficult to find a minimal pair to distinguish /z/ and /ž/, they occur in similar if not identical environments, such as *razor* and *azure*. Consider the same pairs of non-palatalized and palatalized consonants in the following data. (The palatal forms are optional forms that often occur in casual speech.)

Non-Palatalized		**Palatalized**	
[hɪt mi]	"hit me"	[hɪč ju]	"hit you"
[lid hĩm]	"lead him"	[liǰ ju]	"lead you"
[pʰæs ʌs]	"pass us"	[pʰæš ju]	"pass you"
[luz ðẽm]	"lose them"	[luž ju]	"lose you"

State the rule that specifies when /t/, /d/, /s/, and /z/ become palatalized as [č], [ǰ], [š], and [ž]. Use feature notations to reveal generalizations.

4. The following sets of minimal pairs show that English /p/ and /b/ contrast in initial, medial, and final positions.

Initial	**Medial**	**Final**
pit/bit	rapid/rabid	cap/cab

Find similar sets of minimal pairs for each pair of consonants given:

a. /k/–/g/   d. /b/–/v/   g. /s/–/š/
b. /m/–/n/   e. /b/–/m/   h. /č/–/ǰ/
c. /l/–/r/   f. /p/–/f/   i. /s/–/z/

5. Here are some words in Japanese. [č] is the voiceless palatal affricate that occurs in the English word *church*. [ts] is an alveolar affricate that does not occur in English as a single sound but is pronounced as the final sound(s) in *cats*. Japanese words (except for certain loan words) never contain the phonetic sequences *[ti] or *[tu].

tatami	"mat"	tomodači	"friend"	uči	"house"
tegami	"letter"	totemo	"very"	otoko	"male"
čiči	"father"	tsukue	"desk"	tetsudau	"help"
šita	"under"	ato	"later"	matsu	"wait"
natsu	"summer"	tsutsumu	"wrap"	čizu	"map"
kata	"person"	tatemono	"building"	te	"hand"

Consider [č] and [ts] to be a single phone.

a. Based on these data, are [t], [č], and [ts] in complementary distribution?

b.   State the distribution, first in words, then using features, of these phones.

c.   Give a phonemic analysis of these data insofar as [t], [č], and [ts] are concerned. That is, identify the phonemes and the allophones.

d.   Give the phonemic representation of the Japanese words given below. Assume phonemic and phonetic representations are the same except for [t], [č], and [ts].

tatami	tsukue	tsutsumu
tomodači	tetsudau	čizu
uči	šita	kata
tɛgami	ato	koto
totemo	matsu	tatemono
otoko	deguši	te
hiči	natsu	tsuri

6.   Consider the following English verbs. Those in column A have stress on the next-to-last syllable (called the *penultimate syllable* or *penult*), whereas the verbs in column B have the last syllable stressed.

A	B	C
astonish	collapse	explain
exit	exist	erase
imagine	torment	surprise
cancel	revolt	combine
elicit	adopt	careen
practise	insist	atone
solicit	contort	equate

a.   Transcribe the words under columns A, B, and C phonemically. (Use a schwa for the unstressed vowels even if they can be derived from different phonemic vowels. This should make it easier for you.)

Examples: *astonish* /əstonɪš/   *collapse* /kəlæps/   *aflame* /əflem/

b.   Consider the phonemic structure of the stressed syllables in these verbs. What is the difference between the final syllables of the verbs in columns A and B? Formulate a rule that predicts where stress occurs in the verbs in columns A and B.

c.   In the verbs in column C, stress also occurs on the final syllable. What must you add to the rule to account for this fact? (*Hint:* For the forms in columns A and B, consider the final consonants; for the forms in column C, consider the vowels.)

7.   Below are listed the phonetic transcriptions of ten "words." Some are English words, some are not words now but are possible words or nonsense words, and others are definitely "foreign" (they violate English sequential constraints).

Write the English words in regular spelling. Mark the other words "possible" or "foreign." For each word you mark as "foreign," state your reason.

	Word	Possible	"Foreign"	Reason
Example:				
[θrot]	throat			
[slig]		X		
[lsig]			X	No English word can begin with a liquid followed by an obstruent.

a. [pʰril]   e. [gnostɪk]   i. [ŋar]
b. [skrič]   f. [jūnəkɔrn]   j. [æpəpʰlɛksi]
c. [know]   g. [fruit]
d. [maj]   h. [blaft]

*8. The following words are found in Paku, a language spoken by the Pakuni in the NBC television series *Land of the Lost*. (The language was created by V. Fromkin.) v́ = [+stress]

(i)	ótu	"evil" (N)	(viii)	mpósa	"hairless"
(ii)	túsa	"evil" (Adj)	(ix)	ā́mpo	"hairless one"
(iii)	etógo	"cactus" (sg)	(x)	āmpóni	"hairless ones"
(iv)	etogóni	"cactus" (pl)	(xi)	ā́mi	"mother"
(v)	Páku	"Paku" (sg)	(xii)	āmíni	"mothers"
(vi)	Pakū́ni	"Paku" (pl)	(xiii)	áda	"father"
(vii)	épo	"hair"	(xiv)	adā́ni	"fathers"

a. Is stress predictable? If so, what is the rule?
b. Is nasalization a distinctive feature for vowels? Give the reasons for your answer.

*9. Consider these phonetic forms of Hebrew words:

[v]–[b]		[f]–[p]	
bika	"lamented"	litef	"stroked"
mugbal	"limited"	sefer	"book"
šavar	"broke" (masc.)	sataf	"washed"
šavra	"broke" (fem.)	para	"cow"
ʔikev	"delayed"	mitpaxat	"handkerchief"
bara	"created"	haʔalpim	"the Alps"

Assume that these words and their phonetic sequences are representative of what may occur in Hebrew. In your answers below, consider classes of sounds rather than individual sounds.

a. Are [b] and [v] allophones of one phoneme? (Are they in complementary distribution? In what phonetic environments do they occur? Can you formulate a phonological rule stating their distribution?)
b. Does the same rule, or lack of a rule, that describes the distribution of [b] and [v] apply to [p] and [f]? If not, why not?

c.   Here is a word with one phone missing. A blank appears in place of the missing sound: hid____ik. Check the one correct statement.

(1) [b] but not [v] could occur in the empty slot.
(2) [v] but not [b] could occur in the empty slot.
(3) Either [b] or [v] could occur in the empty slot.
(4) Neither [b] nor [v] could occur in the empty slot.

d.   Which one of the following statements is correct about the incomplete word ____ana?

(1) [f] but not [p] could occur in the empty slot.
(2) [p] but not [f] could occur in the empty slot.
(3) Either [p] or [f] could fill the blank.
(4) Neither [p] nor [f] could fill the blank.

e.   Now consider the following possible words (in phonetic transcription):

laval   surva   labal   palar   falu   razif

If these words actually occurred in Hebrew, would they

(1) force you to revise the conclusions about the distribution of labial stops and fricatives you reached on the basis of the first group of words given above?
(2) support your original conclusions?
(3) neither support nor disprove your original conclusions?

*10. In the African language Maninka, the suffix -*li* has more than one pronunciation (like the -*ed* past tense ending on English verbs, as in *reaped* [t], *robbed* [d], and *raided* [əd]). This suffix is similar to the derivational suffix -*ing*, which, when added to the verb *cook*, makes it a noun, as in "Her cooking was great," or the suffix -*ion*, which also derives a noun from a verb, as in *create* + *ion*, permitting "the creation of the word."
   Consider these data from Maninka:

bugo	"hit"	bugoli	"hitting"
dila	"repair"	dilali	"repairing"
don	"come in"	donni	"coming in"
dumu	"eat"	dumuni	"eating"
gwen	"chase"	gwenni	"chasing"

a.   What are the two forms of the "ing" morpheme?
b.   Can you predict which phonetic form will occur? If so, state the rule.
c.   What are the -ing forms for the following verbs?

da	"lie down"
men	"hear"
famu	"understand"
sunogo	"sleep"

*11. Consider the following phonetic data from the Bantu language Luganda. (The data have been somewhat altered to make the problem easier.) In each line, the same root or stem morpheme occurs in both columns A and B, but it has one prefix in column A, meaning "a" or "an," and another prefix in column B, meaning "little."

A		**B**	
ẽnato	"a canoe"	akaato	"little canoe"
ẽnapo	"a house"	akaapo	"little house"
ẽnobi	"an animal"	akaoobi	"little animal"
ẽmpipi	"a kidney"	akapipi	"little kidney"
ẽŋkoosa	"a feather"	akakoosa	"little feather"
ẽmmããmmo	"a peg"	akabããmmo	"little peg"
ẽŋŋõõmme	"a horn"	akagõõmme	"little horn"
ẽnnĩmiro	"a garden"	akadĩmiro	"little garden"
ẽnugẽni	"a stranger"	akatabi	"little branch"

In answering the following questions, base your answers on only these forms. Assume that all the words in the language follow the regularities shown here.

You may need to use scratch paper to work out your analysis before writing your answers. (*Hint:* The phonemic representation of the morpheme meaning "little" is /aka/.)

a. Are nasal vowels in Luganda phonemic? Are they predictable?

b. Is the phonemic representation of the morpheme meaning "garden" /dimiro/?

c. What is the phonemic representation of the morpheme meaning "canoe"?

d. Are [p] and [b] allophones of one phoneme?

e. If /am/ represents a bound prefix morpheme in Luganda, can you conclude that [amdano] is a possible phonetic form for a word in this language starting with this prefix?

f. Is there a phonological homorganic nasal rule in Luganda?

g. If the phonetic representation of the word meaning "little boy" is [aka poobe], give the phonemic and phonetic representations for "a boy."

h. Which of the following forms is the *phonemic* representation for the prefix meaning "a" or "an"?

   (1) /en/   (2) /ẽn/   (3) /ẽm/   (4) /em/   (5) /eŋ/

i. What is the *phonetic* representation of the word meaning "a branch"?

j. What is the *phonemic* representation of the word meaning "little stranger"?

k. State in general terms any phonological rules revealed by the Luganda data.

Works Cited

Chambers, J.K. 1973. "Canadian Raising." *Canadian Journal of Linguistics* 18: 113–35.

Joos, Martin. 1942. "A Phonological Dilemma in Canadian English." *Language* 18: 141–44.

Schane, Sanford. 1968. *French Phonology and Morphology*. Cambridge, MA: MIT Press.
Wells, J.C. 1982. *Accents of English*. Vol. 3. Cambridge, UK: Cambridge University Press.

Further Reading

Anderson, Stephen R. 1974. *The Organization of Phonology*. New York: Academic Press.

Anderson, S.R. 1985. *Phonology in the Twentieth Century: Theories of Rules and Theories of Representations*. Chicago: University of Chicago Press.

Chomsky, N., and M. Halle. 1968. *The Sound Pattern of English*. New York: Harper & Row.

Clark, John, and Colin Yallop. 1990. *An Introduction to Phonetics and Phonology*. Oxford: Basil Blackwell.

Clements, George N., and Samuel Jay Keyser. 1983. *CV Phonology: A Generative Theory of the Syllable*. Cambridge, MA: MIT Press.

Dell, François. 1980. *Generative Phonology*. London: Cambridge University Press.

Goldsmith, John A. 1990. *Autosegmental and Metrical Phonology: A New Synthesis*. Oxford: Basil Blackwell.

Hogg, Richard, and C.B. McCully. 1987. *Metrical Phonology: A Coursebook*. Cambridge, UK: Cambridge University Press.

Hyman, Larry M. 1975. *Phonology: Theory and Analysis*. New York: Holt, Rinehart & Winston.

Kenstowicz, Michael, and Charles Kisseberth. 1979. *Generative Phonology: Description and Theory*. New York: Academic Press.

van der Hulst, Harry, and Norval Smith, eds. 1982. *The Structure of Phonological Representations: Part 1*. Dordrecht, The Netherlands: Foris Publications.

PART 3
Social Aspects of Language

Speech is civilization itself. The word, even the most contradictious word, preserves contact — it is silence which isolates.

Thomas Mann, *The Magic Mountain*

Children raised in isolation do not use language; it is used by human beings in a social context, communicating their needs, ideas, and emotions to one another. . . .

William Labov, *Sociolinguistic Patterns*

CHAPTER 7
Language in Society

Language is a city to the building of which every human being brought a stone.
Ralph Waldo Emerson, *Letters and Social Aims*

Dialects

Within any recognizable speech community, variations are normally found on all levels of linguistic structure — phonological, grammatical, and lexical. Some of the variations are correlated with geographical location ... some ... may ... depend on the identity of the person spoken to or spoken about.... Other variations are correlated with the identity of the speaker. These include cases of difference between men's and women's speech ... linguistic variation may also be correlated with the social status of the speakers [or] with other facts in the social and cultural context.

W. Bright, *Variation & Change in Language* (1976)

All speakers of English can talk to each other and pretty much understand each other; yet no two speak exactly alike. Some differences are due to age, sex, state of health, size, personality, emotional state, and personal idiosyncrasies. That each person speaks somewhat differently from all others is shown by our ability to recognize acquaintances by hearing them talk. The unique characteristics of the language of an individual speaker are referred to as the speaker's **idiolect**. English may then be said to consist of some 400 000 000 idiolects, the approximate number of speakers of English.

Beyond these individual differences, the language of a group of people may show regular variations from that used by other groups of speakers of that language. When the language spoken in different geographical regions and among different social groups shows *systematic* differences, the groups are said to speak different **dialects** of the same language. The dialects of a single language may thus be defined as mutually intelligible forms of a language that differ in systematic ways from each other. Many North Americans encounter British dialects that are so different as to be nearly unintelligible; nevertheless, speakers of all these dialects insist that they are speaking English. Moreover, once the initial shock wears off, speakers begin to detect systematic differences between their dialects. However, as we see in this encounter between the North American and the speaker of a British dialect, it is not always easy to decide whether the systematic differences between two speech communities reflect two dialects or two different languages. A rule-of-thumb definition can be used: "When dialects become mutually unintelligible — when the speakers of one dialect group can no longer understand the speakers of another dialect group — these 'dialects' become different languages." However, to define "mutually intelligible" is itself a difficult task. Danes speaking Danish and Norwegians speaking Norwegian and Swedes speaking Swedish can converse with each other; yet Danish and Norwegian and Swedish are considered separate languages because they are spoken in separate countries and because there are regular differences in their grammars. Similarly, Hindi and Urdu are mutually intelligible "languages" spoken in Pakistan and India, although the differences between them are not much greater than those between the English spoken in North America and that spoken in Australia or, for that matter, between the various dialects of North America. On the other hand, the various languages spoken in China, such as Mandarin and Cantonese, although mutually unintelligible, have been referred to as dialects of Chinese because they are spoken within a single country and have a common writing system.

Because neither mutual intelligibility nor the existence of political boundaries is decisive, it is not surprising that a clear-cut distinction between language and dialects has evaded linguistic scholars. We will use the rule-of-thumb definition, however, and refer to dialects of one language as mutually intelligible versions of the same basic grammar, with systematic differences between them.

Regional Dialects

Phonetics ... the science of speech. That's my profession. ... (I) can spot an Irishman or a Yorkshireman by his brogue. I can place any man within six miles. I can place him within two miles in London. Sometimes within two streets.

George Bernard Shaw, *Pygmalion*

Dialectal diversity develops when people are separated from each other geographically and socially. The changes that occur in the language spoken in one area or group do not necessarily spread to another. Within a single group of speakers who are in regular contact with one another, the changes are spread among the group and "relearned" by their children. When some communication barrier separates groups of speakers — be it a physical barrier such as an ocean or a mountain range or a social barrier of a political, racial, class, or religious kind — linguistic changes are not easily spread, and dialectal differences are reinforced.

Dialect differences tend to increase proportionately to the degree of communicative isolation between the groups. Communicative isolation refers to a situation such as that which existed between North America and England in the eighteenth century. There was some contact through commerce and emigration, but a North American was less likely to talk to an English person than to another North American. Even in countries in close proximity, political separation can lead to the development of dialect differences. Thus, the political separation of Canada and the United States has encouraged dialectal differences. Today, isolation is less pronounced because of the mass media and travel by jet, but even within one country regionalisms persist. In fact, there is no evidence to show that any **dialect levelling** — that is, movement toward a greater uniformity or a decrease in variations — occurs due to the mass media, and recent studies even suggest that dialect variation is increasing, particularly in urban areas.

Changes in the grammar do not take place all at once within the speech community. They take place gradually, often originating in one region and slowly spreading to others and often taking place throughout the lives of several generations of speakers.

A change that occurs in one region and fails to spread to other regions of the language community gives rise to dialect differences. When enough such differences give the language spoken in a particular region (e.g., the city of Boston, Massachusetts, or the province of Newfoundland) its own "flavour," that version of the language is referred to as a **regional dialect**.

Accents

Regional phonological or phonetic distinctions are often referred to as different **accents**. A person is said to have a Boston accent, a Newfoundland or a "down East" accent, a Brooklyn accent, an Ottawa Valley twang, and so on. Thus, *accent* refers to the characteristics of speech that convey information about the speaker's dialect, which may reveal in what country or what part of the country the speaker grew up or — in the case of a **social dialect** — to which sociolinguistic group the speaker belongs. People in the United States often refer to someone as having a British accent or an Australian accent; in Britain, people may refer to an American accent, even when speaking of a Canadian.

The term *accent* is also used to refer to the speech of someone who speaks a language non-natively; for example, a Québécois speaking English may be thought to have a "French accent" by English speakers. In this sense of the word, *accent* refers to phonological differences of "interference" from a different language spoken elsewhere. A native speaker of Parisian French hearing the same speaker, on the other hand, might recognize the regional dialect and conclude that this is not merely a "French accent" but also a "Quebec French accent." Unlike regional dialectal accents, foreign accents do not reflect differences in the language of the community where the language was acquired.

Dialects of North American English

> The educated Southerner has no use for an r except at the beginning of a word.
>
> Mark Twain, *Life on the Mississippi*

The regional dialects of American and Canadian English alike find their roots in the speech of the British colonists who settled North America in the sixteenth through the eighteenth centuries, so it comes as no surprise to discover that they are alike in many respects, so much so that we may speak of Canadian and American English as part of a larger "North American English."

Colonists to the New World brought with them a variety of English dialects, ranging from the Irish and West Country dialects of the Newfoundlanders in the oldest English colony (1583) to the East Anglian speech of the Puritans in New England. As a result, regional dialect differences were apparent even among the settlers of the first American colonies. In addition to the dialects of the fishing settlements of the Newfoundland coast, three major dialect areas can be discerned in the Thirteen Colonies before the outbreak of the American Revolution: a Northern dialect spoken in New England and around the Hudson River, a Midland dialect spoken in Pennsylvania and parts of New York State, and a Southern dialect. These dialects differed from each other — and from the English spoken in England — in systematic ways, for some of the changes that were occurring in British English spread to the colonies, while others did not. And, of course, the colonies themselves were developing dialectal differences that helped to distinguish their speech from that of the "mother country."

How regional differences developed between the dialects of the colonies and between those colonies and Britain may be illustrated in the changes that took place in the pronunciation of words with an *r*. The British in southern England were already dropping their *r*'s before consonants and at the ends of words as early as the eighteenth century. Words such as *farm, farther*, and *father* were pronounced as [fa:m], [fa:ðə], and [fa:ðə], respectively. By the end of the eighteenth century, this practice was a general rule among the early settlers in New England and the southern Atlantic seaboard. Close commercial ties were maintained between the New England colonies and London, and Southerners sent their children to England to be educated, which reinforced the "r-dropping" rule. The "r-less" dialect still spoken today in Boston, New York, and Savannah maintained this characteristic. Later settlers, however, came from northern England, where the *r* had been retained; as the frontier moved westward and northward, so did the *r*. The *r*-less dialect was not, of course, found among the Irish and Scots of Newfoundland and Nova Scotia.

Before the American Revolution, English settlement outside the Thirteen Colonies was largely confined to the Maritimes, for there were few, if any, English settlements in what are now Quebec and Ontario. At the outbreak of war, the population of the Thirteen Colonies was some 2.5 million people, of which a little more than 19 percent (500 000) remained loyal to the Crown, and, as the memoirs of those involved reveal, the conflict between onetime neighbours, friends, and relatives was often brutal, leaving harsh memories for the Loyalist and the Patriot alike. Following the war, many who had remained loyal to the Crown had lands and possessions confiscated, especially if they had been vocal in their opposition to independence or militarily active in the struggle. As many as 100 000 of the Loyalists left or were expelled from the new United States, and of this number between 45 000 and 50 000 migrated to what are now the provinces of Nova Scotia, New Brunswick, Quebec, and Ontario (see Figure 7.1), the remainder returning to Britain or emigrating to the West Indies or to Florida, which at that time was not part of the United States (Stewart 1985).

FIGURE 7.1

Loyalist settlement in Nova Scotia, Lower Canada, and Upper Canada.

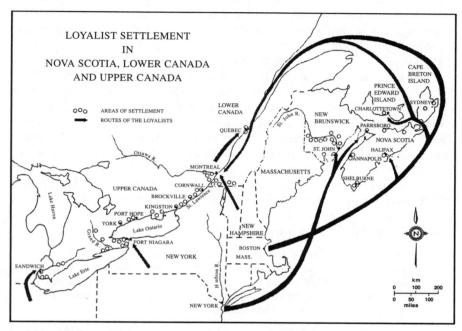

Joan Magee, *Loyalist Mosaic: A Multi-Ethnic Heritage.* Toronto: Dundurn Press, 1984.

Although the American Revolution altered the political map of North America, it had, at the outset at least, little effect on the language spoken by Patriot and Loyalist alike. The dialects that the Loyalists carried northward with them did not differ from those of their former neighbours.

Following the Revolutionary War, citizens of the United States continued to spread westward, and over time their dialects began to change as intermingling "levelled" or "submerged" many of their dialectal differences. This process of levelling is one reason why the English used in large sections of the Midwest and the West of the United States is similar, making up what is sometimes called General American English. A similar levelling occurred among Loyalists in Quebec and Ontario, the majority of whom came from the Midland dialect area. On the other hand, farther east large numbers of Northern dialect speakers moved into Nova Scotia, New Brunswick, and Newfoundland.

In addition to the English settlers, waves of immigration brought speakers of other dialects and other languages to the United States and to British North America, and each group left its linguistic imprint. The Scots and Irish brought their dialects with them into the Maritimes and Ontario, as well as into the Midland dialect area of Pennsylvania; Gaelic Scots came into Cape Breton Island, Nova Scotia, Prince Edward Island, Quebec, and Ontario; and, in the last half of the eighteenth century, Germans settled in the southeastern section of Pennsylvania, from which some subsequently moved into Ontario and still later onto the Canadian Prairies. The place names on a map of North America testify to the many peoples and their languages found on this continent.

The Loyalists who established themselves in British North America were soon joined by other migrants from the United States who were motivated less by politics than by the lure of available land. They came in such numbers, especially to the Ontario peninsula and to Quebec, that by the outbreak of war in 1812 large proportions of those areas were populated by former Americans. Governments on both sides of the border worried over these "Late Loyalists," but the question of their allegiance was quickly resolved when the majority rose in defence of their new homeland. Nevertheless, following the peace, London, wary of this predominance of one-time Americans, despite their proven loyalty, encouraged its own citizens, former soldiers, and other British nationals — the Scots and Irish once more — to settle in Canada. So between 1825 and 1846, more than half a million immigrants came to Canada from Britain (Scargill 1988). It has been argued that,

> because of the Loyalists, the independent nation that emerged had a distinct and different flavor [from that of the United States] — more royalist, more British, more hierarchal and less inclined to kick over the traces. It had a strong penchant for the rule of law and a distaste for vigilante justice. It had less push and more tolerance than the Americans. (Stewart 1985)

As a result of the patterns of settlement, the early social and linguistic history of Canada reflects the strong influence of the "mother country."

Many of those who moved west to settle the Prairies carried with them the speech patterns of Ontario, and the influence of that dialect was ultimately to extend to the foothills of Alberta, if not to the Pacific Ocean.[1]

The provinces of Saskatchewan and Alberta, however, were settled not only by Ontarians but also by many Americans who found their own Great Plains (as the "Prairies" are known in the United States) largely occupied. The influence of Eastern Canada on this region nonetheless remained strong, and, as *The Canadian Encyclopedia* (1988) observes, by the turn of the century it was clear that the area would be, for the time being, "Protestant, English speaking, and British." In the twentieth century, Prairie society began to change because of widespread immigration, and it now reflects a multiculturalism similar to that of other parts of the nation.

The settlement of British Columbia differs from that of the Prairies; because of the landscape, the area had little appeal for farmers from Central Canada. Instead, it attracted a sizable British population, so much so that it has been called the most British region in Canada (Scargill 1988). This influence has been tempered, however, by the strong north–south axis of the Pacific area and by the influence of East Asia. During the 1980s and 1990s, immigration from Hong Kong and other nations of the Pacific Rim, as well as from Central Canada modified the earlier "Englishness" of the area, especially in Vancouver and surrounding cities.

Increased immigration during the last half of the twentieth century has brought people from Africa, Asia, Europe, and Central and South America to North America, some fleeing war and persecution, others seeking, like those who came before them, a better life. As a result, the English language in North America — American and Canadian alike — continues to be enriched by the languages spoken by large numbers of new residents from the Pacific Rim countries of Japan, China, Korea, Malaysia, Vietnam, and Thailand. Eastern Europeans (Russians, Ukrainians, and Armenians), Bermudians, Jamaicans, Portuguese, and Central and South Americans have all added to the richness of the vocabulary of North American English. This cultural diversity is reflected in the various "mother tongues" — a mother tongue is the language first learned as a child and that continues to be understood — of Canadians as recorded in the 1996 census (see Table 7.1). The "Caribana" celebrations of Toronto, once a bastion of "Anglo–Saxon" Canada, the Italian neighbourhoods of Vancouver, the Portuguese clubs scattered across the land, the mosques and the Sikh temples — all have contributed to the "mosaic" of Canadian society. While the designation of "New Canadians" was created by older immigrants

TABLE 7.1
Selected Mother Tongues in Canada, 1996

Language	Numbers of People	Percent of Population
English	16 890 615	59.21
French	6 636 660	23.26
Chinese	715 640	2.51
Italian	484 500	1.70
German	450 140	1.58
Polish	213 410	0.75
Spanish	212 890	0.75
Portuguese	211 290	0.74
Punjabi	201 785	0.71
Ukrainian	162 695	0.57
Arabic	148 555	0.52
Dutch	133 805	0.47
Tagalog (Pilipino)	133 215	0.47
Greek	121 180	0.42
Vietnamese	106 515	0.37
Cree	76 840	0.27
Inuktitut	26 960	0.09

These figures do not include 402 560 people who indicated multiple mother tongues. According to Statistics Canada, 107 945 of this number listed both English and French as their mother tongues; 249 545 indicated English and a non-official language; 35 845 indicated French and a non-official language; and 9225 indicated English, French, and a third language.

Adapted from Statistics Canada, "Population by Detailed Mother Tongue and Home Language, Showing Sex, Immigrant Status and Period of Immigration for Canada, Provinces, Territories and Census Metropolitan Areas," *1996 Census*, Catalogue No. 93FOO24XDB96012.

for these recent immigrants, both "new" and "old" have found a place in Canadian society. The English spoken in regions where new immigrants settle may ultimately be affected by the mother tongues of the settlers, further adding to the variety of the English language. But, despite the variations of Canadian speech, the language of middle-class, urban Canadians remains amazingly homogeneous.

English is the most widely spoken language in the world if one counts all those who use it as a native language or as a second or third language. It is the official national language of a number of countries, such as Australia, the British Isles, Canada, New Zealand, South Africa, and the United States. For many years, it was the official language in countries that were once colonies of Britain, including India, Nigeria, Ghana, Kenya, and the other "Anglophone" countries of Africa. One result of this contact between English and the languages of the onetime colonies has been an enrichment of English through the development of further dialects, each with its own grace and beauty.

Canadian and American English

Wallace Stegner, the son of an American settler in Saskatchewan, was aware of the importance of the border separating the United States and Canada. Despite the apparent similarities between the two countries, that border "exerted uncomprehended pressures upon affiliation and belief, custom and costume. It offered us subtle choices even in language (we stooked our wheat; across the Line they shocked it)" (Stegner 1962). "Subtle choices" continue to characterize the differences between American and Canadian dialects. Walter Avis (1956), one of the pioneering students of Canadian English, defined it as "neither American nor British, but a complex different in many respects from both in vocabulary, grammar and syntax, and pronunciation." With American English, it shares a language that developed out of the Early Modern English dialects of British settlers, joined with borrowings from North American Native languages and the influences of other immigrants from around the world. Indeed, it is often difficult to decide which borrowed specific words from North American Native languages first, Canadian or American English. Canadian English, however, also reflects the effects of continued political, social, and linguistic affiliation with Great Britain. Finally, of course, unique features have, over the centuries, grown up in the country itself. The morphology, phonology, and syntax that Canadians use may not, on the whole, be unique to Canada, but the blending of these elements has produced a distinctive dialect of North American English, even though it may not be immediately recognizable to others. As one account noted,

> Canadian English is difficult to distinguish from some other North American varieties without the tools of the phonetician, yet it is instantly recognisable to other Canadians, if not to the rest of the English-speaking world. In a crowd, where the Englishman or the Australian could not, the Canadian with a good ear will easily spot the other Canadian among the North Americans. (McCrum, Cran, and MacNeil 1992)

Phonological Differences

> I have noticed in traveling about the country a good many differences in the pronunciation of common words. . . . Now what I want to know is whether there is any right or wrong about this matter. . . . If one way is right, why don't we all pronounce that way and compel the other fellow to do the same? If there isn't any right or wrong, why do some persons make so much fuss about it?
>
> Letter quoted in "The Standard American," in J.V. Williamson and V.M. Burke, eds., *A Various Language*

A comparison between the *r*-less dialect and other dialects with *r* was used earlier to illustrate phonological differences between dialects. Similarly, some people in the United States pronounce *caught* as /kɔt/ with the vowel /ɔ/ and *cot* as /kat/, whereas other Americans and most Canadians pronounce them identically. Some Americans pronounce *Mary, marry*, and *merry* identically; others pronounce all three words differently as /meri/, /mæri/, and /mɛri/; and still others pronounce two of them the same. Canadians share this indecision; while few have three distinct pronunciations, a substantial number — especially older speakers — differentiate between /æ/ in *marry* and /ɛ/ in *Mary/merry*. In the southern areas of the United States, *creek* is pronounced with a tense /i/ as /krik/, and in the north Midlands it is pronounced with a lax /ɪ/ as /krɪk/. Both forms are found in Canadian English, but, according to a survey of high school students and their parents, /krik/ predominates (Scargill 1974).[2]

The sound structure of Canadian English, like its vocabulary, further reflects "subtle choices" that distinguish it from American English. The centred and raised diphthongs [ʌj] and [ʌw] (allophones of the phonemes /aj/ and /aw/ appearing before voiceless consonants) have been considered by many to be characteristic of Canadian English. These diphthongs are heard in words such as *light* [lʌjt] and *type* [tʌjp], *house* [hʌws] and *out* [ʌwt], where most Americans — and some Canadians — use a low back diphthong, as in [lajt], [tajp], [haws], and [awt]. This "raising" is triggered by a following voiceless consonant, as is evident in the contrast between words such as *writer* and *rider*. The medial consonant of *writer* may be produced as a voiced flap allophone [D] of /t/ that sounds to many people much like the [d] of *rider*. But speakers of Canadian English make a distinction in the diphthongs, for *writer* is pronounced with the raised vowel [rʌjDər], while *rider* has the lower back vowel [rajdər]. Clearly, speakers are responding to the "voicelessness" of the medial consonant in the first word. Similarly, the initial vowel of the diphthong is raised in words such as *clout* [klʌwt] in contrast with *cloud* [klawd] under the same conditions. However characteristic of Canadian English this raised and centred diphthong may be, a feature much like it has been detected in some dialects of American English (Vance 1987). The appearance of something like **Canadian raising** is apparently a recent development in parts of the northern United States (Thomas 1991), and, curiously, at the same time, it has been seen to be disappearing in the speech of Toronto (Leon 1979).

As the example of *writer* shows, Canadians, like Americans, employ a voiced allophone of /t/ between vowels. Hence, the capital city of Canada, *Ottawa*, is pronounced [ɑDəwə]. British influence may be responsible for the use of voiceless /t/ in the careful speech of some British Columbians, but many of the same speakers employ the voiced allophone in casual speech. Similarly, many Canadians and Americans employ a voiced sound, [ǰ], instead of /č/ in words such as *congratulate* [kəngræǰəlet]. Some Canadians pronounce words such as *tune, duke, news,* and *student* with a /j/ glide between the alveolar consonant and /u/ (called yoddizing), as in British English, thus /tjun/, /djuk/, /njuz/, /stjudənt/, but most pronounce them without /j/ (yod dropping), as /tun/, et cetera. Forms with /j/ seem to have more prestige, presumably because they seem more British. In Ontario, hypercorrection to /ju/ in *moon, noon,* and so on, has been reported along the "middle border" from Thunder Bay to Saskatchewan. Yod coalescence to an affricate, as in *tune* /čjun/, also occurs (Wells 1982).

As this suggests, there is a good deal of variation in Canadian English, even, at times, within the speech of the same person. Some Canadians, for example, use /ajl/ in words such as *hostile* or *futile*, while others employ syllabic [ḷ] or [əl]. Many who say /ajl/ in *futile* also use syllabic /ḷ/ in *missile* ([mɪsḷ]), perhaps because of American news broadcasts over the past 50 years. Some critics have likewise seen the use of [sk] instead of [š] in a word such as *schedule* as the result of American influence. In reality, both forms are evident in the Early Modern English of the settlers of North America. The apparent increase in the use of [əl] and [sk] may, nonetheless, be due to the influence of American films, radio, and television.

Many but not all Canadians use [šɑn] as the past tense of *shine* instead of American [šon], and they may use a high tense vowel in *been*, [bin], instead of the usual lax vowel, [bɪn], of American English. The same vowel may appear in *lever* [livər], though others use [lɛvər]. Similarly, *tomato* is [təmeDə] or [təmeDo] rather than [təmɑto]. It is a mistake to see these examples as an opposition of British versus American forms, for both existed in earlier varieties of English brought to North America.

Stress may follow the British pattern in *coróllary, capíllary,* and *labóratory*, especially in Eastern Canada. But words ending in *-ary* and *-ery* will usually have secondary stress as in American English.

As noted in Chapter 5, the pronunciation of British English differs in systematic ways from that of Central Canadian or General American English. Britain has many regional dialects, and the British vowels described in the phonetics chapter are the ones used by speakers of the most prestigious dialect, often referred to as **RP, Received Pronunciation**, because it was once considered to be the dialect used in court and "received by" the king and queen. In this dialect, /h/ is pronounced at the beginning of both *head* and *herb* (though /r/ in *herb* is not), whereas in the English of North America it is not generally pronounced in the second word (though /r/ is). In some British dialects, the /h/ is regularly dropped from most words in which it is pronounced in both Canadian and American English, such as *house*, pronounced [aws], and *hero*, pronounced [iro]. A similar deletion of [h] occurs in broad Newfoundland English, in which the first word of *Harbour Grace* loses its initial [h]. On the other hand, [h] may be inserted in Newfoundland dialects before initial vowels of stressed syllables, as in *anchor* [hæŋkə]. Both words, *harbour* and *anchor*, illustrate yet another "dropping" in their omission of final *r*. In this dialect, *r*-dropping also occurs between a vowel and a consonant, as one hears in a word such as *scarce*. These are but a few examples of the many regular phonological differences found in the many dialects of English used around the world.

Lexical Differences

People hearing Americans, Britons, and Canadians speaking together probably observe in the Canadian that curious blend of British and "American" elements in Canadian speech that we have been discussing. And it is probably the vocabulary that is first noticed. Americans will hear what they consider to be "Britishisms," while the British will hear "Americanisms." In fact, many "Canadianisms" are of British origin, and those words that perplex the British may be those that are shared with Americans or, indeed, are of American origin. The resulting combination and the way these words are used, however, are uniquely Canadian.

Dialects, national and regional, may differ in the words people use for the same object, as well as in phonology. Hans Kurath (1971), an eminent American dialectologist, asked in an essay entitled "What Do You Call It?"

> Do you call it a *pail* or a *bucket*? Do you draw water from a *faucet* or from a *spigot*? Do you pull down the *blinds*, the *shades*, or the *curtains* when it gets dark? Do you *wheel* the baby, or do you *ride* it or *roll* it? In a *baby carriage*, a *buggy*, a *coach*, or a *cab*?

Some speakers of Canadian English might insist that they use none of Kurath's alternatives; others would suggest that they use some but with differences in meaning. In other instances, they use the word that is commonly attributed to "American" English, and in still other cases they use the "British" form. Canadians pull down the *blinds* to cover a window, as do many Americans. (*Curtains*, on the other hand, are made of cloth and may hang in front of the *blinds*). Canadians and Americans do not take a *lift* to the *first floor* but an *elevator* to the *second floor*; Canadians, like Americans, get *gas* for their cars (not *petrol*, as in Britain); unlike the *gallons* (differing in size, however) of the British and Americans, it is measured in litres. Unlike in North America, a *public school* in Britain is private (you have to pay), and, if a student showed up there wearing *pants* ("underpants") instead of *trousers* ("pants"), he would be sent home to get dressed.

On the other hand, the differences between Canadian and American English are also apparent, and many of these differences reflect British influence. Canadians turn on a *tap* to obtain water, a word that some Americans consider "English." They may *queue up* ("line up") for tickets or the bus, a word that puzzles Americans — and a behaviour that amuses them as "so Canadian." H.B. Allen in his survey of the Upper Midwest of the United States found *chesterfield* to be "uniquely Canadian" even though he noted that it is also used in the San Francisco area. Americans living close to the Canadian border know that the word refers to "a long upholstered seat or couch having back and arms" (Avis et al., *Dictionary of Canadianisms*

1967), but they consider it strictly a Canadianism (Allen 1976). As we might expect, the word is originally English, but in the United Kingdom nowadays it refers primarily to a kind of overcoat. In Canada, *chesterfield* has produced a blend — one that is uniquely Canadian — in *chesterbed*, a "couch" that converts into a bed. It is also an element in compound words such as *chesterfield chair, chesterfield suite*, and even *chesterfield table* (the "coffee table") according to the *Dictionary of Canadianisms*.

Another word, British in origin, but used in a different sense in Canada is *riding* to designate a parliamentary constituency rather than an administrative district (e.g., the "West Riding of Yorkshire") as it does in British English. Originally Scandinavian (a "third"), it is one of the many remains of the Viking occupation of England. Similarly, Canadians speak of electing politicians by *acclamation*, a word defined in both American and English dictionaries as "loud approval" or "cheers" but that in Canada indicates election of a person "without opposition."

Like *chesterfield* and *riding*, the word *serviette* (a "table-napkin" according to the *Concise Oxford Dictionary* to contrast it with "napkin" = "diaper") was originally British. It is widely used in Canada, especially for the paper variety, but *napkin* seems to be gradually replacing it. *Zed* for the last letter of the alphabet is the preferred word in Canadian schools, but every child, influenced by American television, knows that it is called *zee* in the United States.

ANTHONY JENKINS. Reprinted with permission from *The Globe and Mail*.

Many people around the world wear thick-soled canvas shoes for informal or athletic use, but Canadians apparently are singular in calling them *running shoes* or *runners*. Americans refer to them as *sneakers, sneaks*, or *tennis shoes* and Britons as *trainers* or *plimsolls*. In American English, *running shoes*, as Webster attests, are shoes with spikes for track-and-field athletes.

A common belief — it may even be true — is that Customs and Immigration officers on both sides of the 49th parallel distinguish Americans from Canadians by the use of *eh?* in sentences such as "I went over to visit my cousin, eh?" Certainly, parodies of Canadian English such as Mark Orkin's *Canajan, Eh?* (1973) exploit this "tic," as it has been called, as typical of Canadian speech. As with other words and expressions, *eh?* is not, in fact, exclusively Canadian, for it appears in both American and British English as well (Avis 1972). If not uniquely Canadian, *eh?* is used to such an extent by speakers of Canadian English that few question the value of this expression to separate Americans from Canadians.

Dialect Atlases

Dialect atlases and **dialect maps** of various regions have been produced. For instance, in Figure 7.2A, black dots mark communities whose speakers use *settee*, and black squares identify places where the word *chesterfield* occurs. Concentrations of these markings help to define *dialect areas* and, in this case, to mark the border

FIGURE 7.2A

Dialect map of Upper Midwest United States.

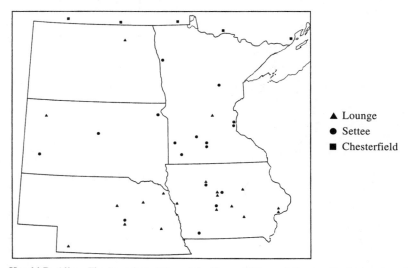

▲ Lounge
● Settee
■ Chesterfield

Harold B. Allen, *The Linguistic Atlas of the Upper Midwest.* Minneapolis: University of Minnesota Press, 1976, Vol. I, p. 165. Reprinted by permission of The Gale Group.

between Canadian and American English. A line drawn on the map (as in Figure 7.2B) separating the areas is called an **isogloss**. When you "cross" an isogloss, you are passing from one dialect area to another. Sometimes several isoglosses will coincide, often at a political boundary or at a natural boundary such as a river or mountain range. Linguists call these groupings a bundle of isoglosses. Such a bundle will define a particular regional dialect.

The first volume of the long-awaited *Dictionary of Regional English* by Frederick G. Cassidy was published in 1985. This work represents years of research and scholarship by Cassidy and other American dialectologists and promises to be a major resource for those interested in American English dialectal differences. Unfortunately, there is at present no work of the same magnitude for Canadian English.

Syntactic Differences

The "standard" dialects of American, British, and Canadian English do not exhibit many syntactic differences. British English, it is true, can delete the verb in a sentence

FIGURE 7.2B

Dialect map of Nova Scotia.

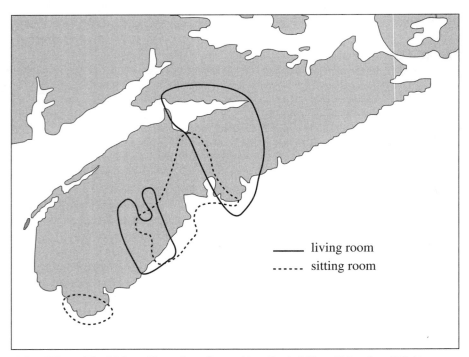

H. Rex Wilson, "The Dialect of Lunenburg County, Nova Scotia." Diss., University of Michigan, 1958, p. 72.

such as *I could have called* and replace it with *done* to form *I could have done*, which is not permitted in North American grammar, where speakers say instead *I could have*. Canadians may be more familiar than Americans with the British construction, but it is seldom used by any but immigrants from the United Kingdom. Like British speakers, Canadians speak of being *in hospital*, while Americans add an article to the expression: *in the/a hospital*. In Canada and Britain, students *go to university*, whereas in the United States they *go to college* as the generic designation. In all three countries, however, criminals end up *in jail*, although in Britain it may be spelled *gaol*.

The syntactic structures of Canadian English, like its vocabulary, thus reflect a unique blend of North American and British elements. A resident of Michigan will ask *Do you have any tea?* while an Ontarian, like British questioners, may well form the question as *Have you any tea?* or *Have you got any tea?* (Avis 1955). Some Americans use *gotten* in a sentence such as *He should have gotten to school on time* and distinguish between *gotten* in the sense of "acquire" ("We've gotten the tickets") and *got* in the sense of "possess" ("We've got the tickets"); in British English only the form *got* occurs. As the question about tea suggests, Canadians generally prefer *got* as a past participle, though *gotten* is becoming more common. Some speakers of Northern American dialects say *They are to home*, while Canadians seldom use such a construction, preferring *They are at home*, as do most other dialects of American English. In some Canadian and American dialects, the pronoun *I* may occur when *me* would be used in other dialects. This is a syntactically conditioned morphological difference.

Dialect 1	**Dialect 2**
between you and I	between you and me
Won't he let you and I swim?	Won't he let you and me swim?

Although often irritated by those who mistake them for "Americans" — a designation that most of the world takes to refer to a resident of the United States — speakers of Canadian English may not stand out from their northern "American" cousins until they are heard to refer to a [lɛftɛnənt], *lieutenant*, ask *Have you got a [hʌws] house in the country?* or speak of a friend *in hospital*. It is this complex of sounds and forms that distinguishes a speaker of Canadian English from a speaker of American or British English.

Even though regional dialects differ as to pronunciation, vocabulary, and syntactic rules, they are minor differences when compared with the totality of the grammar. The largest part of the vocabulary, the sound–meaning relations of words and the syntactic rules, is shared, which is why dialects of one language are mutually intelligible.

The "Standard"

We don't talk fancy grammar and eat anchovy toast. But to live under the kitchen doesn't say we aren't educated.

Mary Norton, *The Borrowers*

> Standard English is the customary use of a community when it is recognized and accepted as the customary use of the community. Beyond this is the larger field of good English, any English that justifies itself by accomplishing its end, by hitting the mark.
>
> George Philip Krapp, *Modern English: Its Growth and Present Use*

Even though every language is a composite of dialects, many people talk and think about a language as if it were a well-defined fixed system with various dialects diverging from this norm. Such was the view of Mario Pei, the author of a number of books on language that were quite popular at one time. He accused the editors of *Webster's Third New International Dictionary*, published in 1961, of confusing "to the point of obliteration the older distinction between standard, substandard, colloquial, vulgar, and slang," erroneously attributing to them the view that "Good and bad, right and wrong, correct and incorrect no longer exist" (Pei 1964).

Language Purists

> A woman who utters such depressing and disgusting sounds has no right to be anywhere — no right to live. Remember that you are a human being with a soul and the divine gift of articulate speech: that your native language is the language of Shakespeare and Milton and The Bible; and don't sit there crooning like a bilious pigeon.
>
> George Bernard Shaw, *Pygmalion*

Prescriptive grammarians, or language "purists," usually consider the dialect used by political leaders, the upper socio-economic classes, and the educated classes, the dialect used for literature or printed documents, and the dialect taught in the schools, as the correct form of the language.

Otto Jespersen (1925), the great Danish linguist, ridiculed the view that a particular dialect is better than any other: "We set up as the best language that which is found in the best writers, and count as the best writers those that best write the language. We are therefore not further advanced than before."

The dominant or prestige dialect is often called the standard dialect. There is not so much a single standard English as several varieties of national standards throughout the world. The chief division is between British English and North American English, the latter including the standard varieties spoken by educated speakers in Canada and the United States. British English includes the standard varieties spoken in England, Scotland, Ireland, and Wales.

Standard British English (SBrE), Standard American English (SAE), and **Standard Canadian English (SCE)** are dialects of English that many English and North Americans *almost* speak; divergences from this "norm" are labelled "Liverpudlian," "Yorkshire," "Chicago dialect," "African American English," and "Newfie." The standard — whether it be SBrE, SAE, or SCE — is an idealization. Nobody speaks this dialect; and, if somebody did, we would not know it, because these dialects are not defined precisely. It used to be the case that the language used by national news broadcasters in Britain (called "Received Pronunciation" [RP]), Canada, and the United States (called "network standard") represented the standard, but today many of these people speak a regional dialect. Several years ago, conferences were held in both the United States and Canada to discuss what Standard American or Standard Canadian might be or, indeed, if there were such a thing as a standard. Neither meeting succeeded in satisfying even its participants. One linguist attending the Kingston, Ontario, conference argued, moreover, that in Canada, a country with two official languages, a country in which a vast number of citizens have neither French nor English as a first language and in which diversity is encouraged, a country strongly influenced by both British and American models, imposition of one standard of correctness is impossible and undesirable (Chambers 1986).

Deviations from "standards" that remain undefined even in the minds of those who are most exasperated by the "errors" they detect on everyone's lips have been seen to reflect a "language crisis." The "Letters to the Editor" in American and Canadian newspapers reflect anxiety over the perilous state of the English language. Edwin Newman (1974), in his bestseller *Strictly Speaking*, asks "Will Americans be the death of English?" and answers "My mature, considered opinion is that they will." All this fuss is reminiscent of Mark Twain's cable to the Associated Press after reading his obituary: "The reports of my death are greatly exaggerated."

The idea that language change equals corruption goes back at least as far as the Greek grammarians at Alexandria of around 200–100 B.C.E. They were concerned that the Greek spoken in their time was different from the Greek of Homer, and they believed that the earlier forms were purer. They also tried to "correct" the imperfections but failed as miserably as do any modern counterparts. Similarly, the Arabic grammarians working at Basra in the eighth and ninth centuries C.E. attempted to purify Arabic to restore it to the perfection of Arabic in the Koran.

During the nineteenth and early twentieth centuries, commentators — both foreign and native — were critical of the English spoken in North America. Often their criticism had a political origin; thus, for many years after the American Revolution,

FOR BETTER OR FOR WORSE copyright Lynn Johnston Prod. Reprinted with permission of United Features Syndicate. All rights reserved.

British writers and journalists railed against American English. The *London Review* chastised Thomas Jefferson for his *Notes on the State of Virginia*:

> For shame, Mr. Jefferson! Why, after trampling upon the honour of the country, and representing it as little better than a land of barbarism — why, we say, perpetually trample also upon the very grammar of our language. . . . Freely, good sir, we will forgive all your attacks, impotent as they are illiberal, upon our *national character*; but for the future spare — O spare, we beseech you, our mother-tongue!

But equally sharp were the self-criticisms of one critic who worried that "Canadian English" was "a corrupt dialect growing up amongst our population . . . until it threatens to produce a language as unlike our noble mother tongue as the negro patua, or the Chinese pidgeon English" (Geike 1857), a comment that reveals the speaker's lack of knowledge about the grammatical complexities of African American English and the social circumstances that led to the development of a pidgin. But the fears of British journalists in 1787 and of Canadian commentators in 1857 have proven to be unfounded, and so will the fears of Edwin Newman and the anxious contributors of Letters to the Editor.

No academy and no guardians of language purity can stem language change, nor should anyone attempt to do so, since change does not mean corruption. The fact that for the great majority of English speakers *criteria* and *data* are now mass nouns, like *information*, is no cause for concern. Information can include one fact or many facts, but one would still say *The information is*. For some speakers, it is equally correct to say *The criteria is* or *The criteria are*. Those who say *The data are* would or could say *The datum* (singular) *is*.

A standard dialect (or prestige dialect) of a particular language may serve a social function — for example, to bind people together or to provide a common written form for multidialectal speakers. The primary function of standard varieties is public (including international) rather than personal and private. The standard or prestige dialect is appropriate to relatively formal styles and genres, for media addressing large numbers of people, and for utterances intended to have permanence (Crystal 1987). It is not, however, more expressive, more logical, more complex, or more regular than any other dialect or language. Any judgements, therefore, as to the superiority or inferiority of a particular dialect or language are social judgements, not linguistic or scientific judgements. It is a matter more of manners than of morals. As Dwight Bolinger (1980) says,

> There will be a prestige variety so long as speakers and writers must take account of needs and desires as hearers and readers. And if producing messages and receiving and decoding them are psychologically opposed operations . . . then that accountability will always be with us. Speakers naturally prefer to sing their half of the duet with no more effort than necessary — to use words and constructions that come first to mind, to speak at low volume, to slur the sounds. Hearers just as naturally want comprehension to require no more effort than necessary — to be favored with background information, unambiguous sentences, and reasonably crisp articulation. The speaker or writer of course is

the one who has to make most of the concessions, especially if he has an audience of more than one and most especially if the audience is remote in space or time. This explains why a prestige variety is so needed in writing.

Banned Languages

Language purists wish to stem change in language or dialect differentiation because of their false belief that some languages are better than others or that change leads to corruption. Languages and dialects have also been **banned** as a means of political control. Russian was the only legal language permitted by the Russian tsars, who banned the use of Ukrainian, Lithuanian, Georgian, Armenian, Azerbaijani, and all the other languages spoken by national groups under the rule of Russia.

For many years, the languages of the First Nations were banned in religious and government schools on the reserves both in Canada and in the United States. Cajun French was banned in southern Louisiana by practice if not by law until about twenty years ago. Individuals over the age of 50 report that they were often punished in school if they spoke in French even though many of them had never heard English before attending school. Japanese movies and songs were once banned in Korea, and Færoese was banned in the Færoe Islands. In a recent discussion among linguists via a computer network called Linguist Net, various degrees of the banning of languages and dialects were reported to exist or to have existed in many countries throughout history.

In France, a notion of the "standard" as the only correct form of the language is propagated by an official academy that determines which usages constitute the "official French language." A number of years ago, this academy enacted a law forbidding the use of "Franglais" words in advertising (words of English origin such as *le parking, le weekend,* and *le hotdog*), but the French continue to use them. Many of the hundreds of local village dialects (called *patois* [pætwɑ] by the academy) are actually separate languages, derived from Latin (as are French, Spanish, and Italian). There were political as well as misguided linguistic motivations behind the efforts to maintain only one official language.

In the past (and to some extent in the present), anyone from the provinces who wished to succeed in French society had to learn Parisian French and be bidialectal. In recent years in France, the regional "nationalist" movements have made a major demand for the right to use their own languages in their schools and for official business. In the section of France known as l'Occitanie, the popular singers sing in the regional language, Languedoc, both as a protest against the official "standard language" policy and as part of the cultural revival movement. Here is the final chorus of a popular song sung in Languedoc (shown below with its French and English translations):

Languedoc	**French**	**English**
Mas perqué, perqué	Mais pourquoi, pourquoi	But why, why
M'an pas dit à	Ne m'a-t-on pas dit à	Did they not speak to me
l'escóla	l'école	at school
La lega de mon pais?	La langue de mon pays?	The language of my country?

In the province of Brittany in France, there has also been a strong movement for the use of Breton in the schools, as opposed to the "standard" French. Breton is not even in the same language family as French, which is a Romance language; Breton is a Celtic language in the same family as Irish, Gaelic, and Welsh. It is not, however, the structure of the language or the genetic family grouping that has led to the Breton movement. It is rather the pride of a people who speak a language or a dialect not considered as good as the "standard" and their efforts to change this political view of language use.

These efforts have proved successful. In 1982, the newly elected French government decreed that the languages and cultures of Brittany (Breton), the southern Languedoc region, and other areas would be promoted through schooling, exhibitions, and festivals. No longer would schoolchildren who spoke Breton be humiliated by having to wear a wooden shoe tied around their necks, as had been the custom.

In recent years in the United States, a movement has arisen in the attempt to establish English as an official language by amending the Constitution. An "Official English" initiative was passed by the electorate in California in 1986, in Colorado, Florida, and Arizona in 1988, and in Alabama in 1990. Such measures have also been adopted by seventeen state legislatures. This kind of linguistic chauvinism is opposed by minority group advocates who point out that such measures prevent large numbers of non-English speakers from participating in the electoral process if ballots and other educational material are printed only in English. Leading educators also oppose such moves, since they could halt programs in bilingual education that are proving to be effective as means both to educate non-native speakers and to aid their acquisition of English.

The Preservation and Restoration of Languages

The attempts to ban certain languages and dialects should not be equated with the efforts by certain peoples to preserve their own languages and cultures. This attempt to slow down or reverse the dying out of a language is evident in the concern of Quebec to preserve and promote the province's French language and heritage. Francophones of Quebec, Acadians of New Brunswick, Franco-Ontarians, and Francophones in scattered communities across Western Canada (where they make up less than 3 percent of the population [Yalden 1984] — islands of French in a sea of English) feel pressure upon their language and culture. The dominance of English, even in an officially bilingual Canada, imposes itself upon the consciousness of Francophones in a way unimaginable to Anglophones.

"Bill 101" of the Quebec National Assembly, which established French as the official language of the province, was designed to defend Francophones — within "la belle province" at least — from assimilation into the "English community" by insisting on French in all official acts, from the laws of the province and agencies down to the use of French on signs and menus. It also directs that all children be educated in French unless one of their parents was educated in English in Quebec. It further mandates the "francization" of businesses with more than 50 employees, and a bureau has been established "to keep a watch on language developments in Quebec with respect to the status and quality of the French language" and to "apprise the Minister of the questions pertaining to language that in its opinion require attention or action by the Government" (*Préfixe du recueil des lois de 1977* 1977).

As one historian of Canadian English has observed, "the relationship between the two languages [French and English] dominates the linguistic and often the political scene throughout the country" (Fee 1992). It is not easy to establish a bilingual and multicultural country, and there are those who might prefer the establishment of two distinct language areas (if not two countries). But, despite the shrillness of some opponents, most Canadians are supportive of bilingualism and, on the whole, believe that the existence of the two official languages adds to the quality of the nation, as a 1991 report discovered (*Annual Report of the Commissioner of Official Languages 1991* 1992).

Efforts have been made in the past half-century not only to secure threatened languages, such as French in Quebec, but also to resurrect languages long dead. A dramatic example of this restoration of a language occurred in Israel. An Academy of the Hebrew Language in Israel was established to accomplish a task never before done in the history of humanity — to revive an ancient written language to serve the daily colloquial needs of the people. Twenty-three lexicologists work with the Bible and the Talmud in order to add new words to the language. While there is some attempt to keep the language "pure," the academy has given way to popular pressure. Thus, a bank cheque is called a *check* /ček/ in the singular and is pluralized by adding the Hebrew suffix to form *check-im*, although the Hebrew word *hamcha* was proposed. Similarly, *lipstick* has triumphed over *faton* and *pajama* over *chalifatsheina*.

African American English

> The language, only the language. . . . It is the thing that black people love so much — the saying of words, holding them on the tongue, experimenting with them, playing with them. It's a love, a passion. Its function is like a preacher's: to make you stand up out of your seat, make you lose yourself and hear yourself. The worst of all possible things that could happen would be to lose that language.
>
> Toni Morrison, interview in *The New Republic*, March 21, 1981

Most of the regional dialects of North America are, to a great extent, free from stigma even though they may be parodied — often quite inexactly — by members of other dialect groups. In the United States, the *r*-less Brooklynese or the "drawl" of Southerners is singled out for "humorous" treatment, as is the Ottawa Valley dialect or the rural speech of Maritimers in Canada. One dialect in the United States, however, has been a victim of prejudice. This dialect, **African American English (AAE),**[3] is spoken by a large number of African Americans who live in urban areas traditionally referred to as *ghettos* but now euphemistically called *inner cities*. African American English is actually a group of closely related dialects also called African American Vernacular English, **Black English (BE)**, Inner City English, and **Ebonics**.

What most Canadians know about African American English — or what passes for this dialect of English — has probably come to them through films in which it is carefully modified to prevent misunderstanding and confusion. The true dialect is found primarily in the large inner cities of the United States.

The distinguishing features of the dialect persist for social, educational, and economic reasons. Discrimination has created ghetto living and segregated schools, and where social isolation exists dialect differences are intensified. In recent years, many Blacks in the United States no longer think of their dialect as inferior, and for them it has become a means of positive identification. Similarly, in England, Jamaican "patois," differing considerably from AAE, has been used by younger people (most of whom also use Received Pronunciation or one of the dialects of British English) as a social and psychological protest against their treatment by society (Edwards 1989).

Some critics attempt to equate the use of AAE with inferior genetic intelligence and cultural deprivation, justifying these notions by stating that AAE is a "deficient, illogical, and incomplete" language. Such epithets cannot be applied to any language, and they are as unscientific in reference to AAE as they would be to Russian, Chinese, Standard American English, or Canadian English.

Some people, of every race, have thought that they could identify race by hearing an unseen person talk, believing that different races inherently speak differently. This assumption is equally false; a Black child raised in an upper-class British neighbourhood will speak that dialect of English, as many British citizens of West Indian background prove daily. A white child raised in an environment where African American English is spoken will speak African American English. Children construct grammar based on the language they hear.

As with any dialect, there are systematic differences between AAE and other forms of English, just as there are systematic differences between Australian and Canadian English or Canadian and American English. AAE is discussed here at some length because it provides an informative illustration of the regularities of a dialect as well as of that dialect's systematic differences from the standard language, differences that are also evident in other dialects less subject to criticism. It is not in the specific phonological and syntactic rules that AAE is unique but in their collective use combined with an imaginative lexicon. In addition, AAE is a unique and powerful dialect — perhaps disturbing at times — well worth study in its own right.

Phonology of African American English

A few of the differences and similarities between AAE and dialects of Canadian English are as follows:

1.   Like a number of dialects of British and American English, AAE includes a rule that deletes /r/ everywhere except before a vowel. Pairs of words such as *guard* and *god, nor* and *gnaw, sore* and *saw, poor* and *pa, fort* and *fought,* and *court* and *caught* are pronounced identically in AAE because of this phonological rule in the grammar and not from indolence or carelessness.

2.   There is also an *l-deletion rule* for some speakers of AAE that creates homophones such as *toll* and *toe, all* and *awe,* and *help* and *hep.* AAE is not unique in this rule, for deletion rules of one form or another are common in English dialects; Torontonians do not demonstrate an inability to grasp the rules of English or expose their intrinsic laziness when they refer to their city as [trʌnə] or [trɑnə] rather than [tʰərɑnto]. They are, in fact, applying a medial cluster simplification rule, one that commonly deletes /t/ after /n/. Moreover, many speakers of Canadian and American English (CE and AE) normally delete nasals before final voiceless stops.

3.   A regular *consonant cluster simplification rule* in AAE reduces a sequence of two or more consonants, particularly those occurring at the ends of words and when one of the two consonants is an alveolar (/t/, /d/, /s/, /z/). The application of this rule may delete the past tense morpheme so that *meant* and *mend* are both pronounced as *men* and *past* and *passed* may both be pronounced as *pass.*

     This deletion rule does not always apply, and studies have shown that it is more likely to apply when the final [t] or [d] does not represent the past tense morpheme, as in nouns such as *paste* [pes] as opposed to verbs such as *chased* [čest], where the final past tense [t] will not always be deleted. This has also been found true with final [s] or [z], which will be retained by speakers of AAE more in words such as *seats* /sit + s/ where the /s/ represents "plural" than in words such as *Keats* /kit/ where it is more likely to be deleted.

     Again, some Newfoundland speakers also simplify final consonant clusters ending in /t/ or /d/ in words such as *loft, sound,* and *field.* As this indicates, deletion and cluster simplification rules of one form or another are not uncommon in English dialects.

4.   AAE shares with many regional dialects the lack of any distinction between /ɪ/ and /ɛ/ before nasal consonants, producing identical pronunciations of *pin* and *pen, bin* and *Ben, tin* and *ten,* and so on. The vowel used in these words is roughly between the [ɪ] of *pit* and the [ɛ] of *pet.*

5.   In AAE the phonemic distinction between /aj/ and /aw/ has been lost, both having become /a/. Thus, *why* and *wow* are pronounced [wa].

6.   Another change has reduced the /ɔj/ (particularly before /l/) to the simple vowel [o] without the glide, so that *boil* and *boy* are pronounced [bo].

7.   A regular feature is the change of a /θ/ to /f/ and /ð/ to /v/, so that *Ruth* is pronounced [ruf] and *brother* is pronounced [brʌvər]. This [θ]–[f] correspondence is also true of some dialects of British English, in which /θ/ is not even a phoneme in the language. *Think* is regularly [fiŋk] in Cockney English.

All these differences are systematic and "rule-governed" and similar to sound changes that have taken place in languages all over the world, including Standard English.

Syntactic Differences between AAE, AE, and CE

Syntactic differences, as noted above, also exist between dialects. It is the syntactic differences that have often been used to illustrate the "illogic" of AAE, yet just such differences point to the fact that AAE is as syntactically complex and as "logical" as AE or CE.

Double Negatives

Following the lead of early prescriptive grammarians, some linguists have concluded that it is illogical to say *he don't know nothing* because two negatives make a positive despite the obvious disagreement of those who use the double negative. Indeed, there are few speakers of English, no matter of what dialect, who would think that the above sentence means *He knows something*. Multiple negation was the standard in an earlier stage of English, and Shakespeare for one was certainly not reluctant to use double negatives. It remains a regular rule for speakers of French and many other languages, and they are seldom accused of being illogical or indolent.

Deletion of the Verb Be

In most cases, if in Standard English the verb can be contracted, in African American English sentences it is deleted, as in the following sentences from Labov (1969):

AE and CE	AAE
He is nice/He's nice.	He nice.
They are mine/They're mine.	They mine.
I am going to do it/I'm gonna do it.	I gonna do it.

Habitual Be

In both AAE and some Newfoundland dialects, a form of the verb *be* is used when a speaker is referring to habitual action. In a sentence such as

> Aidan is happy.

a speaker of Standard Canadian English recognizes at least two possible meanings. It might mean that Aidan is happy at the present moment, or it could mean that he is generally happy. To disambiguate the sentence, a speaker of Standard English would have to employ lexical means, adding a word or two:

> Aidan is generally happy.
> Aidan is happy today.

But both AAE and some Newfoundland dialects can accomplish this disambiguation syntactically by using the verb *be*:

AAE	**Newfoundland**	
Aidan be happy.	Aidan bees happy.	("Aidan is always happy.")
Aidan happy.	⎰ Aidan's happy. ⎱ Aidan is happy now.	("At this moment, Aidan is happy.")

In this Newfoundland dialect, there is no provision for deleting the verb when it refers to an event at the present moment; instead, it employs the standard forms *am*, *is*, and *are*. But *-s* appears in all persons of the verb *be* — *I bes/bees, she bes/bees, they bes/bees* — used for "habitual or continuous action," and consequently it is not, as in Standard English, a marker of the third person, present tense.

This syntactical distinction between habitual and non-habitual aspect occurs in other languages but not in Standard English. It has been suggested that the uninflected *be* in AAE is the result of a convergence of similar rules in African, Creole, and Irish-English sources (Holm 1988). African and Creole sources could not explain the similar use of *be* in Maritime Canada; on the other hand, "habitual *be*" may reflect an important strain in Newfoundland English and point to a common influence in AAE and Newfoundland English, dialects of two otherwise different cultures: the influence of the English of southeastern Ireland. Students of Irish-English, Hiberno-English, or Anglo-Irish, as it is variously called, record a similar "habitual present" tense in that dialect (Adams 1985), and Alan Bliss (1984) notes the common use of *I be, you be*, and *he bees* in this manner, though he reports that *I do be, you do be*, and *he does be* are in more general use. William Kirwin (1993) finds that the "habitual *be*" is "of great frequency" in Newfoundland and that "a variant, *do be*, has been reported very frequently in the negative, for example, 'Don't be talking!' " Perhaps, then, one connection between African American speech (though certainly influenced strongly by the languages of Africa) and the dialects of Newfoundland is found in the speech of immigrants from the Emerald Isle.

There are, of course, other differences and similarities between the dialects we have been discussing, but those listed are enough to show the regularity of AAE (and of the other dialects) and to dispel the notion that there is anything "illogical" or "primitive" about any one of them.

The structure and history of any dialect reveals important information about language change in general, a subject which we discuss in the next chapter. In addition, the history of AAE reveals how social prejudices can distort our perceptions of language. There would be fewer communication breakdowns between teachers and their students if certain dialects were not considered inferior versions of the standard. Children who read *your mother* as *you muvver* or who say *I ain't got no . . .* would be more likely to respond positively to statements such as "In the dialect we are using, the *th* sound is pronounced [ð], not [v], as it is in yours" or that double negatives, though once common in English, are no longer used in the dialect they are learning in school than to a teacher who expresses contempt toward them and their speech.

History of African American English

It is simple to date the beginning of African American English — the first Blacks arrived in Virginia in 1619, and the history of Black slavery in what is now Canada goes back to these early years as well. Ten years after the arrival of Blacks in Virginia, Oliver Le Jeune, one of the first slaves for whom there is a name, was sold into slavery in New France. Many Loyalists were slave holders and brought slaves with them into British North America. But in addition to slaves, a large number of Blacks who earned their freedom through loyalty to the Crown immigrated to Nova Scotia and New Brunswick after the American Revolution. In 1833, Parliament in London abolished slavery in British North America, though the practice had been under severe restrictions in many parts of the country before that date. Upper Canada restricted slavery in 1793, with the intention of abolishing it. Because of such laws, escaping slaves sought refuge in Canada before and during the American Civil War, though many — if not most — returned to their homes in the United States afterward.

With changes in discriminatory immigration laws, the last half of the twentieth century has brought increased immigration from the Caribbean and Africa. Most of these new Canadians continue to speak the English of their former homes, or they — and certainly their children — will have adopted Canadian English after settling in their new country. While AAE in the United States has been subjected to intense study in the past few decades, investigation of the English of Black Canadians has been slight. In part this is due to the smaller size of the Black community (approximately 2 percent of the population), in part to the perception that Black citizens have completely assimilated themselves into the general language community and speak the English of their white neighbours. Like many facets of Canadian English, however, this is an area that remains largely unexplored.

Nonetheless, there are communities, settled by Loyalist Blacks and those fleeing from slavery, that have been largely segregated from the surrounding white neighbourhoods and that may reflect earlier forms of AAE. Linguists have begun to explore the nature of the English spoken in these areas in an effort to determine exactly how these dialects relate to the AAE of the United States (Poplack and Tagliamonte 1993) and to better understand the dialects of Canadian English.

The history and structure of AAE, then, are almost entirely based on a dialect that has been studied in the United States, where at least two views of the origin of that dialect are evident. One view suggests that AAE in North America originated when the African slaves learned English from their colonial masters as a second language. Although the basic grammar was learned, many surface differences persisted, which were reflected in the grammars constructed by the children of the slaves, who heard English primarily from their parents. Had the children been exposed to the English spoken by the whites, their grammars would have been similar if not identical to the general Southern dialect. The dialect differences persisted and grew because Blacks in America were isolated by social and racial barriers. The proponents of this theory point to the fact that the grammars of African American English and Standard American English are basically identical except for a few syntactic and phonological rules, which produce surface differences.

DOONESBURY copyright 1982 and 1984 G.B. Trudeau. Reprinted with permission of Universal Press Syndicate. All rights reserved.

Another view that is receiving increasing support is that many of the unique features of African American English are traceable to influences of the African languages spoken by the slaves. During the seventeenth and eighteenth centuries, Africans who spoke different languages were purposely grouped together to discourage communication and to prevent slave revolts. In order to communicate, the slaves were forced to use the one common language all had access to, namely English. They invented a simplified form — called a pidgin — that incorporated many features from West African languages. According to this view, the differences between AAE and other dialects are due more to basic syntactic differences than to surface distinctions.

It is apparent that African American English of the United States is closer to the Southern dialect of American English than to other dialects. The theory that suggests that the Black slaves learned the English of white Southerners as a second language explains these similarities. They might also be explained by the fact that for many decades a large number of Southern white children were raised by Black women and played with Black children. It is not unlikely that many of the distinguishing features of Southern dialects were acquired from African American English in this way. A publication of the American Dialect Society in 1908–09 makes this point clearly:

> For my part, after a somewhat careful study of east Alabama dialect, I am convinced that the speech of the white people, the dialect I have spoken all my life and the one I tried to record here, is more largely colored by the language of the negroes [sic] than by any other single influence. (Payne 1909)

English, both inside and outside the borders of the United States, has been and continues to be enriched by the words, phrases, and usages originating in AAE. Disseminated through the power of film and television, it affects English throughout the world.

Lingua Francas

Language is a steed that carries one into a far country.

Arab proverb

In medieval times, a trade language came into use in Mediterranean ports based largely on the medieval languages that became modern Italian and Provençal. This language came to be called **lingua franca**, "Frankish language," and was used by common agreement for social or commercial communication between people speaking divergent languages. Subsequently, the term has been generalized to mean any language similarly used. English has been called "the lingua franca of diplomacy," and Latin and Greek were the lingua franca of Christianity in the West and East, respectively, for a millennium. Among Jews, Yiddish has long served as a lingua franca.

More frequently, lingua francas serve as "trade languages." East Africa is populated by hundreds of tribes, each speaking its own language, but most Africans of this area learn at least some Swahili as a second language, and this lingua franca is used and understood in nearly every marketplace. A similar situation exists in West Africa, where Hausa is the lingua franca.

Hindi and Urdu are the lingua francas of India and Pakistan, respectively. The linguistic situation of this area of the world is so complex that there are often regional lingua francas — usually the popular dialects near commercial centres. The same situation existed in Imperial China.

In modern China, the Chinese language as a whole is often referred to as *Zhongwen*, which technically refers to the written language, whereas *Zhongguo hua* refers to the spoken language. Ninety-four percent of the people living in the People's Republic of China are said to speak Han languages, which can be divided into eight major dialects (or language groups) that for the most part are mutually unintelligible. Within each group, there are hundreds of dialects. In addition to these Han languages, there are more than 50 "national minority" languages, including the five principal ones: Mongolian, Uighur, Tibetan, Zhuang, and Korean. The situation is clearly complex, and for this reason an extensive language reform policy was inaugurated to spread a standard language, called *Putonghua*, that embodies the pronunciation of the Beijing dialect, the grammar of Northern Chinese dialects, and the vocabulary of modern colloquial Chinese. The native languages and dialects are not considered inferior; rather, the approach is to spread the "common speech" (the literal meaning of *Putonghua*) so that all may communicate with each other in this lingua franca.

Certain lingua francas arise naturally; others are developed by government policy and intervention. In many places of the world, however, people still cannot speak with neighbours only a few kilometres away.

Pidgins and Creoles

Padi dɛm; kɔntri; una ɔl we de na Rom.
Mɛk una ɔl kak una yes. A Kam bɛr siza,
a nɔ kam prez am.

William Shakespeare, *Julius Caesar*, III.ii, translated to Krio by Thomas Decker

Pidgins

A lingua franca is typically a language with a broad base of native speakers, likely to be used and learned by persons whose native language is in the same language family. Often in history, however, traders and missionaries from one part of the world have visited and attempted to communicate with peoples residing in another area. In such cases, the contact is too specialized and the cultures are too widely separated for the usual kind of lingua franca to arise. Instead, the two (or possibly more) groups use their native languages as a basis for a rudimentary language of few lexical items and less complex grammatical rules. Such a "marginal language" is called a **pidgin**.

There are a number of such languages in the world, including a large number of English-based pidgins. One such pidgin, called Tok Pisin, was originally called Melanesian Pidgin English. It is widely used in Papua New Guinea. Like most pidgins, many of its lexical items and much of its structure are based on only one language of the two or more contact languages, in this case English. The variety of Tok Pisin used as a primary language in urban centres is more highly developed and more complex than the Tok Pisin used as a lingua franca in remote areas. Papers in Tok Pisin have been presented at linguistics conferences in Papua New Guinea, and it is commonly used for debates in the parliament of the country.

Although pidgins are in some sense rudimentary, they are not devoid of grammar. The phonological system is rule-governed, as in any human language. The inventory of phonemes is generally small, and each phoneme may have many allophonic pronunciations. In Tok Pisin, for example, [č], [š], and [s] are all possible pronunciations of the phoneme /s/; [masin], [mašin], and [mačin] all mean "machine."

Tok Pisin has its own writing system, its own literature, and its own newspapers and radio programs, and it has even been used to address a United Nations meeting.

With their small vocabularies, however, pidgins are not good at expressing fine distinctions of meaning. Many lexical items bear a heavy semantic burden, with context being relied upon to remove ambiguity. Much circumlocution and metaphorical extension is necessary. All of these factors combine to give pidgins a unique flavour. What could be a friendlier definition of "friend" than the Australian Aborigine's *him brother belong me* or more poetic than this description of the sun: *lamp belong Jesus*? A policeman is *gubmint catchum-fella*, whiskers are *grass belong face*, and when a man is thirsty *him belly allatime burn*.

Pidgin has come to have negative connotations, perhaps because the best-known pidgins are all associated with European colonial empires. The *Encyclopedia Britannica* once described Pidgin English as "an unruly bastard jargon, filled with nursery imbecilities, vulgarisms and corruptions." It no longer uses such a definition. In recent times, there is greater recognition of the fact that pidgins reflect human creative linguistic ability, as is beautifully revealed by the Chinese servant who asked whether his master's prize sow had given birth to a litter: *Him cow pig have kittens*? Pidgin gives an amusing twist to our view of the monarchy when we hear of Prince Philip, on a visit to New Guinea, referred to as *fella belong Mrs. Queen*.

Some people would like to eradicate pidgins. A pidgin spoken in New Zealand by the Maoris was replaced, through massive education, by Standard English, and the use of Chinese Pidgin English was forbidden by the government of China. Its use had died out by the end of the nineteenth century because the Chinese gained access to learning Standard English, which proved to be more useful in communicating with non-Chinese speakers.

Pidgins have been unjustly maligned; they may serve a useful function (Hall 1955). For example, a New Guinean can learn Tok Pisin well enough in six months to begin many kinds of semiprofessional training. To learn English for the same purpose might require ten times as long. In an area with more than 800 mutually unintelligible languages, Tok Pisin plays a vital role in unifying similar cultures.

From the seventeenth through the nineteenth centuries, many pidgins sprang up along the coasts of China, Africa, and the New World to accommodate the Europeans. Chinook Jargon is a pidginized North American Native language used by various tribes of the Pacific Northwest to carry on trade. Some linguists have suggested that Proto-Germanic (the earliest form of the Germanic languages) was originally a pidgin, arguing that ordinary linguistic change cannot account for certain striking differences between the Germanic tongues and other Indo-European languages. They theorized that in the first millennium B.C.E. the primitive Germanic tribes that resided along the Baltic Sea traded with the more sophisticated, seagoing cultures. The two peoples communicated by means of a pidgin, which either grossly affected Proto-Germanic or actually became Proto-Germanic. If this is true, then English, German, Dutch, and Yiddish had humble beginnings as a pidgin.

Case, tense, mood, and voice are generally absent from pidgins. One cannot, however, speak an English pidgin by merely using English without inflecting verbs or declining pronouns. Pidgins are not "baby talk" or Hollywood's version of North American Natives talking English. *Me Tarzan, you Jane* may be understood, but it is not pidgin as it is used in West Africa.

Pidgins are simple but nonetheless rule-governed. In Tok Pisin, most verbs that take a direct object must have the suffix -*m* or -*im*, even if the direct object is absent; here are some examples of the results of the application of this "rule" of the language:

Tok Pisin:	Mi driman long kilim wanpela snek.
English:	I dreamed that I killed a snake.

Tok Pisin:	Bandarap em i kukim.
English:	Bandarap cooked (it).

Other rules determine word order, which, as in English, is usually quite strict in pidgins because of the lack of case endings on nouns.

The set of pronouns may, in some cases, be simpler in pidgins than in English. In Cameroonian Pidgin (CP), which is also an English-based pidgin, the pronoun system does not show gender or all the case differences that exist in Standard English (data from Todd 1984):

CP			**SE**		
a	mi	ma	I	me	my
yu	yu	yu	you	you	your
i	i/am	i	he	him	his
i	i/am	i	she	her	her
wi	wi	wi	we	us	our
wuna	wuna	wuna	you	you	your
dɛm	dɛm/am	dɛm	they	them	their

Pidgins may also have fewer prepositions than the languages on which they are based. In CP, for example, *fɔ* means "to," "at," "in," "for," "on," and "from," as shown in the following examples:

Gif di buk fɔ mi.	"Give the book to me."
I dei fɔ fam.	"She is at the farm."
Dɛm dei fɔ chɔs.	"They are in the church."
Du dis wan fɔ mi, a bɛg.	"Do this for me, please."
Di mɔni dei fɔ tebul.	"The money is on the table."
You fit muf tɛn frangk fɔ ma kwa.	"You can take ten francs from my bag."

Characteristics of pidgins differ in detail from one pidgin to another and often vary depending on the native language of the pidgin speaker. Thus, the verb generally comes at the end of a sentence for a Japanese speaker of Hawaiian Pidgin English (as in *The poor people all potato eat*), whereas a Filipino speaker of this pidgin puts it before the subject (*Work hard these people*).

Creoles

One distinguishing characteristic of pidgin languages is that no one learns them as native speakers. When a pidgin comes to be adopted by a community as its native tongue, and children learn it as a first language, that language is called a **creole**; the pidgin has become creolized.

The term *creole* comes originally from the Portuguese word meaning "a white man of European descent born and raised in a tropical or semitropical colony.... The term was ... subsequently applied to certain languages spoken ... in and around the Caribbean and in West Africa, and then more generally to other similar languages" (Romaine 1988).

Creoles often arose on slave plantations in certain areas where Africans of many different tribes could communicate only via the plantation pidgin. Haitian Creole, based on French, developed this way, as did the "English" spoken in parts of Jamaica. Gullah is an English-based creole spoken by the descendants of African slaves on islands off the coasts of Georgia and South Carolina. Louisiana Creole, related to Haitian Creole, is spoken by large numbers of Blacks and whites in Louisiana. Krio, the language spoken by as many as 200 000 Sierra Leoneans, developed, at least in part, from an English-based pidgin.

Creoles become fully developed languages, having more lexical items and a broader array of grammatical distinctions than pidgins. In time, they become languages as complete in every way as other languages.

Registers, Slang, and Jargon

Slang is language which takes off its coat, spits on its hands — and goes to work.

Carl Sandburg

Registers

Most speakers of a language know many dialects. They use one dialect when out with friends, another when in a job interview or presenting a report, and yet another when talking with family. These "situational dialects" — that is, those varieties of language one uses in specific social settings — are called **registers** or **styles**.

Nearly everyone has at least an informal and a formal register. Informal registers, although permitting certain abbreviations and deletions not permitted in formal speech, are also rule-governed. The informal register employs the rules of contraction more often than the formal register does, the syntactic rules of negation and agreement may be altered, and many words are used that do not occur in the formal register. Questions are often shortened with the *you* subject and the auxiliary deleted. One can ask *Running the marathon?* or *You running the marathon?* instead of the more formal *Are you running the marathon?*, but one cannot shorten the question to **Are running the marathon?* Everything doesn't go in informal talk, but the rules permit greater deletion than do the rules in the grammar of the formal language.

Many speakers can use a number of different registers, ranging between the two extremes of formal and informal. Speakers of minority dialects sometimes display virtuosic ability to slide back and forth along a continuum of styles from informal to "formal standard." When William Labov was studying the language of Black Harlem youths, he encountered difficulties because the youths (subconsciously) adopted a different style when in the presence of white strangers. It took time and effort to gain their confidence to the point where they would "forget" that their conversations were being recorded and thus use their less formal register.

Many cultures have rules of social behaviour that strictly govern style. In some European languages, there is the distinction between "you (familiar)" and "you (polite)." German *du* and French *tu* are to be used only with "intimates" and children, or the words may be construed as insulting; *Sie* and *vous* are more formal and used with non-intimates. French even has the verb *tutoyer*, which means "to use the *tu* form," and German uses the verb *duzen* to express the informal or less honorific style of speaking.

Other languages have much more elaborate codes of style usage. Speakers of Thai use *kin* "eat" informally with their intimates; but *thaan* "eat" is used informally with strangers, *rabprathaan* "eat" on formal occasions or when conversing with dignitaries or esteemed persons (such as parents), and *chan* "eat" when referring to Buddhist monks. Japanese and Javanese are also languages with elaborate styles that must be adhered to in certain social situations.

Variation in language also depends on what is being talked or written about (called **field of discourse** and **genre**). Fields may be divided into imaginative genres (novels, science fiction, romances, dramas, etc.) and informational genres (scientific, instructional, technical, journalistic, bureaucratic, and the like). Each has its own characteristic use of language that is often immediately recognizable even by those who are not part of the group that employs that language. Thus, public worship may use archaic forms such as *thou* and *thee* and *hath*, while legal language is marked by formal words such as *herein-under* and repetition of noun phrases such as *party of the first part* rather than pronouns. The field of cookbooks includes, of course, terms for food and the preparation of food (*boil, seethe, bake*) and terms for measurements (*teaspoon, cup, millilitre, kilogram*). Cooks put up with abrupt commands (*Bake at 350 degrees for 20 minutes*) that readers might otherwise consider rude were it not that such directions are part of this field of discourse.

Code Switching

Speakers are not confined to one variety of speech, formal or informal, but often move from one variety of English to another or even from one language to another and sometimes do so within the same discourse. This movement between varieties or languages is called **code switching** and may occur in the midst of a sentence. Take, for example, the following sentences:

> Jim asked me to go to the pub with him tonight. He's a nice enough chap, and I like him — but, like, no way!

> The government claims that this bill will easily pass, but I wish to inform my honourable friends across the aisle — it ain't gonna happen!

In both instances, the switch from a more formal variety to "substandard" English serves to underline the speakers' negative responses.

Switching also occurs between languages; a young child, for example, was overheard on a Kitchener, Ontario, bus excitedly exclaiming, "Guck, Mutti, da fahrt ein police car" ("Look, Mummy, there goes a police car"), moving easily from colloquial German to English in the same sentence.

Among the many German-speaking people of the Kitchener–Waterloo area are a large number who employ a low-German dialect similar to that known as "Pennsylvania Dutch" in the United States as their mother tongue. This is not surprising, for their ancestors came to Ontario in the early nineteenth century from Pennsylvania seeking good farming land and freedom to practise their religion. The "Old Order" of Mennonites reject modern ways and modern devices, and their German dialect is the everyday speech of young and old alike. Most also have a working knowledge of English, which they reserve for use in the English-speaking world of town and business. When people employ different varieties of the same language or two distinct languages for different purposes in this fashion, they are said to be **diglossic**. Another instance of diglossia are the Francophones outside the province of Quebec who live among largely English-speaking people; these people will probably restrict their use of their mother tongue, employing French in the home and among French-speaking friends, while using English for business and for the non-Francophone world around them.

Slang

> Police are notorious for creating new words by shortening existing ones, such as *perp* for *perpetrator, ped* for *pedestrian* and *wit* for *witness*. More baffling

to court reporters is the gang member who . . . might testify that he was in his *hooty* around *dimday* when some *mud duck* with a *tray-eight* tried to *take him out of the box*. Translation: The man was in his car about dusk when a woman armed with a .38 caliber gun tried to kill him.

Los Angeles Times, August 11, 1986

One mark of an informal style is the frequent occurrence of **slang**. Almost everyone uses slang on some occasions, but it is not easy to define the word. Slang has been defined as "one of those things that everybody can recognize and nobody can define" (Roberts 1958). The use of slang, or colloquial language, introduces many new words into the language by recombining old words into new meanings. *Spaced out, right on, hangup*, and *rip-off* have all gained a degree of acceptance. Slang may also introduce an entirely new word, such as *barf, flub*, and *pooped*. Finally, slang often consists of ascribing totally new meanings to old words. *Grass* and *pot* widened their meaning to "marijuana"; *pig* and *fuzz* are derogatory terms for "police officer"; *rap, cool, dig, stoned, bread*, and *split* have all extended their semantic domain.

The words we have cited sound "slangy" because they have not gained total acceptability. Words such as *dwindle, freshman, glib*, and *mob* are former slang words that in time overcame their "unsavoury" origin. It is not always easy to know where to draw the line between "slang" words and "regular" words. This confusion seems always to have been around. In 1890, John S. Farmer, co-editor with

FOR BETTER OR FOR WORSE copyright Lynn Johnston Prod. Reprinted with permission of United Features Syndicate. All rights reserved.

W.E. Henley of *Slang and Its Analogues* (1965), remarked that "The borderland between slang and the 'Queen's English' is an ill-defined territory, the limits of which have never been clearly mapped out."

One generation's slang is another generation's standard vocabulary. *Fan* (as in "Leafs' fan"[4]) was once a slang term, short for *fanatic*. *Phone*, too, was once a slangy, clipped version of *telephone*, as *TV* was of *television*. In Shakespeare's time, *fretful* and *dwindle* were slang, and more recently *blimp* and *hotdog* were both "hard-core" slang.

The use of slang varies from region to region, so slang in New York and slang in Vancouver differ. The word *slang* itself is slang in British English for "scold."

Slang words and phrases are often "invented" in keeping with new ideas and customs. They may represent "in" attitudes better than the more conservative items of the vocabulary. Their importance is shown by the fact that it was thought necessary to give the returning American prisoners of war from Vietnam a glossary of 86 new slang words and phrases, from *acid* to *zonked*. The words on this list — prepared by the U.S. Air Force — had come into use during only five years. Furthermore, by the time this book was published, many of the terms had passed out of the language, and many new ones have been added.

A number of slang words have entered English from the "underworld," such as *crack* for a special form of cocaine, *payola, C-note, Horseman, to hang paper* ("to write 'bum' cheques"), *sawbuck*, and so forth.

The now ordinary French word meaning "head," *tête*, was once a slang word derived from the Latin *testa*, which meant "earthen pot." Some slang words seem to hang on and on in the language, though, never changing their status from slang to "respectable." Shakespeare used the expression *beat it* to mean "scram" (or more politely, "leave!"), and *beat it* would be considered by most English speakers still to be a slang expression. Similarly, use of the word *pig* for "police officer" goes back at least as far as 1785, when a writer of the time called a Bow Street police officer a "China Street pig."

Jargon and Argot

> It is common knowledge that students have a language that is quite peculiar to them and that is not understood very well outside student society. . . . But if the code of behaviour somewhere is particularly lively, then the language of the students is all the richer for it — and vice versa.
>
> Friedrich Ch. Laukhard (1792)

Practically every science, profession, trade, and occupation has its own set of words, some of which are considered to be "slang" and others "technical," depending on the status of the people using these "in" words. Such words are sometimes called **jargon** or **argot**. Linguistic jargon, some of which is used in this book, consists of terms such as *phoneme, morpheme, case, lexicon, phrase structure rule*, and so on.

The existence of argots or jargons is illustrated by the story of a seaman witness being cross-examined at a trial who was asked if he knew the plaintiff. Indicating that he did not know what *plaintiff* meant brought a chide from the attorney: "You mean you came into this court as a witness and don't know what 'plaintiff' means?" Later the sailor was asked where he was standing when the boat lurched. "Abaft the binnacle" was the reply, and to the attorney's questioning stare he responded "You mean you came into this court and don't know where 'abaft the binnacle' is?"

The computer age not only ushered in a technological revolution; it also introduced a huge jargon of "computerese," including the words *modem* (a blend of *modulator* and *demodulator*), *bit* (a contraction of *binary digit*), *byte* (a collection of some number of *bits*), *floppy* (a noun or adjective referring to a flexible *disk*), *ROM* (an acronym for *read only memory*), *RAM* (an acronym for *random access memory*), *morf* (an abbreviation for the question *male or female?*), and *OOPS* (an acronym for *object oriented program systems*).

Many jargon terms pass into the standard language. Jargon, like slang, spreads from a narrow group until it is used and understood by a large segment of the population. In fact, it is not always possible to distinguish between what is jargon and what is slang, as illustrated in the book *Slang U: The Official Dictionary of College Slang* (Munro 1990), a collection of slang used on the campus of the University of California, Los Angeles, by Professor Munro and the students in her seminar. One cannot tell from the hundreds of entries in this collection which are used solely by UCLA students, which by the definitions above would make it a UCLA student jargon. It is highly probable that the word *fossil*, meaning a "person who has been a college student for more than four years," is used in this way only on this one campus or on college campuses in general, but certainly the term *prick*, referring to a "mean, offensive, inconsiderate, rude person (usually, a male)," is used as a general slang term on and off university campuses.

Taboo or Not Taboo?

Sex is a four-letter word.

Bumper sticker slogan

A recent item in a newspaper included the following paragraph (the names have been deleted to protect the guilty):

> "This is not a Sunday school, but it is a school of law," the judge said in warning the defendants he would not tolerate the "use of expletives during jury selection." "I'm not going to have my fellow citizens and prospective jurors subjected to filthy language," the judge added.

How can language be filthy? In fact, how can it be clean? The filth or beauty of language must be in the ear of the listener or in the collective ear of society.

There cannot be anything about a particular string of sounds that makes it intrinsically clean or dirty, ugly or beautiful. If you say that you *pricked* your finger when sewing, no one would raise an eyebrow; if you refer to your professor as a *prick*, the judge quoted above would undoubtedly censure this "dirty" word.

Words that are unacceptable in the United States are acceptable in Britain and vice versa. In the 1830s, when Fanny Trollope visited North America, she remarked that

> Hardly a day passed in which I did not discover something or other which I had been taught to consider as natural as eating, was held in abhorrence by those around me; many words to which I had never heard an objectionable meaning attached, were totally interdicted, and the strangest paraphrastic phrases substituted.

Some of the words that were taboo at the time in the United States but not in England were *corset, shirt, leg*, and *woman*. She remarked that the word *woman* was thought to refer "only to the lower or less-refined classes of female human-kind."

Certain words in all societies are considered **taboo** — they are not to be used, at least not in "polite company." The word *taboo* was borrowed from Tongan, a Polynesian language, in which it refers to acts that are forbidden or to be avoided. When an act is taboo, reference to this act may also become taboo. That is, first you are forbidden to do something; then you are forbidden to talk about it.

Which acts or words are forbidden reflect the particular customs and views of the society. Some words may be used in certain circumstances and not in others; for example, among the Zuni Natives of New Mexico, it is improper to use the word *takka*, meaning "frogs," during a religious ceremony; a complex compound word must be used instead, and literally translated it would be "several-are-sitting-in-a-shallow-basin-where-they-are-in-liquid" (Farb 1975).

In certain societies, words that have religious connotations are considered profane if used outside formal or religious ceremonies. Christians are forbidden to "take the Lord's name in vain," and this prohibition has been extended to the use of curses, which are believed to have magical powers. Thus, *hell* and *damn* are changed to *heck* and *darn*, perhaps with the belief or hope that this change will fool the "powers that be."

In England, the word *bloody* has long been and continues to be a taboo word. The 1989 edition of the *Oxford English Dictionary*, quoting from its earlier editions (published as late as 1933), states that it has been in general colloquial use from the Restoration to about 1750; "now [it is] constantly in the mouths of the lowest classes, but by respectable people considered 'a horrid word,' on par with obscene or profane language, and usually printed in the newspapers (in police reports, etc.) 'b—y.' " While some assume that the word may originally have referred to the blood of Christ and others associate it with menstruation, the editors of the *OED* argue that

> it was at first a reference to the habits of the "bloods" or aristocratic rowdies of the end of the 17th and beginning of the 18th C. The phrase "bloody drunk" was apparently = "as drunk as a blood" (cf. "as drunk as a lord"), thence it was extended to kindred expressions, and at length to oaths.

And finally "In later times, its association with bloodshed and murder (cf. a bloody battle, a bloody butcher) ... have recommended it to the rough classes as a word that appeals to their imagination." But as the editors admit at the outset, "the origin is not quite certain." No matter what its origins, when George Bernard Shaw had Liza reject Freddie's offer of a walk across the park with "Walk! Not bloody likely. I am going in a taxi," he caused an uproar among *Pygmalion*'s 1910 audiences, and we are told that "much of the interest in the play was due to the heroine's utterance of this banned word. It was waited for with trembling, heard shudderingly" (Partridge as cited in Johnson 1950).

The uncertainty associated with words such as *bloody* gives us a clue about "dirty" words: people who use them often do not know why they are taboo, only that they are, and to some extent this is why they remain in the language — to give vent to strong emotions.

Words relating to sex, sex organs, and natural bodily functions make up a large part of the set of taboo words in many societies. Some languages have no native words to mean "sexual intercourse" but do borrow such words from neighbouring peoples. Other languages have many words for this common and universal act, most of which are considered taboo.

Two or more words or expressions can have the same linguistic meaning, with one being acceptable and the others causing embarrassment or horror. In English, words borrowed from Latin sound "scientific" and therefore appear to be technical and "clean," whereas native Anglo-Saxon counterparts are taboo. This fact reflects the opinion that the vocabulary used by the upper classes was superior to that used by the lower classes, a distinction going back at least to the Norman Conquest in 1066, when, as Peter Farb (1975) puts it, "a duchess perspired and expectorated and menstruated — while a kitchen maid sweated and spat and bled."

There is no linguistic reason why the word *vagina* is "clean" whereas *cunt* is "dirty," or why *prick* or *cock* is taboo but *penis* is acknowledged as referring to part of the male anatomy, or why everyone *defecates* but only vulgar people *shit*. Many people even avoid words such as *breasts, intercourse*, and *testicles* as much as words such as *tits, fuck*, and *balls*. There is no linguistic basis for such views, but pointing out this fact does not imply advocating the use or non-use of any such words.

Euphemisms

> Banish the use of the four letter words
>> Whose meaning is never obscure.
> The Anglos, the Saxons, those bawdy old birds
>> Were vulgar, obscene, and impure.
> But cherish the use of the weaseling phrase
>> That never quite says what it means;
> You'd better be known for your hypocrite ways
>> Than vulgar, impure, and obscene.

Ogden Nash, "Ode to the Four Letter Words," from *Verses from 1929 On*, by Ogden Nash. Copyright 1931 by Ogden Nash. Copyright © renewed 1985 by Frances Nash, Isabel Nash Eberstadt, and Linnell Nash Smith. By permission of Curtis Brown, Ltd.

The existence of taboo words or taboo ideas stimulates the creation of **euphemisms**. A euphemism is a word or phrase that replaces a taboo word or serves to avoid frightening or unpleasant subjects. In many societies, because death is feared, there are a number of euphemisms related to it. People are less apt to *die* and more apt to *pass on* or *pass away*. Those who take care of your *loved ones* who have passed away are more likely to be *funeral directors* than *morticians* or *undertakers*.

Ogden Nash's poem quoted above exhorts against such euphemisms, as another verse demonstrates:

> When in calling, plain speaking is out;
> > When the ladies (God bless 'em) are milling about,
> You may wet, make water, or empty the glass;
> > You can powder your nose, or the "johnny" will pass.
> It's a drain for the lily, or man about dog
> > When everyone's drunk, it's condensing the fog;
> But sure as the devil, the word with a hiss,
> > It's only in Shakespeare that characters _____.

There are scholars who are as bemused as Nash was with the attitudes revealed by the use of euphemisms in society. A journal, *Maledicta*, subtitled *The International Journal of Verbal Aggression* and edited by Reinhold Aman, "specializes in uncensored glossaries and studies of all offensive and negatively valued words and expressions, in all languages and from all cultures, past and present." A review of this journal by Bill Katz in the *Library Journal* (November 1977) points out that "The history of the dirty word or phrase is the focus of this substantial . . . journal . . . [whose articles] are written in a scholarly yet entertaining fashion by professors . . . as well as by a few outsiders."

A scholarly study of Australian English euphemisms shows the considerable creativity involved (Powell 1972):

urinate:	drain the dragon
	syphon the python
	water the horse
	squeeze the lemon
	drain the spuds
	wring the rattlesnake
	shake hands with wife's best friend
	point Percy at the porcelain
	train Terence on the terracotta
have intercourse:	shag
	root
	dip the wick
	play hospital
	hide the ferret
	play cars and garages
	hide the egg roll (sausage, salami)
	boil bangers
	slip a length

go off like a beltfed motor
go like a rat up a rhododendron
go like a rat up a drain pipe
have a northwest cocktail

These euphemisms, as well as the difference between the accepted Latinate "genteel" terms and the "dirty" Anglo-Saxon terms, show that a word or phrase has not only a linguistic denotative meaning but also a connotative meaning, reflecting attitudes, emotions, value judgements, and so on. In learning a language, children learn which words are "taboo," and these taboo words differ from one child to another, depending on the value system accepted in the family or group in which the child grows up.

Racial and National Epithets

The use of epithets for people of a different religion, nationality, or colour tells us something about the users of these words. The word *boy* is not a taboo word when used generally, but when a 20-year-old white man calls a 40-year-old Black man *boy*, the word takes on an additional meaning; it reflects the racist attitude of the speaker. So also words such as *frog, kike, wop, nigger*, and so forth, which express racist and chauvinist views of society. The use of verbs *to jew* or *to gyp/jip* also reflect the stereotypical views of Jews and Gypsies. Most people do not even realize that *gyp*, which is used to mean cheat, comes from the view that Gypsies are duplicitous charlatans. In time, these words would either disappear or lose their racist connotations if bigotry and oppression ceased to exist, but they show no signs of doing so, and the continued use of such words perpetuates stereotypes and separates one people from another.

Language and Sexism

doctor, n. . . . a man of great learning
The American College Dictionary (1947)

A businessman is aggressive; a businesswoman is pushy. A businessman is good on details; she's picky. . . . He follows through; she doesn't know when to quit. He stands firm; she's hard. . . . His judgments are her prejudices. He is a man of the world; she's been around. He isn't afraid to say what is on his mind; she's mouthy. He exercises authority diligently; she's power mad. He's closemouthed; she's secretive. He climbed the ladder of success; she slept her way to the top.
From "How to Tell a Businessman from a Businesswoman," *The Balloon.*
Graduate School of Management, UCLA.

The discussion of obscenities, blasphemies, taboo words, and euphemisms showed that words of a language cannot be intrinsically good or bad but may reflect individual or societal values. In addition, one speaker may use a word with positive connotations, while another may select a different word with negative connotations, to refer to the same person. For example, the same individual may be referred to as a *terrorist* by one group and as a *freedom fighter* by another. A woman may be called a *castrating female* (or *ballsy women's libber*) or may be referred to as a *courageous feminist advocate*. The words we use to refer to certain individuals or groups reflect our individual non-linguistic attitudes and may also reflect the culture and views of society.

Language reflects sexism in society. Language itself is not sexist, just as it is not obscene, but it can connote sexist attitudes as well as attitudes about social taboos or racism.

Dictionaries often give clues to social attitudes. In the 1969 edition of the *American Heritage Dictionary*, examples used to illustrate the meanings of words include "manly courage" and "masculine charm." Women do not fare as well, as exemplified by "womanish tears" and "feminine wiles." In *Webster's New World Dictionary of the American Language* (1961), *honorarium* is defined as "a payment to a professional man for services on which no fee is set or legally obtainable."

Sections in history textbooks still in use are headed "Pioneers and Their Wives"; children read that "courageous pioneers crossed the country in covered wagons with their wives, children, and cattle." Presumably, wives are not considered to be as courageous as their husbands.

As late as the 1965–68 eleventh edition, Bowker Company (New York) was still publishing *American Men of Science: A Biographical Dictionary*. The editors were much in advance of Columbia University. Until 1972, the women's faculty toilet doors were labelled "Women," whereas the men's doors were labelled "Officers of Instruction."

Language also reflects sexism in society by the way we interpret neutral (non–gender-specific) terms. Most people, hearing *My cousin is a professor* (or *a doctor* or *the chancellor of the university* or *a steel worker*) still assume the cousin is a man. This assumption has nothing to do with the English language but a great deal to do with the fact that, historically, women have not been prominent in these positions. Similarly, if you heard someone say *My cousin is a nurse* (or *elementary school teacher* or *clerk-typist* or *housekeeper*), you would probably conclude that the speaker's cousin is a woman. It is less evident why the sentence *My neighbour is a blonde* is understood as referring to a woman; perhaps the physical characteristics of women in our society assume greater importance than those of men.

Studies analyzing the language used by men in reference to women, which often has derogatory or sexual connotations, indicate that such terms go far back into history and sometimes enter the language with no pejorative implications but gradually gain them. Thus, from Old English *huswif*, "housewife," the word *hussy* was derived. In their original employment, "a laundress made beds, a needlewoman came to sew, a spinster tended the spinning wheel, and a nurse cared for the sick. But all apparently acquired secondary duties in some households, because all became euphemisms for a mistress or a prostitute at some time during their existence" (Schulz 1975).

Words for women — all with abusive or sexual overtones — abound: *dish, tomato, piece, piece of ass, chick, piece of tail, bunny, pussy, pussycat, bitch, doll, slut, cow*, to name just a few. Far fewer such pejorative terms exist for men.

Marked and Unmarked Forms

> Long afterward, Oedipus, old and blinded, walked the roads. He smelled a familiar smell. It was the Sphinx. Oedipus said, "I want to ask one question. Why didn't I recognize my mother?" "You gave the wrong answer," said the Sphinx. "But that was what made everything possible," said Oedipus. "No," she said. "When I asked, 'What walks on four legs in the morning, two at noon, and three in the evening,' you answered, 'Man.' You didn't say anything about woman." "When you say Man," said Oedipus, "you include women too. Everyone knows that." She said, "That's what you think."
>
> Muriel Rukeyser, *Myth*

One striking fact about the asymmetry between male and female terms in many languages is that, when there are male–female pairs, the male form for the most part is **unmarked** and the female term is created by adding a bound morpheme or by compounding. We have many such examples in English:

Male	Female
prince	princess
author	authoress
count	countess
actor	actress
host	hostess
poet	poetess
heir	heiress
hero	heroine
Paul	Pauline

Since the advent of the feminist movement, many of the marked female forms have been replaced by the male forms, which are now used to refer to either sex. Thus, women, as well as men, are authors and actors and poets and heroes and heirs. Women, however, remain countesses if they are among a small group of female aristocrats in England.

Given these asymmetries, folk etymologies arise that misinterpret a number of non-sexist words. **Folk etymology** is the process, normally unconscious, whereby words or their origins are changed through non-scientific speculations or false analogies with other words. When English speakers borrowed the French word *crevisse*, for example, it became *crayfish*. The borrowers did not know that *-isse* was a feminine suffix.

Female is not the feminine form of *male* but came into English from the Latin word *femina*, with the same morpheme *fe* that occurs in the Latin *fecundas*, meaning "fertile" (originally derived from an Indo-European word meaning "to give suck to"). It entered English through the Old French word *femme* and its diminutive form *femelle*, meaning "little woman."

Other male–female gender pairs have interesting differences in meaning. Although a *governor* governs a state, a *governess* takes care of children; a *mistress*, in its most widely used meaning, is not a female master, nor is a *majorette* a female major. We talk of *unwed mothers* but not *unwed fathers*, of *career women* but not *career men*, because historically no stigma was attached to a bachelor who fathered a child, and men were supposed to have careers. It is only recently that the term *househusband* has come into being, again reflecting changes in social customs.

Possibly as a protest against the reference to new and important ideas as being *seminal* (from *semen*), Clare Booth Luce updated Ibsen's drama *A Doll's House* by having Nora tell her husband that she is pregnant "in the way only men are supposed to get pregnant." When he asks "Men pregnant?" she replies, "With ideas. Pregnancies there (she taps her head) are masculine. And a very superior form of labor. Pregnancies here (she taps her stomach) are feminine — a very inferior form of labor."

Neutral non-gender words often become compounds when the base form is associated with either sex. Thus, people talk of a *male nurse* because it is expected that a nurse will be female, and for parallel reasons we have the compound words *lady doctor, career woman*, and *woman athlete*, though these compounds now appear less frequently since women have begun to take more prominent places in formerly male-dominated fields such as medicine, business, and sports.

Other linguistic asymmetries exist, such as the fact that most wives continue to adopt their husbands' names in marriage. This name change can be traced back to early (and, to a great extent, current) legal practices. Thus, we often refer to a woman as Mrs. Jack Fromkin, but seldom do we refer to a man as Mr. Vicki Fromkin, except in an insulting sense. We talk of Professor and Mrs. John Smith but seldom, if ever, of Mr. and Dr. Mary Jones.

It is insulting to a woman to be called a *spinster* or an *old maid*, but it is not insulting to a man to be called a *bachelor*. There is nothing inherently pejorative about the word *spinster*. The connotations reflect the different views society has about an unmarried woman as opposed to an unmarried man. It is not language that is sexist; it is society.

The Generic *He*

When Thomas Jefferson wrote in the Declaration of Independence that "all *men* are created equal" and that "governments are instituted among *men* deriving their just powers from the consent of the governed," he was not using *men* as a general term to include women. His use of the word *men* was precise at a time when women could not vote. In the sixteenth and seventeenth centuries, masculine pronouns were not used as the *generic* terms; the various forms of *he* were used when referring to males and of *she* when referring to females. The pronoun *they* was used to refer to people of either sex even if the referent was a singular noun, as shown by Lord

Chesterfield's statement in 1759: "If a person is born of a gloomy temper . . . they cannot help it."

By the eighteenth century, grammarians (men to be sure) created the rule designating the male pronouns as the general term, and it wasn't until the nineteenth century that the rule was applied widely, after an act of Parliament in Britain in 1850 sanctioned its use. But this generic use of *he* was ignored. In 1879, female doctors were barred from membership in the all-male Massachusetts Medical Society on the basis that the bylaws of the organization referred to members by the pronoun *he*. The unmarked, or male, nouns also serve as general terms, as do the male pronouns. The *brotherhood of man* includes women, but *sisterhood* does not include men.

Changes in English reflect the feminist movement and the growing awareness by both men and women that language may reflect attitudes of society and reinforce stereotypes and bias. More and more the word *people* is replacing *mankind, personnel* is used instead of *manpower, nurturing* instead of *mothering*, and *to operate* instead of *to man*. *Chair* or *moderator* is used instead of *chairman* (particularly by those who do not like the "clumsiness" of *chairperson*), and terms such as *postal worker* and *firefighter* are replacing *mailman* and *fireman*.

Language and Gender

An increasing number of scholars have been conducting research on language and gender and language and sexism since 1973, when the first article specifically concerned with women and language was published in a major linguistics journal (Lakoff 1973). Robin Lakoff's study suggested that women's insecurity due to sexism in society resulted in more "proper" use of the rules of standard grammar than was found in the speech of men. Differences between male and female speech were also investigated.

Variations in the dialects of men and women occur in many countries around the world. In Japanese, women may choose to speak a distinct dialect even though they are fully aware of the standard dialect used by both men and women. It has been said that "seeing-eye" guide dogs in Japan are trained in English because the sex of the owner is not known in advance and because it is easier for a blind person to use English than to train the dog in both language styles.

In the Muskogean language Koasati, spoken in Louisiana, words that end in an /s/ when spoken by men end in /l/ or /n/ when used by women; for example, the word meaning "lift it" is *lakawhol* for women and *lakawhos* for men. Early explorers reported that the men and women of the Carib Aboriginals used different dialects. In Chiquita, a Bolivian language, the grammar of male language includes a noun-class gender distinction, with names for males and supernatural beings morphologically marked in one way and nouns referring to females marked in another.

There is nothing inherently wrong in the development of different styles, which may include intonation, phonology, syntax, and lexicon. It is wrong, however, to continue stereotypes regarding female speech, which are more myths than truths.

For example, a common stereotype is that women talk a lot, yet controlled studies show that just the opposite is true when men and women are together. That is, in mixed groups, women seem to talk less than men.

One characteristic of female speech is the higher pitch used by women, due, to a great extent, to the shorter vocal tracts of women. But a study conducted by the phonetician Caroline Henton showed that the difference in pitch between male and female British voices was, on the average, greater than could be accounted for by physiology alone, suggesting that some social factor must be involved during the acquisition period.

This chapter has stressed the fact that language is neither good nor evil, but its use may be one or the other. If one views women or Blacks as inferior, then special speech characteristics will be viewed as inferior. Furthermore, when society

DENNIS THE MENACE

DENNIS THE MENACE® used by permission of Hank Ketcham and © by North America Syndicate.

itself institutionalizes such attitudes, the language reflects them. If everyone in society were truly equal, and treated as such, then there would be little concern for the asymmetries that exist in language.

Summary

Every person has an individual way of speaking called an **idiolect**. The language used by a group of speakers may also show systematic differences called a **dialect**. The dialects of a language are the mutually intelligible forms of that language that differ in systematic ways from each other. Dialects develop and are reinforced because languages change, and the changes that occur in one group or area may differ from those that occur in another. **Regional dialects** and **social dialects** develop for this reason. Some of the differences in the regional dialects of American and Canadian English may be traced to the different dialects spoken by the settlers from various parts of Britain; those from southern England who arrived first spoke one dialect, those from the north another, and of course those from Ireland and Scotland still others. In addition, the colonists who maintained close contacts with England reflected the changes occurring in British English, while earlier forms were preserved among Americans who spread westward as well as among those Loyalists who, at the conclusion of the American Revolution, moved north and, later, onto the Canadian Prairies. The study of regional dialects has produced **dialect atlases** with **dialect maps** showing the areas where specific dialectal characteristics occur in the speech of the region. Each area is delineated by a boundary line called an **isogloss**.

Dialect differences include phonological or pronunciation differences (often called **accents**), vocabulary distinctions, and syntactic rule differences. The grammar differences between dialects are not as great as their similarities, thus permitting speakers of different dialects to communicate with each other.

In many countries, one dialect or dialect group is viewed as the **standard**, such as **Received Pronunciation (RP)** in England or **Standard American English (SAE)** or **Standard Canadian English (SCE)**. While these particular dialects are not linguistically superior, they may be considered by some language "purists" to be the only "correct" form of the language. Such a view has led to the idea that some non-standard dialects are "deficient," as is erroneously suggested regarding **African American English (AAE)** (recently referred to as **Ebonics**), a dialect used by some African Americans. A study of African American English shows it to be as logical, complete, rule-governed, and expressive as any other dialect and reveals that many of its features are to be found in English dialects from places as distant as Newfoundland.

Attempts to legislate the use of a particular dialect or language have been made throughout history and exist today, even extending to the banning of the use of languages other than the "accepted" one. In Quebec, concern for the preservation of French language and culture has led to strict legal enforcement of the use of French in many spheres of life.

In areas where many languages are spoken, one language may become a **lingua franca** to ease communication among the people. In other cases, where traders or missionaries or travellers need to communicate with people who speak a language unknown to them, a **pidgin** may develop, based on one language that is simplified lexically, phonologically, and syntactically. When a pidgin is widely used and is learned by children as their first language, it is creolized. The grammars of **creole** languages are similar to those of other languages, and languages of creole origin now exist in many parts of the world.

Besides regional and social dialects, speakers may use different **registers** or **styles** of their dialect depending on the context. **Slang** is not often used in formal situations or in writing but is widely used in speech; **argot** and **jargon** refer to the unique vocabulary used by professional or trade groups not shared "outside." Speakers may shift from one register to another in the course of a conversation or a sentence, a process called **code switching**.

In all societies, certain acts or behaviours are frowned on, forbidden, or considered taboo. The words or expressions referring to these **taboo** acts are then also avoided or considered "dirty." Language itself cannot be obscene or clean; the views toward specific words or linguistic expressions reflect the attitudes of a culture or society toward the behaviours and actions of the language users. At times, slang words may be taboo, whereas scientific or standard terms with the same meanings are acceptable in "polite society." Taboo words and acts give rise to **euphemisms**, words or phrases that replace the expressions to be avoided. Thus, *powder room* is a euphemism for *toilet*, which itself started as a euphemism for *lavatory*, which is now more acceptable than its replacement.

Just as the use of some words may reflect society's views toward sex, natural bodily functions, or religious beliefs, so also some words may reflect racist, chauvinist, and sexist attitudes in society. The language itself is not racist or sexist but reflects these views of various sectors of a society. Such terms, however, may perpetuate and reinforce biased views and be demeaning and insulting to those addressed. Popular movements and changes in the institutions of society may then be reflected in changes in the language.

Notes

1. Some students of Canadian English speak of six major dialect areas: Newfoundland, Maritimes, Eastern Ontario, Western Ontario, Prairies, and British Columbia. Others place Ontario and Prairies English in one grouping. Still others include British Columbia in the category, referring to the English spoken from Ontario to the Pacific coast as "General Canadian English."
2. This report is methodologically and statistically flawed, but it remains useful if handled critically.

3. *The Globe and Mail* for November 10, 1999, noted a parallel designation, "European American," as "an alternative to white." The paper cited the Knight-Ridder News Services' comment that "the language of race is constantly evolving, reflecting changing sensitivities and tastes. And in contemporary California, where the population is surging and shifting with breathtaking speed, people are once again grasping for new words to describe new racial realities."
4. Unlike tree leaves (/livz/), this hockey club is always the /lifs/.

Exercises

1. Each pair of words is pronounced as shown phonetically in at least one English dialect. Write in phonetic transcription your pronunciation of each word that you pronounce differently.

a.	horse	[hɔrs]	hoarse	[hors]
b.	morning	[mɔrnĩŋ]	mourning	[mornĩŋ]
c.	ice	[ʌjs]	eyes	[ajz]
d.	knife	[nʌjf]	knives	[najvz]
e.	mute	[mjut]	nude	[njud]
f.	din	[dĩn]	den	[dɛ̃n]
g.	marry	[mæri]	Mary	[meri]
h.	merry	[mɛri]	marry	[mæri]
i.	rot	[rɑt]	wrought	[rɔt]
j.	lease	[lis]	grease (v.)	[griz]
k.	what	[ʍat]	watt	[ʍat]
l.	ant	[ænt]	aunt	[ãnt]
m.	creek	[kʰrɪk]	creak	[kʰrik]

2. Below is a passage from *The Gospel According to St. Mark* in Cameroon English Pidgin. See how much you are able to understand before consulting the English translation given below. State some of the similarities and differences between CEP and CE.

   1. Di fos tok fo di gud nuus fo Jesus Christ God yi Pikin.
   2. I bi sem as i di tok fo di buk fo Isaiah, God yi nchinda (Prophet), "Lukam, mi a di sen man nchinda fo bifo yoa fes weh yi go fix yoa rud fan."
   3. Di vos fo som man di krai fo bush: "Fix di ples weh Papa God di go, mek yi rud tret."

   Translation:

   1. The beginning of the gospel of Jesus Christ, the Son of God.
   2. As it is written in the book of Isaiah the prophet, "Behold, I send my messenger before thy face, which shall prepare thy way before thee."
   3. The voice of one crying in the wilderness, "Prepare ye the way of the Lord, make his paths straight."

3. In the period from 1890 to 1904, *Slang and Its Analogues* by J.S. Farmer and W.E. Henley was published in seven volumes. The following entries are included in this dictionary. For each item, (1) state whether the word or phrase still exists; (2) if not, state what the modern slang term would be; and (3) if the word remains but its meaning has changed, provide the modern meaning.

all out: completely, as in "All out the best." (The expression goes back to as early as 1300.)

to have apartments to let: be an idiot; one who is empty-headed.

been there: in "Oh, yes, I've been there." Applied to a man who is shrewd and who has had many experiences.

belly-button: the navel.

berkeleys: a woman's breasts.

bitch: most offensive appellation that can be given to a woman, even more provoking than that of *whore*.

once in a blue moon: extremely seldom.

boss: master; one who directs.

bread: employment (1785 — "out of bread" = "out of work").

claim: to steal.

cut dirt: to escape.

dog cheap: of little worth. (Used in 1616 by Dekker: "Three things there are Dog-cheap, learning, poorman's sweat, and oathes.")

funeral: as in "It's not my funeral." "It's no business of mine."

to get over: to seduce, to fascinate.

groovy: settled in habit; limited in mind.

grub: food.

head: toilet (nautical use only).

hook: to marry.

hump: to spoil.

hush money: money paid for silence; blackmail.

itch: to be sexually excited.

jam: a sweetheart or a mistress.

to lie low: to keep quiet; to bide one's time.

to lift a leg on: to have sexual intercourse.

looby: a fool.

malady of France: syphilis (used by Shakespeare in 1599).

nix: nothing.

noddle: the head.

old: money. (1900 — "Perhaps it's somebody you owe a bit of the old to, Jack.")

to pill: talk platitudes.

pipe layer: a political intriguer; a schemer.

poky: cramped, stuffy, stupid.

pot: a quart; a large sum; a prize; a urinal; to excel.

puny: a freshman.

puss-gentleman: an effeminate.

4. Suppose someone asked you to help compile items for a new dictionary of slang. List ten "slang" words that you know, and provide a short definition for each.

5. Below are given some words used in British English for which different words are usually used in Canadian English. See if you can match the British and Canadian equivalents.

British

a.	clothes peg	i.	spanner
b.	braces	j.	biscuits
c.	lift	k.	torch
d.	waistcoat	l.	underground
e.	shop assistant	m.	high street
f.	sweets	n.	crisps
g.	boot (of car)	o.	lorry
h.	bobby	p.	knock up

Canadian

A.	candy	I.	elevator
B.	truck	J.	cop
C.	main street	K.	wake up
D.	cookies	L.	trunk
E.	suspenders	M.	vest
F.	wrench	N.	subway
G.	flashlight	O.	clothes pin
H.	potato chips	P.	clerk

*6. In some dialects of English, the following words have different vowels, as is shown by the phonetic transcriptions.

A		B		C	
bite	[bʌjt]	bide	[bajd]	die	[daj]
rice	[rʌjs]	rise	[rajz]	by	[baj]
ripe	[rʌjp]	bribe	[brajb]	sigh	[saj]
wife	[wʌjf]	wives	[wajvz]	rye	[raj]
dike	[dʌjk]	dime	[dajm]	guy	[gaj]
		nine	[najn]		
		rile	[rajl]		
		dire	[dajr]		
		writhe	[rajð]		

a. How may the classes of sounds that end the words in columns A and B be characterized? That is, what feature specifies all the final segments in A and all the final segments in B?

b. How do the words in column C differ from those in columns A and B?

c. Are [ʌj] and [aj] in complementary distribution? Give your reasons.

d. If [ʌj] and [aj] are allophones of one phoneme, should they be derived from /ʌj/ or /aj/? Why?

e. Give the phonetic representations of the following:

life	lives	lie
file	bike	lice

f. State the rule that will relate the phonemic representations to the phonetic representations of the words given above.

7. Compile a list of argot (or jargon) terms from some profession or trade (e.g., lawyer, musician, doctor, longshoreman, and so forth). Give a definition for each term in "non-jargon" language.

8. "Translate" the first paragraph of any well-known document or speech — such as Hamlet's famous soliloquy, "To be, or not to be" — into informal, colloquial language.

Works Cited

Adams, G.B. 1985. "Linguistic Cross-Links in Phonology and Grammar." *Papers on Irish English*. Ed. P. Ó Baoill. N.p.: Irish Association for Applied Linguistics: 27–35.

Allen, H.B. 1976. *The Linguistics Atlas of the Upper Midwest*. Vol. 1. Minneapolis: University of Minnesota Press.

Annual Report of the Commissioner of Official Languages 1991. 1992. Ottawa: Ministry of Supply and Services.

Avis, Walter S. 1955. "Speech Differences along the Ontario–United States Border, II. Grammar and Syntax." *Journal of the Canadian Linguistic Association* 1: 14–19.

———. 1956. "Speech Differences along the Ontario–United States Border, III. Pronunciation." *Journal of the Canadian Linguistic Association* 2: 41–59.

———. 1972. "So Eh? Is Canadian, Eh?" *Canadian Journal of Linguistics* 17.

Avis, Walter, et al. 1967. *Dictionary of Canadianisms on Historical Principles*. Toronto: W.J. Gage.

Bliss, Alan. 1984. "English in the South of Ireland." *Language in the British Isles*. Ed. Peter Trudgill. Cambridge, UK: Cambridge University Press: 135–51.

Bolinger, Dwight. 1980. *Language, the Loaded Weapon. The Use & Abuse of Language Today*. London: Longman.

Bright, W. 1976. *Variation & Change in Language: Essays by William Bright*. Ed. A.S. Dil. Stanford: Stanford University Press.

The Canadian Encyclopedia. 1988. Edmonton: Hurtig Publishers.

Cassidy, Frederick G. 1985. *Dictionary of American Regional English*. Cambridge, MA: Belknap Press.

Chambers, J.K. 1986. "Three Kinds of Standard in Canadian English." *In Search of the Standard in Canadian English*. Ed. W.C. Lougheed. Kingston: Queen's University, Strathy Language Unit: 55–59.

Crystal, David. 1987. *The Cambridge Encyclopedia of Languages*. Cambridge, UK: Cambridge University Press.

Edwards, Vivian. 1989. "Patois and the Politics of Protest: Black English in British Classrooms." *English across Cultures/Cultures across English*. Ed. O. Garcia and R. Otheguy. Berlin: Mouton de Gruyter: 359–72.

Farb, Peter. 1975. *Word Play*. New York: Bantam.

Farmer, J.S., and W.E. Henley. 1965. *Slang and Its Analogues*. 7 vols. 1890–1904. Reprint. New York: Krauss Reprints.

Fee, Margery. 1992. "Canadian English." *The Oxford Companion to the English Language*. Ed. T. McArthur and F. McArthur. Oxford: Oxford University Press: 179–83.

Geike, A. Constable. 1857. "Canadian English." *The Canadian Journal of Industry, Science, and Art*.

Hall, Robert A. 1955. *Hands Off Pidgin English*. New South Wales: Pacific Publications.

Holm, John. 1988–89. *Pidgins and Creoles.* Vols. 1 & 2. Cambridge, UK: Cambridge University Press.

Jespersen, O. 1964. *Mankind, Nation, and Individual.* 1925. Reprint. Bloomington: University of Indiana Press.

Johnson, Falk. 1950. "The History of Some 'Dirty Words.' " *The American Mercury* 71: 538–45.

Kirwin, William J. 1993. "The Planting of Anglo-Irish in Newfoundland." *Focus on Canada.* Ed. Sandra Clarke. Amsterdam: John Benjamins.

Kurath, Hans. 1971. "What Do You Call It?" *A Various Language: Perspective on American Dialects.* Ed. J.V. Williamson and V.M. Burke. New York: Holt, Rinehart and Winston.

Labov, W. 1969. *The Logic of Nonstandard English.* Georgetown University. 20th Annual Round Table, No. 22.

Lakoff, Robin. 1973. "Language and Woman's Place." *Language in Society* 2: 45–80.

Leon, Pierre R. 1979. "Canadian English Pronunciation: From the British to the American Model." *Toronto English: Studies in Phonetics to Honour C.D. Rouillard.* Ed. P.R. Leon and P. Martin. Ottawa: Didier: 1–9.

McCrum, Robert, William Cran, and Robert MacNeil. 1992. *The Story of English.* London: Faber and Faber.

Munro, Pamela. 1990. *Slang U: The Official Dictionary of College Slang.* New York: Harmony Books.

Newman, Edwin. 1974. *Strictly Speaking: Will America Be the Death of English?* Indianapolis: Bobbs-Merrill.

Orkin, Mark. 1973. *Canajan, Eh?* Don Mills, ON: General Publishing.

Payne, L.W. 1909. "A Word-List from East Alabama." *Dialect Notes* 3: 279–328, 343–91.

Pei, M. 1964. "A Loss for Words." *Saturday Review* 14 Nov.: 82–84.

Poplack, S., and S. Tagliamonte. 1993. "African American English in the Diaspora: Evidence from Old-Line Nova Scotians." *Focus on Canada.* Ed. S. Clarke. Amsterdam: John Benjamins: 109–50.

Powell, Jay. 1972. Paper read at the Western Conference of Linguistics, University of Oregon.

Préfixe du recueil des lois de 1977. Lettres patentes/Prefix to the Statutes of 1977. Letters Patent. 1977. Quebec: Charles-Henri Dubé.

Roberts, Paul. 1958. *Understanding English.* New York: Harper & Row.

Romaine, Suzanne. 1988. *Pidgin and Creole Languages.* London: Longman.

Scargill, M.H. 1974. *Modern Canadian Usage.* Toronto: McClelland & Stewart.

———. 1988. "Canadian English." *Canadian Encyclopedia.* Edmonton: Hurtig Publishers.

Schulz, Muriel R. 1975. "The Semantic Derogation of Woman." *Language and Sex.* Ed. B. Thorne and N. Henley. Rowley, MA: Newbury House Publishers: 66–67.

Stegner, Wallace. 1962. *Wolf Willow.* Toronto: Macmillan of Canada.

Stewart, Walter. 1985. *True Blue: The Loyalist Legend.* Toronto: Collins.

Thomas, Erik R. 1991. "The Origin of Canadian Raising in Ontario." *Canadian Journal of Linguistics* 36: 147–70.

Todd, Loreto. 1984. *Modern Englishes: Pidgins & Creoles.* Oxford: Basil Blackwell.

Vance, Timothy J. 1987. " 'Canadian Raising' in Some Dialects of the Northern United States." *American Speech* 62: 195–210.

Wells, J.C. 1982. *Accents of English.* Vol. 3. Cambridge, UK: Cambridge University Press.

Yalden, Maxwell. 1984. "Some Basic Issues." *Language and Society* 14: 6–8.

Further Reading

Alexander, Ken, and Avis Glaze. 1996. *Towards Freedom: The African-Canadian Experience.* Toronto: Umbrella Press.

Allan, Keith, and Kate Burridge. 1991. *Euphemism and Dysphemism.* New York: Oxford University Press.

Andersson, Lars, and Peter Trudgill. 1990. *Bad Language.* Oxford: Basil Blackwell.

Baugh, John. 1983. *Black Street Speech.* Austin: University of Texas.

Bickerton, Derek. 1981. *Roots of Language.* Ann Arbor, MI: Karoma.

Cameron, Deborah. 1992. *Feminism and Linguistic Theory.* 2nd ed. London: Macmillan.

Coates, Jennifer. 1986. *Women, Men, and Language: A Sociolinguistic Account of Sex Differences in Language.* London: Longman.

Dillard, J.L. 1972. *Black English: Its History and Usage in the United States.* New York: Random House.

Ferguson, Charles, and Shirley Brice Health, eds. 1981. *Language in the USA.* Cambridge, UK: Cambridge University Press.

Folb, Edith. 1980. *Runnin' Down Some Lines: The Language and Culture of Black Teenagers.* Cambridge, MA: Harvard University Press.

Frank, Francine, and Frank Ashen. 1983. *Language and the Sexes.* Albany: State University of New York Press.

Jay, Timothy. 1992. *Cursing in America.* Philadelphia: John Benjamins.

King, Ruth. 1991. *Talking Gender: A Guide to Nonsexist Communication.* Toronto: Copp Clark Pitman.

Kinlock, A.M., and W. Avis. 1989. "Central Canadian and Received Standard English: A Comparison of Pronunciation." *English across Cultures/Cultures across English.* Ed. O. García and R. Otheguy. Berlin: Mouton de Gruyter: 403–20.

Lakoff, Robin. 1990. *Talking Power: The Politics of Language.* New York: Basic Books.

Michaels, Leonard, and Christoper Ricks, eds. 1980. *The State of the Language.* Berkeley: University of California Press.

Miller, Casey, and Kate Swift. 1980. *The Handbook of Nonsexist Writing.* New York: Barnes & Noble.

Mulhausler, Peter. 1986. *Pidgin and Creole Linguistics.* Oxford: Basil Blackwell.

Newmeyer, Frederick J., ed. 1988. *Linguistics: The Cambridge Survey, Vol. IV. Language: The Socio-Cultural Context.* Cambridge, UK: Cambridge University Press.

Pringle, I.W.V. 1986. "The Complexity of the Concept of Standard." *In Search of the Standard in Canadian English.* Ed. W.C. Lougheed. Kingston: Queen's University Strathy Language Unit: 20–38.

Reed, Carroll E. 1977. *Dialects of American English.* Rev. ed. Amherst, MA: University of Massachusetts Press.

Rudnýckyi, R.B. 1973. "Immigrant Language, Language Contact, and Bilingualism in Canada." *Current Trends in Linguistics.* Vol. 10. Ed. T.A. Sebeok. The Hague: Mouton.

Shopen, Timothy, and Joseph M. Williams, eds. 1981. *Style and Variables in English.* Cambridge, MA: Winthrop Publishers.

Spears, Richard A. 1981. *Slang and Euphemism: A Dictionary of Oaths, Curses, Insults, Sexual Slang and Metaphor, Racial Slurs, Drug Talk, Homosexual Lingo, and Related Matter.* New York: Jonathan David Publishers.

Talman, James J. 1946. *Loyalist Narratives from Upper Canada.* Toronto: The Champlain Society.

Tannen, Deborah. 1990. *You Just Don't Understand: Women and Men in Conversation.* New York: Ballantine.

Thorne, Barrie, Cheris Kramarae, and Nancy Henley, eds. 1983. *Language, Gender, and Society.* Rowley, MA: Newbury House.

Trahern, Joseph B., ed. 1989. *Standardizing English: Essays in the History of Language Change.* Knoxville: University of Tennessee Press.

Trudgill, Peter. 1977. *Sociolinguistics.* Middlesex, UK: Penguin Books.

Williams, Glyn. 1992. *Sociolinguistics.* Middlesex, UK: Penguin Books.

Williamson, Juanita V., and Virginia M. Burke. 1971. *A Various Language: Perspectives on American Dialects.* New York: Holt, Rinehart and Winston.

Winks, Robin W. 1971. *The Blacks in Canada: A History.* Montreal: McGill–Queen's University Press.

CHAPTER 8
Language Change: The Syllables of Time

> The language of this country being always upon the flux, the Struldbruggs of one age do not understand those of another, neither are they able after two hundred years to hold any conversation (farther than by a few general words) with their neighbors the mortals, and thus they lie under the disadvantage of living like foreigners in their own country.
>
> Jonathan Swift, *Gulliver's Travels*

All living languages change with time, a fact that many have found so disturbing that they have sought to restrict the perceived changes. In 1712, Jonathan Swift insisted on "ascertaining and fixing our language forever. . . . I see no absolute necessity why any language should be perpetually changing." But the only language that does not change is a dead one. Fortunately, however, languages change slowly compared with the human life span, and we are scarcely aware of the changes. If we could turn on a radio and miraculously receive a broadcast in our "native language" from the year 3000, however, we would undoubtedly think we were hearing a foreign language, yet from year to year we hardly notice any change in our language.

We become most aware of linguistic change when we look at documents from the past, for many changes are revealed in those languages with written records. We know, for example, a great deal about the history of English because we have documents reaching back to the seventh and eighth centuries C.E. available to us. **Old English** (actually a group of related dialects spoken in England around the end of the first millennium and the foundation of modern English dialects) is, to a speaker of **Modern English**, largely unintelligible without special study. A few lines from *Beowulf*, an epic poem preserved in a manuscript of the tenth century C.E., may strike us as incomprehensible at first glance:

> Hordweard sōhte
> georne æfter grunde, wolde guman findan
> þone þe him on sweofote sāre getēode.
> (Note that the letter þ, called "thorn," is pronounced, in this instance, like the *th* in *think* — i.e., [θ].)

Clearly, most of us will need a translation to understand much of this text:

> The Guardian of the hoard [i.e., a dragon] sought
> Eagerly along the ground, [he] wanted to find the man
> who sorely harmed him in [his] sleep.

If, at first glance, these lines do not seem to be English, further consideration reveals familiarity behind the surface strangeness: *him*, of course, and *on* are Modern English words, but others — especially once we have looked at the translation — are also familiar if "distorted": *sōhte* (sought), *findan* (find), *grunde* (ground), and perhaps even *sāre* (sorely). This may be English, but clearly it isn't our English.

Some 500 years after the epic of *Beowulf*, Chaucer wrote his *Canterbury Tales* in the London dialect of **Middle English**, spoken from around 1100 to 1500 (the dates are only approximate guides for us; no one woke on January 1, 1100, and began speaking Middle English). Chaucer's language is more easily understood by present-day readers, as we see from the opening of the *Canterbury Tales*:

> Whan that Aprille with his shoures soote
> The droughte of March hath pierced to the roote....

> When April with its sweet showers
> The drought of March has pierced to the root....

Chaucer's English is closer to our own than the language of many of his contemporaries who happened to speak other dialects of English. *Sir Gawain and the Green Knight*, a poem written in a Northwest Midlands dialect about the same time as the *Canterbury Tales*, is "inaccessible to the non-specialist because of the difficulty of its language, a language far more remote from the English of the present than that of Geoffrey Chaucer's London" (Boroff 1967):

> Siþen þe sege and þe assaut watz sesed at Troye
> þe borʒ brittened and brent to brondez and askez
> þe tulk þat þe trammes of tresoun þer wroʒt
> Watz tried for his tricherie, þe trewest on erthe.

> Since the siege and the assault was ceased at Troy
> The city destroyed and burned to brands and ashes
> The knight who the trickery of treason there wrought
> Was tried for his treachery, the truest [greatest] on earth.

Despite the difficulties of this dialect, it is closer to Modern English than the language of the *Beowulf* text, especially if we compare it with many Modern English dialects, some of which are as difficult for us to grasp as the dialect of *Sir Gawain and the Green Knight* — if not more so.

A passage from *Everyman*, a play written about 1485, illustrates why (despite the use of *u* for *v* and *y* for *i* in early printing) it can be claimed that **Early Modern English** was being spoken by 1500:

> The Somonynge of Eueryman called it is,
> That of our lyues and endynge shewes
> How transytory we be all daye.
> The mater is wonders precyous,
> But the entent of it is more gracyous
> And swete to bere awaye.

We no longer need a translation to understand this passage, nor do we have much difficulty with Shakespeare, who, 200 years after Chaucer, has Hamlet say

> "A man may fish with the worme that hath eate of a king, and eate of the fish that hath fedde of that worme."

With these last two examples, we have clearly arrived at a recognizable form — if one with some oddities — of Modern English.

The division of English into Old English (449–1100 C.E.), Middle English (1100–1500), and Modern English (1500–present) is somewhat arbitrary, being marked by the dates of events in English history, such as the Norman Conquest of 1066 C.E. and the introduction of Caxton's printing press into England in 1476, that profoundly influenced the English language. Thus, the history of English and the changes that occurred in the language reflect, to some extent, non-linguistic history.

Changes in a language are changes in the grammars of the speakers of the language and are perpetuated when new generations of children learn the language by acquiring the new grammar. An examination of the changes that have occurred in English during the past 1500 years shows changes in the phonology, morphology, syntax, lexicon, and semantics of the grammar. No part of the grammar remains the same over the course of history. Although most of the examples in this chapter are from English, the histories of all languages show similar changes.

The Regularity of Sound Change

> That's not a regular rule: you invented it just now.
>
> Lewis Carroll, *Alice's Adventures in Wonderland*

In the Ottawa Valley of Ontario, a dialect spoken by some older rural residents differs from Standard Canadian English in the use of a low front vowel [æ] before [r], where speakers of Standard Canadian English would normally use [ɑ]. Thus, words commonly pronounced as [kɑr] "car," [bɑrn] "barn," and [gɑrdən] "garden," appear in this dialect as [kær], [bærn], and [gærdən] (Chambers 1975). This [ɑ]–[æ] correspondence is an example of a **regular sound correspondence** that, in this case, is conditioned by the presence of the [r].

The different pronunciations of *far* and *barn* and so on did not always exist in English. This chapter will discuss how such dialect differences arose and why the sound differences are usually regular and not confined to just a few words.

Sound Correspondences

In Middle English, *mouse* [mʌws] was pronounced *mūs* [mu:s], *house* [hʌws] was *hūs* [hu:s], and *flower* [flawər] was [flu:r]. In general, where we now pronounce [ʌw] or [aw] (depending on the presence or absence of **Canadian raising**), Middle English speakers pronounced [u:]. This is a regular correspondence like the one between [ɑ] and [æ] before [r]. Thus, *out* [ʌwt] was pronounced *ūt* [u:t]. Many such regular correspondences can be found relating older and newer forms of English. Similarly, the North American languages Cree and Ojibwa show a *t–n* correspondence: Cree *atim*, Ojibwa *anim*, "dog"; Cree *nitim*, Ojibwa *ninim*, "my sister-in-law."

The regular sound correspondences we observe between older and modern forms of a language are due to phonological changes that affect certain sounds, or classes of sounds, rather than individual words. Centuries ago, English underwent a phonological change called a **sound shift** in which [u:] became [ʌw]/[aw]. We observe regularity precisely because *sounds* change, not words.

Phonological change can also account for dialect differences. The Ottawa Valley [æ] before [r] in place of the more common Canadian [ɑ] may have had its origin in the Irish dialects of the settlers who migrated into the area after the War of 1812 (Pringle and Padolsky 1981). Because of the area's isolation during much of the nineteenth century, this change did not spread, and the dialect began to die out when outsiders moved into the valley. Its association with "country" and "old-fashioned" ways, joined with the impact of schooling and later the media, may also have restricted its use.

Ancestral Protolanguages

The Romance languages (French, Spanish, Italian, etc.) were once dialects of the Latin spoken in the Roman Empire. Regional dialect differences in pronunciation arose from sound changes that failed to spread. There is nothing degenerate about them. In fact, many of the world's modern languages were at first regional dialects that became widely spoken and highly differentiated, finally becoming separate languages. Because of their common ancestry, the Romance languages are said to be **genetically related**. Early forms of English and German, too, were once dialects of a common ancestor called **Proto-Germanic**. A **protolanguage** is the ancestral language from which related languages have developed. Both Latin and Proto-Germanic themselves were descendants of an older language called **Indo-European** or **Proto–Indo-European**. Thus, **Germanic** languages such as English and German are genetically related to the Romance languages such as French and Spanish. All these national languages were once regional dialects.

Consider a hypothetical language, L, in which the phonemic inventory included the sound A (see Figure 8.1). At some point, the speakers of this language split into two groups with little contact between them. Perhaps half of them migrated to the other side of a mountain, crossed an ocean, or even moved across a political boundary such as that separating Canada and the United States. One group underwent a sound shift of A → B: words in L that were pronounced with an A now were pronounced with a B (e.g., pronouncing /aw/ in the place of /u:/). The other group underwent a different sound shift of A → C. When the sound shifts are complete, there are two languages (or different dialects), L1 and L2, which exhibit the sound correspondence B ↔ C. The B ↔ C correspondence shows that the two languages descended from a common source, the parent language L. Chance alone cannot explain a regular sound correspondence.

FIGURE 8.1

How a regular sound correspondence arises.

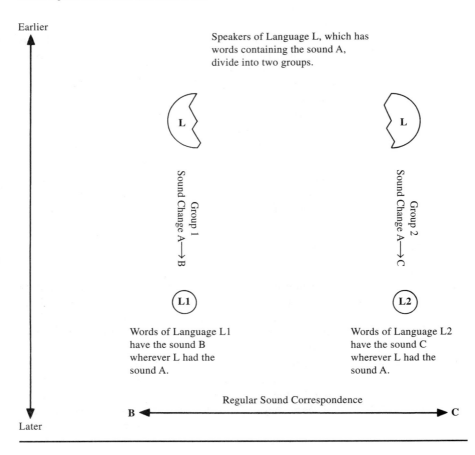

Earlier

Speakers of Language L, which has words containing the sound A, divide into two groups.

L

L

Group 1
Sound Change A→B

Group 2
Sound Change A→C

L1

L2

Words of Language L1
have the sound B
wherever L had the
sound A.

Words of Language L2
have the sound C
wherever L had the
sound A.

Regular Sound Correspondence

B ⟷ C

Later

If records of L were available, it would be possible to observe a regular sound correspondence between L and L1 — namely, A ↔ B — and between L and L2 — namely, A ↔ C. Such observations would confirm the relatedness of L1 and L2.

Now let us turn to actual languages. How do we know that the Germanic and Romance languages have a common ancestor? One clue is the large number of sound correspondences that exist between them. If you speak or have studied a Romance language, you may have noticed that, where an English word begins with *f*, the corresponding word in a Romance language often begins with *p*, as in the following examples:

English /f/	**French /p/**	**Spanish /p/**
father	père	padre
fish	poisson	pescado

This /f/–/p/ correspondence is another example of a regular sound correspondence. There are many correspondences between Germanic and Romance languages, and the prevalence cannot be explained by chance. What, then, accounts for them? A reasonable guess is that a common ancestor language used a /p/ in words for *fish, father,* and so on. A /p/ rather than an /f/ is posited here because more languages show a /p/ in these words. At some point, speakers of this language separated into two groups, retaining little contact. In one of the groups, a sound change of /p/ → /f/ took place. This group eventually became the ancestor of the Germanic languages. This ancient sound change left its trace in the /f/–/p/ sound correspondence that we observe today, as illustrated in the following diagram:

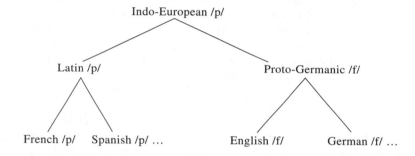

Indo-European /p/

Latin /p/

Proto-Germanic /f/

French /p/   Spanish /p/ ...

English /f/   German /f/ ...

Phonological Change

> Etymologists . . . for whom vowels did not matter and who cared not a jot for consonants.
>
> Voltaire

Regular sound correspondences illustrate changes in the phonological system. In earlier chapters, we discussed speakers' knowledge of their phonological system, including knowledge of the phonemes and phonological rules of the language. Any of these aspects of the phonology is subject to change.

The velar fricative /x/, once common, is no longer part of the phonemic inventory of most Modern English dialects. This phonological change — the loss of /x/ — took place between the times of Chaucer and Shakespeare, except in dialects such as Scottish, which has retained it in words such as *loch* [lɔx], a *lake*. In some cases, the /x/ disappeared altogether: *night* was once pronounced [nɪxt], *drought* was [druxt], and *saw* was [saux]. In other cases, the /x/ became a /k/, as in *elk* (Old English *eolh* [ɛɔlx]). In still other instances, it became a vowel, as in *hollow* (Old English *holh* [hɔlx]) and *sorrow* (Old English *sorh* [sɔrx]).

These examples show that the inventory of sounds can change by the loss of phonemes. The inventory can also change by the addition of new phonemes. Old English did not have the phoneme /ž/ of *leisure* [ližər] — [lɛžər] as some say it — or *confusion* [kɔ̃nfjužən]. Through a process of **palatalization** — a change in the place of articulation to the palatal region — certain occurrences of /z/ were pronounced as [ž]. Eventually, the [ž] sound became a phoneme in its own right, reinforced by the fact that it is a common phoneme in French, a language that exerted a major influence on the English language after the Norman Conquest.

An allophone of a phoneme may become phonemic. For example, Old English did not have the phoneme /v/, but it did have an allophone [v] of /f/. This phoneme was [f] when it occurred initially, finally, and between voiceless elements, but it was [v] when it came between vowels or vowels and voiced consonants. Just as [p] and [pʰ] are allophones of the same /p/ phoneme in Modern English, so too [f] and [v] were variants of the phoneme /f/ in Old English. Thus, *ofer* /ofer/, meaning "over," was pronounced [ɔvɛr] in Old English, while *fisc* was pronounced [fɪš].

Old English also had a geminate phoneme /f:/ that contrasted with /f/ and was pronounced as a long [f:] between vowels. The name *Offa* /of:a/ was pronounced [ɔf:a]. A sound change occurred in which the pronunciation of /f:/ was simplified to [f]. Once the geminate /f:/ was pronounced as [f], it contrasted with the intervocalic [v], and a reinterpretation created a new phoneme /v/.

Phonemes may thus be lost (/x/) or added (/ž/) or result from a change in the status of allophones (the [v] allophone of /f/ becoming /v/).

Similar changes occur in the histories of all languages. Neither /č/ nor /š/ was a phoneme of Latin, but /č/ is a phoneme of modern Italian and /š/ of modern French, both of which evolved from Latin. In an older stage of Russian, the phoneme /æ/ occurred, but in modern Russian [æ] is merely an allophone of /a/.

Phonological Rules

An interaction of phonological rules may result in changes in the lexicon. The nouns *house* and *bath* were once differentiated from the verbs *house* and *bathe* by the fact that the verbs ended with a short vowel sound (still reflected in the spelling). Furthermore, the same rule that realized /f/ as [v] between vowels also realized /s/ and /θ/ as [z] and [ð] between vowels. This was a general rule that voiced intervocalic fricatives. Thus, the /s/, which was followed by a vowel in the verb *house*, was pronounced [z], and the /θ/ in the verb *bathe* was pronounced [ð] for the same reason. Later, a rule was added to the grammar of English deleting unstressed short vowels at the ends of words. Once the unstressed final vowel was deleted, a contrast between voiced and voiceless fricatives resulted, and the new phonemes /z/ and /ð/ were added to the phonemic inventory. Prior to this change, they were simply the allophones of the phonemes /s/ and /θ/ between vowels. The verbs *house* and *bathe* were now represented in the mental lexicon with final voiced consonants. Some speakers of Canadian English, however, do not distinguish phonetically the noun *bath* from the verb in certain utterances: thus, they [bæθ] the baby rather than [beð] it.

Eventually, both the unstressed vowel deletion rule and the intervocalic-voicing rule were lost from the grammar of English. Thus, the set of phonological rules can change by both addition and loss of rules.

Changes in phonological rules often result in dialect differences. In Chapter 7, we discussed the addition of an "*r*-dropping" rule in English that did not spread throughout the language (/r/ is not pronounced unless followed by a vowel). Today we see the effect of that rule in the "*r*-less" pronunciation of British English and of American English dialects spoken in the Boston area and the southern United States.

From the standpoint of the language as a whole, phonological changes occur gradually over the course of many generations of speakers, although a given speaker's grammar may or may not reflect the changes. The changes are not planned any more than we are currently planning which changes will take place in English by the year 2300. Speakers are aware of the changes only through dialect differences.

The Great Vowel Shift

A major change in the history of English that resulted in new phonemic representations of words and morphemes began during Middle English, continued into the eighteenth century, and may still be taking place in some English dialects. It is known as the **Great Vowel Shift**, and it affected the seven long or tense vowels. These vowels underwent the following changes:

	Shift			**Example**		
Middle English		**Modern Canadian English**	**Middle English**		**Modern Canadian English**	
[i:]	→	{ [ʌj] [aj]	[mi:s] [ri:d(ə)]	→ →	[mʌjs] [rajd]	mice ride
[u:]	→	{ [ʌw] [aw]	[mu:s] [flu:r]	→ →	[mʌws] [flawər]	mouse flower
[e:]	→	[i:]	[ge:s]	→	[gi:s]	geese
[o:]	→	[u:]	[go:s]	→	[gu:s]	goose
[ɛ:]	→	[e:]	[brɛ:ken]	→	[bre:k]	break
[ɔ:]	→	[o:]	[brɔ:ken]	→	[bro:k]	broke
[a:]	→	[e:]	[na:mə]	→	[ne:m]	name

By diagramming the Great Vowel Shift on a vowel chart (see Figure 8.2), we can see that the highest vowels [i:] and [u:] "fell off" to become the diphthongs [aj]/[ʌj] and [aw]/[ʌw], while the long vowels underwent an increase in tongue height, as if to fill in the space left when the highest vowels became diphthongs. In addition, [a:] was "fronted."

These changes are among the most dramatic examples of regular sound shift. The phonemic representations of thousands of words changed. Today some reflection of this vowel shift is seen in the alternating forms of morphemes in English: *please, pleasant; serene, serenity; sane, sanity; crime, criminal; sign, signal*; and so on. At one time, the vowels in each pair were the same. In a sound change known as

FIGURE 8.2
The Great Vowel Shift.

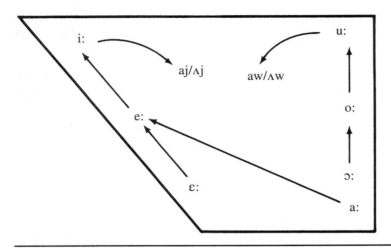

the **Early Middle English Vowel Shortening**, the vowels in the second word of each pair were then shortened, so those words were unaffected by the Great Vowel Shift, which occurred later. Thus, these morphologically related words are pronounced differently today (see Table 8.1).

The Great Vowel Shift is a primary source of many of the spelling inconsistencies of English, because our spelling system still reflects the way words were spelled before the Great Vowel Shift took place.

Morphological Change

Of all the words of witch's doom
There's none so bad as which and whom.
The man who kills both which and whom
Will be enshrined in our Who's Whom.

Fletcher Knebel

Like phonological rules, rules of morphology may be lost, added, or changed. We can observe some of these changes by comparing older and newer forms of the language or by looking at different dialects.

The suffix *-ize* — or, as many British writers and some Canadians prefer to spell it, *-ise* — that changes nouns and adjectives into verbs meaning "to make _____," as in *finalize* "to make final," is becoming more productive. Speakers are attaching this suffix to more words that previously did not take it. Words such as *privatize*

TABLE 8.1
Effect of the Vowel Shift on Modern English

Middle English Vowel	Shifted Vowel	Short Counterpart	Word with Shifted Vowel	Word with Vowel
ī	aj	ɪ	divine	divinity
ū	aw	ʌ	profound	profundity
ē	i	ɛ	serene	serenity
ō	u	ɑ	fool	folly
ā	e	æ	sane	sanity

"to make private" and, perhaps, *rigidize* "to make rigid" are achieving the status of *optimize, stabilize,* and *vitalize.* This change in the morphology of English is reflected in additions to the lexicon.

Extensive changes in rules of morphology have occurred in the history of the Indo-European language. Latin inherited a complex system of **case** endings — suffixes added to the **stem** of the noun based on its grammatical relationship to the verb — from Indo-European. The different forms (the *declension*) of the noun *lupus* "wolf" in classical Latin are as follows:

Case	Noun Stem		Case Ending		
nominative	lup	+	us	lupus	The *wolf* runs. (subject of the verb)
genitive	lup	+	i	lupi	A sheep in *wolf's* clothing. (possession)
dative	lup	+	ō	lupō	Give food *to the wolf.* (indirect object)
accusative	lup	+	um	lupum	I love *the wolf.* (direct object)
ablative	lup	+	ō	lupō	Run *from the wolf.* (*by, with, from, on, in* + noun)
vocative	lup	+	e	lupe	*Wolf,* come here! (the thing/being addressed)

A seventh case, the "locative," referring to "the place where" something occurs, is not given here. These cases are no longer found in the Romance languages.

In *Alice's Adventures in Wonderland,* Lewis Carroll has Alice give us a brief lesson in grammatical case. Alice has become very small and is swimming around in a pool of her own tears with a mouse that she wishes to befriend:

> "Would it be of any use, now," thought Alice, "to speak to this mouse? Everything is so out-of-the-way down here, that I should think very likely it can talk: at any rate, there's no harm in trying." So she began: "O Mouse, do you know the way out of this pool? I am very tired of swimming about here, O Mouse!" (Alice thought this must be the right way of speaking to a mouse: she had never done such a thing before, but she remembered having seen in her brother's Latin Grammar, "A mouse — of a mouse — to a mouse — a mouse — O mouse!")

Alice gives an English "translation" of the nominative, genitive, dative, accusative, and vocative cases.

Ancient Greek and Sanskrit also had extensive case systems expressed morphologically through noun suffixing, as did Old English, as illustrated in the following noun forms:

Case	OE Singular		OE Plural	
nominative	stān	"stone"	stānas	"stones"
genitive	stānes	"stone's"	stāna	"stones'"
dative	stāne	"stone"	stānum	"stones"
accusative	stān	"stone"	stānas	"stones"

The plural nominative and accusative cases of this declension became generalized to all the English regular nouns. In Middle English, a change lengthened the stem vowel and reduced the suffix vowel of certain word classes. Thus, Old English *nama* /nama/, "name," became Middle English /na:mə/. Another phonological rule change, mentioned earlier, resulted in the dropping out of certain short unstressed vowels, and this rule, together with the Great Vowel Shift, applied to the Middle English /na:mə/ gives Modern English /nem/ (with vowel length not indicated because it is not distinctive in Modern English). Similar changes occurred in the development of Old English *stānas* /stā:nas/, "stones," where the stem vowel was raised to /ɔ:/ in Middle English and to /o/ in Modern English and the suffix vowel was reduced and then lost:

OE /stā:nas/ → ME /stɔ:nəs/ → Mod. Eng. /stonz/

This change is representative of thousands of similar changes. When the "weak" syllables representing case endings in the forms of the singular, genitive plural, and dative plural were similarly dropped, only two distinct forms of the noun were left: *stone* and *stones*.

Modern English has preserved more of the case structure of pronouns, but even so the Old English pronoun was more complex, including a "dual" number along with the singular and plural numbers with which we are familiar:

Case	OE Singular		OE Dual		OE Plural	
nominative	ic	"I"	wit	"we two"	we	"we"
genitive	mīn	"my-mine"	uncer	"our two"	ūre	"our-ours"
dative	me	"me"	unc	"us two"	ūs	"us"
accusative	mec/me	"me"	uncit/unc	"us two"	ūsic/ūs	"us"

The dual number, as the translations show, can be expressed in Modern English only with a phrase such as *we two* or *of us two*. The short Old English lyric "Wulf and Eadwacer" illustrates this dual form:

þæt mon ēaþe tōslīteð þætte næfrɛ gesomnad wæs
uncer giedd geador.

One can easily cut asunder that which was never joined together,
The song of *us-two* together.

English has replaced its depleted case system with an equally expressive system of prepositions and with stricter constraints on word order — a trade-off between morphological and syntactic rules. Where once a noun in the dative case could be used, Modern English often employs the preposition *to*, as in *She gave the letter to Mary*. English also retains something of the genitive case, which is written with an apostrophe + *s,* as in *Mary's letter*, but beyond this residual indicator there are no longer any morphological markers suffixed to the English noun to indicate case. Pronouns, as we have seen, retain a few more traces of the case system.

While a few languages, such as Lithuanian and Russian, retain much of the early Indo-European case system, changes have all but obliterated it in most modern Indo-European languages. English and most of the Indo-European languages, then, have undergone extensive morphological changes over time, many of them induced by changes that took place in the phonological rules of the language.

Syntactic Change

The loss of case endings in English occurred together with changes in the rules of syntax governing word order. In Old English, word order was freer because the case endings alone disclosed the thematic or meaning relations in a sentence. Thus, the following sentences were all grammatical in Old English, and all meant "The man slew the king":

> Sē man slōh þone kyning.
> þone kyning slōh sē man.
> Sē man þone kyning slōh.
> þone kyning sē man slōh.
> Slōh sē man þone kyning.
> Slōh þone kyning sē man.

(*Sē* was a definite article used only with the subject noun, and *þone* was the definite article used only with the object noun.)

In Modern English, only the first of the literal translations below means what the original meant, and four of the six are ungrammatical as sentences:

> The man slew the king.
> The king slew the man.
> *The man the king slew.
> *The king the man slew.
> *Slew the man the king.
> *Slew the king the man.

The syntactic rules of Modern English permit less variation in word order. Additionally, Modern English is an SVO (subject–verb–object language), while Old English was both an SVO and an SOV language. (See the discussion of "Types of Languages" later in this chapter.) Consequently, SOV sentences such as *Sē man þone kyning slōh* (*The man the king slew*) were grammatical in Old English. The phrase structure rules that determine the word order of the basic sentences of the language changed in the history of English.

The syntactic rules relating to the English negative construction also underwent a number of changes from Old English to the present. In Modern English, negation is expressed by adding *not* or *do not*. We may also express negation by adding words such as *never* or *no*:

> I am going. → I am not going.
> I went. → I did not go.
> I go to school. → I never go to school.
> I want food. → I don't want any food; I want no food.

In Old English, the main negation element was *ne*. It usually occurred before the *auxiliary verb* or the verb, as illustrated by these examples (Traugott 1972):

> þæt hē *nā*   siþþan geboren *ne* wurde
> that he never after   born   not would-be
> that he should never be born after that

> ac hīe *ne* dorston þǣr on cuman
> but they not dared   there on come
> but they dared not land there

In the first example, the word order is different from that of Modern English, and there are two negatives: *nā* (a contraction of *ne* + *ā*; "not" + "ever" = "never") and *ne*. Double negatives were, as the sentence shows, grammatical in Old English.

In addition to the contraction of *ne* + *ā* → *nā*, other negative contractions occurred in Old English: *ne* could be attached to *habb-* "have," *wes-* "be," *wit-* "know," and *will-* "will" to form *nabb-, nes-, nyt-,* and *nyll-,* respectively.

Similar negative contractions are common in Middle English; toward the end of the period, Chaucer writes:

> She sholde seye   she   *nyste* [i.e., *ne* + *wyste*]   where he was.
> She should say   she   knew not   where he was.

> But he *noot* [*ne* + *wot*]   which the righte wey is thider.
> But he knows not   which the right way is hence.

> And of this cry   they *nolde* [*ne* + *wolde*]   nevere stenten.
> And of this lamentation they wouldn't   never cease.

Other equally common contractions are *nadde* (*ne* + *hadde*), *nam* (*ne* + *am*), *nas* (*ne* + *was*), and *nyl* (*ne* + *wyl*).

The negative force of *ne* before a verb or prefixed to a verb was increased by an additional negative such as *nought* or *not* following the verb, as in *He ne held it noght*. As these examples suggest, double negatives continue to be standard in Middle English. In fact, triple negatives are not unusual: the twelfth-century *Peterborough Chronicle* remarks that *Ne wæren nævre nan martyrs swa pined*, "No martyrs were not never so tortured" (Mossé 1952). But then Chaucer uses four in *He nevere yet no vileynye ne sayde / In al his lif unto no maner wight*, "He never yet no rudeness not said in all his life unto no sort of person" ("He never spoke rudely to any person"). Shakespeare and his contemporaries had no worry about the "illogicality" of multiple negatives. Clearly, the more you say no, the more you mean no.

From around the middle of the fourteenth century, the *ne* appearing before the verb began to be dropped, leaving only the negative *not* following the verb: *cry not so* (Mustanoja 1960). This method of negation was "the norm after any finite verb — I say not, I know not, a pattern which remained colloquial till the late 18c" (Strang 1970).

Modern English has contraction rules that change *do + not* into *don't, will + not* into *won't*, and so on. In these contractions, the phonetic form of the negation element always comes at the *end* of the word, because Modern English word order puts the *not* after the auxiliary. In Modern English, *not* must precede the main verb of the clause, and a *do* or *does* must be present if there is no auxiliary verb. In Old English, the negative element occurs at the beginning of the contraction, because it typically preceded the auxiliary in sentences. The rules determining the placement of the negative morpheme have changed. Such syntactic changes may take centuries to be fully completed, and there are often intermediate stages.

Another syntactic change in English affected the rules of comparative and superlative constructions. Today we form the comparative by adding *-er* to the adjective or by inserting *more* before it; the superlative is formed by adding *-est* or by inserting *most*. In Malory's tales of King Arthur, written in 1470, double comparatives and double superlatives occur, which today are ungrammatical: *more gladder, more lower, moost royallest, moost shamefullest*.

When we study a language solely from written records, as we must with earlier periods, we encounter only those sentences that are grammatical — unless, of course, ungrammatical sentences are used deliberately. In fact, without native speakers to query, we can only infer what was ungrammatical. Such inference leads us to believe that expressions such as *the queen of England's crown* were ungrammatical in former versions of English. The title *The Wife's Tale of Bath* (rather than *The Wife of Bath's Tale*) in *The Canterbury Tales* supports this inference. Modern English, on the other hand, allows rather complex constructions that involve the possessive marker. An English speaker can use possessive constructions such as

> The girl whose sister I'm dating's roommate is pretty.
> The man from Regina's hat fell off.

Older versions of English had to resort to an "*of* construction" to express the same thought (*The hat of the man from Regina fell off*). It is clear that a syntactic change took place that accounts for the extended use of the possessive morpheme *'s*.

Lexical Change

Cul'd minion, dancer, coiner of sweet words.

Matthew Arnold, "Sohrab and Rustum"

Changes in the lexicon also occur, including the addition of new words, changes in the meanings of words, and the loss of words.

New Words

In Chapter 2, we examined some ways in which new words enter a language and noted, for example, that by recombining old words — **compounding** — we can form new words and new meanings. Thousands of common English words have entered the language by this process, including *afternoon, baby bonus, bigmouth, bush pilot, chesterbed, chickenhearted, do in, egghead, force feed, g-string, icecap, jet set, longshoreman, moreover, nursemaid, offshore, pothole, railroad, sailboat, takeover, undergo, water cooler, woodlot, x-ray*, and *zooecology*.

We also saw that new words may be formed by derivational processes, as in *uglification* or *finalize/-se* (from which we get a "bonus," *finalization/-sation*). Other methods for enlarging the vocabulary that were discussed include word coinage, deriving words from names, blends, back-formations, acronyms, and abbreviations or clippings.

Borrowings

Another important source of new words is **borrowing** from other languages. Borrowing occurs when one language takes a word or morpheme from another language and adds it to its lexicon, often altering the pronunciation to fit the phonological rules of the borrowing language. Most languages are borrowers, so the lexicon can be divided into native and non-native words (often called **loan words**). A *native word* is one whose history (or **etymology**) can be traced back to the earliest known stages of the language.

A language may borrow a word *directly* or *indirectly*. A *direct* borrowing means that the borrowed item is a native word in the language from which it is borrowed. *Feast* was borrowed directly from French and can be traced back to Latin *festum*. On the other hand, the word *algebra* was borrowed from Spanish, which in turn had borrowed it from Arabic. Thus, *algebra* was indirectly borrowed from Arabic, with Spanish as an intermediary.

Some languages are heavy borrowers. Albanian has borrowed so heavily that few native words are retained. On the other hand, most Native North American languages borrowed little from their neighbours.

English has borrowed extensively. Of the 20 000 or so words in common use, about three-fifths are borrowed. Of the 500 most frequently used words, however, only two-sevenths are borrowed, and, since these words are used repeatedly in sentences, the frequency of appearance of native words is about 80 percent. Morphemes such as *and, be, have, it, of, the, to, will, you, on, that*, and *is* are all native to English.

The history of the English-speaking peoples can be followed by studying the kinds of loan words in the language and when they entered. Until the Norman Conquest in 1066, England was inhabited chiefly by the Angles, the Saxons, and the Jutes, peoples of Germanic origin who came to England in the fifth century C.E.

and eventually became the English. (The word *England* is derived from *Anglaland* —
i.e., "land of the Angles"). Originally, they spoke Germanic dialects, from which
Old English developed directly. These dialects contained a number of Latin borrowings but were otherwise undiluted by foreign elements. These Germanic tribes
had displaced the earlier Celtic inhabitants, whose influence on Old English was
largely confined to a few Celtic place names. (The modern languages Welsh, Irish,
and Scots Gaelic are descended from the Celtic dialects.)

For three centuries after the Norman Conquest, French was the language used for
affairs of state and for most commercial, social, and cultural matters. The West
Saxon literary language was abandoned, but regional varieties of English continued
to be used in homes, churches, and markets. During these three centuries, vast numbers of French words entered English, of which the following are representative:

government	crown	prince	state	parliament
nation	jury	judge	crime	sue
attorney	property	miracle	charity	court
lechery	virgin	saint	pray	mercy
religion	value	royal	money	society

Until the Norman Conquest, when an Englishman slaughtered an ox for food, he
ate *ox*. If it was a pig, he ate *pig*. If it was a sheep, he ate *sheep*. However, "ox"
served at the Norman tables was *beef (boeuf)*, "pig" was *pork (porc)*, and "sheep"
was *mutton (mouton)*. These words were borrowed from French into English, as
were the food-preparing words *boil* and *fry*. This showed who prepared the food and
who ate it.

English borrowed many "learned" words from foreign sources during the
Renaissance. In 1476, the printing press was introduced in England by William
Caxton, and, by 1640, 55 000 books had been printed in English. The authors of
these books used many Greek and Latin words, and as a result many words of
ancient Greek and Latin entered the language.

From Greek came *drama, comedy, tragedy, scene, botany, physics, zoology*, and
atomic. Greek roots have also provided English with a means for coining new
words, which have been called "neoclassical compounds." *Thermos* "hot" plus *metron*
"measure" give us *thermometer*. From *akros* "topmost" and *phobia* "fear" we get
acrophobia "dread of heights."

Latin loan words in English are numerous and range from obscure learned words
to ordinary words that few nowadays think of as anything but native stock. They
include

candle	street	school	cucumber
describe	noon	exit	bonus
scientific	cedar	supplicate	alumnus
cardiac	lapidary	quorum	orthography

Latin, like Greek, has also provided prefixes and suffixes that are used productively with both native and non-native roots. The prefix *ex-*, as in *ex-student, ex-wife*,
comes from Latin; the suffix *-able/-ible*, a borrowing from Latin through French,
can be attached to almost any English verb:

readable   doable   movable   singable

During the ninth and tenth centuries, the Scandinavians, who first raided and then settled in the British Isles, left their traces on the English language. The pronouns *they, their*, and *them* are loan words from Scandinavian. This period is the only time that English ever borrowed pronouns. Such borrowing was possible only because of the closeness of English and Scandinavian. Over the course of time, Germanic [sk] was palatized to [š] in English but remained [sk] in Scandinavian. Thus *skirt*, a borrowing into English from the Vikings, and *shirt* are derived from the same words in Proto-Germanic.

Bin, flannel, clan, slogan, and *whisky* are all words of Celtic origin, borrowed at various times from Welsh, Scots Gaelic, or Irish.

Dutch was a source of borrowed words, too, many of which are related to shipping: *buoy, freight, leak, pump, yacht.*

From German came *quartz, cobalt, noodle*, and — as we might guess — *sauerkraut.*

From Italian, many musical terms, including words describing opera houses, have been borrowed: *opera, piano, virtuoso, balcony, mezzanine.*

Words having to do with mathematics and chemistry were borrowed — indirectly, for the most part — from Arabic because early Arab scholarship in these, as in other intellectual and scientific fields, was considerably in advance of that found in Europe. Many of the words were initially borrowed by Spanish speakers who had close — often violent — contact with the Arab world. *Alcohol, algebra, cipher*, and *zero* are a representative sample.

Spanish has loaned us (directly) *barbecue, cockroach, guitar*, and *ranch*, as well as *California*, literally "hot furnace."

The English-speaking colonists of North America borrowed from the languages they encountered. First Nations provided them with words such as *pony, hickory, moose, skunk, toboggan, hominy, caribou, squash*, and, of course, *tomahawk, wigwam, papoose*, and *totem*. It is in the realm of place names, however, that English borrowed most extensively from Native North American languages. The names of four provinces — Ontario, Quebec, Manitoba, and Saskatchewan — and the names of innumerable cities, towns, rivers, and natural divisions and formations can be traced to the languages of Canada's First Nations. A few of these names include

Antigonish (NS)	Maniwaki (PQ)
Athabaska (AB)	Nanaimo (BC)
Avayalik (LB)	Niagara (ON)
Coquitlam (BC)	Nipawin (SK)
Inuvik (NWT)	Oka (PQ)
Kamloops (BC)	Ottawa (ON)
Kitimat (BC)	Saskatoon (SK)
Miminegash (PEI)	Toronto (ON)
Miramichi (NB)	Wetaskiwin (AB)
Mississauga (ON)	Winnipeg (MB)

Canada itself has been traced (through French) to Iroquoian *kanata*, "village."

French place names are also found throughout the nation, often marking the paths of French explorers and settlers: Belle Isle (NF), Sault Ste. Marie (ON), Portage-la-Prairie (MB), Souris (MB), Qu'Appelle (SK), Lac La Biche (AB).

Concern about the preservation of French in a largely English-speaking continent and worry over the inroads of anglicisms (e.g., *sandwich au poulet* and *un hot dog*) have led, as we have seen in Chapter 7, to stringent measures by the government of Quebec to restrict borrowing from English and to ensure that immigrants become French speaking. To offset the powerful influence of the English language, Quebec has established an Office de la langue française, which annually prepares a volume, the *Grand dictionnaire terminologique* (now also on the Internet at *www.lgdt.cedrom-sni.com* and on CD-ROM), to provide the public with alternatives to borrowing from English. It provides words for a wide array of items ranging from office furniture to truck axles. It proposes, for example, *courriel*, a compound word formed from *courrier électronique*, literally "electronic mail," in place of "e-mail." But, on the whole, translations — or what appear to be translations — from English are frowned upon; thus, *binette* is recommended for the smiling emoticon employed by computer users, and they are further advised to avoid *souriant*, the equivalent of the English "smiley face." Instead of employing the word *fax*, the *Dictionnaire* suggests *télécopie*; however, as *The Globe and Mail* has observed, "the truth is that plenty of people in Quebec say *fax*, not *télécopie*" (Nolen 1999), and the Office de la langue française is also aware of the fact that, if the public prefers a borrowed word to a "native" word, there is little it can do about it.

But if French shows the inroads of English, English in Quebec has likewise been affected by its contact with French. The vocabulary of "Quebec English" employs, as we might expect, French words and constructions; for example, English speakers may refer to a *depanneur* (a corner store) and discuss the policies of the *Parti Québécois* or the *Bloc Québécois*. More significant, however, is the use of "English" words that are familiar enough on the surface but that, as used in Quebec, seem odd or confusing to English speakers from elsewhere. Some Quebeckers speak, for example, of an *animator*, by which they mean not a creator of TV cartoons but an "organizer or group leader." They offer to *give a conference*, which, it turns out, is not a meeting or series of meetings but a lecture. Speakers of English both in Quebec and on the CBC speak of *sovereignists* instead of *sovereigntists*, reflecting the influence of French *souverainiste*. Other words used in senses different from their usual English meanings include

> collectivity — a community, people as a whole
> confessional schools — denominational schools
> inscription for a course — enrolment in a course
> permanence — permanent employment, tenure
> syndicate — trade union
> scolarity — schooling

(data from McArthur 1989)

The Globe and Mail, Saturday, November 27, 1999.

The meanings of these words reflect the meanings of the equivalent French words.

Three other words, *Anglophone*, *Francophone*, and *allophone* (a speaker of a language other than French or English), have recently become part of general Canadian English, especially following the *Official Languages Act* of 1969 in which both French and English were declared official languages of the country.

A glance at a map provides an insight into the multicultural mosaic that is modern Canada. Edward McCourt noted that, "within a radius of twenty miles [of one small area of eastern Saskatchewan], we find Dubue, Bangor, Stockholm, Esterhazy, Langenburg, Thingvilla, Churchbridge — in origin French, Welsh, Swedish, Hungarian, German, Icelandic, British — intermingled with American and eastern Canadian settlements whose centres bear no distinguishing ethnic labels" (as cited in McConnell 1979).

In 1996, some 21 000 people (0.1 percent of the total population) spoke Yiddish as their mother tongue (*Canadian Global Almanac* 1999), but many Yiddish words are known, if not used, by non-Jews as well as by non–Yiddish-speaking Jews, as is evident from *The Apprenticeship of Duddy Kravitz* by Mordecai Richler. *Lox* "smoked salmon," *bagel* "a hard roll resembling a doughnut," and *matzo* "unleavened cracker" belong to North American English, as do Yiddish expressions such as *chutzpah, schmaltz, schlemiel, schmuck, schmo*, and *kibitz*.

Other languages also borrow words, and many of them have borrowed from English. Twi speakers drank palm wine before Europeans arrived in Africa. Now they also drink [bia] "beer," [hwiski] "whisky," and [gɔrdɔn ǰin] "Gordon's gin."

Italian is filled with "strange" words such as *snack* (pronounced "znak"), *poster*, and *puzzle* ("pootsle"), and Italian girls use *blushes* and are warned by their mothers against *petting*.

Young Russians have incorporated into their language words such as *jazz, rock*, and the *twist*, which they dance in their *blue jeans* to *rock music*. When a former president of the United States, Richard Nixon, was considered for impeachment by the Congress, the official Communist party newspaper *Pravda* used the word *impeechmente* instead of the previously used Russian word *ustraneniye* "removal."

For thousands of years, Japanese borrowed heavily from Chinese (to which it is unrelated). Because Japanese uses Chinese characters in its writing system, many native Japanese words co-exist with a Chinese loan word. Japanese even has two ways of counting, one using native Japanese words and the other using Chinese loan words for the numbers.

In the past 100 years, Japanese has borrowed heavily from European languages, especially English from which it has thousands of loan words, including technical vocabulary, sports terms, and the jargon used in advertising. The Japanese have a special "syllabary" (similar to our alphabet, but see Chapter 9 on writing systems), which is used primarily to transcribe loan words.

Loan translations are compound words or expressions whose parts are translated directly into the borrowing language. *Marriage of convenience* is a loan translation borrowed from French *mariage de convenance*. Spanish speakers eat *perros calientes*, a loan translation of *hot dogs* with an adjustment reversing the order of adjective and noun, as required by the rules of Spanish syntax. And the *Grand dictionnaire terminologique* urges computer users to say *j'ai sauvegardé* and not *j'ai savé*, which it deems a loan translation from English (Nolen 1999).

Loss of Words

Words can also be *lost* from a language, though an old word's departure is never as striking as a new word's arrival. When a new word comes into vogue, its unusual presence draws attention, but a word is lost through inattention — nobody thinks of it; nobody uses it; and it fades out of the language.

A reading of Shakespeare's work shows that English has lost many words, such as these taken from *Romeo and Juliet: beseem* "to be suitable," *mammet* "a doll or puppet," *wot* "to know," *gyve* "a fetter," *fain* "gladly," and *wherefore* "why."

Semantic Change

> His talk was like a stream which runs
> with rapid change from rocks to roses.
> It slipped from politics to puns;
> It passed from Mahomet to Moses.
>
> Winthrop Mackworth Praed, "The Vicar"

We have seen that a language may gain or lose lexical items. Additionally, the meanings or semantic representations of words may change, shifting or becoming broader or narrower.

Broadening

When the meaning of a word becomes broader, that word means everything it used to mean and then some. The Middle English word *dogge* meant a specific breed of dog, but it was eventually **broadened** to encompass all members of the species *canis familiaris*. The word *holiday* originally meant "holy day," a day of religious significance. Today the word signifies any day on which we do not have to work. *Butcher* once meant "slaughterer of goats" (and earlier "of bucks"), but its modern usage is more general. Similarly, *picture* used to mean "painted representation," but today you can take a picture with a camera. A *companion* used to mean a person with whom you shared bread, but today it is a person who accompanies you. *Quarantine* once had the restricted meaning "forty days' isolation," and *bird* once meant "young bird." The invention of steam-powered boats gave the verb *sail* an opportunity to extend its dominion to boats without sails, just as the verb *drive* widened in meaning to encompass self-propelled vehicles.

Narrowing

In the King James Version of the Bible (1611), God says of the herbs and trees, "to you they shall be for meat" (Genesis 1:29). To a speaker of seventeenth-century English, *meat* meant "food," and *flesh* meant "meat." Since that time, semantic change has **narrowed** the meaning of meat to what it is in Modern English. *Deer* once referred to any "beast" or "animal," as its German cognate *Tier* still does. The meaning of *deer* has been narrowed to a particular kind of animal. Similarly, the word *hound* used to be the general term for "dog," like the German *Hund*. Today *hound* means a special kind of dog. The Old English word that occurs as modern *starve* once meant "to die." Its meaning has narrowed to become "to die of hunger" and in colloquial language "to be very hungry," as in "I'm starved." *Token* used to have the broad meaning "sign," but long ago it was specialized to mean a physical object that is a sign, such as a *love token. Liquor* was once synonymous with *liquid, reek* used to mean "smoke" (as it still does in the Scottish dialect), and *girl* once meant "young person of either sex."

Meaning Shifts

The third kind of semantic change that a lexical item may undergo is a shift in meaning. The word *bead* originally meant "prayer." During the Middle Ages, the custom arose of repeating prayers (i.e., *beads*) and counting them by means of little wooden balls on a rosary. The meaning of *bead* shifted from "prayer" to the visible sign of a prayer. The word *knight* once meant "youth" but shifted to a "mounted man-at-arms" and latterly to a person holding a non-hereditary title (which he may have gained through playing in a rock band). *Lust* used to mean simply "pleasure," with no negative or sexual overtones. *Lewd* was merely "ignorant," and *immoral* meant "not customary." *Silly* used to mean "happy" in Old English. By the Middle English period, it had come to mean "naïve," and only in Modern English does it mean "foolish." The overworked Modern English word *nice* meant "ignorant" a thousand years ago. When Juliet tells Romeo "I am too *fond*," she is not claiming she likes Romeo too much. She means "I am too *foolish*."

Reconstructing "Dead" Languages

The branch of linguistics that deals with how languages change, what kinds of change occur, and why they occur is called **historical and comparative linguistics**.

It is *historical* because it deals with the history of particular languages; it is *comparative* because it deals with relationships between languages.

The Nineteenth-Century Comparativists

> When agreement is found in words in two languages, and so frequently that
> rules may be drawn up for the shift in letters from one to the other, then there
> is a fundamental relationship between the two languages.
>
> Rasmus Rask

The nineteenth-century historical and comparative linguists based their theories on observations that there are regular sound correspondences among certain languages and that languages displaying systematic similarities and differences must have descended from a common source language — that is, they were genetically related.

The chief goal of these linguists was to develop and elucidate the genetic relationships that exist among the world's languages. They aimed to establish the major language families of the world and to define principles for the classification of languages. Their work grew out of earlier research.

In 1786, Sir William Jones (an English judge in India) delivered a paper in which he observed that Sanskrit bore to Greek and Latin "a stronger affinity ... than could possibly have been produced by accident." Jones suggested that these three languages had "sprung from a common source" and that probably Germanic and Celtic had the same origin. The classical philologists of the time attempted to disprove the idea that there was any genetic relationship among Sanskrit, Latin, and Greek, because if such a relationship existed it would make their views on language and language development obsolete. A Scottish philosopher, Dugall Stewart, for example, put forth the hypothesis that Sanskrit and Sanskrit literature were inventions of Brahmans, who used Greek and Latin as models. He wrote on this issue without knowing a single Sanskrit character, whereas Jones was an eminent Sanskritist.

About 30 years after Jones delivered his important paper, the German linguist Franz Bopp pointed out the relationships among Sanskrit, Latin, Greek, Persian, and Germanic. At the same time, a young Danish scholar named Rasmus Rask corroborated these results, bringing Lithuanian and Armenian into the relationship as well. Rask was the first scholar to describe formally the regularity of certain phonological differences between related languages.

Rask's investigation of these regularities was followed up by the German linguist Jakob Grimm (of fairy-tale fame), who published a four-volume treatise (1819–22) that specified the regular sound correspondences among Sanskrit, Greek, Latin, and the Germanic languages. It was not only the similarities that intrigued Grimm and the other linguists but also the systematic nature of the differences. Where Latin has a [p], English often has an [f]; where Latin has a [t], English often has a [θ]; where Latin has a [k], English often has an [h].

Grimm pointed out that certain phonological changes that did not take place in Sanskrit, Greek, or Latin must have occurred early in the history of the Germanic languages. Because the changes (illustrated in Figure 8.3) were so strikingly regular, they became known as **Grimm's Law**.

The "earlier stage" referred to in Figure 8.3 is the parent language of Sanskrit, Greek, the Romance and Germanic languages, as well as other languages — namely, Indo-European. The symbols *bh*, *dh*, and *gh* are breathy voiced stop phonemes, often called "voiced aspirates."

Grimm's Law can be expressed in terms of natural classes of speech sounds: voiced aspirates become unaspirated; voiced stops become voiceless; voiceless stops become fricatives.

Cognates

Cognates are words in related languages that developed from the same ancestral root, such as English *horn* and Latin *cornu*. Cognates often, but not always, have similar meanings in the different languages. From cognates, we can observe sound correspondences and from them deduce sound changes. Thus, from the cognates of Sanskrit, Latin, and English (representing Germanic) shown in Figure 8.4, the regular correspondence *p–p–f* indicates that the languages are genetically related. Indo-European *p is posited as the origin of the *p–p–f* correspondence.[2]

A more complete chart of correspondences is given in Figure 8.5, where a single representative example of each regular correspondence is presented. In most cases, many cognate sets exhibit the same correspondence, which leads to the reconstruction of the Indo-European sound shown in the first column.

FIGURE 8.3

Grimm's Law (an early Germanic sound shift).

Earlier stage:[1]	bh	dh	gh	b	d	g	p	t	k
	↓	↓	↓	↓	↓	↓	↓	↓	↓
Later stage:	b	d	g	p	t	k	f	θ	x (or h)

FIGURE 8.4

Cognates of Indo-European ***p**.

Indo-European *p	Sanskrit p	Latin p	English f
	pitar-	pater	father
	pad-	pedis	foot
	No cognate	piscis	fish
	paśu	pecu	fee

FIGURE 8.5

Some Indo-European sound correspondences.

Indo-European	Sanskrit		Latin		English	
*p	p	pitar-	p	pater	f	father
*t	t	trayas	t	trēs	θ	three
*k	ś	śun³	k	canis	h	hound
*b	b	No cognate	b	labium	p	lip
*d	d	dva-	d	duo	t	two
*g	j	ajras	g	ager	k	acre
*bh	bh	bhrātar-	f	frāter	b	brother
*dh	dh	dhā	f	fē-ci	d	do
*gh	h	vah-	h	veh-ō	g	wagon

Sanskrit underwent the fewest consonant changes, while Latin underwent somewhat more, and Germanic (under Grimm's Law) underwent almost a complete restructuring. Still, the fact that it was phonemes and phonological rules that changed, and not individual words, has resulted in the remarkably regular correspondences that allow us to reconstruct much of the sound system of Indo-European.

Exceptions can be found to these regular correspondences, as Grimm was aware: "The sound shift is a general tendency; it is not followed in every case." Karl Verner in 1875 explained some of the exceptions to Grimm's Law. He formulated **Verner's Law** to show why Indo-European *p*, *t*, and *k* failed to correspond to *f*, *θ*, and *x* in certain cases:

> Verner's Law: *When the preceding vowel was unstressed, f, θ, and x underwent a further change to b, d, and g.*

A group of young linguists known as the **Neo-Grammarians** went beyond the idea that such sound shifts represented only a tendency and claimed that sound laws have no exception. They viewed linguistics as a natural science and therefore believed that laws of sound change were unexceptionable natural laws. The "laws" they put forth often had exceptions, however, that could not always be explained as dramatically as Verner's Law explained the exceptions to Grimm's Law. Still, the work of these linguists provided important data and insights into language change and why such changes occur.

The linguistic work of the early nineteenth century had some influence on Charles Darwin, and in turn Darwin's theory of evolution had a profound influence on linguistics and on all science. Some linguists thought that languages have a "life cycle" and develop according to evolutionary laws. In addition, it was believed that each language can be traced to a common ancestor. This theory of biological naturalism, called *Stammbaum* ("family tree") theory, has an element of truth to it, but it is a vast oversimplification of the way languages change and evolve into other languages.

Comparative Reconstruction

> . . . Philologists who chase
> A panting syllable through time and space
> Start it at home, and hunt it in the dark,
> To Gaul, to Greece, and into Noah's Ark.
>
> William Cowper, "Retirement" (1782)

When languages resemble one another in ways not attributable to chance or borrowing, we may conclude that they are related. That is, they evolved via linguistic change from a single ancestral protolanguage. Even if the **parent language** no longer exists, by comparing the **daughter languages** we may deduce many facts about the parent language. The similarities of the basic vocabularies of languages such as English, German, Danish, Dutch, Norwegian, and Swedish are too pervasive for chance or borrowing. In addition to similar vocabularies, the Germanic languages share grammatical properties such as irregularity in the verb *to be* and similar irregular past tense forms of verbs. We therefore conclude that these languages have a common parent, Proto-Germanic. Of course, there are no written records of Proto-Germanic and certainly no native speakers alive today. Proto-Germanic is a hypothetical language whose properties have been deduced based on its descendants.

Once we know — or suspect — that several languages are related, their protolanguage may be partially determined by **comparative reconstruction**. One proceeds by applying the comparative method, which we illustrate with a brief example.

Restricting ourselves to English, German, and Swedish, we find that the word for "man" is *man, Mann*, and *man*, respectively. This is one of many **word sets** in which we can observe the regular sound correspondence [m]–[m]–[m] and [n]–[n]–[n] in the three languages. Using this evidence, we **reconstruct** **mVn* as the word for "man" in Proto-Germanic. The *V* indicates a vowel whose quality we are unsure of since, despite the similar spelling, the vowel is phonetically different in the various Germanic languages, and it is unclear how to reconstruct it without further evidence.

Although we are confident that we can reconstruct much of Proto-Germanic with accuracy, we may never know for sure, and many details remain obscured. To give us confidence in the comparative method, we can apply it to Romance languages such as French, Italian, Spanish, and Portuguese. Their protolanguage is similar to the well-known Latin, so we can verify the method. Consider the following data, focusing on the initial consonant of each word (Lehmann 1973):

French	Italian	Spanish	Portuguese	
cher	caro	caro	caro	"dear"
champ	campo	campo	campo	"field"
chandelle	candela	candela	candeia	"candle"

In French, [š] corresponds to [k] in the three other languages. Note that in these examples *ch* = [š] and *c* = [k]. This regular sound correspondence, [š]–[k]–[k]–[k], along with other facts, supports the view that French, Italian, Spanish, and Portuguese descended from a common language. The comparative method leads to the reconstruction of [k] in "dear," "field," and "candle" of the parent language and shows that [k] underwent a change to [š] in French but not in Italian, Spanish, or Portuguese, which retained the original [k] of the parent language.

To use the comparative method, analysts identify regular sound correspondences (not always easy to do) in what they take to be daughter languages; for each correspondence, they reconstruct a sound of the parent language. In this way, much of the sound system of the parent may be reconstructed. The various phonological changes that occurred in the development of each daughter language as it descended and changed from the parent are then identified. Sometimes the sound that analysts choose in their reconstruction of the parent language will be the sound that appears most frequently in the correspondence. This approach was illustrated above with the four Romance languages.

Other considerations may outweigh the "majority rules" principle. The likelihood of certain phonological changes may persuade the analyst to reconstruct a "minority" sound or even a sound that does not occur in the correspondence. For example, consider data in these four hypothetical languages:

Language A	Language B	Language C	Language D
hono	hono	fono	vono
hari	hari	fari	veli
rahima	rahima	rafima	levima
hor	hor	for	vol

Wherever Languages A and B have an *h*, Language C has an *f*, and Language D has a *v*. Therefore, we have the sound correspondence *h–h–f–v*. We might be tempted by the comparative method to reconstruct *h* in the parent language, but from other data on historical change, and from phonetic research, we know that *h* seldom becomes *f* or *v*. Generally, the reverse is the case: /f/ and /v/ becoming [h] occurs both historically and as a phonological rule with an acoustic explanation. Therefore, linguists reconstruct an **f* in the parent and posit the sound change "*f* becomes *h*" in Languages A and B and "*f* becomes *v*" in Language D. The other correspondences are not problematic insofar as these data are concerned. They are

o–o–o–o   n–n–n–n   a–a–a–e   r–r–r–l   m–m–m–m

They lead to the reconstructed forms **o, *n, *a, *r,* and **m* for the parent language and to the sound changes "*a* becomes *e*" and "*r* becomes *l*" in Language D. They are "natural" sound changes often found in the world's languages. It is now possible to reconstruct the words of the protolanguage. They are *fono, fari, rafima,* and *for.* Language D, in this example, is the most innovative, as it has undergone three sound changes. Language C is the most conservative, being identical to the protolanguage insofar as these data are concerned.

The sound changes seen in the previous illustrations are examples of **unconditioned sound change**. The changes occurred irrespective of phonetic context. Below is an example of **conditioned sound change**, taken from three dialects of Italian:

Standard	Northern	Lombard	
fisso	fiso	fis	"fixed"
kassa	kasa	kasə	"cabinet"

The correspondence sets are

    f–f–f   i–i–i   o–o–<loss of sound>   k–k–k   a–a–a   a–a–ə   s:–s–s

It is a straightforward task to reconstruct *f, *i, and *k. Knowing that a geminate such as s: commonly becomes s (recall that Old English f: became f), we reconstruct *s: for the s–s–s correspondence. A shortening change took place in the Northern and Lombard dialects.

There is evidence in these (very limited) data for a weakening of word-final vowels, a change we discussed earlier for English. We reconstruct *o and *a for o–o–<loss of sound> and a–a–ə. In Lombard, conditioned sound changes took place. The sound o was deleted in word-final position but remained o elsewhere. The sound a became ə in word-final position and remained a elsewhere. The conditioning factor is word-final position as far as we can tell from the data presented.

We reconstruct the protodialect as having had the words *fisso meaning "fixed" and *kassa meaning "cabinet."

It was by means of the comparative method that nineteenth-century linguists, beginning with August Schleicher in 1861, were able to initiate the reconstruction of the long-lost parent language so aptly conceived by Jones, Bopp, Rask, and Grimm. This is the language, which we believe flourished about 6000 years ago, that we have been calling **Indo-European**.

Historical Evidence

> You know my method. It is founded upon the observance of trifles.
>
> Sir Arthur Conan Doyle, "The Boscombe Valley Mystery,"
> *The Memoirs of Sherlock Holmes*

How do we discover phonological changes? How do we know how Shakespeare or Chaucer or the author of *Beowulf* pronounced their versions of English? We have no phonograph records or tape recordings that give us direct knowledge.

For many languages, historical records go back more than a thousand years. These records are studied to find out how languages were once pronounced. The spelling in early manuscripts tells us a great deal about the sound systems of older forms of modern languages. Two words, for example, spelled consistently in a different manner were probably pronounced differently. Once a number of orthographic contrasts are identified, good guesses can be made as to actual pronunciation. These guesses are supplemented by common words that show up in all stages of the language, allowing their pronunciation to be traced from the present, step by step, into the past.

Another clue to earlier pronunciation is provided by non-English words used in the manuscripts of English. Suppose a French word known to contain the vowel [o:]

is borrowed into English. The way the borrowed word is spelled reveals a particular letter–sound correspondence.

Other documents can be examined for evidence. Private letters are an excellent source of data. Linguists prefer letters written by naïve spellers, who will misspell words according to the way they pronounce them. For instance, at one point in English history, all words spelled with -*er* in their stems were pronounced as if they were spelled with -*ar*, just as in Modern British English *clerk* and *derby* are pronounced "clark" and "darby." Some poor spellers kept writing *parfect* for *perfect*, which helped linguists to discover the older pronunciation.

Clues are also provided by the writings of the prescriptive grammarians of the period. Between 1550 and 1750, a group of prescriptivists in England known as **orthoepists** attempted to preserve the "purity" of English. In prescribing how people should speak, they told us how people actually spoke. An orthoepist alive today might write in a manual "It is incorrect to pronounce *Cuba* with a final *r*." Future scholars would know that there were speakers of English who pronounced it that way.

Some of the best clues to earlier pronunciation are provided by puns and rhymes in literature. Two words rhyme if the vowels and final consonants are the same. When a poet rhymes the verb *found* with the noun *wound*, it strongly suggests that the vowels of these two words were identical:

> Benvolio: ... 'tis in vaine to seeke him here
> That meanes not to be found.
> Romeo: He ieasts [jests] at Scarres that neuer felt a wound.

Shakespeare's rhymes are helpful in reconstructing the sound system of Elizabethan English. For example, the rhyming of *convert* with *depart* in Sonnet XI strengthens the conclusion that -*er* was pronounced as -*ar*. Such rhymes were still possible in the eighteenth century when Alexander Pope linked *clerk* with *dark* and *wound* with *bound*.

Dialect differences may provide clues as to what earlier stages of a language were like. There are many dialects of English spoken around the world, and by comparing the pronunciation of various words in several dialects we can arrive at some notion of earlier forms and see what changes took place in the inventory of sounds and in the phonological rules.

For example, since some speakers of English pronounce *Mary, merry*, and *marry* with three different vowels (i.e., [meri], [mɛri], and [mæri], respectively), we suspect that at one time all speakers of English did so. (The different spellings are also a clue.) For some dialects, however, only one of these sounds can occur before /r/ — namely, the sound [ɛ]. Those dialects underwent a sound shift in which both /e/ and /æ/ shifted to /e/ when followed immediately by /r/, another instance of a conditioned sound change. The same change can also be seen in a "drinking song" of the University of California:

> They had to carry Harry to the ferry
> And the ferry carried Harry to the shore
> And the reason that they had to carry Harry to the ferry
> Was that Harry couldn't carry any more.

This song was written by someone who rhymed *Harry, carry*, and *ferry*. It does not sound quite as good to those who do not rhyme *Harry* and *ferry*.

Historical comparativists working with written records have a difficult job, but it is not nearly as difficult as that of scholars who are attempting to discover genetic relationships among languages with no written history. Linguists must first transcribe large amounts of language data from all the languages, analyze them phonologically, morphologically, and syntactically, and establish a basis for relatedness such as similarities in basic vocabulary and regular sound correspondences that could not be due to chance or borrowing. Only then can the comparative method be applied to reconstructing the extinct protolanguage.

The difficulty of this task can be appreciated when we realize the vast number of readily available texts for nearly all the Indo-European languages dating back thousands of years. Even so, Indo-European is far from being completely reconstructed or completely understood. And it is only one of many families of languages around the world. Linguists such as Franz Boas, Edward Sapir, and Mary Haas have discovered many relationships among Native American languages and have successfully reconstructed Native American protolanguages. Similarly, Joseph Greenberg of Stanford University was able to group the large number of languages of Africa into four families: Afro-Asiatic, Nilo-Saharan, Niger-Kordofanian, and Khoisan.

Extinct and Endangered Languages

Any language is the supreme achievement of a uniquely human collective genius, as divine and unfathomable a mystery as a living organism.

Michael Krauss

A language becomes extinct when no children learn it. This situation may come about in two ways: either all the speakers of the language are annihilated by some cataclysm, or, more commonly, the speakers of the language are absorbed by another culture that speaks a different language. Sometimes this absorption is due to political suppression of the language of an oppressed people. Their children, or their children's children, fail to learn the old language, and it passes into oblivion.

This fate has befallen, and is befalling, many First Nations' languages. According to Michael Krauss, only 20 percent of the remaining Native languages in the United States are being learned by children. Already hundreds have been lost. Once widely spoken languages such as Comanche, Apache, and Cherokee have fewer and fewer native speakers every generation. The same situation holds true in Canada. In the recent past, Native children were frequently sent to schools some distance from their home reserves, schools that actively discouraged the children's own languages.

Doomed languages have existed throughout time. The Indo-European languages Hittite and Tocharian no longer exist, Hittite having passed away 3500 years ago and the two dialects of Tocharian during the first millennium C.E. Cornish, a Celtic language akin to Breton, expired in England in the late eighteenth century.

Linguists have placed many languages on an endangered languages list. They attempt to preserve these languages by documenting their grammars — that is, the phonetics, phonology, syntax, and morphology — and by recording for posterity the speech of the last few speakers. Through its grammar, each language provides new evidence about the nature of human cognition. And in its literature, poetry, ritual speech, and word structure, each language stores the collective intellectual achievements of a culture, offering unique perspectives on fundamental problems of the human condition. The disappearance of a language is tragic, for not only are these insights and perspectives lost, but the major medium through which a culture maintains and renews itself is gone as well.

Dialects, too, may become extinct. For example, the dialect spoken on Ocracoke Island off the coast of North Carolina is being studied extensively by the dialectologist Walt Wolfram. One reason for the study is to preserve the dialect, which is in danger of extinction because so many young Ocracokers leave the island and raise their children elsewhere. The dialect-speaking population is also becoming diluted by vacationers and retirees, attracted to the island by its unique character, including, ironically, the quaint speech of the islanders.

Linguists are not alone in their preservation efforts. Under the sponsorship of language clubs, and occasionally even governments, many endangered languages, such as Irish, are learned by adults and children as a symbol of the culture. In Hawaii, a movement is under way to preserve and teach Hawaiian, the native language of the islands.

The United Nations, too, is concerned. In 1991, UNESCO (the United Nations Educational, Scientific, and Cultural Organization) passed a resolution stating that, "As the disappearance of any one language constitutes an irretrievable loss to mankind, it is for UNESCO a task of great urgency to respond to this situation by promoting . . . the description — in the form of grammars, dictionaries, and texts — of endangered and dying languages."

Occasionally, a language is resurrected from written records. For centuries, classical Hebrew was used only in religious ceremonies, but today, with some modernization, and through a great desire among Jews to speak the language of their forebears, it has become the national language of Israel.

The preservation of dying languages and dialects is essential to the study of **Universal Grammar**, an attempt to define linguistic properties shared by all languages. This in turn will help linguists to develop a comprehensive theory of language that will include a specific description of the innate human capacity for language.

The Genetic Classification of Languages

The Sanskrit language, whatever be its antiquity, is of a wonderful structure, more perfect than the Greek, more copious than the Latin, and more exquisitely refined than either, yet bearing to both of them a stronger affinity, both in the roots of verbs and in the forms of grammar, than could possibly be produced by accident; so strong, indeed, that no philologer could examine all three, without believing that they have sprung from some common source, which, perhaps, no longer exists....

Sir William Jones (1786)

We have discussed how different languages evolve from one language and how historical and comparative linguists classify languages into families, such as Germanic or Romance, and reconstruct earlier forms of the ancestral language. When we examine the languages of the world, we perceive that some are closely related, others more distantly related, and still others apparently unrelated.

Counting to five in English, German, and Vietnamese shows similarities between English and German not shared by Vietnamese:

English	German	Vietnamese
one	ein	mot
two	zwei	hai
three	drei	ba
four	vier	bon
five	funf	nam

This similarity between English and German is pervasive. Sometimes it is extremely obvious (*man/Mann*), at other times a little less obvious (*child/Kind*). No regular similarities or differences apart from those due to chance are found between them and Vietnamese.

Pursuing the metaphor of human genealogy, we say that English, German, Norwegian, Danish, Swedish, and Icelandic are sisters in that they descended from one parent and are more closely related to one another than any of them is to non-Germanic languages such as French or Russian.

If we carry the family metaphor further, we might describe the Germanic and Romance languages as cousins since their respective parents, Proto-Germanic and early forms of Latin, were siblings. The Romance languages of French, Spanish, Portuguese, Italian, and Romanian, then, are sister languages to each other and daughter languages of Latin. The numbers from one to three in English and two Romance languages, compared with the unrelated Japanese numbers, reveal something of this relationship:

Spanish	French	English	Japanese
uno	un	one	ichi
dos	deux	two	ni
tres	trois	three	san

As with human families, there are cousins, and then there are distant cousins. If the Germanic and Romance languages are truly cousins, then languages such as Greek, Armenian, Albanian, and even the extinct Hittite and Tocharian are distant cousins. So are Irish, Scots Gaelic, Welsh, and Breton, whose protolanguage, Celtic, was once widespread throughout Europe and the British Isles. Breton is spoken by the people living in the northwest coastal region of France called Brittany. It was brought there by Celts fleeing from Britain in the seventh century and has been preserved as the language of some Celtic descendants in Brittany ever since. Russian is also a distant cousin, as are its sisters, Bulgarian, Serbo-Croatian, Polish, Czech, and Slovak. The Baltic language Lithuanian is related to English, as is its sister language, Latvian. A neighbouring language, Estonian, however, is not a relative. Sanskrit, as was pointed out by Sir William Jones, though far removed geographically and temporally, is nonetheless a relative. Its daughters, Hindi and Bengali, spoken primarily in South Asia, are distantly related to English. Even the Persian spoken in modern Iran is a distant cousin of English.

All the languages mentioned in the previous paragraph, except for Estonian, are related, more or less distantly, because they descended from Indo-European.

Figure 8.6 is an abbreviated "family tree" of the Indo-European languages that gives a genealogical and historical classification of the languages shown. All the languages of the world may be similarly classified. The diagram is, of course, simplified. It may appear from it, for example, that all of the Slavic languages emerged at once, when in fact the nine languages appearing here can be organized hierarchically, showing that some are more closely related than others. In other words, the various separations that resulted in the nine Slavic languages we see today occurred at different times over a long period.

Another simplification in the diagram is that the "dead ends" — languages that evolved and died leaving no offspring, such as Hittite and Tocharian — are not included.

The family tree also fails to show a number of intermediate stages that must have existed in the evolution of modern languages. Languages do not evolve abruptly, which is why comparisons with the genealogical trees of biology have limited usefulness.

Finally, the diagram fails to show a number of Indo-European languages because of lack of space.

Languages of the World

> And the whole earth was of one language, and of one speech.
>
> Genesis 11:1

> Let us go down, and there confound their language, that they may not understand one another's speech.
>
> Genesis 11:7

> There are no primitive languages. The great and abstract ideas of Christianity can be discussed even by the wretched Greenlanders.
>
> Johann Peter Suessmilch (1756)

Most of the world's languages do not belong to the Indo-European family. Linguists have also attempted to classify the non–Indo-European languages according to

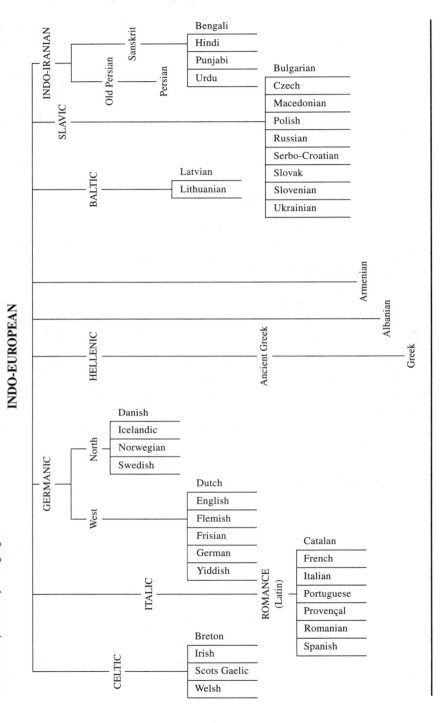

FIGURE 8.6

The Indo–European family of languages.

their genetic relationships. The task is to identify the languages that constitute a family and the relationships that exist among them.

Linguists are frequently asked about the number of languages in the world, but it is hard to ascertain that number because of disagreement over what comprises a language as opposed to a dialect. How different must two dialects be before they become separate languages? One criterion is that of mutual intelligibility. As long as two dialects remain mutually intelligible, it is generally believed that they cannot be considered separate languages. But mutual intelligibility itself lies on a sliding scale, as all of us know who have conversed with persons speaking dialects of our native language whom we do not understand completely.

The Indo-Iranian languages Hindi and Urdu are listed as separate languages in Figure 8.6, yet they are mutually intelligible in their spoken forms and are arguably dialects of one language. However, each uses a different writing system, and each is spoken in communities of differing religious beliefs and nationalities. Hindi, for the most part, is spoken in India by Hindus. Urdu is spoken in Pakistan by Muslims. So what constitutes a separate language is not always determined by linguistic factors alone.

On the other hand, mutually unintelligible languages spoken in China, because they share the same writing system and culture, and are spoken within a single political boundary, are often thought of as dialects.

Estimates of the number of languages in the world vary widely: the minimum has been set at 4000 and the maximum at 8000. It is often surprising to discover which languages are genetically related and which ones aren't. Within the Indo-European family, we find that faraway Punjabi is an Indo-European language, whereas Hungarian, surrounded on all sides by Indo-European languages, is not.

It is not possible in an introductory text such as this to give an exhaustive table of families, subfamilies, and individual languages. Besides, a number of genetic relationships have not yet been firmly established. For example, linguists are divided as to whether Japanese and Turkish are related or not. We will simply mention several language families with a few of their member languages. These families are not thought to be related to one another or to Indo-European. This may be a result, however, of our inability to delve into the past far enough to see commonalities that time has since erased. We can never entirely eliminate the possibility that all the world's languages sprang ultimately from a single source, an "ur-language" lost forever in the depths of the past.

Uralic is the other major family of languages, besides Indo-European, spoken on the European continent. Hungarian, Finnish, and Estonian are the major representatives of the group.

Afro-Asiatic languages are a large family spoken in northern Africa and the Middle East. They include the modern **Semitic** languages of Hebrew and Arabic, as well as languages spoken in biblical times, such as Aramaic, Babylonian, Canaanite, and Moabite.

The **Sino-Tibetan** family includes Mandarin, the most populous language in the world, spoken by about a billion Chinese. It also includes all of the Chinese "dialects" plus Burmese and Tibetan.

Most of the languages of Africa belong to the **Niger-Kordofanian** family. It includes more than 900 languages, such as Swahili, Kikuyu, and Zulu.

Equally numerous, the **Austronesian** family contains about 900 languages, spoken over a wide expanse of the globe, from Madagascar, off the coast of Africa, to Hawaii. Hawaiian itself, of course, is an Austronesian language, as is Maori, spoken in Malaysia and Singapore, to mention only two.

Dozens of language families include hundreds of languages that are, or were, spoken in North and South America. Knowledge of the genetic relationships among these families of languages is often tenuous, and, because so many of the languages are approaching extinction, there may be little hope for as complete an understanding of the Amerindian language families as linguists have achieved for Indo-European.

Types of Languages

> All the Oriental nations jam tongue and words together in the throat, like the Hebrews and Syrians. All the Mediterranean peoples push their enunciation forward to the palate, like the Greeks and the Asians. All the Occidentals break their words on the teeth, like the Italians and Spaniards. . . .
>
> Isidore of Seville, seventh century C.E.

There are many ways to classify languages. One way discussed in this chapter is according to the language "family." This method would be like classifying people according to whether they were Johnsons, Singhs, Cohens, or Liangs. Another way is by certain linguistic traits, regardless of family. With people, this method would be like classifying them according to height and weight or hair and eye colour.

Every language has sentences that include a subject (for this section only, S will be an abbreviation of *subject* rather than of *sentence*), an object (O), and a verb (V), although some sentences do not have all three elements. Languages have been classified according to the basic or most common order in which these elements occur in the language.

There are six possible orders — SOV (subject, object, verb), SVO, VSO, VOS, OVS, OSV — permitting six possible language types. Examples of some of the languages in these classes are

SVO: English, French, Swahili, Hausa, Thai
VSO: Tagalog, Irish, (classical) Arabic, (biblical) Hebrew
SOV: Turkish, Japanese, Persian, Georgian, Inuit
OVS: Apalai (Brazil), Barasano (Columbia), Panare (Venezuela)
OSV: Apurina and Xavante (Brazil)
VOS: Cakchiquel (Guatemala), Huave (Mexico), Coeur d'Alene (Idaho)
(examples of VOS, OVS, OSV from Pullum 1981)

The most frequent word orders found in languages of the world are SVO, VSO, and SOV. The basic VSO and SOV sentences may be illustrated as follows:

VSO (Tagalog):	Sumagot siya sa propesor
	answered he the professor
	"He answered the professor."
SOV (Turkish):	Romalilar barbarlari yendiler
	Romans barbarians defeated
	"The Romans defeated the barbarians."

Languages with OVS, OSV, and VOS basic word order are much rarer.

The order of other sentence components in a language is most frequently correlated with the language type. If a language is of a type in which the verb precedes the object — a VO language, which includes SVO, VSO, and VOS — then the auxiliary verb tends to precede the verb, adverbs tend to follow the verb, and the language utilizes **prepositions**, which precede the noun, among other such ordering relationships. English exhibits all these tendencies.

In OV languages, most of which are SOV, the opposite tendency occurs; auxiliary verbs tend to follow the verb, adverbs tend to precede the verb, and there are postpositions, which function similarly to prepositions but follow the noun. Japanese, an SOV language, has postpositions, as we saw in a previous section. Also in Japanese, the auxiliary verb follows the verb, as illustrated by the following sentence:

Akiko	wa	sakana	o	tabete	iru
Akiko	*topic marker*	fish	*object marker*	eating	is
"Akiko is eating fish."					

We should emphasize that the correlations between language type and the word order of syntactic categories in sentences are "tendencies," not inviolable rules; different languages follow them to a greater or lesser degree.

The knowledge that speakers of the various languages have about word order is revealed in the particular phrase structure rules of the languages. In English, an SVO language, the verb precedes its NP object: VP → V NP. In Turkish and Japanese, SOV languages, the NP object precedes the verb in the corresponding phrase structure rules. Similarly, the rule PP → P NP (the preposition in a prepositional phrase precedes the noun phrase) occurs in SVO languages, whereas the rule PP → NP P is the correlate occurring in SOV languages.

If a language is, say, SVO, this does not mean that SVO is the only possible word order. Yoda, the Jedi Master from the motion picture *Return of the Jedi*, speaks a strange but perfectly understandable style of English that achieves its eccentricity by being OSV. Some of Yoda's utterances are

> Sick I've become.
> Strong with the Force you are.
> Your father he is.
> When 900 years you reach, look as good you will not.

For linguists, the many languages and language families provide essential data for the study of Universal Grammar. Although these languages are diverse in many ways, they are also remarkably similar. We find that the languages of the "wretched

Greenlanders," the Maoris of New Zealand, the Zulus of Africa, and the Aboriginals of North and South America all have similar sounds, similar phonological and syntactic rules, and similar semantic systems.

Why Do Languages Change?

Stability in language is synonymous with rigor mortis.
Ernest Weekley

There is no single explanation for language change, nor can every change be fully explained. No one knows exactly how or why languages change. As we have shown, linguistic changes do not happen suddenly. Speakers of English did not wake up one morning and decide to use the word *beef* for "ox meat"; nor do all the children of one particular generation grow up to adopt a new word. Changes are more gradual, particularly changes in phonology and syntax.

Of course, certain changes may occur instantaneously for any one speaker. When a new word is acquired by a speaker, it is not gradually acquired, although full appreciation of its possible uses may come slowly. When a new rule is incorporated into a speaker's grammar, it is either in or not in the grammar. It may at first be an optional rule, so that sometimes it is used and sometimes it is not, possibly determined by social context or other external factors; however, the rule is either there or not there for use. What is gradual about language change is the spread of certain changes over an entire speech community.

A basic cause of change is the way children acquire the language. No one teaches a child the rules of the grammar; each child constructs a personal grammar alone, generalizing rules from the linguistic input received. The child's language develops in stages until it approximates the adult grammar. The child's grammar is never exactly like that of the adult community, because children receive diverse linguistic input. Certain rules may be simplified or overgeneralized, and vocabularies may show small differences that accumulate over several generations.

The older generation may be using certain rules optionally. For example, at certain times they may say *It's I* and at other times *It's me*. The less formal style is usually used with children, who as the next generation may use only the *me* form of the pronoun in this construction. In such cases, the grammar will have changed.

The reasons for some changes are relatively easy to understand. Before television, there was no such word as *television*. It soon became a common lexical item. Borrowed words, too, generally serve a useful purpose, and their entry into the language is not mysterious. Other changes are more difficult to explain, such as the Great Vowel Shift in English.

One plausible source of change is **assimilation**, a kind of ease-of-articulation process in which one sound influences the pronunciation of another adjacent or nearby sound. Due to assimilation, vowels are frequently nasalized before nasal consonants because it is easiest to lower the velum to produce nasality in advance of the actual consonant articulation. This results in the nasalization of the preceding vowel. Once the vowel is nasalized, the contrast that the nasal consonant provided can be equally well provided by the nasalized vowel alone, and the redundant consonant may be deleted. The contrast between oral and nasal vowels that exists in many languages of the world today results from such a historical sound change.

In French at one time, *bol* "basin," *botte* "high boot," *bog* "a card game," *bock* "Bock beer," and *bon* "good" were pronounced [bɔl], [bɔt], [bɔg], [bɔk], and [bɔ̃n], respectively. Notice that in *bon* there was a final nasal consonant, which *conditioned* the nasalization of the preceding vowel. Due to a **conditioned sound change** that deleted nasal consonants in word-final position, *bon* is pronounced [bɔ̃] in modern French; the nasal vowel alone maintains the contrast with the other words.

Another example from English illustrates how such assimilative processes can change a language. In Old English, word-initial [kʲ] (like the initial sound in *cute*), when followed by /i/, was further palatalized to become our modern palatal affricate /č/, as illustrated by the following words:

Old English (*c* = [kʲ])	Modern English (*ch* = [č])
ciese	cheese
cinn	chin
cild	child

The process of palatalization is found in many languages. In Twi, for example, the word meaning "to hate" was once pronounced [ki]. The [k] became first [kʲ] and then finally [č], so that today "to hate" is pronounced [či].

Ease-of-articulation processes, which make sounds more alike, are countered by the need to maintain contrast. Thus, sound change also occurs when two sounds are acoustically similar, with risk of confusion. We saw a sound change of /f/ to /h/ in an earlier example that can be explained by the acoustic similarity of [f] to other sounds.

Another kind of change that can be thought of as "economy of memory" results in a reduction of the number of exceptional or irregular morphemes. This kind of change has been called **analogic change**. It may be through analogy to *foe/foes* and *dog/dogs* that speakers started saying *cows* as the plural of *cow* instead of the earlier plural *kine*. By analogy to *reap/reaped, seem/seemed*, and *ignite/ignited*, children and adults are now saying *I sweeped the floor* (instead of *swept*), *I dreamed last night* (instead of *dreamt*), and *She lighted the bonfire* (instead of *lit*).

The same kind of analogic change is exemplified by our regularization of exceptional plural forms, which is a kind of morphological change. We have borrowed words such as *datum/data, agendum/agenda, curriculum/curricula, bandit/banditi, memorandum/memoranda, medium/media, criterion/criteria*, and *virtuoso/virtuosi*, to name just a few. The irregular plurals of these nouns have been replaced by regular plurals among many speakers: *agendas, curriculums, memorandums, criterias, virtuosos*. In some cases, the borrowed original plural forms were considered to be singular (as in *agenda* and *criteria*), and the new plural is therefore a "plural-plural." Also, many speakers now regard *data* and *media* as nouns that do not have plural forms, like *information*. All these changes lessen the number of irregular forms that must be remembered.

Some Additional Sound Changes

Old English words that have survived into Modern English provide examples of some additional systematic sound changes that have helped shape language. While some of these processes have been discussed previously, it may be useful to review them and a few others at this point.

The Old English words *ðridda* and *brid* became Modern English *third* and *bird* through a process of **metathesis**, that is, through an interchange and reordering of segments that effectively reverses the order of their sequence. M.L. Samuels (1972) suggested that metathesis may result from an insertion of glide vowels before a consonant; this was subsequently misinterpreted so that Old English *worhte* became *worohte*, for example, which then became *wrohte* (our past tense *wrought*), with a reduction and loss of vowel. Samuels also raised the possibility that metathesis may occur through preference for more common sequences over less common ones. He observed that "English dialects with /wɔps/ as their original form for 'wasp' may also show /krɪps/ 'crisp,' /klaps/ 'clasp' . . . " (Samuels 1972). However metathesis comes about, it has affected many common English words: *r*-metathesis has occurred, for instance, in words such as *þurh, hros, ferse*, and *forst*, giving us *through, horse, fresh*, and *frost*. Metathesis of *ks* to *sk* is evident in *dox* (*dusk*) and *flaxe* (*flask*) (the letter *x* indicates /ks/), and of *ps* to *sp* in *hæpse* (*hasp*).

Epenthesis consists of the insertion of vowels in a word. This frequently serves to break up heavy **consonant clusters**, and a vowel intervening between consonants increases the ease of pronunciation. It has been suggested that the presence of an epenthic sound may be the result of incoordination in the movement from one sound segment to another. Thus, the Old English word *ofen* (our word *oven*) developed from Germanic *ofn* with an inserted vowel. We often hear an epenthetic vowel [ə] between the consonants in modern words such as *elm* and *film*; similarly, *athletic* often becomes [æθəlɛtɪk].

Consonant clusters can also undergo **simplification** by the loss of a segment as in Old English *betst* and *godspell* (Modern English *best* and *gospel*). Initial consonant groupings such as *hl-, hn-, hr-, gn-*, and *kn-* (often spelled *cn-*) were also simplified; thus, Old English *hnappian, hring*, and *hlāf* become *nap, ring*, and *loaf*. In some instances modern spelling preserves older pronunciations as does the *gn-* of *gnæt* (*gnat*) and the *kn-* in *knight* (*cniht*). The rules of Modern English restrict the choice or location of consonant clusters available to speakers, and these initial groupings are no longer permitted, whatever their status might have been in Old and Middle English.

Loss of vowels in all positions in a word is a major process that has affected the grammatical structure of English. **Apocope**, the loss of a final vowel, is common in languages with a strong stress accent on the initial syllables of words such as English and German. This process eliminated final vowels, thereby affecting the markers for case and person. Thus, the past tense, first person singular, of the Old English verb *temman* was *temede* /temədə/, which, as Winfred Lehmann (1973) points out, became the Modern English *tamed* with the loss of final *-e*. Apocope further affected nouns, reducing many to monosyllables as in Old English *nama* /namə/ (Modern English *name* /nem/). The medial vowel of *temede* was also lost, a process known as **syncope**. This process is apparent in our everyday pronunciation of words such as *business, Wednesday, family*, and *evening*.

Aphesis or **aphaeresis** — the loss of initial vowels — as in the pronunciation of *possum* for *opossum* and in the colloquial *cross* in a sentence such as "*I live cross the street*" or *bout* for *about*, "*It's bout time!*" In the thirteenth century, *estate* was borrowed from French and became the English word *state* by the process of aphesis while the French word subsequently lost *s* before *t*, leading to the modern form *état*.

A less common process in the history of English, **hapology**, the loss of repeated identical or nearly identical segments, is apparent in the name of *Engla land*, the land of the Angles, which was reduced to *England*. Hapology occurs among many speakers of modern British dialects who say /tɛmpərɪ/ for *temporary* and /sɛkətrɪ/ for *secretary*.

Many more changes, both conditioned and unconditioned, have taken place in English since the Germanic peoples settled in the British Isles. We have not, for example, discussed the development of excrescent sounds — the /t/ one sometimes hears at the end of *across*, or considered the loss of final nasal consonants in Old English. While these examples have been drawn largely from the history of English, they are by no means unique to English. Every language is historically rich and complex; the changes that mould a language over time can only be touched on in the few paragraphs available to us.

Simplification and regularization of grammars occur, but so does elaboration or complication. Old English rules of syntax became more complex, imposing a stricter word order on the language, at the same time that case endings were being simplified. A tendency toward simplification is counteracted by the need to limit potential ambiguity. Much of language change is a balance between the two.

Many factors contribute to linguistic change: simplification of grammars, elaboration to maintain intelligibility, borrowing, and lexical additions. Changes are actualized by children learning the language, who incorporate them into their grammars. While the exact reasons for linguistic change are still elusive, it is clear that the imperfect learning of the adult dialects by children is a contributing factor. Perhaps language changes for the same reason that all things change: it is the nature of things to change. As Heraclitus pointed out thousands of years ago, "All is flux, nothing stays still. Nothing endures but change."

Summary

All living languages change regularly through time. Evidence of linguistic change is found in the history of individual languages and in the **regular sound**

correspondences that exist between different languages and dialects. **Genetically related** languages "descend" from a common "parent" language through linguistic change. An early stage in the history of related languages is that they are dialects of the same parent.

All parts of the grammar may change. That is, *phonological, morphological, syntactic, lexical,* and *semantic* changes occur. Words, morphemes, phonemes, and rules of all types may be added, lost, or altered. The meanings of words and morphemes may expand, narrow, or shift.

No one knows all the causes for linguistic change. Basically, change comes about through the restructuring of the grammar by children learning the language. Grammars are both simplified and elaborated; the elaborations may arise to counter the simplifications that could lead to unclarity and ambiguity.

Some sound changes result from physiological, **assimilative** processes. Others, such as the **Great Vowel Shift**, are more difficult to explain. Still other changes occur through means such as **simplification of consonant clusters**, reduction of identical or nearly identical groups (**hapology**), and loss of sounds finally (**apocope**), medially (**syncope**), or initially (**aphesis**). Other processes, such as **metathesis** and **epenthesis**, have helped to shape language change. Grammatical changes may be explained, in part, as **analogic changes**, which are simplifications or generalizations. External **borrowing** from other languages also affects the grammar.

The study of linguistic change is called **historical and comparative linguistics**. By examining the internal structures of languages as well as comparing related languages, linguists are able to reconstruct earlier forms of particular language families. A particularly effective technique for reconstructing "dead" languages is the **comparative method**. Through comparison of the various "daughter" languages or dialects, the linguistic history of a language family may be partially reconstructed and represented in a "family tree" similar to that in Figure 8.6.

In spite of the differences among languages, there is a vast number of ways in which languages are alike. That is, there are language universals as well as differences.

Notes

1. This "earlier stage" is the original parent of Sanskrit, Greek, the Romance and Germanic languages, and other languages — namely, Indo-European. The symbols *bh, dh,* and *gh* are "breathy voiced" stop phonemes, often called "voiced aspirate."
2. The **asterisk** before a letter indicates a "reconstructed" sound. It does not mean an unacceptable form. This use of the asterisk occurs only in this chapter.
3. *ś* is a sibilant different from *s*.

Exercises

1. Many changes in the phonological system have occurred in English since 449 C.E. Below are some Old English words (given in their spelling and phonetic forms) and the same words as we pronounce them today. They are typical of regular sound changes that took place in English. What sound changes have occurred in each case?

   Example: OE hlud [xlu:d] → Mod E loud
   Changes: (1) The [x] was lost.
              (2) The long vowel [u:] became [aw].

	OE		**Mod E**
a.	crabbe [krabbə]	→	crab
b.	fisc [fɪsk]	→	fish
c.	fūl [fu:l]	→	foul
d.	gāt [ga:t]	→	goat
e.	lǣfan [læ:van]	→	leave
f.	tēþ [te:θ]	→	teeth

2. The Early Middle English Vowel Shortening and the Great Vowel Shift in English left its traces on Modern English in meaning-related pairs such as

   a. serene/serenity [i]/[ɛ]
   b. divine/divinity [aj]/[ɪ]
   c. sane/sanity [e]/[æ]

   List five such meaning-related pairs that relate [i] and [ɛ] as in example a, [aj] and [ɪ] as in b, and [e] and [æ] as in c.

3. Below are some sentences taken from Old English, Middle English, and early Modern English texts, illustrating some changes that have occurred in the syntactic rules of English grammar. (Note: In the sentences, the earlier spelling forms and words have been changed to conform to Modern English. That is, the OE sentence *His suna twegen mon brohte to þœm cynige* would be written as *His sons two someone brought to that king*, which in Modern English would be *His two sons were brought to the king*.) Underline the parts of each sentence that differ from Modern English. Rewrite the sentence in Modern English. State, if you can, what changes must have occurred.

   Example: It *not* belongs to you. (Shakespeare, *Henry IV*, Part II)
   Mod. Eng.: *It does not belong to you.*
   Change: At one time, a negative sentence could be formed by placing *not* before the main verb. Today the word *do*, in its proper morphological form, must appear before the *not*.

a. It nothing pleased his master.
b. He hath said that we would lift them whom that him please.
c. I have a brother is condemned to die.
d. I bade them take away you.
e. I wish you was still more a Tartar.
f. Christ slept and his apostles.
g. Me was told.

4. It is not unusual to find a yearbook or almanac publishing a "new word list." In the 1980s and 1990s, several new words entered the English language, such as *Teflon* and *liposuction*. From the computer field, we have new or incipient words such as *byte* and *biochip*. Other words have been expanded in meaning, such as *memory* to refer to the storage part of a computer and *crack* to refer to a form of cocaine.

a. Think of five other words or compound words that have entered the language in the past ten years. Describe briefly the source of the word.
b. Think of three words that might be "on the way out." (*Hint:* Consider *flapper, groovy*, and *slay/slew*. Dictionary entries that say "archaic" are a good source.)

*5. Here is a table showing, in phonemic form, the Latin ancestors of ten words in Modern French:

Latin	French	
kor	kør	"heart"
kantāre	šāte	"to sing"
klārus	kler	"clear"
kervus	sɛrf	"hart" (deer)
karbō	šarbɔ̃	"coal"
kwandō	kã	"when"
kentum	sã	"hundred"
kawsa	šoz	"thing"
kinis	sãdrə	"ashes"
kawda ⎱ koda ⎰	kø	"tail"

ø is a mid-front rounded vowel.

Are the following statements true or false?

a. The Modern French word for "thing" shows that a [k], which occurred before the vowel [o] in Latin, became a [š] in French.
b. The French word for "tail" probably derived from the Latin word [koda] rather than from [kawda].
c. One historical change illustrated by these data is that [s] became an allophone of the phoneme /k/ in French.

d.   If there was a Latin word *kertus*, then the Modern French word would probably be *sert*. (Consider only the initial consonant.)

*6.   Here is how to count to five in a dozen languages. Six of these languages are Indo-European, and six are not. Circle the Indo-European ones.

	L1	**L2**	**L3**	**L4**	**L5**	**L6**
1	en	jedyn	i	eka	ichi	echad
2	twene	dwaj	liang	dvau	ni	shnayim
3	thria	tři	san	trayas	san	shlosha
4	fiuwar	štyri	ssu	catur	shi	arba?a
5	fif	pjeć	wu	pañca	go	chamishsha

	L7	**L8**	**L9**	**L10**	**L11**	**L12**
1	mot	ün	hana	yaw	uno	nigen
2	hai	duos	tul	daw	dos	khoyar
3	ba	trais	set	dree	tres	ghorban
4	bon	quatter	net	tsaloor	cuatro	durben
5	nam	tschinch	tasŏt	pindze	cinco	tabon

7.   More than 4000 languages exist in the world today. State one reason why this number might grow larger and one reason why it might grow smaller. Do you think the number of languages will increase or decrease in the next 100 years? Justify your answer.

8.   The vocabulary of English consists of "native" words as well as thousands of loan words. Look up the following words in a dictionary that provides the etymologies (histories) of words. Speculate how each word came to be borrowed from the particular language.

a.	size	h.	robot	o.	skunk	v.	pagoda
b.	royal	i.	check	p.	catfish	w.	khaki
c.	aquatic	j.	banana	q.	hoodlum	x.	shampoo
d.	heavenly	k.	keel	r.	filibuster	y.	kangaroo
e.	skill	l.	fact	s.	astronaut	z.	bulldoze
f.	ranch	m.	potato	t.	emerald		
g.	blouse	n.	muskrat	u.	sugar		

9.   **Analogic change** refers to a tendency to generalize the rules of language, a major cause of language change. We mentioned two instances, the generalization of the plural rule (*cow/kine* becoming *cow/cows*) and the generalization of the past tense formation rule (*light/lit* becoming *light/lighted*). Think of at least three other instances of "non-standard" usage that are analogic; they are indicators of possible future changes in the language. (*Hint:* Consider fairly general rules, and see if you know of dialects or styles that overgeneralize them — e.g., comparative formation by adding *-er*.)

10. Below is a passage from Shakespeare's *Hamlet,* Act IV, scene iii.

> HAMLET: A man may fishe with the worme that hath eate of a king, and eate of the fish that hath fedde of that worme.
>
> KING: What doost thou meane by this?
>
> HAMLET: Nothing but to shew you how a king may goe a progresse through the guts of a beggar.
>
> KING: Where is Polonius?
>
> HAMLET: In heauen, send thither to see, If your messenger finde him not there, seeke him i'th' other place your selfe, but indeed, if you find him not within this month, you shall nose him as you goe up the stayres in the lobby.

Study these lines and identify every difference in expression between Elizabethan and Modern English that is evident (e.g., in line 3, *thou* is now *you*).

*11. Consider these data from two North American Native languages:

Yerington Paviotso = YP	Northfolk Monachi = NM	Gloss
mupi	mupi	"nose"
tama	tawa	"tooth"
piwɨ	piwɨ	"heart"
sawaʔpono	sawaʔpono	"a feminine name"
nɨmɨ	nɨwɨ	"liver"
tamano	tawano	"springtime"
pahwa	pahwa	"aunt"
kuma	kuwa	"husband"
wowaʔa	wowaʔa	"Indians living to the west"
mɨhɨ	mɨhɨ	"porcupine"
noto	noto	"throat"
tapa	tape	"sun"
ʔatapɨ	ʔatapɨ	"jaw"
papiʔi	papiʔi	"older brother"
patɨ	peti	"daughter"
nana	nana	"man"
ʔatɨ	ʔeti	"bow," "gun"

A. Identify each sound correspondence. (*Hint:* There are ten different correspondences of consonants and six different correspondences of vowels — e.g., *p–p, m–w, a–a,* and *a–e.*)

B. a. For each correspondence you identified in A not containing an *m* or *w,* reconstruct a proto-sound (e.g., for *h–h, *h; o–o, *o*).

   b. If the proto-sound underwent a change, indicate what the change is and in which language it took place.

C. a. Whenever a *w* appears in YP, what appears in the corresponding position in NM?

      b.   Whenever an *m* occurs in YP, what two sounds may correspond to it in NM?

      c.   On the basis of the position of *m* in YP words, can you predict which sound it will correspond to in NM words? How?

D. a.   For the three correspondences you discovered in A involving *m* and *w*, should you reconstruct two or three proto-sounds?

      b.   If you chose three proto-sounds, what are they, and what did they become in the two "daughter" languages, YP and NM?

      c.   If you chose two proto-sounds, what are they, and what did they become in the "daughter" languages? What further statement do you need to make about the sound changes? (*Hint:* One proto-sound will become two different pairs, depending on its phonetic environment. It is an example of a **conditioned sound change**.)

E.   Based on the above, reconstruct all the words given in the common ancestor from which both YP and NM descended (e.g., "porcupine" is reconstructed as **mihi*).

Works Cited

Boroff, Marie. 1967. *Sir Gawain and the Green Knight: A New Verse Translation*. New York: W.W. Norton & Co.

Canadian Global Almanac. 1999. Toronto: Macmillan Canada.

Chambers, J.K. 1975. "Ottawa Valley 'Twang.' " *Canadian English: Origins and Structures*. Toronto: Methuen: 55–59.

Lehmann, Winfred P. 1973. *Historical Linguistics*. 2nd ed. New York: Holt, Rinehart and Winston.

McArthur, Tom. 1989. *The English Language as Used in Quebec*. No. 3. Kingston, ON: Queen's University, Strathy Language Unit.

McConnell, R.E. 1979. *Our Own Voice: Canadian English and How It Is Studied*. Toronto: Gage Publishing.

Mossé, Ferdinand. 1952. *A Handbook of Middle English*. Trans. James A. Walker. Baltimore: Johns Hopkins University Press.

Mustanoja, Tauno F. 1960. *A Middle English Syntax. Part I. Parts of Speech*. Helsinki: Société Néophilologique.

Nolen, Stephanie. 1999. "You've Got . . . Courriel?" *The Globe and Mail*. Nov. 15: C1–C2.

Pringle, Ian, and E. Padolsky. 1981. "The Irish Heritage of the English of the Ottawa Valley." *English Studies in Canada* 7: 338–51.

Pullum, G.K. 1981. "Languages with Object before Subject: A Comment and a Catalogue." *Linguistics* 19: 147–55.

Samuels, M.L. 1972. *Linguistic Evolution with Special Reference to English*. Cambridge, UK: Cambridge University Press.

Strang, Barbara M.H. 1970. *A History of English*. London: Methuen.

Traugott, E.C. 1972. *The History of English Syntax*. New York: Holt, Rinehart and Winston.

Further Reading

Aitchison, Jean. 1985. *Language Change: Progress or Decay.* New York: Universe Books.

Anttila, Raimo. 1972. *An Introduction to Historical and Comparative Linguistics.* New York: Macmillan.

Baugh, A.C., and Thomas Cable. 1993. *A History of the English Language.* 4th ed. Englewood Cliffs, NJ: Prentice-Hall.

Cassidy, Frederick G., ed. 1986. *Dictionary of American Regional English.* Cambridge, MA: The Belknap Press of Harvard University Press.

Comrie, Bernard, ed. 1990. *The World's Major Languages.* New York: Oxford University Press.

Cook, Eung-Do. 2000. "Amerindian Languages of Canada." *Contemporary Linguistic Analysis: An Introduction.* 4th ed. Ed. W. O'Grady and J. Archibald. Toronto: Addison Wesley Longman: 358–71.

Hock, Hans Henrich. 1986. *Principles of Historical Linguistics.* New York: Mouton de Gruyter.

Hoenigswald, Henry M. 1960. *Language Change and Linguistic Reconstruction.* Chicago: University of Chicago Press.

Jeffers, Robert J., and Ilse Lehiste. 1979. *Principles and Methods for Historical Linguistics.* Cambridge, MA: MIT Press.

Katzner, Kenneth. 1986. *The Languages of the World.* London: Routledge and Kegan Paul.

Millward, C.M. 1989. *A Biography of the English Language.* New York: Holt, Rinehart and Winston.

Pedersen, H. 1962. *The Discovery of Language.* Bloomington: University of Indiana Press.

Pyles, Thomas. 1982. *The Origins and Development of the English Language.* 3rd ed. New York: Harcourt Brace Jovanovich.

Voegelin, Charles F., and Florence M. Voegelin. 1977. *Classification and Index of the World's Languages.* Amsterdam: Elsevier.

CHAPTER 9
Writing: The ABCs of Language

The Moving Finger writes; and, having writ,
Moves on: nor all thy Piety nor Wit
  Shall lure it back to cancel half a Line,
Nor all thy Tears wash out a Word of it.

Omar Khayyám, *Rubáiyát*

The palest ink is better than the sharpest memory.

Chinese proverb

Throughout this book, we have emphasized the *spoken* form of language. The grammar, which represents one's linguistic knowledge, was viewed as the system for relating the sounds and meanings of one's language. The ability to acquire and use language represents a dramatic evolutionary development. No single individual or people discovered or created language. The human language faculty appears to be biologically and genetically determined. This is not true of the written forms of human languages.

Children learn to speak naturally through exposure to language, without formal teaching. To become literate — to learn to read and write — one must make a conscious effort and receive instruction. A large number of languages spoken today throughout the world lack writing systems, and oral literature still abounds among them. In such societies, crucial lore is passed from older to newer generations orally. However, human memory is short-lived and the brain's storage capacity limited.

Writing overcomes such problems and allows for communication across space and over time. Writing permits a society to record permanently its literature, history, science, and technology. The development of writing systems is indeed one of the greatest human achievements.

By writing, we mean any of the many visual (non-gestural) systems for representing language, including handwriting, printing, and electronic displays of these written forms. It might be argued that writing has become obsolete through electronic means of recording sounds and images. But computers — at least as we now have them and as most people use them — require us to write perhaps even more than before. Moreover, if writing became extinct, there would be no knowledge of electronics for TV technicians to study; there would be, in fact, little technology in years to come. There would be no film or TV scripts, no literature, no books, no mail, no newspapers. There would be some advantages — no bad novels, junk mail, poison-pen letters, or "fine print" — but the losses would far outweigh the gains.

The History of Writing

An Egyptian legend relates that when the god Thoth revealed his discovery of the art of writing to King Thamos, the good King denounced it as an enemy of civilization. "Children and young people," protested the monarch, "who had hitherto been forced to apply themselves diligently to learn and retain whatever was taught them, would cease to apply themselves, and would neglect to exercise their memories."

Will Durant, *The Story of Civilization 1*

There are many legends and stories about the invention of writing. Greek legend has it that Cadmus, prince of Phoenicia and founder of the city of Thebes, invented the alphabet and brought it with him to Greece. (He was later banished to Illyria and changed into a snake.) In one Chinese fable, the four-eyed dragon-god Cang Jie invented writing, but in another fable, writing first appeared to humans in the form of markings on a turtle shell. In an Icelandic saga, Odin was the inventor of the runic script. In other myths, the Babylonian god Nebo and the Egyptian god Thoth gave humans writing as well as speech. The Talmudic scholar Rabbi Akiba believed that the alphabet existed before humans were created; and, according to Islamic teaching, the alphabet was created by Allah himself, who presented it to humans but not to angels.

Although these are delightful stories, it is evident that, before a single word was written, uncountable billions were spoken; it is highly unlikely that a particularly gifted ancestor awoke one morning and decided, "Today I'll invent a writing system." In fact, the invention of writing systems comes relatively late in human history, and its development was gradual.

Pictograms and Ideograms

The seeds out of which writing developed were probably the early drawings made by ancient humans. Cave drawings, called **petroglyphs**, such as those found in the Altamira cave in northern Spain, drawn by humans living more than 20 000 years ago, can be "read" today. They are literal portrayals of life at that time. We have no way of knowing why they were produced; they may be aesthetic expressions rather than pictorial communications. Later drawings, however, are clearly "picture writings" or **pictograms**. Unlike modern writing systems, each picture or pictogram is a direct image of the object it represents. There is a non-arbitrary relationship between the form and the meaning of the symbol. Comic strips minus captions are pictographic — literal representations of the ideas to be communicated. This early form of "writing" did not have any direct relation to the language spoken, because the pictures represented objects in the world rather than the linguistic names given to these objects; they did not represent the sounds of spoken language.

FIGURE 9.1

Canadian Road Signs

fuel	food	accommodation	camping
carburant	restaurant	hébergément	camping

Pictographic "writing" has been found among peoples throughout the world, ancient and modern: among Africans, First Nations of North America, the Inuit, the Incas of Peru, the Yukagirians of Siberia, and the people of Oceania. Pictograms are used today in international road signs and in other places where the native language of the region might not be adequate. The advantage of such symbols is that they can be understood by anyone because they do not depend on the words of any language. To understand many of the signs on Canadian highways, for example, a visitor does not need to know English or French (see Figure 9.1).

Once a pictogram was accepted as the representation of an object, its meaning was extended to attributes of that object or concepts associated with it. Thus, a picture of the sun could represent "warmth," "heat," "light," "daytime," and so on. Pictograms thus began to represent *ideas* rather than objects. Such generalized, abstract pictograms are called **ideograms** ("idea pictures" or "idea writing"). The difference between pictograms and ideograms is not always clear. Ideograms tend to be a less direct representation, and one may have to learn what a particular ideogram means. Pictograms tend to be literal. For example, the "no parking" symbol consisting of a black circle with a slanting red line through it is an ideogram: it represents the idea of no parking abstractly. A "no parking" symbol showing an automobile being towed away is more literal, more like a pictogram.

Pictograms and ideograms became stylized, possibly because of the ambiguities that could result from "poor artists" or creative "abstractionists" of the time. The simplifying conventions that developed so distorted the literal representations that it was no longer easy to interpret symbols without learning the system. The ideograms became *linguistic* symbols as they came to stand for the *sounds* that represented the ideas — that is, for the words of the language. This stage represented a revolutionary step in the development of writing systems.

Cuneiform Writing

> One picture is worth a thousand words.
>
> Chinese proverb

Much of our information on the development of writing stems from the records left by the Sumerians, an ancient people of unknown origin who built a civilization in southern Mesopotamia more than 5000 years ago. They left innumerable clay tablets containing, among other things, business documents, epics, prayers, poems, and proverbs. So copious are these written records that scholars studying the Sumerians are publishing a seventeen-volume dictionary of their written language. The first of these volumes appeared in 1984.

The writing system of the Sumerians is the oldest one known. They were a commercially oriented people, and, as their business deals became increasingly complex, the need for permanent records arose. An elaborate pictography was developed along with a system of "tallies." Some examples are shown here:

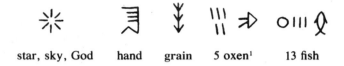

star, sky, God   hand   grain   5 oxen¹   13 fish

Over the centuries, their pictography was simplified and conventionalized. The characters or symbols were produced by using a wedge-shaped stylus that was pressed into soft clay tablets. This form of writing is called **cuneiform** — literally, "wedge-shaped" (from Latin *cuneus* "wedge"). Here is an illustration of how Sumerian pictograms evolved to cuneiform:

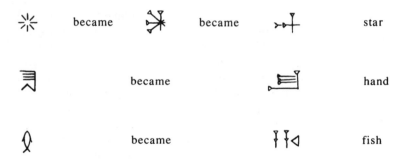

The cuneiform "words" do little to remind us of the meanings represented. As cuneiform evolved, its users began to think of the symbols in terms more of the *name* of the thing represented than of the thing itself. Eventually, cuneiform script came to represent words of the language. Such a system is called **logographic** or **word writing**. In this type of writing, the symbol stands for both the word and the concept, which it may resemble however abstractly. Thus, **logograms**, the symbols of a word-writing system, are ideograms that represent, in addition to the concept, the word or morpheme in the language for that concept.

The cuneiform writing system was borrowed by the Babylonians, Assyrians, and Persians. In adopting cuneiform characters in their own languages, the borrowers used them to represent the *sounds* of the *syllables* in their words. In this way, cuneiform evolved into a **syllabic writing** system.

In a syllabic writing system, each syllable in the language is represented by its own symbol, and words are written syllable by syllable. Cuneiform writing was never purely syllabic; there was always a large residue of symbols that stood for whole words. The Assyrians retained a large number of word symbols, even though every word in their language could be written out syllabically if it were desired. Thus, they could write  *mātu* "country" as

| ma | + | a | + | tu |

The Persians (ca. 600–400 B.C.E.) devised a greatly simplified syllabic alphabet for their language, which made little use of word symbols. By the reign of Darius I (522–468 B.C.E.), this writing system was in wide use. It is illustrated by the following characters:

da

di

fa

ma

tu

The Rebus Principle

B.C. by permission of Johnny Hart and Creators Syndicate, Inc.

When a graphic sign no longer has any visual relationship to the word it represents, it becomes a **phonographic symbol**, standing for the sounds that represent the word. A single sign can then be used to represent all words with the same sounds

— the homophones of the language. If, for example, the symbol ☉ stood for *sun* in English, it could then be used in a sentence such as *My ☉ is a doctor.* This sentence is an example of the **rebus principle**.

A rebus is a representation of words or syllables by pictures of objects whose names *sound like* the intended word or syllable. Thus, ◉ might represent *eye* or the pronoun *I*. The sounds of the two words are identical, even though the meanings are not. In the same way, 🐝🍃 could represent *belief* (*be* + *lief* = *bee* + *leaf* = /biː/ + /liːf/), and 🐝🍃🍃 could be the verb form, *believes*. Similarly, *2* 👄 — /tu/ + /lɪp/ — could represent *tulip*.

Proper names can also be "written" in such a way. If the symbol **/** is used to represent *rod* and the symbol ⚣ represents *man*, then **/** ⚣ could represent *Rodman*, although nowadays the name is unrelated to either rods or men. Such combinations often become stylized or shortened so as to be more easily written. *Rodman*, for example, might be "written" in such a system as **/**⚹ or even ⚼.

This system is not an efficient one, because in many languages words cannot be subdivided into sequences of sounds that have meanings by themselves. It would be difficult, for example, to represent the word *English* (/ɪŋ/ + /glɪš/) in English according to the rebus principle. *Eng* by itself does not "mean" anything, nor does *glish*.

From Hieroglyphs to the Alphabet

At the time that Sumerian pictography was flourishing (ca. 4000 B.C.E.), a similar system was being used by the Egyptians, which the Greeks later called **hieroglyphics** (*hiero* "sacred" + *glyphikos* "carvings"). That the early "sacred carvings" were originally pictography is shown by the following hieroglyphics:

"eye"   "giraffe"   "to rule"[2]   "fresh" or "cool"[3]

Like the Sumerian pictograms, the hieroglyphs came to represent both the concept and the word for the concept. Once this happened, hieroglyphics became a bona fide logographic writing system. Through the rebus principle, hieroglyphics also became a syllabic writing system.

In this "syllabic" stage, hieroglyphics were borrowed by many people, including the Phoenicians, a Semitic people who lived on the eastern shores of the Mediterranean. By 1500 B.C.E., they developed a writing system of 22 syllabic characters, the West Semitic Syllabary. For the most part, the characters stood for consonants alone. The reader provided the vowels, and hence the rest of the syllable, through knowledge of the language. (Cn y rd ths?) Thus, the West Semitic Syllabary was both a **syllabary** and a **consonantal alphabet**.

The ancient Greeks tried to borrow the Phoenician writing system, but it was unsatisfactory as a syllabary because Greek has too complex a syllable structure.

In Greek, unlike in Phoenician, vowels cannot be determined by grammatical context, so a writing system for Greek required that vowels have their own independent representations. Fortuitously, Phoenician had more consonants than Greek, so when the Greeks borrowed the system they used the extra symbols to represent vowel sounds. The result was **alphabetic writing**, a system in which both consonants and vowels are symbolized. (The word *alphabet* is derived from *alpha* and *beta*, the first two letters of the Greek alphabet.)

Alphabetic systems are those in which each symbol typically represents one sound unit. Such systems are primarily *phonemic* rather than *phonetic*, as is illustrated by the fact that the *p* in both *pit* and *spit* in the English alphabet is one rather than two "letters," even though the sounds are phonetically distinct.

A majority of alphabetic systems in use today derive from the Greek system. This alphabet became known to the pre-Latin people of Italy, the Etruscans, and through them to the Romans, who used it for Latin. Thus, the alphabet spread with Western civilization, and eventually most nations of the world were exposed to, and had the option of using, alphabetic writing.

According to one view, the alphabet was not invented; it was *discovered* (Ohman 1969). If language did not include discrete individual sounds, then no one could have invented alphabetic letters to represent such sounds. When humans started to use one symbol for one phoneme, they had merely brought their intuitive knowledge of the language sound system to consciousness; they discovered what they already "knew." Furthermore, children (and adults) can learn an alphabetic system only if each separate sound has some psychological reality.

Modern Writing Systems

... but their manner of writing is very peculiar, being neither from the left to the right, like the Europeans; nor from the right to the left, like the Arabians; nor from up to down, like the Chinese; nor from down to up, like the Cascagians, but aslant from one corner of the paper to the other, like ladies in England.

Jonathan Swift, *Gulliver's Travels*

We have already mentioned the various types of writing systems used in the world: *word* or *logographic writing, syllabic writing, consonantal alphabet writing*, and *alphabetic writing*. Most of the world's written languages use alphabetic writing. Even Chinese and Japanese, whose native writing systems are not alphabetic, have adopted alphabetic transcription systems for special purposes, such as communicating with foreigners.

Word Writing

In a **word writing** or **logographic** system, the written character represents both the meaning and the pronunciation of a word or morpheme. The awkwardness of such a system is obvious. For example, the editors of *Webster's Third New International Dictionary* claim more than 450 000 entries. All these words are written using only 26 alphabetic symbols, a dot, a hyphen, an apostrophe, and a space. It is understandable why, historically, word writing gave way to alphabetic systems in most places in the world.

The major exceptions are the writing systems used in China and Japan. The Chinese system has an uninterrupted history that goes back more than 3500 years. For the most part, it is a word writing system, each character representing an individual word or morpheme. Longer words may be formed by combining two words or morphemes, as shown by the word meaning "business" *măimai*, which is formed by combining the words meaning "buy" and "sell." This system, which could create serious problems if used for English and other Indo-European languages, works for Chinese because *spoken* Chinese has little affixation of bound morphemes (e.g., the *un-* in *unhappy* or the *-fy* in *beautify*).

Chinese writing utilizes a system of **characters**, each of which represents a morpheme or word. Chinese dictionaries and rhyme books contain tens of thousands of these characters, but a person needs to know "only" about 5000 to read a newspaper. In 1956, the Chinese government moved to simplify the characters. This process was first tried in 213 B.C.E., when Li Si published an official list of more than 3000 characters whose written forms were simplified by omitting unneeded strokes. Since that time, successive generations have added new characters and modified old ones, creating redundancy and complexity. The character-simplification efforts that have been under way in the past decades are therefore of major importance. An example of the simplifications is given below (Lehmann 1975):

Original	Simplified	Pronunciation	Meaning
餐	歺	cān	"meal"
酒	氿	jiǔ	"wine"
漆	汔	qī	"paint"
稻	初	dào	"rice crops"
副	付	fù	"deputy"
賽	宭	sài	"to compete"

The Chinese government has adopted a spelling system using the **Roman alphabet**, called **Pinyin**, which is now used for certain purposes along with the regular system of characters. Many city street signs are printed in both systems, which is helpful to foreigners. It is not the government's intent, however, to replace the traditional writing, which is viewed as an integral part of Chinese culture. To the

Chinese, writing is an art — **calligraphy** — and thousands of years of poetry, literature, and history are preserved in the old system.

An additional reason for keeping the traditional system is that it permits all literate Chinese to communicate even though their spoken languages are mutually unintelligible. Thus, writing has served as a unifying factor throughout Chinese history, in an area where hundreds of languages and different dialects exist. A Chinese proverb states that "People separated by a blade of grass cannot understand each other," but the unified writing system cuts across linguistic differences and allows the people to communicate with each other.

This use of written Chinese characters is similar to the use of Arabic numerals, which mean the same in many different countries. The "character" *5*, for example, stands for a different sequence of sounds in English, French, and Finnish. In English it is *five* /fajv/, in French it is *cinq* /sæŋk/, and in Finnish it is *viisi* /viːsi/, but in all these languages, *5*, whatever its phonological form, means "five." Similarly, the spoken word for "rice" is different in the various Chinese languages, but the written character is the same. If the writing system in China were to become alphabetic, then each language would be as different in writing as in speaking, and written communication would no longer be possible among the various language communities.

Syllabic Writing

Syllabic writing systems are more efficient than word writing systems, and they are certainly less taxing on the memory. However, languages with a rich structure of syllables containing many consonant clusters (e.g., *tr* or *spl*) cannot be efficiently written with a **syllabary**. To see this difficulty, consider the syllable structures of English.

I	/aj/	V	an	/æn/	VC
key	/ki/	CV	ant	/ænt/	VCC
ski	/ski/	CCV	ants	/ænts/	VCCC
spree	/spri/	CCCV	pant	/pænt/	CVCC
seek	/sik/	CVC	pants	/pænts/	CVCCC
speak	/spik/	CCVC	stamp	/stæmp/	CCVCC
scram	/skræm/	CCCVC	splints	/splɪnts/	CCCVCCC
striped	/strajpt/	CCCVCC			

With more than 30 consonants and over twelve vowels, the number of different possible syllables is immense, which is why English, and Indo-European languages in general, are unsuitable for syllabic writing systems.

The Japanese language, on the other hand, is more suited for syllabic writing, because all words in Japanese can be phonologically represented by about 100 syllables, mostly of the consonant–vowel (CV) type, and there are no underlying consonant clusters. To write these syllables, the Japanese have two syllabaries, each containing 46 characters, called *kana*. The entire Japanese language can be written using *kana*. One syllabary, *katakana*, is used for loan words and for special effects similar to italics in European writing. The other syllabary, **hiragana**, is used for native words and may occur with Chinese characters, which the Japanese call **kanji**. Thus, Japanese writing is part word writing, part syllable writing.

During the first millennium, the Japanese tried to use Chinese characters to write their language. However, spoken Japanese is totally unlike spoken Chinese (they are genetically unrelated languages). A word writing system alone was not suitable for Japanese, which is a highly inflected language in which verbs may occur in 30 or more different forms. Using modified Chinese characters, the syllabaries were devised to represent the inflectional endings and other grammatical morphemes. Thus, in Japanese writing, Chinese characters will commonly be used for the verb roots and *hiragana* symbols for the inflectional markings.

For example, 行 is the character meaning "go," pronounced [i]. The word for "went" in formal speech is *ikimashita*, written as 行きました, where the *hiragana* symbols きました represent the syllables *ki, ma, shi, ta*. Nouns, on the other hand, are not inflected in Japanese, and they can generally be written using Chinese characters alone.

In theory, all of Japanese could be written in *hiragana*. There are many homophones in Japanese, however, and the use of word characters disambiguates a word that would be ambiguous if written syllabically. Also, like Chinese, Japanese *kanji* writing is an integral part of Japanese culture, and it is unlikely to be abandoned.

Two North American Syllabics

While relatively few originators or developers of scripts around the world are known by name, the same is not true of systems that came to be used among Native North Americans. The majority of North American scripts were created in the nineteenth century by missionaries of European backgrounds who were concerned to make their religious texts available to the First Nations with whom they worked. One of the earliest to establish a workable script was, however, neither a missionary nor a European. Sikwayi was a most remarkable man who, though he himself could neither read nor write, perceived the advantages these abilities would accord his people and set out to devise a system for the Cherokee language.

In 1821, Sikwayi (or Sequoyah), often called the "Cherokee Cadmus," invented a syllabic writing system for his native language, Cherokee. Sequoyah's script, which survives today essentially unchanged, proved useful to the Cherokee people and is justifiably a point of great pride for them. The syllabary contains 85 symbols, many of them derived from Latin characters, which efficiently transcribe spoken Cherokee. A few symbols are shown here:

J   gu

ᒋ   hu

ᏋᏋ   we

An alphabetic character can be used to represent a syllable in some languages. In words such as *OK* and *bar-b-q*, the single letters represent syllables (*b* for [bi] or [bə], *q* for [kju]).

As Albertine Gaur (1984) has observed, creators of scripts have tended to follow similar lines: that is, "an idea script moved towards a word (picture) script and on to the introduction of phonetic elements, mostly on the basis of the rebus principle, to culminate finally in a syllabic script." Sikwayi, however, seems initially to have considered employing a logographic or word writing system but after a time came to the conclusion that such a method would be inappropriate for Cherokee and turned to a syllabic system as more suitable.

By 1824, Sikwayi had established a system of 85 symbols (six vowels, a symbol for /s/, and 78 symbols for CV syllables). For a number of these "letters," he drew on his acquaintance with Roman script — which he nevertheless could not read — while other symbols were modifications of those Roman symbols, both of which he supplemented with his own creations. For this script, see Table 9.1.

Sikwayi's syllabic may not have been a perfect fit for Cherokee — a better system would require 114 symbols instead of 78 — but it was a remarkable achievement and was quickly put into use for books, newspapers, official and religious documents, and personal communication. By 1830, more than half of the adult male population of Cherokees could read and write in Sikwayi's script (Jensen 1969), and while use of the script has subsequently declined there have been attempts to renew its use (DeFrancis 1989).

The first European to devise a system of writing for a First Nations people was James Evans (Diringer 1968). Evans, a young missionary to the Cree in Manitoba, employed his script in 1840 at Norway House on Lake Winnipeg. His script was also a syllabic, a system well suited to Cree, and consisted of 44 geometric symbols in which vowel differences were signalled by the direction in which the symbol was drawn (see Table 9.2).

Evans's system — modified, of course — "spread beyond the Cree to other Algonquian languages in Canada. By 1880 it was even adapted for use in some Eskimo communities and in some Canadian Athapaskan languages" (Silver and Miller 1997).

Some commentators have expressed surprise that American Native scripts did not "progress" to alphabetic systems, but we should keep in mind that, although a syllabry would not fit a language such as English, it functioned well in Cherokee and Cree. In fact, as Shirley Silver and Wick Miller (1997) assure us, syllabics are more appropriate for Cree and Cherokee than the alphabetic system we have inherited for the English language.

TABLE 9.1
Sikwayi's System of 85 Symbols for the Cherokee Writing System

Sign	Value	Sign	Value	Sign	Value	Sign	Value	Sign	Value
Ꭰ	a	Ꭱ	e	Ꭲ	i	Ꭳ	o	Ꭴ	u
Ꭶ	ga	Ꭸ	ge	Ꭹ	gi	Ꭺ	go	Ꭻ	gu
Ꭽ	ha	Ꭾ	he	Ꭿ	hi	Ꮀ	ho	Ꮁ	hu
Ꮃ	la	Ꮄ	le	Ꮅ	li	Ꮆ	lo	Ꮇ	lu
Ꮉ	ma	Ꮊ	me	Ꮋ	mi	Ꮌ	mo	Ꮍ	mu
Ꮎ	na	Ꮑ	ne	Ꮒ	ni	Ꮓ	no	Ꮔ	nu
Ꮖ	gwa	Ꮗ	gwe	Ꮘ	gwi	Ꮙ	gwo	Ꮚ	gwu
Ꮜ	sa	Ꮞ	se	Ꮟ	si	Ꮠ	so	Ꮡ	su
Ꮣ	da	Ꮥ	de	Ꮧ	di	Ꮩ	do	Ꮪ	du
Ꮬ	dla	Ꮮ	dle	Ꮯ	dli	Ꮰ	dlo	Ꮱ	dlu
Ꮳ	dza	Ꮴ	dze	Ꮵ	dzi	Ꮶ	dzo	Ꮷ	dzu
Ꮹ	wa	Ꮺ	we	Ꮻ	wi	Ꮼ	wo	Ꮽ	wu
Ꮿ	ya	Ᏸ	ye	Ᏹ	yi	Ᏺ	yo	Ᏻ	yu
Ꭵ	ö	Ꭼ	gö	Ꮂ	hö	Ꮈ	lö	Ꮕ	nö
Ꮛ	gwö	Ꮢ	sö	Ꮫ	dö	Ꮲ	dlö	Ꮸ	dzö
Ꮾ	wö	Ᏼ	yö	Ꭷ	ka	Ꮏ	hna	Ꮐ	nah
Ꮝ	s	Ꮤ	ta	Ꮦ	te	Ꮨ	ti	Ꮭ	tla

Hans Jensen, *Sign, Symbol, and Script: An Account of Man's Efforts to Write.* Trans. George Unwin. New York: G.P. Putnam's Sons, 1969, p. 242.

Consonantal Alphabetic Writing

Semitic languages, such as Hebrew and Arabic, are written with alphabets that consist only of consonants. Such an alphabet works for these languages because consonants form the roots of most words. For example, the consonants *ktb* in Arabic forms the roots of words associated with "write." Thus, *katab* means "to write," *aktib* means "I write," and *kitab* means "a book." Inflectional and derivational processes can be expressed by different vowels inserted into the tri-consonantal roots.

Because of this structure, vowels can be figured out by a person knowing the spoken language, *jst lk y cn rd ths phrs, prvdng y knw nglsh.* English, however, is unrelated to the Semitic languages, and its structure is such that vowels are crucial for reading and writing much of the time. The English phrase *I like to eat out* would be incomprehensible without vowels: *lk t t t.*

TABLE 9.2
Evans's Syllabic Script for the Cree Language

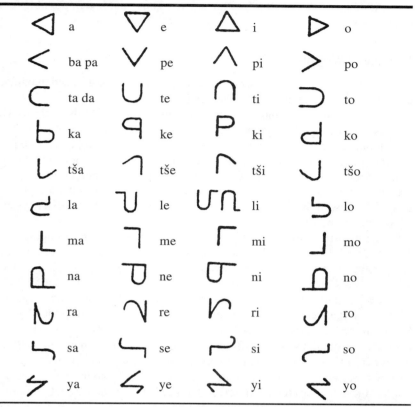

Hans Jensen, *Sign, Symbol, and Script: An Account of Man's Efforts to Write.* Trans. George Unwin. New York: G.P. Putnam's Sons, 1969, p. 244.

Semitic alphabets, primarily to preserve the true pronunciations of religious writings, and secondarily out of deference to children and foreigners learning to read and write, provide a way to express vowels. These vowels come in the form of supplementary marks. In Hebrew, dots or other small figures are placed under, above, or even in the centre of the consonantal letter to indicate the accompanying vowel. For example, ל represents an *l* sound in Hebrew writing. Unadorned, the vowel that follows it would be determined by context. However, לֶ indicates that the vowel that follows is [e], so in effect לֶ represents the syllable [le].

These systems are called consonantal alphabets because only the consonants are fully developed symbols. Sometimes they are considered syllabaries because, once the vowel is perceived by the reader or writer, the consonantal letter appears to stand for a syllable. With a true syllabary, however, a person only needs to know the phonetic value of each symbol to pronounce it correctly and unambiguously. Once you learn a Japanese syllabary, you can read Japanese in a phonetically correct way without any idea of what you are saying. That would be impossible for Arabic or Hebrew.

Alphabetic Writing

Alphabetic writing systems are easy to learn, convenient to use, and maximally efficient for transcribing any human language.

The term **sound writing** is sometimes used in place of **alphabetic writing**, but it does not truly represent the principle involved in the use of alphabets. One sound–one letter is inefficient, because we do not need to represent the [pʰ] in *pit* and the [p] in *spit* by two different letters. It would also be confusing, because the non-phonemic differences between sounds are seldom perceptible to speakers. Except for the phonetic alphabets, whose function is to record the sounds of all languages for descriptive purposes, most, if not all, alphabets have been devised on the **phonemic principle**.

In the twelfth century, an Icelandic scholar developed an orthography derived from the Latin alphabet for the writing of the Icelandic language of his day. Other scholars in this period were also interested in orthographic reform, but the Icelander, who came to be known as "the First Grammarian" (because his anonymous paper was the first entry in a collection of grammatical essays), was the only one of the time who left a record of his principles. The orthography he developed was clearly based on the phonemic principle. He used **minimal pairs** to show the distinctive contrasts; he did not suggest different symbols for voiced and unvoiced [θ] and [ð], nor for [f] and [v], nor for velar [k] and palatal [č], because these pairs, according to him, represented allophones of the phonemes /θ/, /f/, and /k/, respectively. He did not use these modern technical terms, but the letters of this alphabet represent the distinctive phonemes of Icelandic of that century.

King Seijong of Korea (1417–50) realized that the same principles held true for Korean when, with the assistance of scholars, he designed a phonemic alphabet. The king was an avid reader and realized that the more than 30 000 Chinese characters used to write Korean discouraged literacy. The fruit of the king's labour was the Korean alphabet called **Hangul**, which originally had seventeen consonants and eleven vowels.

The Hangul alphabet was designed on the phonemic principle. Although Korean has the sounds [l] and [r], Seijong represented them by a single letter because they are allophonic variants of the same phoneme.[4] The same is true for the sounds [s] and [š] and [ts] and [tš].

Seijong showed further ingenuity in the design of the characters themselves. The consonants are drawn so as to depict the place and manner of articulation. Thus, the letter for /g/ is ㄱ to suggest the raising of the back of the tongue to the velum; /m/ is the closed figure ㅁ to suggest the closing of the lips. Vowels in Hangul are easily distinguished from consonants, being drawn as long vertical or horizontal lines, sometimes with smaller marks attached to them. Thus, | represents /i/, – represents /u/, and ⊢ represents /a/.

In Korean writing, the Hangul characters are grouped into squarish blocks, each corresponding to a syllable. The syllabic blocks, though they consist of alphabetic characters, make Korean look as if it were written in a syllabary. If English were written that way, "Now is the winter of our discontent" would have this appearance:

No	i	th	wi	te	o	ou	di	co	te
w	s	e	n	r	f	r	s	n	nt

The space between letters is less than the space between syllables, which is less than the space between words.

These characteristics make Korean writing unique in the world, unlike that of the Europeans, the Arabians, the Chinese, the Cascagians, or even the "ladies of England."

Many languages have their own alphabet, and each has developed certain conventions for converting strings of alphabetic characters into sequences of sounds (reading) and converting sequences of sounds into strings of alphabetic characters (writing). As we have illustrated with English, Icelandic, and Korean, the rules governing the sound system of the language play an important role in the relationship between sound and character.

Most European alphabets make use of Latin (Roman) letters, making minor adjustments to accommodate individual characteristics of a particular language. For example, Spanish uses ñ to represent the palatal nasal of *señor*, and German has added an "umlaut" for certain vowel sounds that did not exist in Latin (e.g., in *über*). Such "extra" marks are called **diacritics**. The 46 *kana* of the Japanese syllabaries are supplemented by diacritics in order to represent the more than 100 syllables of the language. Diacritic marks are also used in writing systems of tone languages such as Thai to indicate the tone of a syllable.

Some languages use two letters together — called a **digraph** — to represent a single sound. English has many digraphs, such as *sh* /š/ as in *she* /ši/, *ch* /č/ as in *chop* /čap/, *ng* /ŋ/ as in *sing* /sɪŋ/, and *oa* /o/ as in *loaf* /lof/.

Besides the European languages, those such as Turkish, Indonesian, Swahili, and Vietnamese have adopted the Latin alphabet. Other languages that have more recently developed a writing system use some of the IPA phonetic symbols in their alphabets. Twi, a West African language, for example, uses ɔ, ɛ, and ŋ.

The **Cyrillic alphabet**, named for St. Cyril, who brought Christianity to the Slavs, is used by many Slavic languages, including Russian. It is derived directly from the Greek alphabet without Latin mediation.

The contemporary Semitic alphabets, those used for Persian (Iranian), Urdu (spoken in Pakistan), and many languages of the Indian Subcontinent, including Hindi, are ultimately derived from the ancient Semitic syllabaries.

Writing and Speech

> ... Ther is so great diversite
> In English, and in wryting of oure tonge,
> So prey I god that non myswrite thee ...
>
> Geoffrey Chaucer, *Troilus and Cressida*

The development of writing freed us from the limitations of time and geography, but spoken language still has primacy. Writing systems, however, are of interest for their own sake.

The written language reflects, to a certain extent, the elements and rules that together constitute the grammar of the language. The system of phonemes is represented by the letters of the alphabet, though not necessarily in a direct way. The independence of words is revealed by the spaces in the written string; but in languages in which words are composed of more than one morpheme, the writing usually does not show the individual morphemes, even though speakers know what they are. In fact, many languages, such as Japanese or Thai, do not space between words, although speakers and writers are aware of the individual words. The sentences of some languages are indicated in the written form by capitals at the beginning and periods at the end. Other punctuation, such as question marks, italics, commas, and exclamation marks, is used to reveal syntactic structure and to some extent intonation, stress, and contrast; but the written forms of many languages do not use such punctuation.

Consider the difference in meaning between restricted and unrestricted relative clauses illustrated by the following two sentences containing the relative clause *who were philosophers*:

(1) The Greeks, who were philosophers, loved to talk a lot.
(2) The Greeks who were philosophers loved to talk a lot.

Note that the unrestricted relative clause in (1) is set off by commas. This tells us that the sentence may be paraphrased as

(1) The Greeks were philosophers, and they loved to talk a lot.

The meaning of the second sentence, without the commas, can be paraphrased as

(2) Among the Greeks, it was the philosophers who loved to talk a lot.

Similarly, by using an exclamation point or a question mark, the writer can make his or her intention clearer:

(3) The children are going to bed at eight o'clock. (*simple statement*)
(4) The children are going to bed at eight o'clock! (*an order*)
(5) The children are going to bed at eight o'clock? (*a question*)

These punctuation marks reflect the pauses and the intonations that would be used in the spoken language.

In sentence (6), *he* can refer to either John or someone else, but in sentence (7) the pronoun must refer to someone other than John:

(6) John said he's going.
(7) John said, "He's going."

The apostrophe used in contractions and possessives also provides syntactic information not always available in the spoken utterance:

(8) my cousin's friends (*one cousin*)
(9) my cousins' friends (*two or more cousins*)

Writing, then, somewhat reflects the spoken language, and punctuation may even distinguish between two meanings not revealed in the spoken forms, as shown in examples (8) and (9).

In the normal written version of sentence (10),

(10) John whispered the message to Bill, and then he whispered it to Mary.

he can refer to either John or Bill. In the spoken sentence, if *he* receives extra stress (called **contrastive stress**), then it must refer to Bill; if *he* receives normal stress, then it refers to John.

A speaker can usually emphasize any word in a sentence by using contrastive stress. Writers sometimes attempt to show emphasis by using all capital letters, or italics, or by underlining the emphasized word:

(11) *John* kissed Bill's wife. (*Bill didn't*)
(12) John *kissed* Bill's wife. (*rather than hugging her*)
(13) John kissed *Bill's* wife. (*not Dick's or his own*)
(14) John kissed Bill's *wife*. (*not Bill's mother*)

Such devices may serve many functions in written language; for example, italics may indicate reference to the italicized word itself, as in "*The* is an article." Although such visual devices can help in English, it is not clear that they can be used in a language such as Chinese. In Japanese, however, this kind of emphasis can be achieved by writing a word in *katakana*.

Other differences between speech and writing appear lexically in the greater variety of vocabulary in writing, especially in selection of adjectives, longer versus shorter words, and Latin versus Anglo-Saxon words. Syntactically, speech is much less structured than writing, with incomplete sentences, little subordination, active declarative sentences rather than passive ones, or cleft sentences, such as "It was Sam that I saw at the films." Writing makes use of subordination rather than coordination and marks relationships between clauses explicitly with subordinating conjunctions such as *that* or *when/while* and logical connectors such as *moreover, however*, and *besides*, where speech uses coordinating conjunctions such as *and* and *but*. Speech is often much less explicit than writing.

Written language is also more conservative than spoken language. When we write something — particularly in formal writing — we are more apt to obey the "prescriptive rules" taught in school, or to use a more formal style, than when we speak. "Dangling participles" (e.g., *While studying in the library, the fire alarm rang*) and "sentences ending with a preposition" (e.g., *I know what to end a sentence with*) abound in spoken language but may be "corrected" by copy editors, diligent English teachers, and careful writers. A linguist wishing to describe the language that people regularly use cannot depend, therefore, on written records alone.

Spelling

"Do you spell it with a 'v' or a 'w'?" inquired the judge.
    "That depends upon the taste and fancy of the speller, my Lord," replied Sam.

Charles Dickens, *The Pickwick Papers*

If writing represented the spoken language perfectly, then spelling reformers would never have arisen. In Chapter 5, we discussed some of the problems in the English orthographic (**spelling**) system. These problems prompted George Bernard Shaw (1941) to write that

> . . . It was as a reading and writing animal that Man achieved his human eminence above those who are called beasts. Well, it is I and my like who have to do the writing. I have done it professionally for the last sixty years as well as it can be done with a hopelessly inadequate alphabet devised centuries before the English language existed to record another and very different language. Even this alphabet is reduced to absurdity by a foolish orthography based on the notion that the business of spelling is to represent the origin and history of a word instead of its sound and meaning. Thus an intelligent child who is bidden to spell *debt*, and very properly spells it *d-e-t*, is caned for not spelling it with a *b* because Julius Caesar spelt the Latin word for it with a *b*.

The irregularities between **graphemes** (letters) and phonemes have been cited as one reason "why Johnny can't read." **Homographs**, such as *lead* /lid/ and *lead* /lɛd/, have fuelled the flames of spelling reform movements. Different spellings for the same sound, silent letters, and missing letters are also cited as reasons why English needs a new orthographic system. The examples below (and those given in Chapter 5) illustrate the discrepancies between spelling and sounds in English:

Same Sound, Different Spelling	Different Sound, Same Spelling		Silent Letters	Missing Letters
/aj/	thought	/θ/	listen	use /juz/
	though	/ð/	debt	fuse /fjuz/
	Thomas	/t/	gnome	
aye			know	
buy	ate	/e/	psychology	
by	at	/æ/	right	
die	father	/a/	mnemonic	
hi	many	/ɛ/	science	
Thai			talk	
height			honest	
guide			sword	
			bomb	
			clue	
			Wednesday	

Chapters 3 and 8 discussed some of the reasons for the non-phonemic aspects of our spelling system. "Spelling is the written trace of a word. Pronunciation is its linguistic form" (Bolinger 1968). The spelling of most of the words in English today is based on the Late Middle English pronunciation (that used by Chaucer) and on the early forms of Modern English (one of which was used by Shakespeare). The many changes in the sound system of English, such as the Great Vowel Shift, were not always reflected in the spellings of the words that were affected.

When the printing press was introduced in the fifteenth century, archaic and idiosyncratic spellings became widespread and more permanent. Words in print were frequently misspelled outright because many of the early printers were not native speakers of English. But even native spellers in earlier times saw no need to spell the same word consistently. Thus, the first person singular pronoun appears in the texts of Shakespeare's plays as *I, ay*, and *aye*.

Spelling reformers during the Renaissance saw the need for consistent spelling that correctly reflected the pronunciation of words. To that extent, spelling reform was necessary. But many scholars became overzealous. Because of their reverence for classical Greek and Latin, they changed the spellings of English words to conform to their etymologies. Where the Latin had a *b*, they added a *b* even if it was not pronounced; where the original spelling had a *c* or *p* or *h*, these letters were added, as is shown by these few examples:

Middle English Spelling		"Reformed" Spelling
indite	→	indict
dette	→	debt
receit	→	receipt
oure	→	hour

Such spelling habits inspired Robert N. Feinstein (1986) to compose the following poem, entitled "Gnormal Pspelling":

Gnus and gnomes and gnats and such —
Gnouns with just one G too much.
Pseudonym and psychedelic —
P becomes a psurplus relic.
Knit and knack and knife and knocked —
Kneedless Ks are overstocked.
Rhubarb, rhetoric and rhyme
Should lose an H from thyme to time.

Reprinted from *National Forum: The Phi Kappa Phi Journal* LXVI, 3 (Summer 1986). Copyright © by Robert Feinstein. By permission of the publisher.

Current English spellings are based primarily on earlier pronunciations of words. The many changes that have occurred in the sound system of English since then are not reflected in the current spelling system, which was frozen due to the widespread availability of printed material and to scholastic conservatism.

For these reasons, Modern English orthography does not always represent what we know about the phonology of the language. The disadvantage is partially offset by the fact that the writing system allows us to read and understand what people wrote hundreds of years ago without the need for translations. If there were a one-to-one correspondence between our spellings and the sounds of our language, then we would have difficulty reading even fairly recent works such as Catherine Parr Traill's *Backwoods of Canada* (1836).

We do not mean to say that certain reforms would not be helpful. Some "respelling" is already taking place; advertisers often spell *though* as *tho, through* as *thru*, and *night* as *nite*. For a time, the *Chicago Tribune* used such spellings, but it gave up the practice in 1975. Spelling habits are hard to change, and revised spelling is regarded as substandard by many.

Languages change. It is not possible to maintain a perfect correspondence between pronunciation and spelling, nor is it 100 percent desirable to try to do so. For instance, in the case of homophones, it is helpful at times to have different spellings for the same sounds, as in the following pair:

The book was red.   The book was read.

Lewis Carroll once more makes the point with humour:

"And how many hours a day did you do lessons?" said Alice.
"Ten hours the first day," said the Mock Turtle, "nine the next, and so on."
"What a curious plan!" exclaimed Alice.
"That's the reason they're called *lessons*," the Gryphon remarked, "because they *lessen* from day to day."

There are also reasons for using the same spelling for different pronunciations. A morpheme may be pronounced differently when it occurs in different contexts. The identical spelling reflects the fact that the different pronunciations represent the same morpheme. This is the case with the plural morpheme. It is always spelled with an *s* despite being pronounced [s] in *cats* and [z] in *dogs*. The sound of the morpheme is determined by rules in this case.

Similarly, the phonetic realizations of the vowels in the following forms exhibit a regular pattern:

aj/ɪ	**i/ɛ**	**e/æ**
divine/divinity	serene/serenity	sane/sanity
sublime/subliminal	obscene/obscenity	profane/profanity
sign/signature	hygiene/hygienic	humane/humanity

The spelling of such pairs thus reflects our knowledge of the sound pattern of the language and the semantic–morphological relationships between the words. These considerations have led some to suggest that English orthography is **morphophonemic** in addition to being phonemic. To read English with correct pronunciation, morphophonemic knowledge is required. English contrasts with a language such as Spanish, whose orthography is almost purely phonemic.

Other examples provide further motivation for spelling irregularities. The *b* in *debt* may remind us of the related word *debit*, in which the *b* is pronounced. The same principle is true of pairs such as *sign/signal, knowledge/acknowledge, bomb/bombardier,* and *gnosis/prognosis/agnostic.*

There are also different spellings that represent the different pronunciations of a morpheme when confusion would arise from using the same spelling. For example, there is a rule in English phonology that changes a /t/ to an /s/ in certain cases: *democrat → democracy*. The different spellings are due in part to the fact that this rule does not apply to all morphemes, so that *art + y* is *arty*, not **arcy*. Regular phoneme-to-grapheme rules determine in many cases when a morpheme is to be spelled identically and when it is to be changed.

Other subregularities are apparent. A *c* always represents the /s/ sound when it is followed by a *y, i,* or *e,* as in *cynic, citizen,* and *censure*. Because it is always pronounced [k] when it is the final letter in a word or when it is followed by any other vowel (*coat, cat, cut,* and so on), no confusion results. The *th* spelling is usually pronounced voiced as [ð] between vowels (the result of a historical intervocalic voicing rule).

There is another important reason why spelling should not always be tied to phonetic pronunciation. Different dialects of English have divergent pronunciations. Cockneys drop their "(h)aitches," and Bostonians and Southerners drop their "*r*'s"; *neither* is pronounced [niðər] and [niðə] by Americans, [najðə] by the British. Typically, Canadians — sometimes the same person — use alternatively [niðər] and [najðər]. Many Irish, and Canadians from the Maritimes, use still another vowel and say [neðər]. Some Scots pronounce *night* as [nɪxt]; people say *Chicago* and *Chicawgo, hog* and *hawg, bird* and *boyd; four* is pronounced [fɔ:] by the British, [for] in Canada, and [foə] in the South of the United States; *orange* is pronounced in at least two ways in the United States: [arənǰ] and [ɔrənǰ].

While dialectal pronunciations differ, the common spellings indicate the intended word. It is necessary for the written language to transcend local dialects. With a uniform spelling system, a native of Sudbury and a native of Glasgow can communicate through writing. If each dialect were spelled according to its own pronunciation, then written communication among the English-speaking peoples of the world would suffer.

Spelling Pronunciations

> For pronunciation, the best general rule is to consider those as the most elegant speakers who deviate least from written words.
>
> Samuel Johnson (1755)

Despite the primacy of the spoken over the written language, the written word is often regarded with excessive reverence. The stability, permanence, and graphic nature of writing cause some people to favour it over ephemeral and elusive speech. Humpty Dumpty expressed a rather typical attitude: "I'd rather see that done on paper."

Writing has affected speech only marginally, however, most notably in the phenomenon of **spelling pronunciation**. Since the sixteenth century, to some extent spelling has influenced standard pronunciation. The most important of such changes stem from the eighteenth century under the influence of lexicographers and teachers. The struggle between those who demanded that words be pronounced according to spelling and those who demanded that words be spelled according to pronunciation generated great heat in that century. The preferred pronunciations were given in the many dictionaries printed in the eighteenth century, and the authority of the dictionaries influenced pronunciation in this way.

Spelling has also influenced pronunciation in words that are infrequently used in normal daily speech. Many words that were spelled with an initial *h* were not pronounced with any /h/ sound as late as the eighteenth century. Thus, at that time no /h/ was pronounced in *honest, hour, habit, heretic, hotel, hospital*, and *herb*. Frequently used words such as *honest* and *hour* continued to be pronounced without the /h/, despite the spelling, but all those other words were given a "spelling pronunciation." Because people did not hear them often, when they saw them written they concluded that they must begin with an /h/. *Herb* is currently undergoing this change; in Standard British English, the *h* is pronounced, whereas in Standard Canadian and American English it is not.

Similarly, many words now spelled with a *th* were once pronounced /t/, as in *Thomas*; later most of these words underwent a change in pronunciation from /t/ to /θ/, as in *anthem, author*, and *theatre*. "Nicknames" often reflect the earlier pronunciations: "Ka*t*e" for "Ca*th*erine," "Be*tt*y" for "Elizabe*th*," and "Ar*t*" for "Ar*th*ur." The words *often* and *soften*, which are usually pronounced without a /t/ sound, are pronounced with the /t/ by some people because of the spelling.

The clear influence of spelling on pronunciation is observable in the way place names are pronounced. *Berkeley* is pronounced [bʌrkli] in California, although it stems from the British [ba:kli]; *Worcester* is pronounced [wʊstər] or [wʊstə] in England as well as in large parts of Canada and the United States, but in Massachusetts it is often pronounced [wʊrčɛstər]; *Magdalen* is pronounced [mɔdlɪn] in England and [mægdələn] in North America.

Although the written language has some influence on the spoken language, it does not change the basic system — the grammar — of the language. The writing system, conversely, reflects, in a more or less direct way, the grammar that every speaker knows.

Canadian Spelling

Most people who write in the English language employ a common spelling system. No matter how differently they may speak the language, they tend to spell it in the same way. The major difference in English spelling is between those who use "American" forms and those who employ what is called "British spelling," though the latter is used, in part or in whole, in many former British colonies. These two systems are distinguished by a few contrasting practices: the choice of -*our* (*favour*) instead of -*or* (*favor*) and -*ce* (*defence*) as opposed to -*se* (*defense*), the use of double or single consonants in various environments (*fulfil/fulfill; gravelled/graveled*), and the choice of long or short forms of a few words, such as *axe* or *ax* and *plough* or *plow*. Clearly such differences affect only a limited number of words and raise no real difficulties in comprehension. Some of these variations and the environments in which they occur are displayed in Table 9.3:

TABLE 9.3

Examples of British and American Spelling

British Spelling		American Spelling		
colour	neighbour	color	neighbor	-our/-or
harbour	mould	harbor	mold	-ou-/-o-
centre	theatre	center	theater	-re/-er
meagre	kilometre	meager	kilometer	
defence	offence	defense	offense	
practice (noun)		practise		-ce/-se
practise (verb)		practice		-se/-ce
distil	fulfil	distill	fulfill	single/double
omelette	programme	omelet	program	consonant
labelled	travelled	labeled	traveled	before
kidnapped	worshipped	kidnaped	worshiped	inflectional
jewellery	woollen	jewelry	woolen	before
marvellous	enrolment	marvelous	enrollment	derivational
analyse	criticise	analyze	criticize	-se/-ze
judgement	sizeable	judgment	sizable	silent e + suffix
co-operate		cooperate		hyphen
axe	catalogue	ax	catalog	terminal
cheque	plough	check	plow	variation
programme		program		

Adapted from Robert Ireland, "Canadian Spelling: How Much British? How Much American?" *The English Quarterly* 12.4 (1979–80): 64–80.

To many Americans, some spelling choices made by Canadians strike them as distinctly "British," while Britons point to "American" elements in the spelling. In fact, like Canadian English itself, Canadian spelling is a unique hybrid drawn from British and American forms. This blending of systems is apparent in the common Canadian spellings of the words in Table 9.4.

Admittedly, the exact nature and extent of the blend varies regionally. Residents of Nova Scotia, Ontario, and British Columbia, for example, tend to value British over American forms, while the reverse is true for Alberta, Manitoba, and Prince Edward Island (Ireland 1979–80). An Ontarian is more likely to write *honour* and *labour* than an Albertan, who will likely choose *honor* and *labor*.

TABLE 9.4
Examples of Canadian Spelling

Canadian Spelling		
colour	neighbour	-our/-or
harbour	mould	-ou-/-o-
centre	theatre	-re/-er
meager/meagre		
defence/se	offence/se	-ce/-se
practice (noun)	practise (verb)[5]	
distill	fulfill	single/double consonants
omelette		
labelled	travelled	before inflectionals
kidnapped	worshipped	
jewelry	woolen	before derivationals
marvelous	enrollment[6]	
analyze	criticize	-se/-ze
judgement	sizeable	silent e + suffix
co-operate		hyphen
grey	pyjamas	miscellaneous words
gypsy		
axe	catalogue	terminal variation
cheque	plow	
program		

Adapted from L. Burton et al., *Editing Canadian English*. Vancouver and Toronto: Douglas & McIntyre, 1987, pp. 6–13.

Despite regional differences, certain features are generally characteristic of Canadian spelling. Canadians are said to combine the American use of final double consonants (as in *distill*) with the British use of double consonants before inflectionals (as in *travelled*). The *Gage Canadian Dictionary* further suggests that Canadians employ double consonants before derivationals, as in *woollen* (Avis et al. 1983). Long forms such as *axe* (U.S. *ax*) are common, but Canadians seem to prefer the short form in *plow* (British *plough*), and many editors insist on *programme* except where computer programs are concerned (Burton et al. 1987).

It has been suggested that *maneuvre* is an example of a "Canadian compromise" in that it often takes a British final -*re* but rejects the British -*oeu*- in favour of -*eu*, which the *Collins English Dictionary* defines as "the usual U.S. spelling." But it is also an example of the complexity surrounding Canadian English; as long ago as his 1979–80 survey, Robert Ireland found that among "double vowel" words — those that may be spelled with -*ae*- or -*oe*- (*mediaeval, encyclopaedia*) — *manoeuvre* was the most likely to occur, but even so more than half of his secondary school respondents chose *maneuver*, the "American" form.

Canadian newspapers and magazines frequently vacillate in their editorial practices, especially with respect to -*our*/-*or* and -*re*/-*er* forms. In 1962, a report prepared by the Canadian Linguistic Association and the Association of Canadian University Teachers of English predicted that, in such matters, "the tendency to adopt American spellings will spread." This report observed that "this process is already well underway in the newspapers of Canada though the accepted standard is still that of Britain" (*Some Arguments* 1962). Thirty years later, The Canadian Press revealed that the process had not spread far, for it insisted that "we will use -*or* spellings come what may" (Buckley 1992). But by the century's end, CP citations in various newspapers were employing -*our* forms. And in its *1999 Stylebook*, CP admitted that many daily newspapers had already "started switching to 'our' [from -*or* spellings] to reflect the preference of readers," and it bowed to widespread use, announcing that, "In September 1998, The Canadian Press adopted 'our' spelling for words of more than one syllable in which the 'u' is not pronounced. This came after 80 years of writing with *color, ardor* and *rigor*" (Tasko 1999). *The Globe and Mail*, which bills itself as "the National Newspaper," continues to ask for both -*our* and -*re* spellings (McFarlane and Clements 1990).

-*Re* forms remain common in Canada; Burton, who inquired among editors, discovered a majority in favour of it, but Ireland found that high school students preferred -*er* forms. -*Re* forms have also been encouraged by bilingual designations such as "Interpretive Centre d'Interpretation" (McConnell 1979, and Pratt 1993).

Style books and handbooks often suggest that bewildered writers consult "a good Canadian dictionary" for correct spelling, but this advice does not take into account either the conflicting practices of the major dictionaries or strong regional preferences. *The Nelson Canadian Dictionary of the English Language* (1997) (based, as are so many "Canadian" dictionaries, on an American text) lists the following words (from Table 9.4) as "equal variants" — that is, as forms that "occur with virtually equal frequency in edited sources": *jewellery/jewelry, marvellous/marvelous, centre/center, meagre/meager, woollen/woolen, fulfill/fulfil, labelled/labeled, travelled/traveled, worshipped/worshiped, enrolment/enrollment, plough/plow*. It is clear that this dictionary takes issue with the decisions of the editors surveyed by Burton. Moreover, dictionaries do not normally recognize that differing types of writing may require differing spelling forms. More formal genres, such as textbooks, favour British forms, while less formal types, such as newspapers, may follow American practices. The complexity of the situation often leads many style guides to insist only that writers be consistent. If, for example, they choose to use *-our* forms rather than *-or* forms, then they should do so consistently. On the other hand, choosing to mix *between* categories — that is, to use *-re* and at the same time *-or* spellings — "may well constitute the 'Canadian style' " (Burton et al. 1987). Perhaps as a result of regional differences and this tendency to mix categories, there is in general a greater tolerance for spelling diversity in Canada than in Britain or the United States.

Computer Spell-Checkers

Computer programs that check and replace "mis-spellings" are too new for their influence to be fully appreciated. These systems may, in the end, enforce a regularity and consistency across regional boundaries. At present, however, the different word-processing systems themselves reflect those varying choices evident in the published dictionaries. The "Canadian" speller "bundled" with Corel WordPerfect accepts both *fulfil* and *fulfill, distil* and *distill*, but rejects *worshiped*. Microsoft Word's Canadian speller, on the other hand, accepts both *worshiped* and *worshipped* but rejects *fulfill* and *distill*. WordPerfect accepts both *woollen* and *woolen*, while Word rejects *woolen*. The effects of such programs across the various regions of the country are yet to be charted; however, as the number of people employing word-processing programs increases, these checkers may well influence Canadian spelling practices.

Summary

Writing is one of the basic tools of civilization. Without it, the world as we know it could not exist.

The precursor of writing was "picture writing," which used **pictograms** to represent objects directly and literally. Pictograms are called **ideograms** when the drawing becomes less literal and the meaning extends to concepts associated with the object originally pictured. When ideograms become associated with the words for the concepts they signify, they are called **logograms. Logographic** systems are true writing systems in the sense that the symbols stand for words of a language. The Sumerians first developed a pictographic writing system to keep track of commercial transactions. It was later expanded for other uses and eventually evolved into the highly stylized (and stylus-ized) **cuneiform** writing. Cuneiform was generalized to other writing systems by application of the **rebus principle**, which used the symbol of one word or syllable to represent another word or syllable pronounced the same.

The Egyptians also developed a pictographic system, which became known as **hieroglyphics**. This system influenced many peoples, including the Phoenicians, who developed the West Semitic Syllabary. The Greeks borrowed the Phoenician system, and in adapting it to their own language they used the symbols to represent both consonant and vowel sound segments, thus inventing the first alphabet.

There are four types of writing systems still being used in the world: **logographic** or **word writing**, in which every symbol or character represents a word or morpheme (as in Chinese); **syllabic writing**, in which each symbol represents a syllable (as in Japanese); **consonantal alphabetic**, in which each symbol represents a consonant and vowels may be represented by diacritical marks (as in Hebrew); and **alphabetic writing**, in which each symbol represents (for the most part) one phoneme (as in English).

The writing system may have some small effect on the spoken language. Languages change over time, but writing systems tend to be more conservative than spoken forms. Thus, spelling no longer accurately reflects pronunciation. Also, when the spoken and written forms of the language become divergent, some words may be pronounced as they are spelled, sometimes due to the efforts of pronunciation reformers.

There are advantages to a conservative spelling system. A common spelling permits speakers whose dialects have diverged to communicate through writing, as is best exemplified in China, where the "dialects" are mutually unintelligible. We are also able to read and understand the English language as it was written centuries ago. In addition, despite some gross lack of correspondences between sound and spelling, the spelling often reflects speakers' morphological and phonological knowledge.

Canadian spelling reflects both the influence of American spelling practices and the prestige still accorded to English customs. The extent of each influence varies from region to region. The result of these conflicting influences has been a tolerance for diversity in spelling.

Notes

1. The pictograph for "ox" evolved, much later, into our letter *A*.
2. The symbol portrays the Pharaoh's staff.
3. Water trickling out of a vase.
4. See Exercise 1 of Chapter 6 (p. 273).
5. "While variation is recognized for these words, the layman may be unsure of which form is which. Only for *practice* is the choice clearly for the *-ce* ending, especially when the word is used as a noun. Some spelling texts and usage handbooks teach the distinction between the *-ce* ending for the noun and *-se* for the verb. This may account for the higher use of *practise* as a verb" (Ireland

1979–80). Editors who responded to Burton (1987) preferred *defence, practice, pretence*, and *prophecy* as nouns and *practise* and *prophesy* as verbs. It is clear from this survey that Canadian editors and publishers have a strong inclination toward British forms.

6. The *Gage Canadian Dictionary* — like Burton's editors — disagrees with Ireland's findings, giving *jewellery, marvellous, woollen*, and *enrolment* as the first (and, in its eyes, the preferred) Canadian forms. It also prefers *judgment* and *sizable*, as well as *distil* and *fulfil*.

Exercises

1. A. "Write" the following words and phrases, using pictograms that you invent:

a.	eye	e.	tree	i.	ugly
b.	a boy	f.	forest	j.	run
c.	two boys	g.	war	k.	Scotch tape
d.	library	h.	honesty	l.	smoke

   B. Which words are most difficult to symbolize in this way? Why?

   C. How does the following sentence reveal the problems in pictographic writing? "A grammar represents the unconscious, internalized linguistic competence of a native speaker."

2. A *rebus* is a written representation of words or syllables using pictures of objects whose names resemble the sounds of the intended words or syllables. For example, might be the symbol for *eye* or *I* or the first syllable in *idea*.

   A. Using the rebus principle, "write" the following words:

a.	tearing	c.	bareback
b.	icicle	d.	cookies

   B. Why would such a system be a difficult system in which to represent all words in English? Illustrate your answer with an example.

3. A. Construct non-Roman alphabetic letters to replace the letters used to represent the following sounds in English:

   t r s k w č i æ f n

   B. Use these symbols plus the regular alphabet symbols for the other sounds to write the following words in your "new orthography."

a.	character	d.	photo	g.	psychotic
b.	guest	e.	cheat	h.	tree
c.	cough	f.	rang		

4. Suppose the English writing system were a *syllabic* system instead of an *alphabetic* system. Use capital letters to symbolize the necessary syllabic units for the words below, and list your "syllabary." Example: Given the words *mate*, *inmate*, *intake*, and *elfin*, you might use A = *mate*, B = *in*, C = *take*, and D = *elf*. In addition, write the words using your syllabary. Example: *inmate* — BA; *elfin* — DB; *intake* — BC; *mate* — A. (Do not use any more syllable symbols than you absolutely need.)

a.	childishness	e.	likely	i.	jealous
b.	childlike	f.	zoo	j.	witless
c.	Jesuit	g.	witness	k.	lesson
d.	lifelessness	h.	lethal		

*5. In the following pairs of English words, the boldfaced portions are pronounced the same but spelled differently. Can you think of any reason why the spelling should remain distinct? (*Hint: reel* and *real* are pronounced the same, but *reality* shows the presence of a phonemic /æ/ in *real*.)

	A	**B**	**Reason**
a.	I **am**	**iamb**	
b.	**goose**	pro**duce**	
c.	**fashion**	compli**cation**	
d.	New**ton**	or**gan**	
e.	**no**	**know**	
f.	**hymn**	**him**	

6. In the following pairs of words, the boldfaced portions are spelled the same but pronounced differently. State some reasons why the spelling of the words in column B should not be changed.

	A	**B**	**Reason**
a.	mi**ng**le	lo**ng**	The **g** is pronounced in *longer*.
b.	li**ne**	**chi**ldren	
c.	**so**nar	re**so**und	
d.	**c**ent	my**s**tic	
e.	crum**b**le	bom**b**	
f.	cat**s**	dog**s**	
g.	sta**gn**ant	desi**gn**	
h.	se**rene**	ob**sceni**ty	

7. Each of the following sentences is ambiguous in the written form. How can these sentences be made unambiguous when they are spoken?

   Example: John hugged Bill, and then he kissed him.

   For the meaning "John hugged and kissed Bill," use normal stress (*kissed* receives stress). For the meaning "Bill kissed John," contrastive stress is needed on both *he* and *him*.

a. What are we having for dinner, Mother?
b. She's a German language teacher.
c. They formed a student grievance committee.
d. Charles kissed his wife, and George kissed his wife too.

8. In the written form, the following sentences are not ambiguous, but they would be if spoken. State the devices used in writing that make the meanings explicit.

a. They're my brothers' keepers.
b. He said, "He will take the garbage out." *oral* "I will take the garb out."
c. The red book was read.
d. The flower was on the table.

9. Below are ten samples of writing from the ten languages listed. Match the writing to the language. There are enough "hints" in this chapter to get most of them. (The source of these examples, and many others, is Kenneth Katzner. 1975. *Languages of the World*. New York: Funk & Wagnalls.)

a. _____ Cherokee
b. _____ Chinese
c. _____ German (Gothic style)
d. _____ Greek
e. _____ Hebrew
f. _____ Icelandic
g. _____ Japanese
h. _____ Korean
i. _____ Russian
j. _____ Twi

1. 仮に勝手に変えるようなことをすれば。
2. Κι ὁ νοῦς του ἀγκάλιασε πονετικὰ τὴν Κρήτη.
3. «Что это? я падаю? у меня ноги подкашиваются»,
4. וְהָיָה ׀ בְּאַחֲרִית הַיָּמִים נָכוֹן יִהְיֶה הַר
5. Saá sàre yi bèn atɛkyé bí â mpɔtorɔ áhye
6. 既然必须和新的群众的时代相结合.
7. JℰꝄ Dꝿ J5ℰℰ ℭWℾ ℭℰ꜄꜀.
8. Þótt þú langförull legðir sérhvert land undir fót,
9. Pharao's Anblick war wunderbar.
10. 스위스는 독특한 체제

10. Compare the spelling guidelines of Canadian dictionaries and composition handbooks. What do the editors offer as rules for writers who wish to use a "Canadian style"?

Works Cited

Avis, Walter S., et al., eds. 1983. *Gage Canadian Dictionary*. Toronto: Gage Educational Publishing.

Bolinger, D. 1968. *Aspects of Language*. New York: Harcourt Brace Jovanovich.

Buckley, Peter, ed. 1992. *The Canadian Press Stylebook*. Toronto: Canadian Press.

Burton, L., et al. 1987. *Editing Canadian English*. Vancouver and Toronto: Douglas & McIntyre.

DeFrancis, John. 1989. *Visible Speech: The Diverse Oneness of Writing Systems*. Honolulu: University of Hawaii Press.

Diringer, David. 1968. *The Alphabet: A Key to the History of Mankind*. London: Hutchinson.

Feinstein, Robert N. 1986. "Gnormal Pspelling." *National Forum: The Phi Kappa Phi Journal*.

Gaur, Albertine. 1984. *A History of Writing*. London: British Library.

Ireland, Robert J. 1979–80. "Canadian Spelling: How Much British? How Much American?" *The English Quarterly* 12.4: 64–80.

Jensen, Hans. 1969. *Sign, Symbol, and Script: An Account of Man's Efforts to Write*. Trans. George Unwin. New York: Putnam.

Katzner, Kenneth. 1975. *Languages of the World*. New York: Funk & Wagnalls.

Lehmann, Winfred P., ed. 1975. *Language and Linguistics in the People's Republic of China*. Austin: University of Texas Press.

McConnell, R.E. 1979. *Our Own Voice: Canadian English and How It Is Studied*. Toronto: Gage Educational Publishing.

McFarlane, J.A., and Warren Clements. 1990. *The Globe and Mail Style Book*. Toronto: Globe and Mail.

The Nelson Canadian Dictionary of the English Language. 1997. Scarborough, ON: Nelson.

Ohman, Sven. 1969. Paper presented at the International Speech Symposium, Kyoto, Japan.

Pratt, T.K. 1993. "The Hobgoblin of Canadian English Spelling." *Focus on Canada*. Ed. S. Clarke. Amsterdam: John Benjamins Publishing: 45–64.

Shaw, George Bernard. 1941. "Preface to R.A. Wilson." *The Miraculous Birth of Language*. London: British Publishers Guild. Rpt. 1946: 7–33.

Silver, Shirley, and Wick R. Miller. 1997. *American Indian Language: Cultural and Social Contexts*. Tucson: University of Arizona Press.

Some Arguments for & against Reforming English Spelling. A Report Prepared for the Canadian Conference on Education by a Committee Representing the Canadian Linguistic Association and the Association of Canadian University Teachers of English. 1962. Kingston, Ontario.

Tasko, Patti, ed. 1999. *The Canadian Press Stylebook*. Toronto: Canadian Press.

Further Reading

Biber, Douglas. 1988. *Variation across Speech and Writing*. Cambridge, UK: Cambridge University Press.

Clarke, John W. 1965. "American Spelling." In G.A. Vallins, *Spelling*. Rev. D.G. Scragg. London: Andre Deutsch: 184–202.

Coulmas, Florian. 1989. *The Writing Systems of the World*. Oxford: Oxford University Press.

Cummings, D.W. 1988. *American English Spelling*. Baltimore: Johns Hopkins University Press.

Daniels, P.T., and W. Bright, eds. 1996. *The World's Writing Systems*. New York: Oxford University Press.

DeFrancis, John. 1989. *Visible Speech: The Diverse Oneness of Writing Systems*. Honolulu: University of Hawaii Press.

Diringer, D. 1962. *Writing*. New York: Holt, Rinehart and Winston.

Gaur, Albertine. 1984. *A History of Writing.* London: British Library.

Gelb, I.J. 1952. *A Study of Writing.* Chicago: University of Chicago Press.

Jensen, H. 1970. *Sign, Symbol, and Script.* Trans. G. Unwin. London: George Allen and Unwin.

Robertson, S., and F.G. Cassidy. 1954. *The Development of Modern English.* Englewood Cliffs, NJ: Prentice-Hall: 353–74 (on spelling and spelling reform).

Sampson, Geoffrey. 1985. *Writing Systems: A Linguistic Introduction.* Stanford: Stanford University Press.

Wang, William S-Y. 1981. "Language Structure and Optimal Orthography." *Perception of Print: Reading Research in Experimental Psychology.* Ed. O.J.L. Tzeng and H. Singer. Hillsdale, NJ: Erlbaum: 223–36.

PART 4
Biological Aspects of Language

The functional asymmetry of the human brain is unequivocal, and so is its anatomical asymmetry. The structural differences between the left and the right hemispheres are visible not only under the microscope but to the naked eye. The most striking asymmetries occur in language-related cortices. It is tempting to assume that such anatomical differences are an index of the neurobiological underpinnings of language.

Antonio and Hanna Damasio

[The brain is] the messenger of the understanding [and the organ whereby] in an especial manner we acquire wisdom and knowledge.

Hippocratic treatise, "On the Sacred Disease" (c. 377 B.C.E.)

CHAPTER 10
Language Acquisition

The acquisition of language "is doubtless the greatest intellectual feat any one of us is ever required to perform."

Leonard Bloomfield, *Language* (1933)

Every aspect of language is extremely complex; yet very young children — before the age of 5 — already know most of the intricate system we have been calling the grammar of a language. Before they can add 2 + 2, children are conjoining sentences, asking questions, selecting appropriate pronouns, negating sentences, forming relative clauses, and using the syntactic, phonological, morphological, and semantic rules of the grammar.

A normal human being can go through life without learning to read or write, as do millions of people in the world today. Nevertheless, these millions can express, understand, and discuss complex and abstract ideas as effectively as literate speakers can. Learning a language and learning to read and write are different. Similarly, millions of humans never learn algebra or chemistry or how to use a computer. Such skills and systems they must be taught, but they do not have to be taught to talk.

The study of the nature of human language itself has revealed a great deal about language acquisition, about what the child does and does not do when learning or acquiring a language:

1. Children do not learn a language by storing all the words and all the sentences in some giant mental dictionary. The list of words is finite, but no dictionary can hold all the sentences, which are infinite in number.
2. Children learn to construct sentences, most of which they have never produced before.
3. Children learn to understand sentences they have never heard before. They cannot do so by matching the "heard utterance" with some stored sentence.
4. Children must therefore construct the "rules" that permit them to use language creatively.
5. No one teaches them these rules. Their parents are no more aware of the phonological, syntactic, and semantic rules than are the children.

Even if you remember your early years, you will not remember anyone telling you to form a sentence by adding a verb phrase to a noun phrase or to add [s] or [z] to form plurals. Children, then, seem to act like efficient linguists equipped with a perfect theory of language, and they use this theory to construct the grammar of the language they hear.

In addition to acquiring the complex rules of the grammar (i.e., gaining linguistic competence), children learn pragmatics, the appropriate social use of language, what certain scholars have called **communicative competence**. These rules include, for example, the greetings that are to be used, the "taboo" words, the polite forms of address, the various styles that are appropriate to different situations, and so forth.

Stages in Language Acquisition

> ... for I was no longer a speechless infant; but a speaking boy. This I remember; and have since observed how I learned to speak. It was not that my elders taught me words ... in any set method; but I ... did myself ... practice the sounds in my memory. ... And thus by constantly hearing words, as they occurred in various sentences ... I thereby gave utterance to my will.
>
> St. Augustine (trans. F.J. Sheed, 1944), *Confessions* (c. 400 C.E.)

Children do not wake up one morning with a fully formed grammar in their heads or with the rules of social and communicative intercourse. **Linguistic competence** develops by stages, and, it is suggested, each successive stage more closely approximates the grammar of the adult language. Observations of children in different language areas of the world reveal that these stages are similar and possibly universal. Some stages last for a short time; others remain longer. Some stages may overlap for a short period, but the transition between stages is often sudden.

Given the universal aspects of all human languages, signed and spoken, it is not surprising that deaf children of deaf signing parents parallel the **stages of** spoken **language acquisition** in their signing development.

The earliest studies of child language acquisition come from diaries kept by parents. More recent studies include the use of tape recordings, videotapes, and controlled experiments. Spontaneous utterances of children are recorded, and various elicitation techniques have been developed so that the child's production and comprehension can be scientifically studied.

The First Sounds

> An infant crying in the night:
> An infant crying for the light:
> And with no language but a cry.
>
> Alfred Lord Tennyson, *In Memoriam H.H.S.*

Language acquisition can be divided into prelinguistic and linguistic stages. Most scholars agree that the earliest cries, whimpers, and cooing noises of the newborn, or neonate, cannot be considered early language. Such noises are completely stimulus controlled; they are the child's involuntary responses to hunger, discomfort, the desire to be cuddled, or the feeling of well-being. A major difference between human language and the communication systems of other species is that human language is creative in the sense that it is relatively free from either external or internal stimuli. The child's first noises, however, are simply responses to stimuli.

During the earliest period, the noises produced by infants in all language communities sound the same.

The early view that a neonate is born with a mind like a blank slate is countered by the evidence showing that infants are highly sensitive to certain subtle distinctions in their environment and not to others. That is, the mind appears to be "prewired" to receive only certain kinds of information.

By using a specially designed nipple with a pressure-sensitive device that records sucking rate, researchers have found that infants will increase their sucking rate when stimuli (visual or auditory) presented to them are varied, but will decrease the sucking rate when the same stimuli are presented over and over again. Experiments have shown that infants will respond to visual depth and distance distinctions, to differences between rigid versus flexible objects, and to human faces rather than to other visual stimuli.

Similarly, infants respond to phonetic contrasts found in some human languages even when these differences are not phonemic in the language spoken in the baby's home. A baby hearing a human voice over a loudspeaker saying [pa] [pa] [pa] will slowly decrease her rate of sucking; if the sound changes to [ba] or even to [pʰa], the sucking rate increases dramatically. Controlled experiments show that adults find it difficult to differentiate between the allophones of one phoneme, but for infants it is a "piece of cake." Japanese infants can distinguish between [r] and [l], while their parents cannot; babies can hear the difference between aspirated and unaspirated stops even if adults can't. Babies can discriminate between sounds that are phonemic in other languages and non-existent in the language of their parents. For example, in Hindi there is a phonemic contrast between a retroflex [ṭ] and the alveolar [t]. To English-speaking adults, they sound the same; to their infants, they don't.

However, babies will not respond to sound signals that never signal phonemic contrasts in any human language.

A vowel that we perceive as [i] or [u] or [æ] is a different physical sound when produced by a male, female, or child. Yet babies ignore the non-linguistic aspects of the speech signal just as we do. An [i] is an [i] to an infant even if the physical sound is different. Infants do not increase sucking rate when they suddenly hear an [i] spoken by a female after hearing many [i]s spoken by a male. Yet speech communication engineers are having difficulty programming computers to recognize these different signals as the "same."

Infants cannot have learned to perceive the phonetic distinctions and to ignore other non-linguistic differences; they seem to be born with the ability to perceive just those sounds that are phonemic in some language. This partially accounts for the fact that children can learn any human language to which they are exposed.

Children have the sensory and motor abilities to produce and comprehend speech, even in the period of life before language acquisition occurs.

From about 6 months on, babies begin to lose the ability to discriminate between sounds that are not phonemic in their language. Japanese infants can no longer hear the difference between [r] and [l], which do not contrast in Japanese, whereas babies in English-speaking homes retain this perception. These infants have begun to learn the sounds of the language of their parents. Before that, they appear to know the sounds of human language in general.

Babbling

In the first few months, usually around the sixth month, the infant begins to **babble**. Many of the various sounds produced in this period (apart from the continuing stimulus-controlled cries and gurgles) do not occur in the language of the household.

One view suggests that it is during this period that children learn to distinguish between the sounds of their language and the sounds that are not part of the language. During the babbling period, children learn to maintain the "right" sounds and to suppress the "wrong" ones. Babbling, however, does not seem to be a prerequisite for language acquisition. Infants who are unable to produce any sounds at this early stage because of physical motor problems begin to talk properly once the disability has been corrected.

It was once thought that deaf infants produced babbling sounds similar to those of hearing children. This would suggest that the sounds produced do not depend on the presence of auditory input or that they are a first stage in language acquisition.

Studies of vocal babbling of hearing children and manual babbling of deaf children conducted by Laura Petitto of McGill University and her colleagues suggest that babbling is a specifically linguistic ability related to the kind of language input the child receives. She reports that infants from 4 to 7 months produce a restricted set of phonetic forms vocally, if exposed to spoken languages, and manually if exposed to sign language, drawn from the set of possible sounds and possible gestures found in spoken and signed languages.

Babbling illustrates a sensitivity of the human mind to respond to linguistic cues from a very early stage. This is dramatically demonstrated in Petitto's studies (Petitto and Marantette 1991). During the babbling stage of hearing infants, the pitch, or intonation contours, produced by them begin to resemble the intonation contours of sentences spoken by adults. The semantically different intonation contours are among the first linguistic contrasts that children perceive and produce.

During this period, the vocalizations produced by deaf babies are qualitatively different from those produced by hearing infants; they are unsystematic, non-repetitive, and random. In parallel, the manual gestures produced by hearing babies differ greatly from those produced by deaf infants exposed to sign language. The hearing babies move their fingers and clench their fists randomly with little or no repetition of the same gestures; the deaf infants, however, use more than a dozen different hand motions repetitively, all of which are elements of American Sign Language or the other sign languages used by deaf people in all countries.

Petitto's view is that humans are born with a predisposition to discover the units that serve to express linguistic meanings and that, at a genetically specified stage in neural development, the infant will begin to produce these units, sounds, or gestures, depending on the language input the baby receives. Thus, Petitto suggests that babbling is the earliest stage in language acquisition, in opposition to the earlier view that babbling was prelinguistic and simply neuromuscular in origin.

First Words

> From this golden egg a man, Prajapati, was born. . . . A year having passed, he wanted to speak. He said bhur and the earth was created. He said bhuvar and the space of the air was created. He said suvar and the sky was created. That is why a child wants to speak after a year. . . . When Prajapati spoke for the first time, he uttered one or two syllables. That is why a child utters one or two syllables when he speaks for the first time.

Hindu myth

DOONESBURY copyright 1982 & 1984 G.B. Trudeau. Reprinted with permission of Universal Press Syndicate. All rights reserved.

Some time after one year, children begin to use the same string of sounds repeatedly to mean the same thing. By that time, they have learned that sounds are related to meanings, and they are producing their first "words." Most children seem to go through the "one word = one sentence" stage. These one-word "sentences" are called **holophrastic** sentences (from *holo* "complete" or "undivided" plus *phrase* "phrase" or "sentence").

One child, J.P., illustrates how much the young child has learned even before the age of 2 years. J.P.'s words of April 1977, at the age of 16 months, were as follows:[1]

[ʔaw]	"not," "no," "don't"	[s:]	"aerosol spray"
[bʌʔ]/[mʌʔ]	"up"	[sʲu:]	"shoe"
[da]	"dog"	[haj]	"hi"
[iʔo]/[siʔo]	"Cheerios"	[sr]	"shirt,"
[sa]	"sock"		"sweater"
[aj]/[ʌj]	"light"	[sæ:]/[əsæ:]	"What's that?",
[ma]	"mommy"		"Hey, look!"
[baw]/[daw]	"down"		
[dæ]	"daddy"		

J.P.'s mother reports that before April J.P. had also used the words [bʊ] for "book," [ki] for "kitty," and [tsi] for "tree" but seemed to have "lost" them.

What is more interesting than merely the list of J.P.'s vocabulary is the way J.P. used these words. "Up" was originally restricted to mean "Get me up" when he was either on the floor or in his high chair, but later it was used to mean "Get up!" to his mother as well. J.P. used his word for "sock" not only for socks but also for other undergarments that are put on over the feet, or that feet are slipped through, such as underpants. Thus, a child may extend the meaning of a word from a particular referent to encompass a larger class.

When J.P. first began to use these words, the stimulus had to be visible, but soon it was no longer necessary. *Dog*, for example, was first used only when pointing to a real dog but later was used for pictures of dogs in various books. A new word that entered J.P.'s vocabulary at 17 months was *uh-oh*, which J.P. would say after he had an accident such as spilling juice or when he deliberately poured his yogurt over the side of his high chair. His use of this word shows his developing use of language for social purposes. At this time, he also added two new words meaning "no," [do:] and [no]. He used these words frequently when anyone attempted to take something from him that he wanted or tried to make him do something he did not want to do. He used this negative either imperatively (e.g., "Don't do that!") or assertively (e.g., "I don't want to do that!"). Even in his early holophrastic stage, J.P. was using words to convey a variety of ideas, feelings, and social customs.

According to some child-language researchers, the words in the holophrastic stage serve three major functions: they are linked with a child's own action or desire for action (as when J.P. would say *up* to express his wish to be picked up), used to convey emotion (J.P.'s *no*), or serve a naming function (J.P.'s *Cheerios, shoes, dog*, and so on).

At this stage, the child uses only one word to express concepts or predications that will later be expressed by complex phrases and sentences.

Phonologically, J.P.'s first words, like the words of most children at this stage of learning English and other languages, were generally monosyllabic with a CV (consonant–vowel) form; the vowel part may be diphthongal, depending on the language being acquired. His phonemic and phonetic inventory (at this stage, they are equivalent) is much smaller than is found in the adult language. It was suggested by Roman Jakobson (1941) that children will first acquire the sounds found in all languages of the world, no matter what language they are exposed to, and will later acquire the "more difficult" sounds. For example, most languages have the sounds

[p] and [s], but [θ] is a rare sound. J.P. was no exception. His phonological inventory at an early stage included the consonants [b], [m], [d], [k], which are frequently occurring sounds in the world's languages.

Many studies have shown that children in the holophrastic stage can perceive or comprehend many more phonological contrasts than they can produce themselves. Therefore, even at this stage, it is not possible to determine the extent of the grammar of the child simply by observing speech production.

The Two-Word Stage

Before they are 2 years old, children learn a large number of words. According to some estimates, children add a new word to their mental dictionaries every two hours. Then, about the time of their second birthday, something new and exciting occurs. Children begin to put two words together. At first, these utterances appear to be strings of two of the child's earlier holophrastic utterances, each word with its own single-pitch contour. Soon they begin to form actual two-word sentences with clear syntactic and semantic relations. The intonation contour of the two words extends over the whole utterance rather than being separated by a pause between the two words. The following "sentences" illustrate the kinds of patterns that are found in children's utterances at this stage:[2]

allgone sock	hi Mommy
byebye boat	allgone sticky
more wet	beepbeep bang
it ball	Katherine sock
dirty sock	here pretty

During the **two-word stage**, there are no syntactic or morphological markers — that is, no inflections for number, person, tense, and so on. Pronouns are rare, although many children use *me* to refer to themselves, and some children use other pronouns as well. L.M. Bloom (1972) has noted that, in noun + noun sentences such as *Mommy sock*, the two words can express a number of different grammatical relations that will later be expressed by other syntactic devices. Bloom's conclusions were reached by observing the situations in which the two-word sentence was uttered. Thus, for example, *Mommy sock* can be used to show a subject + object relation in the situation when the mother is putting the sock on the child or a possessive relation when the child is pointing to Mommy's sock. Two nouns can also be used to show a subject–locative relation, as in *sweater chair* to mean "The sweater is on the chair," or to show conjunction, to mean "sweater and chair."

From Telegraph to Infinity

There does not seem to be any "three-word" sentence stage. When a child starts stringing more than two words together, the utterances may be two, three, four, or five words or longer. Since the age at which children start to produce words and put words together may vary, chronological age is not a good measure of a child's language development. A child's **mean length of utterances (MLU)** rather than chronological age is thus used in the study of language development. That is, children producing utterances that average 2.3 to 3.5 morphemes in length seem to be at the same stage of grammar acquisition, even though one child may be 2 and another 3 years old.

A child's first utterances longer than two words have a special characteristic. The small function words (or grammatical morphemes) such as *to, the, can, is*, and so on are missing; only the words that carry the main message — the content words — occur. Children often sound as if they are reading a telegram message, which is why such utterances are sometimes called **telegraphic speech**:

> Cat stand up table.
> What that?
> He play little tune.
> Andrew want that.
> Cathy build house.
> No sit there.

J.P.'s early sentences were similar:

Age in Months		
25 months	[danʔiʔtˢɪʔ]	"don't eat (the) chip"
	[bʷaʔtat]	"(the) block (is on) top"
26 months	[mamis tu hæs]	"Mommy's two hands"
	[mo bʌs go]	"where's another bus?"
	[dædi go]	"where's Daddy?"
27 months	[ʔaj gat tu dʲus]	"I got two (glasses of) juice"
	[do baj ʔ mi]	"don't bite (kiss) me"
	[kʌdər sʌni ber]	"Sonny colour(ed a) bear"
28 months	[ʔaj gat pwe dɪs]	"I('m) play(ing with) this"
	[mamis tak mɛns]	"Mommy talk(ed to the) men"

Apart from lacking grammatical morphemes, these utterances appear to be sentence-like — they have hierarchical, constituent structures similar to the syntactic structures found in the sentences produced by the adult grammar. Children's utterances are not simply words that are randomly strung together, but from a very early stage reveal their grasp of the principles of sentence formulation:

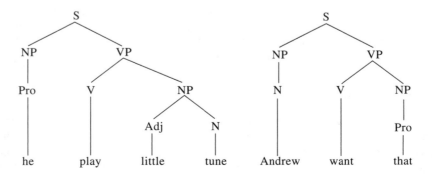

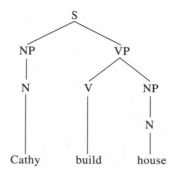

The examples cited above show that children's utterances adhere to the word-order constraints of the language they are acquiring. Children learning English do not say *Mommy men talk* for the sentence that would be *Mommy talked to the men.* On the other hand, in languages in which the regular word order is subject–object–verb (SOV), such as Japanese, children do say *Mommy men talk.*

Although the utterances are described as telegraphic, the child does not deliberately leave out the non-content words as an adult does when sending a telegram. The sentences reflect the child's grammar at that particular stage of language development.

As children produce sentences that more and more closely approximate the adult grammar, they begin to use syntactic or grammatical function words and to acquire the inflectional and derivational morphemes of the language. That these early sentences are constrained by the system of the language is shown by the fact that number agreement and gender agreement in languages such as Italian, Polish, and Turkish occur in early children's utterances where required by the adult language. Children would be unable to inflect the verb to agree with the subject noun phrase if they didn't know what a noun or a noun phrase or a verb was.

Nina Hyams, in her 1986 study of the acquisition of Italian, reports that between the ages of 1 year and 10 months and 2 years and 4 months a number of productive inflectional processes occur in the speech of Italian children. For example, verbs in Italian must be inflected for number and person to agree with the subject. This is similar to the agreement in English for third person subjects. We say *She giggles a lot* but *They giggle a lot*. In Italian, it is more complex, as the following utterances of Italian children show:

Tu leg**gi** il libro	"You read (2nd person singular) the book."
Io va**do** fuori	"I go (1st person singular) outside."
Dor**me** miao dorme	"Sleeps (3rd person singular) cat sleeps."
Leg**giamo** il libro	"(We) read (1st person plural) the book."

Hyams also shows that children at this young age produce sentences in which there is gender and number agreement between the determiner ("the," "a," etc.) and the noun in the noun phrase:

E mi**a** gonna	"(It) is my (feminine singular) skirt."
Questo mi**o** bimbo	"This my (masculine singular) baby."

Guarda **ia** mela piccolin**a**   "Look at the little (feminine singular) apple."
Guarda **il** topo piccolin**o**   "Look at the little (masculine singular) mouse."

Grammatical morphemes enter the language of English-speaking children around the same time. Robert Brown and his associates at Harvard University studied the spontaneous utterances of three children — Adam, Sarah, and Eve — over a long period of time, noting the appearance of grammatical morphemes, free and bound (Brown 1973). They found that the sequences of acquisition of the morphemes were the same for all three children, and this finding has been replicated by others. *-ing*, the ending that represents the present progressive form of the verb, as in *Me going*, was found to be among the earliest inflectional morphemes acquired. The prepositions *in* and *on* next entered the speech of the children studied, and then came the regular plural ending, as in *two doggies*. It is interesting that the third person singular marker (as in *Johnny comes*) and the possessive morpheme (as in *Daddy's hat*), which have the same phonological shape as the plural /s/, entered the children's speech between six months and a year later, showing that acquisition of these morphemes is syntax-dependent.

Eventually, all the other inflections were added, along with the syntactic rules, and finally the child's utterances sounded like those spoken by adults.

This is an incredible feat because of the complexity of the syntactic rules of all languages. Moreover, the child must figure out what these rules are from very "noisy" data. A child hears sentence fragments, false starts, speech errors, and interruptions; no one tells the child "this is a grammatical utterance, and that is not." Yet somehow the adult grammar is acquired. How does the child accomplish this task?

Theories of Child Language Acquisition

Do Children Learn by Imitation?

CHILD: My teacher holded the baby rabbits and we patted them.
ADULT: Did you say your teacher held the baby rabbits?
CHILD: Yes.
ADULT: What did you say she did?
CHILD: She holded the baby rabbits and we patted them.
ADULT: Did you say she held them tightly?
CHILD: No, she holded them loosely.

Courtney Cazden (1972)

Various theories have been proposed to explain how children manage to acquire the adult language. There are those who think that children merely imitate what they hear. Imitation is involved to some extent, of course, but the sentences produced by children show that they are not imitating adult speech. Children do not hear *Cat stand up table* or many of the utterances they produce:

A my pencil.
Two foot.
What the boy hit?
Other one pants.
Mommy get it my ladder.
Cowboy did fighting me.

Even when children are deliberately trying to imitate what they hear, they are unable to produce sentences that cannot be generated by their grammar:

ADULT: He's going out.   CHILD: He go out.
ADULT: That's an old-time train.   CHILD: Old-time train.
ADULT: Adam, say what I say: CHILD: Where I can put them?
        Where can I put them?

The **imitation theory** cannot account for another important phenomenon: children who are unable to speak for neurological or physiological reasons learn the language spoken to them and understand what is said. When they overcome their speech impairment, they immediately use the language for speaking.

Do Children Learn by Reinforcement?

CHILD: Nobody don't like me.
MOTHER: No, say "Nobody likes me."
CHILD: Nobody don't like me.
        (*dialogue repeated eight times*)
MOTHER: Now, listen carefully, say *"Nobody likes me."*
CHILD: Oh, nobody don't likes me.

Another view of language acquisition suggests that children learn to produce grammatical sentences because they are positively reinforced when they say something right and negatively reinforced when they say something wrong (the **reinforcement theory**). This view assumes that children are being constantly corrected when they use "bad grammar" and rewarded when they use "good grammar." Brown and his colleagues report from their studies that reinforcement seldom occurs, and when it does it is usually incorrect pronunciation or incorrect reporting of facts that is corrected. They report, for example, that the ungrammatical sentence *Her curl my hair* was not corrected because Eve's mother was in fact curling Eve's hair. However, when the syntactically correct sentence *Walt Disney comes on on Tuesday* was produced, Eve's mother corrected Eve because the program on television was shown on Wednesday. They conclude that it is "truth value rather than syntactic well-formedness that chiefly governs explicit verbal reinforcement by parents — which renders mildly paradoxical the fact that the usual product of such a training schedule is an adult whose speech is highly grammatical but not notably truthful" (Brown 1973).

Even if syntactic correction occurred more often, it would not explain how or what children learn from such adult responses or how children discover and construct the correct rules.

In fact, attempts to correct a child's language seem to be doomed to failure. Children do not know what they are doing wrong and are unable to make corrections even when they are pointed out, as shown by the example above and by the following one:

CHILD: Want other one spoon, Daddy.
FATHER: You mean, you want *the other spoon.*
CHILD: Yes, I want other one spoon, please, Daddy.
FATHER: Can you say "the other spoon?"
CHILD: Other . . . one . . . spoon.
FATHER: Say . . . "other."
CHILD: Other.
FATHER: Spoon.
CHILD: Spoon.
FATHER: Other . . . spoon.
CHILD: Other . . . spoon. Now give me other one spoon?

Such conversations between parents and children do not occur often. The above conversation was between a linguist studying child language and his child. Mothers and fathers are usually delighted that their young children are talking at all and consider every utterance to be a gem. The "mistakes" children make are cute and repeated endlessly to anyone who will listen.

Do Children Learn Language by Analogy?

It has also been suggested that children learn how to put words together to form phrases and sentences by **analogy**, by hearing a sentence and using it as a sample to form other sentences. But this doesn't work, as Lila Gleitman (1994) points out:

So suppose the child has heard the sentence "I painted a red barn." So now, by analogy, the child can say "I painted a blue barn." That's exactly the kind of theory that we want. You hear a sample and you extend it to all of the new cases by similarity. . . . In addition to "I painted a red barn" you might also hear the sentence "I painted a barn red." So it looks as if you take those last two words and switch them around in their order. . . . So now you want to extend this to the case of seeing, because you want to look at barns instead of painting them. So you have heard, "I saw a red barn." Now you try (by analogy) a . . . new sentence — "I saw a barn red." Something's gone wrong. This is an analogy, but the analogy didn't work. It's not a sentence of English.

The problem we face here of trying to explain how children learn what is or is not a sentence in their language through the use of analogy arises constantly.

Children Form Rules and Construct a Grammar

The analogy theory fails along with the reinforcement and imitation theories. These views cannot account for the non-random mistakes children make, the speed with which the basic rules of grammar are acquired, the ability to learn language *with-*

out any formal instruction, and the regularity of the acquisition process across diverse languages and environmental circumstances.

Between the ages of 5 and 7, children from diverse backgrounds reach the same stage of grammar acquisition whether their parents talk to them constantly or whether they are brought up to be seen and not heard and are seldom spoken to.

A child appears to be equipped from birth with the neural prerequisites for the acquisition and use of human language just as birds are biologically "prewired" to learn the songs of their species. And just as birds of one species cannot learn the songs of other birds, so also children can only learn languages that conform to linguistic principles, such as structural dependencies and universal syntactic categories, that pertain to all human languages and that determine the class of possible languages that can be acquired by children. Thus, children born of Zulu parents and raised in an English-speaking environment will learn English, and vice versa, but no children will acquire a formal language (without specific instruction) that, for example, has a rule to reverse the order of words in a sentence to form its negation. Such a rule is not in keeping with universal linguistic principles.

The different syntactic rules at any stage in acquisition govern the construction of the child's sentences at that period of development. Consider, for example, the increasing complexity of one child's negative sentences. At first, the child simply added a *no* (or some negative morpheme) at the beginning or the end of a sentence:

No heavy.
No singing song.
No want stand head.
No Fraser drink all tea.
No the sun shining.

Fraser did not hear such sentences. He used a simple way to form a negative, but it is not the way negative sentences are constructed in English. At some point, he began to insert a *no* or *can't* or *don't* inside the sentence:

He no bite you.
I no taste them.
That no fish school.
I can't catch you.

The child progressed from simple rules to more complex rules, as is shown below:

		Examples
One-word stage:	Single negative word	No. Allgone.
First sentences:	Negative word added to beginning of sentence	No want food. No Fraser drink all tea.
Later sentences:	Negative element inserted between subject and predicate	Fraser no want some. He no bite you.

(Continued)

(Continued)

Negative auxiliaries *don't*, *can't* appear		I can't catch you.
Negation "spread" — *some* becomes *no*		Fraser don't want no food.
Negative element inserted correctly — *no* changed to *any*		I don't want any food.

Not all children show the same development as the child described above, but they all show similar regular changes. One child studied by Carol Lord first differentiated affirmative from negative sentences by pitch; her negative sentences were all produced with a much higher pitch. When she began to use a negative morpheme, the pitch remained high, but then the intonation became normal as the negative syntactic markers took over.

Similar changes in the grammar are found in the acquisition of questions. One child first formed a question by using a "question intonation" (a rise of pitch at the end of the sentence):

Fraser water?
I ride train?
Sit chair?

At the next stage, the child merely tacked on a question word in front of the sentence; he did not change the word order or insert *do*. This is similar to the negation stage in which *no* or another negation word is put at the front of the sentence.

What he wants?
What he can ride in?
Where I should put it?
Where Ann pencil?
Why you smiling?

Such sentences are perfectly regular. They are not mistakes in the child's language; they reflect the grammar at a specific stage of development.

Errors or Rules?

A final word about the theory of errors. Here it is that the causes are complex and multiple. . . .
Henri Poincaré (1854–1912)

Give me fruitful error any time, full of seeds, bursting with its own corrections.
Vilfredo Pareto (1848–1923)

Language acquisition is a creative process. The grammar develops in stages, and at each stage the child's utterances conform to the rules and regularities acquired at that stage. The mistakes (when looked at from the point of view of the adult grammar) reveal these rules.

Children seem to form the simplest and most general rule they can from the language input they receive and to be so pleased with their "theory" that they use the rule wherever they can.

The Acquisition of Phonology

Children appear to be neurologically prepared to perceive just those sounds that are phonemic in some human language. From the earliest one-word stage, they show an awareness of the phonetic features and properties that characterize natural classes of sounds. Many studies report a similar order of acquisition of classes of sounds characterized by manner of articulation; nasals are acquired first, then glides, stops, liquids, fricatives, and affricates. Natural classes characterized by place of articulation features also appear in children's utterances according to an ordered series: labials, velars, alveolars, and palatals. It is not surprising that *mama* is an early word for many or most children.

In early language, children may not distinguish between voiced and voiceless consonants. When they first begin to contrast one set — that is, when they learn that /p/ and /b/ are distinct phonemes — they also begin to distinguish between /t/ and /d/, /s/ and /z/, and to perceive all the other contrasts between voiceless and voiced consonants. The generalizations refer, as we would expect, to natural classes of speech sounds.

A child's first words show many such substitutions of one feature for another or of one phoneme for another. For example, the word *light* [lajt] is pronounced as *yight* [jajt] in the speech of many children, with the liquid [l] being replaced by the glide [j]; *rabbit* is pronounced with the liquid [r] replaced by the glide [w]. The child's errors in pronunciation are thus not random but rule-governed. Typical phonological rules (or processes) found in children's early utterances (Hyams 1986) include

(1) Consonant cluster simplification: spoon → poon; blue → bu
(2) Devoicing of final consonants: dog → dok
(3) Voicing of initial consonants: truck → druck
(4) Consonant articulation agreement   doggy → goggy, doddy; big → gig
   (called **consonant harmony**)

These rules or constraints on the child's pronunciation of words combine so that *truck* may become *guck*:

truck → **t**uck   by rule (1) — consonant cluster simplification
tuck → **d**uck   by rule (3) — voicing of initial [t]
duck → **g**uck   by rule (4) — consonant harmony

The rules are simplifications of the adult phonological representations. They are natural rules reflecting easier articulations until greater articulatory control is achieved.

It is not that children do not hear the correct pronunciations. They do but are unable in these early years to produce the target pronunciation. We know this from countless stories. The son of one of the authors of this textbook pronounced the word *light* as *yight* [jajt] but would become angry if someone said to him, "Oh, you want me to turn the yight on." "No, no," he would reply, "not yight — yight."

Controlled experiments also show that the child does hear the difference that he seems to be unable to produce. For example, a child who appears to pronounce *wing* and *ring* identically can pick out the correct picture when shown pictures of both. Furthermore, acoustic analysis of children's utterances shows that what sounds to adults like the same sound in a child's pronunciation of *wing* and *ring* are physically different sounds. The differences are not perceived by the adult ear because they are non-linguistic differences.

These phonetic/phonological pronunciations of words, which appear to be mistakes, are actually produced according to the rules at the child's stage of development.

The Acquisition of Morphology

Children's errors in morphology reveal that the child has acquired the regular rules of the grammar and overgeneralizes them. This **overgeneralization** of constructed rules is shown when children treat irregular verbs and nouns as if they were regular. We have probably all heard children say *bringed, goed, singed* or *foots, mouses, sheeps*, and *childs*.

These mistakes tell us more about how children learn language than about the correct forms they use. The child cannot be imitating; children use such forms even when their parents never utter such "bad English." In fact, children may say *brought* or *broke* before they begin to use the incorrect forms. At the earlier stage, they never use any regular past tense forms such as *kissed, walked*, or *helped*. They probably do not know that *brought* is "past" at all. When they begin to say *played* and *hugged* and *helped*, as well as *play, hug*, and *help*, they have worked out how to form a past tense — they have constructed the rule. At that point, they form all past tenses by this rule — they overgeneralize — and they no longer say *brought* but *bring* and *bringed*. The acquisition of the rule overrides previously learned words and is unaffected by "practice" reinforcement. At a later time, children will learn that there are "exceptions" to the rule, and only then will they once more say *brought*. Children look for general patterns, for systematic occurrences.

The child's morphological rules emerge quite early. In 1958, J. Berko conducted a study that has now become a classic in our understanding of child language acquisition. She worked with preschool children and with children in grades one through three. She showed each child a drawing of a nonsense animal such as the funny creature below and gave the "animal" a nonsense name. She would then say to the child, pointing to the picture, "This is a **wug**."

Then she would show the child a picture of two of the animals and say, "Now here is another one. There are two of them. There are two _____?"

The child's "task" was to give the plural form, *wugs* [wʌgz]. Another little make-believe animal was called a *bik*, and when the child was shown two *biks* he or she again was to say the plural form [bɪks]. Berko found that the children applied the regular plural-formation rule to words never heard before. Because the children had never seen a *wug* or a *bik* and had not heard these "words," their ability to add a [z] when the animal's name ended with a voiced sound and an [s] when there was a final voiceless consonant showed that the children were using rules based on an understanding of natural classes of phonological segments and not simply imitating words they had previously heard.

Children also show knowledge of the derivational rules of their language. In English, for example, we can derive verbs from nouns. Some people *xerox* (from the noun *Xerox*, though the verb seems to be in the process of being replaced by *photocopy*). Children acquire this derivational rule early and use it often since there are many gaps in their verb vocabulary (studies show that nouns are usually acquired first). Some further examples are provided by Hyams (1986):

You have to scale it.	"You have to weigh it."
I broomed it up.	"I swept it up."
He's keying the door.	"He's opening the door (with a key)."

Children's utterances reflect their internal grammars, and these grammars include derivational and inflectional rules at a very early age.

The Acquisition of Syntax

Children eventually acquire all the phonological, syntactic, and semantic rules of the grammar. Not only are very young children more successful than the most brilliant linguist but also their grammars, at each stage of their acquisition, are markedly similar and deviate from the adult grammar in highly specific constrained ways.

To account for the ability of children to construct the complex syntactic rules of their grammar, it has been suggested that the child's "grammar" is semantically based. This view holds that the child's early language refers not to syntactic categories and relations (Noun, Noun Phrase, Verb, Verb Phrase, subject, object, and so on) but solely to semantic roles (e.g., agent or theme). Italian children, as we have seen, inflect the verb to agree in person and number with the subject:

(1) Tu leggi il libro	"You read (2nd person singular) the book."
(2) Gira il pallone	"Turns (3rd person singular) the balloon."
	(The balloon turns.)

Subject–verb agreement cannot be semantically based, because the subject is an agent in utterance (1) but not in (2). Instead, agreement must be based on whatever noun phrase is the subject, a syntactic relationship.

Hyams (1986) upholds this position by reference to other kinds of agreement, such as the "modifier–noun agreement" illustrated earlier. There is nothing intrinsically masculine or feminine about nouns marked for such grammatical gender. But children produce the correct forms based on the syntactic classification of these nouns.

Children learning other languages with similar agreement rules, such as Russian, Polish, or Turkish, show the same ability to discover the structures of their language. Their grammars from an early stage reveal their knowledge of the kinds of structure dependencies mentioned in Chapter 3.

In our discussion of telegraphic speech, we noted that at this stage children's utterances consist mainly of content words from the major classes of nouns, verbs, and adjectives and do not include grammatical morphemes — free-standing words or bound inflections. In the course of syntactic development, these categories will change.

Interestingly, utterances produced with these categories missing are all possible in some human language. English-speaking children produce subject-less sentences such as *See ball*, a grammatical sentence in Italian (*Vedo la palla*). Sentences without the copular verb *be* are also produced, and such sentences are common in the adult language in Russian or Hebrew. Languages such as Japanese and Chinese do not have articles; Italian permits an article and a possessive pronoun in a noun phrase, which is not permitted in English — *Il mio libro* but not **The my book*. We see that even the deviant sentences produced by children are within the range of what could be a human language; at an early stage of development, children have not yet discovered which sentences are grammatical, and which are not, in the language they are acquiring. This parallels the fact that in the babbling stage children produce sounds that are possible speech sounds and must learn which sounds are in and which are out of their language.

Just as adult languages are governed by universal characteristics, so too the child's grammar, while differing from the adult grammar in specific ways, follows universal principles.

Learning the Meanings of Words[3]

> Suddenly I felt a misty consciousness as of something forgotten — a thrill of returning thought; and somehow the mystery of language was revealed to me. ... Everything had a name, and each name gave birth to a new thought.
>
> Helen Keller, *My Life*

Most people do not see the acquisition of the meanings of words as posing a great problem. The intuitive view is that children look at an object, the mother or father says a word, and the child connects the sounds with the particular object. However, this is not as easy a task as one might think:

> A child who observes a cat sitting on a mat also observes ... a mat supporting a cat, a mat under a cat, a floor supporting a mat and a cat, and so on. If the adult now says "The cat is on the mat" even while pointing to the cat on the

mat, how is the child to choose among these interpretations of the situation? (Gleitman and Wanner 1982)

Even if the adult simply says *cat*, and the child by accident associates the word with the animal on the mat, the child may interpret *cat* as *Cat*, the name of a particular animal or of an entire species.

Children also overgeneralize the meanings of words. They may learn a word such as *papa* or *daddy* that they first use only for their own father and then extend its meaning to apply to all men. After the child has acquired her first 75 to 100 words, the overgeneralized meanings become narrowed until the meanings of these words are those of the other speakers of the language. How this occurs is also not easy to explain.

The mystery surrounding the acquisition of word meanings has intrigued philosophers and psychologists as well as linguists. It has been observed that children view the world in a similar fashion. They first learn "basic level" terms such as *cat* before learning the larger class word *animal*. Various studies have also shown that, if an experimenter points to an object and uses a nonsense word such as *blick*, saying *That's blick*, the child will interpret the word to refer to the whole object, not to one of its parts or attributes.

Furthermore, as a child is learning the meanings of words, she is also learning the syntax of the language and the syntactic categories. Psycholinguists such as Gleitman suggest that the syntax helps the child to acquire meaning, pointing out that a child will interpret a word such as *blicking* as a verb if the word is used while the investigator points to an action being performed and that she will interpret the word *blick* as a noun if the investigator uses it in the expression *a blick* or *the blick* while looking at the same picture. For example, suppose a child is shown a picture of some funny animal jumping up and down and hears either *See the blicking* or *See the blick*; later, when asked to show *blicking*, the child will jump up and down, but if asked to show a *blick* she will point to the funny animal. Gleitman calls this process **bootstrapping**; children use their knowledge of syntax to learn whether a word is a verb, and thus has a meaning referring to an action, or whether the word is a noun and thus refers to an object.

The Biological Foundations of Language Acquisition

Just as birds have wings, man has language.
George Henry Lewes (1817–1878)

The ability of children to form complex rules and construct the grammars of the languages used around them in a relatively short time is indeed phenomenal. The similarity of the language acquisition stages across diverse peoples and languages shows that children are equipped with special abilities to know what generalizations to look for, what to ignore, and how to discover the regularities of language. Children learn language the way they learn to sit up or walk. They are not taught these things, but all normal children begin to do so at around the same age. "Learning to walk" or "learning language" is different from "learning to read" or "learning to ride a bicycle." Many people never learn to read because they are not taught to do so, and there are large groups of people in many parts of the world who do not have any written language. However, they all have language.

The Innateness Hypothesis

> How comes it that human Beings, whose contacts with the world are brief and personal and limited, are able to know as much as they do know?
>
> Bertrand Russell, *Human Knowledge: Its Scope and Limits* (1948)

A major question concerning the **logical problem of language acquisition** was posed by Noam Chomsky: "What accounts for the ease, rapidity and uniformity of language acquisition in the face of impoverished data?"

The acquisition of language seems to be easy for children. They needn't be taught the complex rules of language. On the other hand, it is far from easy for a student of linguistics trying to solve a syntax problem in another language, so it can't be that the task itself is easy.

Acquisition is rapid: only two years elapse from the time children produce their first word at around the age of 1 until the major part of the grammar is acquired at around 3. Acquisition is uniform across children and languages; children learning the thousands of languages with all their surface differences go through the same stages of phonological, morphological, and syntactic rule acquisition. Although children hear many utterances, the language that is heard is incomplete, noisy, and unstructured. The utterances include slips of the tongue, false starts, ungrammatical and incomplete sentences, and no information as to which utterances heard are well formed and which are not. Yet children seem to learn, or mysteriously know, aspects of the grammar for which they receive no information. This is what is meant by **impoverished data** or the **poverty of the stimulus**. For example, children at an early age learn to form questions such as the following:

Statement	**Question**
Jill is going up the hill.	Is Jill going up the hill?
Jack and Jill are going up the hill.	Are Jack and Jill going up the hill?

That doesn't seem to be too hard a rule to learn: move the auxiliary verb to the beginning of the sentence. But this rule doesn't always work:

Statement	**Question**
Jill, who is my sister, is going up the hill.	*Is Jill, who ___ my sister is, going up the hill?
	Is Jill, who is my sister, ___ going up the hill?

It is not the first auxiliary verb but the auxiliary verb of the main clause that must be moved.

The rules that children construct are **structure dependent**. That is, children use syntactic rules that depend on more than their knowledge of words. They also rely on their knowledge of syntactic structures, which are not overtly marked in the sentences they hear. This is more dramatically shown in the rules for *wh-* question formation.

Statement	Question
<u>Jack</u> went up the hill.	<u>Who</u> went up the hill?
<u>Jack and Jill</u> went up the hill.	<u>Who</u> went up the hill?
Jack and Jill went <u>to school</u>.	Jack and Jill went <u>where</u>?
Jack and <u>Jill</u> went <u>home</u>.	Jack and <u>who</u> went home?
Jill ate <u>bagels and lox</u>.	Jill ate <u>what</u>?
Jill ate cookies and <u>ice cream</u>.	Jill ate cookies and <u>what</u>?

To ask a question, the child learns to replace the Noun Phrase (NP) *Jack, Jill, ice cream,* or *school,* or the coordinate NPs *Jack and Jill* or *bagels and lox,* with the appropriate *wh-* question word, *who, what,* or *where.*

It seems as if the *wh-* phrase can replace any NP subject or object, but in coordinate structures the *wh-* word must stay in the original NP. It can't be moved, as the following sentences show:

*Who did Jack and _____ go up the hill?
*What did Jill eat bagels and _____?

These sentences are starred because they are ungrammatical, yet the following are acceptable:

Statement	Question
Jill ate bagels with lox.	What did Jill eat bagels with _____?
Jack went up the hill with Jill.	Who did Jack go up the hill with _____?

What accounts for the difference between the "and" questions that are ungrammatical and the "with" questions that are well formed? *Bagels and lox* is a coordinate NP — that is, two NPs conjoined with *and* (NP *and* NP). But *bagels with lox* is not a coordinate NP but an NP composed of an NP followed by a Prepositional Phrase (NP + PP), as shown in the following diagrams:

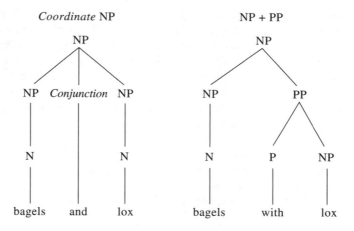

In English and all other languages that have been investigated, there seems to be a **coordinate structure constraint** that prohibits the movement of a *wh-* phrase out of a **coordinate structure**. Children make lots of mistakes in their early sentences, but as mentioned earlier they do not produce sentences that could not be sentences in some human language (e.g., the starred sentences above). No one has told them these sentences are not permitted. No one corrects them since they never utter them.

The factors mentioned above — ease and rapidity of acquisition despite impoverished input and uniformity across children and languages — have led to the **innateness hypothesis** of child language acquisition, which posits not only that the human species is genetically prewired to acquire language but also that the kind of language is determined. The principles referred to as Universal Grammar (UG) determine the class of human languages that can be acquired unconsciously, without instruction, in the early years of life. This Universal Grammar underlies the specific grammars of all languages. It is what we refer to as the genetically determined language faculty of the left hemisphere of the brain.

The innateness hypothesis predicts that all languages will conform to the principles of UG. We are still far from understanding the full nature of the principles of UG. Research on more and more languages provides a way to test principles, such as the coordinate structure constraint that have been posited to be part of our genetic prewiring. If we investigate some language in which posited UG principles are violated, then we will have to correct our theory and substitute other principles. But there seems to be little doubt that the human brain is specially equipped for acquisition of human language grammars.

The Critical Age Hypothesis

It has been suggested that there is a **critical age** for language acquisition or at least for language acquisition without special teaching and without the need for special learning. During this period, language learning proceeds easily, swiftly, and without external intervention. After this period, acquisition of the grammar is difficult and, for some individuals, never fully achieved.

The notion of a critical age is true of many species and seems to pertain to species-specific, biologically triggered behaviour. Ducklings, for example, during the period from nine to 21 hours after hatching, will follow the first moving object they see, whether or not it looks like a duck. Such behaviour is not the result of conscious decision or external teaching or intensive practice. Its emergence unfolds in a maturationally determined order universal across the species.

In a seminal contribution to the study of the biological basis of language, Eric Lenneberg (1967) first proposed that the ability to learn a native language develops within a fixed period, from birth to puberty.

There have been a number of cases of children reared in environments of extreme social isolation who constitute "experiments in nature" for testing the critical age hypothesis. Such reported cases go back at least to the eighteenth century. In 1758, Carl Linnaeus first included *Homo ferus* (wild or feral human) as a subdivision of

Homo sapiens. According to Linnaeus, a defining characteristic of *Homo ferus* was lack of speech or observable language of any kind. All the cases in the literature support his view.

The most dramatic cases of children raised in isolation are those described as "wild" or "feral" children, who have reportedly been reared with wild animals or have lived alone in the wilderness. In 1920, two feral children, Amala and Kamala, were found in India, supposedly having been reared with wolves. A celebrated case, documented in François Truffaut's film *The Wild Child*, is that of Victor, "the wild boy of Aveyron," who was found in 1798. It was ascertained that he had been left in the woods when a very young child and had somehow survived.

There are other cases of children whose isolation resulted from deliberate efforts to keep them from normal social intercourse. As recently as 1970, a child, called Genie in the scientific reports, was discovered confined to a small room under conditions of physical restraint and had received only minimal human contact from the age of 18 months until almost 14 years (Curtiss 1977). None of these children, regardless of the cause of isolation, was able to speak or knew any language at the time of reintroduction to society.

This linguistic inability could simply be because they received no linguistic input, showing that the innate neurological ability of the human brain to acquire language must be triggered by language. In the documented cases of Victor and Genie, however, they were unable to acquire language after exposure and even with deliberate and painstaking linguistic teaching.

Genie did begin to acquire some language, but while she was able to learn a large vocabulary, including colours, shapes, objects, natural categories, and abstract as well as concrete terms, her syntax and morphology never fully developed. Susan Curtiss (1977), who worked with Genie for a number of years after she was found, reports that Genie's utterances were, for the most part, "the stringing together of content words, often with rich and clear meaning but with little grammatical structure." Many of the utterances produced by Genie at the age of 15 and older, a number of years after her emergence from isolation, were like those of children in the telegraphic stage and like those of Paul Pierre Broca's aphasia patients:

> Man motorcycle have.
> Genie full stomach.
> Genie bad cold live father house.
> Want Curtiss play piano.
> Open door key.

Genie's utterances lacked auxiliary verbs, the third person singular agreement marker, the past tense marker, and most pronouns. Genie did not invert subjects and verbs to form questions. She started learning language after the critical age and was never able to acquire fully the morphological and syntactic rules of English, a fact that supports the hypothesis.

The case of Chelsea also supports the critical age hypothesis. She was born deaf and was wrongly diagnosed as retarded. Her devoted and caring family never believed this to be true but did not know that she was deaf. When she was 31, a neurologist finally diagnosed her deafness, and she was fitted with hearing aids. She received extensive language therapy and was able to acquire a large vocabulary but, like Genie, has not yet reached the syntactic level of even a 3-year-old child.

More than 90 percent of children who are born deaf or become deaf before they have acquired language are born to hearing parents. These children have also provided information about the critical age for language acquisition. Because most of their parents do not know sign language at the time of their birth, many of these children receive delayed language exposure. A number of studies have investigated the acquisition of American Sign Language (ASL) among deaf signers exposed to the language at different ages. According to Elissa Newport of the University of Rochester, early learners who received ASL input from birth up to 6 years of age did much better in the production and comprehension of morphologically complex signs than did learners who were not exposed to ASL until after the age of 12. There was little difference, however, in the vocabularies or the word-order constraints (which are very regular in ASL).

Genie, other such isolated children, and deaf children show that children cannot fully acquire any language to which they are exposed unless they are within the critical age. Beyond the critical age, the human brain appears to be unable to acquire much of syntax and inflectional morphology. In humans, then, the critical age for language acquisition pertains not to all of language but to specific components of the grammar.

The Acquisition of Bird Songs

For some bird species, there is no critical age. They do not "learn" at all; the cuckoo will sing a fully developed song even if it never hears another cuckoo sing. These communicative messages are clearly innate. For other species, songs appear to be completely learned; the bullfinch, for example, will learn any song it is exposed to, even that of another species, however "unbullfinch-like" it may be. There do not appear to be any "bullfinch universals."

The chaffinch represents a different acquisition pattern. Certain calls and songs of this species will vary depending on the geographical "dialect" area that the bird inhabits. The message is the same, but the "pronunciation" or form is different. Usually, a young bird will exhibit a basic version of the song shortly after hatching, and later it will undergo further learning in acquiring its final "dialect" version of the song. Since birds from the same brood will acquire different dialects depending on the area in which they finally settle, part of the song must be learned. Since a fledgling chaffinch will sing the song of its species in a simple, degraded form, even if it has never heard it sung, some aspect of "language" is biologically determined — that is, it is innate.

The chaffinch acquires its fully developed song in several stages, just as human children appear to acquire language in several stages. Furthermore, the chaffinch brain may also be lateralized for language, a subject that will be discussed in Chapter 11.

A critical age in the song learning of chaffinches, white-crowned sparrows, zebra finches, and other species has been observed. If these birds are not exposed to the songs of their species during certain fixed periods after their birth (the period differs from species to species), then song acquisition does not occur. The chaffinch is unable to learn new song elements after 10 months of age. If it is isolated from other birds before attaining the full "grammar" and is then re-exposed after ten months, its song will not develop further. If white crowns lose their hearing during a critical period *after* they have learned to sing, then they produce a song that differs from that of other white crowns; they need to hear themselves sing to produce particular whistles and other song features. If, however, the deafness occurs after the critical period, then the songs are normal.

From the point of view of human language research, the relationship between the innate and the learned aspects of bird songs is significant. Apparently, the basic nature of the songs of some species occurs within a critical period. Similarly, it appears that the basic nature of human language is biologically determined, whereas the details of languages that make them different from each other are learned, and the learning must occur within a critical period.

The Acquisition of ASL

Given the universal aspects of **sign languages** and spoken languages, it is not surprising that deaf children of deaf signing parents parallel the stages of spoken language acquisition. They babble, then progress to single signs similar to the single words in the holophrastic stage, and then begin to combine signs. There is also a telegraphic stage in which the grammatical signs are omitted. Grammatical or function signs appear at about the same age for deaf children as function words in spoken languages do for hearing children.

Deaf children's acquisition of the negative morphemes in American Sign Language (ASL) shows much the same pattern as in spoken language (Bellugi and Klima 1976). NO and NEG (a headshake) are frequently used signs in adult ASL, with different restrictions on their use. Children acquiring ASL use them interchangeably in initial position of a signed sentence, in the same way that hearing children start negative sentences with *no*, but not in the ways in which negative signs are used in adult ASL. We see that the acquisition of ASL cannot be simple imitation any more than spoken language is acquired simply by imitation.

Hearing children of deaf parents acquire both sign language and spoken language when exposed to both, although studies have shown that the child's first signs emerge a few months before the first spoken words. It is interesting that deaf children appear to begin producing signs earlier than hearing children begin producing spoken words. It has been suggested that this timing may be because control of hand muscles develops earlier than control of oral and laryngeal muscles.

Deaf children of hearing parents who are not exposed to manual sign language from birth suffer a great handicap in acquiring language, yet language learning ability seems to be so strong in humans that even they begin to develop their own manual gestures to express their thoughts and desires. A study of six such children revealed that they not only developed individual signs but also joined pairs and formed sentences (up to thirteen "words") with definite syntactic order and systematic constraints.

This fact, of course, should not be surprising; sign languages are as grammatical and systematic as spoken languages. We saw in Chapter 1 that the signs are conventional or arbitrary and not imitative. Furthermore, because all languages change over time, just as there are many different spoken languages, so too there are many different sign languages, all of which (spoken and sign) reveal the same linguistic universals. Deaf children often sign themselves to sleep just as hearing children talk themselves to sleep; deaf children report that they dream in sign language, just as French-speaking children dream in French and Hopi-speaking children dream in Hopi. Deaf children sign to their dolls and stuffed animals; slips of the hand occur as do slips of the tongue; finger fumblers amuse signers as tongue twisters amuse speakers. We see that sign languages resemble spoken languages in all major aspects, showing that there truly are universals of language despite differences in the modality in which the language is performed. This universality is predictable because language is biologically based.

Learning a Second (or Third or ...) Language

> He that understands grammar in one language, understands it in another as far as the essential properties of Grammar are concerned. The fact that he can't speak, nor comprehend, another language is due to the diversity of words and their various forms, but these are the accidental properties of grammar.
>
> Roger Bacon (1214–1294)

Those who have attempted to learn a second language in school or when visiting a foreign country know that it is different from learning their native language. Even talented language learners require some instruction, if only from a dictionary and a grammar. Some of us are total failures at second-language learning. We may be extremely fluent in our native language, we may get all As in composition and write beautiful poetry, but still be unable to learn another language.

The younger we are, the easier it seems to be to learn a language. Language is unique in that no other complex system of knowledge is more easily acquired at the age of 2 or 3 than at the age of 13 or 20.

Children who are exposed to more than one language before the age of puberty seem to acquire all the languages equally well. Many bilingual and multilingual speakers acquired their languages early in life. Sometimes one language is the first learned, but if the child is exposed to additional languages at an early age they will also be learned.

The critical age hypothesis discussed above was first proposed to explain the dramatic differences between a child's ease in learning a first language and the difficulty in learning a second language (L2) after puberty. It was believed that these differences could not be fully accounted for by the psychological, physical, and sociological factors present in second-language acquisition that could impede the learning process.

Many adults, for example, who are self-conscious about making mistakes, often find learning L2 very difficult. This is not a problem for children, who are unaware that they are making mistakes. The situation in which second-language learning takes place will also have an influence on one's success. Many individuals attempt to learn an L2 by taking a class in high school or university. The student is exposed to the language only in a formal situation and usually for no more than a few hours a week. Even in intensive courses, the learner does not receive constant input or feedback.

On the other hand, due to the universal characteristics of human language, adults who know one language already know much about the underlying structure of every language. This is shown by the stages in second-language acquisition, which are similar to those in first-language acquisition. For example, Carol Chomsky (1969) found that in the earliest years children learning English naïvely interpret sentences such as *John is easy to see* as *It is easy for John to see*. French speakers learning English seem to go through a similar stage. Yet this cannot be due to any interference from French grammar, because in this sense French is similar to English. The acquisition of grammatical morphemes (both bound and free) in learning English as a second language proceeds in a similar order to children's acquisition no matter what the system is in the native language of the learner. However, interference from one's native phonology, morphology, and syntax can create difficulties that persist as a foreign accent in phonology and in the use of non-native syntactic structures.

Theories of Second-Language Acquisition

There are alternative theories regarding the acquisition of L2. Stephen Krashen (1982) has proposed a distinction between acquisition — the process by which children unconsciously acquire their native language — and learning, which he defines as "conscious knowledge of a second language, knowing the rules, being aware of them, and being able to talk about them."

A similar view suggests that the principles of Universal Grammar hold only during the critical period mentioned above, after which general learning mechanisms, not specific to language acquisition, operate in learning L2.

A second theory proposes that L2 is acquired on the same universal innate principles that govern L1 acquisition, which is why one finds the same stages of development, even if the complete L2 grammar is not acquired because non-linguistic factors are at work.

Children acquire their first language without explicit learning. A second language is usually learned but to some degree may also be acquired or "picked up," depending on the environmental setting and the input received by the second-language learner.

More research and evidence are required before this interesting question can be resolved.

Second-Language Teaching Methods

Many approaches to foreign-language instruction have developed over the years. In one method, **grammar-translation**, the student memorizes words, inflected words, and syntactic rules and uses them to translate from English to L2 and vice versa. The **direct method** abandons memorization and translation; the native language is never used in the classroom, and the structure of L2 or how it differs from the native language is not discussed. The direct method attempts to stimulate learning a language as if the students found themselves in a foreign country without anyone except native speakers to talk to. The direct method seems to assume that adults can learn a foreign language in the way they learned their native language as children. Practically, it is difficult to duplicate the social, psychological, or physical environment of the child or even the number of hours that the learner is exposed to the language to be learned, even if there is no critical age factor.

An **audio-lingual** language-teaching method is based on the assumption that language is acquired mainly through imitation, repetition, and reinforcement. If this is so for second-language acquisition, then it differs vastly from what we know about first-language acquisition.

Most individual methods have serious limitations. Probably a combination of many methods is required as well as motivation on the part of the student, intensive and extensive exposure, native- or near–native-speaking teachers who can serve as models, and instructional material that is based on linguistic analysis of all aspects of the language.

Can Chimps Learn Human Language?

> . . . It is a great baboon, but so much like man in most things . . . I do believe it already understands much English; and I am of the mind it might be taught to speak or make signs.
>
> Entry in Samuel Pepys's Diary, August 1661

In this chapter, the discussion has centred on *human* language acquisition ability. Recently, much effort has been expended to determine whether non-human primates (chimpanzees, monkeys, gorillas, and so on) can learn human language. In their natural habitats, primates communicate with each other in systems that include visual, auditory, olfactory, and tactile signals. Many of these signals seem to have meaning associated with the animals' immediate environment or emotional state. They can signal danger and communicate aggressiveness and subordination. Females of some species emit a specific call indicating that they are anestrous (sexually quiescent), which inhibits attempts by males to copulate. However, the natural sounds and gestures produced by all non-human primates show their signals to be highly stereotyped and limited in the type and number of messages they convey. Their basic vocabularies occur primarily as emotional responses to particular situations. They have no way of expressing the anger they felt yesterday or the anticipation of tomorrow.

Despite their limited natural systems of communication, there has been an interest in whether these animals may have a capacity for acquiring more complex linguistic systems that are similar to human language.

Gua

In the 1930s, Winthrop and Luella Kellogg raised their infant son with an infant chimpanzee named Gua to determine whether a chimpanzee raised in a human environment and given language instruction could learn a human language. Gua understood about 100 words at 16 months, more words than their son at that age, but she never went beyond that. Moreover, comprehension of language involves more than understanding the meanings of isolated words. When their son could understand the difference between *I say what I mean* and *I mean what I say*, Gua could not understand either sentence.

Viki

A chimpanzee named Viki was raised by Keith and Cathy Hayes, and she too learned a number of individual words, even learning to articulate with great difficulty the words *mama, papa, cup*, and *up*. That was the extent of her language production.

Washoe

Allen and Beatrice Gardner recognized that one disadvantage suffered by the primates was their physical inability to pronounce many different sounds. Without a sufficient number of phonemic contrasts, spoken human language is impossible. Many species of primates are manually dexterous, and this fact inspired the Gardners to attempt to teach American Sign Language (ASL) to a chimpanzee whom they named Washoe, after the Nevada county in which they lived. Washoe was brought up in much the same way as a human child in a deaf community, constantly in the presence of people who used ASL. She was deliberately taught to sign, whereas children raised by deaf signers acquire sign language without explicit teaching, just as hearing children learn spoken language.

By the time Washoe was 4 years old (June 1969), she had acquired 85 signs with meanings such as "more," "eat," "listen," "gimme," "key," "dog," "you," "me," "Washoe," and "hurry." According to the Gardners, Washoe was also able to produce sign combinations such as "baby mine," "you drink," "hug hurry," "gimme flower," and "more fruit."

Sarah

At about the same time that Washoe was growing up, David Premack attempted to teach a chimpanzee, named Sarah, an artificial language designed to resemble human languages in some aspects. The "words" of Sarah's "language" were differently shaped and coloured plastic chips that were metal-backed. Sarah and her trainers "talked" to each other by arranging these symbols on a magnetic board. Sarah was taught to associate particular symbols with particular meanings. The form–meaning relationship of these "morphemes" or "words" was arbitrary; a small red square meant "banana," and a small blue rectangle meant "apricot," while the colour red was represented by a grey chip and the colour yellow by a black chip. Sarah learned a number of "nouns," "adjectives," and "verbs" and symbols for abstract concepts, such as "same as" and "different from," "negation," and "question."

There were drawbacks to the experiment. Sarah was not allowed to "talk" spontaneously, only in response to her trainers. There was also the possibility that her trainers unwittingly provided cues and that she responded to these cues rather than to the plastic chips.

Learning Yerkish

To avoid these and other problems, Duane and Sue Rumbaugh and their associates at the Yerkes Regional Primate Research Center began in 1973 to teach a different kind of artificial language, called Yerkish, to three chimpanzees, Lana, Sherman, and Austin. Instead of plastic chips, the words, called lexigrams, are geometric symbols displayed on a computer keyboard. The computer records every button pressed; certain fixed orders of these lexigrams constitute grammatical sentences in Yerkish. The researchers, however, are particularly interested in the ability of primates to communicate using functional symbols.

Koko

Another experiment aimed at teaching sign language to primates involved a gorilla named Koko, who was taught by her trainer, Francine "Penny" Patterson. Patterson claims that Koko has learned several hundred signs, is able to put signs together to make "sentences," and is capable of making linguistic jokes and puns, composing rhymes such as BEAR HAIR (a rhyme in spoken language but not in ASL), and inventing metaphors such as FINGER BRACELET for ring.

Nim Chimpsky

In a project specifically designed to test the linguistic claims that emerged from these primate experiments, another chimpanzee, named Nim Chimpsky, who was taught ASL by an experienced teacher, was studied by H.S. Terrace and his associates (Terrace 1979). Under carefully controlled experimental conditions that included thorough record keeping and many hours of videotaping, Nim's teachers hoped to show beyond a reasonable doubt that chimpanzees have a human-like linguistic capacity, in contradiction to the view put forth by Noam Chomsky (after whom Nim was ironically named) that human language is species-specific. In the nearly four years of study, Nim learned about 125 signs, and during the last two years Nim's teachers recorded more than 20 000 utterances that incorporated two or more signs. Nim produced his first ASL sign (DRINK) after just four months, which greatly encouraged the research team at the start of the study. Their enthusiasm soon diminished when he never seemed to go much beyond the two-word stage. Terrace concluded that "his three-sign combinations do not . . . provide new information. . . . Nim's most frequent two- and three-sign combinations [were] . . . PLAY ME and PLAY ME NIM. Adding NIM to PLAY ME is simply redundant." This kind of redundancy is illustrated by a sixteen-sign utterance of Nim's: GIVE ORANGE ME GIVE EAT ORANGE ME EAT ORANGE GIVE ME EAT ORANGE GIVE ME YOU. This utterance does not sound much like the early sentences of children cited earlier.

Nim rarely signed spontaneously as do children when they begin to use language (spoken or sign). Only 12 percent of his utterances were spontaneous. Most of Nim's signing occurred only in response to prompting by his trainers and was related to eating, drinking, and playing — that is, it was stimulus-controlled. As much as 40 percent of his output was simply repetitions of signs made by the trainer. Children initiate conversations more and more frequently as they grow older, and their utterances repeat less and less of the adult's prior utterance. Some children hardly ever imitate in conversation. Children become increasingly more *creative* in their language use, but Nim showed almost no tendency toward such creativity. Furthermore, children's utterances increase in length and complexity as time progresses, finally mirroring the adult grammar, whereas Nim's "language" did not.

The lack of spontaneity and the excessive non-creative imitative nature of Nim's signing led to the conclusion that Nim's acquisition and use of language are qualitatively different from a child's. After examining the films of Washoe, Koko, and others, Terrace drew similar conclusions regarding the signing of the other primates.

Signing chimpanzees are also unlike humans in that when several of them are together they do not sign to each other as freely as humans would under similar circumstances. There is also no evidence to date that a signing chimp (or one communicating with plastic chips or computer symbols) will teach another chimp language or that its offspring will acquire language from the parent.

Clever Hans

Premack and the Rumbaughs, like Terrace, suggest that the sign language studies were too uncontrolled and that the reported results were thus too anecdotal to support the view that primates are capable of acquiring a human language. They also question whether each of the other studies, and all those attempting to teach sign language to primates, suffer from what has come to be called the Clever Hans phenomenon.

Clever Hans, a horse at the turn of the century, became famous because of his apparent ability to do arithmetic, read and spell, and even solve problems of musical harmony. He answered the questions posed by his interrogators by stamping out numbers with his hoof. It turned out, not surprisingly, that Hans did not know that

2 + 2 = 4, but he was clever enough to pick up subtle cues conveyed unconsciously by his trainer as to when he should stop tapping his hoof.

Sarah, like Clever Hans, took prompts from her trainers and her environment to produce the plastic chip sentences. In responding to the string of chips standing for

SARAH INSERT APPLE PAIL BANANA DISH

all she had to figure out was to place certain fruits in certain containers, and she could decide which by merely seeing that the apple symbol was next to the pail symbol and that the banana symbol was next to the dish symbol. There is no conclusive evidence that Sarah actually grouped strings of words into constituents. There is also no indication that Sarah would understand a *new* compound sentence of this type; the creative ability so integral to human language is not demonstrated by this act.

Problems also exist in Lana's "acquisition" of Yerkish. The Lana project was studied by Thompson and Church (1980), who were able to simulate Lana's behaviour by a computer model. They concluded that the chimp's "linguistic" behaviour can be accounted for by her learning to associate lexigrams with objects, persons, or events and to produce one of several "stock sentences" depending on situational cues (like Clever Hans).

There is another difference between the way Sarah and Lana learned whatever they learned and the way children learn language. In the case of the chimpanzees, each new rule or sentence form was introduced in a deliberate, highly constrained way. As we noted earlier, when parents speak to children they do not confine themselves to a few words in a particular order for months, rewarding the child with a chocolate bar or a banana each time the child correctly responds to a command. Nor do they wait until the child has mastered one rule of grammar before going on to a different structure. Young children require no special training.

Kanzi

Research on the linguistic ability of non-human primates continues. Two investigators, P.M. Greenfield and E. Sue Rumbaugh, studied a male pygmy chimpanzee, named Kanzi, using the same plastic lexigrams and computer keyboard that were used with Lana. They concluded that Kanzi "has not only learned, but also invented grammatical rules that may well be as complex as those used by human 2-year-old children" ("Research Notes" 1990). The grammatical rule referred to was the combination of a lexigram (e.g., that meaning "dog") with a gesture meaning "go." After combining them, Kanzi would go to an area where dogs were located to play with them. Greenfield and Rumbaugh suggest that this "ordering" rule was not an imitation of his caretakers' utterances, for his caretakers used an opposite ordering, in which "dogs" would follow "go." Needless to say, Kanzi could not use the same combination of "go" and "dog" to express the feeling of "going to the dogs."

The investigators do report that Kanzi's acquisition of "grammatical skills" was much slower than that of human children, taking about three years (he was 5 and a half years old when the study began).

Most of Kanzi's so-called sentences are fixed formulas with little if any internal structure. Kanzi has not yet exhibited linguistic knowledge of a complexity equivalent to a 3- or 4-year-old's knowledge of structure dependencies and hierarchical structure.

As often happens in science, the search for answers to one kind of question leads to answers to other questions not originally asked. The linguistic experiments with primates have led to many advances in our understanding of primate cognitive ability. Premack has gone on to investigate other capacities of the chimp mind, such as causality; the Rumbaughs and Greenfield continue to study the ability of chimpanzees to use symbols. These studies also point out how remarkable it is that human children, by the ages of 3 and 4, without explicit teaching or overt reinforcement, create complex sentences never spoken and never heard before.

Summary

When children learn a language, they learn the grammar of that language — the phonological, morphological, syntactic, and semantic rules — as well as the words or vocabulary. No one teaches them these rules; children just pick them up.

Before infants begin to produce words, they produce sounds, some of which will remain if they occur in the language being acquired, while others will disappear. They do not produce sounds that never contrast meanings in any language. Deaf children exposed at birth to sign languages also produce manual babbling, showing that **babbling** is universal in first-language acquisition and is dependent on the linguistic input received.

A child does not learn the language all at once. The grammar is acquired by stages. Children's first utterances are one-word "sentences" (the **holophrastic** stage). After a few months, the **two-word stage** arises, in which the child puts two words together. These two-word sentences are not random combinations of words; the words have definite patterns and express both grammatical and semantic relationships. Later, but still in the very early years, in what has been called the **telegraphic** stage, longer sentences appear, composed primarily of content words and lacking function or grammatical morphemes. The child's early grammar lacks many of the rules of the adult grammar but is not qualitatively different from it, and eventually it mirrors the language used in the community. Deaf children exposed to **sign language** show the same stages of language acquisition as do hearing children exposed to spoken language.

A number of theories have been suggested to explain the acquisition process. The **imitation theory**, which claims that children learn their language by imitating adult speech, the **reinforcement theory**, which hypothesizes that children are conditioned into speaking correctly by being negatively reinforced for "errors" and positively reinforced for correct usage, and the view that children learn by **analogy**, extending one sample structure to others, are not supported by observational and experimental studies. These theories cannot explain the fact that children creatively form new sentences according to the rules of their language.

The ease and rapidity of children's language acquisition and the uniformity of the stages of development for all children and all languages, despite the **poverty of the stimulus** children receive, suggest that the language faculty is innate and that the infant comes to the complex task endowed with a **Universal Grammar** (**UG**). UG is not a grammar like the grammar of English or Arabic; rather, it represents the principles to which all human languages conform.

A **critical age hypothesis** has been proposed, and it suggests that there is a biological period during which a child may acquire the native language without overt teaching. Some songbirds also appear to have a critical period for the acquisition of their calls and songs.

Acquisition of a second or third language parallels acquisition of one's first native language. If a second language is learned early in life, it is usually acquired with no difficulty. The difficulties encountered in attempting to learn languages after puberty may occur because they are learned after the critical age for language learning. One theory of second-language acquisition suggests that the same principles operate that account for first-language acquisition. A second view suggests that, in acquiring a second language after the critical age, general learning mechanisms rather than principles specifically linguistic are used. A number of second-language teaching methods have been proposed, some of them reflecting different theories of the nature of language and language acquisition. These methods, however, do not explain the apparent differences between first- and second-language acquisition.

Questions as to whether language is unique to the human species have led researchers to attempt to teach non-human primates systems of communication that purportedly resemble human language. Chimpanzees such as Sarah and Lana have been taught to manipulate symbols to gain rewards, and other chimpanzees, such as Washoe and Nim Chimpsky, have been taught a number of ASL signs. A careful examination of the "utterances" in ASL by these chimps shows that, unlike the language of children, their language exhibits little spontaneity, is highly imitative (echoic), and reveals little syntactic structure. It has been suggested that the pygmy chimp, Kanzi, shows grammatical ability greater than that of the other chimps studied, but he still does not have the ability of even a 3-year-old child.

The universality of the language acquisition process, of the stages of development, and of the relatively short period in which the child constructs such a complex grammatical system without overt teaching, and the limited results of the chimpanzee experiments, suggest that the human species is innately endowed with special language acquisition abilities, that language is biologically and genetically part of the human neurological system.

All normal children everywhere learn language. This ability is not dependent on race, social class, geography, or even intelligence (within a normal range). This ability is uniquely human.

Notes

1. We specially thank John Peregrine Munro for providing us with such rich data and Drs. Pamela and Allen Munro, J.P.'s parents, for their painstaking efforts in recording these data.
2. All the examples given in this chapter are taken from utterances by children observed by the authors or reported in the literature. The various sources are listed in the Further Reading section at the end of the chapter.
3. We wish to acknowledge the contribution to this section of Lila Gleitman (1991) and her chapter "Language" in *Psychology*, 3rd ed. H. Gleitman, Ed. New York: Norton.

Exercises

1. "Baby talk" is a term used to label the word forms that many adults use when speaking to children. Examples in English are *choo-choo* for "train" and *bow-wow* for "dog." Baby talk seems to exist in every language and culture. At least two things seem to be universal about baby talk: the words that have baby talk forms fall into certain semantic categories (e.g., food and animals), and the words are phonetically simpler than the adult forms (e.g., *tummy* /tʌmi/ for "stomach" /stʌmək/). List all the baby talk words you can think of in your native language; then (1) separate them into semantic categories, and (2) try to state general rules for the kinds of phonological "reductions" or "simplifications" that occur.

2. In this chapter, the way a child learns negation of sentences and question formation was discussed. Can they be considered examples of a process of overgeneralization in syntax acquisition? If so, for each stage indicate *what* is being overgeneralized.

3. With the permission of his or her parents, play with a child between 2 and 4 years of age for about 30 minutes. Keep a list of all words and/or "sentences" that are used inappropriately. Describe what the child's meanings for these words probably are. Describe the syntactic or morphological errors (including omissions). If the child produces multiword sentences, write a grammar that could account for the data you have collected.

4. Chomsky has been quoted as saying,

   > It's about as likely that an ape will prove to have a language ability as that there is an island somewhere with a species of flightless birds waiting for human beings to teach them to fly.

In the light of evidence presented in this chapter, comment on Chomsky's remark. Do you agree or disagree, or do you think the evidence is inconclusive?

*5. Roger Brown and his co-workers at Harvard University (see Brown 1973) studied the language development of three children, referred to in the literature as Adam, Eve, and Sarah. The following are samples of their utterances during the "two-word stage."

see boy	push it
see sock	move it
pretty boat	mommy sleep
pretty fan	bye-bye melon
more taxi	bye-bye hot
more melon	

   A. Assume that the above utterances are grammatical sentences in the children's grammars.

   (1) Write a mini-grammar that would account for these sentences. One rule might apply to more than one sentence.

   Example: One rule might be S → V N.

   (2) Draw phrase structure trees for each utterance.

   Example:

   B. One observation made by Brown was that many of the sentences and phrases produced by the children were ungrammatical from the point of view of the adult grammar. The research group concluded, based on utterances such as those below, that a rule in the children's grammar for a Noun Phrase (NP) was

NP → M N (where M = any modifier)

a coat	my stool	poor man
a celery	that knee	little top
a Becky	more coffee	dirty knee
a hands	more nut	that Adam
my mummy	two tinker-toy	big boot

   (3) Mark with an asterisk any of the above NPs that are ungrammatical in the adult grammar of English. Use a question mark for any that could be grammatical in adult speech under certain circumstances, and define those circumstances.

(4) State the "violation" for each starred item. For example, if one of the utterances were *Lotsa book,* you might say "The modifier *lotsa* must be followed by a plural noun."

*6. In the holophrastic (one-word) stage of child language acquisition, the child's phonological system differs in systematic ways from that in the adult grammar. The inventory of sounds and the phonemic contrasts are smaller, and there are greater constraints on phonotactics. (See Chapter 6 for a discussion on these aspects of phonology.)

A. For each of the following words produced by a child, state what the substitution is.

Example: spook (adult) [spuk], (child) [pʰuk]

Substitution: initial cluster [sp] reduced to single consonant; /p/ becomes aspirated, showing that child has acquired aspiration rule.

1.	don't	[dot]	7.	bath	[bæt]
2.	skip	[kʰɪp]	8.	chop	[tʰap]
3.	shoe	[su]	9.	kitty	[kʰɪdi]
4.	that	[dæt]	10.	light	[wajt]
5.	play	[pʰe]	11.	dolly	[dawi]
6.	thump	[dʌp]	12.	grow	[go]

B. State some general rules that account for the children's deviation from adult pronunciations.

7. Children learn demonstrative words such as *this, that, these,* and *those*; temporal terms such as *now, then,* and *tomorrow*; and spatial terms such as *here, there, right,* and *behind* relatively late. What do all these words have in common? Why might that factor delay their acquisition?

8. We saw in this chapter how children overgeneralize rules such as the plural rule, producing forms such as *mans* and *mouses.* What might a child learning English use instead of the adult words given below?

a.	children	f.	sang
b.	went	g.	geese
c.	better	h.	worst
d.	best	i.	knives
e.	brought	j.	worse

Works Cited

Bellugi, U., and E.S. Klima. 1976. "The Roots of Language in the Sign Talk of the Deaf." *Psychology Today* 6: 60–64.

Berko, J. 1958. "The Child's Learning of English Morphology." *Word* 14: 150–77.

Bloom, L.M. 1972. *Language Development: Form and Function in Emerging Grammar.* Cambridge, MA: MIT Press.

Brown, R.O. 1973. *A First Language: The Early Stages.* Cambridge, MA: Harvard University Press.

Cazden, C. 1972. *Child Language and Education.* New York: Holt, Rinehart and Winston.

Chomsky, Carol. 1969. *The Acquisition of Syntax in Children from Five to Ten.* Cambridge, MA: MIT Press.

Chomsky, Noam. 1965. *Aspects of the Theory of Syntax.* Cambridge, MA: MIT Press.

Curtiss, S. 1977. *Genie: A Linguistic Study of a Modern-Day "Wild Child."* New York: Academic Press.

Gleitman, Lila. 1991. "Language." *Psychology.* 3rd. ed. Ed. H. Gleitman. New York: Norton.

———. 1994. *The Human Language Series: Program 2 by Gene Searchinger.* New York: Equinox Films/Ways of Knowing.

Gleitman, Lila R., and Eric Wanner. 1982. *Language Acquisition: The State of the Art.* Cambridge, UK: Cambridge University Press.

Hyams, Nina. 1986. *Language Acquisition and the Theory of Parameters.* Dordrecht, The Netherlands: Reidel Publishers.

Jakobson, R. 1941. *Kindersprache, Aphasie, und Allgemeine Lautgesetze.* Uppsala, Sweden: Almqvist and Wiksell. (English translation by A. Keiler. *Child Language, Aphasia, and Phonological Universals.* The Hague: Mouton, 1968.)

Krashen, Stephen D. 1982. *Principles and Practice in Second Language Acquisition.* Oxford: Pergamon Press.

Lenneberg, Eric. 1967. *The Biological Foundations of Language.* New York: Wiley.

Petitto, L.A., and P.F. Marantette. 1991. "Babbling in the Manual Mode: Evidence for the Ontogeny of Language." *Science* 251: 1493–96.

"Research Notes." 1990. *Chronicle of Higher Education* 37.

Russell, Bertrand. 1948. *Human Knowledge: Its Scope and Limits.* New York: Simon and Schuster.

Terrace, H.S. 1979. *Nim: A Chimpanzee Who Learned Sign Language.* New York: Knopf.

Thompson, Claudia R., and Russell M. Church. 1980. "An Explanation of the Language of a Chimpanzee." *Science* 208: 313–14.

Further Reading

Atkinson, Martin. 1992. *Children's Syntax: An Introduction to Principles and Parameters Theory.* Oxford: Blackwell.

Bowerman, M. 1973. *Early Syntactic Development.* Cambridge, MA: MIT Press.

Clark, H.H., and E.V. Clark. 1977. *Psychology and Language.* New York: Harcourt Brace Jovanovich.

de Villiers, Peter A., and Jill G. de Villiers. 1978. *Language Acquisition.* Cambridge, MA: Harvard University Press.

Ellis, R. 1985. *Understanding Second Language Acquisition.* Oxford: Oxford University Press.

Feldman, H., S. Goldin-Meadow, and L. Gleitman. 1978. "Beyond Herodotus: The Creation of Language by Linguistically Deprived Deaf Children." *Action, Symbol, and Gesture: The Emergence of Language.* Ed. A. Lock. New York: Academic Press: 351–413.

Fischer, S.D., and P. Siple. 1990. *Theoretical Issues in Sign Language Research, Vol. 1. Linguistics.* Chicago: University of Chicago Press.

Greenfield, Patricia Marks, and E. Sue Savage-Rumbaugh. 1990. *Language and Intelligence in Monkeys and Apes: Comparative Developmental Perspectives.* Cambridge, UK: Cambridge University Press.

Ingram, David. 1989. *First Language Acquisition: Method, Description, and Explanation.* New York: Cambridge University Press.

Landau, Barbara, and Lila R. Gleitman. 1985. *Language and Experience: Evidence from the Blind Child.* Cambridge, MA: Harvard University Press.

Premack, Ann J., and D. Premack. 1972. "Teaching Language to an Ape." *Scientific American* (October): 92–99.

Rumbaugh, D.M. 1977. *Acquisition of Linguistic Skills by a Chimpanzee.* New York: Academic Press.

Sandler, Wendy. 1989. *Phonological Representation of the Sign: Linearity and Nonlinearity in American Sign Language.* Dordrecht, The Netherlands: Foris Publications.

Sebeok, T.A., and Jean Umiker-Sebeok. 1980. *Speaking of Apes: A Critical Anthology of Two-Way Communication with Man.* New York: Plenum Press.

Sebeok, Thomas A., and Robert Rosenthal, eds. 1981. *The Clever Hans Phenomenon: Communication with Horses, Whales, Apes, and People.* Annals of the New York Academy of Sciences, Vol. 364.

White, Lydia. 1989. *Universal Grammar and Second Language Acquisition.* Amsterdam: John Benjamins.

CHAPTER 11
Human Processing: Brain, Mind, and Language

The nervous systems of all animals have a number of basic functions in common, most notably the control of movement and the analysis of sensation. What distinguishes the human brain is the variety of more specialized activities it is capable of learning. The preeminent example is language.

Norman Geschwind (1979)

"Rabbit's clever," said Pooh thoughtfully.
"Yes," said Piglet, "Rabbit's clever."
"And he has Brain."
"Yes," said Piglet, "Rabbit has Brain."
There was a long silence.
"I suppose," said Pooh, "that that's why he never understands anything."

A.A. Milne, *The House at Pooh Corner*

The attempts to understand the complexities of human cognitive abilities and especially the acquisition and use of language are as old and as continuous as history. Three long-standing problems of science include the nature of the brain, the nature of human language, and the relationship between the two. The view that the brain is the source of human language and cognition goes back more than over 2000 years. Assyrian and Babylonian cuneiform tablets mention disorders of intelligence that may develop "when man's brain holds fire." Egyptian doctors in 1700 B.C.E. noted in their papyrus records that "the breath of an outside god" had entered their patients, who had become "silent in sadness." The philosophers of ancient Greece also speculated about the brain–mind relationship, but neither Plato nor Aristotle recognized the brain's crucial function in cognition or language. Aristotle's wisdom failed him when he suggested that the brain is a cold sponge whose function is to cool the blood. But others writing in the same period showed greater insight; the Hippocratic treatises from about 377 B.C.E. define the brain as "the messenger of the understanding [and the organ whereby] in an especial manner we acquire wisdom and knowledge."

A major approach in the study of the brain–mind relationship has been through an investigation of language. Research on the brain in humans and in non-human primates, anatomically, psychologically, and behaviourally, is, for similar reasons, helping to answer the questions concerning the neurological basis for language. The study concerned with the biological and neural foundations of language is called **neurolinguistics**.

The Human Brain

The Two Sides of the Brain

> It only takes one hemisphere to have a mind.
>
> A.W. Wigan (1844)

We have learned a great deal about the brain — the most complicated organ of the body — in the past two millennia. It lies under the skull and consists of approximately ten billion nerve cells (**neurons**) and billions of fibres that interconnect them. The neurons or grey matter form the **cortex**, the surface of the brain, under which is white matter, which consists primarily of connecting fibres. The cortex is the decision-making organ of the body. It receives messages from all the sensory organs, and it initiates all voluntary actions. It is "the seat of all which is exclusively human in the mind" and the storehouse of "memory." Somewhere in this grey matter, the grammar that represents our knowledge of language resides.

The brain is divided into two parts (called **cerebral hemispheres**), one on the right and one on the left. These hemispheres are connected like conjoined twins right down the middle by the **corpus callosum**. This "freeway" between the two brain halves consists of two million fibres connecting the cells of the left and right hemispheres, as shown in Figure 11.1.

In general, the left hemisphere controls the movements of the right side of the body, and the right hemisphere controls the movements of the left side. If you point with your right hand, then it is the left hemisphere that has directed your action. This is referred to as **contralateral** brain function.

Since the middle of the nineteenth century, there has been a basic assumption that it is possible to find a direct relation between language and the brain and a continuous effort to discover direct centres where language capacities (competence and performance) may be localized.

In the early nineteenth century, **Franz Joseph Gall** put forth theories of **localization** — that is, that different human abilities and behaviours are traceable to specific parts of the brain. Some of Gall's views are amusing when looked at from our present state of knowledge. For example, Gall suggested that the frontal lobes of the brain are the locations of language because when he was young he had noticed that the most articulate and intelligent of his fellow students had protruding eyes, which he believed reflected overdeveloped brain material. He also put forth a pseudoscientific theory called "organology" that later came to be known as **phrenology**, the practice of determining personality traits, intellectual capacities, and other matters by examination of the "bumps" on the skull. A disciple of Gall, Johann

FIGURE 11.1

3-D reconstruction of the normal living human brain. The images were obtained from magnetic resonance data using the Brainvox technique. Left panel = view from the top. Right panel = view from the front following virtual coronal section at the level of the dashed line.

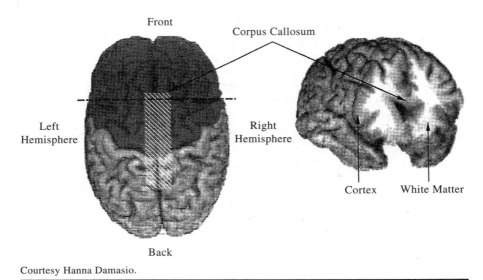

Courtesy Hanna Damasio.

Spurzheim, constructed elaborate maps and skull models, such as the one shown in Figure 11.2, in which language is located directly under the eye.

Although phrenology has long been discarded as a scientific theory, Gall's view that the brain is not a uniform mass and that linguistic capacities are functions of localized brain areas has been upheld. Gall was in fact a pioneer and a courageous scientist in arguing against the prevailing view that the brain is an unstructured organ. He argued instead in favour of **modularity**, with the brain divided into distinct anatomical faculties (referred to as cortical organs) that are directly responsible for specific cognitive functions, including language.

Language was the first distinct cognitive module to be supported by scientific evidence. In 1861, **Paul Broca** specifically related language to the left side of the brain. At a meeting in Paris, he stated that we speak with the left hemisphere on the basis of his finding that damage to the front part of the left hemisphere (now called **Broca's area**) resulted in loss of speech, whereas damage to the right side did not.[1] Language, then, is said to be **lateralized**, a term used to refer to any cognitive functions that are primarily localized to one side of the brain or the other.

Today patients with such damage or lesions in Broca's area are said to have **Broca's aphasia**. **Aphasia** is the neurological term used to refer to language disorders that follow brain lesions caused by strokes, tumours, wounds, and other traumas. The speech output of many of Broca's aphasia patients is characterized by laboured speech,

FIGURE 11.2
Phrenology skull model.

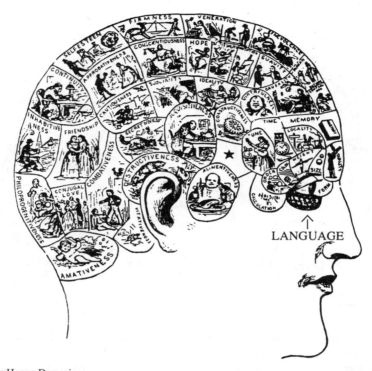

LANGUAGE

Courtesy Hanna Damasio.

word-finding pauses, loss of function words, and, quite often, disturbed word order. Auditory comprehension of colloquial conversation gives the impression of being generally good, although controlled testing reveals considerable impairments when comprehension depends on syntactic structure.

In 1874, **Carl Wernicke** described another variety of aphasia shown by patients with lesions in the back portion of the left hemisphere. Unlike Broca's patients, Wernicke's spoke fluently, with good intonation and pronunciation but with numerous instances of lexical errors (word substitutions), often producing jargon and nonsense words. They also had difficulty in comprehending speech.

The area of the brain that when damaged seems to lead to these symptoms is now, not surprisingly, known as **Wernicke's area**, and the patients are said to suffer from **Wernicke's aphasia**. Figure 11.3, a view of the left side of the brain shows the location of Broca's and Wernicke's areas.

We no longer have to depend on surgical investigations of the brain or wait until patients die to determine where their brain lesions are. New technologies such as

FIGURE 11.3

Lateral (external) view of the left hemisphere of the human brain. Note the position of the Broca and Wernicke regions — two key areas of the cortex related to language processing.

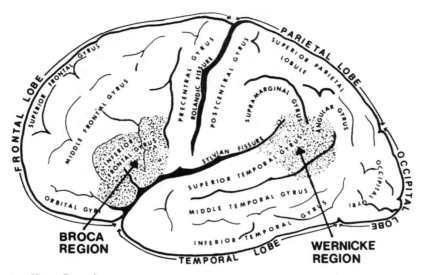

Courtesy Hanna Damasio.

magnetic resonance imaging (MRI) make it possible to see where the sites of lesions are in the living brain. In addition, the new technique called **positron emission tomography (PET)** has revolutionized the study of the brain, making it possible to detect changes in brain activities and relate these changes to focal brain damage and cognitive tasks. PET permits experimenters to look into a living normal brain and see which areas are affected when different stimuli are involved, since degrees of metabolic activity can be viewed and one can see which areas of the brain are more active than others. MRI and PET studies reaffirm the lateralization of language.

Figures 11.4 and 11.5 show the MRI scans of the brains of a Broca's aphasic patient and a Wernicke's aphasic patient. The black areas show the sites of lesions. Each diagram represents a brain "slice."

There is now a consensus that the so-called higher mental functions are greatly lateralized. Research shows that though the nervous system is generally symmetrical — that is, what exists on the left exists on the right and vice versa — the two sides of the brain form an exception.

Evidence from Childhood Brain Lesions

Children who have suffered prenatal, perinatal, or childhood brain lesions provide additional evidence that language is lateralized and that the brain is differentiated in regard to language and non-language abilities.

FIGURE 11.4

3-D reconstruction of the brain of a living patient with Broca's aphasia. Note area of damage in left frontal region (dark grey), which was caused by a stroke.

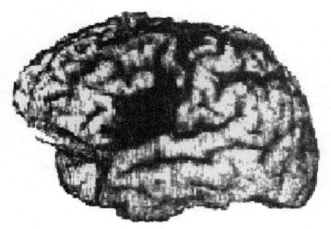

From Hanna Damasio and Antonio Damasio. *Lesion Analysis in Neuropsychology.* New York: Oxford University Press, 1989, p. 53. Courtesy Hanna Damasio.

FIGURE 11.5

3-D reconstruction of the brain of a living patient with Wernicke's aphasia. Note area of damage in left posterior temporal and lower parietal region (dark grey), which was caused by a stroke.

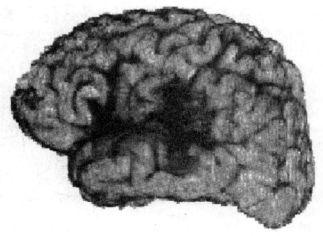

From Hanna Damasio and Antonio Damasio. *Lesion Analysis in Neuropsychology.* New York: Oxford University Press, 1989, p. 107. Courtesy Hanna Damasio.

Studies of **hemiplegic** children, those with acquired unilateral lesions of the brain who retain both hemispheres (one normal and one diseased), show differential cognitive abilities. Those with left-damaged hemispheres show deficiency in language acquisition and performance, with the greatest impairments in their syntactic ability, whereas children with right-hemisphere lesions acquire language as do normal children.

There have also been studies of children with one hemisphere removed (called **hemidecorticates**) either within the first year of life or later in childhood. Although the IQ scores and cognitive skills proved to be equivalent no matter which hemisphere was removed, children whose left hemisphere was removed outperformed in visual and spatial abilities those with the right hemisphere removed. In language, the right hemidecorticates (those with removal of the right hemisphere) surpassed the left hemidecorticates. Both hemispheres appear to be equivalent in the ability to acquire the meanings and referential structures of common words, but the ability to acquire the complex syntactic rules for sentence formation was impaired in left but not in right hemidecorticates.

Split Brains

Aphasia studies and those of early childhood brain lesions provide good evidence that language is primarily processed in the left hemisphere. Other evidence is provided by mature patients who have one of the hemispheres removed. If the right hemisphere is cut out, language remains intact, although other cognitive losses may result. Because language is such an important aspect of daily life, surgical removal of the left hemisphere is performed only in dire cases of malignant brain tumour.

"**Split-brain**" patients provide important evidence for language lateralization and for understanding brain functions. In recent years, it was found that persons suffering from serious epilepsy could be treated by cutting the corpus callosum, the membrane connecting the two hemispheres. When this pathway is split, there is no communication between the "two brains." The corpus callosum is shown in Figure 11.6.

As Michael Gazzaniga (1970) has observed,

> With ... [the corpus callosum] intact, the two halves of the body have no secrets from one another. With it sectioned, the two halves become two different conscious mental spheres, each with its own experience base and control system for behavioural operations.... Unbelievable as this may seem, this is the flavor of a long series of experimental studies first carried out in the cat and monkey.

When the brain is split surgically, certain information from the left side of the body is received only by the right side of the brain and vice versa (because of the crisscross contralateral phenomenon discussed earlier). Suppose, for example, a monkey is trained to respond with its hands to a certain visual stimulus, such as a flashing light. If the brain is split after the training period, and the stimulus is shown only to the left visual field (the right brain), the monkey will perform only with the left hand. Such experiments show the independence of the two sides of the brain.

FIGURE 11.6

Internal view of the left hemisphere of the human brain. Note the position of the corpus callosum, which joins the structures of the left and right hemispheres across the midline.

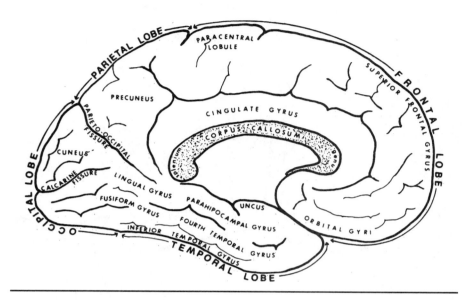

Persons with split brains show that, as in the monkey brain, the two human hemispheres are distinct. However, tests have shown that messages sent to the two sides of the brain result in different responses, depending on which hemisphere receives the message. If an apple is put in the left hand of a split-brain human whose vision is cut off, the person can use it appropriately but cannot name it. The right brain senses the apple and distinguishes it from other objects, but the information cannot be relayed to the left brain for naming. By contrast, if a banana is placed in the right hand, the subject is immediately able to name it as well as describe it (see Figure 11.7).

Various experiments of this sort have been performed, all providing information on the different capabilities of the "two brains." The right brain does better than the left in pattern-matching tasks, in recognizing faces, and in spatial orientation. The left hemisphere is superior for language, for rhythmic perception, for temporal-order judgements, and for mathematical thinking. According to Gazzaniga (1970), "the right hemisphere as well as the left hemisphere can emote and while the left can tell you why, the right cannot."

Studies of human split-brain patients have shown that, when the interhemispheric visual connections are severed, visual information from the right and left visual fields becomes confined to the left and right hemispheres, respectively. Because of the crucial endowment of the left hemisphere for language, written material delivered to the right hemisphere cannot be read if the brain is split, because the information cannot be transferred to the left hemisphere.

FIGURE 11.7

Sensory information is received in the *contralateral* (opposite) side of the brain from the side of the body from which it is sent. In a split-brain patient, the information in the right hemisphere cannot get across to the left hemisphere; for this reason, this patient cannot produce the word *apple*.

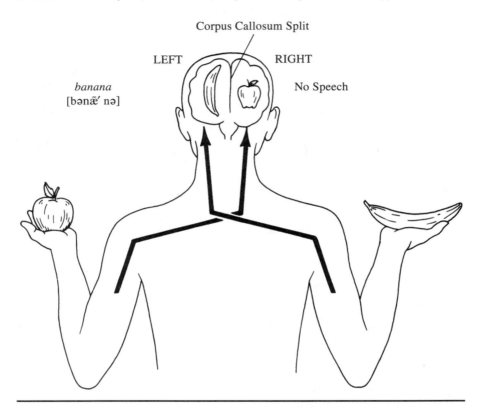

A picture that is flashed to the right visual field of a split-brain patient (and is therefore processed by the left hemisphere) can be named. However, when the picture is flashed in the left visual field and lands in the right hemisphere, it cannot be named.

More Experimental Evidence

Since Broca's proposal that "we speak with the left hemisphere," evidence to support the left lateralization continues to grow. All the early research involved brain-damaged patients. In the past few decades, however, new technologies such as PET and MRI and *f*unctional MRI or *f*MRI permit us to explore the specialized capabilities of the two hemispheres in normal individuals. Another experimental technique that has been used with normal subjects, called **dichotic listening**, uses auditory signals. Subjects hear two different sound signals simultaneously through earphones. For example, a subject may hear *boy* in one ear and *girl* in the other, or *crocodile* in one ear and *alligator* in the other, or the subject may hear a horn tooting in one ear and rushing water in the other. When asked to state what they heard in each ear, subjects are more frequently correct in reporting linguistic stimuli (words, nonsense syllables, and so on) delivered to the right ear, but they are more frequently correct in reporting non-verbal stimuli (musical chords, environmental sounds, and so on) delivered to the left ear. That is, if subjects hear *boy* in the right ear and *girl* in the left ear, they are more likely to report the word heard in the right ear correctly. If they hear coughing in the right ear and laughing in the left, they are more apt to report the laughing stimulus correctly. The same acoustic signal may be processed in one hemisphere or the other depending on whether the subjects perceive it as part of their language system or not. Thai speakers show a right-ear advantage (left hemisphere) in distinguishing between syllables that contrast in tone (pitch contours); Thai is a tone language in which syllables pronounced with different pitch are words with different meanings. English subjects do not show the right-ear advantage when they hear the same stimuli, because English is not a tone language.

Both hemispheres receive signals from both ears, but the "crossed" contralateral stimuli (right to left and vice versa) compete successfully with the "same side" **ipsilateral** stimuli, either because they are received earlier or because they are not weakened by having to cross the corpus callosum. The fact that the left hemisphere has an edge in linguistic processing and the right hemisphere is better at non-verbal material determines the accuracy with which subjects report on what they have heard.

These experiments are important not only because they show that language is lateralized, but also because they show that the left hemisphere is not superior for processing all sounds, only for those that are linguistic. That is, the left side of the brain is specialized for language, not sounds.

Other experimental techniques are also being used to map the brain and to investigate the independence of different aspects of language and the extent of the independence of language from other cognitive systems. Even before the spectacular new technologies were introduced in the 1970s, researchers were taping electrodes to different areas of the skull and investigating the electrical activity of the brain. In such experiments, the electrical signals emitted from the brain in response to different kinds of stimuli (called **event-related brain potentials** or **ERPs**) are measured. For example, electrical differences may result when the subject hears speech sounds and non-speech sounds. One study showed electrical potential differences in timing and area of response when subjects heard sentences that were meaningless, such as

*The man admired Don's headache of the landscape.

(where the asterisk shows that there is something unacceptable about the sentence), as opposed to meaningful sentences such as

The man admired Don's sketch of the landscape.

These experiments show that neuronal activity in different locations varies with different stimuli and different tasks.

The results of these studies, using different techniques and diverse subjects, both normal and brain damaged, are converging to provide the information we seek on the relationship between the brain and various language and non-language cognitive systems.

More Evidence for Modularity

> ... The human mind is not an unstructured entity but consists of components which can be distinguished by their functional properties.
>
> Neil Smith and Ianthi-Maria Tsimpli, *The Mind of a Savant* (1995)

Although neurolinguistics is still in its infancy, our understanding has progressed a great deal since a day in September 1848 when a foreman of a road construction gang named Phineas Gage became a famous figure in medical history. He achieved his "immortality" when an iron rod over a metre long was blown through his head. Despite the gaping tunnel in his brain, Gage maintained the ability to speak and understand and retained whatever intellectual abilities he had prior to the injury, although he suffered major changes in his personality (he became "cranky" and "inconsiderate"), in his sexual behaviour, and in his ability to control his emotions or make plans. Both Gage and science benefited from this explosion. Gage gained monetarily by becoming a one-man touring circus; he travelled all over the country charging money to those curious enough to see him and the iron rod. Nevertheless, he died penniless in an institution twelve years after the accident. Science benefited because brain researchers were stimulated to learn why his intelligence remained intact.

No autopsy was performed when Gage died in 1861. Dr. John Harlowe, the doctor first called after Gage's accident, convinced Gage's sister that his body should be exhumed and his skull preserved for science. This was done, and the skull and the iron bar have been kept in the Harvard Medical School since that time. Dr. Harlowe contributed to scientific knowledge in this way. Approximately 130 years after the exhumation, Dr. Hanna Damasio, a neurologist at the University of Iowa School of Medicine, using the most advanced neuro-imaging techniques and a computer program called Brainvox, was able to reconstruct Gage's brain showing the area through which the bar had travelled. She was able to show unequivocally that the damage was neither to the motor area nor to the language area of the brain but to the section called the prefrontal cortices (H. Damasio et al. 1994). Dr. Antonio Damasio and his colleagues have further shown that patients with damage to this area show the same kind of personality changes as did Gage (A. Damasio 1994).

That damage to some parts of the brain results in language loss whereas damage to other parts of the brain shows intact language with other kinds of deficits supports Gall's view of a structured brain with separate faculties.

Aphasia

The interest in aphasia goes back long before Broca. In the New Testament, St. Luke reports that Zacharias could not speak but could write, showing the early recognition of the **autonomy** of different aspects of linguistic knowledge. And in 30 B.C.E., the Roman writer Valerius Maximus described an Athenian who was unable to remember his "letters" after being hit on the head with a stone. Pliny, who lived from 23 to 79 C.E., refers to the same Athenian, noting that "with the stroke of a stone, he fell presently to forget his letters only, and could read no more; otherwise his memory served him well enough." Recognition of the loss of specific parts of language with the retention of other aspects of linguistic competence or performance and other cognitive abilities has important implications for our understanding of the neural basis for language and cognition and will be discussed further below.

It is primarily in the past 50 years that controlled scientific studies of aphasia have been conducted, providing unequivocal evidence that language is predominantly and most frequently a left-hemisphere function. In the great majority of cases, lesions on the left hemisphere result in aphasia, but injuries to the right do not (although such lesions result in perceptual difficulties, defects in pattern recognition, and other cognitive deficits). If both hemispheres were equally involved with language, this would not be the case. For some people — about a third of all left-handers — there is still lateralization, yet it is the right side that is specialized for language. In other words, the special functions are switched, but asymmetry still exists.

The language impairments suffered by aphasics are not due to any general cognitive or intellectual impairments. Nor are they due to loss of motor or sensory controls of the nerves and muscles of the speech organs or hearing apparatus. Aphasics can produce sounds and hear sounds. Whatever loss they suffer has to do only with the production or comprehension of language (or specific parts of the grammar).

This is dramatically shown by the fact that deaf signers with damage to the left hemisphere show aphasia for sign language similar to the language breakdown in hearing aphasics. Bellugi and her colleagues at the Salk Institute have found that patients with lesions in Broca's area show language deficits similar to those found in hearing patients — severe dysfluent, agrammatic sign production (Poizner, Klima, and Bellugi 1987). While deaf aphasic patients show marked sign language deficits, they have no difficulty in processing non-language visual spatial relationships, just as hearing aphasics have no problem with processing non-linguistic auditory stimuli. Thus, it is not hearing or speech that is lateralized but language.

As shown by the different symptoms of Broca's and Wernicke's aphasias, many aphasias do not show total language loss. Rather, different aspects of language are impaired. Broca's aphasics are often referred to as **agrammatic** because of their particular problems with syntax, as the following sample of the speech of an agrammatic patient with damage to Broca's area illustrates. The patient, asked what brought him back to the hospital, answered:

> Yes — ah — Monday ah — Dad — and Dad — ah — Hospital — and ah — Wednesday — Wednesday — nine o'clock and ah Thursday — ten o'clock ah

doctors — two — two — ah doctors and — ah — teeth — yah. And a doctor
— ah girl — and gums, and I. (Goodglass 1973)

As this patient illustrates, agrammatic aphasics produce non-grammatical utterances, frequently omitting words such as *a* or *the* or *was* and bound inflectional
affixes. They also have difficulty in interpreting sentences correctly when comprehension depends on syntactic structure. Thus, they have a problem with determining "who did what to whom" in passive sentences such as

The cat was chased by the dog.

where either the subject or the object of the sentence can logically be doing the chasing, since in real life cats and dogs can chase each other. But they have less difficulty with

The car was chased by the dog.

where the meaning of the sentence agrees with their non-linguistic knowledge. They
know that cars do not under normal circumstances chase dogs and thus use that
knowledge to interpret the sentence, whereas in the first sentence the interpretation
depends on a knowledge of the English passive construction. Normal speakers will
have no difficulty because they use the syntax for comprehension.

Wernicke's aphasics, on the other hand, produce fluent but often unintelligible
speech, and they have serious comprehension problems and difficulty in lexical
selection. One patient replied to a question about his health with

I felt worse because I can no longer keep in mind from the mind of the minds
to keep me from mind and up to the ear which can be to find among ourselves.

Some aphasics have difficulty naming objects presented to them, which shows a
lexical defect. Others produce semantically anomalous jargon, such as the patient
who described a fork as "a need for a schedule"; another, when asked about his poor
vision, said "My wires don't hire right." While some of these aphasics substitute
words that bear no semantic relationship to the correct word, such as calling a chair
an *engine*, others substitute words that, like normal speech errors, are related semantically, substituting, for example, *table* for *chair* or *boy* for *girl*.

Another kind of aphasia called **jargon aphasia** results in the substitution of one
phoneme for another. Thus, *table* might be pronounced as *sable*. The substituted
segments often share most of the distinctive features of the intended phonemes. An
extreme variety of phonemic jargon results in the production of nonsense forms —
non-occurring but possible words. One patient, a physician prior to his aphasia,
when asked if he was a doctor, replied:

Me? Yes, sir. I'm a male demaploze on my own. I still know my tubaboys what
for I have that's gone hell and some of them go.

The kinds of language impairment found in aphasics provide information on the
nature of the grammar. If we find that damage to different parts of the brain leads
to impairment of different components of the grammar, this is good evidence to support the models proposed by linguistics.

Patients who produce long strings of "jargon" which sound like well-formed grammatical language but which are uninterpretable show that knowledge of the sound sequences by which we represent words in our mental dictionaries can be disassociated from their meanings. That is, we may look at a picture, know what it is, but be unable to produce the string of sounds that relates to the concept.

The substitution of semantically related words provides evidence as to the organization of our mental dictionaries. The aphasics' errors are similar to word substitution errors of normal individuals in that the substituted words are not just randomly selected but are similar to the intended words either in their sounds or in their meanings. Some of the most interesting examples of such substitutions are produced by aphasic patients who become dyslexic after brain damage. Their condition is called **acquired dyslexia** because prior to the brain lesion they were normal readers (unlike developmental dyslexics, who have difficulty learning to read). One group of these patients, when reading aloud words printed on cards, produced the kinds of substitution shown in the following examples taken from Newcombe and Marshall (1984):

Stimulus	Response 1	Response 2
act	*play*	*play*
applaud	*laugh*	*cheers*
example	*answer*	*sum*
heal	*pain*	*medicine*
south	*west*	*east*

Note that these patients did not always substitute the same words in two different testing periods. In fact, at times they would read the correct word, showing that the problem was in performance (accessing the correct phonological form in the lexicon), not in competence, since they could sometimes get to the right word and produce it.

The substitution of phonologically similar words — *pool* for *tool* or *crucial* for *crucible* — also provides information on the organization of the lexicon. Words in the lexicon seem to be connected to other words by phonology and semantics.

The difference between syntactic word classes is revealed in aphasia cases by the omission of grammatical morphemes in the speech of Broca's aphasics and in some cases of acquired dyslexia. Patient G.R., cited above, who produced semantically similar word substitutions, was unable to read grammatical morphemes at all; when presented with words such as *which* or *would*, he just says "No" or "I hate those little words"; but he can read, though with many semantic mistakes, homophones of these words, as shown in the following reading errors:

Stimulus	Response	Stimulus	Response
witch	*witch*	which	*no!*
bean	*soup*	been	*no!*
hour	*time*	our	*no!*
eye	*eyes*	I	*no!*
hymn	*bible*	him	*no!*
wood	*wood*	would	*no!*

These errors suggest that the mental dictionary is divided into sublexicons, one consisting of major lexical content words and the other of grammatical morphemes. Furthermore, it suggests that these two classes of words are processed in different areas or by different neural mechanisms, further supporting the view that the brain has a complex structure. One can think of the grammar as a mental module in the brain with submodular parts.

Most of us have experienced word-finding difficulties in speaking if not in reading, as Alice does when she says

> "And now, who am I? I will remember, if I can. I'm determined to do it!" But being determined didn't help her much, and all she could say, after a great deal of puzzling, was "L, I know it begins with L."

This **tip-of-the-tongue** (**TOT**, as it is often referred to) phenomenon is not uncommon. But if you can never find the word you want, you can imagine how serious a problem aphasics have. Aphasics with such problems are said to suffer from **anomia**.

Distinct Categories of Conceptual Knowledge

Dramatic evidence for a differentiated and structured brain is provided by studies of both normal individuals and patients with lesions in other than Broca's and Wernicke's areas. Some patients have difficulty naming individuals (unique persons), others have problems with naming animals, and still others cannot name tools. The patients in each group have brain lesions in separate and distinct regions of the left temporal lobe. Through use of MRI techniques, the exact shape and location of the brain lesions of these patients were located. No overlap in the lesion sites in the three groups was found. In a follow-up study of normal subjects in a PET word-retrieval experiment, researchers found differential activation of just those sites damaged in the lesion patients when the normal subjects were asked to name persons, animals, or tools (H. Damasio et al. 1996). Further evidence for the separation of cognitive systems is provided by the neurological and behavioural findings that following brain damage some patients lose the ability to recognize sounds or colours or familiar faces while retaining all other perceptual abilities. A patient may not be able to recognize his wife when she walks into the room until she starts to talk; then he will know who she is.

The Autonomy of Language

In addition to brain-damaged individuals who have acquired and lost language, there are cases of children (without brain lesions) who have difficulties acquiring language or are much slower than the average child. These children show no other cognitive deficits; they are not autistic or retarded and have no perceptual problems. They are said to be suffering from a **specific language impairment** (**SLI**). It is only their linguistic ability that is affected.

As children with SLI show, language may be impaired while general intelligence remains intact. But can language develop normally with general intelligence impaired? If such individuals can be found, they would support the view that language does not derive from some general cognitive ability. The question as to whether the language faculty from birth is domain specific — is in our genes — or whether it is derivative of more general intelligence is controversial and receives much attention and debate among linguists, psychologists, and neuropsychologists. There is a growing body of evidence to support the view that the human animal is biologically equipped from birth with an **autonomous language faculty** that itself is highly specific and does not derive from general human intellectual ability.

Asymmetry of Abilities

The psychological literature documents numerous cases of intellectually handicapped individuals, traditionally known as "idiot savants" but more recently simply called **savants**, who, despite their disabilities in certain spheres, show remarkable talents in others. The classic cases include individuals who are superb musicians, or artists, or draftspeople but lack the simple abilities required to take care of themselves. Some of the most famous savants are human calculators who can perform complex arithmetic processes at phenomenal speed or calendrical calculators who can tell you almost instantaneously on which day of the week falls any date in the past or next century.

Until recently, most of the savants have been reported to be linguistically handicapped. They may be good mimics who, like parrots, can repeat speech but show meagre creative language ability.

While such cases strongly argue for domain-specific abilities and suggest that certain talents do not require general intelligence, they do not decisively respond to the suggestion that language is one ability that is derivative of general cognitive abilities.

The more recent literature is now reporting on cases of language savants who have acquired the highly complex grammar of their language (as well as other languages in some cases) without parallel non-linguistic abilities of equal complexity.

Laura

Jeni Yamada (1990) has studied one severely retarded young woman, named Laura, with a non-verbal IQ of 41–44, lacking almost all number concepts, including basic counting principles, drawing at a preschool level, and with a processing auditory memory span limited to three units, who at the age of 16 was asked to name some fruits and responded with *pears, apples*, and *pomegranates* and in this period produced syntactically complex sentences, such as *He was saying that I lost my battery-powered watch that I loved; I just loved that watch* or *Last year at school when I first went there, three tickets were gave out by a police last year.*

Laura cannot add 2 + 2. She is not sure of when "last year" is or whether it is before or after "last week" or "an hour ago," nor does she know how many tickets were "gave out" or whether 3 is larger or smaller than 2. Although Laura produces sentences with multiple embeddings; can conjoin verb phrases, produce passives, and inflect verbs for number and person to agree with the grammatical subject; and forms past tenses when the time adverbial structurally refers to a previous time, she cannot read or write or tell time. She does not know who the president of the United States is or what country she lives in, and she does not know her own age. Her drawings of humans resemble potatoes with stick arms and legs. Yet in a sentence-imitation task, she both detected and corrected surface syntactic and morphological errors (Yamada 1990).

Laura is but one of many examples of children who display well-developed phonological, morphological, and syntactic linguistic abilities; seemingly less developed lexical, semantic, or referential aspects of language; and severe deficits in non-linguistic cognitive development.

In addition, any notion that linguistic ability results simply from communicative abilities or develops to serve communication functions is also negated by studies of children with fully developed structural linguistic knowledge, but with an almost total absence of pragmatic or communicative skills. The ability to communicate in a social setting seems to depend on different cognitive skills than the acquisition of language does.

Christopher

Another dramatic case, that of a 29-year-old linguistic savant named Christopher, has been reported. Christopher has a non-verbal IQ of between 60 and 70 and is institutionalized because he is unable to take care of himself. He finds the tasks of buttoning a shirt, cutting his fingernails, or vacuuming the carpet too difficult. According to the detailed investigation of Christopher, his "linguistic competence in his first language is as rich and as sophisticated as that of any native speaker." Furthermore, when given written texts in some fifteen to twenty languages, he translates them immediately into English. The languages include Germanic languages such as Danish, Dutch, and German; Romance languages such as French, Italian, Portuguese, and Spanish; as well as Polish, Finnish, Greek, Hindi, Turkish, and Welsh. He learned them either from speakers who used the languages in his presence or from grammar books. The investigators of this interesting man conclude that his linguistic ability is independent of his general conceptual or intellectual ability (Smith and Tsimpli 1991).

Such cases argue against the view that linguistic ability derives from more general cognitive "intelligence," since in these cases language develops against a background of deficits in general and non-linguistic intellectual abilities.

Genetic Evidence for Language Autonomy

Studies of genetic disorders also reveal that one cognitive domain can develop normally simultaneous with abnormal development in other domains. Children with

Turner's syndrome (a chromosomal anomaly) reveal normal or advanced language simultaneous with serious non-linguistic cognitive deficits. Similarly, studies of language development in children with Williams syndrome reveal a unique behavioural profile in which there appears to be a selective preservation of linguistic functions in the face of severe general cognitive deficits.

Thus, evidence from aphasia, specific language impairments, and other genetic disorders, along with the asymmetry of abilities as revealed in linguistic savants, supports the view of language as an autonomous, genetically determined, independent, brain (mind) module.

The Linguistic Mind at Work: Human Language Processing

> No doubt a reasonable model of language use will incorporate, as a basic component, the generative grammar that expresses the speaker–hearer's knowledge of the language; but this generative grammar does not, in itself, prescribe the character or functioning of a perceptual model or a model of speech production.
>
> Noam Chomsky, *Aspects of a Theory of Syntax*

Psycholinguistics is the area of linguistics that is concerned with linguistic performance — how we use our linguistic competence, our knowledge of language, in speech (or sign) production and comprehension. The human brain is able not only to acquire and store the mental grammar but also to access that linguistic storehouse to speak and understand what is spoken.

How we process knowledge depends to a great extent on the nature of that knowledge. If, for example, language were not "open-ended," if it consisted of a finite store of fixed phrases and sentences, then speaking might simply consist of finding a sentence that expresses a thought we wish to convey with its phonological representation and producing it; comprehension could be the reverse — matching the sounds to a stored string that has been entered with its meaning. We know this is not possible because of the creativity of language. In Chapter 10, we saw that children do not learn language by imitating and storing sentences but by constructing a grammar. When we speak, we access our grammar to find the words, construct novel sentences, and produce the sounds that express the message we wish to convey. When we listen to someone speak and understand what is being said, we also access the grammar to process the utterances in order to assign a meaning to the sounds we hear.

Speaking and comprehending speech can be viewed as a speech chain linking the speaker's brain with the listener's brain, as shown in Figure 11.8. The grammar relates sounds and meanings and contains the units and rules of the language that make speech production and comprehension possible. But the grammar does not describe the psychological processes that are used in producing and understanding utterances. A theory of linguistic performance describes the relationship between the mental grammar and the psychological mechanisms by means of which this grammar is accessed to permit speech and comprehension.

FIGURE 11.8   The Speech Chain

A spoken utterance starts as a message in the brain/mind of the speaker. It is put into linguistic form and interpreted as articulation commands, emerging as an acoustic signal. The signal is processed by the ear of the listener and sent to the brain/mind, where it is interpreted.

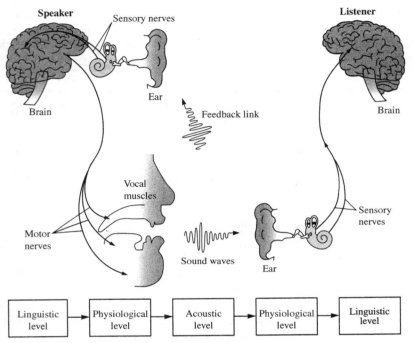

From Jean Berko Gleason and Nan Bernstein Ratner, eds. *Psycholinguistics*. Orlando, FL: Harcourt Brace, 1993, p. 273.

Comprehension

> "I quite agree with you," said the Duchess; "and the moral of that is — 'Be what you would seem to be' — or, if you'd like it put more simply — 'Never imagine yourself not to be otherwise than what it might appear to others that what you were or might have been was not otherwise than what you had been would have appeared to them to be otherwise.' "
>
> "I think I should understand that better," Alice said very politely, "if I had it written down: but I can't quite follow it as you say it."
>
> Lewis Carroll, *Alice's Adventures in Wonderland*

The difficulty Alice has in understanding this sentence is not surprising. What is surprising is that we usually do understand long and complex sentences with multiple embedded relative clauses and many conjoined phrases and modifiers. Even young children can do this automatically and without conscious effort. Once in a while, of course, one stops and asks for clarification, as Christopher Robin does in listening to a story about Winnie-the-Pooh:

> Once upon a time, a very long time ago now, about last Friday, Winnie-the-Pooh lived in a forest all by himself under the name of Sanders.
>
> (*"What does 'under the name' mean?" asked Christopher Robin.*
> *"It means he had the name over the door in gold letters, and lived under it."*) . . .
> (Milne 1926)

If Christopher Robin took the time to think about the meaning of the phrase "under the name of Sanders," then he might realize that it is an ambiguous sentence. In normal conversations, non-linguistic considerations such as word frequency or what we expect to hear or what we are thinking can influence which meaning of an ambiguous sentence we come up with. One aim of psycholinguistic research is to clarify the processes by which speakers match one or more meanings to the strings of sounds they hear.

The Speech Signal

We are not conscious of the complex processes we use to understand speech. One of the first questions concerns the problem of segmentation of the **acoustic signal**. To understand how this is done, some knowledge of the signal itself is helpful.

In Chapter 5, we described speech sounds according to the ways in which they are produced — the position of the tongue, the lips, and the velum; the state of the vocal cords; the airstream mechanisms; whether the articulators obstruct the free flow of air; and so on. All of these articulatory characteristics are reflected in the physical characteristics of the sounds produced.

Speech sounds can also be described in physical or **acoustic** terms. Physically, a sound is produced whenever there is a disturbance in the position of air molecules. The question asked by ancient philosophers as to whether a sound is produced if a tree falls in the middle of the forest with no one to hear it has been answered by the science of acoustics. Objectively, a sound is produced; subjectively, there is no sound. In fact, there are sounds we cannot hear because our ears are not sensitive to all changes in air pressure (which result from the movement of air molecules). **Acoustic phonetics** is concerned only with speech sounds, all of which can be heard by the normal human ear.

When we push air out of the lungs through the glottis, the vocal cords vibrate; this vibration in turn produces pulses of air, which escape through the mouth (and sometimes the nose). These pulses are actually small variations in the air pressure, due to the wavelike motion of the air molecules.

The sounds we produce can be described in terms of how fast the variations of the air pressure occur, which determines the **fundamental frequency** of the sounds and is perceived by the hearer as **pitch**. We can also describe the magnitude or **intensity** of the variations, which determines the **loudness** of the sound. The **quality of sound** is determined by the kind of vibrations, or **wave form**, which is determined by the shape of the vocal tract when the air is flowing through it.

An important tool in acoustic research is a computer program that decomposes the speech signal into its frequency components. When you speak into a microphone plugged into the back of the computer (or when a tape recording is played through the computer), an image of the speech sound is displayed. The patterns produced are called **spectrograms, sound spectograms**, or, more vividly, **voiceprints**. A spectrogram of the words *heed, head, had*, and *who'd* is shown in Figure 11.9.

Time in milliseconds moves horizontally from left to right; vertically, the graph represents pitch (or, more technically, frequency). Notice that for each vowel there are a number of dark bands that differ in their placement according to pitch. They represent the strongest harmonics (the **overtones**) produced by the shape of the vocal tract and are called the **formants** of the vowels. Because the tongue is in a different position for each vowel, the formant frequencies, or overtone pitches, differ for each vowel. It is the different frequencies of these formants that account for the different vowel qualities you hear. The pitch of the entire utterance (intonation contour) is shown by the voicing bar marked *P* on the spectrogram. When the striations are far apart, the vocal cords are vibrating slowly, and the pitch is low; when the striations are close together, the vocal cords are vibrating rapidly, and the pitch is high.

By studying spectrograms of all speech sounds and many different utterances, acoustic phoneticians have learned a great deal about the basic acoustic components that reflect the articulatory features of speech sounds.

Speech Perception and Comprehension

The comprehension of speech involves many psychological operations. Speech perception — analyzing the speech signal into strings of phonemes — is a necessary but not sufficient first step in comprehension. Some of the complexities of the speech per-

FIGURE 11.9

A spectrogram of the words *heed, head, had*, and *who'd*, as spoken with a British accent by Peter Ladefoged, February 16, 1973.

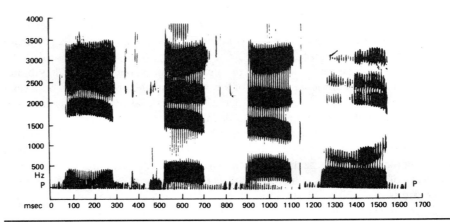

ception process were discussed in Chapter 6 and will be further discussed in Chapter 12. To see how complex speech processing is, suppose you heard someone say

> A sniggle blick is procking a slar.

and were able to perceive the sounds as

> /əsnɪgəlblɪkɪzprakɪŋəslar/

You would still be unable to assign a meaning to the sounds, because the meaning of a sentence depends on the meanings of its words, and the only English lexical items in the string are the morphemes *a, is,* and *-ing.* The sentence lacks any English content words. You would, however, accept it as a grammatically formed sentence in English because it conforms to the rules of English syntax.

You can know that the sentence has no meaning only if you attempt (unconsciously or consciously) to search your mental lexicon for the phonological strings you decide are possible words. This process is called **lexical access** and **word recognition**. Finding that there are no entries for *sniggle, blick, prock,* or *slar,* you can conclude that the sentence includes nonsense strings.

If instead you heard someone say *The cat chased the rat,* through a lexical lookup process you would conclude that an event concerning a cat, a rat, and the activity of chasing had occurred. You could know this by segmenting the words in the continuous speech signal, analyzing them into their phonological word units, and matching these units with similar strings stored in your lexicon, which also includes the meanings attached to these phonological representations. This still would not enable you to tell who chased whom, since that is determined by syntactic processing. Processing speech to get at the meaning of what is said requires syntactic analysis as well as knowledge of lexical semantics.

Stress and intonation provide some clues to syntactic structure. We know, for example, that the different meanings of the sentences *He lives in the white house* and *He lives in the White House* can be signalled by differences in their stress patterns. Such prosodic aspects of speech also help to segment the speech signal into words and phrases; syllables at the end of a phrase are longer in duration than at the beginning. Intonation contours mark boundaries of clauses. Relative loudness, pitch, and duration of syllables thus provide information in the comprehension process.

Speech comprehension is very fast and automatic. We understand an utterance as we hear it or read it. We don't wait for a pause and then say "Hold on. I have to analyze the speech sounds, look the words up in my dictionary, and parse (provide a syntactic analysis of) your utterance." But how do we understand a sentence?

Comprehension Models and Experimental Studies

> I have experimented and experimented until now I know that . . . [water] never does run uphill, except in the dark. I know it does in the dark, because the pool never goes dry; which it would, of course, if the water didn't come back in the night. It is best to prove things by experiment; then you know; whereas if you depend on guessing and supposing and conjecturing, you will never get educated.
>
> Mark Twain, *Eve's Diary*

In this laboratory the only one who is always right is the cat.
Motto in laboratory of Arturo Rosenblueth

The psychological stages and processes that a listener goes through in comprehending the meaning of an utterance are very complex. Alternative models of speech processing have been proposed in the attempt to clarify the stages involved. Some psycholinguists suggest that speech perception and comprehension involve both **top-down** and **bottom-up** processing.

Top-down processes proceed from semantic and syntactic information to the sensory input. Using such higher-level information, it is suggested, we can predict what is to follow in the signal.

Bottom-up processes move step by step from the incoming acoustic signal to semantic interpretation, building each part of the structure on the basis of the sensory data alone.

Evidence for at least partial top-down processing is provided in a number of experiments. For example, subjects make fewer identification errors of words when the words occur in sentences than when they are presented in isolation. This suggests that subjects use knowledge of syntactic structures in addition to the acoustic input signal. This is true even when the stimuli are presented in the presence of noise. Subjects also do better if the words occur in grammatically meaningful sentences as opposed to grammatically anomalous sentences; identification of words in ungrammatical sentences produced the most errors. This supports the idea that subjects are not responding simply to the input word by word.

Top-down processing is also supported by the fact that, when subjects hear recorded sentences in which some part of the signal is removed and a cough substituted, they "hear" the sentence without a missing phoneme and, in fact, are unable to say which phonemic segment the cough replaced. Context plays a major role in determining which sounds the subjects replace. Thus, "[cough] eel" is heard as *wheel, heel, peel*, or *meal* depending on whether the sentence in which the distorted word occurs refers to an axle, shoe, orange, or food, respectively. We have also seen that context plays a role in word segmentation. If we heard [n a j t r e t] while checking into a motel, then we would interpret it as *night rate*, whereas in a chemistry lab we would think we heard *nitrate*. Similarly, the phonetic string [w a j t š u z] would be heard as *white shoes* rather than *why choose* in a shoe store.

Lexical Access and Word Recognition

There has been a great deal of research by psycholinguists on *lexical access* or *word recognition*, the process by which we obtain information about the meaning of a word from our mental lexicons. A number of experimental techniques have been used in studies of lexical access.

One technique asks subjects to decide whether a string of sounds (or letters if printed stimuli are used) is or is not a word. They must respond by pressing a button if the stimulus is an actual word. In these **lexical decision** experiments, **response time** or **reaction time** measurements (often referred to as RTs) are taken.

The assumption is that, the longer it takes to respond to a particular task, the more processing is involved. Using such measurements, it has been found that lexical access depends to some extent on word **frequency** — that is, RT is faster to words that occur more frequently in speech and writing. This is evidence that comprehension performance involves both linguistic and non-linguistic factors. Another finding is that ambiguous sentences take longer to process than unambiguous sentences. It appears that, even if subjects are not aware of the multiple meanings of an ambiguous sentence, both meanings are evoked and interfere with each other. This is true of sentences that are lexically ambiguous (with words that have more than one meaning) and of sentences that are syntactically ambiguous.

Reaction time is also measured in experiments using a **priming** technique. It has been found, for example, that if subjects hear a word such as *nurse* their response to *doctor* will be faster than to a semantically unrelated word such as *flower*. This may be due to the fact that semantically related words are located in the same part of the lexicon, and once the "path" to that section has been taken it is easier to travel that way a second time. It may also be due to the fact that other words are triggered when we "look up" a semantically related word.

An interesting finding in such experiments is that a lexically ambiguous word can be primed by a word referring to either meaning, even if the context of the ambiguous word disambiguates it. For example, either *harbour* or *wine* will prime the word *port* (result in faster response time) in the sentence

> The ship is in port.

This suggests that, in listening to speech, all the meanings represented by a phonological form will be triggered. This argues, however, against top-down processing, since both words are accessed even when the preceding sentence disambiguates the ambiguous word. That is, if we use information other than what is contained in the incoming signal, then the sentence that was heard earlier should influence which word is accessed.

Another experimental technique, called the **naming** task, asks the subject to read aloud a printed word. Subjects read real words faster than non-words and irregularly spelled words such as *dough* and *enough* as fast as regularly spelled words such as *doe* and *stuff* and even faster than regularly spelled nonsense forms such as *cluff*. This shows that the subjects first go to the lexicon to see if the word is there, access the phonological representation, and produce the word. They can use spelling-to-pronunciation rules only if they cannot find the string of letters listed.

In naming, frequency also has an effect. That is, frequent words are read more quickly than infrequent ones. One model of word recognition proposed by Kenneth Forster of the University of Arizona, called the **search model**, accounts for the frequency effect by suggesting that in lexical access the most recent words are accessed first.

Syntactic Processing

There has been more psycholinguistic research dealing with lexical access than with syntactic processing, possibly because the available experimental techniques can be more easily directed toward this question. In recent years, an increasing number of studies have concentrated on sentence processing.

One class of sentences that involves syntactic processing as distinguished from syntactic competence has been referred to as *garden path sentences*, illustrated by the following:

> The horse raced past the barn fell.

Many individuals, on hearing this sentence, will judge it to be ungrammatical, yet they will judge a sentence with the same syntactic structure as grammatical, such as

> The bus driven past the school stopped.

Similarly, subjects will have no problem with

> The horse that was raced past the barn fell.

The first sentence is called a garden path sentence because, as the idiom implies, we are incorrectly led to interpret the word *raced* as the **main verb** of the verb phrase since it immediately follows the first noun phrase. To interpret the sentence correctly, we have to retrace our processing when we come to the main sentence verb *fell*, which becomes very confusing. Such backtracking seems to put a burden on short-term memory and syntactic processors that creates comprehension errors. Such sentences highlight the distinction between syntactic competence and syntactic performance strategies.

There are a number of other techniques used experimentally in the study of speech perception and comprehension. In a **shadowing** task, subjects are asked to repeat what they hear as rapidly as possible. A few exceptionally good shadowers can follow what is being said only about a syllable behind (300 milliseconds). Most of us, however, shadow with a delay of about a second (500 to 800 milliseconds). This is still quite fast. Shadowers often correct speech errors or mispronunciations unconsciously and even add inflectional endings if they are absent. Even when they are told that the speech they are to shadow includes errors and that they should repeat the errors, they are unable to do so. Lexical corrections are more likely to occur when the target word is predictable from what has been said previously. These shadowing experiments show that speech perception involves more than simply processing the incoming signal.

The ability to understand and comprehend what is said to us is a complex psychological process involving the internal grammar, motivation, frequency factors, memory, and both linguistic and non-linguistic context.

Speech Production

> And has the reader never asked himself what kind of a mental fact is his intention of saying a thing before he has said it? . . . How much of it consists of definite sensorial images, either of words or of things? Hardly anything! Linger, and the words and things come to mind. . . . The intention welcomes them.
>
> William James (1890)

The speech chain starts with a speaker who, through some complicated set of neuromuscular processes, produces an acoustic signal that represents a thought, idea, or message to be conveyed to a listener, who must then decode the signal to arrive at a similar message. It is more difficult to devise experiments that provide information on how the speaker proceeds than to do so from the listener's side of the process. The best information has come from observing and analyzing spontaneous speech.

Planning Units

We might suppose that the thoughts of the speaker are simply translated into words one after the other through a semantic mapping process. Grammatical morphemes would be added as demanded by the syntactic rules of the language. The phonetic representation of each word in turn would then be mapped onto the neuromuscular commands to the articulators to produce the acoustic signal representing it.

We know, however, that this supposition is not a true picture of speech production. Although, when we speak, the sounds we produce and the words we use are linearly ordered, speech errors show that the pre-articulation stages involve units larger than the single phonemic segment or even the word. Phrases and even whole sentences are constructed prior to the production of a single sound. Errors show that features, segments, and words can be anticipated — that is, produced earlier than intended or reversed (as in typical spoonerisms) — so the later words or phrases in which they occur must already be conceptualized. This point is illustrated in the following examples (the intended utterance to the left of the arrow, the actual utterance, including the error, to the right of the arrow):

(1) The **h**iring of minority **f**aculty. → The **f**iring of minority faculty.
(The intended *h* is replaced by the *f* of *faculty*, which occurs later in the intended utterance.)
(2) **ad hoc** → **o**dd h**a**ck
(The vowels /æ/ of the first word and /a/ of the second are exchanged or reversed.)
(3) **big** and **fat** → **p**ig and **v**at
(The values of a single feature are switched: [+voiced] becomes [–voiced] in *big* and [–voiced] becomes [+voiced] in *fat*.)
(4) There are many ministers in our church. → There are many churches in our minister.
(The stem morphemes *minister* and *church* are exchanged; the grammatical plural morpheme remains in its intended place in the phrase structure.)
(5) Seymour sliced the salami with a knife. → Seymour sliced a knife with the salami.
(The two entire noun phrases — article + noun — are exchanged.)

In these errors, the intonation contour (primary stressed syllables and variations in pitch) remained the same as in the intended utterances, even when the words were disordered. In the intended utterance of (5), the highest pitch would be on *knife*. In the disordered sentence, the highest pitch occurred on the second syllable of *salami*.

The pitch rise and increased loudness are thus determined by the syntactic structure of the sentence and are independent of the individual words. Thus, syntactic structures are also units in linguistic performance.

Errors like those cited above are constrained in interesting ways. Phonological errors involving segments or features, as in (1), (2), and (3), primarily occur in content words, not in grammatical morphemes, again showing the distinction between these lexical classes. In addition, while words and lexical morphemes may be interchanged, grammatical morphemes and free or bound inflectional affixes may not be. As example (4) illustrates, the inflectional endings are "stranded," left behind, and subsequently attached, in proper phonological form, to the moved lexical morpheme.

Such errors show that speech production involves different kinds of units — features, segments, morphemes, words, phrases, the very units that exist in the grammar. They also show that, when we speak, words are structured into larger syntactic phrases that are stored in a kind of buffer memory before segments or features or words are disordered. This storage must occur prior to the articulatory stage. Thus, we do not select one word from our mental dictionaries and say it, then select another word and say it. We organize an entire phrase and in many cases an entire sentence.

The constraints on which units can be exchanged or moved also suggest that grammatical morphemes are added at a stage after the lexical morphemes are selected. This provided one of the motivations for a two-lexicon grammatical model, one with lexical and derivational morphemes listed, the other with inflectional and grammatical morphemes listed.

Lexical Selection

> . . . Humpty Dumpty's theory, of two meanings packed into one word like a portmanteau, seems to me the right explanation for all. For instance, take the two words "fuming" and "furious." Make up your mind that you will say both words but leave it unsettled which you will say first. Now open your mouth and speak. If . . . you have that rarest of gifts, a perfectly balanced mind, you will say "frumious."
>
> Lewis Carroll, "Preface," *The Hunting of the Snark*

In Chapter 4, word substitution errors were used to illustrate the semantic properties of words. Such substitutions are seldom random; they show that in speaking, in our attempts to express our thoughts through words in the lexicon, we may make an incorrect lexical selection based on partial similarity or relatedness of meanings.

Blends, in which we produce part of one word and part of another, further illustrate the lexical selection process in speech production; we may select two or more words to express our thoughts and, instead of deciding between them, produce them as "portmanteaus," as Humpty Dumpty calls them. Such blends are illustrated in the following errors:

(1) splinters/blisters → splisters
(2) edited/annotated → editated

(3) a swinging/hip chick → a swip chick
(4) frown/scowl → frowl

Application and Misapplication of Rules

> I thought . . . four rules would be enough, provided that I made a firm and con-
> stant resolution not to fail even once in the observance of them.
>
> René Descartes (1596–1650)

Spontaneous errors show that the rules of morphology and syntax, discussed in earlier chapters as part of competence, may also be applied (or misapplied) when we
speak. It is hard to see this process in normal error-free speech; however, when
someone says *groupment* instead of *grouping, ambigual* instead of *ambiguous*, or
bloodent instead of *bloody*, it shows that regular rules are applied to morphemes to
form possible but non-existent words.

Inflectional rules also surface. The professor who said *We swimmed in the pool*
knows that the past tense of *swim* is *swam* but mistakenly applied the regular rule
to an irregular form.

Morphophonemic rules appear to be performance rules as well as rules of competence. Consider the *a/an* alternation rule in English. Errors such as *an istem* for
the intended *a system* or *a burly bird* for the intended *an early bird* show that, when
segmental disordering changes a noun beginning with a consonant to a noun beginning with a vowel, or vice versa, the indefinite article is also changed so that it conforms to the grammatical rule.

Such utterances also reveal that in speech production internal "editing" or moni-
toring attempts to prevent errors. When an error slips by the editor, such as the disordering of phonemes, the editor prevents a compounding of errors. Thus, when the
/b/ of *bird* was anticipated and added to the beginning of *early*, the result was not *an
burly bird*. The editor applied (or reapplied) the *a/an* rule to produce *a burly bird*.

An examination of such data also tells us something about the stages in the production of an utterance. Disordering of phonemes must occur before the indefinite
article is given its phonological form, or the morphological rule must reapply after
the initial error has occurred. An error such as *bin beg* for the intended *Big Ben*
shows that phonemes are disordered before phonetic allophones are determined.
That is, the intended *Big Ben* phonetically is [bɪg bɛ̃n] with an oral [ɪ] before the
[g] and a nasal [ɛ̃] before the [n]. In the utterance that was produced, however, the
[ɪ̃] is nasalized because it now occurs before the disordered [n], whereas the [ɛ] is
oral before the disordered [g]. If the disordering occurred after the phonemes had
been replaced by phonetic allophones, then the result would have been the phonetic
utterance [bɪn bɛ̃g].

Non-Linguistic Influences

The discussion of speech comprehension suggested that non-linguistic factors are
involved in and sometimes interfere with linguistic processing. They also affect
speech production. The individual who said *He made hairlines* instead of *He made*

headlines was referring to a barber. The facts that the two compound nouns start with the same sound, are composed of two syllables, have the same stress pattern, and contain identical second morphemes undoubtedly played a role in producing the error, but the relationship between hairlines and barbers may also have been a contributing factor.

Other errors show that thoughts unrelated structurally to the intended utterance may have an influence on what is said. One speaker said "I've never heard of classes *on April 9*" instead of the intended *on Good Friday*. Good Friday fell on April 9 that year. The two phrases are not similar phonologically or morphologically, yet the non-linguistic association seems to have influenced what was said. This influence is a further example of the distinction between linguistic competence and performance.

Looking at both normal conversational data and experimentally elicited data provides the psycholinguist with evidence in the construction of models of both speech production and comprehension, the beginning and end points of the speech chain of communication.

Summary

The attempt to understand what makes human language acquisition and use possible has led to research on the brain–mind–language relationship. **Neurolinguistics** studies the brain mechanisms and anatomical structures underlying language representation and use.

The brain is the most complicated organ of the body, controlling motor and sensory activities and thought processes. Research conducted for more than a century reveals that different parts of the brain control different bodily functions. The nerve cells that form the surface of the brain are called the **cortex**, which serves as the intellectual decision maker, receiving messages from the sensory organs and initiating all voluntary actions. The brain of each higher animal is divided into two parts called the **cerebral hemispheres**, which are connected by the **corpus callosum**, a pathway that permits the left and right hemispheres to communicate with each other.

Although each hemisphere appears to be a mirror image of the other, the left hemisphere controls the right hand, leg, visual field, and so on, and the right brain controls the left side of the body; this is referred to as **contralateral** control of function. Despite this general symmetry of the human body, there is much evidence that the left and right hemispheres are specialized for different functions. Evidence from **aphasia** — language dysfunction as a result of brain injuries — and from surgical removal of parts of the brain, electrical stimulation studies, emission tomography results, dichotic listening, and experiments measuring brain electrical activity shows a lack of symmetry of function of the two hemispheres. These results are further supported by studies of **split-brain** patients, who, for medical reasons, have had the corpus callosum severed. In the past, studies of the brain and language depended on surgery or autopsy. Today new technologies such as **magnetic reso-**

nance imaging (MRI) and **positron emission tomography (PET)** make it possible to see the sites of lesions in the living brain, to detect changes in brain activities, and to relate these changes to focal brain damage and cognitive tasks.

For normal right-handers and many left-handers, the left side of the brain appears to be specialized for language. This **lateralization** of functions is genetically and neurologically conditioned. Lateralization refers to any cognitive functions that are primarily localized to one side of the brain or the other.

In addition to aphasia, other evidence supports the lateralization of language. Children with early brain lesions in the left hemisphere, resulting in the surgical removal of parts or the whole of the left brain, show specific linguistic deficits with other cognitive abilities remaining intact. If the right brain is damaged, however, language is not disordered, but other cognitive disorders may result.

Aphasia studies show impairment of different parts of the grammar. Patients with **Broca's aphasia** exhibit impaired syntax and speech problems, whereas **Wernicke's aphasia** patients are fluent speakers who produce semantically empty utterances and have difficulty in comprehension. **Anomia** is a form of aphasia in which the patient has word-finding difficulties. **Jargon aphasia** patients may substitute words unrelated semantically to their intended messages; others produce phonemic substitution errors, sometimes resulting in nonsense forms, making their utterances uninterpretable.

The **modularity** of the language faculty — its independence from other cognitive systems with which it interacts — is supported by brain-damage studies and studies of children with a **specific language impairment (SLI)** who are normal in all other respects. The ability to acquire language seems to be genetically determined, as shown by the cases of linguistic **savants** — individuals who are fluent in language and deficient in general intelligence. Given such individuals, linguistic ability does not seem to be derived from some general cognitive ability.

Psycholinguistics is concerned with **linguistic performance** or processing, the use of linguistic knowledge (competence) in speech production and comprehension.

Comprehension, the process of understanding an utterance, requires the ability to access the mental lexicon to match the words in the utterance we are listening to with their meanings. It starts with the perception of the **acoustic speech signal**. The speech signal can be described in terms of the **fundamental frequency**, perceived as **pitch**; the **intensity**, perceived as loudness; and the **quality**, perceived as differences in speech sounds, such as an [i] from an [u]. The speech wave can be displayed as a **spectrogram**, sometimes called a **voiceprint**. In a spectrogram, vowels exhibit dark bands where frequency intensity is greatest. They are called **formants** and result from the emphasis of certain *harmonics* of the fundamental frequency, as determined by the shape of the vowel tract. Each vowel has a characteristic formant pattern different from that of other vowels.

Perception of the speech signal is necessary but not sufficient for the understanding of speech. To get the full meaning of an utterance, we must **parse** the string into syntactic structures, since meaning depends on word order, constituent structure, and so on, in addition to the meanings of words. Some psycholinguists believe we utilize both **top-down** and **bottom-up** processes during comprehension. Top-down processing uses semantic and syntactic information in addition to the incoming **acoustic signal**; bottom-up processes utilize only information contained in the sensory input.

Psycholinguistic experimental studies are aimed at uncovering the units, stages, and processes involved in linguistic performance. A number of experimental techniques have proved to be very helpful. In a **lexical decision** task, subjects are asked to respond to spoken or written stimuli by pressing a button if they consider the stimulus to be a word. In **naming** tasks, subjects read from printed stimuli. The measurement of **response times (RTs)** in naming and lexical decision tasks shows that it takes longer to comprehend ambiguous utterances, ungrammatical compared with grammatical sentences, and nonsense forms as opposed to real words. Response time is also measured in experiments using a **priming** technique, which presents a subject with a word followed by another word or a sentence. The first word primes what follows if it is semantically related. A word such as *nurse* will prime the word *doctor* such that the response to it will be faster than to a semantically unrelated word such as *flower*. Such experiments also show that all the meanings of a word are accessed despite the context of a previously heard sentence that should disambiguate the meanings.

Another technique used is **shadowing**, in which subjects repeat what is being said to them as fast as possible; they often correct errors in the stimulus sentence, suggesting that they use linguistic knowledge rather than simply echoing the sounds they hear. Other experiments reveal the processes involved in accessing the mental grammar and the influence of non-linguistic factors in comprehension.

The units and stages in speech production have been studied by analyzing spontaneously produced speech errors. Anticipation errors, in which a sound is produced earlier than in the intended utterance, and **spoonerisms**, in which sounds or words are exchanged or reversed, show that we do not produce one sound or one word or even one phrase at a time, but construct and store larger units with their syntactic structures specified prior to mapping these linguistic structures onto neuromuscular commands to the articulators. In producing speech, we select words from the mental lexicon whose meanings partially express the thoughts we wish to convey. Word substitutions and **blends** may occur, showing that words are connected to other words phonologically and semantically. The production of ungrammatical utterances also shows that morphological, inflectional, and syntactic rules may be wrongly applied or fail to apply when we speak, but at the same time it shows that such rules are actually involved in speech production.

Note

1. Broca also held extremely racist and sexist views based on incorrect measurements of the brains of men and women and different races. His correlation of brain size with intelligence is thoroughly demolished by Stephen Jay Gould in *The Mismeasure of Man* (New York: W.W. Norton, 1981).

Exercises

1. **A.** Some aphasic patients, when asked to read a list of words, substitute other words for those printed. In many cases, there are similarities between the printed words and the substituted words. The data given below are from actual aphasic patients. In each case, state what the two words have in common and how they differ.

	Printed Word	Word Spoken by Aphasic
a.	liberty	freedom
	canary	parrot
	abroad	overseas
	large	long
	short	small
	tall	long
b.	decide	decision
	conceal	concealment
	portray	portrait
	bathe	bath
	speak	discussion
	remember	memory

B. What do the words in groups a and b reveal about how words are likely to be stored in the brain?

2. The following sentences, spoken by aphasic patients, were collected and analyzed by Dr. Harry Whitaker of the University of Maryland. In each case, state how the sentence deviates from normal non-aphasic language.

a. There is under a horse a new sidesaddle.
b. In girls we see many happy days.
c. I'll challenge a new bike.
d. I surprise no new glamour.
e. Is there three chairs in this room?
f. Mike and Peter is happy.
g. Bill and John likes hotdogs.
h. Proliferate is a complete time about a word that is correct.
i. Went came in better than it did before.

*3. A young patient at the Division of Neuropsychology of the Radcliffe Infirmary, Oxford, England, following a head injury, appears to have lost the spelling-to-pronunciation and phonetic-to-spelling rules that most of us can use to read and write new words or nonsense strings. He is also unable to get to the phonemic representations of words in his lexicon. Consider the following examples of his reading pronunciation and his writing from dictation.

Reading	Pronunciation	Writing from Dictation
fame	/fæmi/	FAM
café	/sæfi/	KAFA
time	/tajmi/	TIM
note	/noti/ or /nɔti/	NOT
praise	/pra-aj-si/	PRAZ
treat	/tri-æt/	TRET
goes	/go-ɛs/	GOZ
float	/flɔ-æt/	FLOT

His reading and writing errors are not random but rule-governed. See if you can figure out the rules he uses to relate standard (spelling) orthography to his pronunciation and spelling.

4. Speech errors, commonly referred to as "slips of the tongue" or "bloopers," illustrate a difference between linguistic competence and performance, since our very recognition of them as errors shows that we have knowledge of well-formed sentences. Furthermore, errors provide information about the grammar. The utterances listed below were actually produced deviations from the speakers' intended utterances. They are part of the University of California at Los Angeles corpus of over 15 000 speech errors, plus a few from Dr. Spooner.

   a. For each speech error, state what kind of linguistic unit or rule is involved — that is, phonological, morphological, syntactic, lexical, or semantic.
   b. State, to the best of your ability, the nature of the error or the mechanisms that produced it.

   (Note: The intended utterance is to the left of the arrow, the actual utterance to the right.)

   example: ad hoc → odd hack
   　　　　a. phonological vowel segment　　　b. reversal or exchange of segments

   example: she gave it away → she gived it away
   　　　　a. inflectional morphology　　　b. incorrect application of regular past tense rule to exceptional verb

   example: When will you leave? → When you will leave?
   　　　　a. syntactic rule　　　b. failure to "move the auxiliary" to form a question

   (1) brake fluid → blake fruid
   (2) Drink is the curse of the working classes. → Work is the curse of the drinking classes. (Spooner)
   (3) We have many ministers in our church. → . . . many churches in our minister.

(4) untactful → distactful
(5) an eating marathon → a meeting arathon
(6) executive committee → executor committee
(7) lady with the dachshund → lady with the Volkswagen
(8) stick in the mud → smuck in the tid
(9) He broke the crystal on my watch. → He broke the whistle on my crotch.
(10) a phonological rule → a phonological fool
(11) pitch and stress → piss and stretch
(12) big and fat → pig and vat
(13) speech production → preach seduction
(14) He's a New Yorker. → He's a New Yorkan.
(15) I'd forgotten about that. → I'd forgot abouten that.

Works Cited

Damasio, A. 1994. *Descarte's Error: Emotion, Reason, and the Human Brain.* New York: G.P. Putnam.

Damasio, Hanna, and Antonio Damasio. 1989. *Lesion Analysis in Neuropsychology.* New York: Oxford University Press.

Damasio, H., T. Grabowski, R. Frank, A.M. Galaburda, and A.R. Damasio. 1994. "The Return of Phineas Gage: The Skull of a Famous Patient Yields Clues about the Brain." *Science* 264: 1102–05.

Damasio, H., T. Grabowski, D. Tranel, R.D. Hichwa, and A.R. Damasio. 1996. "A Neural Basis for Lexical Retrieval." *Nature* 380: 499–505.

Gazzaniga, Michael. 1970. *The Bisected Brain.* New York: Appleton-Century-Crofts.

Goodglass, Harold. 1973. "Studies on the Grammar of Aphasics." *Psycholinguistics and Aphasia.* Ed. H. Goodglass and S. Blumstein. Baltimore: Johns Hopkins University Press: 183–215.

Milne, A.A. 1926. *Winnie-the-Pooh.* New York: E.P. Dutton.

Newcombe, F., and J. Marshall. 1984. "Varieties of Acquired Dyslexia: A Linguistic Approach." *Seminars in Neurology* 4.2: 181–95.

Poizner, H., E. Klima, and U. Bellugi. 1987. *What the Hands Reveal about the Brain.* Cambridge, MA: MIT Press.

Smith, Neil, and Ianthi-Maria Tsimpli. 1995. *The Mind of a Savant.* Oxford: Blackwell.

Smith, Neil, and Ianthi Tsimpli. 1991. "Linguistic Modularity: A Case-Study of a 'Savant' Linguist." Paper presented to the meeting of Generative Linguistics of the Old World, Spain.

Yamada, J. 1990. *Laura: A Case for the Modularity of Language.* Cambridge, MA: MIT Press, a Bradford Book.

Further Reading

Blumstein, S. 1973. *A Phonological Investigation of Aphasic Speech.* Janua Linguarum Series 153. The Hague: Mouton.

Caplan, D. 1987. *Neurolinguistics and Linguistic Aphasiology.* Cambridge, UK: Cambridge University Press.

Carroll, D.W. 1986. *Psychology of Language.* Monterey, CA: Brooks/Cole Publishing.

Coltheart, M., K. Patterson, and J.C. Marshall, eds. 1980. *Deep Dyslexia.* London: Routledge and Kegan Paul.

Damasio, H. 1981. "Cerebral Localization of the Aphasias." *Acquired Aphasia.* Ed. M. Taylor Sarno. New York: Academic Press: 27–65.

Fodor, J.A., M. Garrett, and T.G. Bever. 1986. *The Psychology of Language.* New York: McGraw-Hill.

Fromkin, V.A., ed. 1980. *Errors in Linguistic Performance.* New York: Academic Press.

Gardner, H. 1978. "What We Know (and Don't Know) about the Two Halves of the Brain." *Harvard Magazine* 80: 24–27.

Garnham, A. 1985. *Psycholinguistics: Central Topics.* London: Methuen.

Garrett, M.F. 1988. "Processes in Sentence Production." *The Cambridge Linguistic Survey.* Vol. 3. Ed. F. Newmeyer. Cambridge, UK: Cambridge University Press.

Geschwind, N. 1979. "Specializations of the Human Brain." *Scientific American* 206: 180–99.

Grodzinsky, Y. 1990. *Theoretical Perspectives on Language Deficits.* Cambridge, MA: MIT Press, a Bradford Book.

Lenneberg, Eric H. 1967. *Biological Foundations of Language.* New York: Wiley.

Lesser, R. 1978. *Linguistic Investigation of Aphasia.* New York: Elsevier.

Lieberman, P. 1975. *On the Origins of Language.* New York: Macmillan.

Newcombe, F., and J.C. Marshall. 1972. "Word Retrieval in Aphasia." *International Journal of Mental Health* 1: 38–45.

Springer, S.P., and G. Deutsch. 1981. *Left Brain, Right Brain.* San Francisco: W.H. Freeman.

PART 5
Language in the Computer Age

We should acknowledge that computers are not just another product of industrial society. They are not like automobiles, cameras, or telephones, which represent extensions of human physical or sensory capabilities. Computers are information processing systems. They manipulate symbols, and thus resemble us more closely in what we see as our essential being: a thinking person. In computers ... we recognize ... a new kind of intelligence different from ours, in some ways more powerful and in others much more limited. ... We did not ask for this new world. But it is the opportunity of our generation to seize the computer revolution, make it ours, and bring it forth for the good of all humanity.

Heinz R. Pagels, "Introduction," *Annals of the New York Academy of Sciences* 426 (1984)

Further information processing must be able to handle Japanese, English, and other natural languages. This is one of the core themes of artificial intelligence and at the same time, an area of linguistics: deep relations exist between theoretical linguistics and computers.

Kazuhiro Fuchi, "Fifth Generation Computers: Some Theoretical Issues," *Annals of the New York Academy of Sciences* 426 (1984)

CHAPTER 12
Computer Processing of Human Language

BIZARRO by Dan Piraro is reprinted courtesy of Universal Press Syndicate.

Throughout history, only human beings have had the capability to process language. Today, it is common for computers to process language. **Computational linguistics** is a subfield of linguistics and computer science that is concerned with computer processing of human language. It includes automatic machine translation of one language into another, the analysis of written texts and spoken discourse, the use of language for communication between people and computers, computer modelling of linguistic theories, and the role of human language in artificial intelligence.

Machine Translation

Egad, I think the interpreter is the hardest to be understood of the two!

R.B. Sheridan, *The Critic*

. . . There exist extremely simple sentences in English — and . . . for any other natural language — which would be uniquely . . . and unambiguously translated into any other language by anyone with a sufficient knowledge of the two languages involved, though I know of no program that would enable a machine to come up with this unique rendering. . . .

Yeshua Bar-Hillel

The first use of computers for natural language processing began in the 1940s with the attempt to develop **automatic machine translation**. During World War II, U.S. scientists without the assistance of computers deciphered coded Japanese military communications and proved their skill in coping with difficult language problems. The idea of using deciphering techniques to translate from one language into another was expressed in a letter written to Norbert Wiener by Warren Weaver, a pioneer in the field of computational linguistics: "When I look at any article in Russian, I say: 'This is really written in English, but it has been coded in some strange symbols. I will now proceed to decode' " (Locke and Boothe 1955).

The aim in automatic translation is to "feed" into the computer a written passage in the **source language** (the input) and to receive a grammatical passage of equivalent meaning in the **target language** (the output). In the early days of machine translation, it was believed that this task could be accomplished by entering into the memory of a computer a dictionary of a source language and a dictionary with the corresponding morphemes and words of a target language. The translating program consisted of matching the morphemes of the input sentence with those of the target language. Unfortunately, what often happened was a process called by early machine translators "language in, garbage out." A classic example of such "translation" was that for *out of sight, out of mind* as *invisible idiot*.

Translation is more than word-for-word replacement. Often there is no equivalent word in the target language, and the order of words may differ, as in translating from a subject–verb–object (SVO) language such as English to a subject–object–verb (SOV) language such as Japanese. There is also difficulty in translating idioms, metaphors, jargon, and so on.

These problems are dealt with by human translators because they know the grammars of the two languages and draw on general knowledge of the subject matter and the world to arrive at the intended meaning. Machine translation is often impeded by lexical and syntactic ambiguities, structural disparities between the two languages, morphological complexities, and other cross-linguistic differences. It is often difficult to get good translations even when humans do the translating, as is illustrated by some of the "garbage" printed on signs in non–English-speaking countries as "aids" to tourists:

Utmost of chicken with smashed pot (restaurant in Greece)
Nervous meatballs (restaurant in Bulgaria)
The nuns harbour all diseases and have no respect for religion (Swiss nunnery hospital)
All the water has been passed by the manager (German hotel)
Certified midwife: entrance sideways (Jerusalem)

Such "translations" represent the difficulties of just finding the "equivalent" words, but word choice is a minor problem in automatic translation. The syntactic problems are more complex.

Greater recognition of the role of syntax and application of linguistic principles over the past 40 years have made it possible to use computers to translate simple texts — those in a constrained context such as a mathematical proof — systematically between well-studied languages such as English and Russian. More complex texts require human intervention if the translation is to be grammatical and semantically faithful. The use of computers to aid the human translator can improve efficiency by a factor of ten or more, but the day when travellers can whip out a "pocket translator," hold it up to the mouth of a native speaker, and receive a translation in their own language is as yet beyond the horizon.

Text Processing

[The professor had written] all the words of their language in their several moods, tenses, and declensions [on tiny blocks of wood, and had] emptied the whole vocabulary into his frame, and made the strictest computation of the general proportion there is in books between the numbers of particles, nouns, and verbs, and other parts of speech.

Jonathan Swift, *Gulliver's Travels*

Jonathan Swift prophesied one way computers would be put to work in linguistics — in the statistical analysis of language. Computers can be programmed to reveal properties of language, such as the distribution of sounds, allowable word orders, permitted combinations of morphemes, relative frequencies of words and morphemes (i.e., their "general proportion"), and so on.

Such analyses can be conducted on existing texts (e.g., the works of Shakespeare or the Bible) or on a collection of utterances gathered from spoken or written sources, called a **corpus**. One such corpus, compiled at Brown University, consists of more than one million words from fifteen sources of written American English, including passages from daily newspapers, magazines, and literary material (Kučera and Francis 1967). Because this corpus is available in computer-readable form, many scholars are able to use it in their research.

A corpus of *spoken* American English, similar in size to the Brown Corpus, was also collected (Dahl 1979). A computer analysis of this corpus was conducted, and the result was compared with the Brown Corpus, which provided a contrast between written and spoken American English. Not surprisingly, the pronoun *I* occurs ten times more frequently in the spoken corpus. Profane and taboo words are, as expected, more frequent in spoken language; *shit* occurs 128 times in the spoken corpus but only four times in the written one. All of the prepositions except *to* occur more frequently in written than in spoken English, suggesting that different syntactic structures are used in written English than in spoken English.

The Lancaster–Oslo/Bergen Corpus provides about a million words of British English — largely in their written form — for analysis, while the London–Lund Corpus and the Spoken English Corpus give examples from spoken British English. The Spoken English Corpus provides information about the pronunciation, spelling, and grammatical status of the words it includes.

Still other corpora, most of which are modelled on the Brown Corpus, are being compiled for Australian English (Maquarie Corpus), for Indian English (Kolhapur Corpus), and for an International Corpus of English (ICE) that will include spoken and written material from countries, including Canada, where English is spoken as a second or foreign language.

More powerful computers, improved scanning devices for transferring texts from print to computer, and computer-assisted photo composition have made the collection of these huge bodies of machine-readable texts available for linguistic and literary analysis. Thus, one retrieval service, NEXIS, has a data bank containing the full texts of articles from some 135 publications — more than 14 billion words of text. The Birmingham Corpus contains some 20 million words of spoken and written British English, the Longman/Lancaster English Corpus has 30 million words from various sources of the language, and even larger projects were initiated in the last half of the 1990s. In England, the British National Corpus compiled 100 million words of spoken and written British English in 1995, and in the United States the Association for Computational Linguists is preparing another 100-million-word corpus. In the future, we expect that similar collections will become available for analysis through agencies such as the World Wide Web.

These corpora have already been used to test linguistic hypotheses for the *Comprehensive Grammar of the English Language* (1985) prepared by Randolph Quirk, Sidney Greenbaum, Geoffrey Leach, and Jan Svartvik and as an aid in constructing the *Collins COBUILD English Language Dictionary* (Sinclair 1987) and grammar (1990). Computerized corpora have also proved fruitful in stylistic analysis. W. Nelson Francis and H. Kučera (1982) used the Brown Corpus to illustrate the characteristic features of imaginative and informative genres of English. They found that verbs and adverbs are more characteristic of imaginative genres and nouns and adjectives of informative genres. As we might expect, interjections are used exclusively in imaginative genres, while numerals are almost restricted to informative ones. Another student, Douglas Biber (1988), used these corpora to study various genres and found characteristic linguistic features for each, features such as the use of present tenses in contrast with past tenses or relative clauses as opposed to time and place adverbials.

In the early 1990s, a group of universities and companies collaborated to form the Linguistic Data Consortium (LDC), whose headquarters are at the University of Pennsylvania in Philadelphia. This group makes available vast quantities of language data, both written and spoken, from dozens of Indo- and non–Indo-European languages. These databases are being used extensively for research into language itself and for testing computer language-processing systems such as automatic speech recognition. LDC's home page at *http://www.ldc.upenn.edu* may be consulted for further information.

A computer can also be used to produce a **concordance** of a literary text, which gives the frequency of every word in a text and the line and page numbers of each occurrence with its context. Such analyses, once carried out painstakingly over many years, were produced for only the most eminent texts (e.g., the Bible). Now a concordance can be accomplished in a short time on any text that has been entered into a computer. The use of concordances on *The Federalist Papers* helped to ascribe the authorship of a disputed paper to James Madison rather than to Alexander Hamilton by comparing the concordance of the paper in question with those of known works by the two writers. For example, the information that Hamilton favoured *while* and Madison *whilst*, as well as Hamilton's fondness for *enough* helped to identify who wrote what. Generally, choice of function words is more useful for author attribution than content words.

A concordance of *sounds* by computer may reveal patterns in poetry that would be nearly impossible for a human to detect. Such an analysis on the *Iliad* showed that many of the lines with an unusual number of etas (/ɛ/) related to youth and lovemaking; the line with the most alphas (/a/) was interpreted as being an imitation of stamping feet.

Poetic and prosaic features such as assonance, alliteration, metre, and rhythm have always been studied by literary scholars. Today computers can do the tedious mechanical work of such analyses, making it possible to analyze even such minute details as distinctive features of sounds in whole texts of poetry and prose. This leaves the researcher with more time to contemplate new ideas — once the texts have been input and transcribed.

Electronic Dictionaries and Lexicons

Large corpora and concordances are now routinely used in making commercial dictionaries. Many dictionaries themselves have become machine readable. The earliest were desk dictionaries prepared for photocomposition with codes for typesetting. Later some dictionaries such as *COBUILD* and the *Oxford English Dictionary* added codes for linguistic information. This information was explicitly coded for computer access and retrieval. The second edition of the *OED* was published in twenty volumes (Simpson and Weiner 1989), but the machine-readable dictionary is available in electronic form for the mainframe, on a CD-ROM, and on the World Wide Web. This makes it possible to find all the words quoted from a particular author or work or in a particular year or range of years (Logan 1991).

Machine-readable dictionaries provide material for constructing lexical databases or electronic lexicons. A lexicon is a highly formalized dictionary, what we have called a "mental dictionary." Work has focused on abstracting information from available machine-readable desk dictionaries prepared for printing, such as *Webster's Seventh New Collegiate*. This is available on UNIX systems and the NeXT machine. Lexical databases are especially valuable in natural language processing, the automation of the processes of language comprehension, production, and acquisition in both written and spoken media (Boguraev and Briscoe 1989).

Computers That Talk and Listen

> The first generations of computers had received their inputs through glorified typewriter keyboards, and had replied through high-speed printers and visual displays. Hal could do this when necessary, but most of his communication with his shipmates was by means of the spoken word. Poole and Bowman could talk to Hal as if he were a human being, and he would reply in the perfect idiomatic English he had learned during the fleeting weeks of his electronic childhood.
>
> Arthur C. Clarke, *2001, A Space Odyssey*

The ideal computer is multilingual; it should "speak" computer languages such as C, FORTRAN, and Java as well as languages such as English and Japanese. For many purposes, it would be helpful if we could communicate with computers as we communicate with other humans, through our native language, but the computers portrayed in films and on television as capable of speaking and understanding human language do not yet exist.

Computers at present are severely limited in their ability to comprehend and produce spoken language, and programming them to do so is one of the most difficult and challenging goals of computational linguistics. Properly programmed, a computer can "understand" language fragments with vocabularies of 100 to 1000 words in an extremely narrow context (simple syntax and a limited semantic field — e.g., weather reports).[1] (The vocabulary can be larger for written language or for language spoken with pauses between individual words.) Computers can produce synthetic speech that imitates the human voice fairly well, but humans must program them to do it and tell them what to say.

Just as human speech production and comprehension differ in the psychological mechanisms involved (although they access the same mental grammar), comprehension and production of speech by computers require entirely different programs. In some cases, the attempt is to model the human processor; in others, the goal is to get the computer to speak and understand rather than to shed light on human performance.

Computer comprehension consists of **speech recognition**, the perception of sounds and words, and **speech understanding**, the interpretation of words recognized. Some comprehension programs bypass speech recognition by processing written text. These texts may be typed at a keyboard, in which case they are entered directly into the computer. Optical scanners and interpretive programs are able to convert printed text into an electronic form suitable for computers, but the process is error-prone and highly dependent on such mundane features as the quality of the paper and ink used to create the printed page originally.

Speech production consists of **language generation** — deciding what to say — and **speech synthesis** — the actual creation of speech sounds. As in attempts at computer comprehension, different research groups with different purposes concentrate on one aspect or another of speech production.

Talking Machines (Speech Synthesis)

Machines which, with more or less success, imitate human speech, are the most difficult to construct, so many are the agencies engaged in uttering even a single word — so many are the inflections and variations of tone and articulation, that the mechanician finds his ingenuity taxed to the utmost to imitate them.

Scientific American, January 14, 1871

Early efforts toward building "talking machines" were concerned more with machines that could produce sounds that imitated human speech than with machines that could figure out what to say. In 1779, Christian Gottlieb Kratzenstein won a prize for building such a machine ("an instrument constructed like the *vox humana* pipes of an organ which . . . accurately express the sounds of the vowels") and for answering a question posed by the Imperial Academy of St. Petersburg: "What is the nature and character of the sounds of the vowels *a, e, i, o, u* [that make them] . . . different from one another?" Kratzenstein (1782) constructed a set of "acoustic resonators" similar to the shapes of the mouth when these vowels are articulated and set them resonating by a vibrating reed that produced pulses of air similar to those coming from the lungs through the vibrating vocal cords.

Twelve years later, Wolfgang von Kempelen of Vienna constructed a more elaborate machine with bellows to produce a stream of air like that produced by the lungs and with other mechanical devices to simulate the different parts of the vocal tract. Von Kempelen's machine so impressed the young Alexander Graham Bell, who saw a replica of it in Edinburgh in 1850, that he, together with his brother Melville, attempted to construct a "talking head," making a cast from a human skull. They used various materials to form the velum, palate, teeth, lips, tongue, cheeks, and so on, and they installed a metal larynx with vocal cords made by stretching a slotted piece of rubber. They used a keyboard control system to manipulate all the parts with an intricate set of levers. This ingenious machine produced vowel sounds and some nasal sounds and even a few short combinations of sounds.

With advances in the acoustic theory of speech production and technological developments in electronics, machine production of speech sounds has made great progress. We no longer have to build physical models of the speech-producing mechanism; we can now imitate the process by producing the physical signals electronically.

Research on speech has shown that all speech sounds can be reduced to a small number of acoustic components. One way to produce **synthetic speech** is to mix these important parts together in the proper proportions, depending on the speech sounds to be imitated. It is rather like following a recipe for making soup, which might read "Take two litres of water, add one onion, three carrots, a potato, a teaspoon of salt, a pinch of pepper, and stir it all together." This method of producing synthetic speech would include a "recipe" that might read

(1) Start with a tone at the same frequency as vibrating vocal cords (higher if a woman's or child's voice is being synthesized, lower if a man's).
(2) Add overtones corresponding to the formants required for a particular vowel quality.
(3) Add hissing or buzzing for fricatives.
(4) Add nasal resonances for any nasal sounds.
(5) Temporarily cut off sound to produce stops and affricates.
(6) And so on. . . .

All these "ingredients" are blended together electronically, using computers to produce highly intelligible, more or less natural-sounding speech.

Most synthetic speech still has a machine-like quality or "accent" due to small inaccuracies in simulation and because suprasegmental factors such as changing intonation and stress patterns are not yet fully understood. Still, speech synthesizers today are no harder to understand than a person speaking with a slight "accent." Thus, for instance, *flower* might be pronounced [floɚ] (as *flow* + *er*) but *flour* as [flawr].

Of course, the machine used to produce synthetic speech does not "know" what it is saying. It may be reading a text, a useful function for persons unable to read for some reason, but it employs no linguistic knowledge of syntax or semantics.

When a computer produces synthetic speech, it produces speech sounds corresponding to the input text it is "reading." It must be programmed with a complex set of text-to-speech rules that translate texts written in English orthography into a phonetic transcription from which speech sounds are synthesized and produced. Since, in its synthesis program, the computer uses no semantic or syntactic knowledge (even if such information has been put into its memory), it will read ungrammatical and nonsensical texts in the same way as grammatical ones.

Speech synthesis has important applications. It benefits blind persons in the form of "reading machines," now commercially available. Mute patients with laryngectomies or other medical conditions that prevent normal speech can use synthesizers to express themselves. For example, Eva K. Simmons at North Carolina State University developed a communication system for an individual with so severe a form of multiple sclerosis that he could utter no sound and was totally paralyzed except for nodding his head. Using a head movement for "yes" and no head movement for "no," this individual could select words displayed on a computer screen and assemble sentences expressing his thoughts, which were then "spoken" by a synthesizer.

Most of us these days hear synthesized speech when we call our bank and an "automatic bank clerk" tells us our bank balance or when a telephone information "operator" gives us a requested phone number. Most airlines offer up-to-the-minute arrival and departure information via automatic processing using a synthetic voice. Many information services now available, such as those listing stock prices, are automated and deliver timely information over the telephone via synthesized speech. Although some people find the speech unpleasant, even unnerving, it does make current information available over the telephone to millions of people.

Knowing What to Say

> Speech was given to the ordinary sort of men whereby to communicate their mind; but to wise men, whereby to conceal it.
>
> Robert South, *Sermon* (1676)
>
> PATIENT: Men are all alike.
>   ELIZA: In what way?
> PATIENT: They're always bugging me about something or other.
>   ELIZA: Can you think of a specific example?
> PATIENT: Well, my boyfriend made me come here.
>   ELIZA: Your boyfriend made you come here?
> PATIENT: He says I'm depressed much of the time.
>   ELIZA: I am sorry to hear you are depressed.
>
> Joseph Weizenbaum, *Eliza*

When a computer is "reading" a text, it knows what to say, but in many applications the computer is called on not only to speak but also to decide what to say and to do so grammatically. This is the problem called **language generation**.

In the dialogue at the head of this section, ELIZA is a computer program designed to simulate a non-directive psychiatrist talking to a patient. ELIZA has a collection of prepared phrases stored in memory such as "In what way?" or "Tell me more" that help to keep the conversation going when it doesn't "understand" the patient. When ELIZA recognizes certain syntactic patterns, however, it turns them around to make a sensible response, as when it echoes "Your boyfriend made you come here?" ELIZA was programmed with a bit of syntactic knowledge, allowing it to make grammatical utterances based on the patient's statements, but no semantic knowledge. If a patient says "My sniggle is untherible," then ELIZA would respond with "How long has your sniggle been untherible?"

In other applications, the computer is given bits of knowledge in computer-digestible form (e.g., the day's baseball scores) and then programmed to state that knowledge in fluent, grammatically and semantically correct language (e.g., a report of the baseball scores on the news). This program requires adherence to the rules of syntax and semantics, as well as morphology and phonetics. In some sense, the machine "knows" what it is saying, because if you changed the bits of knowledge fed to it the statement of that knowledge would change too, provided it had been correctly programmed. The most sophisticated language generation programs allow the computer to converse with a human.

One such application is for repairing electronic circuits. The computer is programmed with knowledge of the circuit and a method to enable it to understand and speak phrases and sentences within the context of the repair problem. The following dialogue was observed on one such system developed at Duke University in collaboration with North Carolina State University:

> COMPUTER: This is the circuit fix-it shop. How may I help you?
> TECHNICIAN: I need to fix the RS111 circuit.
> COMPUTER: I am familiar with that circuit. The LED is supposed to be displaying alternately blinking one and seven.
> TECHNICIAN: Where is the LED?
> COMPUTER: In the middle right of the blue region is the LED.
> TECHNICIAN: No light.
> COMPUTER: What is the switch at when the LED is off?
> TECHNICIAN: The switch is down.
> COMPUTER: Put the switch up.

Once the computer has understood the technician's utterance, it uses rules of semantics and syntax, together with a lexicon of words and morphemes, to formulate a grammatical, sensible response, which its synthesizer program then speaks. The rules in many cases are similar to the phrase structure rules seen in Chapter 3, such as form a noun phrase from a determiner followed by a noun. It also has semantic rules that tell it to use *the* with the word *switch* since its "world knowledge" tells it that there is only one switch in that particular circuit.

Unlike a human, though, if the technician used unusual or complex syntax, the computer would be unable to answer the question because the grammar with which it is programmed is incomplete, as is any computer grammar. Similarly, if the technician suddenly changed the subject and asked the computer "Who won the game last night?" or "How much is 2 plus 2?" the computer would be stumped since both its world knowledge and its linguistic knowledge are confined to the narrow realm of repairing circuits.

Machines for Understanding Speech

Understanding is a relative concept. We often complain that our parents or mates or children don't understand what we say, and we are probably at least partially right: 100 percent understanding is an ideal goal toward which we strive in communication, including human–computer communication.

For a machine to understand speech, it must process the speech signal into sounds, morphemes, and words, which is **speech recognition**, and at the same time comprehend the meanings of the words as they occur in phrases and sentences, which is **speech understanding**. In many machine-understanding systems, these are separate stages, with recognition preceding comprehension. In human language processing, these two stages blend together smoothly as listeners recognize some words based on the speech signal alone, while other words have to be figured out from the meanings of words already understood.

Speech Recognition

Speech recognition is far more difficult than speech synthesis. It is comparable to trying to transcribe a spectrogram with only phonetic knowledge of the language spoken. As we have seen, the speech signal is not physically divided into discrete sounds. Human ability to segment the signal arises from knowledge of the grammar, which tells us how to pair certain sounds with certain meanings, which sounds or words may be deleted or pushed together, and when two different speech signals are linguistically the same and when two similar signals are linguistically different. The difficulty of programming a computer to have and use such linguistic knowledge in recognizing speech is enormous.

There are two kinds of speech recognizers. One recognizes speech at the word level, the other at the phoneme level. A word-level recognizer keeps the acoustic patterns of its vocabulary in its memory. When it receives spoken input, it matches the acoustic pattern of the input signal with all of its previously stored acoustic patterns. The best match is chosen as the word or words are recognized.

A phoneme-level recognizer operates in a similar manner, pre-storing acoustic patterns of the sounds of the language and attempting to match them to incoming sound patterns. Phoneme-level recognition is more error-prone than word-level recognition because individual sounds can be confused more easily than individual words. That is, the machine is more likely to confuse the sound [b] with the sound [d] than it is to confuse the word *boy* with the word *dog*; words contain more redundant information than sounds, which helps to resolve confusions and ambiguities.

To ease the difficulties of recognition in some speech-recognizer systems, the user must insert a short pause of about one-third of a second after each word spoken. (The pause between words must exceed the pause that occurs within words during stop and affricate articulation.) This pause shifts the burden of word boundary detection to the human speaker and makes the machine-recognition process more accurate, but it is inconvenient to speak in this manner and reveals that the computer is not capable of "perceiving" in the way a human perceives.

Other speech recognizers accept continuously spoken speech, provided the speaker articulates carefully and clearly. In this case, the speaker may not apply certain optional rules, such as vowel reduction to schwa, vowel and/or consonant deletion, consonant assimilation at word boundaries, and so on; so *did you* is pronounced [dɪd ju], not [dɪǰə]. Natural, rapid, continuous speech — the kind that humans usually use — is not yet machine recognizable with a useful degree of accuracy.

Speech Understanding

> A computer understands a subset of English if it accepts input sentences which are members of this subset, and answers questions based on information contained in the input.
>
> Daniel Bobrow

Computer comprehension of spoken language is so difficult that it is often divided into two stages: recognition and understanding. Even when recognition is successful, and a transcription of the utterance is obtained, understanding is still an exacting task. Words may have several meanings, the syntactic structure of the utterance must be ascertained, and the meaning of the entire utterance must be built up using rules of syntax and the meanings of its parts. In cases of ambiguity, contextual knowledge may be needed to arrive at the intended meaning.

Understanding is also done in stages. One stage is parsing, which is discovering the syntactic structure, or structures, of the utterance. Another stage is semantic processing, which combines the meanings of words, looked up in the computer's lexicon, into phrasal meanings, and so on, until the entire utterance meaning is assembled. A third stage is applying contextual or world knowledge to disambiguate any utterances.

Parsing   To understand a sentence, you must know its syntactic structure. If you didn't know the structure of *Dogs that chase cats chase birds*, you wouldn't know whether dogs or cats chase birds. Similarly, machines that understand language must determine syntactic structure. A **parser** is a computer program that uses a grammar to assign a phrase structure to a string of words. Parsers may use a phrase structure grammar and lexicon similar to those discussed in Chapter 3.

For example, a parser may use a grammar containing the following rules: S→NP VP, NP→Det N, and so on. Suppose the machine is asked to parse *The child found the kittens*. A **top-down parser** proceeds by first consulting the grammar rules and then examining the input string to see if the first word could begin an S. If the input string begins with a Det, as in the example, the search is successful, and the parser continues by looking for an N and then a VP. If the input string happened to be *child found the kittens*, then the parser would be unable to assign it a structure because it doesn't begin with a Det, which is required by this grammar to begin an S.

A **bottom-up parser** takes the opposite tack. It looks first at the input string and finds a Det (*the*) followed by an N (*child*). The rules tell it that this phrase is an NP. It would continue to process *found, the*, and *kittens* to construct a VP, and it would finally combine the NP and VP to make an S.

Occasionally, a parser may have to **backtrack**. In a sentence such as *The little orange rabbit hopped*, the parser might mistakenly assume that *orange* is a noun. Later in the parse, when the error is apparent, the parser can return to *orange* and process it as an adjective. To avoid backtracking, Mitch Marcus at MIT invented the **look-ahead parser**, which is capable of scanning ahead. In the above example, a look-ahead parser will find that the word following *orange* is not a verb, so that *orange* cannot be a noun and must be an adjective. Even look-ahead parsers may have to backtrack when parsing garden path sentences such as *The horse raced past the barn fell*, discussed in Chapter 11, because the amount of structure that must be scanned ahead is too great.

In general, humans are far more capable of understanding sentences than computers. But there are some interesting cases in which computers outperform humans. For example, try to figure out what the sentence *Buffalo buffalo buffalo buffalo* means. Most people have trouble determining its sentence structure and are thus unable to understand it. A computer parser, with four simple rules and a lexicon in which *buffalo* has three entries as a noun, verb, and adjective, will easily parse this sentence as follows:

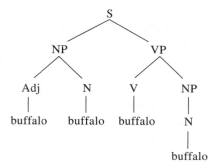

It means "Bison from the city of Buffalo deceive bison." Alternatively, the first NP could be N (*buffalo*), and the second NP could be Adj N (*buffalo buffalo*), with the resulting string N–V–Adj–N, hence "Bison deceive bison from the city of Buffalo."

Regardless of details, every parser uses some kind of grammar to assign phrase structures to input strings. If a structure cannot be found, then the input string is ungrammatical relative to that grammar.

A **morphological parser** uses rules of word formation, such as those studied in Chapters 2 and 6, to decompose words into their component morphemes. A morphological parser decomposes a word such as *kittens* into *kitten + s*.

Morphological parsers also operate on morphologically complex words, such as *uncomfortably*, to decompose them into the bound morphemes *un-*, *-able*, and *-ly* and the free morpheme *comfort*, all of which have regular meanings that may be looked up in the lexicon and rules that determine the meanings of the combinations.

As suggested, just as humans store information about words and morphemes in their mental lexicons, so too a machine must store such information in a lexicon in its "memory." Information such as syntactic category (parts of speech), pronunciation, spelling, subcategorization, plurality if irregular like *men*, tense if irregular like *found*, and elements of meaning are usually included in the computer's lexicon. Thus, when a parser encounters *found*, it can use the spelling to look the word up in the lexicon, at which point the computer would know, among other things, that it is a verb, that it is the past tense of *find*, and that it is transitive.

A parser may use as its grammar **transition networks** that represent the grammar as a complex of **nodes** (circles) and **arcs** (arrows). A network that is the equivalent of the phrase structure rule S→NP VP may be illustrated as

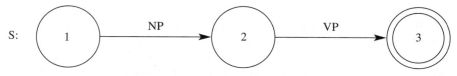

Transition Network for S → NP VP

The nodes are numbered to distinguish them; the double circle is the "final" node.

The parser would start at node 1, examine an input string of words, and, if the string began with a noun phrase, "move" to node 2. (If it did not find a noun phrase, then it would decide that the input string was not a sentence, unless there were other S networks in the grammar to try.) The parser would then look for a verb phrase, and if one were found the VP arc could be traversed to node 3. Because node 3 is a final node, the parser would indicate that the input string was a sentence consisting of a noun phrase and a verb phrase. The program would also, of course, have to specify which string of words constitutes an NP, VP, and so on.

Augmented transition networks (ATN) are transition networks in which each arrow not only indicates a syntactic category but may carry other information essential to accurate parsing as well. For example, an ATN extension to the above example might carry a condition on the VP arc to ensure subject–verb agreement, as shown below:

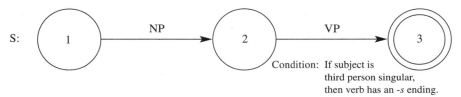

Augmented Transition Network for S → NP VP

Semantic Processing Once a sentence is parsed, the machine can try to find the meaning or semantic representation. This task requires a dictionary with the meaning of each word, and rules for combining meanings, as discussed in Chapter 4. The question of how to represent meaning is one that has been debated for thousands of years, and it continues to engender much research in linguistics, philosophy, psychology, cognitive science, and computer science.

One approach common to several semantic-processing methods first locates the verb of the sentence — based on the sentence parse — and then identifies the thematic roles of noun phrases such as agent, theme, location, instrument, any complements, and so on.

Another approach is based on mathematical logic and represents the sentence *Zachary loves sushi* as

LOVE (ZACHARY, SUSHI)

where LOVE is a two-place predicate, or function, with arguments ZACHARY and SUSHI. Rules of semantic interpretation indicate that the reference of ZACHARY is the person named *Zachary*, that the reference of SUSHI is something in the world called *sushi*, and that *Zachary* is the subject loving and *sushi* is the object loved. The lexicon will indicate that *Zachary* is usually the name of a human male and that *sushi* is a combination of rice with things such as raw fish, cooked egg, and vegetables.

Two well-known natural language-processing systems from the 1970s used this **logical** approach of semantic representation. One, named SHRDLU by its developer, Terry Winograd, demonstrated a number of abilities, such as being able to interpret questions, draw inferences, learn new words, and even explain its actions. It operated within the context of a "blocks world," consisting of a table, blocks of various shapes, sizes, and colours, and a robot arm for moving the blocks. Using simple sentences, one could ask questions about the blocks and give commands to have blocks moved from one location to another.

The second system is called LUNAR, developed by William Woods. The LUNAR program was capable of answering questions phrased in simple English about the lunar rock samples brought back from the moon by the astronauts. LUNAR translated English questions into a logical representation, which it then used to query a database of information about the lunar samples.

Semantic networks are also used to represent meaning. They are similar to ATNs in appearance, consisting of nodes and arcs, but they function differently. Here is how *Zachary loves sushi* might be represented using semantic networks:

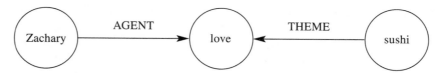

Semantic Network for *Zachary loves sushi*

Semantic networks make thematic roles explicit, which is a crucial part of semantic interpretation.

Both logical expressions and semantic networks are convenient for machine representation of meaning because they are easily programmed and because the meanings thus represented can be used linguistically. For example, if the computer is asked "Who loves sushi?" it can search through its knowledge base for a node labelled *love*, look to see if an arc labelled THEME is connected to *sushi*, and if so find the answer by looking for an arc labelled AGENT.

Pragmatic Processing

When a sentence is structurally ambiguous, such as *He sells synthetic buffalo hides*, the parser will compute each structure. Semantic processing may eliminate some of the structures if they are anomalous, but often some ambiguity remains. For example, the structurally ambiguous sentence *John found a book on the Oregon Trail* is semantically acceptable in both its meanings. To decide which meaning is intended, situational knowledge is needed. If John is in the library researching history, then the "book *about* the Oregon Trail" meaning is most likely; if John is on a two-week hike to Oregon, then the "book *upon* the Oregon Trail" meaning is more plausible.

Many language-processing systems have a **knowledge base** containing contextual and world knowledge. The semantic-processing routines can refer to the knowledge base in cases of ambiguity. For example, the linguistic component of the electronic repair task system, referred to earlier, will have two meanings for *The LED is in the middle of the blue region at the top.* Its knowledge base, however, disambiguates the meanings because it "knows" that the LED is in the middle of the blue region, and the blue region is at the top of the work area, rather than that the LED is in the middle top of the blue region.

Computer Models of Grammars

I am never content until I have constructed a . . . model of the subject I am studying. If I succeed in making one, I understand; otherwise I do not.

William Thomson (Lord Kelvin), *Molecular Dynamics and the Wave Theory of Light*

A theory has only the alternative of being right or wrong. A model has a third possibility: it may be right, but irrelevant.

Manfred Eigen, *The Physicist's Conception of Nature*

The grammars used by computers for parsing may not be the same as the grammars linguists construct for human languages, which are models of linguistic competence, nor are they similar, for the most part, to models of linguistic performance. Computers are different from people, and they achieve similar ends differently. Just as an efficient flying machine is not a replica of any bird, so too efficient grammars for computers do not resemble human language grammars in every detail.

Computers are often used to model physical or biological systems, which allows researchers to study those systems safely and sometimes even cheaply. For example, the performance of a new aircraft can be simulated and the test pilot informed as to safe limits in advance of actual flight.

Computers can also be programmed to model the grammar of a language. An accurate grammar — one that is a true model of a speaker's mental grammar — should be able to generate *all* and *only* the sentences of the language. Failure to generate a grammatical sentence indicates the presence of an error in the grammar, because the human mental grammar has the capacity to generate all possible grammatical sentences — an infinite set. In addition, if the grammar produces a string that speakers consider to be ungrammatical, that also indicates a defect in the grammar; although in actual speech performance we often produce ungrammatical strings — such as sentence fragments, slips of the tongue, word substitutions, and blends — we judge them to be ill formed if we notice them. Our grammars cannot generate these strings.

One computer model of a grammar was developed in the 1960s by Joyce Friedman to test a generative grammar of English. More recently, computational linguists have been developing computer programs to generate the sentences of a language and to simulate human parsing of these sentences using the rules included in various linguistic theories, such as Noam Chomsky's government and binding theory. The computational models developed by Ed Stabler, Robert Berwick, Amy

Weinberg, and Mark Johnson, among other computational linguists, show that it is possible, in principle, to use a transformational grammar, for example, in speech and comprehension, but it is still controversial whether human language processing works in this way. That is, even if we can get a computer program to produce sentences as output and to parse sentences fed into the machine as input, we still need psycholinguistic evidence that this is the way the human mind stores and processes language.

It is because linguistic competence and performance are so complex that computers are being used as a tool in the attempt to understand human language and its use. We have emphasized some of the differences between the way humans process language and the way computers process language. For example, humans appear to do speech recognition, parsing, semantic interpretation, and contextual disambiguation more or less simultaneously and smoothly while comprehending speech. Computers, on the other hand, usually have different components, loosely connected, and perform these functions individually.

One reason for this is that, typically, computers have only a single, powerful processor capable of performing one task at a time. Currently, computers are being designed with multiple processors, albeit less powerful ones, that are interconnected. The power of these computers lies both in the individual processors and in the connections. Such computers are capable of **parallel processing**: carrying out several tasks simultaneously.

With a parallel architecture, computational linguists may be better able to program machine understanding in ways that blend all the stages of processing together, from speech recognition to contextual interpretation, and hence approach more closely the way humans process language.

Summary

Computers can process language. They can be programmed to translate from a **source language** into a **target language**, and they can aid scholars analyzing a literary text or a **corpus** of linguistic data. They can also communicate with people via spoken human language.

Speech synthesis is accomplished by programming computers to imitate the human voice electronically. **Language generation** is the problem of determining *what* the computer should say. Sometimes canned or prepared speech is used. At other times, the computer uses rules of grammar to assemble sentences from a lexicon of words and morphemes that express the intended meaning.

Speech understanding is a far more difficult task because the physical speech signal alone is insufficient for understanding a spoken message; much linguistic knowledge is required. Machine comprehension of speech begins with **speech recognition**, which attempts to identify phonemes and words from the raw acoustic signal. To understand a string of recognized words, the machine must first **parse** the string to determine its syntactic structure. **Parsers** are computer programs that use a grammar to determine the structure of an input string. Parsers may operate **top-down** or **bottom-up**. **Look-ahead parsers** scan forward to avoid the need to **backtrack**. **Morphological parsers** decompose words into their component morphemes according to rules of word formation.

Once parsed, an utterance is analyzed semantically using **logical representations, semantic networks,** or other devices to represent meaning.

Computers may be programmed to model a grammar of a human language and thus rapidly and thoroughly test that grammar. Modern computer architectures include **parallel-processing** machines that can be programmed to process language more as humans do, insofar as they can carry out many linguistic tasks simultaneously.

Note

1. See *Spoken Natural Language Dialog Systems* (Smith and Hipp 1994) for an excellent, detailed description of what is involved in getting a computer to understand and respond correctly to spoken input.

Exercises

1. The use of spectrograms or "voiceprints" for speaker identification is based on the fact that no two speakers have the same speech characteristics. List some of the differences you have noticed in the speech of several individuals. Can you think of any possible reason why such differences exist?

2. Using a bilingual dictionary of some language you do not know, attempt to translate the following English sentences by looking up each word.

   The children will eat the fish.
   Send the professor a letter from your new school.
   The fish will be eaten by the children.
   Who is the person that is hugging that dog?
   The spirit is willing, but the flesh is weak.

   A. Using your own knowledge, or someone else's, give a *grammatically correct* translation of each sentence. What difficulties are brought to light by comparing the two translations? Briefly mention five of them.
   B. Have a person who knows the target language translate the grammatical translation back into English. What problems do you observe? Are they related to any of the difficulties you mentioned in part A?

3. Suppose you were given a manuscript of a play and were told that it is by either Christopher Marlowe or William Shakespeare (both born in 1564). Suppose

further that this work, and all of the works of Marlowe and Shakespeare, were in a computer. Describe how you would use the computer to help determine the true authorship of the mysterious play.

4. Speech synthesis is useful because it allows computers to convey information to the blind. Think of five other uses for speech synthesis in our society.

5. Some advantages of speech recognition are similar to those of speech synthesis. A computer that understands speech does not require a person to use hands or eyes in order to convey information to the computer. Think of five other possible uses for speech recognition in our society.

6. Consider the following ambiguous sentences. Explain the ambiguity, give the most likely interpretation, and state what a computer would have to know to achieve that interpretation.

> Example: A cheesecake was on the table. It was delicious and was soon eaten.
> Ambiguity: "It" can refer to the cheesecake or the table.
> Likely: "It" refers to the cheesecake.
> Knowledge: Tables aren't usually eaten.

   a.   John gave the boys five dollars. One of them was counterfeit.
   b.   The police were asked to stop drinking in public places.
   c.   John went to the bank to get some cash.
   d.   He saw the Grand Canyon flying to New York.
   e.   Do you know the time? (*Hint:* This is a pragmatic ambiguity.)
   f.   Concerned with spreading violence, the premier called a press conference.

*7. Here is a transition network similar to the one on page 507 for the Noun Phrase (NP) rule given in Chapter 3.

NP → (Det) (Adj)* N (PP)

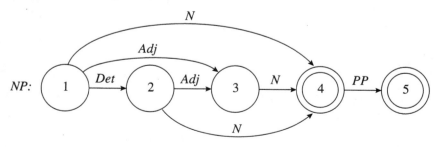

Using this as a model, draw a transition network for the verb phrase rules VP→V (NP) (PP)

(*Hint:* Recall from Chapter 3 that the above rule abbreviates four rules.)

*8. Here are some sentences along with a possible representation in predicate logic notation.

(i)   Birds fly. FLY (BIRDS)
(ii) The student understands the question. UNDERSTAND (THE STUDENT, THE QUESTION)
(iii) Penguins do not fly. NOT (FLY [PENGUINS])
(iv) The wind is in the willows. IN (THE WIND, THE WILLOWS)
(v)   Kathy loves her cat. LOVE (KATHY, [POSS (KATHY, CAT)])

A. Based on the examples in the text, and those in part B of this exercise, give a possible semantic network representation for each of these examples.

B. Here are five more sentences and a possible semantic network representation for each. Give a representation of each using the predicate logic notation. (*Hint:* Review Chapter 4 for the meanings of *agent, theme, patient, goal*, and so on.)

(i)   Seals swim swiftly.

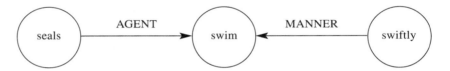

(ii) The student doesn't understand the question.

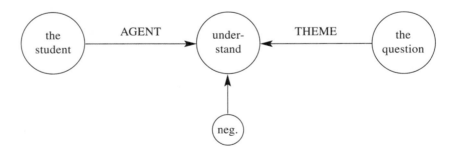

(iii) The pen is on the table.

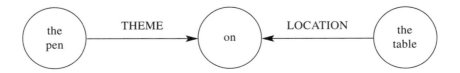

(iv) My dog eats bones.

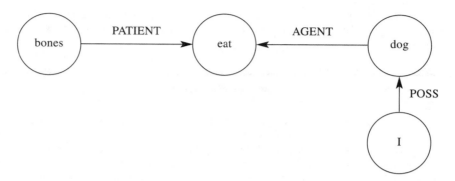

(v) Emily gives money to charity. (*Hint: Give* is a three-place predicate.)

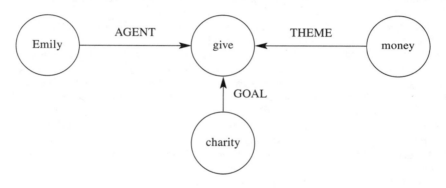

Works Cited

Biber, Douglas. 1988. *Variation across Speech and Writing.* Cambridge, UK: Cambridge University Press.

Boguraev, Branimir, and Ted Briscoe, eds. 1989. *Computational Lexicography for Natural Language Processing.* London: Longman.

Dahl, H. 1979. *Word Frequencies of Spoken American English.* Essex, CT: Verbatim.

Francis, W.N., and H. Kučera. 1982. *Frequency Analysis of English Usage: Lexicon and Grammar.* Boston: Houghton Mifflin.

Kučera, H., and W.N. Francis. 1967. *Computational Analysis of Present-Day American English.* Providence, RI: Brown University Press.

Locke, W.N., and A.D. Boothe, eds. 1955. *Machine Translation of Languages.* New York: Wiley.

Logan, Harry M. 1991. "Electronic Lexicography." *Computers and the Humanities* 25: 351–61.

Quirk, R., et al. 1985. *A Comprehensive Grammar of the English Language.* London: Longman.

Simpson, J.A., and E.S.C. Weiner, eds. 1989. *Oxford English Dictionary.* 2nd ed. Oxford: Oxford University Press.

Sinclair, J.M., ed. 1987. *Collins COBUILD English Language Dictionary.* London: Collins.

Smith, R., and R. Hipp. 1994. *Spoken Natural Language Dialog Systems.* New York: Oxford University Press.

Further Reading

Aijmer, Karin, and Bengt Attenberg, eds. 1991. *English Corpus Linguistics: Studies in Honour of Jan Svartvik.* London: Longman.

Allen, J. 1987. *Natural Language Understanding.* Menlo Park, CA: Benjamin/Cummings.

Armstrong, Susan, ed. 1994. *Using Large Corpora.* Cambridge, MA: MIT Press.

Barr, A., and E.A. Feigenbaum, eds. 1981. *The Handbook of Artificial Intelligence.* Los Altos, CA: I. William Kaufmann.

Berwick, R.C., and A.S. Weinberg. 1984. *The Grammatical Basis of Linguistic Performance: Language Use and Acquisition.* Cambridge, MA: MIT Press.

Carlson, Greg N., and Michael K. Tanenhaus, eds. 1989. *Linguistic Structure in Language Processing.* Dordrecht: Kluwer Academic Publishers.

Gazdar, G., and C. Mellish. 1989. *Natural Language Processing PROLOG: An Introduction to Computational Linguistics.* Reading, MA: Addison-Wesley.

Hockey, S. 1980. *A Guide to Computer Applications in the Humanities.* London: Duckworth.

Johnson, M. 1989. "Parsing as Deduction: The Use of Knowledge in Language." *Journal of Psycholinguistic Research* 18.1: 105–28.

Kratzenstein, C.G. "Sur la naissance de la formation des voyelles." *Acta. Acad. Petrograd. Trans.* 1782. *J. Phys. Chim. Hist. Nat. Arts* 21: 358–81.

Ladefoged, P. 1981. *Elements of Acoustic Phonetics.* 2nd ed. Chicago: University of Chicago Press.

Lea, W.A. 1980. *Trends in Speech Recognition.* Englewood Cliffs, NJ: Prentice-Hall.

Marcus, M.P. 1980. *A Theory of Syntactic Recognition for Natural Language.* Cambridge, MA: MIT Press.

Slocum, J. 1985. "A Survey of Machine Translation: Its History, Current Status, and Future Prospects." *Computational Linguistics* 11.1.

Sowa, J., ed. 1991. *Principles of Semantic Networks.* San Mateo, CA: Morgan Kaufmann.

Stabler, E.P., Jr. 1992. *The Logical Approach to Syntax: Foundations, Specifications, and Implementations of Theories of Government and Binding.* Cambridge, MA: MIT Press, Bradford Books.

Weizenbaum, J. 1976. *Computer Power and Human Reason.* San Francisco, CA: W.H. Freeman.

Winograd, T. 1972. *Understanding Natural Language.* New York: Academic Press.

———. 1983. *Language as a Cognitive Process.* Reading, MA: Addison-Wesley.

Witten, I.H. 1986. *Making Computers Talk.* Englewood Cliffs, NJ: Prentice-Hall.

GLOSSARY

Abbreviation Shortened form of a word (e.g., *prof* from *professor*). Cf. **clipping**.

Accent (1) Prominence. Cf. **stressed syllable**; (2) the phonology or pronunciation of a specific regional dialect (e.g., Newfoundland or Southern United States); (3) the pronunciation of a language by a non-native speaker (e.g., French accent).

Accidental gaps Phonological or morphological forms that constitute possible but non-occurring lexical items (e.g., *blick* or *unsad*).

Acoustic Pertaining to physical aspects of sound.

Acoustic phonetics The study of the physical properties of speech sounds.

Acoustic signal The sound waves produced by any sound source, including speech.

Acquired dyslexia Loss of ability to read correctly following brain damage in persons who were previously literate.

Acronym Word composed of the initials of several words (e.g., *PET scan* from *positron emission tomography scan*).

Active sentence A sentence in which the noun phrase subject in deep structure is also the noun phrase subject in surface structure. Cf. **passive sentence**.

Adjective (Adj) The syntactic category of words that may precede a noun in a noun phrase and have the semantic effect of qualifying the noun. In many languages adjectives are inflected to agree with the nouns they modify in gender, number, and case. In English some adjectives may be inflected to indicate comparative or superlative degree (e.g., *-er, -est*). Also a **lexical category**.

Adjective Phrase (AdjP) The syntactic category containing an adjective as its head that may be modified by an intensifier, such as *very, rather,* or *quite*. It appears in noun phrases before the noun (e.g., *the very good life*) and in verb phrases following a copular verb, such as *be*, as a predicate adjective (e.g., *life is very good*).

Adverb (Adv) The syntactic category, also lexical category, of words that may occur last within a verb phrase in deep structure, and qualify the verb in that verb phrase. A transformation that moves adverbs allowing them to occur in many positions in surface structure (e.g., *John wept* silently, *John* silently *wept,* Silently *John wept*).

Adverb Phrase (AdvP) The syntactic category containing an adverb as its head that may be modified by an intensifier, such as *very, rather,* or *quite*. It may occur last within a verb phrase (e.g., *very quietly* in *told the story very quietly*).

Affix Bound morpheme attached to a stem or root morpheme. Cf. **prefix, suffix, infix, circumfix**.

Affricate Sound produced by a stop closure followed immediately by a slow release, characteristic of a fricative; phonemically, a sequence of stop + fricative.

African American English (AAE) A dialect of English spoken by some African Americans, largely in the United States; formerly known as Black English.

Afro-Asiatic A family of languages spoken in northern Africa and the Middle East. They include the Semitic languages of Hebrew and Arabic, as well as languages spoken in biblical times, such as Aramaic, Babylonian, Canaanite, and Moabite.

Agent The thematic role of the noun phrase whose referent deliberately performs the action described by the verb (e.g., *George* in *George hugged Martha*).

Agrammatism Language disorder usually resulting from damage to Broca's area in which the patient has difficulty with syntax. Cf. **Broca's area**.

Agreement A relationship between words of a sentence in which the choice of one restricts the choice of the other (e.g., the choice of a pronoun is restricted by the person, number, and gender of its antecedent). See also **subject–verb agreement**.

Airstream mechanisms The ways in which air from the lungs or mouth is moved to produce speech sounds.

Allomorph Alternative phonetic forms of a morpheme — for example, /s/, /z/, and /ɪz/ are allomorphs of the English plural morpheme.

Allophones Predictable phonetic variants of phonemes (e.g., [p] and [pʰ] of the phoneme /p/ in English).

Alphabetic writing A writing system in which each symbol typically represents one sound segment.

Alveolar ridge The part of the hard palate directly behind the front teeth.

Alveolars Sounds produced by raising the tongue to the alveolar ridge (the bony tooth ridge).

Alveopalatals Sounds whose place of articulation is the hard palate immediately behind the alveolar ridge.

Ambiguous The term used to describe a word, phrase, or sentence with multiple meanings.

American Sign Language (ASL; AMESLAN) The sign language used by the deaf community in North America. Cf. **sign languages**.

Analogic change A language change in which a rule generalizes to forms hitherto unaffected (e.g., the plural of *cow* changed from the earlier *kine* to *cows* by the generalization of the plural formation rule). Also called **internal borrowing**.

Analogy The use of one form as a sample by which other forms can be similarly constructed. One theory of language acquisition suggests that children learn how to put words together to form phrases and sentences by analogy.

Analytic Sentences or propositions that are necessarily true by virtue of meaning alone (e.g., *Kings are monarchs*).

Anaphor A pronominal expression such as a reflexive pronoun whose reference is determined by an antecedent in the same sentence or discourse (e.g., *herself* is an anaphor coreferential with its antecedent *Sue* in the sentence *Sue bit herself*).

Anaphora The process of replacing a longer expression with a shorter one, especially with a pronoun, that is coreferential with the longer expression.

Anomalous Semantically ill formed (e.g., *Colourless green ideas sleep furiously*).

Anomaly A violation of semantic rules resulting in expressions that give the impression of being nonsense (e.g., *The verb crumpled the milk*).

Anomia A form of aphasia in which patients have word-finding difficulties.

Antecedent The noun phrase in a sentence or discourse with which a pronoun is coreferential (e.g., the antecedent of *he* in *John said he was tired* is John).

Anterior A phonetic feature of consonants whose place of articulation is in front of the palato-alveolar area, including labials, interdentals, and alveolars.

Antonyms Words that are opposite in meaning. Cf. **gradable pairs, complementary pairs, relational opposites**.

Aphasia Language loss or disorders following damage to the left cerebral hemisphere of the brain.

Aphesis/Aphaeresis Loss of initial vowels as in the common pronunciation of *possum* for *opossum*.

Apocope Loss of final sounds in a word so that, for example, Old English *nama* /namə/ became *name* /nem/.

Arbitrary The property of language, including sign language, whereby there is no natural or intrinsic relationship between the way a word is pronounced (or signed) and its meaning (e.g., the sounds represented by *casa* in Spanish, *house* in English, *dom* in Russian, etc., have the same meaning).

Arc Part of the graphical depiction of a transition network represented as an arrow labelled with syntactic category and connecting two nodes. Cf. **node, transition network**.

Argot The set of words used by a particular occupational group, such as scientists, artists, musicians, bricklayers, etc. Also called **jargon**.

Article (Art) One of several subclasses of determiners (e.g., *the, a, an*).

Articulators The tongue and lips, which change the shape of the vocal tract to produce different speech sounds.

Articulatory phonetics The study of how the vocal tract produces speech sounds; the physiological characteristics of speech sounds.

Aspirated A term that refers to voiceless consonants in which the vocal cords remain open for a brief period after the release of the constriction, resulting in a puff of air (e.g., the [pʰ] in *pit*). Cf. **unaspirated**.

Assimilation The change or spread of phonetic feature values that makes segments more alike; a process in which one phone assumes features of a neighbouring phone (e.g., the vowel of *man* assumes the nasal quality of the surrounding consonants).

Assimilation rules Phonological rules that change feature values of segments to make them more similar.

Asterisk The symbol [*] used to indicate ungrammatical or anomalous examples (e.g., *cried the baby*, *sincerity dances*). Also used in historical and comparative linguistics to represent a reconstructed form.

Audio-lingual A language teaching method based on the assumption that language is acquired mainly through imitation, repetition, and reinforcement.

Auditory phonetics The study of the perception of speech sounds.

Augmented transition network (ATN) A transition network in which the arcs carry information necessary to parsing over and above their syntactic category label. Cf. **transition network, arc, node**.

Austronesian A family of languages spoken over a wide expanse of the globe, from Madagascar to Hawaii, including Hawaiian itself, as well as Maori, spoken in Malaysia and Singapore.

Automatic machine translation The use of computers to translate from one language to another. Cf. **source language, target language**.

Autonomy of language The independence of language as a genetically conditioned cognitive system that is not derived from the general intellectual capacities of the human species.

Auxiliary Verbs (Aux) Verbal elements, traditionally called "helping verbs," that co-occur with and qualify the main verb in a verb phrase with regard to tense, aspect, modality, etc. (e.g., *have, be, will, may, must*).

Babbling Sounds produced in the first few months after birth, including sounds that do and do not occur in the language of the household. Deaf children "babble" with hand gestures paralleling the vocal babbling of hearing children.

Back vowels Vowel sounds involving the back of the tongue.

Back-formation A new word created by removing what is mistakenly considered to be an affix (e.g., *edit* from *editor*).

Backtrack The action in which a parser returns to a decision point where it went wrong and makes a different choice.

Banned languages Languages or dialects that are by law not permitted in an attempt to maintain one official language.

Bilabials Sounds articulated by bringing both lips together.

Binary-valued The two values of a distinctive feature (e.g., a segment is either nasal [+nasal] or oral [–nasal]).

Bird calls One or more short notes that convey messages associated with the immediate environment, such as danger, feeding, nesting, flocking, etc.

Bird songs Complex patterns of notes with no internal structure used to mark territory and to attract mates.

Black English (BE) See **African American English**.

Blend Word composed of the parts of more than one word (e.g., *smog* from *smoke* + *fog*).

Bootstrapping Children's use of their knowledge of syntax to learn the meanings of words. Experiments have shown that knowing a word is a verb or a noun informs children that it has a meaning referring to an action or to an object, respectively.

Borrowing The incorporation of a loan word from one language into another (e.g., English borrowed *buoy* from Dutch). Cf. **loan words**.

Bottom-up parser A parser that first examines the input sequence of words and then determines whether it conforms to the rules of grammar stored in the computer's memory. Cf. **parser, top-down parser**.

Bound Describes a pronoun that is coreferential with a noun phrase under at least one interpretation of the sentence or discourse (e.g., *she* in *Jane believes she loves Tarzan*). Cf. **free**.

Bound morphemes Morphemes that can occur only in words attached to other morphemes; prefixes, suffixes, infixes, circumfixes, and some roots, such as *cran* in *cranberry*. Cf. **free morphemes**.

Broadening A semantic change in which the meaning of a word changes over time to become more encompassing (e.g., *dog* once meant a particular breed of dog).

Broca, Paul A French neurologist who in 1861 suggested that the left side of the brain is the language hemisphere.

Broca's aphasia A language disorder following damage to Broca's area in which speech is non-fluent, lacking in grammatical morphemes, and agrammatic. Comprehension is fairly good except for difficulties in comprehending sentences that depend on syntactic structures.

Broca's area or region A front part of the left hemisphere of the brain, damage to which causes telegraphic, agrammatic speech (Broca's aphasia).

Calligraphy Originally referred to the art of drawing Chinese characters; the profession or art of elegant writing.

Canadian raising An allophonic variation typical of many speakers of Canadian English (and some speakers of American English) whereby /aj/ and /aw/ become [ʌj] and [ʌw] before voiceless consonants. The centred and raised diphthongs are considered typical of Canadian English.

Case The morphological form of nouns and pronouns, and in some languages articles and adjectives, indicating the grammatical relationship to the verb (e.g., *I* is the *nominative* case of the first person singular pronoun in English and functions as a subject; *me* is in the *accusative* case and can only function as an object).

Case endings Suffixes on the noun based on its grammatical relationship to the verb.

Case theory The study of thematic roles and grammatical case in languages of the world.

Causative The thematic role of the noun phrase referring to a natural force that brings about a change.

Cause The thematic role of the noun phrase whose referent is a natural force that causes a change (e.g., *The wind* in *The wind damaged the roof*).

Cerebral hemispheres The two parts of the brain, the left hemisphere controlling the movements of the right side of the body, the right hemisphere those of the left side.

Characters (Chinese) The units of Chinese writing, each of which represents a morpheme or word. Cf. **ideogram, ideograph, logogram**.

Circumfix Bound morpheme, parts of which occur in a word both before and after the root (e.g., *ge---t* in German *geliebt*, "loved," from the root *lieb*).

Clause A sentence containing a noun phrase and a verb phrase which may be embedded in another sentence.

Cleft sentence A sentence of the type *it is XP who/that YP*, where XP is a constituent noun phrase and YP the rest of the sentence from which the XP was moved. In a cleft sentence, we cut ("cleave") one constituent (represented by XP) out of the sentence and place it in a position in which it will function as a contrasting force in the sentence (e.g., in the sentence *Romeo loves Juliet*, we can say *It is Romeo who loves Juliet* or *It is Juliet who loves Romeo*).

Click A speech sound produced by a velaric airstream mechanism found in certain African languages. (One of the clicks is similar to the sound of disapproval made by speakers of non-click languages, often spelled *tsk, tsk*.)

Clipping The morphological process whereby a word is shortened, or abbreviated, while still keeping the same meaning and word class (e.g., *prof* is a clipped form of *professor*). Cf. **abbreviation**.

Closed class words Function words; a category of words that rarely if ever has new words added to it (e.g., prepositions, pronouns, conjunctions).

Coarticulation The spreading of phonetic features either in anticipation of sounds or in the perseveration of articulatory processes.

Coda One or more phonological segments that follow the nucleus of a syllable (e.g., the /st/ in /prist/ *priest*).

Code-switching The insertion of a word or phrase of a language other than that being spoken or from varieties of a language into a single sentence, or the movement back and forth between two languages or dialects.

Cognates Words in related languages that developed from the same ancestral root, such as English *horn* and Latin *cornú*.

Coherent A series of sentences that "hang together" is coherent. Coherence is the principle of organization that accounts for the connectedness or identity of a text.

Coinage The construction and addition of new words to the lexicon.

Communication A system for conveying information. Language is a linguistic system of communication; there are also non-linguistic systems of human communication, as well as systems used by other species.

Communicative competence Knowledge of the appropriate social uses of language, such as greetings, taboo words, polite forms of address, and various styles that are suitable to different situations.

Comparative linguistics The branch of linguistics that deals with language change by comparing related languages.

Comparative method The technique used by linguists to deduce forms in an earlier stage of a language by examining corresponding forms in several of its daughter languages.

Comparative reconstruction The deduction of an earlier form of genetically related languages by application of the comparative method.

Competence, linguistic The knowledge of a language represented by the mental grammar that accounts for speakers' linguistic creativity. For the most part, linguistic competence is unconscious knowledge.

Complementary distribution Phones that never occur in the same phonetic environment (e.g., [p] and [pʰ] in English). Cf. **allophones**.

Complementary pairs Two antonyms related in such a way that the negation of one is the meaning of the other (e.g., *alive* means not *dead*). Cf. **gradable pairs, relational opposites**.

Compound A word composed of two words (e.g., *washcloth*).

Computational linguistics A subfield of linguistics and computer science that is concerned with computer processing of human language.

Concordance An alphabetical index of all the words of a text that gives the frequency of every word and the location of each occurrence in the text with its verbal context.

Conditioned sound change Phonological change that occurs in specific phonetic contexts only.

Connotative meaning/connotation The evocation or affective meaning associated with a word. Two words may have the same referential, denotative meaning but different connotations.

Consonant (C) A speech sound produced with some constriction of the airstream.

Consonant cluster Two or more consonants in sequence (e.g., /str/ in the word *string*).

Consonant harmony Consonant articulation agreement within a word. This often occurs in children's first words (e.g., *doggy* may be pronounced as *goggy* or *doddy*).

Consonantal Phonetic feature distinguishing the class of obstruents, liquids, and nasals, which are [+consonantal], from other sounds that are [–consonantal].

Consonantal alphabet The symbols of a consonantal writing system.

Consonantal alphabetic writing A writing system in which only symbols representing consonants are used; vowels are inferred from context (as in Arabic).

Constituent A syntactic unit in a phrase structure tree (e.g., *The girl* is a noun phrase constituent in the sentence *The boy loves the girl*).

Constituent structure The hierarchically arranged syntactic units such as noun phrase and verb phrase that underlie every sentence.

Constituent structure tree Cf. **phrase structure tree**.

Content words The nouns, verbs, adjectives, and adverbs constituting the major part of the vocabulary. Cf. **open class words**.

Continuants Sounds in which the airstream continues without complete interruption through the mouth.

Contour tones Tones in which the pitch glides from one level to another (e.g., from low to high as a rising tone).

Contradiction Negative entailment: the truth of one sentence necessarily implies the falseness of another sentence (e.g., *He opened the door* and *The door is closed*). Cf. **entailment**.

Contradictory A sentence that is false by virtue of its meaning alone (e.g., *My aunt is a man*).

Contralateral The control of one side of the body by the cerebral hemisphere on the opposite side.

Contrast The difference between two speech sounds that can result in a difference in meaning. Contrasting sounds are allophones — that is, they represent distinct phonemes.

Contrastive stress Additional stress placed on a word to highlight it or to clarify the referent of a pronoun (e.g., in *Joe hired Bill and **he** hired Sam*, with a contrastive stress on *he*, it is usually understood that Bill rather than Joe hired Sam).

Convention (conventional) The agreed-on arbitrary relationship between the form and the meaning of a word.

Cooperative Principle A broad principle within whose scope fall the various maxims of conversation. It states that, in order to communicate effectively, speakers should agree to be informative and relevant.

Coordinate structure A syntactic structure in which two or more constituents of the same syntactic category are joined together with a conjunction such as *and* or *or* (e.g., *bread and butter, the big dog or the small cat, huffing and puffing*).

Coordinate structure constraint A constraint on all languages that prohibits the movement of constituents out of a coordinate structure.

Copula A verb, usually a form of *to be*, that equates the expressions on either side of it (e.g., *is* in *Bob is the professor*).

Coreference The relation between two noun phrases that refer to the same entity.

Coreferential Refers to noun phrases (including pronouns) that refer to the same entity.

Coronals The class of sounds including labials, alveolars, and palatals.

Corpus A collection of utterances, gathered from spoken or written sources, used for linguistic research and analysis.

Corpus callosum The nerve fibres connecting the right and left cerebral hemispheres.

Cortex The approximately ten billion neurons forming the outside surface of the brain; also referred to as the *grey matter*.

Count nouns Nouns that can be enumerated; nouns that may appear with an indefinite article or in the plural form (e.g., *one book/a book, two books*). Cf. **mass nouns**.

Cover symbol A symbol that represents a class of sounds (e.g., C for consonants; V for vowels).

Creativity of language, creative aspect of linguistic knowledge Speakers' ability to combine the finite number of linguistic units of their language to produce and understand an infinite range of novel sentences never produced or heard previously.

Creole A pidgin language adopted by a community as its native tongue and learned by children as their first language.

Critical age, critical age hypothesis The period between early childhood and puberty during which, it is hypothesized, a child can acquire language without instruction. During this period, language learning proceeds easily, swiftly, and without external intervention. After this period, the acquisition of the grammar is difficult and, for some individuals, never fully achieved.

Cuneiform A form of writing in which the characters are produced using a wedge-shaped stylus. It was developed by the Sumerians in the fourth millennium B.C.E. and was borrowed by several civilizations, including the Assyrians and the Babylonians. It was in use as late as the fifth century B.C.E.

Cyrillic alphabet The alphabet used by many Slavic languages, including Russian.

Daughter language A descendant of an earlier form of a language (e.g., French is a daughter language of Latin, which is the parent).

Deep structure Any phrase structure tree generated by the phrase structure rules of a transformational grammar. The basic syntactic structures of the grammar.

Definite A noun phrase that refers to a unique object insofar as the speaker and listener are concerned.

Deictic, deixis Describes words or expressions whose reference relies entirely on context (e.g., *I, now, here*). Cf. **person deixis, time deixis, place deixis, demonstrative articles**.

Deletion A process that removes phonemic segments in certain contexts, (e.g., in contractions, such as *he is* becoming *he's* or *I will* becoming *I'll*).

Demonstrative articles, demonstratives Words such as *this, that, those*, and *these* that function syntactically as articles but are semantically deictic because context is needed to determine the referent of the noun phrase in which they occur.

Denotative meaning The referential meaning of a word.

Derivation The steps in the application of phonological rules to a phonemic representation ending with a phonetic representation.

Derivational morphemes Morphemes added to stem morphemes to form new stems or words that may not change the syntactic category of a word.

Derived structure Any structure resulting from the application of transformational rules — that is, any underlying structure except deep structure.

Descriptive grammar A linguist's description or model of the mental grammar, including the units, structures, and rules. The attempt to state what speakers unconsciously know about their language.

Determiner (Det) The syntactic category (also lexical category) of words and expressions that, when combined with a noun form, form a noun phrase; a category of expressions that can directly qualify the noun in a noun phrase. Includes the articles *the* and *a*, demonstratives such as *this* and *that*, quantifiers such as *each* and *every*, and expressions such as *John Smith's*.

Diacritics Additional markings on written symbols to specify various phonetic properties such as length, tone, stress, and nasalization; extra marks added to written characters that change their usual value (e.g., the tilde [~] drawn over the letter *n* in Spanish represents a palatalized nasal rather than an alveolar nasal).

Dialect A language variety used by a particular group of speakers. Cf. **regional dialect**, **social dialect**. Dialects are the mutually intelligible forms of a language that differ in systematic ways from each other.

Dialect atlas A book of dialect maps showing the areas where specific dialectal characteristics occur in the speech of the region.

Dialect levelling Movement toward a greater uniformity or decrease in variations among dialects.

Dialect map A map showing the areas where specific dialectal characteristics occur in the speech of the region.

Dichotic listening Experimental method for testing brain lateralization in which subjects hear different auditory signals in the left and right ears.

Diglossic Speakers who employ different varieties of the same language or two distinct languages for different purposes (e.g., Francophones outside Quebec who restrict French to the home and friends while employing English for business in the community at large).

Digraph Two letters used to represent a single sound (e.g., *gh* represents [f] in *enough*).

Diphthong Vowel + glide (e.g., [aj], [aw], [ɔj] as in *bide, bout, boy*).

Direct method Second-language teaching without any reference to the native language and without use of translation or grammar instructions. It is an attempt to stimulate learning a foreign language in the way children learn their native language.

Direct object The grammatical relation of a noun phrase when it appears immediately below the verb phrase (VP) in deep structure.

Discontinuous dependency A situation in which two syntactic elements that are adjacent in deep structure, and function together to give a certain meaning, are separated in surface structure by a transformation (e.g., *They ran a big bill up*. The deep structure is *They ran up a big bill*. *Ran* and *up* depend on each other for the meaning of "ran up").

Discontinuous morpheme A morpheme with multiple parts that occur in more than one place in a word or sentence. Cf. **circumfix**.

Discourse Linguistic units composed of several sentences.

Discourse analysis The study of discourse.

Dissimilation rules Phonological rules that change feature values of segments to make them less similar.

Distinctive Describes linguistic elements that contrast.

Distinctive features Phonetic properties of phonemes that account for their ability to contrast meanings of words (e.g., *voice, nasal, labial*).

Ditransitive verb A verb that appears to take two noun-phrase objects (e.g., *give* in *He gave Sally the gift*). Ditransitive verb phrases often have an alternative form with a prepositional phrase in place of the first noun phrase, as in *He gave the gift to Sally*.

Dominate In a phrase structure tree, when a continuous downward path can be traced from a node labelled *A* to a node labelled *B*, *A* dominates *B*.

Downdrift The lowering of pitch (and tones) of a phrase or utterance.

Early Middle English Vowel Shortening A sound change that shortened vowels, such as the first *i* in *criminal*. As a result, *criminal* was unaffected by the Great Vowel Shift, leading to word pairs, such as *crime/criminal*. Other similar alternations occur in Modern English for the same reason.

Early Modern English The dialects of English spoken between c. 1500 and 1800.

Ease of articulation Expression referring to the tendency when we speak to make it easier to move the articulators.

Ebonics An alternative term for the various dialects of African American English, first used in 1997.

Egressive See **egressive airstream mechanism**.

Egressive airstream mechanism Method by which lung air is pushed out of the mouth.

Egressive sounds Produced by air moving out of the mouth.

Ejective A speech sound produced with a glottalic airstream mechanism.

Embedded sentence A sentence occurring within a sentence in a phrase structure tree (e.g., *You know that sheepdogs cannot swim*).

Entailment The relationship between two sentences where the truth of one necessarily implies the truth of the other (e.g., such a relationship holds between *Corday assassinated Marat* and *Marat is dead* since, if the first is true, the second must be true).

Entails One sentence entails another if the truth of the first necessarily implies the truth of the second (e.g., *The sun melted the ice* entails *The ice melted* since, if the first is true, the second must be true).

Environment The phonemic context in which a sound occurs.

Epenthesis The insertion of consonants or vowels in a word that often serves to break up heavy consonant clusters.

Eponym A word taken from a proper name, such as *john* for "toilet."

Etymeme A bound base that has etymological relevance (e.g., *-ceive* in *receive*).

Etymology The history of words; the study of the history of words.

Euphemism A word or phrase that replaces a taboo word or is used to avoid reference to certain acts or subjects (e.g., *powder room* for *toilet*).

Event-related brain potentials (ERPs) The electrical signals emitted from different areas of the brain in response to different kinds of stimuli.

Experiencer The thematic role of the noun phrase referring to one who receives sensory input or who perceives something (e.g., *Helen* in *Helen heard Robert playing the piano*).

Extension The reference of an expression.

Feature, phonetic feature The smallest articulatory characteristics into which speech sounds may be analyzed.

Feature matrix A representation of phonological segments in which the columns represent segments and the rows represent features, each cell being marked with a + or – to designate the value of the feature for that segment.

Feature-changing rules, feature-spreading rules Phonological rules that change feature values of segments to make them more similar (cf. **assimilation rules**) or less similar (cf. **dissimilation rules**).

Field of discourse Variation in language depending on what is being talked or written about; fields may be divided into imaginative genres (novels, science fiction, romances, dramas, etc.) and informational genres (scientific, instructional, technical, journalistic, bureaucratic, etc.), each with a characteristic use of language.

Finger spelling Hand gestures symbolizing the letters of the alphabet used when there is no sign in the sign language.

Flap See **tap**.

Folk etymology The process, normally unconscious, whereby words or their origins are changed through non-scientific speculations or false analogies with other words.

Form, linguistic Phonological or gestural representation of a morpheme or word.

Formants The principal frequencies of a speech sound; the overtones of the speech signal. They are depicted by dark bands on spectrograms.

Free Describes a pronoun that refers to an object not explicitly mentioned in the sentence or discourse (e.g., *it* in *Everyone saw it*).

Free morphemes Single morphemes that constitute words.

Free variation Alternative pronunciations of a word in which one sound is substituted for another without changing the word's meaning (e.g., pronunciation of *bottle* with a glottal stop as the medial consonant).

Frequency effect Influence on response time of how often words are used in speech and writing.

Fricatives Sounds produced in which the constriction in the mouth or at the lips is very narrow, creating a hiss or friction; sometimes called spirants.

Front vowels Vowel sounds in which the tongue is positioned forward in the mouth.

Function words Grammatical words, including conjunctions, prepositions, articles, etc. Cf. **closed class words**.

Fundamental frequency In speech, the rate at which the vocal cords vibrate, symbolized as F_0, called F-zero, perceived by the listener as pitch.

Gall, Franz Joseph A nineteenth-century physiologist who proposed a theory of brain localization — that is, that different parts of the brain are responsible for different abilities and actions.

Gapping The syntactic process of deletion in which subsequent occurrences of a verb are omitted in similar contexts (e.g., *Bill washed the grapes and Mary the cherries*).

Geminates A sequence of two identical sounds; an alternative way of representing long segments.

Generic term A general term that applies to a whole class; the use of a word that ordinarily has the semantic feature [+male] to refer to both sexes (e.g., *mankind* meaning "the human race"; the use of the [+male] pronoun as the neutral form, as in *Everyone should do his duty*).

Genetically related Describes two or more languages that developed from a common earlier language (e.g., French, Italian, and Spanish, which all developed from Latin).

Genre A category of speech or writing characterized by a particular style and content, such as imaginative genres (novels, science fiction) and informational genres (scientific, journalistic).

Germanic The family of languages that includes German, English, Dutch, the Scandinavian languages, and related dialects.

Glides (G) Sounds produced with little or no obstruction of the airstream that are always preceded or followed by a vowel (e.g., /w/ and /j/ in *we* and *you*).

Gloss A word in one language given to express the meaning of a word in another language (e.g., "house" is the gloss for the French word *maison*); a brief definition of a difficult word or expression.

Glottalic airstream mechanism Air in the pharynx moved through action of the glottis; it is the articulatory method for the production of implosive and ejective sounds.

Glottals/glottal stop Sounds produced with constriction at the glottis; when the air is stopped completely at the glottis by tightly closed vocal cords, a glottal stop is produced.

Glottis The opening between the vocal cords.

Goal The thematic role of the noun phrase toward whose referent the action of the verb is directed (e.g., *the theatre* in *The kids went to the theatre*).

Gradable pairs Two antonyms related in such a way that more of one is less of the other (e.g., *warm* and *cool*, where more warm is less cool and vice versa). Cf. **complementary pairs, relational opposites**.

Grammar The mental representation of a speaker's linguistic competence; what a speaker knows about a language, including its phonology, morphology, syntax, semantics, and lexicon. A linguistic description of a speaker's mental grammar.

Grammar-translation The method for teaching a second language (L2) by which the student memorizes words, inflected words, and syntactic rules and uses them to translate from English to L2 and vice versa.

Grammatical Describes a well-formed sequence of words, one conforming to rules of syntax.

Grammatical case See **case**.

Grammatical categories Traditionally called "parts of speech"; expressions that can substitute for one another without loss of grammaticality (e.g., noun phrases).

Grammatical morpheme/word Free function word or bound morpheme required by the syntactic rules (e.g., *to* and *-s* in *He wants to go*). Cf. **inflectional morphemes**.

Grammatical relation Any one of several structural positions that a noun phrase may assume in a sentence. Cf. **subject, direct object**.

Grammaticality The degree to which a string of words conforms to the syntactic rules for sentences.

Graphemes The symbols of an alphabetic writing system; the letters of an alphabet.

Great Vowel Shift A sound change in many dialects of English that took place sometime after the fourteenth century and continued into the eighteenth century in which the Middle English long vowels changed qualities.

Grimm's Law The description formulated by Jacob Grimm of regular phonological changes between Indo-European and Germanic consonants.

Hangul An alphabet for writing the Korean language designed in the fifteenth century around the phonemic principle.

Hapology The loss of repeated identical or nearly identical segments (e.g., Old English *Engla land* became *England*).

Head The lexical category always present in the corresponding phrasal category (e.g., the noun of a noun phrase).

Hemidecorticates Individuals with one brain hemisphere removed.

Hemiplegics Individuals (including children) with acquired unilateral lesions of the brain who retain both hemispheres (one normal and one diseased).

Heteronyms Different words that are spelled the same but pronounced differently, such as *sow*, a female pig, and *sow*, meaning "to scatter seeds."

Hierarchical structure The groupings, subgroupings, etc., of words in a phrase or sentence.

Hieroglyphics A pictographic writing system used by the Egyptians around 4000 B.C.E.

High (vowels) Vowels formed with the tongue raised high in the mouth accompanied by raised jaw and closed mouth, as in *beat, bit, boot,* and *book.*

Hiragana A Japanese syllabary used to write native words of the language; may co-occur with ideographic characters.

Historical and comparative linguistics The branch of linguistics that deals with how languages change, what kinds of change occur, and why they occur.

Holophrastic The stage of child language acquisition in which one word equals one sentence.

Homographs Different words spelled identically and possibly pronounced the same (e.g., *lead*, the metal, and *lead*, what leaders do; or *bear,* the animal, and *bear*, to carry or endure).

Homonyms Different words pronounced, and possibly spelled, the same (e.g., *to, too, two* or *bat* the animal, *bat* the stick, and *bat* as in *bat the eyelashes*).

Homophones Different words that are pronounced the same (e.g., *rose* and *rows*).

Homorganic consonants Two sequential consonants that are articulated with the same organs and agree in their place of articulation.

Hypernym See **superordinate**. A more general word that includes other more specific words in it (e.g., *tree* is a hypernym of *oak, birch*, and *maple,* called hyponyms).

Hyponym A word whose sense is included in that of a more general or superordinate word, sometimes called a hypernym. *Oak, birch*, and *maple* are co-hyponyms of the superordinate *tree.* Hyponymy is a "kind of" relationship, as in "An oak is a kind of tree."

Iconic relationship, iconicity A non-arbitrary relationship between form and meaning, such as the male and female symbols on toilet doors.

Ideogram, ideograph A character of a word writing system, often highly stylized, that represents a concept or the pronunciation of the word representing that concept.

Idiolect An individual's way of speaking, reflecting that person's grammar.

Idiom An expression whose meaning may be unrelated to the meanings of its parts (e.g., *to kick the bucket* meaning "to die").

Ill formed An ungrammatical or anomalous sequence of words.

Illocutionary force The effect of a speech act, such as a warning, a promise, a threat, a bet, etc. (e.g., the illocutionary force of *I resign!* is the act of resignation).

Imitation theory A theory of child language acquisition that claims that children learn their language by imitating adult speech.

Immediately dominate If a node labelled *A* is the first node above a node labelled *B* in a phrase structure tree, then *A* immediately dominates *B*.

Implication See **entailment**.

Implosive Sounds produced with a glottalic ingressive airstream.

Impoverished data The incomplete, noisy, and unstructured utterances that children hear, including slips of the tongue, false starts, and ungrammatical or incomplete sentences; the lack of evidence as to which utterances are well formed and which are not. Also referred to as the **poverty of the stimulus**.

Indexicality See **deixis**.

Indo-European The descriptive name given to the ancestor language of many modern language families, including Germanic, Slavic, Romance, etc.

Inference The derivation of additional knowledge from facts already known.

Infix A bound morpheme that is inserted in the middle of a word or stem.

Inflectional morphemes Bound grammatical morphemes that are added to complete words according to rules of syntax (e.g., third person singular verbal suffix -*s*).

Ingressive airstream mechanism The method of producing speech sounds in which air is sucked into the vocal tract through the mouth during part of the articulation.

Initialism A type of acronym that is pronounced as separate letters (e.g., *MP* for *Member of Parliament*).

Innateness hypothesis Scientific hypothesis that posits that the human species is genetically equipped to acquire universal grammar, which is the basis for all human languages. Cf. **Universal Grammar (UG)**.

Instrument The thematic role of the noun phrase whose referent is the means by which an action is performed (e.g., *a paper clip* in *Houdini picked the lock with a paper clip*).

Intension The non-referential part of the meaning of an expression. Cf. **sense, extension**.

Intensity The magnitude of sound waves, perceived by the listener as loudness.

Interdentals Sounds produced by inserting the tip of the tongue between the upper and lower teeth.

Internal borrowing A language change in which the effect of a rule spreads to forms hitherto unaffected. Cf. **analogic change**.

International Phonetic Alphabet The phonetic alphabet designed by the International Phonetic Association to be used to represent the sounds found in all human languages.

International Phonetic Association (IPA) The organization founded in 1888 to further phonetic research and develop the International Phonetic Alphabet.

Intonation Pitch contour of a phrase or sentence.

Intransitive Verb A verb that may not be followed by a noun phrase direct object in deep structure (e.g., *sleep*).

Inventory of sounds The phonetic segments of a language.

Ipsilateral Refers to the processing of auditory signals by the same side of the brain in which the signal is received. Cf. **contralateral**.

Isogloss The boundary separating one regional dialect or dialectal characteristic from another.

Jargon Special words peculiar to the members of a profession or group. Cf. **argot**.

Jargon aphasia Form of aphasia in which phonemes are substituted, often producing nonsense words.

Kana The characters of either of the two Japanese syllabaries, *Katakana* and *Hiragana*.

Kanji The Japanese term for the Chinese characters used in Japanese writing.

Katakana A Japanese syllabary generally used for writing loan words and to achieve the effect of italics.

Knowledge base Contextual and word knowledge built into many language-processing systems.

Labials Sounds articulated with the lips.

Labiodentals Sounds produced by touching the bottom lip to the upper teeth.

Language faculty That part of human biological and genetic makeup specifically designed for language acquisition and use.

Language generation A computer process in which grammatical sentences and discourses are constructed as part of a human–computer interaction.

Language purists Prescriptivists who attempt to establish a particular dialect or usage as the only correct one.

Larynx The structure of muscles and cartilage in the throat that contains the vocal cords; often called the "voice box."

Lateral A sound produced with air flowing past one or both sides of the tongue.

Lateralization Term used to refer to any cognitive functions localized to one or the other side of the brain.

Lax vowels Short vowels produced with very little tension in the vocal cords.

Length A prosodic feature referring to duration of segment. Two sounds may contrast in length (e.g., *long* versus *short*).

Level tones Relatively stable (non-gliding) pitch on syllables of tone languages. Also called **register tones**.

Lexical access The process by which we obtain information about the meaning of a word from our mental lexicon. A number of experimental techniques have been used in studies of lexical access.

Lexical ambiguity Ambiguity — multiple meanings — due to an ambiguous word (e.g., *He was lying on a stack of bibles*).

Lexical category A syntactic category whose members are words (e.g., noun, verb, article); those categories occurring only on the right side of phrase structure rules; those categories occurring just above the words in a phrase structure tree.

Lexical content morpheme word Morphemes that constitute the major word classes — nouns, verbs, adjectives, adverbs. Cf. **open class**.

Lexical decision Task of subjects in psycholinguistic experiments who on presentation of a spoken or printed stimulus must decide whether it is a word or not.

Lexical gap Possible but non-occurring words; forms obeying the phonological rules of a language for which as yet there is no meaning (e.g., *blick* in English).

Lexical insertion The collection of principles governing the positions of words and morphemes in deep structure phrase structure trees.

Lexical paraphrases Paraphrases based on synonyms (e.g., *She lost her purse* and *She lost her handbag*).

Lexical semantics The subfield of semantics concerned with the meanings of words and the meaning relationships among words.

Lexicographer One who edits or works on a dictionary.

Lexicography The editing or making of a dictionary.

Lexicon The component of the grammar containing speakers' knowledge about morphemes and words; a speaker's mental dictionary.

Lingua franca The major language used in an area where speakers of more than one language live to permit communication and commerce among them.

Linguistic competence The knowledge of a language represented by the mental grammar that accounts for speakers' linguistic creativity. For the most part, linguistic competence is unconscious knowledge.

Linguistic context The meaning of a sentence or utterance based solely on its grammatical structure.

Linguistic performance The use of linguistic competence in the production and comprehension of language; behaviour as distinguished from knowledge.

Linguistic theory The principles that characterize all human languages, the discovery of which is the goal of modern linguistics.

Liquids (L) Sounds such as /r/ and /l/ in which there is obstruction of the air but not sufficient to cause friction.

Loan translation Compound words or expressions whose parts are translated directly into the borrowing language. *Marriage of convenience* is a loan translation from the French *mariage de convenance*. Also called *calque*.

Loan words Words in one language whose origins are in another language (in Japanese, *besiboru [baseball]* is a loan word from English). Cf. **borrowing**.

Localization The term used to refer to the fact that different areas of the brain appear to be responsible for representation and processing of distinct cognitive systems.

Location The thematic role of the noun phrase whose referent is the place where the action of the verb occurs (e.g., *her office* in *Vicki graded exams in her office*).

Logical problem of language acquisition The question posed by Noam Chomsky when he asked "What accounts for the ease, rapidity and uniformity of language acquisition in the face of impoverished data?"

Logical representation Method of representing semantic information that utilizes notations from symbolic logic.

Logograms The symbols of a word or logographic writing system.

Logographic writing See **word writing**.

Look-ahead parser A parser capable of scanning forward in a sequence of words to avoid mistaken assumptions.

Loudness The listener's perception of the magnitude of sound waves.

Low (vowels) Vowels produced by lowering the tongue from a central position in the oral cavity accompanied by a lowered jaw and open mouth, such as *bat* and *bother*.

Magnetic resonance imaging (MRI) A technique used to investigate the sites of brain lesions.

Main clause See **matrix sentence**.

Main verb The non-auxiliary verb in the verb phrase in the deep structure of a sentence.

Manner of articulation The way the airstream is obstructed as it travels through the vocal tract. Stop, nasal, affricate, and fricative are some manners of articulation. Cf. **place of articulation**.

Marked That member of a gradable pair of antonyms that is not used in questions of degree (e.g., *low* is the marked member of the pair *high/low* because we ask *How high is the mountain?* not **How low is the mountain?*); in a male–female pair of words, the word that contains a derivational morpheme, usually the female word (e.g., *princess* is marked, whereas *prince* is unmarked). Cf. **unmarked**.

Mass nouns Nouns that cannot ordinarily be enumerated (e.g., *milk, water; *two milks* is grammatical only when it means "two kinds of milk," "two containers of milk," etc.).

Matrix sentence The larger sentence (S) in which other sentences or clauses may be embedded (e.g., in the sentence *Mary knew that he was wrong*, the matrix sentence is *Mary knew that he was wrong* and the embedded sentence or clause is *that he was wrong*).

Maxim of manner A conversational convention that states that a speaker's discourse should be brief and orderly and should avoid ambiguity and obscurity.

Maxim of quality A conversational convention that states that a speaker should not lie or make unsupported claims.

Maxim of quantity A conversational convention that states that a speaker's contribution to the discourse should be as informative as is required — neither more nor less.

Maxim of relevance A conversational convention that states that a speaker's contribution to a discourse should always have a bearing on, and a connection with, the matter under consideration.

Maxims of conversation Conversational conventions such as the maxim of quantity that people appear to obey so as to give coherence to discourse.

Mean length of utterances (MLU) A measure used by child language researchers to refer to the number of words or morphemes in a child's utterance; a more accurate measure of the acquisition stage than chronological age of the child.

Meaning Refers to the conceptual or semantic aspect of a word or sentence that permits us to comprehend the message being conveyed. The linguistic sign has both a form (its pronunciation) and a meaning.

Meaning shift A semantic change in which the meaning of a word changes over time (e.g., *silly* once meant "happy").

Mental grammar The rules (largely unconscious) that speakers of a language have in their brain that allows them to understand and use that language.

Meronym A part-to-whole relationship in which the meronym is "part of" a larger entity.

Metaphor Non-literal meaning (e.g., *The walls have ears*, meaning "You may be overheard").

Metathesis A phonological rule that reorders segments, often by transposing two sequential sounds.

Metonym A word used in place of another word or expression to convey the same meaning (e.g., the use of *Ottawa* to indicate the federal government).

Mid (vowels) Vowels produced by raising the tongue from a position midway between high and low vowels, as in *bait, bet, boat*, and *butt*.

Middle English The dialects of English spoken between 1100 and 1500 C.E.

Mimetic Similar to imitating, acting out, or miming.

Minimal pair (or set) A pair (or set) of words that are identical except for one phoneme, occurring in the same place in the string (e.g., *pain* /pen/, *bane* /ben/, *main* /men/).

Modal verbs or modals (M) Another term for auxiliary verbs.

Modern English The dialects of English spoken from 1500 C.E. to the present.

Modularity The organization of the brain and the mind into distinct, independent, and autonomous parts that interact with each other.

Monogenetic theory of language origin The belief that all languages originated from a single source.

Monomorphemic word A word consisting of one morpheme.

Monophthong Simple vowel. Cf. **diphthong**.

Monosyllabic Having one syllable (e.g., words such as *boy, through*).

Morpheme Smallest unit of linguistic meaning.

Morphological parser A parser that uses rules of word formation to decompose words into their component morphemes.

Morphological rules Rules for the combination of morphemes to form stems and words.

Morphology The study of the structure of words; the component of the grammar that includes the rules of word formation.

Morphophonemic orthography A writing system, usually alphabetic, in which knowledge of how different forms of a word are pronounced is needed to read 100 percent correctly. For example, one needs to know English to know that the *ea* in *please* represents a high front tense vowel, whereas in *pleasant ea* represents a mid front lax vowel.

Morphophonemic rules Rules that specify the pronunciation of morphemes; a morpheme may have more than one pronunciation determined by such rules (e.g., the plural morpheme in English is regularly pronounced /s/, /z/, or /əz/).

Naming task An experimental technique asking subjects to read aloud printed stimuli and measuring their response times. The naming task is also used in studies of aphasics, who are asked to name the object shown in a picture.

Narrow transcription A detailed phonetic transcription. Cf. **transcription, phonetic**.

Narrowing A semantic change in which the meaning of a word changes over time to become less extensive (e.g., *deer* once meant "animal").

Nasal passages The passageways between the throat and the nose through which air passes if the velum is open.

Nasal sounds Speech sounds produced with an open nasal passage permitting air to go through the nose as well as the mouth (e.g., /m, n, ŋ/). Cf. **oral sounds**.

Nasalization The process of assimilation by which a vowel becomes or is nasalized in the environment before a nasal segment.

Natural class A class of sounds characterized by a phonetic property or feature pertaining to all members of the set (e.g., class of stops).

Neo-Grammarians A group of nineteenth-century linguists who claimed that sound shifts (i.e., changes in phonological systems) took place without any exceptions.

Neurolinguistics That branch of linguistics concerned with the brain mechanisms underlying the acquisition and use of human language; the study of the neurobiology of the language.

Neuron Nerve cell.

Neutralization rules Phonological rules that obliterate the contrast between two phonemes in certain environments (e.g., in some dialects of English, /t/ and /d/ are both pronounced as voiced flaps intervocalically as in *writer, rider*).

Niger-Kordofanian A family of languages including most of the languages of Africa, such as Swahili, Kikuyu, and Zulu.

Node A labelled branch point in a phrase structure tree; part of the graphical depiction of a transition network represented as a circle, pairs of which are connected by arcs. Cf. **arc, phrase structure tree, transition network**.

Non-continuants Sounds in which air is totally constricted as it passes through the vocal tract. Cf. **stops, affricates**.

Non-count noun See **mass nouns**.

Non-distinctive features Phonetic features of phonemes that are predictable by rule (e.g., aspiration in English).

Non-phonemic A difference in sounds (phones) that is predictable, redundant, or non-distinctive, such as the aspiration of a voiceless stop at the beginning of a word.

Non-redundant A distinctive or phonemic feature of English consonants, contrasting nasal consonants and oral consonants, whereas nasality is a redundant feature of English vowels.

Nonsense word A permissable phonological form without meaning (e.g., *slithy*).

Noun (N) The syntactic and lexical category of words that can comprise the core of a noun phrase (e.g., *book, Jean, sincerity*). In many languages, nouns have grammatical alternations for number, case, and gender and are modified by determiners.

Noun phrase (NP) The syntactic category of expressions containing some form of a noun or pronoun and capable of functioning as the subject or as various objects in a sentence.

Nucleus That part of the syllable that has the greatest acoustic energy; usually the vowel portion of a syllable (e.g., /i/ in /prist/ *priest*).

Obligatory transformation A transformation that must apply in order for the derived sentence to be grammatical (e.g., the transformation that, in some grammatical theories, enforces subject–verb agreement).

Obstruents (O) The class of sounds consisting of non-nasal stops, fricatives, and affricates. Cf. **sonorants**.

Occupational deixis See **social and occupational deixis**.

Old English The dialects of English spoken between 449 and 1100 C.E.

Onomatopoeic, onomatopoetic Terms used to describe words whose pronunciations suggest their meanings (e.g., *meow, buzz*).

Onset One or more phonemes that precede the syllable nucleus (e.g., /pr/ in /prist/ *priest*).

Open class words Lexical content words; a category of words that commonly adds new words (e.g., nouns, verbs).

Optional transformation A transformation whose application is immaterial insofar as the grammaticality of the derived sentence is concerned (e.g., the transformation that moves adverbs).

Oral cavity The mouth area through which air passes during the production of speech.

Oral sounds Non-nasal sounds produced by raising the velum to close the nasal passages so that air can escape only through the mouth. Cf. **nasal sounds**.

Orthoepists Prescriptivist grammarians in the sixteenth to eighteenth centuries who were concerned with the pronunciation of words and the spelling–pronunciation relationship.

Orthography The written form of a language; spelling.

Overgeneralization Children's treatment of irregular verbs and nouns as if they were regular (e.g., *bringed, goed, singed or foots, mouses, sheeps, childs*). This shows that the child has acquired the regular rules but has not yet learned that there are exceptions. Overgeneralization also refers to the process used by children to extend the meaning of a word (e.g., *papa* to refer to all men). Cf. **undergeneralization**.

Overtones The harmonics of an acoustic signal; the formants of a speech signal.

Palatalization A change in the place of articulation to the palatal region.

Palatals Sounds produced by raising the front part of the tongue to the palate.

Palate The section of the roof of the mouth behind the alveolar ridge.

Palato-alveolar See **alveopalatals**.

Paradigm A set of forms derived from a single root morpheme (e.g., *give, gives, given, gave, giving* or *woman, women, woman's, women's*).

Parallel processing The ability of a computer to carry out several tasks simultaneously due to the presence of multiple central processors.

Paraphrases Sentences with the same meaning, except possibly for minor differences in emphasis (e.g., *He ran up a big bill* and *He ran a big bill up*).

Parent language An earlier form of a language (e.g., Latin is the parent language of French, which is the daughter).

Parse The act of determining the grammaticality of sequences of words according to certain rules of grammar and assigning a linguistic structure to the grammatical ones.

Parser A computer program that determines the grammaticality of sequences of words according to whatever rules of grammar are stored in the computer's memory and assigns a linguistic structure to the grammatical ones.

Participle The form of a verb that occurs after the auxiliary verb *have* (e.g., *kissed* in *John has kissed many girls* or *seen* in *I have seen trouble*).

Passive sentence A sentence in which the verbal complex contains a form of *to be* followed by a verb in its participle form (e.g., *The girl was kissed by the boy; The robbers must not have been seen*). In a passive sentence, the direct object of a transitive verb in deep structure functions as the subject in surface structure. Cf. **active sentence**.

Patient The thematic role of the noun phrase whose referent undergoes the action of the verb, usually called the theme (e.g., *Martha* in *George hugged Martha*).

Performance, linguistic The use of linguistic competence in the production and comprehension of language; behaviour as distinguished from linguistic knowledge.

Performative sentence A sentence containing a performative verb used to accomplish some act. Performative sentences are affirmative and declarative and are in first person, present tense (e.g., *I now pronounce you husband and wife*, when spoken by an empowered person in the appropriate situation, is an act of marriage).

Performative verb A verb, certain usages of which comprise a speech act (e.g., *resign* when the sentence *I resign!* is interpreted as an act of resignation).

Person deixis The use of terms to refer to persons whose reference relies entirely on context (pronouns such as *I, he, you* and expressions such as *this child*). Cf. **deictic, time deixis, place deixis, demonstrative articles**.

Petroglyph A drawing on rock.

Pharynx The tube or cavity in the vocal tract through which the air passes during speech production.

Phone A phonetic realization of a phoneme.

Phoneme A contrastive phonological segment whose phonetic realizations are predictable by rule (e.g., /p/ in *pit* and /b/ in *bit*).

Phonemic environment The phonemic context of a phone; this is represented in the formal statement of a phonological rule by a slash mark (/).

Phonemic principle The principle underlying alphabetic writing systems in which one symbol typically represents one phoneme.

Phonemic representation The phonological representation of words and sentences prior to the application of phonological rules.

Phonetic alphabet Alphabetic symbols used to represent the phonetic segments of speech, in which there is a one-to-one relationship between sound and symbol.

Phonetic features Phonetic properties of segments (e.g., *voice, nasal, labial*) that distinguish one segment from another.

Phonetic representation The representation of words and sentences after the application of phonological rules; symbolic transcription of the pronunciation of words and sentences.

Phonetic similarity Sounds that share most of the same phonetic features.

Phoneticization The process by which a pictographic writing system came to represent the sounds of the words it depicted.

Phonetics The study of linguistic sounds, how they are produced (articulatory phonetics), how they are perceived (auditory or perceptual phonetics), and the physical aspects of speech sounds (acoustic phonetics).

Phonographic symbol A symbol in a writing system that stands for the sounds of a word.

Phonological rules Rules that state what speakers know about the predictable aspects — the phonological regularities — of the speech sounds in their language; rules in the phonological component of a grammar that apply to phonemic representations to derive phonetic representations or pronunciation.

Phonology The sound system of a language; the component of a grammar that includes the inventory of sounds (phonetic and phonemic units) and rules for their combination and pronunciation; the study of the sound systems of all languages.

Phonotactics Sequential constraints; rules stating permissible strings of phonemes.

Phrasal categories Syntactic categories that are composed of other syntactic categories; those categories occurring on the left side of phrase structure rules. Cf. **lexical category**.

Phrasal (sentential) semantics The study of how word meanings combine into phrase and sentence meanings and the meaning relationships among these larger units.

Phrasal verb A verb complex consisting of a lexical verb and a verbal particle (e.g., *look up*). The phrasal verb may be discontinuous, as in *look the number up*.

Phrase structure rules Principles of grammar that specify the constituency of syntactic categories in the language (e.g., NP→Det N).

Phrase structure tree A tree diagram with syntactic categories at each node that reveals both the linear and the hierarchical structures of phrases and sentences.

Phrenology A pseudoscience developed by Spurzheim in the nineteenth century; the practice of determining personality traits and intellectual ability by examination of the bumps on the skull.

Pictogram A form of writing in which the symbols resemble the objects represented; a nonarbitrary form of writing.

Pidgin A simple but rule-governed language developed for communication among speakers of mutually unintelligible languages, often based on one of the languages spoken.

Pinyin An alphabetic writing system for Mandarin Chinese using a Western-style alphabet to represent individual sounds.

Pitch The fundamental frequency as perceived by the listener.

Pitch contour The "melody" or movement from one pitch to another in a speech utterance (e.g., the pattern of falling and rising pitch in an English expression).

Place deixis The use of terms to refer to places whose reference relies entirely on context (e.g., *here, there, next door*). Cf. **deictic, time deixis, person deixis, demonstrative articles**.

Place of articulation The part of the vocal tract at which constriction occurs during the production of speech sounds. Cf. **manner of articulation**.

Plosives Oral or non-nasal stop consonants, so called because the air that is stopped "explodes" with the release of the closure.

Polymorphemic A word consisting of more than one morpheme.

Polysemous A single word with several closely related but slightly different meanings (e.g., *face*, as in the face of a person, a building, or a clock).

Positron emission tomography (PET) Method to detect changes in brain activities and relate these changes to focal brain damage and cognitive tasks.

Possessor The thematic role of the noun phrase referring to one who owns or has something (e.g., *the dog* in *The tail of the dog got caught in the door*).

Possible word A word that conforms to the morphological and phonetic rules of a given language and thus is "possible" even if not used (e.g., *blick* is a possible English word).

Poverty of the stimulus See **impoverished data**.

Pragmatics The study of how context and situation affect meaning.

Predictable feature A non-distinctive, non-contrastive, redundant phonetic feature of a phone (e.g., aspiration is a predictable feature of voiceless stops that occur initially in stressed syllables in English).

Prefix Bound morpheme that occurs before a root or stem of a word; affix that is attached to the beginning of a morpheme or word.

Preposition (P) The syntactic and lexical category of words that occur first in a prepositional phrase.

Prepositional object The grammatical relation of the noun phrase that occurs immediately below a prepositional phrase in deep structure.

Prepositional Phrase (PP) The syntactic category occurring within both noun phrases and verb phrases consisting of a preposition followed by a noun phrase in deep structure.

Prescriptive grammar Rules of grammar brought about by grammarians' attempts to legislate what speakers' grammatical rules should be rather than what they are.

Prestige dialect That dialect that is usually spoken by those in positions of power and the one deemed most correct by prescriptive grammarians.

Presupposition Implicit assumptions about the world required to make an utterance meaningful or appropriate (e.g., *Take some more tea!* presupposes that you already had some tea).

Primary stress The main or predominant *stress* in a word; the primary stress is normally indicated in transcription by an acute accent (e.g., *rèsignátion*).

Primes The basic formal units of sign languages corresponding to phonological elements of spoken language (originally called *cheremes*).

Priming The effect on response time of a previously read or heard related word on the accessing of subsequent words.

Productivity Any process may be said to be productive to the extent that it can be used in the production of new forms in the language. In morphology, processes that can be used freely to form new words from the list of free and bound morphemes. In general, productivity is that property of a language that allows a speaker to produce and understand an infinitely large number of sentences.

Pronoun A word that may be used in place of a Noun Phrase and refers to an entity presumably known to participants in the discourse.

Proper names Names of persons, places, and other entities with unique reference insofar as the speaker and listener are concerned. Usually capitalized in writing.

Prosodic feature Duration (length), pitch, or loudness of vowel sounds.

Proto-Germanic The name given by linguists to the language that was an ancestor of English, German, and other Germanic languages.

Proto–Indo-European See **Indo-European**.

Protolanguage The first identifiable language from which genetically related languages developed.

Psycholinguistics The branch of linguistics concerned with linguistic performance, language acquisition, and speech production and comprehension.

Pulmonic egressive Speech sounds produced by movement of lung air flowing through the vocal tract and out of the mouth or nose. Cf. **glottalic airstream mechanism, ingressive airstream mechanism, velaric airstream mechanism**.

Quality of sound Determined by the kinds of vibrations, or wave form, that are perceived by a listener as differences in speech sounds (e.g., the difference between [i] and [o]).

Raising See **Canadian raising**.

Rebus principle Using a pictogram for its phonetic value (e.g., using a picture of a bee to represent the verb *be* or the sound [b]).

Received Pronunciation (RP) A prestige dialect of southern British English supposedly "received" in court and thus approved by those in authority and by linguistic purists.

Reconstruction Using the comparative method to establish the forms of words in a parent language. Cf. **comparative method**.

Recursion The property of human language in which phrases of the same type occur within themselves, giving rise to the limitless and creative aspects of language.

Recursive Phrase structure rules in which the same syntactic category occurs on the left and right sides (e.g., NP→Det N PP, PP→P NP) and that give rise to recursion.

Reduced vowels Unstressed vowels. In English, all unstressed non-final vowels are reduced to [ə] schwa.

Redundancy rules Principles in the lexicon stating generalizations between semantic features (e.g., a word that is [+human] is [+animate]).

Redundant A non-distinctive, non-phonemic feature of a phone; the value (+ or –) of a phonetic feature that is predictable either from its context or from other feature values of the segment (e.g., [+voicing] is redundant for any nasal phoneme in English since all nasals are voiced).

Reduplication A morphological process that repeats or copies all or part of a word to change its meaning — that is, to derive a new word.

Reference That part of the meaning of a noun phrase that associates it with some entity. That part of the meaning of a declarative sentence that associates it with a truth value, either *true* or *false*. Also called extension. Cf. **referent, sense**.

Reference grammar, scholarly grammar A description of a language that attempts to be as thorough and comprehensive as possible; it can serve as a reference for those interested in establishing grammatical facts.

Referent The entity designated by a noun phrase (e.g., the referent of *John* in *John knows Sue* is the actual person named John under discussion).

Reflexive pronoun A pronoun ending with *-self* that requires a noun-phrase antecedent within the same S (e.g., *A gnome bit himself*).

Regional dialect The dialect spoken by people in a particular area of the language community.

Register A stylistic variant of a language appropriate to a particular social setting. Also called **style**.

Register tones Level tones; high, mid, or low tones.

Regular sound correspondence The occurrence of a phoneme in a word in one language or dialect with a corresponding phoneme in the same position of the word in another dialect or language with this parallel holding for a significant number of words in the two dialects or languages (e.g., /aj/ in non-Southern American English corresponds to /a/ in Southern American English). Also found between new and older forms of the same language.

Reinforcement theory A theory of child language acquisition that claims that children are conditioned into speaking correctly by being negatively reinforced for "errors" and positively reinforced for "correct" usage.

Relational opposites Pairs of antonyms in which one describes a relationship between two objects and the other describes the same relationship when the two objects are mentioned in the opposite order (e.g., *parent* and *child; John is the parent of Susie* describes the same relationship between John and Susie as *Susie is the child of John*).

Response or reaction time (RTs) The measurement of the time it takes subjects to respond in psycholinguistic experiments (e.g., in making lexical decisions, naming objects). RT is assumed to reflect processing time.

Retroflex Refers to sounds produced by curling the tip of the tongue back behind the alveolar ridge.

Retronym Words or expressions that once were redundant but that changes in society or technology have made non-redundant (e.g., *silent films*, for at one time all movies were silent).

Rhyme The nucleus + coda of a syllable (e.g., the /en/ of /ren/ *rain*).

Roman alphabet The characters used in many of the alphabetic writing systems of the world (e.g., English, French, etc.).

Root A morpheme that cannot be further analyzed into other morphemes. It is that part of the word that remains after all other affixes have been removed (e.g., *mean* is the root of the word *meaningfulness*). It carries the lexical content of the word. Also called **lexical content morpheme**.

Rounded vowels Vowel sounds produced with rounding of the lips (e.g., /o, u/).

Rules of syntax Principles of grammar that account for the grammaticality of sentences, word order, structural ambiguity, and much more.

Savants Individuals who show special abilities in one cognitive area while being deficient in others. Linguistic savants may be fluent in language and deficient in general intelligence.

Search model A model of word recognition which suggests that the most recent words are accessed first in lexical access.

Segment (1) An individual sound that occurs in a language; (2) The act of dividing utterances into individual sounds, morphemes, words, and phrases.

Semantic features A notational device for expressing the presence or absence of semantic properties by pluses and minuses (e.g., *baby* is [+young], [–abstract]).

Semantic network A network of arcs and nodes used to represent semantic information about sentences.

Semantic properties The components of meaning of a word (e.g., "young" is a semantic property of *baby, colt*, and *puppy*).

Semantic substitutions Common reading errors by one group of acquired dyslexic patients who produce semantically similar word substitutions (e.g., *hour* is read as *time*).

Semantics The study of the linguistic meanings of words and sentences; the component of the grammar that specifies these meanings.

Semitic A family of languages which includes modern Arabic and Hebrew, as well as the historical languages of Aramaic, Babylonian, Canaanite, and Moabite.

Semivowel A phone that shares features of both consonant and vowel; a glide such as /w/ or /j/ and sometimes /r/.

Sense That part of the meaning of an expression which, together with context, determines its referent. Also called intension. For example, knowing the sense or intension of a noun phrase such as *the prime minister of Canada in 2000* allows one to determine that Jean Chrétien is the referent. Cf. **reference**.

Sentence (S) A syntactic category of expressions consisting minimally of a noun phrase followed by a verb phrase in deep structure.

Sentential (phrasal) semantics See **phrasal semantics**.

Shadowing Studies of speech perception and recognition in which subjects are asked to repeat ("shadow") whatever they hear as rapidly as possible.

Sibilants The class of sounds that includes alveolar and palatal fricatives, and affricates, characterized acoustically by a hissing sound.

Signed English See **Siglish**.

Siglish The name used for Signed English, consisting of the replacement of each spoken English word (and morpheme) by a sign.

Sign Term used in traditional linguistics to refer to a form arbitrarily related to a meaning — that is, a word; a single gesture (possibly with complex meaning) in the sign languages used by the deaf equivalent to the term *word* in spoken languages.

Sign languages The languages used by the deaf in which hand and body gestures are the forms of morphemes and words.

Simplification of consonant clusters The reduction of two or more consonants in sequence, such as *best* from Old English *betst*.

Sino-Tibetan The family of languages that consists of the various Chinese "dialects," including Mandarin, Burmese, and Tibetan.

Situational context Knowledge of who is speaking, who is listening, which objects are being discussed, and general facts about the world we live in; used to interpret meaning.

Slang Words and phrases used in casual speech often invented and spread by close-knit social or age groups.

Slip of the tongue Speech error; involuntary deviation of intended utterance. Cf. **spoonerism**.

Sluicing The syntactic process in which material following a *wh-* word is deleted when it is identical to previous material (e.g., *John is talking with* is deleted from the second clause in *John is talking with someone, but nobody knows who _____*).

Social and occupational deixis Words and expressions such as "Teacher says to do the exercises" or "Mother says so" in which the meanings of "Teacher" or "Mother" depends on who is speaking.

Social dialect The variety of a language spoken by a class or group.

Sonorants The class of sounds that includes vowels, glides, liquids, and nasals; non-obstruents. Cf. **obstruents**.

Sound shift Historical phonological change.

Sound spectrogram Picture of a physical sound showing the harmonics (formants), amplitude (loudness), and fundamental frequency (pitch).

Sound spectrograph A device for depicting the wave forms of speech in the form of spectrograms.

Sound symbolism Certain sound combinations that occur in semantically similar words, such as *gl* in *gleam, glisten*, and *glitter*, which all relate to sight.

Sound writing A term sometimes used to mean a writing system in which one sound is represented by one letter. Sound writing systems do not employ the phonemic principle and are similar to phonetic transcriptions.

Source The thematic role of the noun phrase whose referent is the place from which an action originates (e.g., *Quebec* in *Wolfe sent news from Quebec*).

Source language In automatic machine translation, the language being translated. Cf. **target language**.

Specific language impairment (SLI) Difficulty faced by certain children with no other cognitive deficits in acquiring language; they are much slower than the average child, but only their linguistic ability is affected.

Specifier Function words that help to identify the head of a phrase and mark off the limits of the phrase. They include determiners of NPs (*the*), qualifiers of VPs (*seldom*), and intensifiers or degree words of AdjPs, AdvPs, and PPs (*more*).

Spectrograms, speech spectrograms Graphical depictions of speech, plotting frequency (on the y-axis) as a function of time (on the x-axis). The intensity of the sound is represented by darker (more intensity) and lighter (less intensity) areas on the graph. Sometimes called "visible speech" or voiceprints.

Speech act The non-linguistic accomplishments of an utterance, such as a warning or a promise, as determined in part by context (e.g., *There is a bear behind you* is a warning in certain contexts).

Speech recognition Computer processing for transcribing speech.

Speech synthesis An electronic process in which speech is reproduced.

Speech understanding A computer process in which speech is interpreted semantically.

Spelling The alphabetic representation of words. Cf. **orthography**.

Spelling pronunciation Pronouncing a word as it is spelled, irrespective of its actual pronunciation by native speakers (e.g., pronouncing *Wednesday* as "wed-ness-day").

Spirant See **fricative**.

Split brain The result of an operation for epilepsy in which the corpus callosum is cut, thus separating the brain into its two halves; split-brain patients are studied to determine the role of each hemisphere in cognitive and language processing.

Spoonerism Slip of the tongue in which phonemic segments are reversed or exchanged as in *tip of the slongue*; named for Reverend William Archibald Spooner, head of New College, Oxford, in the nineteenth century, who was purported to have made many such errors.

Stages in language acquisition Periods from infancy to the age of five or six through which all children learning languages pass in acquiring their first language. Cf. **babbling, holophrastic, two-word stage, telegraphic speech**.

Standard The dialect (regional or social) considered to be the norm.

Standard American English (SAE) A dialect of American English employed by those in positions of authority and valued by linguistic purists.

Standard British English (SBrE) A dialect of English spoken in the British Isles employed by those in authority and valued by linguistic purists.

Standard Canadian English (SCE) A dialect of Canadian English employed by those in positions of authority and valued by linguistic purists.

Stem A root morpheme combined with affix morphemes; other affixes can be added to a stem to form a more complex stem.

Stops Sounds in which the air flow is briefly but completely stopped in the oral cavity (e.g., /p/, /n/, /g/).

Stressed syllable, stress Syllable with relatively greater length, loudness, and/or higher pitch. Also called **accent**.

Structural ambiguity The phenomenon in which the same sequence of words has two or more meanings based on different phrase structure analyses.

Structure dependent (1) Describes the fact that the application of transformational rules is determined by phrase structure properties as opposed to structureless sequences of words or specific sentences; (2) Describes how children construct rules using their knowledge of syntactic structure irrespective of the specific words in the structure or their meaning.

Style See **register**.

Subcategorization That part of the lexical entry of a verb specifying which syntactic categories can and cannot occur with it (e.g., specification that the verb *sleep* may not be followed by a noun phrase but that the verb *find* must be followed by a noun phrase).

Subject The noun phrase immediately below the S in the phrase structure tree of a sentence.

Subject–verb agreement The addition of an inflectional morpheme to the main verb required by some property of the noun phrase subject, such as number or gender. In English, whenever the subject of a sentence is third person singular, the main verb must have an -*s* or -*es* added to it (orthographically) — for example, *The boys I know think* but *The boy I know thinks*.

Suffix Bound morpheme that occurs after the root or stem of a word; affix that is attached to the end of a morpheme or word.

Superordinate A structure that may include other structures within it, as a superordinate clause may include within it a subordinate clause. In semantics, the superordinate word, or hypernym, is a more general word that may include more specific words, called hyponyms, in it (e.g., *tree* is the superordinate of *oak, birch*, and *maple*).

Suppletive forms A term used to refer to inflected morphemes in which the regular rules do not apply (e.g., *went* as the past tense of *go*).

Supraglottal cavities Those parts of the vocal tract lying above the glottis.

Suprasegmentals Prosodic features (e.g., length, tone).

Surface structure The final transformationally derived structure, which is the result of applying transformational rules to a deep structure and all but the last derived structure. It is syntactically closest to actual utterances.

Syllabary The inventory of symbols used in a syllabic writing system.

Syllabic A phonetic feature present in sounds that constitute the nucleus of syllables; all vowels are syllabic, and liquids and nasals may be syllabic in words such as *towel, button*, and *bottom*.

Syllabic writing A writing system in which each syllable in the language is represented by its own symbol.

Syllable A unit of phonological structure consisting of a nucleus (generally a vowel) which may or may not be preceded and/or followed by various consonants. See **nucleus, onset, coda**.

Syncope The loss of a medial vowel, as is exemplified in the everyday pronunciation of words such as *Wednesday* and *family*.

Synonyms Different words with the same or nearly the same meaning (e.g., *purse* and *handbag*).

Syntactic category Units of phrase structure that can substitute for one another without loss of grammaticality (e.g., noun phrase). Traditionally called "parts of speech."

Syntactic label A term used for indicating the syntactic categories in a phrase structure tree.

Syntax The rules of sentence formation; the component of the mental grammar that represents speakers' knowledge of the structure of phrases and sentences.

Synthetic sentences Unlike analytic sentences, synthetic sentences require more than linguistic knowledge to determine their truth value; they depend on our knowing something of the events and conditions in the world.

Synthetic speech Speech that attempts to replicate human speech by mechanical or electronic means.

Taboo A descriptive term used in reference to words (or acts) that are not to be used (or performed) in "polite society."

Tap Sound in which the tongue touches the alveolar ridge, as in some British pronunciations of /r/. Also called **flap**.

Target language In automatic machine translation, the language into which the source language is translated.

Teaching grammar A set of language rules written to help speakers learn a foreign language or a different dialect of their language.

Telegraphic speech Utterances of children after the two-word stage when many grammatical morphemes are omitted.

Tense vowels Feature of vowels that are often slightly longer in duration and higher in tongue position and pitch than the corresponding lax vowels.

Thematic role The semantic relationship between the verb and the noun phrases of a sentence, such as agent, theme, location, instrument, goal, and source.

Theme The thematic role of the noun phrase whose referent undergoes the action of the verb (e.g., *Martha* in *George hugged Martha*). Sometimes called **patient**.

Theta-criterion A proposed universal principle stating that a particular thematic role may occur only once in a sentence.

Time deixis Expressions such as *now, then,* and *last week* for which context is needed to determine the actual time being referred to. Cf. **deixis**.

Tip-of-the-tongue (TOT) The difficulty encountered from time to time in finding a particular word. Anomic aphasics suffer from an extreme form of this problem.

Tone Contrastive pitch of syllables in languages where two words may be identical except for such differences in pitch. Cf. **register tones, contour tones**.

Top-down parser A parser that operates by first consulting the rules of grammar and then determining whether the input sequence of words conforms to those rules. Cf. **parser, bottom-up parser**.

Topicalization A transformation that moves a syntactic element to the front of a sentence, deriving, for example, *dogs I love* from *I love dogs*.

Transcription, phonemic The phonemic representation of speech sounds using phonetic symbols, ignoring phonetic details that are predictable by rule, usually given between slashes (e.g., /pul/ for *pool*).

Transcription, phonetic The representation of speech sounds using phonetic symbols between square brackets. They may reflect non-distinctive predictable features (e.g., [pʰæt] *pat*).

Transformational rule, transformation A structurally based formal statement relating two phrase structure trees, one of which is basic — nearer to deep structure — and the other of which is derived — nearer to surface structure (e.g., the passive transformation relates the basic structure underlying *Fido bit Lee* to the derived structure of *Lee was bitten by Fido*).

Transformationally induced ambiguity An ambiguity that results when two different deep structures with two different meanings are transformed into a single surface structure (e.g., *Jim wants the sports car more than Judy*).

Transition network A method for representing rules of grammar that can be graphically depicted by means of nodes connected by arcs.

Transitive Verb A verb that must be followed by a noun phrase direct object in deep structure.

Tree diagram A graphical representation of the hierarchical structure of a phrase or sentence.

Trill Sounds in which the tip of the tongue vibrates against the roof of the mouth.

Truth conditions The circumstances that must be known to determine whether a sentence is true and therefore part of the meaning of declarative sentences.

Turn-taking A conversational principle involving our knowing when to speak and when to listen.

Two-word stage About the beginning of the second year, children produce sentences of two words with clear syntactic and semantic relations.

Unaspirated Voiceless sounds in which the vocal cords start vibrating immediately upon release of constriction (e.g., /p/ in *spit*). Cf. **aspirated**.

Unbound Describes a pronoun lacking an antecedent. Also called **free**. Cf. **free, bound**.

Unconditioned sound change Phonological change that occurs in all phonetic contexts.

Undergeneralize, undergeneralization Children's use of a general term such as *dog* to refer only to a single instance (e.g., the family pet).

Underlying representation Phonemic representation.

Underlying structure (1) The phrase structure tree manifestation of a grammatical sequence of words; (2) Deep structure and any structure resulting from the application of transformational rules except surface structure.

Underspecification The omission of the values of predictable features in a phonemic matrix, revealing the redundancy of such features.

Ungrammatical Describes an ill-formed sequence of words, one not conforming to rules of syntax. Cf. **ill formed**.

Uninterpretable A condition whereby a sentence cannot be interpreted because of nonsense words (e.g., *All mimsy were the borogoves*).

Universal Grammar (UG) The principles or properties that pertain to the grammars of all human languages; the initial state of the language faculty. Cf. **language faculty**. The principles of Universal Grammar that determine the class of human languages that can be acquired unconsciously, without instruction, in the early years of life.

Unmarked The term used to describe that member of a gradable pair of antonyms used in questions of degree (e.g., *high* is the unmarked member of *high/low*). In a male–female pair of words, the word that does not contain a derivational morpheme, usually the male word (e.g., *prince* is unmarked, whereas *princess* is marked). Cf. **marked**.

Uralic The family of languages including Hungarian, Finnish, and Estonian, all of which are spoken on the European continent.

Uvula The fleshy appendage hanging from the end of the velum or soft palate.

Uvular A sound produced by raising the back of the tongue to the uvula.

Velaric airstream mechanism Method by which clicks are produced in which there is a slight inflow of air into the mouth.

Velars Sounds produced by raising the back of the tongue to the soft palate or velum.

Velum The soft palate; the part of the roof of the mouth behind the hard palate.

Verb (V) The syntactic and lexical category of words that can occur as the first syntactic unit in a verb phrase in deep structure.

Verb Phrase (VP) A syntactic category of expressions containing a verb and, possibly, other syntactic units, such as a noun phrase and prepositional phrases (e.g., *gave the book to the child*).

Verbal particle A word that resembles a preposition in form and co-occurs with a particular verb to give a phrasal verb that has a meaning different from the meaning of the verb without the particles (e.g., *ran up* in *They ran up a big bill*). Unlike true prepositions, verbal particles may occur after a direct object, as in *They ran a big bill up*. Cf. *They ran a big hill up*. Cf. **phrasal verb**.

Verner's Law The description of a phonological change in the sound system of certain Indo-European languages formulated by Karl Verner as an explanation of some of the exceptions to Grimm's Law. Cf. **Grimm's Law**.

Voiced sounds Speech sounds produced with closed and vibrating vocal cords.

Voiceless sounds Speech sounds produced with open and non-vibrating vocal cords.

Voiceprint The visual image of the speech signal.

Vowel (V) A sound produced without significant constriction of the air flowing through the mouth.

Wave form Vibrations determined by the shape of the vocal tract when air is flowing through it.

Well formed A term used to describe a sequence of words conforming to the rules of syntax; grammatical sequence.

Wernicke, Carl Neurologist who showed that damage to different parts of the left cerebral hemisphere cause differential language disorders.

Wernicke's area or region Back (posterior) part of the left brain that if damaged causes fluent but semantically empty speech production (Wernicke's aphasia).

Wh- words Words in English typified by those beginning with *wh* that may function as question words (e.g., *who, what, when, which, where, whose*).

Word A free sound–meaning lexical unit, which may be simple (monomorphemic) or complex (polymorphemic) (e.g., *boy, boys*).

Word recognition See **lexical access**.

Word sets Words related by virtue of including the same root morpheme or stem — that is, the same content morpheme (e.g., *phone, phonetic, phonetician, phonic, phoneme*, etc.).

Word writing A system of writing in which each character represents a word or morpheme of the language (e.g., Chinese). Sometimes called ideographic or logographic writing.

Wug An imaginary animal created by Jean Berko Gleason to test children's acquisition of morphological and phonological rules.

Zero-form A morpheme that has no phonological representation (e.g., *sheep + plural* is *sheep*).

ANSWERS TO SELECTED EXERCISES

Chapter 1   What Is Language?

2. *Judgements.* Some judgements may vary across dialects.

   a. **Robin forced the sheriff go.*
      The word *to* is missing in front of the verb *go*. The verb *force* requires a *to* infinitival in the embedded clause.

   f. **He came a large sum of money by.*
      Some (but not all) verb–particle pairs (e.g., *put away* or *look up*) can be split, with the particle going to the right of the direct object. *Pass by* can be split in this way, but *come by* is one of the verb–particle pairs that cannot be split.

   g. **Did in a corner little Jack Horner sit?*
      A yes–no question must start with an auxiliary verb, such as *did*, but the element following the auxiliary verb must be the subject of the sentence. Here the second element is the prepositional phrase *in a corner.*

   h. **Elizabeth is resembled by Charles.*
      The verb *resemble* does not occur in passive sentences.

   k. **It is eager to love a kitten.*
      If the word *it* refers to an animate (but non-human) thing (e.g., a dog), then the sentence is grammatical. If the word *it* is the non-referential expletive, then the sentence is ungrammatical because the adjective *eager* must have a referential subject.

   l. **That birds can fly amazes.*
      Amaze is a transitive verb; it requires a direct object. Compare *That birds can fly amazes Fred.*

   n. **Has the nurse slept the baby yet?*
      The verb *sleep* is intransitive; it cannot take a direct object.

   o. **I was surprised for you to get married.*
      The adjective *surprised* requires a tensed sentential complement (i.e., *that you got married*) and cannot take an infinitival one.

p. *I wonder who and Mary went swimming.*
The verb *wonder* requires a *wh-* phrase in the embedded clause. *Who* is a *wh-* phrase; *I wonder who went swimming* is grammatical. *Who and Mary* is not a *wh-* phrase.

q. *Myself bit John.*
Reflexive noun phrases such as *myself* need a coreferent antecedent (another NP that refers to the same person or object) in the same clause. There is no antecedent for *myself* in this sentence.

Chapter 2   Morphology: The Words of Language

5. *Zulu morphology.*

   A. Zulu nouns

      a. um-
      b. aba-
      c. Zulu   English

          fazi   "married woman"
          fani   "boy"
          zali   "parent"
          fundisi   "teacher"
          bazi   "carver"
          limi   "farmer"
          dlali   "player"
          fundi   "reader"

   B. Zulu verbs

      d. -a
      e. -i
      f. A noun is formed by adding the suffix *-i* to the stem (and adding a singular or plural prefix). Schematically,

          Noun = Stem + *i*

      g. fund
      h. baz

8. *Swahili.*

   a. -toto   "child"
       -fika   "arrive"
       m-   noun prefix attached to singular Class I nouns
       wa-   noun prefix attached to plural Class I nouns

a-	prefix attached to verbs when subject is a singular Class I noun
wa-	prefix attached to verbs when subject is a plural Class I noun
me-	prefix attached to verbs to indicate past tense
na-	prefix attached to verbs to indicate present progressive tense
ta-	prefix attached to verbs to indicate future tense
-tu	man
-lala	sleep
-su	knife
-anguka	fall
ki-	noun prefix attached to singular nouns of Class II
vi-	noun prefix attached to plural nouns of Class II
ki-	prefix attached to verbs when subject is a singular Class II noun
vi-	prefix attached to verbs when subject is a plural Class II noun
-kapu	basket

b. The verb is constructed by stringing together, in order from left to right, (1) the verbal prefix indicating the noun class, (2) the verbal prefix indicating the tense, and (3) the verbal stem. Schematically,

Verb = Class prefix + Tense prefix + Stem

c. (1) mtoto anaanguka
   (2) vikapu vimefika
   (3) mtu ataanguka

Chapter 3   Syntax: The Sentence Patterns of Language

4. *Phrase structure trees.*

a. The puppy found the child.

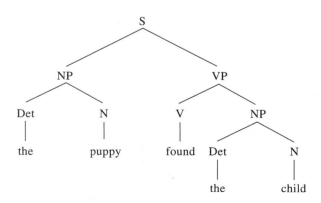

b. The house on the hill collapsed in the wind.

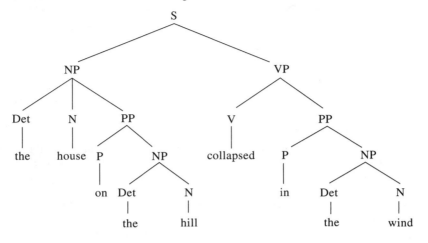

c. A quaint house appeared.

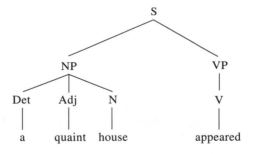

d. The children put the toy in the box.

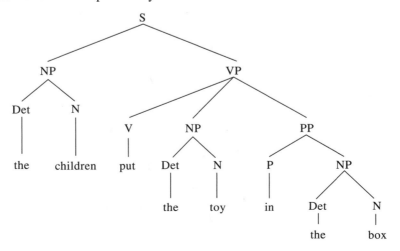

5. *Representing structural ambiguity.*

<u>The magician touched the child with the wand.</u>

Meaning 1: The magician used a wand to touch the child.

Tree 1:

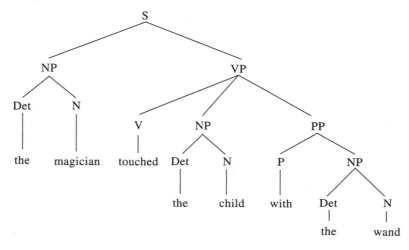

Meaning 2: The magician touched the child who had a wand.

Tree 2:

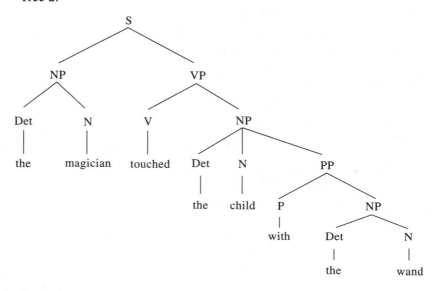

11. *Recursion.*

a.   Noun Phrase recursion: sample answer

(i) The boy in the house on the corner sneezed.

(ii) The boy in the house on the corner of the street sneezed.

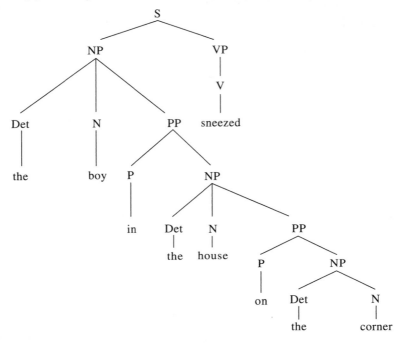

b. Verb Phrase recursion: sample answer

(i) You know that she read the book.

(ii) We believe that you know that she read the book.

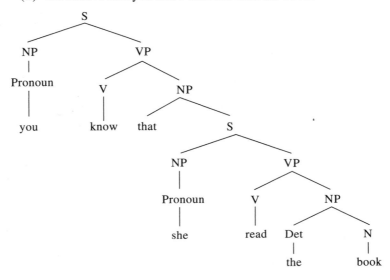

c. Sentence recursion: sample answer

The same samples can be used here as in b, since VP recursion and S recursion are both illustrated in b.

13. *Subcategorization.*

a. *The man located.* The verb *locate* is transitive: it requires an NP object.
<u>locate</u>: Verb, [__ NP]

b. *Jesus wept the apostles.* The verb *weep* is intransitive: it does not allow an object.
<u>weep</u>: Verb, [__]

c. *Robert is hopeful of his children.* The adjective *hopeful* allows an S complement (*that his children will succeed*) or no complement, but it cannot take a PP complement with *of*.
<u>hopeful</u>: Adjective, [__ (S)]

d. *Robert is fond that his children love animals.* The adjective *fond* subcategorizes for a PP complement with *of*, but does not allow an S complement.
<u>fond</u>: Adjective, [__ PP[of]]

e. *The children laughed the man.* Like *weep*, the verb *laugh* is intransitive and may not take a direct object; however, unlike *weep*, *laugh* allows a PP with *at*.
<u>laugh</u>: Verb, [__(PP[at])]

Chapter 4   Semantics: The Meanings of Language

3. *Complementary, gradable, and relational opposites.*

A	B	C
good	bad	g
expensive	cheap	g
parent	offspring	r
beautiful	ugly	g
false	true	c
lessor	lessee	r
pass	fail	c
hot	cold	g
legal	illegal	c
larger	smaller	r
poor	rich	g
fast	slow	g
asleep	awake	c
husband	wife	r
rude	polite	g

4. *Thematic relations.*

           a   t   l
a.   Mary found a ball in the house.

            a   s   g
b.   The children ran from the playground to the wading pool.

             a   t   i
c.   One of the men unlocked all the doors with a paper clip.

          a   t   i
d.   John melted the ice with a blowtorch.

          i   t
e.   The sun melted the ice.

          t
f.   The ice melted.

           a   t   g
g.   The farmer loaded hay onto the truck.

           a   t   i
h.   The farmer loaded the hay with a pitchfork.

          t   g   a
i.   The hay was loaded onto the truck by the farmer.

6. *Analytic versus circumstantial truth.*

a.	Queens are monarchs.	A
b.	Queens are female.	A
c.	Queens are mothers.	N
d.	Dogs are four-legged.	N
e.	Dogs are animals.	A
f.	Cats are felines.	A
g.	Cats are stupid.	N
h.	Audrey MacLaughlin is Audrey MacLaughlin.	A
i.	Audrey MacLaughlin was the first woman to lead a federal political party in Canada.	N
j.	Uncles are male.	A

10. *Presuppositions.*

    b.   Presupposition: You have taken me out to the ball game before.
    c.   Presupposition: Valerie did not receive a new T-bird for Labour Day.
    d.   Presupposition: Emily's pet turtle ran away.
    e.   Presupposition: The professors support the students.
    f.   Presupposition: Canada entered World War II in 1939.

g. Presupposition: Canada entered World War II in 1939.
h. Presupposition: Disa has had some popcorn already.
i. Presupposition: Pigs don't have wings.
j. Presupposition: Somebody discovered America in 1492.

13. *Pronouns.* The following judgements are based on the assumptions that *John* refers to a male and *Louise* and *Maria* to females.

a. herself — bound; I — free
b. he — free; her — bound or free
c. I — free; you — free; her — free
d. himself — bound; him — bound or free; her — free
e. it — expletive (bound); she — free; he — free; them — free
f. their own — bound

Chapter 5 Phonetics: The Sounds of Language

1. *Initial sound.*

a.	judge	[ǰ]	f.	thought	[θ]
b.	Thomas	[tʰ]	g.	contact	[kʰ]
c.	though	[ð]	h.	phone	[f]
d.	easy	[i]	i.	civic	[s]
e.	pneumonia	[n]	j.	usury	[j]

2. *Final sound.*

a.	fleece	[s]	f.	cow	[aw]
b.	neigh	[e]	g.	rough	[f]
c.	long	[ŋ]	h.	cheese	[z]
d.	health	[θ]	i.	bleached	[t]
e.	watch	[č]	j.	rags	[z]

3. *Phonetic transcription.* Note: transcriptions will vary across dialects. For example, the *marry–merry–Mary* distinction is neutralized in many dialects.

a.	physics	[fɪzɪks]	f.	marry	[mæri]
b.	merry	[mɛri]	g.	tease	[tʰiz]
c.	weather	[wɛðər]	h.	heath	[hiθ]
d.	coat	[kʰot]			
e.	yellow	[jɛlo]			

4. *Correcting major errors in transcription.*

a.	cʌ̃m	should be	kʰʌ̃m
b.	sed	should be	sɛd

c. tʰɑlk   should be   tʰɑk
d. āND   should be   ænd
e. wæx   should be   wæks
f. kʰæbəgəz   should be   kʰæbəǰəz
g. ɪs   should be   ɪz
h. wɛθər   should be   wɛðər

6. *Phonetic properties.*

    a.   bath–bathe: The **th** in *bath* is voiceless; the **th** in *bathe* is voiced. Both are interdental fricatives.

    b.   reduce–reduction: The **c** in *reduce* is an alveolar fricative; the **c** in *reduction* is a velar stop. Both are voiceless obstruents.

    c.   cool–cold: The **oo** in *cool* is high; the **o** in *cold* is mid. Both are tense, back, and rounded.

    d.   wife–wives: The **f** in *wife* is voiceless; the **v** in *wives* is voiced. Both are labiodental fricatives.

    e.   cats–dogs: The **s** in *cats* is voiceless; the **s** in *dogs* is voiced. Both are alveolar fricatives.

    f.   impolite–indecent: The **m** in *impolite* is bilabial; the **n** in *indecent* is alveolar. Both are nasals.

7. *Transcription.*

Word	Transcription	Alternates
know	no	
tough	tʰʌf	
bough	baw	
cough	kʰɑf	kʰɔf
dough	do	
you	ju	
hiccough	hɪkəp	
thorough	θəro	θərə, θṛo
slough	slʌf	slu, slaw
through	θru	
heard	hʌrd	hṛd
word	wʌrd	wṛd
beard	bird	
bird	bʌrd	bṛd
dead	dɛd	
said	sɛd	
bed	bɛd	
bead	bid	
deed	did	
meat	mit	
great	gret	
threat	θrɛt	

suite	swit	
straight	stret	
debt	dɛt	
moth	mɑθ	mɔθ
mother	mʌðər	mʌðr̩
both	boθ	
bother	bɑðər	bɔðr̩
broth	brɑθ	brɔθ
brother	brʌðər	brʌðr̩

8. *Shared features.*

a. stop, consonant   d. voiceless, consonant
b. back, round, non-low, vowel   e. voiced, consonant
c. front, vowel   f. coronal, consonant

11. *Phonetic features distinguishing sets of sounds.*

a. back   d. high
b. voicing   e. continuant
c. labial   f. back

Chapter 6   Phonology: The Sound Patterns of Language

1. *Korean.* [r] and [l] are allophones of one phoneme.

a. They do not appear in minimal pairs.
b. They are in complementary distribution.
c. [r] occurs syllable initially, and [l] occurs syllable finally. (Alternatively, [r] occurs before vowels, and [l] occurs before consonants or at the end of a word.)
d. The rule can be written as follows:

$$/l/ \rightarrow \begin{cases} [l] & /\_\_\_ \text{ (C)\#} \\ [r] & /\_\_\_ \text{ V} \end{cases}$$

2. *Southern Kongo.*

a. Distributions:
[t]–[č]: [t] occurs before the back vowels [o, a, u]; [č] occurs before [i].
[s]–[š]: [s] occurs before [o], [u], and [e]; [š] occurs before [i].
[z]–[ž]: [z] occurs before [u], [e], and [w]; [ž] occurs before [i].

b. In each pair, the non-palatal segment should be used as the basic phoneme (e.g., [t] and [č] derived from /t/). Non-palatal segments have a wider distribution, so the rule will be simpler with the non-palatal segment as the "elsewhere" (default) case.

c.
$$\begin{bmatrix} +\text{consonantal} \\ -\text{sonorant} \\ +\text{coronal} \\ +\text{anterior} \end{bmatrix} \rightarrow [-\text{anterior}] \Big/ \underline{\qquad} \begin{bmatrix} +\text{syllabic} \\ +\text{high} \\ -\text{back} \end{bmatrix}$$

8. *Paku.*

a. Yes. Stress falls on the penultimate (next to last) syllable.

b. Nasalization is not a distinctive feature for vowels. It is predictable. A vowel is nasalized if it precedes a nasal consonant.

9. *Hebrew.*

a. Yes, they are in complementary distribution: [v] occurs only after vowels; [b] occurs word initially and after consonants.

b. Yes; [f] occurs only after vowels; [p] occurs word initially and after consonants.

c. The correct statement is (1): [b] but not [v] could occur in the empty slot.

d. The correct statement is (2): [p] but not [f] could occur in the empty slot.

e. The correct statement is (1): These words would force you to revise conclusions reached on the basis of the first group of words, since they show [b] occurring after a vowel, [v] occurring after a consonant, and [f] occurring word initially. If the statements in b are correct, then these words would be impossible.

10. *Maninka.*

a. (1) li   (2) ni

b. Yes. The form is *ni* if the last consonant of the stem is a nasal and *li* otherwise. Notice that the last consonant of the stem is not always the last segment of the stem.

c. dali   "lying down"
   menni   "hearing"
   famuni   "understanding"
   sunogoli   "sleeping"

11. *Luganda.*

a. *Are nasal vowels in Luganda phonemic?* No.
   Are they predictable? Yes. Vowels are nasalized before nasal consonants.

b. Yes.

c. /ato/

d. No. They represent separate phonemes. While there are no minimal pairs, both [p] and [b] occur before [i] and after [a]; their distribution is not predictable.

e. No, because a voiced stop assimilates in nasality to a preceding nasal. Sequences of nasal consonants followed by voiced oral consonants do not occur.
f. Yes.
g. Phonemic: /enpoobe/   Phonetic: [ẽmpoobe]
h. The answer is (1) /en/.
i. [ẽntabi]
j. /akaugeni/
k. (i) Vowel nasalization: a vowel is nasalized when it precedes a nasal consonant.
 (ii) Homorganic nasal rule: /n/ assimilates to the place of articulation of a following consonant.
 (iii) Voiced stop assimilation: A voiced stop becomes a nasal if preceded by a nasal consonant.

Chapter 7   Language in Society

6. *English [aj]–[ʌj].*

a. The sounds that end the words in columns A and B are all consonants ([+consonantal]).
b. The words in column C end in a vowel.
c. Yes. The distribution of [ʌj] and [aj] is predictable: [ʌj] occurs before voiceless segments, and [aj] occurs before voiced segments or word finally.
d. They should be derived from /aj/. [aj] has a wider distribution. Also, it is easier to characterize the distribution of [ʌj] than the distribution of [aj], so the rule will be simpler if [aj] is the sound occurring "elsewhere."
e. life [lʌjf]   lives [lajvz]   lie [laj]
   file [fajl]   bike [bʌjk]   lice [lʌjs]
f. /aj/ → [ʌj]/___[−voice]

Chapter 8   Language Change: The Syllables of Time

5. *Latin–French correspondences.*

a. False.
b. True.
c. False.
d. True.

6. *Indo-European.* The Indo-European languages are 1, 2, 4, 8, 10, and 11.

11. *Historical Reconstruction.*

A. m–m   p–p   t–t   m–w
    w–w   s–s   ʔ–ʔ   n–n
    h–h   k–k   u–u   i–i
    a–a   ɨ–ɨ   o–o   a–e

B. a.   Proto-sounds:

p–p: *p   t–t: *t
s–s: *s   ʔ–ʔ: *ʔ
n–n: *n   h–h: *h
k–k: *k   u–u: *u
i–i: *i   a–a: *a
ɨ–ɨ: *ɨ   o–o: *o
a–e: *e

   b.   The last item above shows a change: proto *e became *a* in YP.

C. a.   w
    b.   m, w
    c.   Yes. A YP *m* corresponds to an NM *m* word initially and an NM *w* between vowels.

D. a.   Two.
    b.   If you chose 3, they would have to be *m, *w, and an abstract sound representing both of them, perhaps *b. Then *m corresponds to *m* in both languages, *w corresponds to *w* in both languages, and *b corresponds to *m* word initially and *w* between vowels in NM. But this solution is unmotivated; the simpler solution below is better.
    c.   The proto-sounds are *m and *w. Proto *m becomes *m* in YP. In NM, proto *m becomes *m* word initially and *w* between vowels. Proto *w becomes *w* in both YP and NM.

E. The proto forms are as in YP except for the words with a proto *e* sound:

*mupi   *pahwa   *ʔatapɨ
*tama   *kuma   *papiʔi
*piwɨ   *wowaʔa   *petɨ
*sawaʔpono   *mɨhɨ   *nana
*nɨmɨ   *noto   *ʔetɨ
*tamano   *tape

Chapter 9   Writing: The ABCs of Language

---

5. *Pronounced the same, spelled differently.* The key to this exercise is to think of cognates in which the letters are pronounced differently.

	A	**B**	**Reason**
a.	I a**m**	ia**mb**	The *b* is pronounced in words such as *iambic*.
b.	goo**se**	produ**ce**	The *c* is pronounced [k] in *production*.

c. fashion   complication   The *t* is pronounced [t] in *complicate*.
d. Newton   organ   The *a* is pronounced [æ] in *organic*; the *o* is
                              pronounced [o] in *Newtonian*.
e. **no**   **kn**ow   The *k* is pronounced in words such as *acknowledge*.
f. hy**mn**   hi**m**   The *n* is pronounced in *hymnal*.

Chapter 10   Language Acquisition

5. *Adam, Eve, and Sarah.*

A. (1) Mini-grammar (sample answer):

      i.   S → V N
     ii. S → Adj N
   iii. S → more N
   iv. S → V it
    v. S → N V
   vi. S → bye-bye N
  vii. S → bye-bye Adj

(2) Trees — sample answer. Students' trees should follow their own
     phrase structure rules from part (1).

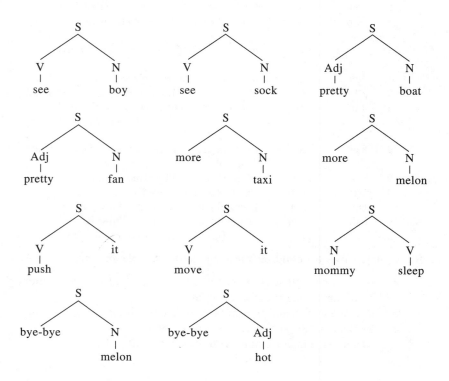

B. (3)

a coat	my stool	poor man
*a celery	that knee	little top
? a Becky	more coffee	dirty knee
*a hands	*more nut	? that Adam
my mummy	*two tinker-toy	big boot

(4) *a celery: Celery is a mass noun, and a must be followed by something countable and singular: a piece/stalk/bite of celery.

? a Becky: Names, especially names of people, do not usually occur with determiners in English. However, note that this phrase is well formed in certain contexts (e.g., My name is Becky, and I live next door to a Becky [someone whose name is also Becky]).

*a hands: The article a must be followed by a singular noun.

*more nut: More must be followed by a mass noun (coffee) or a plural noun (nuts).

*two tinker-toy: Numerals greater than one must be followed by a plural (and countable) noun.

? that Adam: See the response to a Becky above. This phrase is also fine in certain contexts.

6. *Holophrastic stage phonology.*

A.

	Adult	**Child**	**Substitution**
1.	dont	dot	final cluster [nt] reduced to single [t]
2.	skɪp	kʰɪp	initial cluster [sk] reduced to single consonant; /k/ aspirated
3.	šu	su	palato-alveolar fricative replaced by alveolar fricative
4.	ðæt	dæt	interdental fricative replaced by alveolar stop
5.	pʰle	pʰe	initial cluster [pʰl] replaced by single aspirated stop
6.	θʌmp	dʌp	initial voiceless interdental fricative replaced by voiced alveolar stop; final [mp] cluster replaced by single [p]
7.	bæθ	bæt	final interdental fricative replaced by voiceless alveolar stop
8.	čap	tʰap	affricate replaced by alveolar stop
9.	kʰɪDi	kʰɪdi	flap replaced by voiced alveolar stop
10.	lajt	wajt	lateral liquid replaced by labiovelar glide
11.	dali	dawi	lateral liquid replaced by labiovelar glide
12.	gro	go	initial [gr] cluster reduced to single consonant

B. General rules for children's pronunciation (sample answer):

a. In consonant clusters consisting of a stop and a fricative, liquid, or nasal, delete the fricative or nasal.

b. Replace interdental fricatives with alveolar stops.

c. Replace palato-alveolars with alveolars.

d. Replace the lateral liquid with the labiovelar glide.

Chapter 11   Human Processing: Brain, Mind, and Language

3. *Rules relating spelling to pronunciation.* In the patient's system of spelling-to-pronunciation, the following are true:

Written *a* corresponds to /a/ or /æ/.
Written *e* corresponds to /ɛ/ or /i/.
Written *i* corresponds to /aj/.
Written *o* corresponds to /o/ or /ɔ/.
Written *c* corresponds to /s/.
Every letter is pronounced separately, and there is one vowel per syllable. There are no "silent" letters in this system.

In the patient's system of pronunciation-to-spelling, the same rules hold as itemized above. In addition, the sound [k] is always written K, and the third person singular verb ending in -*s* (as in *goes*), when realized as [z], is written Z. This indicates that the patient is not doing lexical lookup or morphological analysis.

Chapter 12   Computer Processing of Human Language

7. *Transition Network.*

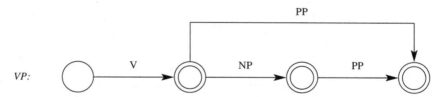

8. *Semantic Networks.*

A. (i) Birds fly.
FLY (BIRDS)

(ii) The student understands the question.
UNDERSTAND (THE STUDENT, THE QUESTION)

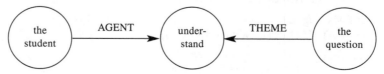

(iii) Penguins do not fly.
NOT (FLY [PENGUINS])

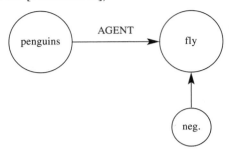

(iv) The wind is in the willows.
IN (THE WIND, THE WILLOWS)

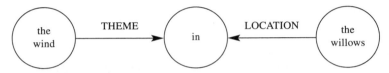

(v) Kathy loves her cat.
LOVE (KATHY, [POSS (KATHY, CAT)])

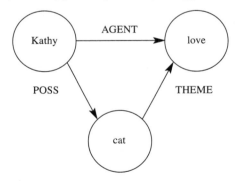

B. (i) Seals swim swiftly.
SWIFTLY (SWIM [SEALS])

(ii) The student doesn't understand the question.
NOT (UNDERSTAND [THE STUDENT, THE QUESTION])

(iii) The pen is on the table.
ON (THE PEN, THE TABLE)

(iv) My dog eats bones.
EAT ([POSS (I, DOG)], BONES)

(v) Emily gives money to charity.
GIVE (EMILY, MONEY, CHARITY)

INDEX